Eighth Edition

Leadership Roles and Management Functions in Nursing

Theory and Application

Bessie L. Marquis, RN, MSN
Professor Emeritus of Nursing
California State University
Chico, California

Carol J. Huston, RN, MSN, DPA, FAAN
Director, School of Nursing
California State University
Chico, California

 Wolters Kluwer
Health

Philadelphia · Baltimore · New York · London
Buenos Aires · Hong Kong · Sydney · Tokyo

Acquisitions Editor: Christopher Richardson
Product Development Editor: Maria McAvey
Production Project Manager: Joan Sinclair
Editorial Assistant: Zachary Shapiro
Senior Designer: Joan Wendt
Manufacturing Coordinator: Karin Duffield
Prepress Vendor: Integra Software Services Pvt. Ltd.

BLACKBURN COLLEGE LIBRARY

BB 65122	
Askews & Holts	27-Jan-2016
UCL362.173 MAR	

8th edition
Copyright © 2015 Wolters Kluwer Health | Lippincott Williams & Wilkins

Copyright © 2012 by Wolters Kluwer Health | Lippincott Williams & Wilkins, Copyright ©, 2009, 2006, 2003, and 2000 by Lippincott Williams & Wilkins. Copyright © 1996 by Lippincott-Raven Publishers. Copyright © 1992 by J. B. Lippincott Company. All rights reserved. This book is protected by copyright. No part of this book may be reproduced or transmitted in any form or by any means, including as photocopies or scanned-in or other electronic copies, or utilized by any information storage and retrieval system without written permission from the copyright owner, except for brief quotations embodied in critical articles and reviews. Materials appearing in this book prepared by individuals as part of their official duties as U.S. government employees are not covered by the above-mentioned copyright. To request permission, please contact Lippincott Williams & Wilkins at Two Commerce Square, 2001 Market Street, Philadelphia, PA 19103, via e-mail at permissions@lww.com, or via our Web site at lww.com (products and services).

9 8 7 6 5 4 3 2 1

Printed in China

Not authorised for sale in United States, Canada, Australia, New Zealand, Puerto Rico or the U.S. Virgin Islands.

Library of Congress Cataloging-in-Publication Data
Marquis, Bessie L., author.
    Leadership roles and management functions in nursing: theory and application/Bessie L. Marquis, Carol J. Huston.—8th edition.
        p. ; cm.
Includes bibliographical references and index.
    ISBN 978-1-4511-9281-0 — ISBN 1-4511-9281-9
I. Huston, Carol Jorgensen, author.   II. Title.
    [DNLM: 1. Leadership.   2. Nursing, Supervisory.   3. Nurse Administrators.   4. Nursing—organization & administration. WY 105]
    RT89
    362.17'3068—dc23
                                                                    2013036678

Care has been taken to confirm the accuracy of the information presented and to describe generally accepted practices. However, the author(s), editors, and publisher are not responsible for errors or omissions or for any consequences from application of the information in this book and make no warranty, expressed or implied, with respect to the currency, completeness, or accuracy of the contents of the publication. Application of this information in a particular situation remains the professional responsibility of the practitioner; the clinical treatments described and recommended may not be considered absolute and universal recommendations.

The author(s), editors, and publisher have exerted every effort to ensure that drug selection and dosage set forth in this text are in accordance with the current recommendations and practice at the time of publication. However, in view of ongoing research, changes in government regulations, and the constant flow of information relating to drug therapy and drug reactions, the reader is urged to check the package insert for each drug for any change in indications and dosage and for added warnings and precautions. This is particularly important when the recommended agent is a new or infrequently employed drug.

Some drugs and medical devices presented in this publication have Food and Drug Administration (FDA) clearance for limited use in restricted research settings. It is the responsibility of the health-care provider to ascertain the FDA status of each drug or device planned for use in his or her clinical practice.

LWW.com

I dedicate this book to the two most important partnerships in my life: my husband, Don Marquis, and my colleague, Carol Huston.

BESSIE L. MARQUIS

I dedicate this book to my mother Marilyn Jorgensen. You are one of the reasons I have become the capable woman I am today.

CAROL JORGENSEN HUSTON

Reviewers

Carol Amann, MSN, RN-BC, CDP
Instructor
Gannon University
Erie, Pennsylvania

Joanne Casatelli, DNP
Molloy College
Rockville Centre, New York

Joanne Clements, MS, RN, ACNP
Assistant Professor of Clinical Nursing
University of Rochester
Rochester, New York

Margaret Decker, MS, RN, CNE
Clinical Assistant Professor
Binghamton University
Binghamton, New York

Hobie Feagai, EdD, MSN, FNP-BC, APRN-Rx
Chair
Department of Baccalaureate Nursing Program
Hawaii Pacific University
Kaneohe, Hawaii

Lisa Marie Greenwood, MSN, RN, APRN-BC, CWOCN, CNS
Nursing Instructor
Madison Area Technical College
Reedsburg, Wisconsin

Vonna Henry, BSN, MPH, RN
Assistant Professor
St. Cloud State University
St. Cloud, Minnesota

Debora Kirsch, RN, MS, CNS
Director of Undergraduate Nursing Studies
SUNY Upstate Medical University
Syracuse, New York

Carole McCue, RN, MS, CNE
Instructor
Cochran School of Nursing
Yonkers, New York

Jennifer Douglas Pearce, MSN, RN, CNE
Professor and Chairperson
University of Cincinnati
Blue Ash, Ohio

Tawna Pounders, RN, MNSc
Coordinator and Medical-Surgical Theory Faculty
Baton Rouge Community College
Baton Rouge, Louisiana

Loretta Quigley, MSN
Academic Dean
St. Joseph's College of Nursing
Syracuse, New York

Elaine Rose, RN, BN, MHS, DM(c)
Assistant Professor
Mount Royal University
Calgary, Alberta, Canada

Charlotte Sortedahl, DNP, MPH, MS, RN
Assistant Professor
University of Wisconsin
Eau Claire, Wisconsin

Patricia Varga, MSN, RN
Assistant Professor
Alverno College
Milwaukee, Wisconsin

Preface

This book's philosophy has evolved over the past 30+ years of teaching leadership and management. We entered academe from the acute care sector of the health-care industry, where we held nursing management positions. In our first effort as authors, *Management Decision Making for Nurses: 101 Case Studies*, published in 1987, we used an experiential approach and emphasized management functions appropriate for first- and middle-level managers. The primary audience for this text was undergraduate nursing students.

Our second book, *Retention and Productivity Strategies for Nurse Managers*, focused on leadership skills necessary for managers to decrease attrition and increase productivity. This book was directed at the nurse-manager rather than the student. The experience of completing research for the second book, coupled with our clinical observations, compelled us to incorporate more leadership content in our teaching and to write this book.

Leadership Roles and Management Functions in Nursing was also influenced by national events in business and finance that led many to believe that a lack of leadership in management was widespread. It became apparent that if managers are to function effectively in the rapidly changing health-care industry, enhanced leadership and management skills are needed.

What we attempted to do, then, was to combine these two very necessary elements: leadership and management. We do not see leadership as merely one role of management nor management as only one role of leadership. We view the two as equally important and necessarily integrated. We have attempted to show this interdependence by defining the leadership components and management functions inherent in all phases of the management process. Undoubtedly, a few readers will find fault with our divisions of management functions and leadership roles; however, we felt it was necessary to first artificially separate the two components for the reader, and then to reiterate the roles and functions. We do believe strongly, however, that adoption of this integrated role is critical for success in management.

The second concept that shaped this book was our commitment to developing critical-thinking skills through the use of experiential learning exercises and the promotion of whole-brain thinking. We propose that integrating leadership and management and using whole-brain thinking can be accomplished through the use of learning exercises. The majority of academic instruction continues to be conducted in a teacher-lecturer–student-listener format, which is one of the least effective teaching strategies. Few individuals learn best using this style. Instead, most people learn best by methods that utilize concrete, experiential, self-initiated, and real-world learning experiences.

In nursing, theoretical teaching is almost always accompanied by concurrent clinical practice that allows concrete and real-world learning experience. However, the exploration of leadership and management theory may have only limited practicum experience, so learners often have little first-hand opportunity to observe middle- and top-level managers in nursing practice. As a result, novice managers frequently have little chance to practice their skills before assuming their first management position, and their decision making thus reflects trial-and-error methodologies. For us, then, there is little question that vicarious learning, or learning through mock experience, provides students the opportunity to make significant leadership and management decisions in a safe environment and to learn from the decisions they make.

Having moved away from the lecturer–listener format in our classes, we lecture for only a small portion of class time. A Socratic approach, case study debate, and problem solving are emphasized. Our students, once resistant to the experiential approach, are now our most enthusiastic supporters. We also find this enthusiasm for experiential learning apparent in the workshops and seminars we provide for registered nurses. Experiential learning enables management and leadership theory to be fun and exciting, but most important, it facilitates retention of didactic material. The research we have completed on this teaching approach supports these findings.

Although many leadership and management texts are available, our book meets the need for an emphasis on both leadership and management and the use of an experiential approach. Two hundred and fifty-nine learning exercises, taken from various health-care settings and a wide variety of learning modes, are included to give readers many opportunities to apply theory, resulting in internalized learning. In Chapter 1, we provide guidelines for using the experiential learning exercises. We strongly urge readers to use them to supplement the text.

We also provide guidelines for instructors on thePoint, Wolters Kluwer Health's trademarked web-based course and content management system that is available to instructors who adopt the text. We recommend its use. The Web site includes a test bank, an image collection, suggestions for using the learning exercises, a glossary, and a large number of PowerPoint slides with images.

TEXT ORGANIZATION

The first edition of *Leadership Roles and Management Functions in Nursing* presented the symbiotic elements of leadership and management, with an emphasis on problem solving and critical thinking. This eighth edition maintains this precedent with a balanced presentation of a strong theory component along with a variety of real-world scenarios in the experiential learning exercises. Nineteen new learning exercises have been added to this edition, further strengthening the problem-based element of this text. Almost 200 displays, figures, and tables (46 of which are new) help readers to visualize important concepts.

Responding to reviewer recommendations, we have added and deleted content. In particular, we have attempted to strengthen the leadership component of the book while maintaining a balance of management content. We have also added a chapter crosswalk (pp. 15–22) of content based on the American Association of Colleges of Nursing (AACN) *Essentials of Baccalaureate Education for Professional Nursing Practice* (2008); the AACN *Essentials of Master's Education in Nursing (2011)*; the *American Organization of Nurse Executive (AONE) Competencies*; and the *Quality and Safety Education for Nurses (QSEN) Competencies*. This crosswalk shows how content in each chapter draws from or contributes to content identified as essential for baccalaureate and graduate education, for practice as a nurse administrator, and for safety and quality in clinical practice.

We have also retained the strengths of earlier editions, reflecting content and application exercises appropriate to the issues faced by nurse-leader-managers as they practice in an era increasingly characterized by limited resources and emerging technologies. The eighth edition also includes contemporary research and theory to ensure accuracy of the didactic material.

Unit I provides a foundation for the decision-making, problem-solving, and critical-thinking skills, as well as management and leadership skills needed to address the management–leadership problems presented in the text. Unit II covers ethics, legal concepts, and advocacy, which we see as core components of leadership and management decision making. The remaining units are organized using the management processes of planning, organizing, staffing, directing, and controlling.

LEARNING TOOLS

The eighth edition contains many pedagogical features designed to benefit both the student and the instructor:

Examining the Evidence, appearing in each chapter, depicts new research findings, evidence-based practice, and best practices in leadership and management.

Learning Exercises interspersed throughout each chapter foster readers' critical-thinking skills and promote interactive discussions. Additional learning exercises are also presented at the end of each chapter for further study and discussion.

Breakout Comments are highlighted throughout each chapter, visually reinforcing key ideas.

Tables, displays, figures, and illustrations are liberally supplied throughout the text to reinforce learning as well as to help clarify complex information.

Key Concepts summarize important information within every chapter.

NEW AND EXPANDED CONTENT

Additional content that has been added or expanded in this edition includes:
- Increased focus on evidence-driven leadership and management decision making
- New models for ethical problem solving and an increased emphasis on patient, professional, and subordinate advocacy
- Expanded discussion of full-range leadership theory, transformational leadership, and leadership competency identification
- Emerging leadership theories such as Strengths-Based Leadership and the Positive Psychology Movement, Level 5 leadership, thought leadership, authentic leadership, and servant leadership
- Introduction to *Affordable Care Act* in 2010, and the new Patient's Bill of Rights
- Key components of the *Patient Protection and Affordable Care Act* (PPACA) as well as its implementation plan between 2010 and 2014
- Health-care reform and financing mechanisms, including bundled payments, accountable care organizations, value-based purchasing, medical homes, and health insurance marketplaces
- The shifting in health-care reimbursement from *volume* to *value*
- Reflective practice and the professional portfolio
- Transition-to-practice programs/residencies for new graduate nurses
- Civility, incivility, bullying, mobbing, and workplace violence
- Visioning of health care's future
- A broad discussion of social media as a communication tool and cause for work distraction and the ethical issues encompassed in the topic
- Continuing competence, lifelong learning, nurse residencies, reflective practice, and the professional portfolio
- Interprofessional collaboration including the Multidisciplinary Team Leader, Interprofessional Primary Healthcare Teams, and Interprofessional Primary Health Care Teams (PHCTs)
- The unique needs of a culturally diverse workforce as well as a workforce representing up to four generations at the same time
- Nurse navigators
- Patient- and family-centered care
- Importance of self-care for nurses

- The use of *ISBAR* (Introduction, *Situation, Background, Assessment, Recommendation*) as a tool to promote communication between care providers or between care providers and patients/families
- Social media and organizational communication
- New mergers of collective bargaining agents to form super unions for nurses
- Leapfrog initiatives including electronic health records, computerized provider order entry, evidence-based hospital staffing, and ICU physician staffing
- New Joint Commission core measures and National Patient Safety Goals
- The Hospital Consumer Assessment of Healthcare Providers and Systems (HCAHPS) survey
- Patient safety and quality of care

thePoint

thePoint (http://thepoint.lww.com), a trademark of Wolters Kluwer Health, is a web-based course and content management system providing every resource that instructors and students need in one easy-to-use site.

Instructor Resources

Advanced technology and superior content combine at thePoint to allow instructors to design and deliver online and off-line courses, maintain grades and class rosters, and communicate with students.

In addition, instructors will find the following content designed specifically for this edition:

- Test bank
- Image bank
- Instructor's guide, including guidelines for using the experiential learning exercises in the text
- PowerPoint slides with images

Student Resources

Students can visit thePoint to access supplemental multimedia resources to enhance their learning experience, download content, upload assignments, and join an online study group. Students will also find a glossary that defines the italicized terms in the text.

THE CROSSWALK

New to this edition is a chapter crosswalk of content based on the AACN *Essentials of Baccalaureate Education for Professional Nursing Practice* (2008); the AACN *Essentials of Master's Education in Nursing (2011)*; the *AONE Competencies*; and the *QSEN Competencies*. A crosswalk is a table that shows elements from different databases or criteria that interface. This edition then attempts to show how content in each chapter draws from or contributes to content identified as essential for baccalaureate and graduate education, for practice as a nurse administrator, and for safety and quality in clinical practice.

Without doubt, some readers will disagree with the author's determinations of which Essential or Competency has been addressed in each chapter, and certainly, an argument could be made that most chapters address many, if not all, of the Essentials or Competencies in some way. The crosswalks in this book then are intended to note the primary content focus in each chapter although additional Essentials or Competencies may well be a part of the learning experience with each chapter.

The American Association of Colleges of Nursing Essentials of Baccalaureate Education for Professional Nursing Practice

The AACN *Essentials of Baccalaureate Education for Professional Nursing Practice* (commonly called the BSN Essentials) were released in 2008 and identified the following nine outcomes expected of graduates of baccalaureate nursing programs (Table 1). Essential IX describes generalist nursing practice at the completion of baccalaureate nursing education and includes practice-focused outcomes that integrate the knowledge, skills, and attitudes delineated in Essentials I to VIII. Achievement of the outcomes identified in the BSN Essentials will enable graduates to practice within complex health-care systems and to assume the roles of provider of care; designer/manager/coordinator of care'; and member of a profession (AACN, 2008) (Table 1).

TABLE 1	American Association of Colleges of Nursing Essentials of Baccalaureate Education for Professional Nursing Practice

Essential I: Liberal education for baccalaureate generalist nursing practice

- A solid base in liberal education provides the cornerstone for the practice and education of nurses

Essential II: Basic organizational and systems leadership for quality care and patient safety

- Knowledge and skills in leadership, quality improvement, and patient safety are necessary to provide high-quality health care.

Essential III: Scholarship for evidence-based practice

- Professional nursing practice is grounded in the translation of current evidence into one's practice.

Essential IV: Information management and application of patient-care technology

- Knowledge and skills in information management and patient-care technology are critical in the delivery of quality patient care

Essential V: Health-care policy, finance, and regulatory environments

- Health-care policies, including financial and regulatory, directly and indirectly influence the nature and functioning of the health-care system and thereby are important considerations in professional nursing practice.

Essential VI: Interprofessional communication and collaboration for improving patient health outcomes

- Communication and collaboration among health-care professionals are critical to delivering high quality and safe patient care.

Essential VII: Clinical prevention and population health

- Health promotion and disease prevention at the individual and population level are necessary to improve population health and are important components of baccalaureate generalist nursing practice.

Essential VIII: Professionalism and professional values

- Professionalism and the inherent values of altruism, autonomy, human dignity, integrity, and social justice are fundamental to the discipline of nursing.

Essential IX: Baccalaureate generalist nursing practice

- The baccalaureate graduate nurse is prepared to practice with patients, including individuals, families, groups, communities, and populations across the lifespan and across the continuum of health-care environments.

- The baccalaureate graduate understands and respects the variations of care, the increased complexity, and the increased use of health-care resources inherent in caring for patients.

The American Association of Colleges of Nursing Essentials of Master's Education in Nursing

The AACN *Essentials of Master's Education in Nursing* (commonly called the MSN Essentials) were published in March 2011 and identified the following nine outcomes expected of graduates of master's nursing programs, regardless of focus, major, or intended practice setting (Table 2). Achievement of these outcomes will prepare graduate nurses to lead change to improve quality outcomes, advance a culture of excellence through lifelong learning, build and lead collaborative interprofessional care teams, navigate and integrate care services across the health-care system, design innovative nursing practices, and translate evidence into practice (AACN, 2011).

TABLE 2	American Association of Colleges of Nursing Essentials of Master's Education in Nursing

Essential I: Background for practice from sciences and humanities

- Recognizes that the master's-prepared nurse integrates scientific findings from nursing, biopsychosocial fields, genetics, public health, quality improvement, and organizational sciences for the continual improvement of nursing care across diverse settings.

Essential II: Organizational and systems leadership

- Recognizes that organizational and systems leadership are critical to the promotion of high quality and safe patient care. Leadership skills are needed that emphasize ethical and critical decision making, effective working relationships, and a systems perspective.

Essential III: Quality improvement and safety

- Recognizes that a master's-prepared nurse must be articulate in the methods, tools, performance measures, and standards related to quality, as well as prepared to apply quality principles within an organization.

Essential IV: Translating and integrating scholarship into practice

- Recognizes that the master's-prepared nurse applies research outcomes within the practice setting, resolves practice problems, works as a change agent, and disseminates results.

Essential V: Informatics and health-care technologies

- Recognizes that the master's-prepared nurse uses patient-care technologies to deliver and enhance care and uses communication technologies to integrate and coordinate care

Essential VI: Health policy and advocacy

- Recognizes that the master's-prepared nurse is able to intervene at the system level through the policy development process and to employ advocacy strategies to influence health and health care.

Essential VII: Interprofessional collaboration for improving patient and population health outcomes

- Recognizes that the master's-prepared nurse, as a member and leader of interprofessional teams, communicates, collaborates, and consults with other health professionals to manage and coordinate care.

Essential VIII: Clinical prevention and population health for improving health

- Recognizes that the master's-prepared nurse applies and integrates broad, organizational, client-centered, and culturally appropriate concepts in the planning, delivery, management, and evaluation of evidence-based clinical prevention and population care and services to individuals, families, and aggregates/identified populations.

Essential IX: Advanced generalist nursing practice

- Recognizes that nursing practice, at the master's level, is broadly defined as any form of nursing intervention that influences health-care outcomes for individuals, populations, or systems. Master's-level nursing graduates must have an advanced level of understanding of nursing and relevant sciences as well as the ability to integrate this knowledge into practice. Nursing practice interventions include both direct and indirect care components.

The Quality and Safety Education for Nurses Competencies

Using the Institute of Medicine (2003) competencies for nursing, the QSEN Institute defined six pre-licensure and graduate quality and safety competencies for nursing (Table 3) and proposed targets for the knowledge, skills, and attitudes to be developed in nursing programs for each of these competencies. Led by a national advisory board and distinguished faculty, QSEN pursues strategies to develop effective teaching approaches to assure that future graduates develop competencies in patient-centered care, teamwork and collaboration, evidence-based practice, quality improvement, safety, and informatics.

TABLE 3	Quality and Safety Education for Nurses Competencies

Patient-centered care
- Definition: Recognize the patient or designee as the source of control and full partner in providing compassionate and coordinated care based on respect for patient's preferences, values, and needs.

Teamwork and collaboration
- Definition: Function effectively within nursing and interprofessional teams, fostering open communication, mutual respect, and shared decision making to achieve quality patient care.

Evidence-based practice
- Definition: Integrate best current evidence with clinical expertise and patient/family preferences and values for delivery of optimal health care.

Quality improvement
- Definition: Use data to monitor the outcomes of care processes and use improvement methods to design and test changes to continuously improve the quality and safety of health-care systems.

Safety
- Definition: Minimizes the risk of harm to patients and providers through both system effectiveness and individual performance.

Informatics
- Definition: Use information and technology to communicate, manage knowledge, mitigate error, and support decision making.

The American Organization of Nurse Executives - Nurse Executive Competencies

In 2004, the AONE published a paper describing skills common to nurses in executive practice regardless of their educational level or titles in different organizations. While these *Nurse Executive Competencies* differed depending on the leader's specific position in the organization, the AONE suggested that managers at all levels must be competent in the five areas noted in Table 4 (AONE, 2011). These competencies suggest that nursing leadership/management is as much a specialty as any other clinical nursing specialty and as such, it requires proficiency and competent practice specific to the executive role (AONE).

TABLE 4	American Organization of Nurse Executive Competencies

I. Communication and relationship building
- Communication and relationship building includes effective communication; relationship management; influence of behaviors; ability to work with diversity; shared decision making; community involvement; medical staff relationships; and academic relationships.

II. A knowledge of the health-care environment
- Knowledge of the health-care environment includes clinical practice knowledge; patient-care delivery models and work design knowledge; health-care economics knowledge; health-care policy knowledge; understanding of governance; understanding of evidence-based practice; outcome measurement; knowledge of, and dedication to patient safety; understanding of utilization/case management; knowledge of quality improvement and metrics; and knowledge of risk management.

III. Leadership
- Leadership skills include foundational thinking skills; personal journey disciplines; the ability to use systems thinking; succession planning; and change management.

IV. Professionalism
- Professionalism includes personal and professional accountability; career planning; ethics; evidence-based clinical and management practice; advocacy for the clinical enterprise and for nursing practice; and active membership in professional organizations.

V. Business skills
- Business skills include understanding of health-care financing; human resource management and development; strategic management; marketing; and information management and technology.

REFERENCES

American Association of Colleges of Nursing (AACN). (2008, October 20). *The essentials of baccalaureate education for professional nursing practice.* Retrieved June 20, 2013, from http://www.aacn.nche .edu/education-resources/baccessentials08.pdf

American Association of Colleges of Nursing (AACN). (2011, March 21) *The essentials of master's education in nursing.* Retrieved June 20, 2013, from http://www.aacn.nche.edu/education-resources/ MastersEssentials11.pdf

American Organization of Nurse Executives (2011). *The AONE nurse executive competencies.* Retrieved June 20, 2013, from http://www.aone.org/resources/ leadership%20tools/nursecomp.shtml

Institute of Medicine. (2003). *Health professions education: A bridge to quality.* Washington, DC: National Academies Press.

Quality and Safety Education for Nurses Institute (2013). *Competencies.* Retrieved June 20, 2013, from http:// qsen.org/competencies/

Contents

UNIT II

Foundation for Effective Leadership and Management Ethics, Law, and Advocacy 69

UNIT III

Roles and Functions in Planning 137

UNIT V

Roles and Functions in Staffing 333

UNIT VI

Roles and Functions in Directing 413

18 Creating a Motivating Climate 414

19 Organizational, Interpersonal, and Group Communication 436

UNIT VII

Roles and Functions in Controlling 541

UNIT I

The Critical Triad: Decision Making, Management, and Leadership

1

Decision Making, Problem Solving, Critical Thinking, and Clinical Reasoning: Requisites for Successful Leadership and Management

... again and again, the impossible problem is solved when we see that the problem is only a tough decision waiting to be made.
—Robert H. Schuller

... in any moment of decision the best thing you can do is the right thing, the next best thing is the wrong thing, and the worst thing you can do is nothing.
—Theodore Roosevelt

CROSSWALK THIS CHAPTER ADDRESSES:

BSN Essential I: Liberal education for baccalaureate generalist nursing practice
BSN Essential III: Scholarship for evidence-based practice
BSN Essential IV: Information management and application of patient care technology
BSN Essential VI: Interprofessional communication and collaboration for improving patient health outcomes
MSN Essential I: Background for practice from sciences and humanities
QSEN Competency: Informatics
MSN Essential IV: Translating and integrating scholarship into practice
AONE Nurse Executive Competency I: Communication and relationship building
AONE Nurse Executive Competency III: Leadership
QSEN Competency: Evidence-based practice

LEARNING OBJECTIVES The learner will:

- differentiate between problem solving, decision making, critical thinking, and clinical reasoning
- describe how case studies, simulation, and problem-based learning can be used to improve the quality of decision making
- explore strengths and limitations of using intuition and heuristics as adjuncts to problem solving and decision making
- identify characteristics of successful decision makers
- select appropriate models for decision making in specific situations
- describe the importance of the individual in the decision-making process
- identify critical elements of decision making
- explore his or her personal propensity for risk taking in decision making
- discuss the effect of organizational power on decision making
- differentiate between the economic man and the administrative man in decision making

- select appropriate management decision-making tools that would be helpful in making specific decisions
- differentiate between autocratic, democratic, and laissez-faire decision styles and identify situation variables that might suggest using one decision style over another

Decision making is often thought to be synonymous with management and is one of the criteria on which management expertise is judged. Much of any manager's time is spent critically examining issues, solving problems, and making decisions. The quality of the decisions that leader-managers make is the factor that often weighs most heavily in their success or failure.

Decision making, then, is both an innermost leadership activity and the core of management. This chapter explores the primary requisites for successful management and leadership: decision making, problem solving, and critical thinking. Also, because it is the authors' belief that decision making, problem solving, and critical thinking are learned skills that improve with practice and consistency, an introduction to established tools, techniques, and strategies for effective decision making is included. This chapter also introduces the learning exercise as a new approach for vicariously gaining skill in management and leadership decision making. Finally, evidence-based decision making is introduced as an imperative for both personal and professional problem solving.

DECISION MAKING, PROBLEM SOLVING, CRITICAL THINKING, AND CLINICAL REASONING

Decision making is a complex, cognitive process often defined as choosing a particular course of action. BusinessDictionary.com (2013, para 1) defines decision making as "the thought process of selecting a logical choice from the available options." This implies that doubt exists about several courses of action and that a choice is made to eliminate uncertainty.

Problem solving is part of decision making and is a systematic process that focuses on analyzing a difficult situation. Problem solving always includes a decision-making step. Many educators use the terms problem solving and decision making synonymously, but there is a small yet important difference between the two. Although decision making is the last step in the problem-solving process, it is possible for decision making to occur without the full analysis required in problem solving. Because problem solving attempts to identify the root problem in situations, much time and energy are spent on identifying the real problem.

Decision making, on the other hand, is usually triggered by a problem but is often handled in a manner that does not focus on eliminating the underlying problem. For example, if a person decided to handle a conflict when it occurred but did not attempt to identify the real problem causing the conflict, only decision-making skills would be used. The decision maker might later choose to address the real cause of the conflict or might decide to do nothing at all about the problem. The decision has been made *not* to problem solve. This alternative may be selected because of a lack of energy, time, or resources to solve the real problem. In some situations, this is an appropriate decision. For example, assume that a nursing supervisor has a staff nurse who has been absent a great deal over the last 3 months. Normally, the supervisor would feel compelled to intervene. However, the supervisor has reliable information that the nurse will be resigning soon to return to school in another state. Because the problem will soon no longer exist, the supervisor *decides* that the time and energy needed to correct the problem are not warranted.

Critical thinking, sometimes referred to as *reflective thinking*, is related to evaluation and has a broader scope than decision making and problem solving. Dictionary.com (2013) defines critical thinking as "the mental process of actively and skillfully conceptualizing, applying, analyzing, synthesizing, and evaluating information to reach an answer or conclusion" (para 1). Critical thinking also involves reflecting upon the meaning of statements, examining the offered evidence and reasoning, and forming judgments about facts.

Whatever definition of critical thinking is used, most agree that it is more complex than problem solving or decision making, involves higher-order reasoning and evaluation, and has both cognitive and affective components. The authors believe that insight, intuition, empathy, and the willingness to take action are additional components of critical thinking. These same skills are necessary to some degree in decision making and problem solving. See Display 1.1 for additional characteristics of a critical thinker.

DISPLAY 1.1	Characteristics of a Critical Thinker	
Open to new ideas	Flexible	Creative
Intuitive	Empathetic	Insightful
Energetic	Caring	Willing to take action
Analytical	Observant	Outcome directed
Persistent	Risk taker	Willing to change
Assertive	Resourceful	Knowledgeable
Communicator	"Outside-the-box" thinker	Circular thinking

Insight, intuition, empathy, and the willingness to take action are components of critical thinking.

Nurses today must have higher-order thinking skills to identify patient problems and to direct clinical judgments and actions that result in positive patient outcomes. When nurses integrate and apply different types of knowledge to weigh evidence, critically think about arguments and reflect upon the process used to arrive at a diagnosis; this is known as *clinical reasoning* (Linn, Khaw, Kildea, & Tonkin, 2012). Thus, clinical reasoning uses both knowledge and experience to make decisions at the point of care.

VICARIOUS LEARNING TO INCREASE PROBLEM-SOLVING AND DECISION-MAKING SKILLS

Decision making, one step in the problem-solving process, is an important task that relies heavily on critical thinking and clinical reasoning skills. How do people become successful problem solvers and decision makers? Although successful decision making can be learned through life experience, not everyone learns to solve problems and judge wisely by this trial-and-error method because much is left to chance. Some educators feel that people are not successful in problem solving and decision making because individuals are not taught how to reason insightfully from multiple perspectives.

Moreover, information and new learning may not be presented within the context of real-life situations, although this is changing. For example, in teaching clinical reasoning, nurse educators strive to see that the elements of clinical reasoning, such as noticing crucial changes in patient status, analyzing these changes to decide on a course of action, and evaluating responses to modify care, are embedded at every opportunity throughout the nursing curricula (Russell, Geist, & Maffett, 2013). In addition, time is included for meaningful reflection on the decisions that are made and the outcomes that result. Such learning can occur in both real-world settings and through vicarious learning, where students problem solve and make decisions based on simulated situations that are made real to the learner.

Case Studies, Simulation, and Problem-Based Learning

Case studies, simulation, and problem-based learning (PBL) are some of the strategies that have been developed to vicariously improve problem solving and decision making. *Case studies* may be thought of as stories that impart learning. They may be fictional or include real persons and events, be relatively short and self-contained for use in a limited amount of time, or be longer with significant detail and complexity for use over extended periods of time. Case studies, particularly those that unfold or progress over time, are becoming much more common in nursing education since they provide a more interactive, learning experience for students than the traditional didactic approach.

Similarly, *simulation* provides learners opportunities for problem solving that have little or no risk to patients or to organizational performance. For example, some organizations are now using computer simulation (known as *discrete event simulation*) to imitate the operation of a real-life system such as a hospital. Based on chosen alternatives, the simulation can determine the relative performance of patient throughputs, the timeliness of care, and the appropriateness of resource utilization, thus integrating management priorities and operational decision making (Hamrock, Paige, Parks, Scheulen, & Levin, 2013).

In addition, simulation models are increasingly being used by schools of nursing to allow students the opportunity to gain skill mastery before working directly with acutely ill and vulnerable clients. In addition, simulation allows students to apply and improve the critically important "nontechnical" skills of communication, teamwork, leadership, and decision making (Lewis, Strachan, & Smith, 2012). (See Examining the Evidence 1.1.)

Examining the Evidence 1.1

Source: Lewis, R., Strachan, A., & Smith, M. (2012). Is high fidelity simulation the most effective method for the development of non-technical skills in nursing? A review of the current evidence. Open Nursing Journal, 6, 82–89.

This literature review suggested that simulation was positively associated with significantly improved interpersonal communication skills at patient handover as well as improved team performance in the management of crisis situations. It also appeared to enable the development of transferable, transformational leadership skills, improved students' critical thinking and clinical reasoning in complex care situations, and aided in the development of students' self-efficacy and confidence in their own clinical abilities. The authors concluded that simulation provides a learning environment in which both technical and nontechnical skills can be improved without fear of compromising patient safety.

PBL also provides opportunities for individuals to address and learn from authentic problems vicariously. Typically, in PBL, learners meet in small groups to discuss and analyze real-life problems. Thus, they learn by problem solving. The learning itself is collaborative as the teacher guides the students to be self-directed in their learning, and many experts suggest that this type of active learning helps to develop critical thinking skills.

The Marquis-Huston Critical Thinking Teaching Model

The desired outcome for teaching and learning decision making and critical thinking in management is an interaction between learners and others that results in the ability to critically examine management and leadership issues. This is a learning of appropriate social/professional behaviors rather than a mere acquisition of knowledge. This type of learning occurs best in groups, using a PBL approach.

In addition, learners retain didactic material more readily when it is personalized or when they can relate to the material being presented. The use of case studies that learners can identify with assists in retention of didactic materials.

Also, while formal instruction in critical thinking is important, using a formal decision-making process improves both the quality and consistency of decision making. Many new leaders and managers struggle to make quality decisions because their opportunity to practice making management and leadership decisions is very limited until they are appointed to a management position. These limitations can be overcome by creating opportunities for vicariously experiencing the problems that individuals would encounter in the real world of leadership and management.

The *Marquis-Huston model for teaching critical thinking* assists in achieving desired learner outcomes (Fig. 1.1). Basically, the model comprises four overlapping spheres, each being an essential component for teaching leadership and management. The first is a didactic theory component, such as the material that is presented in each chapter; second, a formalized approach to problem solving and decision making must be used. Third, there must be some use of the group process, which can be accomplished through large and small groups and classroom discussion. Finally, the material must be made real for the learner so that the learning is internalized. This can be accomplished through writing exercises, personal exploration, and values clarification, along with risk taking, as case studies are examined.

 Experiential learning provides mock experiences that have tremendous value in applying leadership and management theory.

This book was developed with the perspective that experiential learning provides mock experiences that have tremendous value in applying leadership and management theory. The text includes numerous opportunities for readers to experience the real world of leadership and management. Some of these learning situations, called *learning exercises*, include case studies, writing exercises, specific management or leadership problems, staffing and budgeting calculations, group discussion or problem-solving situations, and assessment of personal attitudes and values. Some exercises include opinions, speculation, and value judgments. All of the learning exercises, however, require some degree of critical thinking, problem solving, decision making, or clinical reasoning.

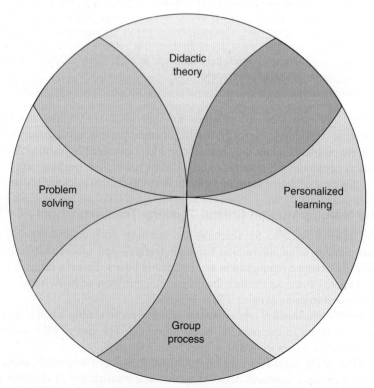

FIGURE 1.1 • The Marquis-Huston critical thinking teaching model.

Some of the case studies have been solved (solutions are found at the back of the book) so that readers can observe how a systematic problem-solving or decision-making model can be applied in solving problems common to nurse-managers. The authors feel strongly, however, that the problem solving suggested in the solved cases should not be considered the only plausible solution or "the right solution" to that learning exercise. Most of the learning exercises in the book have multiple solutions that could be implemented successfully to solve the problem.

THEORETICAL APPROACHES TO PROBLEM SOLVING AND DECISION MAKING

Most people make decisions too quickly and fail to systematically examine a problem or its alternatives for solution. Instead, most individuals rely on discrete, often unconscious processes known as *heuristics*, which allows them to solve problems more quickly and to build upon experiences they have gained in their lives. Thus, heuristics use trial-and-error methods or a rule-of-thumb approach to problem solving, rather than set rules.

For example, a study by Muoni (2012) found that nurse midwives often use heuristics (which are defined as shortcut mental strategies that help simplify information), coupled with intuition, to make clinical decisions. While Muoni notes that the use of such heuristics does allow midwives to make decisions more quickly, she questions the reliability of heuristics and suggests that clinical decisions should always be evidence based and follow a systematic continuum that clearly portrays the process used to make the decision.

Formal process and structure can benefit the decision-making process, as they force decision makers to be specific about options and to separate probabilities from values. A structured approach to problem solving and decision making increases clinical reasoning and is the best way to learn how to make quality decisions because it eliminates trial and error and focuses the learning on a proven process. A structured or professional approach involves applying a theoretical model in problem solving and decision making. Many acceptable problem solving models exist, and most include a decision-making step; only four are reviewed here.

A structured approach to problem solving and decision making increases clinical reasoning.

Traditional Problem-Solving Process

One of the most well-known and widely used problem-solving models is the *traditional problem-solving model*. The seven steps follow in Display 1.2. (Decision-making occurs at step 5.)

DISPLAY 1.2   Traditional Problem Solving Process

1. Identify the problem.
2. Gather data to analyze the causes and consequences of the problem.
3. Explore alternative solutions.
4. Evaluate the alternatives.
5. Select the appropriate solution.
6. Implement the solution.
7. Evaluate the results.

Although the traditional problem-solving process is an effective model, its weakness lies in the amount of time needed for proper implementation. This process, therefore, is less effective when time constraints are a consideration. Another weakness is lack of an initial objective-setting step. Setting a decision goal helps to prevent the decision maker from becoming sidetracked.

Managerial Decision-Making Models

To address the weaknesses of the traditional problem-solving process, many contemporary models for management decision making have added an objective-setting step. These models are known as *managerial decision-making models* or *rational decision-making models*. One such model suggested by Decision-making-confidence.com (2006–2013) includes the six steps shown in Display 1.3.

DISPLAY 1.3	Managerial Decision Making Model

1. Determine the decision and the desired outcome (set objectives).
2. Research and identify options.
3. Compare and contrast these options and their consequences.
4. Make a decision.
5. Implement an action plan.
6. Evaluate results.

In the first step, problem solvers must identify the decision to be made, who needs to be involved in the decision process, the timeline for the decision, and the goals or outcomes that should be achieved. Identifying objectives to guide the decision making helps the problem solver determine which criteria should be weighted most heavily in making their decision. Most important decisions require this careful consideration of context.

In step 2, problem solvers must attempt to identify as many alternatives as possible. Alternatives are then analyzed in step 3, often using some type of *SWOT* (strengths, weaknesses, opportunities, and threats) analysis. Decision makers may choose to apply quantitative decision-making tools, such as decision-making grids and payoff tables (discussed further later in this chapter), to objectively review the desirability of alternatives.

In step 4, alternatives are rank ordered on the basis of the analysis done in step 3 so that problem solvers can make a choice. In step 5, a plan is created to implement desirable alternatives or combinations of alternatives. In the final step, challenges to successful implementation of chosen alternatives are identified and strategies are developed to manage those risks. An evaluation is then conducted of both process and outcome criteria, with outcome criteria typically reflecting the objectives that were set in step 1.

The Nursing Process

The *nursing process*, developed by Ida Jean Orlando in the late 1950s, provides another theoretical system for solving problems and making decisions. Originally a four-step model (assess, plan, implement, and evaluate) diagnosis was delineated as a separate step, and most contemporary depictions of this model now include at least five steps. (See Display 1.4.)

DISPLAY 1.4	Nursing Process

1. Assess
2. Diagnose
3. Plan
4. Implement
5. Evaluate

As a decision-making model, the greatest strength of the nursing process may be its multiple venues for feedback. The arrows in Figure 1.2 show constant input into the process.

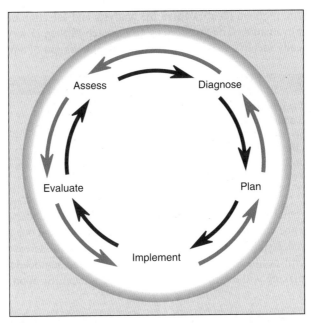

FIGURE 1.2 • Feedback mechanism of the nursing process.

When the decision point has been identified, initial decision making occurs and continues throughout the process via a feedback mechanism.

Although the process was designed for nursing practice with regard to patient care and nursing accountability, it can easily be adapted as a theoretical model for solving leadership and management problems. Table 1.1 shows how closely the nursing process parallels the decision-making process.

The weakness of the nursing process, like the traditional problem-solving model, is in not requiring clearly stated objectives. Goals should be clearly stated in the planning phase of the process, but this step is frequently omitted or obscured. However, because nurses are familiar with this process and its proven effectiveness, it continues to be recommended as an adapted theoretical process for leadership and managerial decision making.

Integrated Ethical Problem-Solving Model

A more contemporary model for effective thinking and problem solving was developed by Park (2012) upon review of 20 existing models for ethical decision making (Display 1.5). While developed primarily for use in solving ethical problems, the model also works well as a general problem-solving model. Similar to the three models already discussed, this model provides a structured approach to problem solving that includes an assessment of

TABLE 1.1 Comparing the Decision-Making Process with the Nursing Process	
Decision-Making Process	*Simplified Nursing Process*
Identify the decision	Assess
Collect data	
Identify criteria for decision	Plan
Identify alternatives	
Choose alternative	Implement
Implement alternative	
Evaluate steps in decision	Evaluate

the problem, problem identification, the analysis and selection of the best alternative, and a means for evaluation. The model does go one step further, however, in requiring the learner to specifically identify strategies that reduce the likelihood of a problem recurring.

DISPLAY 1.5   Integrated Ethical Problem Solving Model

1. State the problem.
2. Collect additional information and analyze the problem.
3. Develop alternatives and analyze and compare them.
4. Select the best alternative and justify your decision.
5. Develop strategies to successfully implement a chosen alternative and take action.
6. Evaluate the outcomes and prevent a similar occurrence.

Many other excellent problem analysis and decision models exist. The model selected should be one with which the decision maker is familiar and one appropriate for the problem to be solved. Using models or processes consistently will increase the likelihood that critical analysis will occur. Moreover, the quality of management/leadership problem solving and decision making will improve tremendously via a scientific approach.

LEARNING EXERCISE 1.1

Applying Scientific Models to Decision Making

You are a registered nurse who graduated 3 years ago. During the last 3 years, your responsibilities in your first position have increased. Although you enjoy your family (spouse and one preschool-aged child), you realize that you love your job and that your career is very important to you. Recently, you and your spouse decided to have another baby. At that time, you and your spouse reached a joint decision that if you had another baby, you wanted to reduce your work time and spend more time at home with the children. Last week, your supervisor told you that the charge nurse is leaving. You were thrilled and excited when she said that she wants to appoint you to the position. Yesterday, you found out that you and your spouse are expecting a baby.

Last night, you spoke with your spouse about your career future. Your spouse is an attorney whose practice has suddenly gained momentum. Although the two of you have shared child rearing equally until this point, your spouse is not sure how much longer this can be done if the law practice continues to expand. If you take the position, which you would like to do, it would mean full-time work. You want the decision that you and your spouse reach to be well thought out, as it has far-reaching consequences and concerns many people.

Assignment: Determine what you should do. After you have made your decision, get together in a group (four to six people) and share your decisions. Were they the same? How did you approach the problem solving differently from others in your group? Was a rational systematic problem-solving process used, or was the chosen solution based more on intuition? How many alternatives were generated? Did some of the group members identify alternatives that you had not considered? Was a goal(s) or objective identified? How did your personal values influence your decision?

Intuitive Decision-Making Models

There are theorists who suggest that intuition should always be used as an adjunct to empirical or rational decision-making models. Experienced nurses often report that gut-level feelings encourage them to take appropriate strategic action that impacts patient outcomes, although intuition should generally serve as an adjunct to decision making founded on nurse's scientific knowledge base.

Pearson (2013) agrees, suggesting that intuition can and should be used in conjunction with evidence-based practice and that it deserves to be acknowledged as a factor in achieving good outcomes within clinical practice. Pearson goes on to say that intuition is, in reality, often a rapid, automatic process of recognizing familiar problems instantly and using experience to identify solutions. Thus, intuition may be perceived as a cognitive skill rather than a perception or knowing without knowing how.

This recognition of familiar problems and the use of intuition to identify solutions is a focus of contemporary research on intuitive decision-making research. Klein and his colleagues (Klein, 2008) developed the *recognition-primed decision (RPD) model* for intuitive decision making in the mid-1980s to explain how people can make effective decisions under time pressure and uncertainty. Considered a part of *naturalistic decision making*, the RPD model attempts to understand how humans make relatively quick decisions in complex, real-world settings such as firefighting and critical care nursing without having to compare options.

Klein's work suggests that instead of using classical rational or systematic decision-making processes, many individuals act on their first impulse if the "imagined future" looks acceptable. If this turns out not to be the case, another idea or concept is allowed to emerge from their subconscious and is examined for probable successful implementation. Thus, the RPD model blends intuition and analysis, but pattern recognition and experience guide decision makers when time is limited or systematic rational decision making is not possible.

CRITICAL ELEMENTS IN PROBLEM SOLVING AND DECISION MAKING

Because decisions may have far-reaching consequences, some problem solving and decision making must be of high quality. Using a scientific approach alone for problem solving and decision making does not, however, ensure a quality decision. Special attention must be paid to other critical elements. The elements in Display 1.6, considered crucial in problem solving, must occur if a high-quality decision is to be made.

DISPLAY 1.6   Critical Elements in Decision Making
1. Define objectives clearly.
2. Gather data carefully.
3. Take the time necessary.
4. Generate many alternatives.
5. Think logically.
6. Choose and act decisively.

Define Objectives Clearly

Decision makers often forge ahead in their problem-solving process without first determining their goals or objectives. However, it is especially important to determine goals and objectives when problems are complex. Even when decisions must be made quickly, there is time to pause and reflect on the purpose of the decision. A decision that is made without a clear objective in mind or a decision that is inconsistent with one's philosophy is likely to be a poor-quality decision. Sometimes the problem has been identified but the wrong objectives are set.

If a decision lacks a clear objective or if an objective is not consistent with the individual's or organization's stated philosophy, a poor-quality decision is likely.

For example, it would be important for the decision maker in Learning Exercise 1.1 to determine whether their most important objective is career advancement, having more time with family, or meeting the needs of their spouse. None of these goals is more "right" than the others, but not having clarity about which objective(s) is paramount makes decision making very difficult.

Gather Data Carefully

Because decisions are based on knowledge and information available to the problem solver at the time the decision must be made, one must learn how to process and obtain accurate information. The acquisition of information begins with identifying the problem or the occasion for the decision and continues throughout the problem-solving process. Often the information is unsolicited, but most information is sought actively. Acquiring information always involves people, and no tool or mechanism is infallible to human error. Questions that should be asked in data gathering are shown in Display 1.7.

DISPLAY 1.7   Questions to Examine in Data Gathering

1. What is the setting?
2. What is the problem?
3. Where is it a problem?
4. When is it a problem?
5. Who is affected by the problem?
6. What is happening?
7. Why is it happening? What are the causes of the problem? Can the causes be prioritized?
8. What are the basic underlying issues? What are the areas of conflict?
9. What are the consequences of the problem? Which is the most serious?

In addition, human values tremendously influence our perceptions. Therefore, as problem solvers gather information, they must be vigilant that their own preferences and those of others are not mistaken for facts.

Facts can be misleading if they are presented in a seductive manner, if they are taken out of context, or if they are past oriented.

How many parents have been misled by the factual statement, "Johnny hit me"? In this case, the information seeker needs to do more fact finding. What was the accuser doing before Johnny hit him? What was he hit with? Where was he hit? When was he hit? Like the parent, the manager who becomes expert at acquiring adequate, appropriate, and accurate information will have a head start in becoming an expert decision maker and problem solver.

LEARNING EXERCISE 1.2

Gathering Necessary Information

Identify a poor decision that you recently made because of faulty data gathering. Have you ever made a poor decision because necessary information was intentionally or unintentionally withheld from you?

Take the Time Necessary

Moxley, Anders Ericsson, Charness, and Krampe (2012) suggest that most current problem-solving and decision-making theories argue that human decision making is largely based on the quick, automatic, and intuitive processes that are a part of heuristics, and that these are only occasionally supplemented by slow controlled deliberation. Moxley et al. (2012) argue that slow deliberation results in improved decision making for both experts and those less skilled, regardless of whether the problem is easy or difficult.

Use an Evidence-Based Approach

To gain knowledge and insight into managerial and leadership decision making, individuals must reach outside their current sphere of knowledge in solving the problems presented in this text. Some data-gathering sources include textbooks, periodicals, experts in the field, colleagues, and current research. Indeed, most experts agree that the best practices in nursing care and decision making are also *evidence-based practices* (Prevost, 2014).

While there is no one universally accepted definition for an evidence-based approach, most definitions suggest the term evidence based can be used synonymously with research based or science based. Others suggest that evidence based means that the approach has been reviewed by experts in the field using accepted standards of empirical research and that reliable evidence exists that the approach or practice works to achieve the desired outcomes. Typically, a *PICO* (patient or population, intervention, comparison, and outcome) format is used in evidence-based practice to guide the search for the current best evidence to address a problem.

Given that human lives are often at risk, nurses, then, should feel compelled to use an evidence-based approach in gathering data to make decisions regarding their nursing practice. Yet, Prevost (2014) suggests that many practicing nurses feel they do not have the time, access, or expertise needed to search and analyze the research literature to answer clinical questions. In addition, most staff nurses practicing in clinical settings have less than a baccalaureate degree and therefore may not have been exposed to a formal research course. Findings from research studies may also be technical, difficult to understand, and even more difficult to translate into practice. Strategies the new nurse might use to promote evidence-based practice are shown in Display 1.8.

DISPLAY 1.8   Strategies for the New Nurse to Promote Evidence-Based Best Practice

1. Keep abreast of the evidence—subscribe to professional journals and read widely.
2. Use and encourage use of multiple sources of evidence.
3. Use evidence not only to support clinical interventions but also to support teaching strategies.
4. Find established sources of evidence in your specialty—do not reinvent the wheel.
5. Implement and evaluate nationally sanctioned clinical practice guidelines.
6. Question and challenge nursing traditions and promote a spirit of risk taking.
7. Dispel myths and traditions not supported by evidence.
8. Collaborate with other nurses locally and globally.
9. Interact with other disciplines to bring nursing evidence to the table.

Source: Reprinted from Prevost, S. (2014). Evidence-based practice. In C. Huston (Ed.), Professional issues in nursing *(3rd ed.). Philadelphia, PA: Lippincott Williams & Wilkins.*

Evidence-based decision making and evidence-based practice should be viewed as imperatives for all nurses today as well as for the profession in general.

It is important to recognize that the implementation of evidence-based best practices is not just an individual, staff nurse–level pursuit (Prevost, 2014). Too few nurses understand what best practices and evidence-based practice are all about, and many organizational cultures do not support nurses who seek out and use research to change long-standing practices rooted in tradition rather than in science. Administrative support is needed to access the resources, provide the support personnel, and sanction the necessary changes in policies, procedures, and practices for evidence-based data gathering to be a part of every nurse's practice (Prevost, 2014). This approach to care is even being recognized as a standard expectation of accrediting bodies, such as the Joint Commission as well as an expectation for magnet hospital designation.

Generate Many Alternatives

The definition of decision making implies that there are at least two choices in every decision. Unfortunately, many problem solvers limit their choices to two when many more options usually are available. Remember that one alternative in each decision should be the choice not to do anything. When examining decisions to be made by using a formal process, it is often found that the status quo is the right alternative.

 The greater the number of alternatives that can be generated, the greater the chance that the final decision will be sound.

Several techniques can help to generate more alternatives. Involving others in the process confirms the adage that two heads are better than one. Because everyone thinks uniquely, increasing the number of people working on a problem increases the number of alternatives that can be generated.

Brainstorming is another frequently used technique. The goal in brainstorming is to think of all possible alternatives, even those that may seem "off target." By not limiting the possible alternatives to only apparently appropriate ones, people can break through habitual or repressive thinking patterns and allow new ideas to surface. Although most often used by groups, people who make decisions alone also may use brainstorming.

LEARNING EXERCISE 1.3

Possible Alternatives in Problem Solving

In the personal-choice scenario presented in Learning Exercise 1.1, some of the following alternatives could have been generated:

- Do not take the new position.
- Hire a full-time housekeeper, and take the position.
- Ask your spouse to quit working.
- Have an abortion.
- Ask one of the parents to help.
- Take the position, and do not hire child care.
- Take the position, and hire child care.
- Have your spouse reduce the law practice and continue helping with child care.
- Ask the supervisor if you can work 4 days a week and still have the position.
- Take the position and wait and see what happens after the baby is born.

Assignment: How many of these alternatives did you or your group generate? What alternatives did you identify that are not included in this list?

Think Logically

During the problem-solving process, one must draw inferences from information. An *inference* is part of deductive reasoning. People must carefully think through the information and the alternatives. Faulty logic at this point may lead to poor-quality decisions. Primarily, people think illogically in three ways.

1. *Overgeneralizing*: This type of "crooked" thinking occurs when one believes that because *A* has a particular characteristic, every other *A* also has the same characteristic. This kind of thinking is exemplified when stereotypical statements are used to justify arguments and decisions.
2. *Affirming the consequences*: In this type of illogical thinking, one decides that if *B* is good and he or she is doing *A*, then *A* must not be good. For example, if a new method is heralded as the best way to perform a nursing procedure and the nurses on your unit are not using that technique, it is illogical to assume that the technique currently used in your unit is wrong or bad.
3. *Arguing from analogy*: This thinking applies a component that is present in two separate concepts and then states that because *A* is present in *B*, then *A* and *B* are alike in all respects. An example of this would be to argue that because intuition plays a part in clinical and managerial nursing, then any characteristic present in a good clinical nurse also should be present in a good nurse-manager. However, this is not necessarily true; a good nurse-manager does not necessarily possess all the same skills as a good nurse-clinician.

Various tools have been designed to assist managers with the important task of analysis. Several of these tools are discussed in this chapter. In analyzing possible solutions, individuals may want to look at the following questions:

1. What factors can you influence? How can you make the positive factors more important and minimize the negative factors?
2. What are the financial implications in each alternative? The political implications? Who else will be affected by the decision and what support is available?
3. What are the weighting factors?
4. What is the best solution?
5. What are the means of evaluation?
6. What are the consequences of each alternative?

Choose and Act Decisively

It is not enough to gather adequate information, think logically, select from among many alternatives, and be aware of the influence of one's values. In the final analysis, one must act. Many individuals delay acting because they do not want to face the consequences of their choices (e.g., if managers granted all employees' requests for days off, they would have to accept the consequences of dealing with short staffing).

Many individuals choose to delay acting because they lack the courage to face the consequences of their choices.

It may help the reluctant decision maker to remember that even though decisions often have long-term consequences and far-reaching effects, they are not usually cast in stone. Often, judgments found to be ineffective or inappropriate can be changed. By later evaluating decisions, managers can learn more about their abilities and where the problem solving was faulty. However, decisions must continue to be made, although some are of poor quality, because through continued decision making, people develop improved decision-making skills.

INDIVIDUAL VARIATIONS IN DECISION MAKING

If each person receives the same information and uses the same scientific approach to solve problems, an assumption could be made that identical decisions would result. However, in practice, this is not true. Because decision making involves perceiving and evaluating, and people perceive by sensation and intuition and evaluate their perception by thinking and feeling, it is inevitable that individuality plays a part in decision making. Because everyone has different values and life experiences, and each person perceives and thinks differently, different decisions may be made given the same set of circumstances. No discussion of decision making would, therefore, be complete without a careful examination of the role of the individual in decision making.

Gender

New research suggests that gender may play a role in how individuals make decisions, although some debate continues as to whether these differences are more gender role based than gender based. Research does suggest, however, that men and women do have different structures and wiring in the brain and that men and women may use their brains differently (Edmonds, 1998–2013). For example, Harvard researchers have found that parts of the frontal lobe, responsible for problem solving and decision making, and the limbic cortex, responsible for regulating emotions, are larger in women (Hoag as cited by Edmonds). Men also have approximately 6.5 times more gray matter in the brain than women, but women have about 10 times more white matter than men (Carey as cited by Edmonds). Researchers believe that men may think more with their gray matter, while women think more with the white matter. This use of white matter may allow a woman's brain to work faster than a man's (Hotz as cited by Edmonds).

Values

Individual decisions are based on each person's value system. No matter how objective the criteria, value judgments will always play a part in a person's decision making, either consciously or subconsciously. The alternatives generated and the final choices are limited by each person's value system. For some, certain choices are not possible because of a person's beliefs. Because values also influence perceptions, they invariably influence information gathering, information processing, and final outcome. Values also determine which problems in one's personal or professional life will be addressed or ignored.

 No matter how objective the criteria, value judgments will always play a part in a person's decision making, either consciously or subconsciously.

Life Experience

Each person brings to the decision-making task past experiences that include education and decision-making experience. The more mature the person and the broader his or her background, the more alternatives he or she can identify. Each time a new behavior or decision is observed, that possibility is added to the person's repertoire of choices.

In addition, people vary in their desire for autonomy, so some nurses may want more autonomy than others. It is likely that people seeking autonomy may have much more experience at making decisions than those who fear autonomy. Likewise, having made good or poor decisions in the past will influence a person's decision making.

Individual Preference

With all the alternatives a person considers in decision making, one alternative may be preferred over another. The decision maker, for example, may see certain choices as involving greater personal risk than others and therefore may choose the safer alternative. Physical, economic, and emotional risks and time and energy expenditures are types of personal risk and costs involved in decision making. For example, people with limited finances or a reduced energy level may decide to select an alternative solution to a problem that would not have been their first choice had they been able to overcome limited resources.

Brain Hemisphere Dominance and Thinking Styles

Our way of evaluating information and alternatives on which we base our final decision constitutes a thinking skill. Individuals think differently. Some think systematically—and are often called analytical thinkers—whereas others think intuitively. It is believed that most people have either right- or left-brain hemisphere dominance. Analytical, linear, *left-brain thinkers* process information differently from creative, intuitive, *right-brain thinkers*. Left-brain thinkers are typically better at processing language, logic, numbers, and sequential ordering while right-brain thinkers excel at nonverbal ideation and holistic synthesizing (Rigby, Gruver, & Allen, 2009). The end result is that individuals with left-brain dominance do well in mathematics, reading, planning, and organizing while right-brain dominant individuals are better at handling images, music, colors, and patterns (Rigby et al., 2009). Although the authors encourage whole-brain thinking, and studies have shown that people can strengthen the use of the less dominant side of the brain, most people continue to have a dominant side.

Some researchers, including Nobel Prize winner Roger Sperry, suggest that there are actually four different thinking styles based on brain dominance. Ned Herrmann, a researcher in critical thinking and whole-brain methods, also suggested that there are four brain hemispheres and that decision making varies with brain dominance (12 Manage: The Executive Fast Track, 2013). For example, Herrmann suggested that individuals with upper-left-brain dominance truly are analytical thinkers who like working with factual data and numbers. These individuals deal with problems in a logical and rational way. Individuals with lower-left-brain dominance are highly organized and detail oriented. They prefer a stable work environment and value safety and security over risk taking.

Individuals with upper-right-brain dominance are big picture thinkers who look for hidden possibilities and are futuristic in their thinking. They also frequently rely on intuition to solve problems and are willing to take risks to seek new solutions to problems. Individuals with lower-right-brain dominance experience facts and problem solve in a more emotional way than the other three types. They are sympathetic, kinesthetic, and empathetic and focus more on interpersonal aspects of decision making (12 Manage: The Executive Fast Track, 2013).

In the past, some organizations more openly valued their logical, analytical thinkers but more recently have recognized that intuitive thinking is also a valuable managerial resource. Indeed, organizations need all types of thinkers, and in fact, smart leaders will see that teams are composed of individuals with different types of brain dominance. Rigby et al. (2009, p. 79) agree, suggesting that when resources are constrained, "the key to growth is pairing an analytic left-brained thinker with an imaginative right-brain partner." The right-brained thinker will be creative in producing innovation, and the left-brained thinker will give the idea structure so that it can become a reality.

 There is no evidence that any one thinking style or that having either right- or left-brain dominance is better.

LEARNING EXERCISE 1.4

Thinking Styles

In small groups, examine how each individual in the group thinks. Did you have a majority of individuals with right- or left-brain dominance? Did group members self-identify with one or more of the four thinking styles noted by Herrmann (12 Manage: The Executive Fast Track, 2013)? Did gender seem to influence thinking style or brain hemisphere dominance? What types of thinkers were represented in group members' families? Did most group members view variances in a positive way?

OVERCOMING INDIVIDUAL VULNERABILITY IN DECISION MAKING

How do people overcome subjectivity in making decisions? This can never be completely overcome, nor should it. After all, life would be boring if everyone thought alike. However, managers and leaders must become aware of their own vulnerability and recognize how it influences and limits the quality of their decision making. Using the following suggestions will help decrease individual subjectivity and increase objectivity in decision making.

Values

Being confused and unclear about one's values may affect decision-making ability. Overcoming a lack of self-awareness through values clarification decreases confusion. People who understand their personal beliefs and feelings will have a conscious awareness of the values on which their decisions are based. This awareness is an essential component of decision making and critical thinking. Therefore, to be successful problem solvers, managers must periodically examine their values. Values clarification exercises are included in Chapter 7.

Life Experience

It is difficult to overcome inexperience when making decisions. However, a person can do some things to decrease this area of vulnerability. First, use available resources, including current research and literature, to gain a fuller understanding of the issues involved. Second, involve other people, such as experienced colleagues, mentors, trusted friends, and experts, to act as sounding boards and advisors. Third, analyze decisions later to assess their success. By evaluating decisions, people learn from mistakes and are able to overcome inexperience.

In addition, novice nurse-leaders of the future may increasingly choose to improve the quality of their decision making by the use of commercially purchased *expert networks*—communities of top thinkers, managers, and scientists—to help them make decisions. Such network panels are typically made up of researchers, health-care professionals, attorneys, and industry executives.

Individual Preference

Overcoming this area of vulnerability involves self-awareness, honesty, and risk taking. The need for self-awareness was discussed previously, but it is not enough to be self-aware; people also must be honest with themselves about their choices and their preferences for those choices. In addition, the successful decision maker must take some risks. Nearly every decision has some element of risk, and most decisions involve consequences and accountability.

Those who can do the right but unpopular thing and who dare to stand alone will emerge as leaders.

Individual Ways of Thinking

People making decisions alone are frequently handicapped because they are not able to understand problems fully or make decisions from both analytical and intuitive perspectives. However, most organizations include both types of thinkers. Using group process, talking management problems over with others, and developing whole-brain thinking also are methods for ensuring that both intuitive and analytical approaches will be used in solving problems and making decisions. Use of heterogeneous rather than homogeneous groups will usually result in better-quality decision making. Indeed, learning to think "outside the box" is often accomplished by including a diverse group of thinkers when solving problems and making decisions.

Although not all experts agree, many consider the following to be qualities of a successful decision maker:

- *Courage*: Courage is particularly important and involves the willingness to take risks.
- *Sensitivity*: Good decision makers seem to have some sort of antenna that makes them particularly sensitive to situations and others.
- *Energy*: People must have the energy and desire to make things happen.
- *Creativity*: Successful decision makers tend to be creative thinkers. They develop new ways to solve problems.

 # DECISION MAKING IN ORGANIZATIONS

In the beginning of this chapter, the need for managers and leaders to make quality decisions was emphasized. The effect of the individual's values and preferences on decision making was discussed, but it is important for leaders and managers to also understand how the organization influences the decision-making process. Because organizations are made up of people with differing values and preferences, there is often conflict in organizational decision dynamics.

Effect of Organizational Power

Powerful people in organizations are more likely to have decisions made (by themselves or their subordinates) that are congruent with their own preferences and values. On the other hand, people wielding little power in organizations must always consider the preference of the powerful when they make management decisions. In organizations, choice is constructed and constrained by many factors, and therefore choice is not equally available to all people.

In addition, not only do the preferences of the powerful influence decisions of the less powerful, but the powerful also can inhibit the preferences of the less powerful. This occurs because individuals who remain and advance in organizations are those who feel and express values and beliefs congruent with the organization. Therefore, a balance must be found between the limitations of choice posed by the power structure within the organization and totally independent decision making that could lead to organizational chaos.

 The ability of the powerful to influence individual decision making in an organization often requires adopting a private personality and an organizational personality.

For example, some might believe they would have made a different decision had they been acting on their own, but they went along with the organizational decision. This "going along" in itself constitutes a decision. People choose to accept an organizational decision that differs from their own preferences and values. The concept of power in organizations is discussed in more detail in Chapter 13.

Rational and Administrative Decision Making

For many years, it was widely believed that most managerial decisions were based on a careful, scientific, and objective thought process and that managers made decisions in a rational manner. In the late 1940s, Herbert A. Simon's work revealed that most managers made many decisions that did not fit the objective rationality theory. Simon (1965) delineated two types of management decision makers: the *economic man* and the *administrative man*.

Managers who are successful decision makers often attempt to make rational decisions, much like the economic man described in Table 1.2. Because they realize that restricted knowledge and limited alternatives directly affect a decision's quality, these managers

TABLE 1.2   Comparing the Economic Man with the Administrative Man

Economic	Administrative
Makes decisions in a very rational manner	Makes decisions that are good enough
Has complete knowledge of the problem or decision situation	Because complete knowledge is not possible, knowledge is always fragmented
Has a complete list of possible alternatives	Because consequences of alternatives occur in the future, they are impossible to predict accurately
Has a rational system of ordering preference of alternatives	Usually chooses from among a few alternatives, not all possible ones
Selects the decision that will maximize utility	The final choice is satisficing rather than maximizing

Source: Adapted from Simon, H. A. (1965). The shape of automation for man and management. New York, NY: Harper Textbooks.

gather as much information as possible and generate many alternatives. Simon believed that the economic model of man, however, was an unrealistic description of organizational decision making. The complexity of information acquisition makes it impossible for the human brain to store and retain the amount of information that is available for each decision. Because of time constraints and the difficulty of assimilating large amounts of information, most management decisions are made using the administrative man model of decision making.

Most management decisions are made by using the administrative man model of decision making.

The administrative man never has complete knowledge and generates fewer alternatives. Simon argued that the administrative man carries out decisions that are only *satisficing*, a term used to describe decisions that may not be ideal but result in solutions that have adequate outcomes. These managers want decisions to be "good enough" so that they "work," but they are less concerned that the alternative selected is the optimal choice. The "best" choice for many decisions is often found to be too costly in terms of time or resources, so another less costly but workable solution is found.

DECISION-MAKING TOOLS

There is always some uncertainty in making decisions. However, management analysts have developed tools that provide some order and direction in obtaining and using information or that are helpful in selecting who should be involved in making the decision. Because there are so many decision aids, this chapter presents selected technology that would be most helpful to beginning- or middle-level managers, including decision grids, payoff tables, decision trees, consequence tables, logic models, and program evaluation and review technique (PERT). It is important to remember, though, that any decision-making tool always results in the need for the person to make a final decision and that all such tools are subject to human error.

Decision Grids

A *decision grid* allows one to visually examine the alternatives and compare each against the same criteria. Although any criteria may be selected, the same criteria are used to analyze each alternative. An example of a decision grid is depicted in Figure 1.3. When many alternatives have been generated or a group or committee is collaborating on the decision, these grids are particularly helpful to the process. This tool, for instance, would be useful when changing

Alternative	Financial effect	Political effect	Departmental effect	Time	Decision
#1					
#2					
#3					
#4					

FIGURE 1.3 • A decision grid.

the method of managing care on a unit or when selecting a candidate to hire from a large interview pool. The unit manager or the committee would evaluate all of the alternatives available using a decision grid. In this manner, every alternative is evaluated using the same criteria. It is possible to weight some of the criteria more heavily than others if some are more important. To do this, it is usually necessary to assign a number value to each criterion. The result would be a numeric value for each alternative considered.

Payoff Tables

The decision aids known as *payoff tables* have a cost–profit–volume relationship and are very helpful when some quantitative information is available, such as an item's cost or predicted use. To use payoff tables, one must determine probabilities and use historical data, such as a hospital census and a report on the number of operating procedures performed. To illustrate, a payoff table might be appropriately used in determining how many participants it would take to make an in-service program break even in terms of costs.

If the instructor for the class costs $500, the in-service director would need to charge each of the 20 participants $25 for the class, but for 40 participants, the class would cost only $12.50 each. The in-service director would use attendance data from past classes and the number of nurses potentially available to attend to determine probable class size and thus how much to charge for the class. Payoff tables do not guarantee that a correct decision will be made, but they assist in visualizing data.

Decision Trees

Because decisions are often tied to the outcome of other events, management analysts have developed *decision trees*.

The decision tree in Figure 1.4 compares the cost of hiring regular staff with the cost of hiring temporary employees. Here, the decision is whether to hire extra nurses at regular salary to perform outpatient procedures on an oncology unit or to have nurses available to the unit on an on-call basis and pay them on-call and overtime wages. The possible consequences of a decreased volume of procedures and an increased volume must be considered. Initially, costs would increase in hiring a regular staff, but over a longer time, this move would mean greater savings if the volume of procedures does not dramatically decrease.

Consequence Tables

Consequence tables demonstrate how various alternatives create different consequences. A consequence table lists the objectives for solving a problem down one side of a table and rates how each alternative would meet the desired objective.

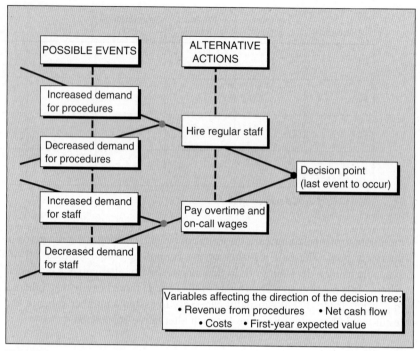

FIGURE 1.4 • A decision tree.

For example, consider this problem: "The number of patient falls has exceeded the benchmark rate for two consecutive quarters." After a period of analysis, the following alternatives were selected as solutions:

1. Provide a new educational program to instruct staff on how to prevent falls.
2. Implement a night check to ensure that patients have side rails up and beds in low position.
3. Implement a policy requiring soft restraint orders on all confused patients.

The decision maker then lists each alternative opposite the objectives for solving the problem, which for this problem might be (a) reduces the number of falls, (b) meets regulatory standards, (c) is cost-effective, and (d) fits present policy guidelines. The decision maker(s) then ranks each desired objective and examines each of the alternatives through a standardized key, which allows a fair comparison between alternatives and assists in eliminating undesirable choices. It is important to examine long-term effects of each alternative as well as how the decision will affect others. See Table 1.3 for an example of a consequence table.

TABLE 1.3   A Consequence Table

Objectives for Problem Solving	Alternative 1	Alternative 2	Alternative 3
1. Reduces the number of falls	X	X	X
2. Meets regulatory standards	X	X	X
3. Is cost-effective		X	X
4. Fits present policy guidelines			X
Decision Score			

Logic Models

Logic models are schematics or pictures of how programs are intended to operate. The schematic typically includes resources, processes, and desired outcomes and depicts exactly what the relationships are between the three components. For example, Allmark, Baxter, Goyder, Guillaume, and Crofton-Martin (2013) used logic models to depict causal pathways between the provision of advice services and improvements in health. Data and discussion from 87 documents were used to construct a model describing interventions, primary outcomes, secondary and tertiary outcomes following advice interventions.

Program Evaluation and Review Technique

PERT is a popular tool to determine the timing of decisions. Developed by the Booz-Allen-Hamilton organization and the U.S. Navy in connection with the Polaris missile program, PERT is essentially a flowchart that predicts when events and activities must take place if a final event is to occur. Figure 1.5 shows a PERT chart for developing a new outpatient treatment room for oncology procedures. The number of weeks to complete tasks is listed in optimistic time, most likely time, and pessimistic time. The critical path shows something that must occur in the sequence before one may proceed. PERT is especially helpful when a group of people is working on a project. The flowchart keeps everyone up-to-date, and problems are easily identified when they first occur. Flowcharts are popular, and many people use them in their personal lives.

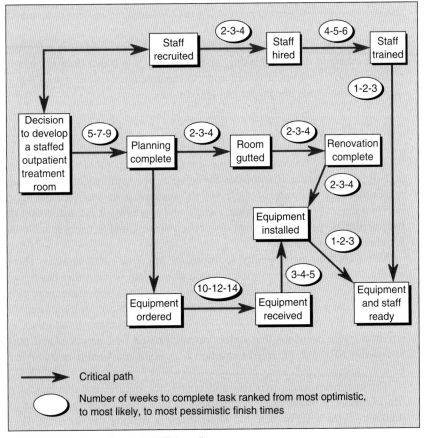

FIGURE 1.5 • Example of a PERT flow diagram.

LEARNING EXERCISE 1.5

Using a Flowchart for Project Management

Think of a project that you are working on; it could be a dance, a picnic, remodeling your bathroom, or a semester schedule of activities in a class.

Assignment: Draw a flowchart, inserting at the bottom the date that activities for the event are to be completed. Working backward, insert critical tasks and their completion dates. Refer to your flowchart throughout the project to see if you are staying on target.

PITFALLS IN USING DECISION-MAKING TOOLS

A common flaw in making decisions is to base decisions on first impressions. This then typically leads to *confirmation biases*. A confirmation bias is a tendency to affirm one's initial impression and preferences as other alternatives are evaluated. So, even the use of consequence tables, decision trees, and other quantitative decision tools will not guarantee a successful decision.

It is also human nature to focus on an event that leaves a strong impression, so individuals may have preconceived notions or biases that influence decisions. Too often, managers allow the past to unduly influence current decisions.

Many of the pitfalls associated with management decision-making tools can be reduced by choosing the correct decision-making style and involving others when appropriate.

Although there are times when others should be involved, it is not always necessary to involve others in decision making, and frequently a manager does not have time to involve a large group. However, it is important to separate out those decisions that need input from others and those that a manager can make alone.

SUMMARY

This chapter has discussed effective decision making, problem solving, critical thinking, and clinical reasoning as requisites for being a successful leader and manager. The effective leader-manager is aware of the need for sensitivity in decision making. The successful decision maker possesses courage, energy, and creativity. It is a leadership skill to recognize the appropriate people to include in decision making and to use a suitable theoretical model for the decision situation.

Managers who make quality decisions are effective administrators. The manager should develop a systematic, scientific approach to problem solving that begins with a fixed goal and ends with an evaluation step. Decision tools exist to help make more effective decisions; however, leader-managers must remember that they are not foolproof and that they often do not adequately allow for the human element in management. In addition, managers should strive to make decisions that reflect research-based best practices and nursing's scientific knowledge base. Yet, the role of intuition as an adjunct to quality decision making should not be overlooked.

The integrated leader-manager understands the significance that gender, personal values, life experience, preferences, willingness to take risks, brain hemisphere dominance, and thinking styles have on selected alternatives in making the decision. The critical thinker pondering a decision is aware of the areas of vulnerability that hinder successful decision making and will expend his or her efforts to avoid the pitfalls of faulty logic and data gathering.

Both managers and leaders understand the impact that the organization has on decision making and that some of the decisions that will be made in the organization will be only satisficing. However, leaders will strive to problem solve adequately in order to reach optimal decisions as often as possible.

KEY CONCEPTS

- Successful decision makers are self-aware, courageous, sensitive, energetic, and creative.
- The rational approach to problem solving begins with a fixed goal and ends with an evaluation process.
- Naturalistic decision making blends intuition and analysis, but pattern recognition and experience guide decision makers when time is limited or systematic rational decision making is not possible.
- Evidence-based nursing practice integrates the best evidence available to achieve desirable outcomes.
- The successful decision maker understands the significance that gender, personal, individual values, life experience, preferences, willingness to take risks, brain hemisphere dominance, and predominant thinking style have on alternative identification and selection.
- The critical thinker is aware of areas of vulnerability that hinder successful decision making and makes efforts to avoid the pitfalls of faulty logic in his or her data gathering.
- The act of making and evaluating decisions increases the expertise of the decision maker.
- There are many models for improving decision making. Using a systematic decision-making or problem-solving model reduces heuristic trial-and-error or rule-of-thumb methods and increases the probability that appropriate decisions will be made.
- Left- and right-brain dominance as well as thinking styles influences, at least to some degree, how individuals think.
- Two major considerations in organizational decision making are how power affects decision making and whether management decision making needs to be only satisficing.
- Management science has produced many tools to help decision makers make better and more objective decisions, but all are subject to human error, and many do not adequately consider the human element.

ADDITIONAL LEARNING EXERCISES AND APPLICATIONS

LEARNING EXERCISE 1.6

Evaluating Decision Making

A. Describe the two best decisions that you have made in your life and the two worst. What factors assisted you in making the wise decisions? What elements of critical thinking went awry in your poor decision making? How would you evaluate your decision-making ability?

B. Examine the process that you used in your decision to become a nurse. Would you describe it as fitting a profile of the economic man or the administrative man?

LEARNING EXERCISE 1.7

18 question How Good Are Your Decision-Making Skills? Quiz and Key

Instructions:

For each statement, click the button in the column that best describes you. Please answer questions as you actually are (rather than how you think you should be), and do not worry if some questions seem to score in the "wrong direction." When you are finished, please click the "Calculate My Total" button at the bottom of the test.

	Statement	Not at all	Rarely	Some times	Often	Very often
1	I evaluate the risks associated with each alternative before making a decision.	▢	▢	▢	▢	▢
2	After I make a decision, it is final—because I know my process is strong.	▢	▢	▢	▢	▢
3	I try to determine the real issue before starting a decision-making process.	▢	▢	▢	▢	▢
4	I rely on my own experience to find potential solutions to a problem.	▢	▢	▢	▢	▢
5	I tend to have a strong "gut instinct" about problems, and I rely on it in decision making.	▢	▢	▢	▢	▢
6	I am sometimes surprised by the actual consequences of my decisions.	▢	▢	▢	▢	▢
7	I use a well-defined process to structure my decisions.	▢	▢	▢	▢	▢
8	I think that involving many stakeholders to generate solutions can make the process more complicated than it needs to be.	▢	▢	▢	▢	▢
9	If I have doubts about my decision, I go back and recheck my assumptions and my process.	▢	▢	▢	▢	▢
10	I take the time needed to choose the best decision-making tool for each specific decision.	▢	▢	▢	▢	▢
11	I consider a variety of potential solutions before I make my decision.	▢	▢	▢	▢	▢
12	Before I communicate my decision, I create an implementation plan.	▢	▢	▢	▢	▢
13	In a group decision-making process, I tend to support my friends' proposals and try to find ways to make them work.	▢	▢	▢	▢	▢
14	When communicating my decision, I include my rationale and justification.	▢	▢	▢	▢	▢
15	Some of the options I've chosen have been much more difficult to implement than I had expected.	▢	▢	▢	▢	▢
16	I prefer to make decisions on my own, and then let other people know what I've decided.	▢	▢	▢	▢	▢

17	I determine the factors most important to the decision, and then use those factors to evaluate my choices.	☐	☐	☐	☐	☐
18	I emphasize how confident I am in my decision as a way to gain support for my plans.	☐	☐	☐	☐	☐

Total = 0

Score Interpretation

Score	Comment
18–42	Your decision making has not fully matured. You are not objective enough, and you rely too much on luck, instinct, or timing to make reliable decisions. Start to improve your decision-making skills by focusing more on the process that leads to the decision, rather than on the decision itself. With a solid process, you can face any decision with confidence. We will show you how.
43–66	Your decision-making process is OK. You have a good understanding of the basics, but now you need to improve your process and be more proactive. Concentrate on finding lots of options and discovering as many risks and consequences as you can. The better your analysis, the better your decision will be in the long term. Focus specifically on the areas where you lost points, and develop a system that will work for you across a wide variety of situations.
67–90	You have an excellent approach to decision making! You know how to set up the process and generate lots of potential solutions. From there, you analyze the options carefully, and you make the best decisions possible based on what you know. As you gain more and more experience, use that information to evaluate your decisions, and continue to build on your decision-making success. Think about the areas where you lost points, and decide how you can include those areas in your process.

As you answered the questions, did you see some common themes? We based our quiz on six essential steps in the decision-making process:

1. Establishing a positive decision-making environment.
2. Generating potential solutions.
3. Evaluating the solutions.
4. Deciding.
5. Checking the decision.
6. Communicating and implementing.

If you are aware of these six basic elements and improve the way you structure them, this will help you develop a better overall decision-making system. Let us look at the six elements individually.

Establishing a Positive Decision-Making Environment (Statements 3, 7, 13, and 16)

If you have ever been in a meeting where people seem to be discussing different issues, then you have seen what happens when the decision-making environment has not been established. It is so important for everyone to understand the issue before preparing to make a decision. This includes agreeing on an objective, making sure the right issue is being discussed, and agreeing on a process to move the decision forward.

You also must address key interpersonal considerations at the very beginning. Have you included all the stakeholders? And do the people involved in the decision agree to respect one another and engage in an open and honest discussion? After all, if only the strongest opinions are heard, you risk not considering some of the best solutions available.

(Continued)

Generating Potential Solutions (Statements 4, 8, and 11)

Another important part of a good decision process is generating as many good alternatives as sensibly possible to consider. If you simply adopt the first solution you encounter, then you are probably missing a great many even better alternatives.

Evaluating Alternatives (Statements 1, 6, and 15)

The stage of exploring alternatives is often the most time-consuming part of the decision-making process. This stage sometimes takes so long that a decision is never made! To make this step efficient, be clear about the factors you want to include in your analysis. There are three key factors to consider:

1. **Risk**—Most decisions involve some risk. However, you need to uncover and understand the risks to make the best choice possible.

2. **Consequences**—You cannot predict the implications of a decision with 100% accuracy. But you can be careful and systematic in the way that you identify and evaluate possible consequences.

3. **Feasibility**—Is the choice realistic and implementable? This factor is often ignored. You usually have to consider certain constraints when making a decision. As part of this evaluation stage, ensure that the alternative you have selected is significantly better than the status quo.

Deciding (Statements 5, 10, and 17)

Making the decision itself can be exciting and stressful. To help you deal with these emotions as objectively as possible, use a structured approach to the decision. This means taking a look at what is most important in a good decision.

Take the time to think ahead and determine exactly what will make the decision "right." This will significantly improve your decision accuracy.

Checking the Decision (Statements 2 and 9)

Remember that some things about a decision are not objective. The decision has to make sense on an intuitive, instinctive level as well. The entire process we have discussed so far has been based on the perspectives and experiences of all the people involved. Now, it is time to check the alternative you have chosen for validity and "making sense."

If the decision is a significant one, it is also worth auditing it to make sure that your assumptions are correct, and that the logical structure you have used to make the decision is sound.

Communicating and Implementing (Statements 12, 14, and 18)

The last stage in the decision-making process involves communicating your choice and preparing to implement it. You can try to force your decision on others by demanding their acceptance. Or you can gain their acceptance by explaining how and why you reached your decision. For most decisions—particularly those that need participant buy-in before implementation—it is more effective to gather support by explaining your decision.

Have a plan for implementing your decision. People usually respond positively to a clear plan—one that tells them what to expect and what they need to do.

Source: How Good Is Your Decision-Making? Retrieved February 6, 2013, from http://www.mindtools.com/pages/article/ newTED_79.htm. Reproduced with permission from MindTools. © Mind Tools Ltd, 1996–2013.

LEARNING EXERCISE 1.8

Considering Critical Elements in Decision Making

You are a college senior and president of your nursing organization. You are on the committee to select a slate of officers for the next academic year. Several of the current officers will be graduating, and you want the new slate of officers to be committed to the organization. Some of the brightest members of the junior class involved in the organization are not well liked by some of your friends in the organization.

Assignment: Looking at the critical elements in decision making, compile a list of the most important points to consider in making the decision for selecting a slate of officers. What must you guard against, and how should you approach the data gathering to solve this problem?

LEARNING EXERCISE 1.9

Examining the Decision-Making Process

You have been a staff nurse for the 3 years since your graduation from nursing school. There is a nursing shortage in your area and many openings at other facilities. In addition, you have been offered a charge nurse position by your present employer. Last, you have always wanted to do community health nursing and know that this is also a possibility. You are self-aware enough to know that it is time for a change, but which change, and how should you make the decision?

Assignment: Examine both the individual aspects of decision making and the critical elements in making decisions. Make a plan including a goal, a list of information, and data that you need to gather and areas where you may be vulnerable to poor decision making. Examine the consequences of each alternative available to you. After you have done this, as an individual, form a small group and share your decision-making planning with members of your group. How was your decision making like others in the group, and how was it different?

LEARNING EXERCISE 1.10

Using Models in Decision Making

Do you use a problem-solving or decision-making model to solve problems? Have you ever used an intuitive model? Think of a critical decision that you have made in the last year. What model, if any, did you use?

Assignment: Write a one-page essay about a problem that you solved or a decision that you made this year. Describe what theoretical model, if any, you used to assist you in the process. Determine if you consciously used the model or if it was purely by accident. Did you enlist the help of other experts in solving the problem?

LEARNING EXERCISE 1.11

Decision Making and Risk Taking

You are a new graduate nurse just finishing your 3-month probation period at your first job in acute care nursing. You have been working closely with a preceptor; however, he has been gradually transitioning you to more independent practice. You now have your own patient care

(Continued)

assignment and have been giving medications independently for several weeks. Today, your assignment included an elderly confused patient with severe coronary disease. Her medications include antihypertensives, antiarrhythmics, and beta-blockers. It was a very busy morning, and you have barely had a moment to reorganize and collect your thoughts.

It is now 2:30 PM, and you are preparing your handoff report. When you review the patient's 2:00 PM vital signs, you note a significant rise in this patient's blood pressure and heart rate. The patient, however, reports no distress. You remember that when you passed the morning medications, the patient was in the middle of her bath and asked that you just set the medications on the bedside table and that she would take them in a few minutes. You meant to return to see that she did but were sidetracked by a problem with another patient.

You now go to the patient's room to see if she indeed did take the pills. The pill cup and pills are not where you left them, and a search of the wastebasket, patient bed, and bedside table yields nothing. The patient is too confused to be an accurate historian regarding whether she took the pills. No one on your patient care team noticed the pills.

At this point, you are not sure what you should do next. You are frustrated that you did not wait to give the medications in person but cannot change this now. You charted the medications as being given this morning when you left them at the bedside. You are reluctant to report this as a medication error since you are still on probation and you are not sure that the patient did not take the pills as she said she would. Your probation period has not gone as smoothly as you would have liked anyway, and you are aware that reporting this incident will likely prolong your probation and that a copy of the error report will be placed in your personnel file. The patient's physician is also frequently short-tempered and will likely be agitated when you report your uncertainty about whether the patient received her prescribed medications. The reality is that if you do nothing, it is likely that no one will ever know about the problem.

You do feel responsible, however, for the patient's welfare. The physician might want to give additional doses of the medication if indeed the patient did not take the pills. In addition, the rise in heart rate and blood pressure has only just become apparent, and you realize that her heart rate and blood pressure could continue to deteriorate over the next shift. The patient is not due to receive the medications again until 9 PM tonight (b.i.d. every 12 hours).

Assignment: Decide how you will proceed. Determine whether you will use a systematic problem-solving model, intuition, or both in making your choices. How did your values, preferences, life experiences, willingness to take risks, and individual ways of thinking influence your decision?

LEARNING EXERCISE 1.12

Determining a Need to Know

You are a nursing student. You are also HIV positive as a result of some high-risk behaviors you engaged in a decade ago. (It seems like a lifetime ago.) You are now in a committed, monogamous relationship and your partner is aware of your HIV status. You have experienced relatively few side effects from the antiretroviral drugs you take and you appear to be healthy. You have not shared your sexual preferences, past history, or HIV status with any of your classmates, primarily because you do not feel that it is their business and because you fear being ostracized in the local community, which is fairly conservative.

Today, in the clinical setting, one of the students accidentally stuck herself with a needle right before she injected it into a patient. Laboratory follow-up was ordered to ensure that the patient was not exposed to any blood-borne disease from the student. Tonight, for the first time, you recognize that no matter how careful you are, there is at least a small risk that you could inadvertently expose patients to your bodily fluids and thus to some risk.

Assignment: Decide what you will do. Is there a need to share your HIV status with the school? With future employers? With patients? What determines whether there is "a need to tell" and a "need to know"? What objective weighted most heavily in your decision?

REFERENCES

Allmark, P., Baxter, S., Goyder, E., Guillaume, L., & Crofton-Martin, G. (2013). Assessing the health benefits of advice services: Using research evidence and logic model methods to explore complex pathways. *Health & Social Care in the Community, 21*(1), 59–68.

BusinessDictionary.com (2013). *Decision making. Definition.* Retrieved January 26, 2013, from http://www .businessdictionary.com/definition/decision-making .html

Decision-making-confidence.com (2006–2013). *Six step decision making process.* Retrieved January 24, 2013, from http://www.decision-making-confidence.com/ six-step-decision-making-process.html

Dictionary.com (2013). *Critical thinking. Definition.* Retrieved January 26, 2013, from *http://dictionary .reference.com/browse/critical+thinking?s=t*

Edmonds, M. (1998–2013). *Do men and women have different brains? How stuff works.* Retrieved January 25, 2013, from http://science.howstuffworks.com/life/ men-women-different-brains.htm

Hamrock, E., Paige, K., Parks, J., Scheulen, J., & Levin, S. (2013). Discrete event simulation for healthcare organizations: A tool for decision making. *Journal of Healthcare Management, 58*(2), 110–124.

How Good Is Your Decision-Making? (1996–2013). *Mind tools.* Retrieved February 6, 2013, from http://www .mindtools.com/pages/article/newTED_79.htm

Klein, G. (2008). Naturalistic decision making. *Human Factors, 50,* 456–460.

Lewis, R., Strachan, A., & Smith, M. (2012). Is high fidelity simulation the most effective method for the development of non-technical skills in nursing? A review of the current evidence. *Open Nursing Journal, 6,* 82–89.

Linn, A., Khaw, C., Kildea, H., & Tonkin, A. (2012, January/ February). Clinical reasoning. A guide to improving

teaching and practice. *Australian Family Physician, 41*(1/2), 18–20. Retrieved January 26, 2013, from http://www.racgp.org.au/download/documents/ AFP/2012/JanFeb/201201linn.pdf

Moxley, J., Anders Ericsson, K., Charness, N., & Krampe, R. (2012). The role of intuition and deliberative thinking in experts' superior tactical decision-making. *Cognition, 124*(1), 72–78.

Muoni, T. (2012). Decision-making, intuition, and the midwife: Understanding heuristics. *British Journal of Midwifery, 20*(1), 52–56.

Park, E. (2012). An integrated ethical decision-making model for nurses. *Nursing Ethics, 19*(1), 139–159.

Pearson, H. (2013). Science and intuition: Do both have a place in clinical decision making? *British Journal of Nursing, 22*(4), 212–215.

Prevost, S. (2014). Evidence-based practice. In C. Huston (Ed.), *Professional issues in nursing* (3rd ed.). Philadelphia, PA: Lippincott Williams & Wilkins.

Rigby, D. K., Gruver, K., & Allen, J. (2009, July/August). Innovation in turbulent times. *Harvard Business Review,* 79–86.

Russell, B. H., Geist, M. J., & Maffett, J. H. (2013, January). Safety: An integrated clinical reasoning and reflection framework for undergraduate nursing students. *Journal of Nursing Education, 52*(1), 59–62. Retrieved January 27, 2013, from http://www.healio .com/nursing/journals/jne/%7Bd04983cb-e91a- 4272-82d1-f44f5eab3e12%7D/safety-an-integrated -clinical-reasoning-and-reflection-framework-for -undergraduate-nursing-students

Simon, H. A. (1965). *The shape of automation for man and management.* New York, NY: Harper Textbooks.

12 Manage: The Executive Fast Track. (2013). *Whole brain model (Herrmann).* Retrieved May 14, 2013, from http://www.12manage.com/methods_herrmann _whole_brain.html

2

Classical Views of Leadership and Management

... management is efficiency in climbing the ladder of success; leadership determines whether the ladder is leaning against the right wall.
—Stephen R. Covey

... no executive has ever suffered because his subordinates were strong and effective.
—Peter Drucker

CROSSWALK THIS CHAPTER ADDRESSES:

BSN Essential II: Basic organizational and systems leadership for quality care and patient safety

BSN Essential VI: Interprofessional communication and collaboration for improving patient health outcomes

BSN Essential IX: Baccalaureate generalist nursing practice

MSN Essential II: Organizational and systems leadership

MSN Essential VII: Interprofessional collaboration for improving patient and population health outcomes

MSN Essential IX: Advanced generalist nursing practice

AONE Nurse Executive Competency I: Communication and relationship building

AONE Nurse Executive Competency II: A knowledge of the health-care environment

AONE Nurse Executive Competency III: Leadership

QSEN Competency: Teamwork and collaboration

LEARNING OBJECTIVES *The learner will:*

- discuss the evolution of management theory in relationship to changing society
- correlate management theorists with their appropriate theoretical contributions
- discuss the need for health-care managers to have highly integrated, well-developed leadership and management skills
- define the components of the management process
- differentiate between leadership roles and management functions
- identify common leadership styles and describe situations in which each leadership style could be used appropriately
- describe the differences between interactional and transformational leadership theories
- analyze the historical development of leadership theory
- differentiate between authoritative, democratic, and laissez-faire leadership styles
- identify contextual factors impacting the relationship between leaders and followers, based on full-range leadership theory
- delineate variables suggested in situational and contingency theories

The relationship between leadership and management continues to prompt some debate, although there clearly is a need for both. "Psychologists tend to define leadership in terms of interpersonal behavior, while management thinkers emphasize how leaders shape structural features of organizations" (Kaiser, Lindberg McGinnis, & Overfield, 2012, p. 120). Leadership is also viewed by some as one of management's many functions; others maintain that leadership requires more complex skills than management and that management is only one role of leadership. Still others suggest that management emphasizes *control*—control of hours, costs, salaries, overtime, use of sick leave, inventory, and supplies—whereas leadership increases productivity by maximizing workforce *effectiveness*.

But if a manager guides, directs, and motivates and a leader empowers others, then it could be said that every manager should be a leader. Similarly, leadership without management results in chaos and failure for both the organization and the individual executive.

Thompson (2012) agrees, suggesting that good management, as defined by strong planning, organizational skills, and control, allows managers to intervene when goals are threatened. But it is leadership skill that is needed to implement the planned change that is a part of system improvement. Thus, the integration of both leadership and management skills is critical to goal attainment.

Dignam et al. (2012) also agree, suggesting that since change is a primary feature of contemporary health-care environments, managers must be able to shift from a traditional focus on operational task completion to the leadership skills of visioning, motivating, and inspiring others before desired outcomes can be achieved. MacLeod (2012) echoes similar thoughts in his assertion that in the face of significant change, *both* sound management and strong leadership skills are essential to the long-term viability of today's health-care organizations.

Yet, we are all aware of individuals in leadership positions who cannot manage and individuals in management roles who cannot lead. This chapter first artificially differentiates between management and leadership, focusing on how theory development in each field of study has changed over time, and then concludes with a discussion of how closely integrated the two roles must actually be for individuals in contemporary leadership or management roles.

MANAGERS

Dictionary.com (2013, para 1) defines *management* as "the act or manner of guiding or taking charge" or "handling, direction, or control." Both definitions imply that management is the process of leading and directing all or part of an organization, often a business, through the deployment and manipulation of resources. Managers then typically:

- Have an assigned position within the formal organization.
- Have a legitimate source of power due to the delegated authority that accompanies their position.
- Are expected to carry out specific functions, duties, and responsibilities.
- Emphasize control, decision making, decision analysis, and results.
- Manipulate people, the environment, money, time, and other resources to achieve organizational goals.
- Have a greater formal responsibility and accountability for rationality and control than leaders.
- Direct willing and unwilling subordinates.

 Management is the process of leading and directing all or part of an organization through the deployment and manipulation of resources.

LEADERS

Although the term *leader* has been in use since the 1300s, the word *leadership* was not known in the English language until the first half of the 19th century. Despite its relatively new addition to the English language, leadership has many meanings and there is no single definition broad enough to encompass the total leadership process.

To examine the word *leader*, however, is to note that leaders lead. Leaders are those individuals who are out front, taking risks, attempting to achieve shared goals, and inspiring others to action. Those individuals who choose to follow a leader do so by choice, not because they have to. Kaiser et al. (2012) agree, suggesting that the essence of leadership is a social influence process where leaders use interpersonal behaviors to motivate followers to commit and give their best effort to contribute to group goals.

Leaders are in the front, moving forward, taking risks, and challenging the status quo.

It is important to remember though that a job title alone does not make a person a leader. Only a person's behavior determines if he or she holds a leadership role. The manager is the person who brings things about—the one who accomplishes, has the responsibility, and conducts. A leader is the person who influences and guides direction, opinion, and course of action. Display 2.1 includes a partial list of common leadership roles.

DISPLAY 2.1	Leadership Roles	
Decision maker	Coach	Forecaster
Communicator	Counselor	Influencer
Evaluator	Teacher	Creative problem solver
Facilitator	Critical thinker	Change agent
Risk taker	Buffer	Diplomat
Mentor	Advocate	Role model
Energizer	Visionary	Innovator

Other characteristics of leaders include the following:

- Leaders often do not have delegated authority but obtain their power through other means, such as influence.
- Leaders have a wider variety of roles than do managers.
- Leaders may or may not be part of the formal organization.
- Leaders focus on group process, information gathering, feedback, and empowering others.
- Leaders emphasize interpersonal relationships.
- Leaders direct willing followers.
- Leaders have goals that may or may not reflect those of the organization.

LEARNING EXERCISE 2.1

Leadership Roles and Management Functions

In small or large groups, discuss your views of management and leadership. Do you believe they are the same or different? If you believe that they are different, do you think that they have the same importance for the future of nursing? Do you feel that one is more important than the other? How can novice nurse-managers learn important management functions and develop leadership skills?

It is important to remember that all it takes to stop being a leader is to have others stop following you. Leadership then is more dynamic than management and leaders do make mistakes that can result in the loss of their followers. For example, Zenger and Folkman (2009), using 360-degree feedback data from more than 450 Fortune 500 executives, identified 10 fatal flaws that derail leaders (see Display 2.2). Although these flaws seem fairly obvious, many ineffective leaders are unaware that they exhibit these behaviors.

DISPLAY 2.2   Ten Fatal Leadership Flaws

1. A lack of energy and enthusiasm
2. Acceptance of their own mediocre performance
3. Lack of a clear vision and direction
4. Having poor judgment
5. Not collaborating
6. Not walking the talk
7. Resisting new ideas
8. Not learning from mistakes
9. A lack of interpersonal skills
10. Failing to develop others

Source: Zenger, J., & Folkman, J. (2009). Ten fatal flaws that derail leaders. Harvard Business Review. *18.*

HISTORICAL DEVELOPMENT OF MANAGEMENT THEORY

Management science, like nursing, develops a theory base from many disciplines, such as business, psychology, sociology, and anthropology. Because organizations are complex and varied, theorists' views of what successful management is and what it should be have changed repeatedly in the last 100 years.

Theorists' views of what successful management is and what it should be have changed repeatedly in the last 100 years.

Scientific Management (1900 to 1930)

Frederick W. Taylor, the "father of scientific management," was a mechanical engineer in the Midvale and Bethlehem Steel plants in Pennsylvania in the late 1800s. Frustrated with what he called "systematic soldiering," where workers achieved minimum standards doing the least amount of work possible, Taylor postulated that if workers could be taught the "one best way to accomplish a task," productivity would increase. Borrowing a term coined by Louis Brandeis, a colleague of Taylor's, Taylor called these principles *scientific management*. The four overriding principles of scientific management as identified by Taylor (1911) are:

1. Traditional "rule of thumb" means of organizing work must be replaced with scientific methods. In other words, by using time and motion studies and the expertise of experienced workers, work could be scientifically designed to promote greatest efficiency of time and energy.
2. A scientific personnel system must be established so that workers can be hired, trained, and promoted based on their technical competence and abilities. Taylor thought that each employee's abilities and limitations could be identified so that the worker could be best matched to the most appropriate job.
3. Workers should be able to view how they "fit" into the organization and how they contribute to overall organizational productivity. This provides common goals and

a sharing of the organizational mission. One way Taylor thought that this could be accomplished was by the use of financial incentives as a reward for work accomplished. Because Taylor viewed humans as "economic animals" motivated solely by money, workers were reimbursed according to their level of production rather than by an hourly wage.

4. The relationship between managers and workers should be cooperative and interdependent, and the work should be shared equally. Their roles, however, were not the same. The role of managers, or *functional foremen* as they were called, was to plan, prepare, and supervise. The worker was to do the work.

What was the result of scientific management? Productivity and profits rose dramatically. Organizations were provided with a rational means of harnessing the energy of the industrial revolution. Some experts have argued that Taylor lacked humanism and that his scientific principles were not in the best interest of unions or workers. However, it is important to remember the era in which Taylor did his work. During the Industrial Revolution, laissez-faire economics prevailed, optimism was high, and a Puritan work ethic prevailed. Taylor maintained that he truly believed managers and workers would be satisfied if financial rewards were adequate as a result of increased productivity. As the cost of labor rises in the United States, many organizations are taking a new look at scientific management with the implication that we need to think of new ways to do traditional tasks so that work is more efficient.

LEARNING EXERCISE 2.2

Strategies for Efficiency

In small groups, discuss some work routines carried out in health-care organizations that seem to be inefficient. Could such routines or the time and motion involved to carry out a task be altered to improve efficiency without jeopardizing quality of care? Make a list of ways that nurses could work more efficiently. Do not limit your examination to only nursing procedures and routines, but examine the impact that other departments or the arrangement of the nurse's work area may have on preventing nurses from working more efficiently. Share your ideas with your peers.

About the same time that Taylor was examining worker tasks, Max Weber, a well-known German sociologist, began to study large-scale organizations to determine what made some workers more efficient than others. Weber saw the need for legalized, formal authority and consistent rules and regulations for personnel in different positions; he thus proposed *bureaucracy* as an organizational design. His essay "Bureaucracy" was written in 1922 in response to what he perceived as a need to provide more rules, regulations, and structure within organizations to increase efficiency. Much of Weber's work and bureaucratic organizational design are still evident today in many health-care institutions. His work is discussed further in Chapter 12.

Management Functions Identified (1925)

Henri Fayol (1925) first identified the management functions of planning, organization, command, coordination, and control. Luther Gulick (1937) expanded on Fayol's management functions in his introduction of the "seven activities of management"—planning, organizing, staffing, directing, coordinating, reporting, and budgeting—as

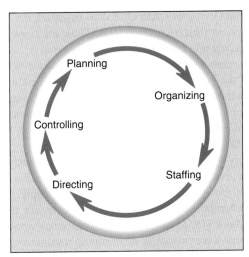

FIGURE 2.1 • The management process.

denoted by the mnemonic POSDCORB. Although often modified (either by including staffing as a management function or renaming elements), these functions or activities have changed little over time. Eventually, theorists began to refer to these functions as the management process.

The *management process*, shown in Figure 2.1, is this book's organizing framework. Brief descriptions of the five functions for each phase of the management process follow:

1. *Planning* encompasses determining philosophy, goals, objectives, policies, procedures, and rules; carrying out long- and short-range projections; determining a fiscal course of action; and managing planned change.
2. *Organizing* includes establishing the structure to carry out plans, determining the most appropriate type of patient care delivery, and grouping activities to meet unit goals. Other functions involve working within the structure of the organization and understanding and using power and authority appropriately.
3. *Staffing* functions consist of recruiting, interviewing, hiring, and orienting staff. Scheduling, staff development, employee socialization, and team building are also often included as staffing functions.
4. *Directing* sometimes includes several staffing functions. However, this phase's functions usually entail human resource management responsibilities, such as motivating, managing conflict, delegating, communicating, and facilitating collaboration.
5. *Controlling* functions include performance appraisals, fiscal accountability, quality control, legal and ethical control, and professional and collegial control.

Human Relations Management (1930 to 1970)

During the 1920s, worker unrest developed. The Industrial Revolution had resulted in great numbers of relatively unskilled laborers working in large factories on specialized tasks. Thus, management scientists and organizational theorists began to look at the role of worker satisfaction in production. This *human relations era* developed the concepts of participatory and humanistic management, emphasizing people rather than machines.

Mary Parker Follett (1926) was one of the first theorists to suggest basic principles of what today would be called *participative decision making* or *participative management*.

In her essay "The Giving of Orders," Follett espoused her belief that managers should have authority with, rather than over, employees. Thus, solutions could be found that satisfied both sides without having one side dominate the other.

The human relations era also attempted to correct what was perceived as the major shortcoming of the bureaucratic system—a failure to include the "human element." Studies done at the Hawthorne Works of the Western Electric Company near Chicago between 1927 and 1932 played a major role in this shifting focus. The studies, conducted by Elton Mayo and his Harvard associates, began as an attempt to look at the relationship between light illumination in the factory and productivity.

Mayo and his colleagues discovered that when management paid special attention to workers, productivity was likely to increase, regardless of the environmental working conditions. This *Hawthorne effect* indicated that people respond to the fact that they are being studied, attempting to increase whatever behavior they feel will continue to warrant the attention. Mayo (1953) also found that informal work groups and a socially informal work environment were factors in determining productivity, and Mayo recommended more employee participation in decision making.

Douglas McGregor (1960) reinforced these ideas by theorizing that managerial attitudes about employees (and, hence, how managers treat those employees) can be directly correlated with employee satisfaction. He labeled this *Theory X* and *Theory Y*. Theory X managers believe that their employees are basically lazy, need constant supervision and direction, and are indifferent to organizational needs. Theory Y managers believe that their workers enjoy their work, are self-motivated, and are willing to work hard to meet personal and organizational goals.

Chris Argyris (1964) supported McGregor and Mayo by saying that managerial domination causes workers to become discouraged and passive. He believed that if self-esteem and independence needs are not met, employees will become discouraged and troublesome or may leave the organization. Argyris stressed the need for flexibility within the organization and employee participation in decision making.

The human relations era of management science brought about a great interest in the study of workers. Many sociologists and psychologists took up this challenge, and their work in management theory contributed to our understanding about worker motivation, which will be discussed in Chapter 18. Table 2.1 summarizes the development of management theory up to 1970. By the late 1960s, however, there was growing concern that the human relations approach to management was not without its problems. Most people continued to work in a bureaucratic environment, making it difficult to always apply a participatory approach to management. The human relations approach was time consuming and often resulted in unmet organizational goals. In addition, not every employee liked working in a less structured environment. This resulted in a greater recognition of the need to intertwine management and leadership than ever before.

TABLE 2.1   Management Theory Development 1900 to 1970

Theorist	Theory
Taylor	Scientific management
Weber	Bureaucratic organizations
Fayol	Management functions
Gulick	Activities of management
Follett	Participative management
Mayo	Hawthorne effect
McGregor	Theories X and Y
Argyris	Employee participation

HISTORICAL DEVELOPMENT OF LEADERSHIP THEORY (1900 TO PRESENT)

Because strong management skills were historically valued more than strong leadership skills, the scientific study of leadership did not begin until the 20th century. Early works focused on broad conceptualizations of leadership, such as the traits or behaviors of the leader. Contemporary research focuses more on leadership as a process of influencing others within an organizational culture and the interactive relationship of the leader and follower. To better understand newer views about leadership, it is necessary to look at how leadership theory has evolved over the last century.

 Like management theory, leadership theory has been dynamic; that is, what is "known" and believed about leadership continues to change over time.

The Great Man Theory/Trait Theories (1900 to 1940)

The *Great Man theory* and *trait theories* were the basis for most leadership research until the mid-1940s. The Great Man theory, from Aristotelian philosophy, asserts that some people are born to lead, whereas others are born to be led. It also suggests that great leaders will arise when the situation demands it.

Trait theories assume that some people have certain characteristics or personality traits that make them better leaders than others. To determine the traits that distinguish great leaders, researchers studied the lives of prominent people throughout history. The effect of followers and the impact of the situation were ignored. Although trait theories have obvious shortcomings (e.g., they neglect the impact of others or the situation on the leadership role), they are worth examining. Many of the characteristics identified in trait theories (Display 2.3) are still used to describe successful leaders today.

Contemporary opponents of these theories argue that leadership skills can be developed, not just inherited. Avolio, Walumbwa, and Weber (2009) suggest, however, that very little work has been done in the last 100 years to determine whether leadership can actually be developed. A recent meta-analytic review suggested that only about one-third of the 201 interventional leadership studies focused on developing leadership skills rather than manipulating it for impact.

 Perhaps leaders are both born and made that way.

LEARNING EXERCISE 2.3

Effective Leadership

In groups or individually, list additional characteristics that you believe an effective leader possesses. Which leadership characteristics do you have? Do you believe that you were born with leadership skills, or have you consciously developed them during your lifetime? If so, how did you develop them?

Behavioral Theories (1940 to 1980)

During the human relations era, many behavioral and social scientists studying management also studied leadership. For example, McGregor's (1960) theories had as much influence on leadership research as they did on management science. As leadership theory developed, researchers moved away from studying what traits the leader had and placed emphasis on what he or she did—the leader's style of leadership.

DISPLAY 2.3	Characteristics Associated with Leadership	
Intelligence	Adaptability	Ability
Knowledge	Creativity	Able to enlist cooperation
Judgment	Cooperativeness	Interpersonal skills
Decisiveness	Alertness	Tact
Oral fluency	Self-confidence	Diplomacy
Emotional intelligence	Personal integrity	Prestige
Independence	Emotional balance and control	Social participation
Personable	Risk taking	Charisma

A major breakthrough occurred when Lewin (1951) and White and Lippitt (1960) isolated common *leadership styles*. Later, these styles came to be called authoritarian, democratic, and laissez-faire.

The *authoritarian* leader is characterized by the following behaviors:

- Strong control is maintained over the work group.
- Others are motivated by coercion.
- Others are directed with commands.
- Communication flows downward.
- Decision making does not involve others.
- Emphasis is on difference in status ("I" and "you").
- Criticism is punitive.

Authoritarian leadership results in well-defined group actions that are usually predictable, reducing frustration in the work group and giving members a feeling of security. Productivity is usually high, but creativity, self-motivation, and autonomy are reduced. Authoritarian leadership is frequently found in very large bureaucracies such as the armed forces.

The *democratic* leader exhibits the following behaviors:

- Less control is maintained.
- Economic and ego awards are used to motivate.
- Others are directed through suggestions and guidance.
- Communication flows up and down.
- Decision making involves others.
- Emphasis is on "we" rather than "I" and "you."
- Criticism is constructive.

Democratic leadership, appropriate for groups who work together for extended periods, promotes autonomy and growth in individual workers. In fact, Wong (2012) suggests that *relational leadership styles* such as democratic leadership are related to both positive nurse and patient outcomes since they emphasize the leader's ability to create positive relationships within the organization. Democratic leadership is particularly effective when cooperation and coordination between groups are necessary. Studies have shown, however, that democratic leadership may be less efficient quantitatively than authoritative leadership.

Because many people must be consulted, democratic leadership takes more time and, therefore, may be frustrating for those who want decisions made rapidly.

The *laissez-faire* leader is characterized by the following behaviors:

- Is permissive, with little or no control.
- Motivates by support when requested by the group or individuals.
- Provides little or no direction.
- Uses upward and downward communication between members of the group.
- Disperses decision making throughout the group.
- Places emphasis on the group.
- Does not criticize.

Because it is nondirected leadership, the laissez-faire style can be frustrating; group apathy and disinterest can occur. However, when all group members are highly motivated and self-directed, this leadership style can result in much creativity and productivity. Laissez-faire leadership is appropriate when problems are poorly defined and brainstorming is needed to generate alternative solutions.

 A person's leadership style has a great deal of influence on the climate and outcome of the work group.

LEARNING EXERCISE 2.4

What Is Your Leadership Style?

Define your predominant leadership style. Ask those who work with you if in their honest opinion this is indeed the leadership style that you use most often. What style of leadership do you work best under? What leadership style best describes your present or former managers?

For some time, theorists believed that leaders had a predominant leadership style and used it consistently. During the late 1940s and early 1950s, however, theorists began to believe that most leaders did not fit a textbook picture of any one style but rather fell somewhere on a continuum between authoritarian and laissez-faire. They also came to believe that leaders moved dynamically along the continuum in response to each new situation. This recognition was a forerunner to what is known as *situational* or *contingency* leadership theory.

Situational and Contingency Leadership Theories (1950 to 1980)

The idea that leadership style should vary according to the situation or the individuals involved was first suggested almost 100 years ago by Mary Parker Follett, one of the earliest management consultants and among the first to view an organization as a social system of contingencies. Her ideas, published in a series of books between 1896 and 1933, were so far ahead of their time that they did not gain appropriate recognition in the literature until the 1970s. Her *law of the situation*, which said that the situation should determine the directives given after allowing everyone to know the problem, was *contingency leadership* in its humble origins.

Fiedler's (1967) *contingency approach* reinforced these findings, suggesting that no one leadership style is ideal for every situation. Fiedler felt that the interrelationships between the group's leader and its members were most influenced by the manager's ability to be a good leader. The task to be accomplished and the power associated with the leader's position also were cited as key variables.

In contrast to the continuum from autocratic to democratic, Blake and Mouton's (1964) grid showed various combinations of concern or focus that managers had for or on productivity, tasks, people, and relationships. In each of these areas, the leader-manager may rank high or low, resulting in numerous combinations of leadership behaviors. Various formations can be effective depending on the situation and the needs of the worker.

Hersey and Blanchard (1977) also developed a situational approach to leadership. Their tridimensional leadership effectiveness model predicts which leadership style is most appropriate in each situation on the basis of the level of the followers' maturity. As people mature, leadership style becomes less task focused and more relationship oriented.

Tannenbaum and Schmidt (1958) built on the work of Lewin and White, suggesting that managers need varying mixtures of autocratic and democratic leadership behavior. They believed that the primary determinants of leadership style should include the nature of the situation, the skills of the manager, and the abilities of the group members.

Although situational and contingency theories added necessary complexity to leadership theory and continue to be applied effectively by managers, by the late 1970s, theorists began arguing that effective leadership depended on an even greater number of variables, including organizational culture, the values of the leader and the followers, the work, the environment, the influence of the leader-manager, and the complexities of the situation. Efforts to integrate these variables are apparent in more contemporary interactional and transformational leadership theories.

INTERACTIONAL LEADERSHIP THEORIES (1970 TO PRESENT)

The basic premise of interactional theory is that leadership behavior is generally determined by the relationship between the leader's personality and the specific situation. Schein (1970), an interactional theorist, was the first to propose a model of humans as complex beings whose working environment was an open system to which they responded. A *system* may be defined as a set of objects, with relationships between the objects and between their attributes. A system is considered open if it exchanges matter, energy, or information with its environment. Schein's model, based on systems theory, had the following assumptions:

- People are very complex and highly variable. They have multiple motives for doing things. For example, a pay raise might mean status to one person, security to another, and both to a third.
- People's motives do not stay constant but change over time.
- Goals can differ in various situations. For example, an informal group's goals may be quite distinct from a formal group's goals.
- A person's performance and productivity are affected by the nature of the task and by his or her ability, experience, and motivation.
- No single leadership strategy is effective in every situation.

To be successful, the leader must diagnose the situation and select appropriate strategies from a large repertoire of skills. Hollander (1978) was among the first to recognize that both leaders and followers have roles outside of the leadership situation and that both may be influenced by events occurring in their other roles.

With leader and follower contributing to the working relationship and both receiving something from it, Hollander (1978) saw leadership as a dynamic two-way process. According to Hollander, a leadership exchange involves three basic elements:

- The leader, including his or her personality, perceptions, and abilities.
- The followers, with their personalities, perceptions, and abilities.
- The situation within which the leader and the followers function, including formal and informal group norms, size, and density.

Leadership effectiveness, according to Hollander, requires the ability to use the problem-solving process; maintain group effectiveness; communicate well; demonstrate leader fairness, competence, dependability, and creativity; and develop group identification.

Ouchi (1981) was a pioneer in introducing interactional leadership theory in his application of Japanese style management to corporate America. *Theory Z*, the term Ouchi used for this type of management, is an expansion of McGregor's Theory Y and supports democratic leadership. Characteristics of Theory Z include consensus decision making, fitting employees to their jobs, job security, slower promotions, examining the long-term consequences of management decision making, quality circles, guarantee of lifetime employment, establishment of strong bonds of responsibility between superiors and subordinates, and a holistic concern for the workers (Ouchi, 1981). Ouchi was able to find components of Japanese-style management in many successful American companies.

In the 1990s, Theory Z lost its favor with many management theorists. American managers are unable to put these same ideas into practice in the United States. Instead, they continue to boss-manage workers in an attempt to make them do what they do not want to do. Although Theory Z is more comprehensive than many of the earlier theories, it too neglects some of the variables that influence leadership effectiveness. It has the same shortcomings as situational theories in inadequately recognizing the dynamics of the interaction between the worker and the leader.

One of the pioneering leadership theorists of this time was Kanter (1977), who developed the theory that the structural aspects of the job shape a leader's effectiveness. She postulated that the leader becomes empowered through both formal and informal systems of the organization. A leader must develop relationships with a variety of people and groups within the organization in order to maximize job empowerment and be successful. The three major work empowerment structures within the organization are opportunity, power, and proportion. Kanter asserts that these work structures have the potential to explain differences in leader responses, behaviors, and attitudes in the work environment.

Nelson and Burns (1984) suggested that organizations and their leaders have four developmental levels and that these levels influence productivity and worker satisfaction. The first of these levels is *reactive*. The reactive leader focuses on the past, is crisis driven, and is frequently abusive to subordinates. In the next level, *responsive*, the leader is able to mold subordinates to work together as a team, although the leader maintains most decision-making responsibility. At the *proactive* level, the leader and followers become more future oriented and hold common driving values. Management and decision making are more participative. At the last level, *high-performance teams*, maximum productivity and worker satisfaction are apparent.

Brandt's (1994) interactive leadership model suggests that leaders develop a work environment that fosters autonomy and creativity through valuing and empowering followers. This leadership "affirms the uniqueness of each individual," motivating them to "contribute their unique talents to a common goal." The leader must accept the responsibility for quality of outcomes and quality of life for followers. Brandt states that this type of leadership affords the leader greater freedom while simultaneously adding to the burdens of leadership. The leader's responsibilities increase because priorities cannot be limited to the organization's goals, and authority confers not only power but also responsibility and obligation. The leader's concern for each worker decreases the need for competition and fosters an atmosphere of collegiality, freeing the leader from the burden of having to resolve follower conflicts.

Wolf, Boland, and Aukerman (1994) also emphasized an interactive leadership model in their creation of a *collaborative practice matrix*. This matrix highlights the framework for the development and ongoing support of relationships between and among professionals working together. The "social architecture" of the work group is emphasized, as is how expectations, personal values, and interpersonal relationships affect the ability of leaders and followers to achieve the vision of the organization.

Kanter (1989) perhaps best summarized the work of the interactive theorists by her assertion that title and position authority were no longer sufficient to mold a workforce where subordinates are encouraged to think for themselves, and instead managers must learn to work synergistically with others.

Transactional and Transformational Leadership

Similarly, Burns (2003), a noted scholar in the area of leader–follower interactions, was among the first to suggest that both leaders and followers have the ability to raise each other to higher levels of motivation and morality. Identifying this concept as *transformational leadership*, Burns maintained that there are two primary types of leaders in management. The traditional manager, concerned with the day-to-day operations, was termed a *transactional leader*. The manager who is committed, has a vision, and is able to empower others with this vision was termed a *transformational leader*. A composite of the two different types of leaders is shown in Table 2.2.

Transactional leaders focus on tasks and getting the work done. Transformational leaders focus on vision and empowerment.

Similarly, Bass and Avolio (1994) suggested that transformational leadership leads followers to levels of higher morals because such leaders do the right thing for the right reason, treat people with care and compassion, encourage followers to be more creative and innovative, and inspire others with their vision. This new shared vision provides the energy required to move toward the future.

Doody and Doody (2012) agree, suggesting that traditionally, nurses have been overmanaged and inadequately led, and that contemporary health-care organizations need increasingly adaptive and flexible leadership. Doody and Doody suggest that transformational leadership "motivates followers by appealing to higher ideas and moral values, where the leader has a deep set of internal values and ideas. This leads followers acting to sustain the greater good, rather than their own interests, and supportive environments where responsibility is shared" (p. 1212).

Kouzes and Posner (2007) are perhaps the best known authors to further the work on transformational leadership in the past decade. Kouzes and Posner suggest that exemplary leaders foster a culture in which relationships between aspiring leaders and willing followers can thrive. This requires the development of the five practices shown in Display 2.4. Kouzes and Posner suggest that when these five practices are employed, anyone can further their ability to lead others to get extraordinary things done.

TABLE 2.2 Transactional and Transformational Leaders	
Transformational Leader	*Transactional Leader*
Focuses on management tasks	Identifies common values
Is committed	Is a caretaker
Uses trade-offs to meet goals	Inspires others with vision
Does not identify shared values	Has long-term vision
Examines causes	Looks at effects
Uses contingency reward	Empowers others

DISPLAY 2.4   Kouzes and Posner's Five Practices for Exemplary Leadership

1. **Modeling the way:** Requires value clarification and self-awareness so that behavior is congruent with values.
2. **Inspiring a shared vision:** Entails visioning which inspires followers to want to participate in goal attainment.
3. **Challenging the process:** Identifying opportunities and taking action.
4. **Enabling others to act:** Fostering collaboration, trust, and the sharing of power.
5. **Encouraging the heart:** Recognize, appreciate, and celebrate followers and the achievement of shared goals.

Source: Kouzes, J., & Posner, B. (2007). The leadership challenge (4th ed.). San Francisco, CA: Jossey Bass.

Although the transformational leader is held as the current ideal, many management theorists sound a warning about transformational leadership. Although transformational qualities are highly desirable, they must be coupled with the more traditional transactional qualities of the day-to-day managerial role. In addition, both sets of characteristics need to be present in the same person in varying degrees. The transformational leader will fail without traditional management skills. Indeed, Avolio et al. (2009, p. 428) note that much of the disillusionment with leadership theory and research in the early 1980s was related to "the fact that most models of leadership and measures accounted for a relatively small percentage of variance in performance outcomes such as productivity and effectiveness."

Although transformational qualities are highly desirable, they must be coupled with the more traditional transactional qualities of the day-to-day managerial role or the leader will fail.

In addition, Badaracco cautions that "because we admire heroes, it is easy to overlook the inconvenient fact that some leaders are effective without being either visionary or very inspiring. There must be a place for leading by example and other forms of quiet leadership" (McCrimmon, n.d., para 2). Similarly, the North Carolina Center for Student Leadership in Ethics & Public Service (2009) warns that transformational leaders must be careful not to mistake passion and confidence for truth and reality. "Whilst it is true that great things have been achieved through enthusiastic leadership, it is also true that many passionate people have led the charge right over the cliff and into a bottomless chasm. Just because someone *believes* they are right, it does not mean they *are* right" (para 14).

Finally, recent research by Braun, Peus, and Frey (2012) suggests another potential limitation to holding transformational leadership as the ideal. Their attempt to test the interaction effects of leader gender, leader attractiveness, and leadership style on followers' trust and loyalty found that attractive females using transformational leadership skills struggled more than less attractive females to gain follower support and trust; the so-called *beauty is beastly effect.* The same results did not occur for attractive males. It also did not occur when transactional leadership skills were used. These study results hold implications for female leaders, for followers, and for anyone who evaluates leaders and their effectiveness in organizational contexts. (See Examining the Evidence 2.1.)

Full-Range Leadership Theory

It is this idea that context is an important mediator of transformational leadership that led to the creation of *full-range leadership theory* early in the 21st century. This theory, originally developed by Antonakis, Avolio, and Sivasubramaniam (2003), suggests that there are nine

Examining the Evidence 2.1

Source: Braun, S., Peus, C., & Frey, D. (2012). Is beauty beastly?: Gender-specific effects of leader attractiveness and leadership style on followers' trust and loyalty. Zeitschrift Für Psychologie, 220(2), 98–108.

Two hundred and fifty-three undergraduate students (127 female and 126 male) with an average age of 21.9 years from a German university participated in this study. Leader gender (male versus female), leader attractiveness (attractive versus unattractive), and leadership style (transformational versus transactional) were varied in a 2 × 2 × 2 between-subjects design. Participant gender (male versus female) was accounted for as a quasi-experimental factor. Participant evaluations of trust, loyalty, and ascribed leader communion were collected as measures of dependent and mediating variables, respectively.

   Attractive when compared with unattractive female leaders elicited lower levels of trust and loyalty in their followers when they displayed a transformational leadership style, but not when they displayed a transactional leadership style. The researchers suggested that these study findings had important implications in at least four regards: (1) The study raised the awareness of the potential impact of physical appearance on the ability of female leaders to successfully employ transformational leadership strategies; (2) to counteract biased evaluations toward attractive female leaders, leadership assessments must be conducted in a structured manner, primarily based on behavioral criteria with relevance to their effectiveness as a leader as opposed to aspects related to candidates' gender role; (3) the practice of attaching portraits to application materials challenges the fairness of selection procedures for male and female applications; and (4) enhanced training of all (future) female leaders and young professionals in general is needed with regard to the pitfalls of biased perceptions and evaluations based on gender stereotypes in organizational settings.

factors impacting leadership style and its impact on followers; five are transformational, three are transactional, and one is a nonleadership or laissez-faire leadership factor (Rowold & Schlotz, 2009) (see Display 2.5).

DISPLAY 2.5   Nine Factors of Full-Range Leadership Theory

Factor 1	Inspirational motivation	Transformational
Factor 2	Idealized influence (attributed)	Transformational
Factor 3	Idealized influence (behavior)	Transformational
Factor 4	Intellectual stimulation	Transformational
Factor 5	Individualized consideration	Transformational
Factor 6	Contingent reward	Transactional
Factor 7	Active management-by-exception	Transactional
Factor 8	Management-by-exception passive	Transactional
Factor 9	Nonleadership	Laissez-faire

   In describing these factors, Rowold and Schlotz (2009) suggest that the first factor, *inspirational motivation*, is characterized by the leader's articulation and representation of vision. *Idealized influence (attributed)*, the second factor, relies on the charisma of the leader to create emotional ties with followers that build trust and confidence. The third factor, *idealized influence (behavior)*, results in the leader creating a collective sense of mission and values and prompting followers to act upon these values. With the fourth factor, *intellectual stimulation*, leaders challenge the assumptions of followers' beliefs as well as analyze subordinates' problems and possible solutions. The final transformational factor, *individualized consideration*, occurs when the leader is able to individualize his or her followers, recognizing and appreciating their unique needs, strengths, and challenges.

The first transactional factor, as described by Rowold and Schlotz (2009), is *contingent reward*. Here, the leader is task oriented in providing followers with meaningful rewards based on successful task completion. *Active management-by-exception*, the second transactional factor, suggests that the leader watches and searches actively for deviations from rules and standards and takes corrective actions when necessary. In contrast, the third transactional factor, *management-by-exception passive*, describes a leader who intervenes only after errors have been detected or standards have been violated. Finally, the ninth factor of full-range leadership theory is the *absence of leadership*. Thus, laissez-faire is a contrast to the active leadership styles of transformational and transactional leadership exemplified in the first eight factors.

Leadership Competencies

Just as Fayol and Gulick identified management functions, contemporary leadership experts suggest that there are certain competencies (skills, knowledge, and abilities) health-care leaders need to be successful. The American College of Healthcare Executives, the American College of Physician Executives, the American Organization of Nurse Executives, the Healthcare Information and Management Systems Society, the Healthcare Financial Management Association, and the Medical Group Management Association have collaborated to identify leadership competencies, which included leadership skills and behavior; organizational climate and culture; communicating vision; and managing change (Esparza and Rubino, 2014).

 ## INTEGRATING LEADERSHIP AND MANAGEMENT

Because rapid, dramatic change will continue in nursing and the health-care industry, it has grown increasingly important for nurses to develop skill in both leadership roles and management functions. For managers and leaders to function at their greatest potential, the two must be integrated.

Gardner (1990) asserted that *integrated leader-managers* possess six distinguishing traits:

1. *They think longer term*: They are visionary and futuristic. They consider the effect that their decisions will have years from now as well as their immediate consequences.
2. *They look outward, toward the larger organization*: They do not become narrowly focused. They are able to understand how their unit or department fits into the bigger picture.
3. *They influence others beyond their own group*: Effective leader-managers rise above an organization's bureaucratic boundaries.
4. *They emphasize vision, values, and motivation*: They understand intuitively the unconscious and often nonrational aspects that are present in interactions with others. They are very sensitive to others and to differences in each situation.
5. *They are politically astute*: They are capable of coping with conflicting requirements and expectations from their many constituencies.
6. *They think in terms of change and renewal*: The traditional manager accepts the structure and processes of the organization, but the leader-manager examines the ever-changing reality of the world and seeks to revise the organization to keep pace.

Leadership and management skills can and should be integrated as they are learned. Table 2.3 summarizes the development of leadership theory through the end of the 20th century. Newer (21st century) and emerging leadership theories are discussed in Chapter 3.

TABLE 2.3	Leadership Theorists and Theories
Theorist	*Theory*
Aristotle	Great Man theory
Lewin and White	Leadership styles
Follett	Law of the situation
Fiedler	Contingency leadership
Blake and Mouton	Task versus relationship in determining leadership style
Hersey and Blanchard	Situational leadership theory
Tannenbaum and Schmidt	Situational leadership theory
Kanter	Organizational structure shapes leader effectiveness
Burns	Transactional and transformational leadership
Bass and Avolio	Transformational leadership
Gardner	The integrated leader-manager

In examining leadership and management, it becomes clear that these two concepts have a symbiotic or synergistic relationship. Every nurse is a leader and manager at some level, and the nursing role requires leadership and management skills. The need for visionary leaders and effective managers in nursing preclude the option of stressing one role over the other. Highly developed management skills are needed to maintain healthy organizations. So too are the visioning and empowerment of subordinates through an organization's leadership team. Because rapid, dramatic change will continue in nursing and the health-care industry, it continues to be critically important for nurses to develop skill in both leadership roles and management functions and to strive for the integration of leadership characteristics throughout every phase of the management process.

KEY CONCEPTS

- Management functions include planning, organizing, staffing, directing, and controlling. These are incorporated into what is known as the management process.

- Classical, or traditional, management science focused on production in the workplace and on delineating organizational barriers to productivity. Workers were assumed to be motivated solely by economic rewards, and little attention was given to worker job satisfaction.

- The human relations era of management science emphasized concepts of participatory and humanistic management.

- Three primary leadership styles have been identified: authoritarian, democratic, and laissez-faire.

- Research has shown that the leader-manager must assume a variety of leadership styles, depending on the needs of the worker, the task to be performed, and the situation or environment. This is known as situational or contingency leadership theory.

- Leadership is a process of persuading and influencing others toward a goal and is composed of a wide variety of roles.

- Early leadership theories focused on the traits and characteristics of leaders.

- Interactional leadership theory focuses more on leadership as a process of influencing others within an organizational culture and the interactive relationship of the leader and follower.

- The manager who is committed, has a vision, and is able to empower others with this vision is termed a transformational leader, whereas the traditional manager, concerned with the day-to-day operations, is called a transactional leader.

- Full-range leadership theory suggests that context is an important mediator of transformational leadership.

- Integrating leadership skills with the ability to carry out management functions is necessary if an individual is to become an effective leader-manager.

ADDITIONAL LEARNING EXERCISES

LEARNING EXERCISE 2.5

When Culture and Policy Clash

You are the nurse-manager of a medical unit. Recently, your unit admitted a 16-year-old East Indian boy who has been newly diagnosed with insulin-dependent diabetes. The nursing staff has been interested in his case and has found him to be a delightful young man—very polite and easygoing. However, his family has been visiting in increasing numbers and bringing him food that he should not have.

The nursing staff has come to you on two occasions and complained about the family's noncompliance with visiting hours and unauthorized food. Normally, the nursing staff on your unit has tried to develop a culturally sensitive nursing care plan for patients with special cultural needs, so their complaints to you have taken you by surprise.

Yesterday, two of the family members visited you and complained about hospital visitor policies and what they took to be rudeness by two different staff members. You spent time talking to the family, and when they left, they seemed agreeable and understanding.

Last night, one of the staff nurses told the family that according to hospital policy only two members could stay (this is true) and if the other family members did not leave, she would call hospital security. This morning the boy's mother and father have suggested that they will take him home if this matter is not resolved. The patient's diabetes is still not controlled, and you feel that it would be unwise for this to happen.

Assignment: Leadership is needed to keep this situation from deteriorating further. Divide into groups. Develop a plan of action for solving this problem. First, select three desired objectives for solving the problem and then proceed to determine what you would do that would enable you to meet your objectives. Be sure that you are clear as to who you consider your followers to be and what you expect from each of them.

LEARNING EXERCISE 2.6

Delineating Leadership Roles and Management Functions

Examine the scenario in Learning Exercise 2.5. How would you divide the management functions and leadership roles in this situation? For example, you might say that having the nurse-manager adhere to hospital policy was a management function and that counseling staff was a leadership role.

Assignment: List at least five management functions and five leadership roles that you could also delineate in this scenario. Share these with your group.

LEARNING EXERCISE 2.7

What Is Your Management Style?

Recall times when you have been a manager. This does not only mean a nursing manager. Perhaps you were a head lifeguard or an evening shift manager at a fast-food restaurant. During those times, do you think you were a good manager? Did you involve others in your management decision making appropriately? How would you evaluate your decision-making ability? Make a list of your management strengths and a list of management skills that you felt you were lacking.

Thompson, J. (2012). Transformational leadership can improve workforce competencies. *Nursing Management (Harrow), 18*(10), 21–24.

White, R. K., & Lippitt R. (1960). *Autocracy and democracy: An experimental inquiry.* New York, NY: Harper & Row.

Wolf, G. A., Boland, S., & Aukerman, M. (1994, May). A transformational model for the practice of professional nursing. Part 2, Implementation of the model. *Journal of Nursing Administration, 24*(5), 38–46.

Wong, C. A. (2012). Advancing a positive leadership orientation: From problem to possibility. *Nursing Leadership, 25*(2), 51–55.

Zenger, J., & Folkman, J. (2009). Ten fatal flaws that derail leaders. *Harvard Business Review, 18.*

Twenty-First-Century Thinking about Leadership and Management

... 21st century leaders are less reliant on "how things should be" and instead approach business challenges and opportunities with an enquiring mind—one that makes room for new possibilities.
—Shirlaws Pty Ltd

... we are not creatures of circumstance; we are creators of circumstance.
—Benjamin Disraeli

CROSSWALK THIS CHAPTER ADDRESSES:

BSN Essential II: Basic organizational and systems leadership for quality care and patient safety
BSN Essential VI: Interprofessional communication and collaboration for improving patient health outcomes
BSN Essential IX: Baccalaureate generalist nursing practice
MSN Essential II: Organizational and systems leadership
MSN Essential IX: Advanced generalist nursing practice
MSN Essential VII: Interprofessional collaboration for improving patient and population health outcomes
AONE Nurse Executive Competency I: Communication and relationship building
AONE Nurse Executive Competency II: A knowledge of the health-care environment
AONE Nurse Executive Competency III: Leadership
QSEN Competency: Teamwork and collaboration

LEARNING OBJECTIVES *The learner will:*

- analyze how current and future paradigm shifts in healthcare may affect the leadership skills needed by nurses in the 21st century
- compare *strengths-based leadership*, which focuses on the development or empowerment of workers' strengths, with the traditional management practices of identifying problems, improving underperformance, and addressing weaknesses and obstacles
- Identify Level 5 Leadership skills (as espoused by Jim Collins) which differentiate great companies from good companies
- identify the characteristics of a servant leader and suggest strategies for encouraging a service inclination in others
- explore elements of human and social capital which impact resource allocation in organizations
- describe situations where followers (agents) might not be inherently motivated to act in the best interest of the principal (leader or employer)
- describe components of emotional intelligence which promote the development of productive work teams

- identify characteristics of authentic leadership and discuss the consequences to the leader–follower relationship when leaders are not authentic
- identify contemporary nurse-leaders who exemplify thought leadership and the innovative ideas they have suggested
- describe why quantum leaders need flexibility in responding to the complex relationships that exist between environment and context in work environments
- describe complexities that exist in the relationship between followers and leaders
- provide examples of the 21st-century shift from *industrial age leadership* to *relationship age leadership*
- develop insight into his or her individual leadership strengths

Throughout history, nursing has been required to respond to changing technological and social forces. In the last decade alone, a growing elderly population, health-care reform, reductions in federal and state government reimbursement as well as commercial insurance, and new quality imperatives such as value-based purchasing and pay for performance have resulted in major redesigns of most health-care organizations. In addition, the locus of care continues to shift from acute-care hospitals to community and outpatient settings, innovation and technological advances are transforming the workplace, and organizational cultures are increasingly shifting to externally regulated, safety-driven, customer-focused care. All of these changes have brought about a need for leader-managers to learn new roles and develop new skills.

The new managerial responsibilities placed on organized nursing services call for nurse administrators who are knowledgeable, skilled, and competent in all aspects of management. Now more than ever, there is a greater emphasis on the business of health care, with managers being involved in the financial and marketing aspects of their respective departments. Managers are expected to be skilled communicators, organizers, and team builders and to be visionary and proactive in preparing for emerging new threats such as domestic terrorism, biological warfare, and global pandemics.

In addition, the need to develop nursing leadership skills has never been greater. At the national level, nurse-leaders and nurse-managers are actively involved in implementing health-care reform and in addressing a potential international nursing shortage. At the organizational and unit levels, nurse-leaders are being directed to address high turnover rates by staff, an emerging shortage of qualified top-level nursing administrators, growing trends toward unionization, and intensified efforts to legislate minimum staffing ratios and eliminate mandatory overtime, while maintaining cohesive and productive work environments. Moreover, ensuring successful recruitment, creating shared governance models, and maintaining high-quality practice depends on successful interprofessional team building, another critical leadership skill in contemporary health-care organizations. This challenging and changing health-care system requires leader-managers to use their scarce resources appropriately and to be visionary and proactive in planning for challenges yet to come.

In confronting these expanding responsibilities and demands, many leader-managers turn to the experts for tools or strategies to meet these expanded role dimensions. What they have found is some new and innovative thinking about how best to manage organizations and lead people as well as some reengineered interactive leadership theories from the later 20th century. This chapter explores this contemporary thinking about leadership and management, with specific attention given to emergent 21st-century thinking.

NEW THINKING ABOUT LEADERSHIP AND MANAGEMENT

Japsen (2012) suggests that new leadership will be required to build bridges and find solutions to the complex health-care problems that will be faced in the next 20 years. This leadership must embrace community needs and new roles to care and guide individuals across a more data-driven, accountable US health system.

Zinni and Koltz (2009) suggest, however, that there is a profound leadership crisis in America in the 21st century and that contemporary leaders have failed to change with the times. They argue that this has occurred because the world is changing quickly and the traditional top-down hierarchical leadership approach has not evolved quickly enough to match the complexity of the 21st-century world. Single directive approaches to leading will no longer work and participatory enterprise models, which are not easy to develop, must replace them (Zinni and Koltz, 2009).

New research on leadership, including *full-range leadership theory* (see Chapter 2), is rediscovering the importance of organizational context, levels of analysis, and potential boundary conditions on transformational leadership. Indeed, many recent leadership and management concepts focus on the complexity of the relationship between the leader and the follower and much of the leadership research emerging in the second decade of the 21st century builds upon the interactive leadership theories developed in the latter part of the 20th century. As a result, concepts such as strengths-based leadership, Level 5 Leadership, servant leadership, principal agent theory, human and social capital theory, emotional intelligence (EI), authentic leadership, quantum leadership, and thought leadership have emerged as part of the leader-manager's repertoire for the 21st century.

Strengths-Based Leadership and the Positive Psychology Movement

Strengths-based leadership, which grew out of the positive psychology movement (began in the late 1990s), focuses on the development or empowerment of workers' strengths as opposed to identifying problems, improving underperformance, and addressing weaknesses and obstacles (Wong, 2012). For example, paying attention to multiple points of view, searching for common ground, making continuous learning in the workplace a priority, and promoting collaborative relationships represent strengths-based leadership activities (Wong, 2012). Wong suggests that strengths-based leadership is part of the development of *positive organizational scholarship*, which focuses on successful performance that exceeds the norm and embodies an orientation toward strengths and developing collective efficacy in organizations.

While the types of activities encompassed in strengths-based leadership may vary, Gottlieb, Gottlieb, and Shamian (2012) suggest that there are eight *strengths-based leadership* principles that create the sustainable changes needed in health care and which provide a vision for current and future nursing leadership. These eight leadership principles are shown in Display 3.1. Gottlieb et al. argue that consistently using these leadership principles will allow nurses to step forward and create a more holistic, humanistic, integrated, health-based, 21st-century health-care system that focuses on what is best, what works, and what has potential.

DISPLAY 3.1   Principles of Strengths-Based Leadership

STRENGTHS-BASED NURSING LEADERSHIP

- Works with the whole, while appreciating the interrelationships among its parts
- Recognizes the uniqueness of staff, nurse-leaders, and the organization
- Creates work environments that promote nurses' health and facilitates their development
- Understands the significance of subjective reality and created meaning
- Values self-determination
- Recognizes that person and environment are integral and that nurses function best in environments where there is a "goodness of fit" that capitalizes on their strengths
- Creates environments that promote learning and recognizes the importance of readiness and timing
- Invests in collaborative partnerships

Source: Adapted from Gottlieb, L. N., Gottlieb, B., & Shamian, J. (2012). Principles of strengths-based nursing leadership for strengths-based nursing care: A new paradigm for nursing and healthcare for the 21st century. Nursing Leadership, 25(2), 38–50.

Level 5 Leadership

The concept of *Level 5 Leadership* was developed by Jim Collins and published in his classic (2001) book, *From Good to Great*. Collins studied 1,435 companies to determine what separates great companies from good companies. What he found was that five levels of leadership skill (see Display 3.2) may be present in any organization. Truly great organizations, however, typically have leaders who possess the qualities found in all five levels. Thus, not only do Level 5 leaders have the knowledge to do the job, but they also have team building skills and can help groups achieve shared goals. They also though demonstrate humility and seek success for the team, rather than for self-serving purposes, a core component of another 21st-century leadership theory known as *Servant Leadership*. Level 5 leaders also know when to ask for help, accept responsibility for the errors they or their team make, and are incredibly disciplined in their work.

DISPLAY 3.2   Jim Collin's Level 5 Leadership

LEVEL 1: HIGHLY CAPABLE INDIVIDUAL

Leader makes high-quality contributions to their work; possesses useful levels of knowledge; and has the talent and skills needed to do a good job

LEVEL 2: CONTRIBUTING TEAM MEMBER

Leader uses knowledge and skills to help their team succeed; works effectively, productively, and successfully with other people in their group

LEVEL 3: COMPETENT MANAGER

Leader is able to organize a group effectively to achieve specific goals and objectives

LEVEL 4: EFFECTIVE LEADER

Leader is able to galvanize a department or organization to meet performance objectives and achieve a vision

LEVEL 5: GREAT LEADER

Leader has all of the abilities needed for the other four levels, plus a unique blend of humility and will that is required for true greatness

Source: Adapted from Mindtools (1996–2013). Level 5 Leadership. Achieving "greatness" as a leader. Retrieved May 14, 2013, from http://www.mindtools.com/pages/article/level-5-leadership.htm

Servant Leadership

Although Greenleaf (1977) developed the idea of servant leadership more than 35 years ago, it continues to greatly influence leadership thinking in the 21st century. In more than four decades of working as director of leadership development at AT&T, Greenleaf noticed that most successful managers lead in a different way from traditional managers. These managers, which he termed *servant leaders*, put serving others, including employees, customers, and the community, as the number-one priority. In addition, servant leaders foster a service inclination in others that promotes collaboration, teamwork, and collective activism.

Greenleaf argued that to be a great leader, one must be a servant first.

Sutton (2009) notes that many individuals placed in positions of authority become less mindful of others' feelings and needs. Meanwhile, their subordinates devote tremendous energy to watching and interpreting the actions of their leaders and the end result is a toxic tandem where employees feel underappreciated and overcontrolled. Sutton suggests that good leaders find ways to provide employees with more predictability, understanding, control, and compassion and the reward is long-term employee loyalty. Other defining qualities of servant leadership are shown in Display 3.3.

| DISPLAY 3.3 | Defining Qualities of Servant Leaders |

- The ability to listen on a deep level and to truly understand
- The ability to keep an open mind and hear without judgment
- The ability to deal with ambiguity, paradoxes, and complex issues
- The belief that honestly sharing critical challenges with all parties and asking for their input is more important than personally providing solutions
- Being clear on goals and good at pointing the direction toward goal achievement without giving orders
- The ability to be a servant, helper, and teacher first and then a leader
- Always thinking before reacting
- Choosing words carefully so as not to damage those being led
- The ability to use foresight and intuition
- Seeing things whole and sensing relationships and connections

LEARNING EXERCISE 3.1

Creating a Service Inclination

An important part of servant leadership is the servant leader's ability to create a service inclination in others. In doing so, more leaders are created for the organization.

Assignment: Identify servant leaders who you have worked with. Did they motivate followers to be service oriented? If so, what strategies did they use? Does servant leadership result in a greater number of leaders within an organization? If so, why do you think that this happens?

LEARNING EXERCISE 3.2

Servant Leadership in Nursing and Medicine

Assignment: Write a one-page essay that addresses the following:

1. Both nursing and medicine are helping, service-oriented professions. Do you believe there are inherent differences in service inclination between individuals who choose nursing for a profession rather than medicine?

2. Do you believe that nursing education fosters a greater service inclination than medical education?

3. Do you believe the female majority (gender) of the nursing profession influences nursing's propensity to be service oriented?

New Thinking about Leaders and Followers

Many contemporary scholars have expanded on Greenleaf's work, particularly in terms of how followers influence the actions of the leader. While the positive effect of followers on leaders has been fairly well described in most discussions of transformational leadership, less has been said about potential negative impacts. For example, followers can and do mislead leaders, whether intentionally or not, as noted in *principal agent*

have a rational thinking mind and an emotional feeling mind and that both influence action. The goal, then, in EI is *emotional literacy*—being self-aware about one's emotions and recognizing how they influence subsequent action. Unlike Mayer and Salovey, however, Goleman argued that EI could be learned, although he too felt that it improves with age.

While many proponents of EI have suggested that having EI may be even more critical to leadership success than intellectual intelligence (IQ), Sadri (2012) warns that the concept has not yet been fully vetted in peer-reviewed research. It is a bit disconcerting then that some employers and even Schools of Nursing have begun using EI evaluation tools as a criterion for employability or admission (see Examining the Evidence 3.1).

Examining the Evidence 3.1

Source: Kendall-Raynor, P. (2012). Prospective nursing students tested for emotional intelligence. Nursing Standard, 26(24), 5.

The University of Dundee in Scotland is now using EI assessments as part of its screening criteria for admission to its nursing program. Students are asked to look at photographs of people's faces and match them with seven emotions—anger, sadness, surprise, disgust, fear, happiness, and neutrality. In addition, students must complete a self-assessment questionnaire comprising 33 questions about emotions. The university suggests its decision to use EI assessment as a screening tool is based on research that links EI with high academic performance, lower attrition rates, and positive clinical practice outcomes. Yet, these same academic administrators note their concern that some students may be able to answer in a way that they think is correct, without having any significant degree of EI.

LEARNING EXERCISE 3.4

Emotions and Decision Making

Think back on a recent decision you made that was more emotionally laden than usual. Were you self-aware about what emotions were influencing your thinking and how your emotions might have influenced the course(s) of action you chose? Were you able to objectively identify the emotions that others were experiencing and how these emotions may have influenced their actions?

Authentic Leadership

Another emerging leadership theory for the contemporary leader-manager's arsenal is that of *authentic leadership* (also known as *congruent leadership*). Authentic leadership suggests that in order to lead, leaders must be true to themselves and their values and act accordingly.

It is important to remember that authentic or congruent leadership theory differs somewhat from more traditional transformational leadership theories, which suggest that the leader's vision or goals are often influenced by external forces and that there must be at least some "buy-in" of that vision by followers. In authentic leadership, it is the leaders' principles and their conviction to act accordingly that inspire followers. Thus, authentic followers realize their own true nature.

In authentic leadership, it is the leaders' principles and their conviction to act accordingly that inspire followers.

Authentic leadership is not easy. It takes great courage to be true to one's convictions when external forces or peer pressure encourages an individual to do something he or she feels morally would be inappropriate. For example, there is little doubt that some nurse-leaders experience intrapersonal value conflicts between what they believe to be morally appropriate and a need to deliver results in a health-care system increasingly characterized by pay for performance and rewarded by cost containment.

A number of theorists have attempted to further define the theoretical construct of authentic leadership in the past decade. Shirey (2006) suggests that there are five distinguishing characteristics of authentic leaders: *purpose, values, heart, relationships,* and *self-discipline* (see Display 3.5). Avolio, Walumbwa, and Weber (2009) suggest, however, that the general agreement in the literature is that there are four factors that cover the components of authentic leadership: balanced processing, internalized moral perspective, relational transparency, and self-awareness. *Balanced processing* refers to analyzing data rationally before making decisions. *Internalized moral perspective* suggests that the authentic leader is guided by internal moral standards that then guide his or her behavior. *Relational transparency* refers to openly sharing feelings and information appropriate to a situation, and *self-awareness* alludes to a knowing of self so as to make sense of the world (Avolio et al., 2009). Avolio et al. (2009) suggest, however, that work on defining and measuring authentic leadership is in its early stages of development and that further research is needed to assess the validity of this construct.

DISPLAY 3.5   Five Distinguishing Characteristics of the Authentic Leader

1. *Purpose*: Authentic leaders understand their own purposes and passions as a result of ongoing self-reflection and self-awareness.
2. *Values*: Authentic leaders link between purpose and passion by having congruence in beliefs and actions.
3. *Heart*: Authentic leaders care for themselves and the people they lead, and their compassion is genuine.
4. *Relationships*: Authentic leaders value building relationships and establishing connections with others, not to receive rewards but rather to strengthen the human connection.
5. *Self-discipline*: Authentic leaders practice self-discipline by incorporating balance into their personal and professional lives.

Source: Shirey, M. R. (2006). Fostering leadership through collaboration. Reflections on nursing leadership *(3rd quarter).* Indianapolis, IN: *Sigma Theta Tau International.*

LEARNING EXERCISE 3.5

Inconsistency in Word and Action

There are many examples of internationally or nationally recognized leaders who have lost their followers because of their actions being inconsistent with personally stated convictions. An example might be a world-class athlete and advocate for healthy lifestyles who is found to be using steroids to enhance physical performance. Or it might be a political figure who preaches morality and becomes involved in an extramarital affair or a religious leader who promotes celibacy and then becomes involved in a sex scandal.

Assignment: Think of a leader who espoused one message and then acted in a different manner. How did it affect the leader's ability to be an effective leader? How did it change how you personally felt about that leader? Do you feel that leaders who have lost their "authenticity" can ever regain the trust of their followers?

Finally, one must not be so idealistic as to assume that all leaders strive to be authentic. Indeed, many are flawed, at least at times. Leaders may be deceitful and trustworthy, greedy and generous, cowardly and brave. To assume that all good leaders are good people is foolhardy and makes us blind to the human condition. Future leadership theory may well focus on why leaders behave badly and why followers continue to follow bad leaders.

Thought Leadership

Another relatively new leadership theory to emerge in the 21st century is that of *thought leadership*, which applies to a person who is recognized among his or her peers for innovative ideas and who demonstrates the confidence to promote those ideas. Thus, thought leadership refers to any situation in which one individual convinces another to consider a new idea, product, or way of looking at things.

Thought leaders challenge the status quo and attract followers not by any promise of representation or empowerment, but by their risk taking and vision in terms of being innovative.

The ideas put forth by thought leaders typically are future oriented and make a significant impact. In addition, they are generally problem oriented, which increases their value to both individuals and organizations.

Organizations can also be thought leaders. For example, Blue Cross and Blue Shield were early thought leaders in the development of private health insurance in the late 1920s. Johnson and Johnson launched the *Discover Nursing* campaign earlier this decade to champion the nursing profession and promote the recruitment and retention of nurses. Thought leaders in the coming decade will likely focus on enduring issues that continue to be of critical importance to nursing and health care, and address new, emerging problems of significance. For example, thought leadership is still greatly needed in identifying and adopting innovative safety and quality improvement approaches that actually reduce the risk of harm to patients and health-care workers. In addition, the threat of an international nursing shortage continues to loom and an inadequate number of innovative solutions have been suggested for addressing the dire nursing faculty shortage that is expected to occur in the next 5 to 10 years.

LEARNING EXERCISE 3.6

Technological Innovation and Thought Leadership

Technological innovations continue to change the face of health care, and the pace of such innovations continues to increase exponentially. For example, wireless communication, computerized charting, and the barcode scanning of medications have all greatly affected the practice of nursing.

Assignment: Choose at least one of the following technological innovations, and write a one-page report on how this technology is expected to impact nursing and health care in the coming decade. See if you can identify the thought leader(s) credited with developing these technologies and explore the process that they used to both develop and market their innovations.

- Biometrics to ensure patient confidentiality
- Computerized physician order entry
- Point-of-care testing
- Bluetooth technology
- Electronic health records
- Nursebots (prototype nurse robots)
- Genetic and genomic testing

Quantum Leadership

Quantum leadership is another relatively new leadership theory that is being used by leader-managers to better understand dynamics of environments, such as health care. This theory, which emerged in the 1990s, builds upon transformational leadership and suggests that leaders must work together with subordinates to identify common goals, exploit opportunities, and empower staff to make decisions for organizational productivity to occur. This is especially true during periods of rapid change and needed transition.

Building on quantum physics, which suggests that reality is often discontinuous and deeply paradoxical, quantum leadership suggests that the environment and context in which people work is complex and dynamic and that this has a direct impact on organizational productivity. The theory also suggests that change is constant. Today's workplace is a highly fluid, flexible, and mobile environment, and this calls for an entirely innovative set of interactions and relationships as well as the leadership necessary to create them (Porter-O'Grady & Malloch, 2011).

Quantum leadership suggests that the environment and context in which people work is complex and dynamic and that this has a direct impact on organizational productivity.

Because the health-care industry is characterized by rapid change, the potential for intra-organizational conflict is high. Porter-O'Grady and Malloch (2011) suggest that because the unexpected is becoming the normative, the quantum leader must be able to address the unsettled space between present and future and resolve these conflicts appropriately. In addition, they suggest that the ability to respond to the dynamics of crisis and change is not only an inherent leadership skill, it must now be inculcated within the very fabric of the organization and its operation.

TRANSITION FROM INDUSTRIAL AGE LEADERSHIP TO RELATIONSHIP AGE LEADERSHIP

In considering all of these emerging leadership theories, it becomes apparent that a paradigm shift has taken place early in the 21st century—a transition from *industrial age leadership* to *relationship age leadership* (Scott, 2006). Scott contends that industrial age leadership focused primarily on traditional hierarchical management structures, skill acquisition, competition, and control. These are the same skills traditionally associated with management. Relationship age leadership focuses primarily on the relationship between the leader and his or her followers, on discerning common purpose, working together cooperatively, and seeking information rather than wealth (Table 3.1). Servant leadership, authentic leadership, human and social capital, and EI are all relationship-centered theories that address the complexity of the leader–follower relationship.

TABLE 3.1 Comparing Industrial and Relationship Age Leadership		
	Industrial Age Leadership	*Relationship Age Leadership*
Skills	Technical skills	People skills
Authority	Command and control	Invitation and interdependence
Strategy	Gaining advantage	Discerning purpose
Methodology	Competition	Cooperation
Focus	Gathering facts	Finding meaning
Value	What you have (wealth)	What you know (information)
Structure	Hierarchy (top-down)	Circular (egalitarian)
Meaning of leadership	Leadership: position	Leadership: trusteeship

Source: Adapted from Scott (2006). © Ki ThoughtBridge, LLC 2000. Author, Katherine Taylor Scott. All rights reserved. Permission for use in this publication granted by Ki ThoughtBridge.

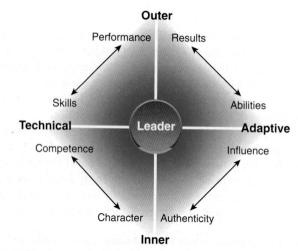

FIGURE 3.1 • Integrated model of leadership. (Reproduced with permission from Ki ThoughtBridge & Scott, K. T. (2006, September 29). *The gifts of leadership*. Keynote presented at the Sigma Theta Tau International Chapter Leader Academy, Indianapolis, IN.)

 A paradigm shift is taking place early in the 21st century—a transition from industrial age leadership to relationship age leadership.

Covey (2011) concurs, noting that the primary drivers of economic prosperity in the industrial age were machines and capital—in other words, things. People were necessary, but replaceable. Covey argues that many current management practices come from the industrial age where the focus was on controlling workers, fitting them into a slot and using reward and punishment for external motivation. In contrast, relationship age leadership is all about leading people who have the power to choose. It is about requiring leaders to embrace the whole person paradigm (Covey, 2011).

Yet the leader-manager in contemporary health-care organizations cannot and must not focus solely on relationship building. Ensuring productivity and achieving desired outcomes are essential to organizational success. The key, then, likely lies in integrating the two paradigms. Scott (2006) suggests that such integration is possible (Fig. 3.1).

Technical skills and competence seeking must be balanced with the adaptive skills of influencing followers and encouraging their abilities. Performance and results priorities must be balanced with authentic leadership and character. In other words, leader-managers must seek the same tenuous balance between leadership and management that has existed since time began.

LEARNING EXERCISE 3.7

Balancing the Focus between Productivity and Relationships

You are a top-level nursing administrator in a large, urban medical center in California. As in many acute-care hospitals, your annual nursing turnover rate is more than 25%. At this point, you have many unfilled licensed nursing positions, and local recruitment efforts to fill these positions have been largely unsuccessful. The problem has been exacerbated by the recent passage of legislated minimum licensed staffing ratios in your state.

During a meeting with the CEO today, you are informed that the hospital vacancy rate for licensed nurses is expected to rise to 35% with the implementation of the new minimum staffing ratios in 3 months. The CEO states that you must reduce turnover or increase recruitment efforts immediately or the hospital will have to consider closing units or reducing available beds when the new ratios take effect.

You consider the following "industrial leadership" paradigm options:

1. You could aggressively recruit international nurses to solve at least the immediate staffing problem.

2. You could increase sign-on bonuses and offer other incentives for recruiting new nurses.

3. You could expand the job description for unlicensed assistive personnel and LVNs to relieve the registered nurses of some of their duties.

4. You could make newly recruited nurses sign a minimum 2-year contract upon hire.

You also consider the following "relationship leadership" paradigm options:

1. You could hold informal meetings with current staff to determine major variables affecting their current satisfaction levels and attempt to increase those variables that increase worker satisfaction.

2. You could develop an open-door policy in an effort to be more accessible to workers who wish to discuss concerns or issues about their work environment.

3. You could implement a shared governance model to increase worker participation in decision making on the units in which they work.

4. You could make daily rounds on all the units in an effort to get to know your nursing staff better on a one-to-one basis.

Assignment: Decide which of the options you would select. Rank order them in terms of what you would do first. Then look at your list. Did it reflect more of the industrial leadership paradigm or a relationship leadership paradigm? What inferences might you draw from your rank ordering in terms of your leadership skills? Do you think that your rank ordering might change with your age? Your experience?

LEADERSHIP AND MANAGEMENT FOR NURSING'S FUTURE

Seemingly insurmountable problems, a lack of resources to solve these problems, and individual apathy have been and will continue to be issues that contemporary leader-managers face. Effective leadership is absolutely critical to organizational success in the 21st century. Becoming a better leader-manager begins with a highly developed understanding of what leadership and management are and how these skills can be developed. The problem is that these skills are dynamic, and what we know and believe to be true about leadership and management changes constantly in response to new research and visionary thinking.

Contemporary leader-managers, then, are challenged not only to know and be able to apply classical leadership and management theory but also to keep abreast of new insights, new management decision-making tools, and new research in the field. It is more important than ever that leader-managers be able to integrate leadership roles and management functions and that some balance be achieved between industrial age leadership and relationship age leadership skills. Leading and managing in the 21st century promises to be more complex than ever before, and leader-managers will be expected to have a greater skill set than ever before. The key to organizational success will likely be having enough highly qualified and visionary leader-managers to steer the course.

KEY CONCEPTS

- Many new leadership and management theories have emerged in the 21st century to explain the complexity of the leader–follower relationship and the environment in which work is accomplished and goals are achieved.

- *Strengths-based leadership* focuses on the development or empowerment of workers' strengths as opposed to identifying problems, improving underperformance, and addressing weaknesses and obstacles.

- *Level 5 leadership* is characterized by knowledge, team building skills, the ability to help groups achieve goals, humility, and the empowerment of others through servant leadership.

- *Servant leadership* is a contemporary leadership model that puts serving others as the first priority.

- Followers can and do influence leaders in both positive and negative ways.

- *Principal agent theory* suggests that followers may have an informational (expertise or knowledge) advantage over the leader as well as their own preferences, which may deviate from those of the principal. This may lead to a misalignment of goals.

- *Human capital* represents the capability of the individual. Social capital represents what a group can accomplish together.

- *Emotional intelligence* refers to the ability to use emotions effectively and is considered by many to be critical to leadership and management success.

- *Authentic leadership* suggests that in order to lead, leaders must be true to themselves and their values and act accordingly.

- *Thought leadership* refers to any situation whereby one individual convinces another to consider a new idea, product, or way of looking at things.

- Thought leaders attract followers not by any promise of representation or empowerment but by their risk taking and vision in terms of being innovative.

- *Quantum leadership* suggests that the environment and context in which people work is complex and dynamic and that this has a direct impact on organizational productivity.

- A transition has occurred in the 21st-century from *industrial age leadership* to *relationship age leadership*.

ADDITIONAL LEARNING EXERCISES AND APPLICATIONS

LEARNING EXERCISE 3.8

Reflecting on Emotional Intelligence in Self

Do you feel that you have emotional intelligence? Do you express appropriate emotions such as empathy when taking care of patients? Are you able to identify and control your own emotions when you are in an emotionally charged situation?

Assignment: Describe a recent emotional experience. Write two to four paragraphs reporting how you responded in this experience. Were you able to read the emotions of the other individuals involved? How did you respond, and were you later able to reflect on this incident?

LEARNING EXERCISE 3.9

Self-Regulation and Emotional Intelligence

You have just come from your 6-month performance evaluation as a new charge nurse. While your supervisor stated that he was very pleased in general with how you are performing in this new role, one area that he suggested you work on was to learn to be calmer in hectic clinical situations. He suggested that your anxiety could be transmitted to coworkers and subordinates who look to you to be their role model. He feels that you are especially anxious when staffing is short and that at times you vent your frustrations to your staff, which only adds to the general anxiety level on the unit.

Assignment: Create a specific plan of 6 to 10 things you can do to bolster your emotional intelligence in terms of self-regulation during stressful times.

LEARNING EXERCISE 3.10

Human and Social Capital

Examine the institution in which you work or go to school. Assess both the human capital and social capital present. Which is greater? Which do you believe contributes most to this institution in being able to accomplish its stated mission and goals?

REFERENCES

About.com-Economics. (2013). *Definition of human capital.* Retrieved May 14, 2013, from http://economics.about .com/cs/economicsglossary/g/human_capital.htm

Aiken, L., Clarke, S. P., Sloane, D. M., Lake, E. T., & Cheney, T. (2008, May). Effects of hospital care environment on patient mortality and nurse outcomes. *Journal of Nursing Administration, 38*(5), 223–229.

American Association of Colleges of Nursing. (2013). *Fact sheet. Creating a more highly qualified nursing workforce.* Retrieved May 13, 2013, from, http://www .aacn.nche.edu/Media/FactSheets/NursingWrkf.htm

Avolio, B., Walumbwa, F., & Weber, T. (2009). Leadership: Current theories, research, and future directions. *Annual Review of Psychology, 60*, 421–449.

Collins, J. (2001). Good to great: Why some companies make the leap … and others don't. New York, NY: Harper Collins.

Covey, S. (2011, September). Lighthouse principles and leadership. *UC Morning in America* (adaptation from a speech presented at University of the Cumberlands on April 8, 2008, in the "Principle-Centered Leadership Series" sponsored by the Forcht Group of Kentucky Center for Excellence in Leadership). Retrieved May 14, 2013, from http://www .ucumberlands.edu/academics/history/downloads/ MorningInAmericaVol2i3.pdf

Ford, B., & Tamir, M. (2012). When getting angry is smart: Emotional preferences and emotional intelligence. *Emotion, 12*(4), 685–689.

Goleman, D. (1998). *Working with emotional intelligence.* New York, NY: Bantam Books.

Gottlieb, L.N., Gottlieb, B., & Shamian, J. (2012). Principles of strengths-based nursing leadership for strengths-based nursing care: A new paradigm for nursing and healthcare for the 21st century. *Nursing Leadership, 25*(2), 38–50.

Greenleaf, R. K. (1977). *Servant leadership: A journey in the nature of legitimate power and greatness.* New York, NY: Paulist.

Japsen, B. (2012, June 22). *Health leaders look to 2032 for opportunities to improve the health of the nation.* Robert Wood Johnson Foundation. Retrieved February 25, 2013, from http://www.rwjf.org/en/about-rwjf/ newsroom/newsroom-content/2012/06/health-leaders -look-to-2032-for-opportunities-to-improve-the-hea.html

Kendall-Raynor, P. (2012). Prospective nursing students tested for emotional intelligence. *Nursing Standard, 26*(24), 5.

Mayer, J. D., & Salovey, P. (1997). What is emotional intelligence? In P. Salovey & D. Sluyter (Eds.), *Emotional development and emotional intelligence: Implications for educators* (pp. 3–31). New York, NY: Basic Books.

Mindtools (1996–2013). Level 5 leadership. *Achieving "greatness" as a leader*. Retrieved Sept. 26, 2013, from http://www.mindtools.com/pages/article/level-5 -leadership.htm

Porter-O'Grady, T., & Malloch, K. (2011). *Quantum leadership: Advancing information, transforming healthcare* (3rd ed.). Sudbury, MA: Jones & Bartlett.

Sadri, G. (2012). Emotional intelligence and leadership development. *Public Personnel Management, 41*(3), 535–548.

Scott, K. T. (2006, September 29). *The gifts of leadership*. Keynote presented at the Sigma Theta Tau International Chapter Leader Academy, Indianapolis, IN.

Shirey, M. R. (2006). Promoting sustainability through collaboration. *Reflections on nursing leadership* (3rd quarter) Indianapolis, IN:.

Sutton, R. I. (2009, June). How to be a good boss in a bad economy. *Harvard Business Review*, 42–50.

Wong, C. A. (2012). Advancing a positive leadership orientation: From problem to possibility. *Nursing Leadership, 25*(2), 51–55.

Zinni, T., & Koltz, T. (2009). *Leading the charge: Leadership lessons from the battlefield to the boardroom*. New York, NY: Palgrave Macmillan.

Foundation for Effective
Leadership and Management
Ethics, Law, and Advocacy

4

Ethical Issues

... when organizations and their leaders become fixated on the bottom line and ignore values, an environment conducive to ethics failure is nurtured.

–J. G. Bruhn

... All my growth and development led me to believe that if you really do the right thing, and if you play by the rules, and if you've got good enough, solid judgment and common sense, that you're going to be able to do whatever you want to do with your life.

–Barbara Jordan

CROSSWALK THIS CHAPTER ADDRESSES:

BSN Essential II: Basic organizational and systems leadership for quality care and patient safety

BSN Essential VIII: Professionalism and professional values

BSN Essential IX: Baccalaureate generalist nursing practice

MSN Essential II: Organizational and systems leadership

MSN Essential VI: Health policy and advocacy

MSN Essential IX: Advanced generalist nursing practice

AONE Nurse Executive Competency III: Leadership

AONE Nurse Executive Competency IV: Professionalism

QSEN Competency: Patient-centered care

LEARNING OBJECTIVES *The learner will:*

- define ethics and ethical dilemmas
- compare and contrast the utilitarian, duty-based, rights-based, and intuitionist frameworks for ethical decision making
- identify and define six different principles of ethical reasoning
- use a systematic problem-solving or decision-making model to determine appropriate action for select ethical problems
- describe the limitations of using outcome as the sole criterion for the evaluation of ethical decision making
- distinguish between legal and ethical obligations in decision making
- describe how differences in personal, organizational, subordinate, and patient obligations increase the risk of intrapersonal conflict in ethical decision making
- demonstrate self-awareness regarding the ethical frameworks and ethical principles that most strongly influence his or her personal decision making.
- role model ethical decision making congruent with the American Nurses Association (ANA) Code of Ethics and Interpretive Statements and professional standards

Unit II examines ethical, legal, and legislative issues affecting leadership and management as well as professional advocacy. This chapter focuses on applied ethical decision making as a critical leadership role for mangers. Chapter 5 examines the impact of legislation and the law on leadership and management and Chapter 6 focuses on advocacy for patients and subordinates and for the nursing profession in general.

Ethics is the systematic study of what a person's conduct and actions should be with regard to self, other human beings, and the environment; it is the justification of what is right or good and the study of what a person's life and relationships should be, not necessarily what they are. Ethics is a system of moral conduct and principles that guide a person's actions in regard to right and wrong and in regard to oneself and society at large.

Ethics is concerned with doing the right thing and with being a certain kind of person, in terms of conduct and character (Gallagher & Hodge, 2012).

Applied ethics requires application of normative ethical theory to everyday problems. The normative ethical theory for each profession arises from the purpose of the profession. The values and norms of the nursing profession, therefore, provide the foundation and filter from which ethical decisions are made. The nurse-manager, however, has a different ethical responsibility than the clinical nurse and does not have as clearly defined a foundation to use as a base for ethical reasoning.

In addition, because management is a discipline and not a profession, it does not have a defined purpose, such as medicine and the law; therefore, it lacks a specific set of norms to guide ethical decision making. Instead, the organization reflects norms and values to the manager, and the personal values of managers are reflected through the organization. The manager's ethical obligation is tied to the organization's purpose, and the purpose of the organization is linked to the function that it fills in society and the constraints society places on it. So, the responsibilities of the nurse-manager emerge from a complex set of interactions. Society helps define the purposes of various institutions, and the purposes, in turn, help ensure that the institution fulfills specific functions. However, the specific values and norms in any particular institution determine the focus of its resources and shape its organizational life. The values of people within institutions influence actual management practice. In reviewing this set of complex interactions, it becomes evident that arriving at appropriate ethical management decisions is a difficult task.

Not only are *nursing management ethics* distinct from *clinical nursing ethics*, they are also distinct from other areas of management. Although there are many similar areas of responsibility between nurse-managers and non-nurse-managers, many leadership roles and management functions are specific to nursing. These differences require the nurse-manager to deal with unique obligations and ethical dilemmas that are not encountered in non-nursing management.

In addition, because personal, organizational, subordinate, and consumer responsibilities differ, there is great potential for nursing managers to experience intrapersonal conflict about the appropriate course of action. Multiple advocacy roles and accountability to the profession further increase the likelihood that all nurse-managers will be faced with ethical dilemmas in their practice. Nurses often find themselves viewed simultaneously as advocates for physicians, patients, and the organization—all of whose needs and goals may be dissimilar.

Nurses are often placed in situations where they are expected to be agents for patients, physicians, and the organization simultaneously, all of which may have conflicting needs, wants, and goals.

To make appropriate ethical decisions then, the manager must have knowledge of ethical principles and frameworks, use a professional approach that eliminates trial and error and focuses on proven decision-making models, and use available organizational processes to assist in making such decisions. Such organizational processes include institutional review boards (IRBs), ethics committees, and professional codes of ethics. Using both a systematic approach and proven ethical tools and technology allows managers to make better decisions and increases the probability that they will feel confident about the decisions they have made. Leadership roles and management functions involved in management ethics are shown in Display 4.1.

DISPLAY 4.1   Leadership Roles and Management Functions Associated with Ethics

LEADERSHIP ROLES

1. Is self-aware regarding own values and basic beliefs about the rights, duties, and goals of human beings.
2. Accepts that some ambiguity and uncertainty must be a part of all ethical decision making.
3. Accepts that negative outcomes occur in ethical decision making despite high-quality problem solving and decision making.
4. Demonstrates risk taking in ethical decision making.
5. Role models ethical decision making, which is congruent with the American Nurses Association (ANA) Code of Ethics and Interpretive Statements and professional standards.
6. Clearly communicates expected ethical standards of behavior.
7. Role models behavior that eliminates theory–practice–ethics gaps.

MANAGEMENT FUNCTIONS

1. Uses a systematic approach to problem solving and decision making when faced with management problems with ethical ramifications.
2. Identifies outcomes in ethical decision making that should always be sought or avoided.
3. Uses established ethical frameworks to clarify values and beliefs.
4. Applies principles of ethical reasoning to define what beliefs or values form the basis for decision making.
5. Is aware of legal precedents that may guide ethical decision making and is accountable for possible liabilities should they go against the legal precedent.
6. Continually reevaluates the quality of personal ethical decision making, based on the process of decision making or problem solving used.
7. Recognizes and rewards ethical conduct of subordinates.
8. Takes appropriate action when subordinates use unethical conduct.

TYPES OF ETHICAL ISSUES

There are many terms used to describe moral issues faced by nurses, including moral indifference, moral uncertainty, moral conflict, moral distress, moral outrage, and ethical dilemmas. *Moral indifference* occurs when an individual questions why morality in practice is even necessary. *Moral uncertainty* or *moral conflict* occurs when an individual is unsure which moral principles or values apply and may even include uncertainty as to what the moral problem is.

On the other hand, *moral distress* occurs when the individual knows the right thing to do but organizational constraints make it difficult to take the right course of action. Pauly, Varcoe, and Storch (2012) suggest that moral distress in health care is a growing concern and that it impacts satisfaction, the recruitment and retention of health-care providers, as well as the delivery of safe and competent quality patient care. Nalley (2013) agrees, suggesting that the intense patient situations (e.g., end-of-life care), lack of collaboration, and disrespectful communication that are often a part of nursing can lead to emotional exhaustion, increased absenteeism, low morale, chronic discontent, and job dissatisfaction.

To identify which influencers nurses perceived as having the greatest impact on their ethical beliefs and moral distress, Davis, Schrader, and Belcheir (2012) surveyed 1144 Idaho nurses. Approximately 35% of the nurses reported experiencing moral distress in the workplace at least once a month and 27.7% reported leaving a job due to moral distress. Nurses with strong religious beliefs had significantly higher moral distress than those who identified the nurses' Code of Ethics, family values, or work/life experiences as the compass for their ethical beliefs. The researchers concluded that because religion and spiritual beliefs may pose additional moral distress for nurses in dealing with ethical dilemmas (see Examining the Evidence 4.1).

Examining the Evidence 4.1

Source: Davis, S., Schrader, V., & Belcheir, M. (2012). Influencers of ethical beliefs and the impact on moral distress and conscientious objection. Nursing Ethics, 19(6), 738–749.

The aim of this exploratory study was to identify influencers that had the greatest impact on the development of nurses' ethical beliefs and to determine whether these influencers might impact levels of moral distress and the potential for conscientious objection. One thousand one hundred forty-four registered nurses from throughout Idaho participated in this study by completing a 30-item survey on the Idaho State Board of Nursing online license renewal website.

Thirty-four percent of the sample claimed that their work and/or life experience was the most important influence in the development of their ethical beliefs, followed by religious beliefs (29.4%), family values (24%), and the Nursing Code of Ethics (9%). A small percentage of the sample claimed to have developed their ethical beliefs from governing laws (3.2%), and even fewer from political views (0.3%). The religious beliefs group had significantly higher moral distress scores compared with those who identified the nurses' Code of Ethics, family values, or work/life experiences as influencing the development of their ethical beliefs. Those who chose governing laws or political views had a mean which did not differ from any other group.

This study supported previous findings that nurses' ethical beliefs are influenced less by their professional codes of ethics and more by work or life experiences, religious beliefs, and family values. The researchers noted that how one's ethical beliefs are influenced may determine how they will react to ethical dilemmas and that religion and spiritual beliefs often influence how nurses and health-care providers in general make ethical decisions. Because these values are often strongly engrained from childhood, the authors concluded that it may be unrealistic to expect nurses to ignore these belief systems when faced with ethical dilemmas.

Moral outrage occurs when an individual witnesses the immoral act of another but feels powerless to stop it. For example, in a high-profile whistle-blower case in New Mexico, six nurses at Memorial Medical Center in Las Cruces independently voiced concerns to their nurse-managers over a 6-year period, regarding inadequate and inappropriate care being given by an osteopathic physician on staff (Bitoun Blecher, 2001–2013). In addition, the nurses brought the alleged shortcomings of this particular doctor to the attention of other physicians. The doctor in this case was later accused of negligence and incompetence after one of her patients died from sepsis and another suffered a serious injury.

But for reasons that are still unclear, the hospital allegedly failed to act on the nurses' complaints. Instead, the hospital challenged the nurses' actions and disciplined them, citing state regulations that forbid sharing patient information for any reason. The hospital also retaliated after the case was filed and the nurses agreed to testify against the doctor. "Sometimes the atmosphere in a hospital is set up so that you cannot work through the system, and that's what happened here—the system failed" (Bitoun Blecher, 2001–2013, para 28).

Lastly, the most difficult of all moral issues is termed a *moral* or *ethical dilemma*, which may be described as being forced to choose between two or more undesirable alternatives. For example, a nurse might experience a moral or ethical dilemma if he or she was required to provide care or treatments, which were in conflict with his or her own religious beliefs. In this case, the nurse would likely experience an intrapersonal moral conflict about whether his or her values, needs, and wants can or should supersede those of the patient. Because ethical dilemmas are so difficult to resolve, many of the learning exercises in this chapter are devoted to addressing this type of moral issue.

 Individual values, beliefs, and personal philosophy play a major role in the moral or ethical decision making that is part of the daily routine of all managers.

How do managers decide what is right and what is wrong? What does the manager do if no right or wrong answer exists? What if all solutions generated seem to be wrong? Remember that the way managers approach and solve ethical issues is influenced by their values and basic beliefs about the rights, duties, and goals of all human beings. Self-awareness, then, is a vital leadership role in ethical decision making, just as it is in so many other aspects of management.

No rules, guidelines, or theories exist that cover all aspects of the ethical problems that managers face. However, it is the manager's responsibility to understand the ethical problem-solving process, to be familiar with ethical frameworks and principles, and to know ethical professional codes. It is these tools that will assist managers in effective problem solving and prevent ethical failure within their organization. Critical thinking occurs when managers are able to engage in an orderly process of ethical problem solving to determine the rightness or wrongness of courses of action.

ETHICAL FRAMEWORKS FOR DECISION MAKING

Ethical frameworks guide individuals in solving ethical dilemmas. These frameworks do not solve the ethical problem but assist the manager in clarifying personal values and beliefs. Four of the most commonly used ethical frameworks are utilitarianism, duty-based reasoning, rights-based reasoning, and intuitionism (Table 4.1).

 Ethical frameworks do not solve ethical problems but do assist decision makers in clarifying personal values and beliefs.

The *teleological* theory of ethics is also called *utilitarianism* or *consequentialist* theory. Using an ethical framework of utilitarianism encourages decision making based on what provides the greatest good for the greatest number of people. In doing so, the needs and wants of the individual are diminished. Utilitarianism also suggests that the end can justify the means. For example, a manager using a utilitarian approach might decide to use travel budget money to send many staff to local workshops rather than to fund one or two people to attend a national conference. Another example would be an insurance program that meets

TABLE 4.1	Ethical Frameworks
Framework	**Basic Premise**
Utilitarian (teleological)	Provide the greatest good for the greatest number of people
Rights based (deontological)	Individuals have basic inherent rights that should not be interfered with
Duty based (deontological)	A duty to do something or to refrain from doing something
Intuitionist (deontological)	Each case weighed on a case-by-case basis to determine relative goals, duties, and rights

the needs of many but refuses coverage for expensive organ transplants. As illustrated in Learning Exercise 4.5, the organization uses utilitarianism to justify lying to employee applicants because their hiring would result in good for many employees by keeping several units in the hospital open.

Deontological ethical theory judges whether the action is right or wrong regardless of the consequences and is based on the philosophy of Emanuel Kant in the 18th century. Primarily, this theory uses both duty-based reasoning and rights-based reasoning as the basis for its philosophy. *Duty-based reasoning* is an ethical framework stating that some decisions must be made because there is a duty to do something or to refrain from doing something. In Learning Exercise 4.5, the supervisor feels a duty to hire the most qualified person for the job, even if the personal cost is high.

Rights-based reasoning is based on the belief that some things are a person's just due (i.e., each individual has basic claims, or entitlements, with which there should be no interference). Rights are different from needs, wants, or desires. The supervisor in Learning Exercise 4.5 believes that both applicants have the right to fair and impartial consideration of their application. In Learning Exercise 4.6, Sam believes that all people have the right to truth and, in fact, that he has the duty to be truthful.

The *intuitionist framework* allows the decision maker to review each ethical problem or issue on a case-by-case basis, comparing the relative weights of goals, duties, and rights. This weighting is determined primarily by intuition—what the decision maker believes is right for that particular situation. Recently, some ethical theorists have begun questioning the appropriateness of intuitionism as an ethical decision-making framework because of the potential for subjectivity and bias. All of the cases solved in this chapter involve some degree of decision making by intuition.

Other more recent theories of ethical philosophy include *ethical relativism* and *ethical universalism*. Ethical relativism suggests that individuals make decisions based only on what seems right or reasonable according to their value system or culture. Conversely, universalism holds that ethical principles are universal and constant and that ethical decision making should not vary as a result of individual circumstances or cultural differences.

PRINCIPLES OF ETHICAL REASONING

Both teleological and deontological theorists have developed a group of moral principles that are used for ethical reasoning. These principles of ethical reasoning further explore and define what beliefs or values form the basis for decision making. Respect for people is the most basic and universal ethical principle. The major *ethical principles* stemming from this basic principle are discussed in Display 4.2.

The most fundamental universal principle is respect for people.

DISPLAY 4.2	Ethical Principles

Autonomy: Promotes self-determination and freedom of choice
Beneficence: Actions are taken in an effort to promote good
Nonmaleficence: Actions are taken in an effort to avoid harm
Paternalism: One individual assumes the right to make decisions for another
Utility: The good of the many outweighs the wants or needs of the individual
Justice: Seek fairness; treat "equals" equally and treat "unequals" according to their differences
Veracity: Obligation to tell the truth
Fidelity: Need to keep promises
Confidentiality: Keep privileged information private

Autonomy (Self-Determination)

A form of personal liberty, *autonomy*, is also called freedom of choice or accepting the responsibility for one's choice. The legal right of *self-determination* supports this moral principle. The use of progressive discipline recognizes the autonomy of the employee. The employee, in essence, has the choice to meet organizational expectations or to be disciplined further. If the employee's continued behavior warrants termination, the principle of autonomy says that the employee has made the choice to be terminated by virtue of his or her actions, not by that of the manager. Therefore, nurse-managers must be cognizant of the ethical component present whenever an individual's decisional capacity is in question. To take away a person's right to self-determination is a serious but sometimes necessary action.

Beneficence (Doing Good)

This principle states that the actions one takes should be done in an effort to promote good. The concept of *nonmaleficence*, which is associated with *beneficence*, says that if one cannot do good, then one should at least do no harm. For example, if a manager uses this ethical principle in planning performance appraisals, he or she is much more likely to view the performance appraisal as a means of promoting employee growth.

Paternalism

This principle is related to beneficence in that one person assumes the authority to make a decision for another. Because *paternalism* limits freedom of choice, most ethical theorists believe that paternalism is justified only to prevent a person from coming to harm. Unfortunately, some managers use the principle of paternalism in subordinates' career planning. In doing so, managers assume that they have greater knowledge of what an employee's short- and long-term goals should be than the employee does.

Utility

This principle reflects a belief in utilitarianism—what is best for the common good outweighs what is best for the individual. Utility justifies paternalism as a means of restricting individual freedom. Managers who use the principle of utility need to be careful not to become so focused on desired group outcomes that they become less humanistic.

Justice (Treating People Fairly)

This principle states that equals should be treated equally and that unequals should be treated according to their differences. This principle is frequently applied when there are scarcities or competition for resources or benefits. The manager who uses the principle of *justice* will work to see that pay raises reflect performance and not just time of service.

Woods (2012) notes that in the last few decades, a growing number of commentators have questioned the appropriateness of the "justice view" of ethics as a suitable approach in healthcare ethics, and most certainly in nursing. Woods noted that nurses do not readily adopt the high degree of impartiality and objectivity that is associated with a justice view; instead their moral practices are more accurately reflected through the use of alternative approaches such as relational or care-based ethics. This observation suggests the need for a more ethically refined nursing response to an increasingly complex set of sociocultural inequalities such as a combined social justice and relational care-based approach. Woods maintains that such an approach is not only possible, but crucial if nurses are to realize their full potential as ethical agents for individual and social good.

LEARNING EXERCISE 4.1

Are Some More Equal than Others

Research suggests that individuals with health insurance in this country have better access to health-care services and better health-care outcomes than those who do not. This does not mean, however, that all individuals with health insurance receive "equal treatment." Medicaid recipients (the financially indigent) often complain that although they have public insurance, many private providers refuse to accept them as patients. Patients enrolled in managed care suggest that their treatment options are more limited than traditional private insurance because of the use of gatekeepers, required authorizations, and queuing. Even individuals with private insurance suggest that copayments and out-of-pocket costs for deductibles place the cost of care beyond the reach of many.

Assignment: Using the ethical principle of justice, determine whether health care in this country should be a right or a privilege. Are the uninsured and the insured "unequals" that should be treated according to their differences? Does the type of health insurance that one has also create a system of "unequals"? If so, are the unequals being treated according to their differences?

Veracity (Truth Telling)

This principle is used to explain how people feel about the need for truth telling or the acceptability of deception. A manager who believes that deception is morally acceptable if it is done with the objective of beneficence may tell all rejected job applicants that they were highly considered whether they had been or not.

LEARNING EXERCISE 4.2

Weighing Veracity versus Nonmaleficence

You are a second-year nursing student. During the first year of the nursing program, you formed a close friendship with Susan, another nursing student, and the two of you spend many of your free evenings and weekends together doing fun things. The only thing that drives you a bit crazy about your friend is that she is incredibly messy. When you go to her home, you usually see dirty dishes piled in the sink, dog hair over all the furniture, clothing strewn all over the apartment, and uneaten pizza or other half spoiled food sitting on the floor. You attempt to limit your time at her apartment since it is so bothersome to you, so it has not been a factor in your friendship.

Today, when Susan and you are sitting at the dining table in your apartment, your current roommate tells you that she is unexpectedly vacating her lease at the end of the month. Susan becomes excited and shares that her lease will end at the end of this month as well and suggests how much fun it would be if the two of you could move in together. She immediately begins talking about when she could move in, where she would locate her furniture in the apartment, and where her dog might stay when the two of you are in clinical. While you value Susan's friendship and really enjoy the time you spend together, the idea of living with someone as untidy as Susan is not something you want to do. Unfortunately, your current lease does not preclude pets or subleases.

Assignment: Decide how you will respond to Susan. Will you tell her the truth? Are your values regarding veracity stronger or weaker than your desire to cause no harm to Susan's feelings (nonmaleficence)?

Fidelity (Keeping Promises)

Fidelity refers to the moral obligation that individuals should be faithful to their commitments and promises. Breaking a promise is believed by many ethicists to be wrong regardless of the consequences. In other words, even if there were no far-reaching negative results of the broken promise, it is still wrong because it would render the making of any promise meaningless. However, there are times when keeping a promise (fidelity) may not be in the best interest of the other party, as discussed below under confidentiality. Although nurses have multiple fidelity duties (patient, physician, organization, profession, and self) that at times may be in conflict, the ANA Code of Ethics is clear that the nurse's primary commitment is to the patient (ANA, 2001).

Confidentiality (Respecting Privileged Information)

The obligation to observe the privacy of another and to hold certain information in strict confidence is a basic ethical principle and a foundation of both medical and nursing ethics. However, as in deception, there are times when the presumption against disclosing information must be overridden. For example, health-care managers are required by law to report certain cases, such as drug abuse in employees, elder abuse, and child abuse.

LEARNING EXERCISE 4.3

Family Values

You are the evening shift charge nurse of the recovery room. You have just admitted a 32-year-old woman who 2 hours ago was thrown from a Jeep in which she was a passenger. She was rushed to the emergency department and subsequently to surgery, where cranial burr holes were completed and an intracranial monitor was placed. No further cranial exploration was attempted because the patient sustained extensive and massive neurologic damage. She will probably not survive your shift. The plan is to hold her in the recovery room for 1 hour and, if she is still alive, transfer her to the intensive care unit.

Shortly after receiving the patient in the recovery room, you are approached by the evening house supervisor, who says that the patient's sister is pleading to be allowed into the recovery room. Normally, visitors are never allowed into the recovery room but occasionally exceptions are made. Tonight, the recovery room is empty except for this patient. You decide to bend the rules and allow the young woman's sister into the recovery room. The visiting sister is near collapse; it is obvious that she had been the driver of the Jeep. As the visitor continues to speak to the comatose patient, her behavior and words make you begin to wonder if she is indeed the sister.

Within 15 minutes, the house supervisor returns and states, "I have made a terrible mistake. The patient's family just arrived, and they say that the visitor we just allowed into the recovery room is not a member of the family but is the patient's lover. They are very angry and demand that this woman not be allowed to see the patient."

You approach the visitor and confront her in a kindly manner regarding the information that you have just received. She looks at you with tears streaming down her face and says, "Yes, it is true. Mary and I have been together for 6 years. Her family disowned her because of it, but we were everything to each other. She has been my life, and I have been hers. Please, please let me stay. I will never see her again. I know the family will not allow me to attend the funeral. I need to say my goodbyes. Please let me stay. It is not fair that they have the legal right to be family when I have been the one to love and care for Mary."

Assignment: You must decide what to do. Recognize that your own value system will play a part in your decision. List several alternatives that are available to you. Identify which ethical frameworks or principles most affected your decision making.

AMERICAN NURSES ASSOCIATION CODE OF ETHICS AND PROFESSIONAL STANDARDS

"Professional ethics relates to the values and standards of a particular profession, which are generally made explicit in professional codes of conduct or practice" (Grob, Leng, & Gallagher, 2012, p. 36). A *professional code of ethics* is a set of principles, established by a profession, to guide the individual practitioner. The first Code of Ethics for Nurses was adopted by the ANA in 1950 and has been revised five times since then. The ANA Center for Ethics and Human Rights again began seeking public input in the review of the *Code of Ethics for Nurses with Interpretative Statements* (the Code) in early 2013 with suggested revisions again in 2013.

This code outlines the important general values, duties, and responsibilities that flow from the specific role of being a nurse. While not legally binding, the code functions as a guide to the highest ethical practice standards for nurses and as an aid for moral thinking. See Display 4.3.

| DISPLAY 4.3 | American Nurses Association Code of Ethics for Nurses |

The ANA House of Delegates approved these nine provisions of the new *Code of Ethics for Nurses* at its June 30, 2001, meeting in Washington, DC. In July 2001, the Congress of Nursing Practice and Economics voted to accept the new language of the interpretive statements, resulting in a fully approved revised *Code of Ethics for Nurses with Interpretive Statements.*

1. The nurse, in all professional relationships, practices with compassion and respect for the inherent dignity, worth, and uniqueness of every individual, unrestricted by considerations of social or economic status, personal attributes, or the nature of health problems.
2. The nurse's primary commitment is to the patient, whether an individual, family, group, or community.
3. The nurse promotes, advocates for, and strives to protect the health, safety, and rights of the patient.
4. The nurse is responsible and accountable for individual nursing practice and determines the appropriate delegation of tasks consistent with the nurse's obligation to provide optimum patient care.
5. The nurse owes the same duties to self as to others, including the responsibility to preserve integrity and safety, to maintain competence, and to continue personal and professional growth.
6. The nurse participates in establishing, maintaining, and improving health-care environments and conditions of employment conducive to the provision of quality health care and consistent with the values of the profession through individual and collective action.
7. The nurse participates in the advancement of the profession through contributions to practice, education, administration, and knowledge development.
8. The nurse collaborates with other health professionals and the public in promoting community, national, and international efforts to meet health needs.
9. The profession of nursing, as represented by associations and their members, is responsible for articulating nursing values, for maintaining the integrity of the profession and its practice, and for shaping social policy.

Professional codes of ethics function as a guide to the highest standards of ethical practice for nurses. They are not legally binding.

The 2001 Code of Ethics for Nurses departs from previous versions in several important ways. The newest code returns to the use of the term *patient* rather than *client*, as *patient* more accurately reflects what the majority of nurses do—care for individuals with health problems. The code also explicitly details that the nurse's most fundamental accountability is to the patient, whether an individual, family, group, or community (No. 2). The 2001 code also addresses the responsibility of the nurse for assuring that the work environment is safe, even in an era of cutting costs and reduced revenues (No. 6). Finally, there is a provision (No. 5) that addresses duties of nurses to themselves.

Another document that may be helpful specifically to the nurse-manager in creating and maintaining an ethical work environment is *The Scope and Standards of Practice of Nursing Administration Practice* published by the ANA. These standards, revised in 2009, specifically delineate professional standards in management ethics, and these appear in Display 4.4.

DISPLAY 4.4   Standards of Practice for Nurse Administrators

STANDARD 12. ETHICS

The nurse administrator integrates ethical provisions in all areas of practice.

MEASUREMENT CRITERIA

1. Incorporates Code of Ethics for Nurses with Interpretive Statements (ANA, 2001) to guide practice.
2. Assures the preservation and protection of the autonomy, dignity, and rights of individuals.
3. Maintains confidentiality within legal and regulatory parameters.
4. Assures a process to identify and address ethical issues within nursing and the organization.
5. Participates on multidisciplinary and interdisciplinary teams that address ethical risks, benefits, and outcomes.
6. Demonstrates a commitment to practicing self-care, managing stress, and connecting with self and others.

Source: American Nurses Association. (2009). Nursing administration: Scope and standards of practice. Silver Springs, MD: American Nurses Publishing.

ETHICAL PROBLEM SOLVING AND DECISION MAKING

"Cutting edge medical research, coupled with rapid advances in the delivery of health care, has far surpassed society's ability to predict, comprehend, and/or resolve the ethical dilemmas confronting modern health care. These dilemmas resist fast and easy solutions" (Alichnie, 2012, p. 3). Therefore, ethical concepts and their utility in clinical practice must be taught along with the problem-solving skills that are a part of all decision making.

Some of the difficulty people have in making ethical decisions can be attributed to a lack of formal education about problem solving. Other individuals lack the thinking skills or risk taking needed to solve complex ethical problems. Still other nurses erroneously use decision-making outcomes as the sole basis for determining the quality of the decision making. Although decision makers should be able to identify desirable and undesirable outcomes, outcomes alone cannot be used to assess the quality of the problem solving. Many variables affect outcome, and some of these are beyond the control or foresight of the problem solver. Even the most ethical courses of action can have undesirable and unavoidable consequences. The quality of ethical problem solving should be evaluated in terms of the process used to make the decision. The best possible decisions stem from structured problem solving, adequate data collection, and examination of multiple alternatives—even if outcomes are poor.

If a structured approach to problem solving is used, data gathering is adequate, and multiple alternatives are analyzed, even with a poor outcome, the nurse should accept that the best possible decision was made at that time with the information and resources available.

In addition, Mortell (2012) suggests that some decision making by nurses reflects a *theory–practice–ethics gap* despite the moral obligation nurses have to ensure theory and practice are integrated. For example, Mortell notes that noncompliance exists in hand hygiene among practitioners despite ongoing infection prevention education and training; easy access to facilities such as wash basins; antiseptic/alcohol hand gels that are convenient, effective, and skin- and user-friendly; and organizational recognition and support for clinicians in hand washing and hand gel practices. Thus, despite nurses having knowledge of best practices based on current research, they continue to fail to achieve the required and desired compliance in hand hygiene. Mortell concludes that more emphasis should be placed on clinicians' moral and ethical obligations as part of training and orientation and that organizations must continue to emphasize the duty of care toward patients in nurses' decision making.

Kearney and Penque (2012) provide another example of a theory–practice–ethics gap in their suggestion that while nurses recognize that checklists can reduce episodes of patient harm by ensuring that procedures are being carried out appropriately, that some providers will indicate that an intervention has been undertaken when it has not. This occurs because of the mantra "If it wasn't documented, it wasn't done" and an increasing emphasis and reliance on documentation that demands that "all boxes must be ticked" to ensure complete care has been provided. Kearney and Penque suggest then that checklists present a context for ethical decision making in that when providers do not take ethics into account, checklists could actually perpetuate rather than prevent unsafe practices or errors.

The Traditional Problem-Solving Process

Although not recognized specifically as an ethical problem-solving model, one of the oldest and most frequently used tools for problem solving is the traditional problem-solving process. This process, which is discussed in Chapter 1, consists of seven steps, with the actual decision being made at step 5 (review the seven steps under "Traditional Problem-Solving Process" in Chapter 1). Although many individuals use at least some of these steps in their decision making, they frequently fail to generate an adequate number of alternatives or to evaluate the results—two essential steps in the process.

LEARNING EXERCISE 4.4

A Nagging Uneasiness

You are a nurse on a pediatric unit. One of your patients is a 15-month-old girl with a diagnosis of failure to thrive. The mother says that the child is emotional, cries a lot, and does not like to be held. You have been taking care of the infant for 2 days since her admission, and she has smiled and laughed and held out her arms to everyone. She has eaten well. There is something about the child's reaction to the mother's boyfriend that bothers you. The child appears to draw away from him when he visits. The mother is very young and seems to be rather immature but appears to care for the child.

This is the second hospital admission for this child. Although you were not on duty for the first admission 6 weeks ago, you check the records and see that the child was admitted with the same diagnosis. While you are on duty today, the child's father calls and inquires about her condition. He lives several hundred miles away and requests that the child be hospitalized until the weekend (it is Wednesday) so that he can "check things out." He tells you that he believes the child is mistreated. He says he is also concerned about his ex-wife's 4-year-old child from another marriage and is attempting to gain custody of that child in addition to his own child. From what little the father said, you are aware that the divorce was bitter and that the mother has full custody.

(Continued)

You talk with the physician at length. He says that after the last hospitalization, he requested that the community health agency and Child Protective Services call on the family. Their subsequent report to him was that the 4-year-old child appeared happy and well and that the 15-month-old child appeared clean, although underweight. There was no evidence to suggest child abuse. However, the community health agency plans to continue following the children. He says that the mother has been good about keeping doctor appointments and has kept the children's immunizations up to date. The pediatrician proceeds to write an order for discharge. He says that although he also feels somewhat uneasy, continued hospitalization is not justified, and the state medical aid will not pay for additional days. He also says that he will follow up once again with Child Protective Services to make another visit.

When the mother and her boyfriend come to take the baby home, the baby clings to you and refuses to go to the boyfriend. She also seems reluctant to go to the mother. All during the discharge, you are extremely uneasy. When you see the car drive away, you feel very sad.

After returning to the unit, you talk with your supervisor, who listens carefully and questions you at length. Finally, she says, "It seems as if you have nothing concrete on which to act and are only experiencing feelings. I think you would be risking a lot of trouble for yourself and the hospital if you acted rashly at this time. Accusing people with no evidence and making them go through a traumatic experience is something I would hesitate to do."

You leave the supervisor's office still troubled. She did not tell you that you must do nothing, but you believe that she would disapprove of further action on your part. The doctor also felt strongly that there was no reason to do more than was already being done. The child will be followed by community health nurses. Perhaps the ex-husband was just trying to make trouble for his ex-wife and her new boyfriend. You would certainly not want anyone to have reported you or created problems regarding your own children. You remember how often your 5-year-old bruised himself when he was that age. He often looked like an abused child. You go about your duties and try to shake off your feeling. What should you do?

Assignment:

1. Solve the case in small groups by using the traditional problem-solving process. Identify the problem and several alternative solutions to solve this ethical dilemma. What should you do and why? What are the risks? How does your value system play a part in your decision? Justify your solution. After completing this assignment, solve Part 2.

2. Assume that this was a real case. Twenty-four hours after the child's discharge, she is readmitted with critical head trauma. Police reports indicate that the child suffered multiple skull fractures after being thrown up against the wall by her mother's boyfriend. The child is not expected to live. Does knowing the outcome change how you would have solved the case? Does the outcome influence how you feel about the quality of your group's problem solving?

The Nursing Process

Another problem-solving model not specifically designed for ethical analysis but appropriate for it is the nursing process. Most nurses are aware of the nursing process and the cyclic nature of its components of assessment, diagnosis, planning, implementation, and evaluation (see Fig. 1.2). However, most nurses do not recognize its use as a decision-making tool. The cyclic nature of the process allows for feedback to occur at any step. It also allows the cycle to repeat until adequate information is gathered to make a decision. It does not, however, require clear problem identification. Learning Exercise 4.4 shows how the nursing process might be used as an ethical decision-making tool.

LEARNING EXERCISE 4.5

One Applicant Too Many

The reorganization of the public health agency has resulted in the creation of a new position of community health liaison. A job description has been written, and the job opening has been posted. As the chief nursing executive of this agency, it will be your responsibility to select the best person for the position. Because you are aware that all hiring decisions have some subjectivity, you want to eliminate as much personal bias as possible. Two people have applied for the position; one of them is a close personal friend.

Analysis

Assess: As the nursing executive, you have a responsibility to make personnel decisions as objectively as you can. This means that the hiring decision should be based solely on which employee is best qualified for the position. You do recognize, however, that there may be a personal cost in terms of the friendship.

Diagnose: You diagnose this problem as a potential intrapersonal conflict between your obligation to your friend and your obligation to your employer.

Plan: You must plan how you are going to collect your data. The tools you have selected are applications, resumes, references, and personal interviews.

Implement: Both applicants are contacted and asked to submit resumes and three letters of reference from recent employers. In addition, both are scheduled for structured formal interviews with you and two of the board members of the agency. Although the board members will provide feedback, you have reserved the right to make the final hiring decision.

Evaluate: As a result of your plan, you have discovered that both candidates meet the minimal job requirements. One candidate, however, clearly has higher-level communication skills, and the other candidate (your friend) has more experience in public health and is more knowledgeable regarding the resources in your community. Both employees have complied with the request to submit resumes and letters of reference; they are of similar quality.

Assess: Your assessment of the situation is that you need more information to make the best possible decision. You must assess whether strong communication skills or public health experience and familiarity with the community would be more valuable in this position.

Plan: You plan how you can gather more information about what the employee will be doing in this newly created position.

Implement: If the job description is inadequate in providing this information, it may be necessary to gather information from other public health agencies with a similar job classification.

Evaluate: You now believe that excellent communication skills are essential for the job. The candidate who had these skills has an acceptable level of public health experience and seems motivated to learn more about the community and its resources. This means that your friend will not receive the job.

Assess: Now you must assess whether a good decision has been made.

Plan: You plan to evaluate your decision in 6 months, basing your criteria on the established job description.

Implement: You are unable to implement your plan because this employee resigns unexpectedly 4 months after she takes the position. Your friend is now working in a similar capacity in another state. Although you correspond infrequently, the relationship has changed as a result of your decision.

(Continued)

Evaluate: Did you make a good decision? This decision was based on a carefully thought-out process, which included adequate data gathering and a weighing of alternatives. Variables beyond your control resulted in the employee's resignation, and there was no apparent reason for you to suspect that this would happen. The decision to exclude or minimize personal bias was a conscious one, and you were aware of the possible ramifications of this choice. The decision making appears to have been appropriate.

THE MORAL DECISION-MAKING MODEL

Crisham (1985) developed a model for ethical decision making incorporating the nursing process and principles of biomedical ethics. This model is especially useful in clarifying ethical problems that result from conflicting obligations. This model is represented by the mnemonic MORAL as shown in Display 4.5. Learning Exercise 4.6 demonstrates the MORAL modeling in solving an ethical issue.

DISPLAY 4.5   The MORAL Decision-Making Model

Massage the dilemma: Collect data about the ethical problem and who should be involved in the decision-making process.
Outline options: Identify alternatives, and analyze the causes and consequences of each.
Review criteria and resolve: Weigh the options against the values of those involved in the decision. This may be done through a weighting or grid.
Affirm position and act: Develop the implementation strategy.
Look back: Evaluate the decision making.

Source: Crisham, P. (1985). MORAL: How can I do what is right? Nursing Management, 16(3), 42A–42N.

LEARNING EXERCISE 4.6

Little White Lies

Sam is the nurse recruiter for a metropolitan hospital that is experiencing an acute nursing shortage. He has been told to do or say whatever is necessary to recruit professional nurses so that the hospital will not have to close several units. He also has been told that his position will be eliminated if he does not produce a substantial number of applicants in the nursing career days to be held the following week. Sam loves his job and is the sole provider for his family. Because many organizations are experiencing severe personnel shortages, the competition for employees is keen. After his third career day without a single prospective applicant, he begins to feel desperate. On the fourth and final day, Sam begins making many promises to potential applicants regarding shift preference, unit preference, salary, and advancement that he is not sure he can keep. At the end of the day, Sam has a lengthy list of interested applicants but also feels a great deal of intrapersonal conflict.

Massage the Dilemma

In a desperate effort to save his job, Sam finds he has taken action that has resulted in high intrapersonal value conflict. Sam must choose between making promises he cannot keep and losing his job. This has far-reaching consequences for all involved. Sam has the ultimate responsibility for knowing his values and acting in a manner that is congruent with his value system. The organization is, however, involved in the value conflict in that its values and expectations conflict with those of Sam. Sam and the organization have some type of responsibility to these applicants, although the exact nature of this responsibility is one of the values in conflict. Because this is Sam's problem and an intrapersonal conflict, he must decide the appropriate course of action. His primary role is to examine his values and act in accordance.

Outline Options

Option 1. Quit his job immediately. This would prevent future intrapersonal conflict, provided that Sam becomes aware of his value system and behaves in a manner consistent with that value system in the future. It does not, however, solve the immediate conflict about the action Sam has already taken. This action takes away Sam's livelihood.

Option 2. Do nothing. Sam could choose not to be accountable for his own actions. This will require Sam to rationalize that the philosophy of the organization is in fact acceptable or that he has no choice regarding his actions. Thus, the responsibility for meeting the needs and wants of the new employees is shifted to the organization. Although Sam will have no credibility with the new employees, there will be only a negligible impact on his ability to recruit at least on a short-term basis. Sam will continue to have a job and be able to support his family.

Option 3. If after value clarification Sam has determined that his values conflict with the organization's directive to do or say whatever is needed to recruit employees, he could approach his superior and share these concerns. Sam should be very clear about what his values are and to what extent he is willing to compromise them. He also should include in this meeting what, if any, action should be taken to meet the needs of the new employees. Sam must be realistic about the time and effort usually required to change the values and beliefs of an organization. He also must be aware of his bottom line if the organization is not willing to provide a compromise resolution.

Option 4. Sam could contact each of the applicants and tell them that certain recruitment promises may not be possible. However, he will do what he can to see that the promises are fulfilled. This alternative is risky. The applicants will probably be justifiably suspicious of both the recruiter and the organization, and Sam has little formal power at this point to fulfill their requests. This alternative also requires a time and energy commitment by Sam and does not prevent the problem from recurring.

Review the Options

In value clarification, Sam discovered that he valued truth telling. Alternative 3 allows Sam to present a recruiting plan to his supervisor that includes a bottom line that this value will not be violated.

Affirm Position and Act

Sam approached his superior and was told that his beliefs were idealistic and inappropriate in an age of severe worker shortages. Sam was terminated. Sam did, however, believe that he made an appropriate decision. He did become self-aware regarding his values and attempted to communicate these values to the organization in an effort to work out a mutually agreeable plan.

(Continued)

Look Back

Although Sam was terminated, he knew that he could find some type of employment to meet his immediate fiscal needs. He did become self-aware regarding his values and used what he had learned in this decision-making process, in that he planned to evaluate more carefully the recruitment philosophy of the organization in relation to his own value system before accepting another job.

WORKING TOWARD ETHICAL BEHAVIOR AS THE NORM

The concerns about ethical conduct in American institutions are documented by many news articles in the national press. Many individuals believe that organizational and institutional ethical failure has become the norm. Governmental agencies, both branches of Congress, the stock exchange, oil companies, and savings and loan institutions have all experienced problems with unethical conduct. Many members of society wonder what has gone wrong. Nurse-managers, then, have a responsibility to create a climate in their organizations in which ethical behavior is not only the expectation but the norm.

In an era of markedly limited physical, human, and fiscal resources, nearly all decision making by nurse-managers will involve some ethical component. Indeed, the following forces ensure that ethics will become an even greater dimension in management decision making in the future: increasing technology, regulatory pressures, and competitiveness among health-care providers; workforce shortages; an imperative to provide better care at less cost; spiraling costs of supplies and salaries; and the public's increasing distrust of the health-care delivery system and its institutions. The following actions, as shown in Display 4.6, can help the manager in ethical problem solving.

DISPLAY 4.6	Strategies Leader-Managers Can Use to Promote Ethical Behavior as the Norm

1. Separate legal and ethical issues
2. Collaborate through ethics committees
3. Use IRBs appropriately
4. Foster an ethical work environment

Separate Legal and Ethical Issues

Although they are not the same, separating legal and ethical issues is sometimes difficult. Legal controls are generally clear and philosophically impartial; ethical controls are much less clear and individualized. In many ethical issues, courts have made a decision that may guide managers in their decision making. Often, however, these guidelines are not comprehensive, or they differ from the manager's own philosophy. Managers must be aware of established legal standards and cognizant of possible liabilities and consequences for actions that go against the legal precedent.

In general, legal controls are clearer and philosophically impartial; ethical controls are much less clear and individualized.

Legal precedents are frequently overturned later and often do not keep pace with the changing needs of society. In addition, certain circumstances may favor an illegal course of action as the "right" thing to do. If a man were transporting his severely ill wife to the hospital, it might be morally correct for him to disobey traffic laws. Therefore, the manager should think of the law as a basic standard of conduct, whereas ethical behavior requires a greater examination of the issues involved.

The manager may confront several particularly sensitive legal–ethical issues, including termination or refusal of treatment, durable power of attorney, abortion, sterilization, child abuse, and human experimentation. Most health-care organizations have legal counsel to assist managers in making decisions in such sensitive areas. Because legal aspects of management decision making are so important, Chapter 5 is devoted exclusively to this topic.

Collaborate Through Ethics Committees

The new manager must consult with others when solving sensitive legal–ethical questions because a person's own value system may preclude examining all possible alternatives. Many institutions have ethics committees to assist with problem solving in ethical issues. These ethics committees typically are interprofessional and are organized to consciously and reflectively consider significant and often difficult or ambiguous value issues related to patient care or organizational activities. Ethics committees are a core element of collaborative ethical decision making and should include representatives of all stakeholders, including patients when they are involved in the ethical issue.

Use Institutional Review Boards Appropriately

IRBs are primarily formed to protect the rights and welfare of research subjects. They provide oversight to ensure that individuals conducting research adhere to ethical principles that were articulated by the National Commission for the Protection of Human Subjects of Biomedical and Behavioral Research. The primary role of the manager regarding IRBs is to make sure that such a board is in place in the organization where the manager works and that any research performed within his or her sphere of responsibility has been approved by such a board.

Foster an Ethical Work Environment

Perhaps the most important thing a leader-manager can do to foster an ethical work environment, however, is to role model ethical behavior. Silén, Kjellström, Christensson, Sidenvall, and Svantesson (2012) note this can be done as simply as meeting the needs of patients and next of kin in a considerate way, as well as receiving and giving support and information within the work group. Likewise, working as a team with a standard for behavior can promote a positive ethical climate. Other important interventions include encouraging staff to openly discuss ethical issues that they face daily in their practice. This allows subordinates to gain greater perspective on complex issues and provides a mechanism for peer support.

Sorbello (2008), however, notes the challenge faced by some nurse administrators in both retaining the essence of nurses who "live caring" at the same time they are "challenged to make wise and ethical decisions for what is best for the organization" (p. 48). She recommends that nurse-leaders seek to balance the competing demands for resources within the organization within the context of the ethical problems they face. She also suggests that in sharing these challenges with staff, managers are often able to nurture meaningful relationships, foster honest dialogue, and role model caring.

ETHICAL DIMENSIONS IN LEADERSHIP AND MANAGEMENT

The need for ethical decisions occurs in every phase of the management process, and many of the learning exercises in this book have an ethical component that must be considered in problem solving. In fact, each section in this book could appropriately include a section on ethical issues, such as the following:

Unit III

- At what point do the needs of the organization become more important than those of the individual worker?
- Should employees ever be coerced into changing their stated values so that they more closely align with those of the organization?
- How can managers fairly allocate resources when virtually all resources are limited?

Unit IV

- Should quality or cost be the final determinant when selecting the most appropriate type of patient care delivery system?
- Should licensed vocational nurses and licensed professional nurses be allowed to function in the primary nursing role?
- How should the manager protect clients from an inadequately trained nurse?
- Which should be more important to the organization—human relations or productivity?
- Which is more corrupting—power or powerlessness?

Unit V

- At what point does short staffing become unsafe?
- Should shift scheduling be used as a means of reward and punishment?
- Is luring or recruiting employees from other agencies ever ethical?
- How far can the truth be stretched in recruitment advertising before it becomes deceptive?
- Should preemployment testing be required as a condition of employment?
- Is it ethical for employees to take a position in an organization if they know that they are planning to leave in a short time?
- Is it ever justified for an employee to lie in an interview?
- Who has the responsibility for socializing the new graduate into the professional nursing role—the nursing school, the hospital, or is it a joint process?
- What commitment does the organization have to the nurse who is reentering the profession after not practicing for many years?

Unit VI

- To whom do managers owe their primary allegiance—the organization or their subordinates?
- When is it appropriate to use money as the primary motivator?
- If employees are producing at acceptable or higher levels, what new rewards and incentives should be introduced?

- Is it ethical to promote antiunion organizers to management roles to reduce the possibility of union formation?
- Is affirmative action hiring to compensate for past discrimination ethically justifiable, or does it promote reverse discrimination?
- Is it ethical for nurses to strike?
- Should the national nursing organization also be a collective bargaining agent?

Unit VII

- Is it necessary for each employee to be assisted to achieve at optimal levels? Can the manager be selective in determining which employees are assisted to reach optimal productivity?
- At what point does the power to evaluate the work of others become dangerous?
- Should the individual be allowed total self-determination in short- and long-term career planning?
- Is it ethical to promote or transfer a less-qualified person to keep a valuable employee on a unit?
- Does the organization have an obligation to reemploy the chemically impaired employee who seeks rehabilitation?
- When does the employee's right to privacy regarding drug or alcohol use stop and the manager's right to that information begin?
- Is it ever ethical to file a grievance against another person for the purpose of harassment?
- Can discipline administered in anger ever be fair?
- In pursuing beneficence, is it more appropriate to discipline marginal employees progressively or to terminate them?

INTEGRATING LEADERSHIP ROLES AND MANAGEMENT FUNCTIONS IN ETHICS

Leadership roles in ethics focus on the human element involved in ethical decision making. Leaders are self-aware regarding their values and basic beliefs about the rights, duties, and goals of human beings. As self-aware and ethical people, they role model confidence in their decision making to subordinates. They also are realists and recognize that some ambiguity and uncertainty must be a part of all ethical decision making. Leaders are willing to take risks in their decision making despite the fact that negative outcomes can occur even with quality decision making.

In ethical issues, the manager is often the decision maker. Because ethical decisions are so complex and the cost of a poor decision may be high, management functions focus on increasing the chances that the best possible decision will be made at the least possible cost in terms of fiscal and human resources. This usually requires that the manager becomes expert at using systematic approaches to problem solving or decision making, such as theoretical models, ethical frameworks, and ethical principles. By developing expertise, the manager can identify universal outcomes that should be sought or avoided.

The integrated leader-manager recognizes that ethical issues pervade every aspect of leadership and management. Rather than being paralyzed by the complexity and ambiguity of these issues, the leader-manager seeks counsel as needed, accepts his or her limitations, and makes the best possible decision at that time with the information and resources available.

KEY CONCEPTS

● Ethics is the systematic study of what a person's conduct and actions should be with regard to self, other human beings, and the environment; it is the justification of what is right or good and the study of what a person's life and relationships should be—not necessarily what they are.

● In an era of markedly limited physical, human, and fiscal resources, nearly all decision making by nurse-managers involves some ethical component. Multiple advocacy roles and accountability to the profession further increase the likelihood that managers will be faced with ethical dilemmas in their practice.

● Many systematic approaches to ethical problem solving are appropriate. These include the use of theoretical problem-solving and decision-making models, ethical frameworks, and ethical principles.

● Outcomes should never be used as the sole criterion for assessing the quality of ethical problem solving, because many variables affect outcomes that have no reflection on whether the problem solving was appropriate. Quality, instead, should be evaluated both by the outcome and the process used to make the decision. If a structured approach to problem solving is used, data gathering is adequate, and multiple alternatives are analyzed, then, regardless of the outcome, the manager should feel comfortable that the best possible decision was made at that time with the information and resources available.

● Four of the most commonly used ethical frameworks for decision making are utilitarianism, duty-based reasoning, rights-based reasoning, and intuitionism. These frameworks do not solve the ethical problem but assist individuals involved in the problem solving to clarify their values and beliefs.

● Principles of ethical reasoning explore and define what beliefs or values form the basis for our decision making. These principles include autonomy, beneficence, nonmaleficence, paternalism, utility, justice, fidelity, veracity, and confidentiality.

● Professional codes of ethics and standards for practice are guides to the highest standards of ethical practice for nurses.

● Sometimes it is very difficult to separate legal and ethical issues, although they are not the same. Legal controls are generally clear and philosophically impartial. Ethical controls are much more unclear and individualized.

ADDITIONAL LEARNING EXERCISES AND APPLICATIONS

LEARNING EXERCISE 4.7

The Impaired Employee

Beverly, a 35-year-old, full-time nurse on the day shift, has been with your facility for 10 years. There are rumors that she comes to work under the influence of alcohol. Staff report the smell of alcohol on her breath, unexcused absences from the unit, and an increase in medication errors. Although the unit supervisor suspected that Beverly was chemically impaired, she was unable to observe directly any of these behaviors.

After arriving at work last week, the supervisor walked into the nurses' lounge and observed Beverly covertly drinking from a dark-colored flask in her locker. She immediately confronted Beverly and asked her if she was drinking alcohol while on duty. Beverly tearfully admitted that she was drinking alcohol but stated this was an isolated incident and begged her to forget it. She promised never to consume alcohol at work again.

In an effort to reduce the emotionalism of the event and to give herself time to think, the supervisor sent Beverly home and scheduled a conference with her for later in the day. At this conference, Beverly was defensive and stated, "I do not have a drinking problem, and you are overreacting." The supervisor shared data that she had gathered supporting her impression that Beverly was chemically impaired. Beverly offered no explanation for these behaviors.

The plan for Beverly was a referral to the State Board of Nursing Diversion Program and a requirement that she complete the program as they direct her. Beverly again became very tearful and begged the supervisor to reconsider. She stated that she was the sole provider for her four small children and that her frequent sick days had taken up all available vacation and sick pay. The supervisor stated that she believed her decision was appropriate and again encouraged Beverly to seek guidance for her drinking. Four days later, the supervisor read in the newspaper that Beverly committed suicide the day after this meeting.

Assignment: Evaluate the problem solving of the supervisor. Would your actions have differed if you were the manager? Are there conflicting legal and ethical obligations? To whom does the manager have the greatest obligation—patients, subordinates, or the organization? Could the outcome have been prevented? Does this outcome reflect on the quality of the problem solving?

LEARNING EXERCISE 4.8

Everything Is Not What It Seems

You are a perinatal unit coordinator at a large teaching hospital. In addition to your management responsibilities, you have been asked to fill in as a member of the hospital promotion committee, which reviews petitions from clinicians for a step-level promotion on the clinical specialist ladder. You believe that you could learn a great deal on this committee and could be an objective and contributing member.

The committee has been convened to select the annual winner of the Outstanding Clinical Specialist Award. In reviewing the applicant files, you find that one file from a perinatal clinical specialist contains many overstatements and several misrepresentations. You know for a fact that this clinician did not accomplish all that she has listed, because she is a friend and close colleague. She did not, however, know that you would be a member of this committee and thus would be aware of this deception.

When the entire committee met, several members commented on this clinician's impressive file. Although you were able to dissuade them covertly from further considering her nomination, you are left with many uneasy feelings and some anger and sadness. You recognize that she did not receive the nomination and thus there is little real danger regarding the deceptions in the file being used inappropriately at this time. However, you will not be on this committee next year, and if she were to submit an erroneous file again, she could be highly considered for the award. You also recognize that even with the best of intentions and the most therapeutic of communication techniques, confronting your friend with her deception will cause her to lose face and will probably result in an unsalvageable friendship. Even if you do confront her, there is little you can do to stop her from doing the same in future nomination processes other than formally reporting her conduct.

Assignment: Determine what you will do. Do the potential costs outweigh the potential benefits? Be realistic about your actions.

LEARNING EXERCISE 4.9

The Valuable Employee

Gina has been the supervisor of a 16-bed intensive care unit/critical care unit (ICU/CCU) in a 200-bed urban hospital for 8 years. She is respected and well liked by her staff. Her unit's staff retention level and productivity are higher than any other unit in the hospital. For the last 6 years, Gina has relied heavily on Mark, her permanent charge nurse on the day shift. He is bright and motivated and has excellent clinical and managerial skills. Mark seems satisfied and challenged in his current position, although Gina has not had any formal career planning meetings with him to discuss his long-term career goals. It would be fair to say that Mark's work has greatly increased Gina's scope of power and has enhanced the reputation of the unit.

Recently, one of the physicians approached Gina about a plan to open an outpatient cardiac rehabilitation program. The program will require a strong leader and manager who is self-motivated. It will be a lot of work but also provides many opportunities for advancement. He suggests that Mark would be an excellent choice for the job, although he has given Gina full authority to make the final decision.

Gina is aware that Lynn, a bright and dynamic staff nurse from the open-heart surgery floor, also would be very interested in the job. Lynn has been employed at the hospital for only 1 year but has a proven track record and would probably be very successful in the job. In addition, there is a staffing surplus right now on the open-heart surgery floor because two of the surgeons have recently retired. It would be difficult and time-consuming to replace Mark as charge nurse in the ICU/CCU.

Assignment: What process should this supervisor pursue to determine who should be hired for the position? Should the position be posted? When does the benefit of using transfers/promotions as a means of reward outweigh the cost of reduced productivity?

LEARNING EXERCISE 4.10

To See or Not to See

For the last few days, you have been taking care of Mr. Cole, a 28-year-old patient with end-stage cystic fibrosis. You have developed a caring relationship with Mr. Cole and his wife. They are both aware of the prognosis of his disease and realize that he has only a short time left to live.

When Dr. Jones made rounds with you this morning, she told the Coles that Mr. Cole could be discharged today if his condition remains stable. They were both excited about the news because they had been urging the doctor to let him go home to enjoy his remaining time surrounded by things he loves.

When you bring in Mr. Cole's discharge orders to his room in order to review his medications and other treatments, you find Mrs. Cole assisting Mr. Cole as he coughs up bright red blood. When you confront them, they both beg you not to tell the doctor or chart the incident because this is the first time this has happened. They believe that it is their right to go home and let Mr. Cole die surrounded by his family. They said that they know that they can leave against their physician's wishes and go home AMA (against medical advice), but if they do, their insurance will not pay for home care.

Assignment: What is your duty in this case? What are Mr. Cole's rights? Is it ever justified to withhold information from the physician? Will you chart the incident and will you report it to anyone? Solve this case, justifying your decision by using ethical principles.

REFERENCES

Alichnie, C. (2012). Ethics and nursing. *Pennsylvania Nurse*, *67*(2), 5–26.

American Nurses Association. (2001). *Code of ethics for nurses with interpretive statements*. Washington, DC: American Nurses Publishing.

American Nurses Association. (2009). *Nursing administration: Scope and standards of practice*. Silver Springs, MD: American Nurses Publishing.

Bitoun Blecher, M. (2001–2013). *What color is your whistle?* Minoritynurse.com. Retrieved February 24, 2013, from http://www.minoritynurse.com/workplace-issues/what-color-your-whistle

Crisham, P. (1985). MORAL: How can I do what is right? *Nursing Management*, *16*(3), 42A–42N.

Davis, S., Schrader, V., & Belcheir, M. (2012). Influencers of ethical beliefs and the impact on moral distress and conscientious objection. *Nursing Ethics*, *19*(6), 738–749.

Gallagher, A., & Hodge, S. (Eds.) (2012). *Ethics, law and professional issues: A practice-based approach for health professionals*. Basingstoke: Palgrave MacMillan.

Grob, C., Leng, J., & Gallagher, A. (2012). Educational responses to unethical healthcare practice. *Nursing Standard*, *26*(41), 35–41.

Kearney, G., & Penque, S. (2012). Ethics of everyday decision making. *Nursing Management – UK*, *19*(1), 32–36.

Mortell, M. (2012). Hand hygiene compliance: Is there a theory-practice-ethics gap? *British Journal of Nursing*, *21*(17), 1011–1014.

Nalley, C. (2013, February 8). *Moral distress takes toll on nurses*. *Advance for nurses*. Retrieved February 25, 2013, from http://nursing.advanceweb.com/Features/Articles/Moral-Distress-Takes-Toll-on-Nurses.aspx

Pauly, B. M., Varcoe, C., & Storch, J. (2012, March). Framing the issues. Moral distress in health care. *HEC Forum, 24*(1), 1–11.

Silén, M., Kjellström, S., Christensson, L., Sidenvall, B., & Svantesson, M. (2012). What actions promote a positive ethical climate? A critical incident study of nurses' perceptions. *Nursing Ethics*, *19*(4), 501–512.

Sorbello, B. (2008, December). The nurse administrator as caring person: A synoptic analysis applying caring philosophy, Ray's ethical theory of existential authenticity, the ethic of justice, and the ethic of care. *International Journal for Human Caring*, *12*(1), 44–49.

Woods, M. (2012). Exploring the relevance of social justice within a relational nursing ethic. *Nursing Philosophy*, *13*(1), 56–65.

5

Legal and Legislative Issues

... It may seem a strange principle to enunciate as the very first requirement in a hospital that it should do the sick no harm.
—Florence Nightingale

... Laws or ordinances unobserved, or partially attended to, had better never have been made.
—George Washington, letter to James Madison, March 31, 1787

CROSSWALK THIS CHAPTER ADDRESSES:

BSN Essential II: Basic organizational and systems leadership for quality care and patient safety
BSN Essential V: Health-care policy, finance, and regulatory environments
BSN Essential VIII: Professionalism and professional values
MSN Essential II: Organizational and systems leadership
MSN Essential VI: Health policy and advocacy
AONE Nurse Executive Competency II: A knowledge of the health-care environment
AONE Nurse Executive Competency V: Business skills
QSEN Competency: Safety

LEARNING OBJECTIVES *The learner will:*

- correlate the legal authority of nursing practice and the nursing process
- select appropriate legal nursing actions in sensitive clinical situations
- explain how increased consumer awareness of patient rights has affected the actions of the health-care team
- evaluate the significance of professional and institutional licensure
- describe appropriate methods of ensuring informed consent
- analyze the impact of civil law on nursing practice
- differentiate between legal and ethical accountability

Chapter 4 presented ethics as an internal control of human behavior and nursing practice. Therefore, ethics has to do with actions that people should take, not necessarily actions that they are legally required to take. On the other hand, ethical behavior written into law is no longer just desired, it is mandated. This chapter focuses on the external controls of legislation and law. Since the first mandatory *Nurse Practice Act* was passed in North Carolina in 1903, nursing has been legislated, directed, and controlled to some extent.

The primary purpose of law and legislation is to protect the patient and the nurse. Laws and legislation define the scope of acceptable practice and protect individual rights. Nurses who are aware of their rights and duties in legal matters are better able to protect themselves against liability or loss of professional licensure.

This chapter has five sections. The first section presents the primary sources of law and how each affects nursing practice. The nurse's responsibility to be proactive in establishing and revising laws affecting nursing practice is emphasized. The second section presents the types of legal cases in which nurses may be involved and differentiates between the burden of proof and the consequences for each if the nurse is found to have broken the law. The third section identifies specific doctrines used by the courts to define legal boundaries for nursing practice. The role of state boards in professional licensure and discipline is examined. The fourth section deals with the components of malpractice for the individual practitioner and the manager or supervisor. Legal terms are defined. The fifth and final section discusses issues such as informed consent, medical records, intentional torts, the Patient Self-Determination Act (PSDA), the Good Samaritan Act, and the Health Insurance Portability and Accountability Act (HIPAA).

This chapter is not meant to be a complete legal guide to nursing practice. There are many excellent legal textbooks and handbooks that accomplish that function. The primary function of this chapter is to emphasize the widely varying and rapidly changing nature of laws and the responsibility that each manager has to keep abreast of legislation and laws affecting both nursing and management practice. Leadership roles and management functions inherent in legal and legislative issues are shown in Display 5.1.

| DISPLAY 5.1 | Leadership Roles and Management Functions Associated with Legal and Legislative Issues |

LEADERSHIP ROLES

1. Serves as a role model by providing nursing care that meets or exceeds accepted standards of care.
2. Updates knowledge and skills in the field of practice and seeks professional certification to increase expertise in a specific field.
3. Reports substandard nursing care to appropriate authorities following the established chain of command.
4. Fosters nurse–patient relationships that are respectful, caring, and honest, thus reducing the possibility of future lawsuits.
5. Creates an environment that encourages and supports diversity and sensitivity.
6. Prioritizes patient rights and patient welfare in decision making.
7. Demonstrates vision, risk taking, and energy in determining appropriate legal boundaries for nursing practice, thus defining what nursing is and what should be in the future.

MANAGEMENT FUNCTIONS

1. Increases knowledge regarding sources of law and legal doctrines that affect nursing practice.
2. Delegates to subordinates wisely, looking at the manager's scope of practice and that of the individuals he or she supervises.
3. Understands and adheres to institutional policies and procedures.
4. Minimizes the risk of product liability by assuring that all staff are appropriately oriented to the appropriate use of equipment and products.
5. Monitors subordinates to ensure they have a valid, current, and appropriate license to practice nursing.
6. Uses foreseeability of harm in delegation and staffing decisions.
7. Increases staff awareness of intentional torts and assists them in developing strategies to reduce their liability in these areas.
8. Provides educational and training opportunities for staff on legal issues affecting nursing practice.

SOURCES OF LAW

The US legal system can be somewhat confusing because there are not only four sources of the law but also parallel systems at the state and federal levels. The sources of law include constitutions, statutes, administrative agencies, and court decisions. A comparison is shown in Table 5.1.

A *constitution* is a system of fundamental laws or principles that govern a nation, society, corporation, or other aggregate of individuals. The purpose of a constitution is to establish the

TABLE 5.1	Sources of Law	
Origin of Law	*Use*	*Involvement with Nursing Practice*
The Constitution	The highest law in the United States; interpreted by the U.S. Supreme Court; gives authority to other three sources of the law	Little direct involvement in the area of malpractice
Statutes	Also called *statutory law* or *legislative law*; laws that are passed by the state or federal legislators and that must be signed by the president or governor	Before 1970s, very few state or federal laws dealt with malpractice. Since the malpractice crisis, many statutes affect malpractice
Administrative agencies	The rules and regulations established by appointed agencies of the executive branch of the government (governor or president)	Some of these agencies, such as the National Labor Relations Board and health and safety boards, can affect nursing practice
Court decisions	Also called *tort law*; this is court mode law and the courts interpret the statutes and set precedents; in the United States, there are two levels of court: trial court and appellate court	Most malpractice law is addressed by the courts

basis of a governing system for the future and the present. The U.S. Constitution establishes the general organization of the federal government and grants and limits its specific powers. Each state also has a constitution that establishes the general organization of the state government and grants and limits its powers.

The second source of law is *statutes*—laws that govern. Legislative bodies, such as the U.S. Congress, state legislatures, and city councils, make these laws. Statutes are officially enacted (voted on and passed) by the legislative body and are compiled into codes, collections of statutes, and ordinances. The 51 *Nurse Practice Acts* representing the 50 states and the District of Columbia are examples of statutes. These Nurse Practice Acts define and limit the practice of nursing, thereby stating what constitutes authorized practice as well as what exceeds the scope of authority. Although Nurse Practice Acts may vary among states, all must be consistent with provisions or statutes established at the federal level.

The 51 Nurse Practice Acts (one for each state and the District of Columbia) define and limit the practice of nursing, thereby stating what constitutes authorized practice as well as what exceeds the scope of authority.

Administrative agencies, the third source of law, are given authority to act by the legislative bodies and create rules and regulations that enforce statutory laws. For example, State Boards of Nursing are administrative agencies set up to implement and enforce the state Nurse Practice Act by writing rules and regulations and by conducting investigations and hearings to ensure the law's enforcement. Administrative laws are valid only to the extent that they are within the scope of the authority granted to them by the legislative body.

The fourth source of law is *court decisions*. Judicial or decisional laws are made by the courts to interpret legal issues that are in dispute. Depending on the type of court involved, judicial or decisional law may be made by a single justice, with or without a jury, or by a panel of justices. Generally, initial trial courts have a single judge or magistrate, intermediary appeal courts have three justices, and the highest appeal courts have nine justices.

TYPES OF LAWS AND COURTS

Although most nurses worry primarily about being sued for malpractice, they may actually be involved in three different types of court cases: criminal, civil, and administrative (Table 5.2). The court in which each is tried, the burden of proof required for conviction, and the resulting punishment associated with each is different.

TABLE 5.2	Types of Laws and Courts	
Type	*Burden of Proof Required for Guilty Verdict*	*Likely Consequences of a Guilty Verdict*
Criminal	Beyond a reasonable doubt	Incarceration, probation, and fines
Civil	Based on a preponderance of the evidence	Monetary damages
Administrative	Clear and convincing standard	Suspension or loss of licensure

In *criminal* cases, the individual faces charges generally filed by the state or federal attorney general for crimes committed against an individual or society. In criminal cases, the individual is always presumed to be innocent unless the state can prove his or her guilt beyond a reasonable doubt. Incarceration and even death are possible consequences for being found guilty in criminal matters. Nurses found guilty of intentionally administering fatal doses of drugs to patients would be charged in a criminal court.

In *civil* cases, one individual sues another for money to compensate for a perceived loss. The burden of proof required to be found guilty in a civil case is described as a *preponderance of the evidence*. In other words, the judge or jury must believe that it was more likely than not that the accused individual was responsible for the injuries of the complainant. Consequences of being found guilty in a civil suit are monetary. Most malpractice cases are tried in civil court.

In *administrative* cases, an individual is sued by a state or federal governmental agency assigned the responsibility of implementing governmental programs. State Boards of Nursing are one such governmental agency. When an individual violates the state Nurse Practice Act, the Boards of Nursing may seek to revoke licensure or institute some form of discipline. The burden of proof in these cases varies from state to state. When the *clear and convincing standard* is not used, the preponderance of the evidence standard may be used. Clear and convincing involves higher burdens of proof than preponderance of evidence but significantly lower burdens of proof than beyond a reasonable doubt.

 The burden of proof required for conviction as well as the type of punishment given differs in criminal, civil, and administrative cases.

LEARNING EXERCISE 5.1

Both Guilty and Not Guilty

Think of celebrated cases where defendants have been tried in both civil and criminal courts. What were the verdicts in both cases? If the verdicts were not the same, analyze why this happened. Do you agree that taking away an individual's personal liberty by incarceration should require a higher burden of proof than assessing for monetary damages?

Assignment: Also complete a literature search to see if you can find cases where a nurse faced both civil and administrative charges. Were you able to find cases where the nurse was found guilty in a civil court but did not lose his or her license? Did you find the opposite?

 ## LEGAL DOCTRINES AND THE PRACTICE OF NURSING

Two important legal doctrines frequently guide all three courts in their decision making. The first of these, *stare decisis*, means to let the decision stand. *Stare decisis* uses precedents as a guide for decision making. This doctrine gives nurses insight into ways that the court has previously fixed liability in given situations. However, the nurse must avoid two pitfalls in determining if *stare decisis* should apply to a given situation.

 Precedent is often used as a guide for legal decision making.

The first is that the previous case must be within the jurisdiction of the court hearing the current case. For example, a previous Florida case decided by a state court does not set precedent for a Texas appellate court. Although the Texas court may model its decision after the Florida case, it is not compelled to do so. The lower courts in Texas, however, would rely on Texas appellate decisions.

The other pitfall is that the court hearing the current case can depart from the precedent and set a landmark decision. Landmark decisions generally occur because societal needs have changed, technology has become more advanced, or following the precedent would further harm an already injured person. Roe versus Wade, the 1973 landmark decision to allow a woman to seek and receive a legal abortion during the first two trimesters of pregnancy, is an example. Given the influence of politics and varying societal views about abortion, this precedent may change again in the future.

The second doctrine that guides courts in their decision making is *res judicata*, which means a "thing or matter settled by judgment." It applies only when a competent court has decided a legal dispute and when no further appeals are possible. This doctrine keeps the same parties in the original lawsuit from retrying the same issues that were involved in the first lawsuit.

When using doctrines as a guide for nursing practice, the nurse must remember that all laws are fluid and subject to change. An example of changing law regarding professional nursing occurred in an Illinois Supreme Court case just over a decade ago when the law finally recognized nursing as an independent profession with its own unique body of knowledge. In this case (Sullivan versus Edward Hospital, 2004), the Illinois Supreme Court decided that physicians could not serve as expert witnesses regarding nursing standards (Find Law for Legal Professionals, 2013). This demonstrates how the law is ever evolving. Laws cannot be static; they must change to reflect the growing autonomy and responsibility desired by nurses. It is critical that all nurses be aware of and sensitive to rapidly changing laws and legislation that affect their practice. Nurses must also recognize that state laws may differ from federal laws and that legal guidelines for nursing practice in the organization may differ from state or federal guidelines.

Boundaries for practice are defined in the Nurse Practice Act of each state. These acts are general in most states to allow for some flexibility in the broad roles and varied situations in which nurses practice. Because this allows for some interpretation, many employers have established guidelines for nursing practice in their own organization. These guidelines regarding scope of practice cannot, however, exceed the requirements of the state Nursing Practice Acts. Managers need to be aware of their organization's specific practice interpretations and ensure that subordinates are aware of the same and follow established practices. All nurses must understand the legal controls for nursing practice in their state.

PROFESSIONAL NEGLIGENCE

Historically, physicians were the health-care providers most likely to be held liable for nursing care. As nurses have gained authority, autonomy, and accountability, they have assumed responsibility, accountability, and liability for their own practice. As roles have expanded, nurses have begun performing duties traditionally reserved for medical practice. As a result of an increased scope of practice, many nurses now carry individual malpractice insurance. This is a double-edged sword. Nurses need malpractice insurance in basic practice as well as in expanded practice roles. They do incur a greater likelihood of being sued, however, if they have malpractice insurance, since injured parties will always seek damages from as many individuals with financial resources as possible.

In addition, some nurses count on their employer-provided professional liability policies to protect them from malpractice claims, but such policies often have limitations. For example, employers may not provide coverage once an employee has terminated their employment, even if the situation which led to the complaint occurred while the nurse was employed there and some employer-provided policies have inadequate limits of liability for the individual employee. Nurses then are advised to obtain their own personal liability policy.

Unfortunately, both the enhanced role of nurses and the increase in the number of insured nurses have led to a great increase in the number of liability suits seeking damages from nurses as individuals over the past few decades. In particular, malpractice has become of great concern to *advanced practice nurses* such as nurse practitioners and nurse midwives. Nurse practitioners are not only paying high costs for their insurance premiums, they generally are subject to strict professional liability (malpractice) insurance requirements.

Elements of Malpractice

All liability suits involve a plaintiff and a defendant. In malpractice cases, the *plaintiff* is the injured party and the *defendant* is the professional who is alleged to have caused the injury. *Negligence* is the omission to do something that a reasonable person, guided by the considerations that ordinarily regulate human affairs, would do—or as doing something that a reasonable and prudent person would not do. *Reasonable and prudent* generally means the average judgment, foresight, intelligence, and skill that would be expected of a person with similar training and experience. *Malpractice*—the failure of a person with professional training to act in a reasonable and prudent manner—also is called *professional negligence*. Five elements must be present for a professional to be held liable for malpractice (Table 5.3).

First, a *standard of care* must have been established that outlines the level or degree of quality considered adequate by a given profession. Standards of care outline the duties a defendant has to a plaintiff or a nurse to a client. These standards represent the skills and learning commonly possessed by members of the profession and generally are the minimal requirements that define an acceptable level of care. Standards of care, which guarantee clients safe nursing care, include organizational policy and procedure statements, job descriptions, and student guidelines.

TABLE 5.3   Components of Professional Negligence

Elements of Liability	*Explanation*	*Example: Giving Medications*
1. Duty to use due care (defined by the standard of care)	The care that should be given under the circumstances (what the reasonably prudent nurse would have done)	A nurse should give medications accurately, completely, and on time
2. Failure to meet standard of care (breach of duty)	Not giving the care that should be given under the circumstances	A nurse fails to give medications accurately, completely, or on time
3. Foreseeability of harm	The nurse must have reasonable access to information about whether the possibility of harm exists	The drug handbook specifies that the wrong dosage or route may cause injury
4. A direct relationship between failure to meet the standard of care (breach) and injury can be proved	Patient is harmed because proper care is not given	Wrong dosage causes the patient to have a convulsion
5. Injury	Actual harm results to the patient	Convulsion or other serious complication occurs

Second, after the standard of care has been established, it must be shown that the standard was violated—there must have been a *breach of duty*. This breach is shown by calling other nurses who practice in the same specialty area as the defendant to testify as expert witnesses.

Third, the nurse must have had the knowledge or availability of information that not meeting the standard of care could result in harm. This is called *foreseeability of harm*. If the average, reasonable person in the defendant's position could have anticipated the plaintiff's injury as a result of his or her actions, then the plaintiff's injury was foreseeable. Ignorance is not an excuse, but lack of information may have a negative effect on the ability to foresee harm.

Being ignorant is not a justifiable excuse, but not having all the information in a situation may impede one's ability to foresee harm.

For example, a charge nurse assigns another registered nurse (RN) to care for a critically ill patient. The assigned RN makes a medication error that injures the patient in some way. If the charge nurse had reason to believe that the RN was incapable of adequately caring for the patient or failed to provide adequate supervision, foreseeability of harm is apparent, and the charge nurse also could be held liable. If the charge nurse was available as needed and had good reason to believe that the RN was fully capable, he or she would probably not be held liable.

A number of malpractice cases have hinged on whether the nurse was persistent enough in attempting to notify health-care providers of changes in a patient's conditions or to convince the providers of the seriousness of a patient's condition. Because the nurse has foreseeability of harm in these situations, the nurse who is not persistent can be held liable for failure to intervene because the intervention was below what was expected of him or her as a patient advocate.

The fourth element is that *failure to meet the standard of care must have the potential to injure the patient*. There must be a provable correlation between improper care and injury to the patient.

The final element is that *actual patient injury* must occur. This injury must be more than transitory. The plaintiff must show that the action of the defendant directly caused the injury and that the injury would not have occurred without the defendant's actions. It is important to remember here, however, that not taking action is an action.

LEARNING EXERCISE 5.2

Who Is Responsible for Harm to This Patient? You Decide

You are a surgical nurse at Memorial Hospital. At 4 PM, you receive a patient from the recovery room who has had a total hip replacement. You note that the hip dressings are saturated with blood but are aware that total hip replacements frequently have some postoperative oozing from the wound. There is an order on the chart to reinforce the dressing as needed, and you do so. When you next check the dressing at 6 PM, you find the reinforcements saturated and drainage on the bed linen. You call the physician and tell her that you believe the patient is bleeding too heavily. The physician reassures you that the amount of bleeding you have described is not excessive but encourages you to continue to monitor the patient closely. You recheck the patient's dressings at 7 and 8 PM. You again call the physician and tell her that the bleeding still looks too heavy. She again reassures you and tells you to continue to watch the patient closely. At 10 PM, the patient's blood pressure becomes nonpalpable, and she goes into shock. You summon the doctor, and she comes immediately.

Assignment: What are the legal ramifications of this case? Using the components of professional negligence outlined in Table 5.3, determine who in this case is guilty of malpractice. Justify your answer. At what point in the scenario should each character have altered his or her actions to reduce the probability of a negative outcome?

AVOIDING MALPRACTICE CLAIMS

Interactions between nurses and clients that are less businesslike and more personal are more satisfying to both. It has been shown that despite technical competence, nurses who have difficulty establishing positive interpersonal relationships with patients and their families are at greater risk for being sued. Communication that proceeds in a caring and professional manner has been shown repeatedly to be a major reason that people do not sue, despite adequate grounds for a successful lawsuit.

In addition, many experts have suggested a need to create safer environments for care so that less patients are injured during the course of their care. This has especially been true since the 1999 release of *To Err Is Human* by the Institute of Medicine (IOM), a congressionally chartered independent organization. The IOM report indicated that errors are simply a part of the human condition and that the health-care system itself needs to be redesigned so that fewer errors can occur. For example, even though there are unit-dose systems in play, nurse-leaders often look the other way when staff dump all the medications into a soufflé cup and hand them to patients, thus increasing the possibility of medication errors.

Strategies recommended by the Joint Commission, in its 2005 seminal report, *Healthcare in the Crossroads*, can be viewed in Display 5.2. The three major areas of focus in the call to action are to prevent injuries, improve communication, and examine mechanisms for injury compensation.

Nurses then can reduce the risk of malpractice claims by taking the following actions:

- Practice within the scope of the Nurse Practice Act.
- Observe agency policies and procedures.
- Model practice after established standards by using evidence-based practice.
- Always put patient rights and welfare first.
- Be aware of relevant law and legal doctrines and combine such with the biological, psychological, and social sciences that form the basis of all rational nursing decisions.
- Practice within the area of individual competence.
- Upgrade technical skills consistently by attending continuing education programs and seeking specialty certification.

Nurses should also purchase their own liability insurance and understand the limits of their policies. Although this will not prevent a malpractice suit, it should help protect a nurse from financial ruin should there be a malpractice claim.

LEARNING EXERCISE 5.3

Discussing Lawsuits and Liability

In small groups, discuss the following questions:

1. Do you believe that there are unnecessary lawsuits in the health-care industry? What criteria can be used to distinguish between appropriate and unnecessary lawsuits?

2. Have you ever advised a friend or family member to sue to recover damages that you believed they suffered as a result of poor-quality health care? What motivated you to encourage them to do so?

3. Do you think that you will make clinical errors in judgment as a nurse? If so, what types of errors should be considered acceptable (if any), and what types are not acceptable?

4. Do you believe that the recent national spotlight on medical error identification and prevention will encourage the reporting of medical errors when they do occur?

| DISPLAY 5.2 | Summary of Recommendations from the Executive Summary of "Healthcare in the Crossroads: Strategies for Improving the Medical Liability System and Preventing Injury" |

1. *Pursue patient safety initiatives that prevent medical injury by:*
   - Strengthening oversight and accountability mechanisms to better ensure the competencies of physicians and nurses
   - Encouraging appropriate adherence to clinical guidelines to improve quality and reduce liability risk
   - Supporting team development through team training
   - Continuing to leverage patient safety initiatives through regulatory and oversight bodies
   - Building an evidence-based information and technology system that impacts patient safety and pursue proposals to offset implementation costs
   - Promoting the creation of cultures of patient safety in health-care organizations
   - Establishing a federal leadership locus for advocacy of patient safety and health-care quality
   - Pursuing "pay-for-performance" strategies that provide incentives to improve patient safety and health-care quality

2. *Promote open communication between patients and practitioners by:*
   - Involving health-care consumers as active members of the health-care team
   - Encouraging open communication between practitioners and patients when adverse events occur
   - Pursuing legislation that protects disclosure and apology from being used as evidence against practitioners in litigation
   - Encouraging nonpunitive reporting of errors to third parties that promote information and data analysis as a basis for developing safety improvement
   - Enacting federal safety legislation that provides legal protection for when information is reported to patient safety organizations

3. *Create an injury compensation system that is patient centered and serves the common good by:*
   - Conducting demonstration projects of alternatives to medical liability that promote patient safety and transparency and provide swift compensation for injured patients
   - Encouraging continued development of mediation and early-offer initiatives
   - Prohibiting confidential settlements that prevent learning from events
   - Redesigning the National Practitioner Data Bank
   - Advocating for court-appointed, independent expert witnesses to mitigate bias in expert witness testimony

Source: Joint Commission on Accreditation of Healthcare Organizations. (2005). Health care in the crossroads: Strategies for improving the medical liability system and preventing patient injury. Oakbrook Terrace, IL: Author.

EXTENDING THE LIABILITY

In recent years, the concept of *joint liability*, in which the nurse, physician, and employing organization are all held liable, has become the current position of the legal system. This probably more accurately reflects the higher level of accountability now present in the nursing profession. Before 1965, nurses were rarely held accountable for their own acts, and hospitals were usually exempt due to *charitable immunity*. However, following precedent-setting cases in the 1960s, employers are now held liable for the nurse's acts under a concept known as *vicarious liability*. One form of vicarious liability is called *respondeat superior*, which means "the master is responsible for the acts of his servants." The theory behind the doctrine is that an employer should be held legally liable for the conduct of employees whose actions he or she has a right to direct or control.

The difficulty in interpreting *respondeat superior* is that many exceptions exist. The first and most important exception is related to the state in which the nurse practices. In some states, the *doctrine of charitable immunity* applies, which holds that a charitable (nonprofit) hospital cannot be sued by a person who has been injured as a result of a hospital employee's negligence. Thus, liability is limited to the employee.

Another exception to *respondeat superior* occurs when the state or federal government employs the nurse. The common-law rule of *governmental immunity* provides that governments cannot be held liable for the negligent acts of their employees while carrying out government activities. Some states have changed this rule by statute, however, and in these particular jurisdictions, *respondeat superior* continues to apply to the acts of nurses employed by the state government.

Nurses must remember that the purpose of *respondeat superior* is not to shift the burden of blame from the employee to the organization but rather to share the blame, increasing the possibility of larger financial compensation to the injured party. Some nurses erroneously assume that they do not need to carry malpractice insurance because their employer will in all probability be sued as well and thus will be responsible for financial damages. Under the doctrine of *respondeat superior*, any employer required to pay damages to an injured person because of an employee's negligence may have the legal right to recover or be reimbursed that amount from the negligent employee.

One rule that all nurses must know and understand is that of *personal liability*, which says that every person is liable for his or her own conduct. The law does not permit a wrongdoer to avoid legal liability for his or her own wrongdoing, even though someone else also may be sued and held legally liable. For example, if a manager directs a subordinate to do something that both know to be improper, the injured party can recover damages against the subordinate even if the supervisor agreed to accept full responsibility for the delegation at the time. In the end, each nurse is always held liable for his or her own negligent practice.

Managers are not automatically held liable for all acts of negligence on the part of those they supervise, but they may be held liable if they were negligent in the supervision of those employees at the time that they committed the negligent acts. Liability for negligence is generally based on the manager's failure to determine which of the patient needs can be assigned safely to a subordinate or the failure to supervise a subordinate adequately for the assigned task (Huston, 2014a). Both the abilities of the staff member and the complexity of the task assigned must be considered when determining the type and amount of direction and supervision warranted.

Hospitals have also been found liable for assigning personnel who were unqualified to perform duties as shown by their evaluation reports. Managers, therefore, need to be cognizant of their responsibilities in assigning and appointing personnel because they could be found liable for ignoring organizational policies or for assigning employees duties that they are not capable of performing. In such cases, though, the employee must provide the supervisor with the information that he or she is not qualified for the assignment. The manager does have the right to reassign employees as long as they are capable of discharging the anticipated duties of the assignment.

In addition, there has been a push to have more in-depth background checks when health-care employees are hired, with some states already mandating such checks. For example, California, as of 2009, determined that it would no longer issue temporary or permanent licenses to nurses without a criminal background check. Indeed, many states are now requiring a criminal background check on all license renewals, and federal legislation has recently been introduced along these lines.

At present, except in a few states, personnel directors in hospitals (those making hiring decisions) are required to request information from the National Practitioner Data Bank for those individuals who seek clinical privileges, and many states now require nursing students to be fingerprinted before they are allowed to work with vulnerable populations. In the future, hiring someone without an adequate background check, who later commits a crime involving a patient, could be another area of liability for the manager. This is an example of the type of pending legislation with which a manager must keep abreast so that if it becomes law, its impact on future management practices will be minimized.

LEARNING EXERCISE 5.4

Understanding Limitations and Rules

Have you ever been directed in your nursing practice to do something that you believed might be unsafe or that you felt inadequately trained or prepared to do? What did you do? Would you act differently if the situation occurred now? What risks are inherent in refusing to follow the direct orders of a physician or superior? What are the risks of performing a task that you believe may be unsafe?

 ## INCIDENT REPORTS

Incident reports or *adverse event* forms are records of unusual or unexpected incidents that occur in the course of a client's treatment. Because attorneys use incident reports to defend the health agency against lawsuits brought by clients, the reports are generally considered confidential communications and cannot be subpoenaed by clients or used as evidence in their lawsuits in most states. (Be sure, however, that you know the law for the state in which you live, as this does vary.) However, incident reports that are inadvertently disclosed to the plaintiff are no longer considered confidential and can be subpoenaed in court. Thus, a copy of an incident report should not be left in the chart. In addition, no entry should be made in the patient's record about the existence of an incident report. The chart should, however, provide enough information about the incident or occurrence so that appropriate treatment can be given.

 ## INTENTIONAL TORTS

Torts are legal wrongs committed against a person or property, independent of a contract, that render the person who commits them liable for damages in a civil action. Whereas professional negligence is considered to be an *unintentional tort*, assault, battery, false imprisonment, invasion of privacy, defamation, and slander are intentional torts. *Intentional torts* are a direct invasion of someone's legal rights. Managers are responsible for seeing that staff members are aware of and adhere to laws governing intentional torts. In addition, the manager must clearly delineate policies and procedures about these issues in the work environment.

Nurses can be sued for assault and battery. *Assault* is conduct that makes a person fearful and produces a reasonable apprehension of harm. Essentially then, assault is "threatening a person, with the present ability to carry out the threat" (Frederick, 2012, para 1). *Battery* is an intentional and wrongful physical contact with a person that entails an injury or offensive touching. "If there was a threat but no physical contact, the charge is *simple assault*. When there is a physical injury, no matter how slight, the charge is simple assault and battery" (Frederick, 2012, para 1).

Unit managers must be alert to patient complaints of being handled in a rough manner or complaints of excessive force in restraining patients. In fact, performing any treatment without patient's permission or without receiving an informed consent might constitute both assault and battery. In addition, many battery suits have been won based on the use of restraints when dealing with confused patients.

The use of physical restraints also has led to claims of *false imprisonment*. False imprisonment is the restraint of a person's liberty of movement by another party who lacks the legal authority or justification to do so (Criminal Law Lawyers Source, 2003–2013). Practitioners are liable for false imprisonment when they unlawfully restrain the movement of their patients. Physical restraints should be applied only with a physician's direct order. Likewise, the patient who wishes to sign out against medical advice should not be held against his or her will. This tort also is frequently applicable to involuntary commitments to mental health facilities. Managers in mental health settings must be careful to institutionalize patients in accordance with all laws governing commitment.

Another intentional tort is defamation. *Defamation* is communicating to a third party, false information that injures a person's reputation. When defamation is written, it is called *libel*. When it is spoken, it is called *slander*.

OTHER LEGAL RESPONSIBILITIES OF THE MANAGER

Managers also have some legal responsibility for the quality control of nursing practice at the unit level, including such duties as reporting dangerous understaffing, checking staff credentials and qualifications, and carrying out appropriate discipline. Health-care facilities may also be held responsible for seeing that staff know how to operate equipment safely. Sources of liability for managers vary from facility to facility and from position to position.

For example, standards of care as depicted in policies and procedures may pose a liability for the nurse if such policies and procedures are not followed. The chain of command in reporting inadequate care by a physician is another area in which management liability may occur if employees are not taught proper protocols. Managers have a responsibility to see that written protocols, policies, and procedures are followed in order to reduce liability. In addition, the manager, like all professional nurses, is responsible for reporting improper or substandard medical care, child and elder abuse, and communicable diseases, as specified by the Centers for Disease Control and Prevention.

Individual nurses also may be held liable for *product liability*. When a product is involved, negligence does not have to be proved. This strict liability is a somewhat gray area of nursing practice. Essentially, strict liability holds that a product may be held to a higher level of liability than a person. In other words, if it can be proved that the equipment or product had a defect that caused an injury, then it would be debated in court by using all the elements essential for negligence, such as duty and breach. Therefore, equipment and other products fall within the scope of nursing responsibility. In general, if they are aware that equipment is faulty, nurses have a duty to refuse to use the equipment. If the fault in the equipment is not readily apparent, risks are low that the nurse will be found liable for the results of its use.

Informed Consent

Many nurses erroneously believe that they have obtained informed consent when they witness a patient's signature on a consent form for surgery or procedure. Strictly speaking, *informed consent* (Display 5.3) can be given only after the patient has received a complete explanation of the surgery, procedure, or treatment and indicates that he or she understands the risks and benefits related to it.

DISPLAY 5.3   Guidelines for Informed Consent

THE PERSON(S) GIVING CONSENT MUST FULLY COMPREHEND:
1. The procedure to be performed
2. The risks involved
3. Expected or desired outcomes
4. Expected complications or side effects that may occur as a result of treatment
5. Alternative treatments that are available

CONSENT MAY BE GIVEN BY:
1. A competent adult
2. A legal guardian or individual holding durable power of attorney
3. An emancipated or married minor
4. Mature minor (varies by state)
5. Parent of a minor child
6. Court order

Informed consent is obtained only after the patient receives full disclosure of all pertinent information regarding the surgery or procedure and only if the patient understands the potential benefits and risks associated with doing so.

The information must be in a language that the patient can understand and should be conveyed by the individual who will be performing the procedure. Patients must be invited to ask questions and have a clear understanding of the options as well.

Only a competent adult can legally sign the form that shows informed consent. To be considered competent, patients must be capable of understanding the nature and consequences of the decision and of communicating their decision. Spouses or other family members cannot legally sign unless there is an approved guardianship or conservatorship or unless they hold a durable power of attorney for health care. If the patient is younger than 16 years (18 in some states), a parent or guardian must generally give consent.

In an emergency, the physician can invoke *implied consent*, in which the physician states in the progress notes of the medical record that the patient is unable to sign but that treatment is immediately needed and is in the patient's best interest. Usually, this type of implied consent must be validated by another physician.

Nurses frequently seek *express consent* from patients by witnessing patients sign a standard consent form. In express consent, the role of the nurse is to be sure that the patient has received informed consent and to seek remedy if he or she has not.

Informed consent does pose ethical issues for nurses. Although nurses are obligated to provide teaching and to clarify information given to patients by their physicians, nurses must be careful not to give new information that contradicts information given by the physician, thus interfering in the physician–patient relationship. The nurse is not responsible for explaining the procedure to be performed. The role, rather, is to be a patient advocate by determining their level of understanding and seeing that the appropriate person answers their questions. At times, this can be a cloudy issue both legally and ethically.

Informed Consent for Clinical Research

The intent of informed consent in clinical research is to give patients adequate information, through a full explanation of a proposed treatment, including any possible harms, so they can make an informed decision. Studies, however, repeatedly suggest that participants often have incomplete understanding of various features of clinical trials and issues associated with written informed consent are common. (See Examining the Evidence 5.1.)

Examining the Evidence 5.1

Source: Braude, H., & Kimmelman, J. (2012). The ethics of managing affective and emotional states to improve informed consent: Autonomy, comprehension, and voluntariness. Bioethics, 26*(3), 149–156.*

An individual's right to self-determination and autonomy is a core consideration in research. Braude and Kimmelman, however, argue that surveys consistently show that patient-subjects involved in clinical research frequently harbor inflated expectations of benefit (therapeutic overestimation) or conflate trial participation with care (therapeutic misconception). Many commentators argue that such misunderstandings raise important concerns about consent validity.

In addition, Braude and Kimmelman suggest that while consent should be free from undue influence, that some correction, persuasion, or manipulation often exists. Both directive and nondirective affective interventions raise similar ethical concerns regarding the manipulation of consent practices. A paradoxical tension exists in that affective interventions intended to enhance autonomy may achieve their end through bypassing conscious cognition. Thus, the increasing impact of affective interventions on the lives of researchers and subjects, who experience real affect and emotions in considering difficult decisions, is a phenomenon that requires continued rigorous and sophisticated moral reflection.

Banner and Zimmer (2012) also underscore the importance of nurses understanding and applying ethical principles for obtaining a valid informed consent in research. This includes the clear and accurate disclosure of information, assessment of decisional capacity, and the promotion of voluntarism. Understanding and responding to these issues and criteria are important in maintaining client safety, dignity, and respect and are essential to the development of high-quality, ethically sound research that improves health outcomes.

LEARNING EXERCISE 5.5

Is It Really Informed Consent?

You are a staff nurse on a surgical unit. Shortly after reporting for duty, you make rounds on all your patients. Mrs. Jones is a 36-year-old woman scheduled for a bilateral salpingo-oophorectomy and hysterectomy. In the course of conversation, Mrs. Jones comments that she is glad she will not be undergoing menopause as a result of this surgery. She elaborates by stating that one of her friends had surgery that resulted in "surgical menopause" and that it was devastating to her. You return to the chart and check the surgical permit and doctor's progress notes. The operating room permit reads "bilateral salpingo-oophorectomy and hysterectomy," and it is signed by Mrs. Jones. The physician has noted "discussed surgery with patient" in the progress notes.

You return to Mrs. Jones's room and ask her what type of surgery she is having. She states, "I'm having my uterus removed." You phone the physician and relate your information to the surgeon who says, "Mrs. Jones knows that I will take out her ovaries if necessary; I've discussed it with her. She signed the permit. Now, please get her ready for surgery—she is the next case."

Assignment: Discuss what you should do at this point. Why did you select this course of action? What issues are involved here? Be able to discuss legal ramifications of this case.

Medical Records

One source of information that people seek to help them make decisions about their health care is their medical record. Nurses have a legal responsibility for accurately recording appropriate information in the client's medical record. The alteration of medical records can result in license suspension or revocation.

Although the patient owns the information in that medical record, the actual record belongs to the facility that originally made the record and is storing it. Although patients must have "reasonable access" to their records, the method for retrieving the record varies greatly from one institution to another. Generally, a patient who wishes to inspect his or her records must make a written request and pay reasonable clerical costs to make such records available. The health-care provider generally permits such inspection during business hours within several working days of the inspection request. Nurses should be aware of the procedure for procuring medical records for patients at the facilities where they work. Often, a patient's attempt to procure medical records results from a lack of trust or a need for additional teaching and education. Nurses can do a great deal to reduce this confusion and foster an open, trusting relationship between the patient and his or her health-care providers. Collaboration between health-care providers and patients, and documentation thereof, is a good indication of well-provided clinical care.

If it is not documented in the health-care record. ... it did not happen.

LEARNING EXERCISE 5.6

Mrs. Brown's Chart

Mrs. Brown has been diagnosed with invasive cancer. She has been having daily radiation treatments. Her husband is a frequent visitor and seems to be a devoted husband. They are both very interested in her progress and prognosis. Although they have asked many questions and you have given truthful answers, you know little because the physician has not shared much with the staff. Today, you walk into Mrs. Brown's room and find Mr. Brown sitting at Mrs. Brown's bedside reading her chart. The radiation orderly had inadvertently left the chart in the room when Mrs. Brown returned from the X-ray department.

Assignment: Identify several alternatives that you have. Discuss what you would do and why. Is there a problem here? What follow-up is indicated? Attempt to solve this problem on your own before reading the sample analysis that follows.

Analysis

The nurse needs to determine the most important goal in this situation. Possible goals include (a) getting the chart away from Mr. Brown as soon as possible, (b) protecting the privacy of Mrs. Brown, (c) gathering more information, or (d) becoming an advocate for the Browns.

In solving the case, it is apparent that not enough information has been gathered. Mr. Brown now has the chart, and it seems pointless to take it away from him. Usually, the danger in patients' families reading the chart lies in the direction of their not understanding the chart and thereby obtaining confusing information or the patient's privacy being invaded because the patient has not consented to family members' access to the chart.

Using this as the basis for rationale, the nurse should use the following approach:

1. Clarify that Mr. Brown has Mrs. Brown's permission to read the chart by asking her directly.

2. Ask Mr. Brown if there is anything in the chart that he did not understand or anything that he questions. You may even ask him to summarize what he has read. Clarify the things that are appropriate for the nurse to address, such as terminology, procedures, and nursing care.

3. Refer questions that are inappropriate for the nurse to answer to the physician, and let Mr. Brown know that you will help him in talking with the physician regarding the medical plan and prognosis.

4. When finished talking with Mr. Brown, the nurse should request the chart and place it in the proper location. The incident should be reported to the immediate supervisor.

5. The nurse should follow through by talking with the physician about the incident and Mr. Brown's concerns and by assisting the Browns to obtain the information that they have requested.

Conclusion

The nurse first gathered more information before becoming the adversary or advocate. It is possible that the Browns had only simple questions to ask and that the problem was a lack of communication between staff and their patients rather than a physician–patient communication deficit. Legally, patients have a right to understand what is happening to them, and that should be the basis for the decisions in this case.

The Patient Self-Determination Act

The PSDA, enacted in 1991, required health-care organizations that received federal funding (Medicare and Medicaid) to provide education for staff and patients on issues concerning treatment and end-of-life issues. This education included the use of *advance directives* (ADs), written instructions regarding desired end-of-life care. Most ADs address the use of dialysis and respirators; if you want to be resuscitated if breathing or heartbeat stops; tube feeding; and organ or tissue donation (Medline Plus, 2013). They also likely include a *durable power of attorney* for health care, which names your *health-care proxy*, someone you trust to make health decisions if you are unable to do so (Medline Plus).

The PSDA requires acute care facilities to document on the medical record whether a patient has an AD and to provide written information to patients who do not. However, despite mechanisms within most health-care institutions to provide this information, the AD completion rate remains low and many patients do not understand what is included in the AD or whether this is something important they should have. Examining the Evidence 5.2 reveals evidence found in one study.

Examining the Evidence 5.2

Source: Johnson, R. W., Zhao, Y., Newby, L., Granger, C. B., & Granger, B. B. (2012). *Reasons for noncompletion of advance directives in a cardiac intensive care unit.* American Journal of Critical Care, 21 (5), 311–320.

This semistructured cross-sectional study asked all ($n = 505$) eligible patients 18 years or older admitted to the cardiac intensive care unit at Duke University Medical Center, Durham, North Carolina, the standard question required by the PSDA—Do you have an AD?—and three open-ended questions to ascertain the patient's understanding of ADs. Most patients (64.4%; $n = 325$) did not have an AD before admission to the unit. Of the patients who initially declined the opportunity to complete an AD ($n = 213$), 33.8% ($n = 72$) said they did not understand the question when initially asked and therefore just said no.

The researchers concluded that simply asking patients if they have an AD does not elicit an accurate reflection of a patient's understanding of ADs and that confusion about ADs makes it difficult for patients to communicate their end-of-life wishes to the appropriate person. The researchers suggest a need to restructure the current implementation of the PSDA and to move beyond simply checking a box to providing more meaningful discussion with each patient and their family.

Good Samaritan Laws

Nurses are not required to stop and provide emergency services as a matter of law although most health-care workers feel ethically compelled to stop if they believe they can help. *Good Samaritan laws* suggest that health-care providers are typically protected from potential liability if they volunteer their nursing skills away from the workplace (generally limited to emergencies), provided that actions taken are not grossly negligent and if the health-care worker does not exceed his or her training or scope of practice in performing the emergency services. Hasley (2012) warns, however, that not being paid for your services alone will not provide Good Samaritan law protection. For example, nurses who volunteer at clinics or summer camps would typically not be covered since this does not constitute emergency assistance.

Good Samaritan laws apply only if the health-care worker does not exceed his or her training or scope of practice in performing the emergency services.

Protection under Good Samaritan laws varies tremendously from state to state. In some states, the law grants immunity to RNs but does not protect licensed vocational nurses (LVNs) or licensed professional nurses (LPNs). Other states offer protection to anyone who offers assistance, even if they do not have a health-care background. Nurses should be familiar with the Good Samaritan laws in their state.

Health Insurance Portability and Accountability Act of 1996

Another area of the law that nurses must understand is the right to confidentiality. Unauthorized release of information or photographs in medical records may make the person who discloses the information civilly liable for invasion of privacy, defamation, or slander. Written authorization by the patient to release information is needed to allow such disclosure.

Many nurses have been caught unaware by the telephone call requesting information about a patient's condition. It is extremely important that the nurse does not give out unauthorized information, regardless of the urgency of the person making the request. In addition, nurses must be careful not to discuss patient information in venues where it can be inadvertently overheard, read, transmitted, or otherwise unintentionally disclosed. For example, nurses talking in elevators, the hospital gift shop, or in a restaurant for lunch need to be aware of their surroundings and remain alert about not revealing any patient information in a public place.

Efforts to preserve patient confidentiality increased tremendously with the passage of the *Health Insurance Portability and Accountability Act* (*HIPAA*) *of 1996* (also known as the Kassebaum–Kennedy Act). HIPAA gave Congress a deadline of August 1999 to pass legislation protecting the privacy of health information and to improve the portability and continuity of health insurance coverage. When this did not happen, the Department of Health and Human Services stepped in and issued the appropriate regulations. The first version of the privacy rule was issued in December 2000 under the Clinton administration, but it was modified by the Bush administration before it was ever implemented, and it continues to be modified on a regular basis.

HIPAA essentially represents two areas for implementation. The first is the *Administrative Simplification plan*, and the second area includes the *Privacy Rules*. The Administrative Simplification plan is directed at restructuring the coding of health information to simplify the digital exchange of information among health-care providers and to improve the efficiency of health-care delivery. The privacy rules are directed at ensuring strong privacy protections for patient without threatening access to care.

The Privacy Rule applies to health plans, health-care clearinghouses, and health-care providers. It also covers all patient records and other individually identifiable health information. Although there are many components to HIPAA, key components of the Privacy Rule are that direct treatment providers must make a good faith effort to obtain written acknowledgment of the notice of privacy rights and practices from patients. In addition, health-care providers must disclose protected health information to patients requesting their own information or when oversight agencies request the data. Reasonable efforts must be taken, however, to limit the disclosure of personal health information to the minimum information necessary to complete the transaction. There are situations, however, when limiting the information is not required. For example, a minimum of information is not required for treatment purposes, since it is clearly better to have too much information than too little. The HIPAA Privacy Rule and Common Rule also require that individuals participating in research studies should be assured privacy, particularly regarding personal health information.

 The Privacy Rule attempts to balance the need for the protection of personal health information with the need for disclosure of that information for patient care.

Because of the complexity of the HIPAA regulations, it is not expected that a nursing manager would be responsible for compliance alone. Instead, it is most important that the manager work with the administrative team to develop compliance procedures. For example, managers must ensure that unauthorized people do not have access to patient charts or medical records and that unauthorized people are not allowed to observe procedures.

It is equally important that managers remain cognizant of ongoing changes to the guidelines and are aware of how rules governing these issues may differ in the state in which they are employed. Some provisions of the Privacy Rules mention "reasonable efforts" toward achieving compliance, but being reasonable is provision specific. The American Recovery and Reinvestment Act (ARRA) applies several of HIPAA's security and privacy requirements to business associates and changes data restrictions, disclosure, and reporting requirements.

LEGAL CONSIDERATIONS OF MANAGING A DIVERSE WORKFORCE

Diversity has been defined as the differences among groups or between individuals and comes in many forms, including age, gender, religion, customs, sexual orientation, physical size, physical and mental capabilities, beliefs, culture, ethnicity, and skin color (Huston, 2014b). Demographic data from the U.S. Census Bureau continue to show increased diversification of the US population, a trend that began almost 35 years ago.

As will be discussed in later chapters, a primary area of diversity is language, including word meanings, accents, and dialects. Problems arising from this could be misunderstanding or reluctance to ask questions. Staff from cultures in which assertiveness is not promoted may find it difficult to disagree with or question others. How the manager handles these manifestations of cultural diversity is of major importance. If the manager's response is seen as discriminatory, the employee may file a complaint with one of the state or federal agencies that oversee civil rights or equal opportunity enforcement. Such things as overt or subtle discrimination are prohibited by Title VII (Civil Rights Act of 1964). Managers have a responsibility to be fair and just. Lack of promotions and unfair assignments may occur with minority employees just because they are different.

In addition, English-only rules in the workplace may be viewed as discriminatory under Title VII. Such rules may not violate Title VII if employers require English only during certain periods of time. Even in these circumstances, the employees must be notified of the rules and how they are to be enforced.

Clearly, managers should be taught how to deal sensitively and appropriately with an increasingly diverse workforce. Enhancing self-awareness and staff awareness of personal cultural biases, developing a comprehensive cultural diversity program, and role modeling cultural sensitivity are some of the ways that managers can effectively avoid many legal problems associated with discriminatory issues. However, it is hoped that future goals for the manager would go beyond compliance with Title VII and move toward understanding of and respect for other cultures.

PROFESSIONAL VERSUS INSTITUTIONAL LICENSURE

In general, a *license* is a legal document that permits a person to offer special skills and knowledge to the public in a particular jurisdiction when such practice would otherwise be unlawful. Licensure establishes standards for entry into practice, defines a scope of practice, and allows for disciplinary action. Currently, licensing for nurses is a responsibility of State Boards of Nursing or State Boards of Nurse Examiners, which also provide discipline as necessary. The manager, however, is responsible for monitoring that all licensed subordinates have a valid, appropriate, and current license to practice.

Professional licensure is a privilege and not a right.

All nurses must safeguard the privilege of licensure by knowing the standards of care applicable to their work setting. Deviation from that standard should be undertaken only when nurses are prepared to accept the consequences of their actions, in terms of both liability and loss of licensure.

Nurses who violate specific norms of conduct, such as securing a license by fraud, performing specific actions prohibited by the Nurse Practice Act, exhibiting unprofessional or illegal conduct, performing malpractice, and abusing alcohol or drugs, may have their licenses suspended or revoked by the licensing boards in all states. Frequent causes of license revocation are shown in Display 5.4.

DISPLAY 5.4	Common Causes of Professional Nursing License Suspension or Revocation

- Professional negligence
- Practicing medicine or nursing without a license
- Obtaining a nursing license by fraud or allowing others to use your license
- Felony conviction for any offense substantially related to the function or duties of an RN
- Participating professionally in criminal abortions
- Not reporting substandard medical or nursing care
- Providing patient care while under the influence of drugs or alcohol
- Giving narcotic drugs without an order
- Falsely holding oneself out to the public or to any health-care practitioner as a "nurse practitioner"

Typically, suspension and revocation proceedings are administrative. Following a complaint, the Board of Nursing completes an investigation. Most of these investigations reveal no grounds for discipline. If the investigation supports the need for discipline, nurses are notified of the charges and are allowed to prepare a defense. At the hearing, which is very similar to a trial, the nurse is allowed to present evidence. Based on the evidence, an administrative law judge makes a recommendation to the State Board of Nursing, which makes the final decision. The entire process, from complaint to final decision, may take up to 2 years.

Some professionals have advocated shifting the burden of licensure, and thus accountability, from individual practitioners to an institution or agency. Proponents for this move believe that *institutional licensure* would provide more effective use of personnel and greater flexibility. Most professional nursing organizations oppose this move strongly because they believe that it has the potential for diluting the quality of nursing care.

An alternative to institutional licensure has been the development of *certification programs* by the American Nurses Association (ANA). By passing specifically prepared written examinations, nurses are able to qualify for certification in most nurse practice areas. This voluntary testing program represents professional organizational certification. In addition to ANA certification, other specialties, such as cardiac care, offer their own certification examinations. Many nursing leaders today strongly advocate professional certification as a means of enhancing the profession. However, certification is really only helpful in determining a nurse's continued competence if that nurse is functioning in the areas of his or her certified competence (Huston, 2014c).

INTEGRATING LEADERSHIP ROLES AND MANAGEMENT FUNCTIONS IN LEGAL AND LEGISLATIVE ISSUES

Legislative and legal controls for nursing practice have been established to clarify the boundaries of nursing practice and to protect clients. The leader uses established legal guidelines to role model nursing practice that meets or exceeds accepted standards of care. Leaders also are role models in their efforts to expand expertise in their field and to achieve specialty certification. Perhaps the most important leadership roles in law and legislation are those of vision, risk taking, and energy. The leader is active in professional organizations and groups that define what nursing is and what it should be in the future. This is an internalized responsibility that must be adopted by many more nurses if the profession is to be a recognized and vital force in the political arena.

Management functions in legal and legislative issues are more directive. Managers are responsible for seeing that their practice and the practice of their subordinates are in accord with current legal guidelines. This requires that managers have a working knowledge of current laws and legal doctrines that affect nursing practice. Because laws are not static, this is an active and ongoing function. The manager has a legal obligation to uphold the laws, rules, and regulations affecting the organization, the patient, and nursing practice.

Managers have a responsibility to be fair and nondiscriminatory in dealing with all members of the workforce, including those whose culture differs from their own. The effective leader goes beyond merely preventing discriminatory charges and instead strives to develop sensitivity to the needs of a culturally diverse staff.

The integrated leader-manager reduces the personal risk of legal liability by creating an environment that prioritizes patient needs and welfare. In addition, caring, respect, and honesty as part of nurse–patient relationships are emphasized. If these functions and roles are truly integrated, the risks of patient harm and nursing liability are greatly reduced.

KEY CONCEPTS

- Sources of law include constitutions, statutes, administrative agencies, and court decisions.

- The burden of proof required to be found guilty and the punishment for the crime varies significantly between criminal, civil, and administrative courts.

- Nurse Practice Acts define and limit the practice of nursing in each state.

- Professional organizations generally espouse standards of care that are higher than those required by law. These voluntary controls often are forerunners of legal controls.

- Legal doctrines such as stare decisis and res judicata frequently guide courts in their decision making.

- Currently, licensing for nurses is a responsibility of State Boards of Nursing or State Boards of Nurse Examiners. These state boards also provide discipline as necessary.

- Some professionals have advocated shifting the burden of licensure, and thus accountability, from individual practitioners to an institution or agency. Many professional nursing organizations oppose this move.

- Malpractice or professional negligence is the failure of a person with professional training to act in a reasonable and prudent manner. Five components must be present for an individual to be found guilty of malpractice.

- Employers of nurses can now be held liable for an employee's acts under the concept of vicarious liability.

- Each person, however, is liable for his or her own tortuous conduct.

- Managers are not automatically held liable for all acts of negligence on the part of those they supervise, but they may be held liable if they were negligent in supervising those employees at the time that they committed the negligent acts.

- While professional negligence is considered to be an unintentional tort, assault, battery, false imprisonment, invasion of privacy, defamation, and slander are intentional torts.

- Consent can be informed, implied, or expressed. Nurses need to understand the differences between these types of consents and use the appropriate one.

- Although the patient owns the information in a medical record, the actual record belongs to the facility that originally made it and is storing it.

- It has been shown that despite good technical competence, nurses who have difficulty establishing positive interpersonal relationships with clients and their families are at greater risk for being sued.

- Each nurse should be aware of how laws such as Good Samaritan immunity or legal access to incident reports are implemented in the state in which they live.

- New legislation pertaining to confidentiality (HIPAA) and patient rights (e.g., PSDA) continues to shape nurse–client interactions in the health-care system.

ADDITIONAL LEARNING EXERCISES AND APPLICATIONS

LEARNING EXERCISE 5.7

Where Does Your Responsibility Lie?

Mrs. Shin is a 68-year-old patient with liver cancer. She has been admitted to the oncology unit at Memorial Hospital. Her admitting physician has advised chemotherapy, even though she believes that there is little chance of it working. The patient asks her doctor, in your presence, if there is an alternative treatment to chemotherapy. She replies, "Nothing else has proved to be effective. Everything else is quackery, and you would be wasting your money." After the doctor leaves, the patient and her family ask you if you know anything about alternative treatments. When you indicate that you do have some current literature available, they beg you to share your information with them.

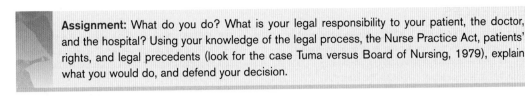

Assignment: What do you do? What is your legal responsibility to your patient, the doctor, and the hospital? Using your knowledge of the legal process, the Nurse Practice Act, patients' rights, and legal precedents (look for the case Tuma versus Board of Nursing, 1979), explain what you would do, and defend your decision.

LEARNING EXERCISE 5.8

Legal Ramifications for Exceeding One's Duties

You have been the evening charge nurse in the emergency department at Memorial Hospital for the last 2 years. Besides yourself, you have two LVNs and four RNs working in your department. Your normal staffing is to have two RNs and one LVN on duty Monday through Thursday and one LVN and three RNs on during the weekend.

It has become apparent that one of the LVNs, Maggie, resents the recently imposed limitations of LVN duties because she has had 10 years of experience in nursing, including a tour of duty as a medic in the first Gulf War. The emergency department physicians admire her and are always asking her to assist them with any major wound repair. Occasionally, she has exceeded her job description as an LVN in the hospital, although she has done nothing illegal of which you are aware. You have given her satisfactory performance evaluations in the past, even though everyone is aware that she sometimes pretends to be a "junior physician." You also suspect that the physicians sometimes allow her to perform duties outside her licensure, but you have not investigated this or actually seen it yourself.

Tonight, you come back from supper and find Maggie suturing a deep laceration while the physician looks on. They both realize that you are upset, and the physician takes over the suturing. Later, the doctor comes to you and says, "Don't worry! She does a great job, and I'll take the responsibility for her actions." You are not sure what you should do. Maggie is a good employee, and taking any action will result in unit conflict.

Assignment: What are the legal ramifications of this case? Discuss what you should do, if anything. What responsibility and liability exist for the physician, Maggie, and yourself? Use appropriate rationale to support your decision.

LEARNING EXERCISE 5.9

To Float or Not to Float

You have been an obstetrical staff nurse at Memorial Hospital for 25 years. The obstetrical unit census has been abnormally low lately, although the patient census in other areas of the hospital has been extremely high. When you arrive at work today, you are told to float to the thoracic surgery critical care unit. This is a highly specialized unit, and you feel ill prepared to work with the equipment on the unit and the type of critically ill patients who are there. You call the staffing office and ask to be reassigned to a different area. You are told that the entire hospital is critically short staffed, that the thoracic surgery unit is four nurses short, and that you are at least as well equipped to handle that unit as the other three staff who also are being floated. Now your anxiety level is even higher. You will be expected to handle a full RN patient load. You also are aware that more than half of the staff on the unit today will have no experience in thoracic surgery. You consider whether to refuse to float. You do not want to place your nursing license in jeopardy, yet you feel conflicting obligations.

Assignment: To whom do you have conflicting obligations? You have little time to make this decision. Outline the steps that you use to reach your final decision. Identify the legal and ethical ramifications that may result from your decision. Are they in conflict?

REFERENCES

Banner, D. D., & Zimmer, L. L. (2012). Informed consent in research: An overview for nurses. *Canadian Journal of Cardiovascular Nursing, 22*(1), 26–30.

Braude, H., & Kimmelman, J. (2012). The ethics of managing affective and emotional states to improve informed consent: Autonomy, comprehension, and voluntariness. *Bioethics, 26*(3), 149–156.

Criminal Law Lawyers Source. (2003–2013). *Terms. False imprisonment.* Retrieved February 5, 2013, from http://www.criminal-law-lawyer-source.com/terms/false-imprisonment.html

Find Law for Legal Professionals. (2013). Docket No. 95409-Agenda 9-November 2003. JUANITA SULLIVAN, Indiv. and as Special Adm'r of the Estate of Burns Sullivan, Deceased, Appellant, v. EDWARD HOSPITAL et al. Appellees. Opinion filed February 5, 2004. Retrieved February 4, 2013, from http://caselaw.findlaw.com/il-supreme-court/1367447.html

Frederick, B. G. (2012). *Assault and battery.* Retrieved February 4, 2013, from http://www.grandstrandlaw.com/lawyer-attorney-1266243.html

Hasley, J. (2012). Good Samaritan Law: Am I covered? *ASBN Update, 16*(1), 16.

Huston, C. J. (2014a). Unlicensed assistive personnel and the registered nurse. In C. J. Huston (Ed.), *Professional issues in nursing* (2nd ed.). Philadelphia, PA: Lippincott Williams & Wilkins 107–120.

Huston, C. J. (2014b). Diversity in the nursing workforce. In C. J. Huston (Ed.), *Professional issues in nursing* (2nd ed.). Philadelphia, PA: Lippincott Williams & Wilkins 136–155.

Huston, C. J. (2014c). Assuring provider competence through licensure, continuing education and certification. In C. J. Huston (Ed.), *Professional issues in nursing* (2nd ed.). Philadelphia, PA: Lippincott Williams & Wilkins 292–307.

Institute of Medicine. (1999, November). *To err is human.* Retrieved June 26, 2013, from http://www.iom.edu/˜/media/Files/Report%20Files/1999/To-Err-is-Human/To%20Err%20is%20Human%201999%20%20report%20brief.pdf

Joint Commission on Accreditation of Healthcare Organizations. (2005). *Health care in the crossroads: Strategies for improving the medical liability system and preventing patient injury.* Oakbrook Terrace, IL: Author.

Johnson, R. W., Zhao, Y., Newby, L., Granger, C. B., & Granger, B. B. (2012). Reasons for noncompletion of advance directives in a cardiac intensive care unit. *American Journal of Critical Care, 21*(5), 311–320.

Medline Plus. (2013). *Advance directives.* Retrieved November 9, 2009, from http://www.nlm.nih.gov/medlineplus/advancedirectives.html

6

Patient, Subordinate, and Professional Advocacy

... to see what is right, and not do it, is want of courage, or of principles.
—Confucius

... in our imperfect state of conscience and enlightenment, publicity and the collision resulting from publicity are the best guardians of the interest in the sick.
—Florence Nightingale

CROSSWALK THIS CHAPTER ADDRESSES:

BSN Essential II: Basic organizational and systems leadership for quality care and patient safety
BSN Essential V: Health-care policy, finance, and regulatory environments
BSN Essential VI: Interprofessional communication and collaboration for improving patient health outcomes
BSN Essential VIII: Professionalism and professional values
MSN Essential II: Organizational and systems leadership
MSN Essential VI: Health policy and advocacy
AONE Nurse Executive Competency II: A knowledge of the health-care environment
AONE Nurse Executive Competency III: Leadership
AONE Nurse Executive Competency I: Professionalism
QSEN Competency: Patient-centered care
QSEN Competency: Teamwork and collaboration

LEARNING OBJECTIVES *The learner will:*

- differentiate between the manager's responsibility to advocate for patients, subordinates, the organization, the profession, and for self
- identify values central to advocacy
- differentiate between controlling patient choices and assisting patients to choose
- select an appropriate response that exemplifies advocacy in given situations
- identify how the Patient's Bill of Rights protects patients
- describe ways a manager can advocate for subordinates
- identify ways individual nurses can become advocates for the profession
- identify both the risks and potential benefits of becoming a whistleblower
- specify both direct and indirect strategies to influence legislation
- describe strategies nurses can use to successfully interact with the media

Advocacy—helping others to grow and self-actualize—is a critically important leadership role. Many of the leadership skills that will be described in the following chapters, such as risk taking, vision, self-confidence, ability to articulate needs, and assertiveness, are used in the advocacy role.

Managers, by virtue of their many roles, must be advocates for the profession, subordinates, and patients. The actions of an *advocate* are to inform others of their rights and to ascertain that they have sufficient information on which to base their decisions. The term *advocacy* can be stated in its simplest form as protecting and defending what one believes in for both self and others (The Free Dictionary, 2013). Nurses often are expected to advocate for patients when they are unable to speak for themselves. Indeed, advocacy has been recognized as one of the most vital and basic roles of the nursing profession since the time of Florence Nightingale.

Nurses may act as advocates by helping others make informed decisions, by acting as an intermediary in the environment, or by directly intervening on behalf of others.

This chapter examines the processes through which advocacy is learned as well as the ways in which leader-managers can advocate for their patients, subordinates, and the profession. The role of "whistleblower" as an advocacy role is discussed. Specific suggestions for interacting with legislators and the media to influence health policy are also included. Leadership roles and management functions essential for advocacy are shown in Display 6.1.

BECOMING AN ADVOCATE

Although advocacy is present in all clinical practice settings, the nursing literature contains only limited descriptions of how nurses learn the advocacy role and some experts have even questioned whether advocacy can be taught at all. Some students learn about the advocacy role as part of ethics or policy content in their nursing education, and while most undergraduate and graduate programs likely include some type of advocacy instruction, the extent or impact of this education is largely unknown.

DISPLAY 6.1	Leadership Roles and Management Functions Associated with Advocacy

LEADERSHIP ROLES

1. Creates a climate where advocacy and its associated risk taking are valued.
2. Seeks fairness and justice for individuals who are unable to advocate for themselves.
3. Seeks to strengthen patient and subordinate support systems to encourage autonomous, well-informed decision making.
4. Influences others by providing information necessary to empower them to act autonomously.
5. Assertively advocates on behalf of patients and subordinates when an intermediary is necessary.
6. Participates in professional nursing organizations and other groups that seek to advance the profession of nursing.
7. Role models proactive involvement in health-care policy through both formal and informal interactions with the media and legislative representatives.
8. Works to establish the creation of a national, legally binding Bill of Rights for Patients.
9. Speaks up when appropriate to advocate for health-care practices necessary for safety and quality improvement.
10. Advocates for social justice in addition to individual patient advocacy.
11. Appropriately differentiates between controlling patient choices (domination and dependence) and in assisting patient choices (allowing freedom).

MANAGEMENT FUNCTIONS

1. Assures that subordinates and patients have adequate information to make informed decisions.
2. Prioritizes the rights and values of patients.
3. Seeks appropriate consultation when advocacy results in intrapersonal or interpersonal conflict.
4. Promotes and protects the workplace safety and health of subordinates and patients.
5. Encourages subordinates to bring forth concerns about the employment setting and seeks impunity for whistleblowers.
6. Demonstrates the skills needed to interact appropriately with the media and legislators regarding nursing and health-care issues.
7. Is aware of current legislative efforts affecting nursing practice and organizational and unit management.
8. Assures that the work environment is both safe and conducive to professional and personal growth for subordinates.
9. Creates work environments that promote subordinate empowerment so that workers have the courage to speak up for patients, themselves, and their profession.
10. Takes immediate action when illegal, unethical, or inappropriate behavior occurs that can endanger or jeopardize the best interests of the patient, the employee, or the organization.

Regardless of how or when advocacy is learned, there are nursing values central to advocacy. These values emphasize caring, autonomy, respect, and empowerment (Display 6.2).

The nursing values central to advocacy emphasize caring, autonomy, respect, and empowerment.

DISPLAY 6.2   Nursing Values Central to Advocacy

1. Each individual has a right to autonomy in deciding what course of action is most appropriate to meet his or her health-care goals.
2. Each individual has a right to hold personal values and to use those values in making health-care decisions.
3. All individuals should have access to the information they need to make informed decisions and choices.
4. The nurse must act on behalf of patients who are unable to advocate for themselves.
5. Empowerment of patients and subordinates to make decisions and take action on their own is the essence of advocacy.

LEARNING EXERCISE 6.1

Values and Advocacy

How important a role do you believe advocacy to be in nursing? Do you believe that your willingness to assume this role is a learned value? Were the values of caring and service emphasized in your family and/or community when you were growing up? Have you identified any role models in nursing who actively advocate for patients, subordinates, or the profession? What strategies might you use as a new nurse to impart the need for advocacy to your peers and to the student nurses who work with you?

PATIENT ADVOCACY

Standard VII of the American Nurses Association (ANA) Scope and Standards of Practice (2010) states that the registered nurse practices ethically. As such, the registered nurse is expected to take appropriate action regarding instances of illegal, unethical, and inappropriate behavior that can endanger or jeopardize the best interests of the health-care consumer or situation; speak up when appropriate to question health-care practice when necessary for safety and quality improvement; and advocate for equitable health-care consumer care.

This patient advocacy is necessary because disease almost always results in decreased independence, loss of freedom, and interference with the ability to make choices autonomously. In addition, aging, as well as physical, mental, or social disability, may make individuals more vulnerable and in need of advocacy. This certainly was the case in research conducted by Jenkins (2012) who found that advocacy has a role in the prevention and detection of abuse in safeguarding vulnerable adults as well as ensuring that those abused can achieve justice. Thus, advocacy becomes the foundation and essence of nursing, and nurses have a responsibility to promote human advocacy.

Managers also must advocate for patients with regard to distribution of resources and the use of technology. The advances in science and limits of financial resources have created new problems and ethical dilemmas. For example, although diagnosis-related groupings may have eased the strain on government fiscal resources, they have created ethical problems, such as patient dumping, premature patient discharge, and inequality of care.

O'Mahony Paquin (2011) agrees, suggesting that nurses must advocate for social justice in addition to individual patient advocacy. When nurses focus their assessment and advocacy skills solely at the individual level, they risk overlooking the underlying systematic problems and injustices which lead to disease and thus implementing limited interventions that provide only Band-Aid solutions. Common areas in which nurses must advocate for patients are shown in Display 6.3.

DISPLAY 6.3   Common Areas Requiring Nurse–Patient Advocacy

1. End-of-life decisions
2. Technological advances
3. Health-care reimbursement
4. Access to health care
5. Provider–patient conflicts regarding expectations and desired outcomes
6. Withholding of information or blatant lying to patients
7. Insurance authorizations, denials, and delays in coverage
8. Medical errors
9. Patient information disclosure (privacy and confidentiality)
10. Patient grievance and appeals processes
11. Cultural and ethnic diversity and sensitivity
12. Respect for patient dignity
13. Inadequate consents
14. Incompetent health-care providers
15. Complex social problems including AIDS (acquired immunodeficiency syndrome), teenage pregnancy, violence, and poverty
16. Aging population

Yet at times, individual rights must be superseded to ensure the safety of all parties involved. It is important, however, for the patient advocate to know the difference between controlling patient choices and assisting patients to choose. Lavelle and Tusaie (2011) note that the assumption that health-care professionals are the best judges of what treatment would be most effective is actually very narcissistic and, in fact, this assumption may strip patients of their right to self-determination. Nurses must not use paternalism as a means to reduce patient autonomy.

It is important for the patient advocate to be able to differentiate between controlling patient choices (domination and dependence) and in assisting patient choices (allowing freedom).

LEARNING EXERCISE 6.2

Culture and Decisions

You are a staff nurse on a medical unit. One of your patients, Mr. Dau, is a 56-year-old Hmong immigrant to the United States. He has lived in the United States for 4 years and became a citizen 2 years ago. His English is marginal, although he understands more than he can verbalize. He was admitted to the hospital with sepsis resulting from urinary tract infection. His condition is now stable.

Today, Mr. Dau's physician informed him that his computed tomography scan shows a large tumor in his prostrate that is likely cancer. The physician wants to do immediate follow-up testing and surgical resection of the tumor to relieve his symptoms of hesitancy and urinary retention. Although the tumor is probably cancerous, the physician believes that it will respond well to traditional oncology treatments. The expectation is that Mr. Dau should recover fully.

One hour later, when you go in to check on Mr. Dau, you find him sitting on his bed with his suitcase packed, waiting for a ride home. He informs you that he is checking out of the hospital. He states that he believes he can make himself better at home with herbs and through prayers by the Hmong shaman. He concludes by telling you, "if I am meant to die, there is little anyone can do." When you reaffirm the hopeful prognosis reported by his physician that morning, Mr. Dau says "The doctor is just trying to give me false hope. I need to go home and prepare for my death."

Assignment: What should you do? How can you best advocate for this patient? Is the problem a lack of information? How does culture play a role in the patient's decision? Does a lack of understanding on this patient's part justify paternalism?

PATIENT RIGHTS

Until the 1960s, patients had few rights; in fact, patients often were denied basic human rights during a time when they were most vulnerable. This changed with the adoption of the *Consumer Bill of Rights and Responsibilities*, also known as the *Patient's Bill of Rights* in 1998. This document had three key goals: (1) to help patients feel more confident in the US healthcare system, (2) to stress the importance of a strong relationship between patients and their health-care providers, and (3) to stress the key role patients play in staying healthy by laying out rights and responsibilities for all patients and health-care providers (American Cancer Society, 2013).

Since that time, the National League for Nursing, the American Hospital Association, and many other organizations have created documents outlining the rights of patients. While not legally binding, these documents do guide health-care organizations and practitioners in terms of professional expectations for patient advocacy. Some federal laws do exist though in

The bottom line is that patients are increasingly aware that they have rights, and as a result, they are more assertive and involved in their health care. They want to know and understand their treatment options and to be participants in decisions about their health care. This right to information and participation in medical care decisions has led to some conflicts in the areas of informed consent and access to medical records. Leader-managers, however, have a responsibility to see that all patient rights are met, including the right to privacy and personal liberty, which are guaranteed by the constitution.

SUBORDINATE AND WORKPLACE ADVOCACY

Subordinate advocacy is a neglected concept in management theory but is an essential part of the leadership role. Standard 16 of the ANA Scope and Standards for Nursing Administration (2009) suggests that nurse administrators should advocate for other health-care providers (including subordinates) as well as patients, especially when this is related to health and safety.

For example, *workplace advocacy* is a critical role managers assume to promote subordinate advocacy. In this type of advocacy, the manager works to see that the work environment is both safe and conducive to professional and personal growth for subordinates. Unfortunately, workplace violence is an ever increasing problem in contemporary society. The Occupational Safety and Health Administration (OSHA) reports that over 2 million American workers are victims of workplace violence each year and the second leading cause of death from women while at work is workplace homicides from assaults and other violent acts (Papa & Venella, 2013).

Survey results from a descriptive study of experiences of 3,465 registered nurse members of the Emergency Nurses Association noted that approximately 25% of the respondents had experienced physical violence greater than 20 times in the previous 3 years and nearly 20% reported encountering verbal abuse more than 200 times in that same time frame. Respondents suggested these incidents were often not reported due to fear of retaliation and fear of a lack of support from their employer. The researchers concluded that one factor important to mitigating this type of workplace violence then is a commitment by upper management to ensuring a safer workplace by hospital administrators, emergency department managers, and hospital security.

In addition, occupational health and safety must be assured by interventions such as reducing worker exposure to workplace violence, needle sticks, or blood and body fluids. Subordinates should also be able to have the expectation that their work hours and schedules will be reasonable, that staffing ratios will be adequate to support safe patient care, that wages will be fair and equitable, and that nurses will be allowed participation in organizational decision making. When these working conditions do not exist, managers must advocate to higher levels of the administrative hierarchy to correct the problems.

In addition, when the health-care industry has faced the crisis of inadequate human resources and nursing shortages, many organizations have made quick, poorly thought-out decisions to find short-term solutions to a long-term and severe problem. New workers have been recruited at a phenomenally high cost, yet the problems that caused high worker attrition were not solved. Upper-level managers must advocate for subordinates in solving problems and making decisions about how best to use limited resources. These decisions must be made carefully, following a thorough examination of the political, social, economic, and ethical costs.

Another way leaders advocate for subordinates is in creating a work environment that promotes risk taking and leadership. For example, administrators should foster work environments that promote subordinate empowerment so that workers have the courage to speak up for patients, themselves, and their profession. In addition, managers must help members of their health-care team resolve ethical problems and live with the solutions at the unit level.

The following are suggestions for creating an environment that promotes subordinate advocacy:

- Invite collaborative decision making.
- Listen to staff needs.
- Get to know staff personally.
- Take time to understand the challenges faced by the staff in delivering care.
- Face challenges and solve problems together.
- "Go to bat" for staff when needed.
- Promote shared governance.
- Empower staff.
- Promote nurse autonomy.
- Provide staff with workable systems.

Managers must recognize what subordinates are striving for and the goals and values that subordinates consider appropriate. The leader-manager should be able to guide subordinates toward actualization while defending their right to autonomy. To help nurses deal with ethical dilemmas in their practice, nurse-managers should establish and utilize appropriate support groups, ethics committees, and channels for dealing with ethical problems.

LEARNING EXERCISE 6.4

How Can You Best Advocate?

You are a unit supervisor in a skilled nursing facility. One of your aides, Martha Greenwald, recently reported that she suffered a "back strain" several weeks ago when she was lifting an elderly patient. She did not report the injury at the time because she did not think it was serious. Indeed, she finished the remainder of her shift and has performed all of her normal work duties since that time.

Today, Martha reports that she has just left her physician's office and that he has advised her to take 4 to 6 weeks off from work to fully recover from her injury. He has also prescribed physical therapy and electrical nerve stimulation for the chronic pain. Martha is a relatively new employee, so she has not yet accrued enough sick leave to cover her absence. She asks you to complete the paperwork for her absence and the cost of her treatments to be covered as a work-related injury.

When you contact the workers' compensation case manager for your facility, she states that the claim will be investigated; however, with no written or verbal report of the injury at the time it occurred, there is great likelihood that the claim will be rejected.

Assignment: How best can you advocate for this subordinate?

WHISTLEBLOWING AS ADVOCACY

The public has become much more aware of ethical malfeasance within its institutions and corporate organizations as a result of various scandals that have occurred in the last 50 years. From Watergate to Morgan Stanley to Bernard Madoff's ponzi scheme, the American public has been fed a diet of wrongdoing that has led to an increase in moral awareness.

Wrongdoing does not stop at large corporations or political activity, it also occurs within health-care organizations. Huston (2014a) states, "In an era of managed care, declining reimbursements and the ongoing pressure to remain fiscally solvent, the risk of fraud, misrepresentation, and ethical malfeasance in healthcare organizations has never been higher. As a result, the need for *whistle-blowing* has also likely never been greater" (p. 251).

Huston (2014a) states that there are basically two types of whistleblowing. *Internal whistleblowing* occurs within an organization, reporting up the chain of command. *External whistleblowing* involves reporting outside the organization such as the media and an elected official. An example of whistleblowing by a nurse might be to report abuse to a patient by one another care provider.

It is interesting to note that while much of the public wants wrongdoing or corruption to be reported, such behavior is often looked upon with distrust, and whistleblowers may be considered disloyal or experience repercussions for their actions, even if the whistleblowing was done with the best of intentions. The whistleblower cannot even trust that other health-care professionals, with similar belief systems about advocacy, will value their efforts, because the public's feelings about whistleblowers are so mixed (Huston, 2014a). Leader-managers then must be willing to advocate for whistleblowers so that they feel assured, that if they are acting within the scope of their expertise, and that remedy can be sought through appropriate channels without fear of retaliation.

Speaking out as a whistleblower is often honored more in theory than in fact.

Huston (2014a) suggests that nurses as health-care professionals have a responsibility to uncover, openly discuss, and condemn shortcuts which threaten the clients they serve. Yet clearly, there has been a collective silence in many such cases. The reality is that whistleblowing offers no guarantee that the situation will change or the problem will improve, and the literature is replete with horror stories regarding negative consequences endured by whistleblowers (see Examining the Evidence 6.1). For all these reasons, it takes tremendous courage to come forward as a whistleblower. It also takes a tremendous sense of what is right and what is wrong as well as a commitment to follow a problem through until an acceptable level of resolution is reached (Huston).

Examining the Evidence 6.1

Source: Thomas, M., & Willmann, J. (2012). Why nurses need whistleblower protection. Journal of Nursing Regulation, 3(3), 19–23.

Thomas and Willmann shared the case of two Winkler County, Texas, nurses who voiced concerns about a physician's dangerous practices including unprofessional conduct, via what they thought was a confidential report to the State Board for Medicine. One nurse was the compliance officer for the hospital and the other was the performance improvement officer. Instead of the physician being investigated, the nurses found themselves indicted for unprofessional conduct charges (misuse of official information, a third-degree felony) brought by the local Sheriff and County Attorney, who were friends and business associates of the reported physician. In the end, the nurses who had a combined 47 years of experience at the hospital were fired. The charges for the two nurses were eventually dropped and the Sherriff, County Attorney, and hospital administrator were indicted (violation of the nurses' civil rights under Federal Law as well as violation of the Texas Public Employee Whistleblower Law) for retaliating against the whistleblowers. All four of the indictments resulted in convictions. In addition, the nurses sued the county and settled for a shared $750,000.

Leader-managers must be willing to advocate for *whistleblowers*, who speak out about organizational practices that they believe may be harmful or inappropriate.

Although whistleblower protection has been advocated at the federal level and has passed in some states, many employees are reluctant to report unsafe conditions for fear of retaliation. Nurses should check with their state association to assess the status of whistleblower protection in their state. At present, there is no universal legal protection for whistleblowers in the United States.

PROFESSIONAL ADVOCACY

Managers also must be advocates for the nursing profession. This type of advocacy has a long history in nursing. It was nurses who pushed for accountability through state Nurse Practice Acts and state licensing, although this was not accomplished until 1903. Beyers (as cited in Huston, 2014b) suggests that nurse leaders collaborated on defining the profession, achieving legal recognition of the profession, and establishing a culture for professional nursing which has continued to the present time. Advocating for professional nursing is a leadership role.

Joining a profession requires making a personal decision to involve oneself in a system of socially defined roles. Thus, entry into a profession involves a personal and public promise to serve others with the special expertise that a profession can provide and that society legitimately expects it to provide.

Professional issues are always ethical issues. When nurses find a discrepancy between their perceived role and society's expectations, they have a responsibility to advocate for the profession. At times, individual nurses believe that the problems of the profession are too big for them to make a difference; however, their commitment to their profession obligates them to ask questions and think about problems that affect the profession. They cannot afford to become powerless or helpless or claim that one person cannot make a difference. Often, one voice is all it takes to raise the consciousness of colleagues within a profession.

A professional commitment means that people cannot shrink from their duty to question and contemplate problems that face the profession.

If nursing is to advance as a profession, practitioners and managers must broaden their sociopolitical knowledge base to better understand the bureaucracies in which they live. This includes speaking out on consumer issues, continuing and expanding attempts to influence legislation, and increasing membership on governmental health policy-making boards and councils. Only then will nurses be able to influence the tremendous problems facing society today in terms of the homeless, teenage pregnancy, drug and alcohol abuse, inadequate health care for the poor and elderly, and medical errors. These are essential advocacy roles for the profession.

LEARNING EXERCISE 6.5

Write It Down. What Would You Change?

List five things that you would like to change about nursing or the health-care system. Prioritize the changes that you have identified. Write a one-page essay about the change that you believe is most needed. Identify the strategies that you could use individually and collectively as a profession to make the change happen. Be sure that you are realistic about the time, energy, and fiscal resources you have to implement your plan.

Nursing's Advocacy Role in Legislation and Public Policy

A distinctive feature of American society is the manner in which citizens can participate in the political process. People have the right to express their opinions about issues and candidates by voting. People also have relatively easy access to lawmakers and policy makers and can make their individual needs and wants known. Theoretically, then, any one person can influence those in policy-making positions. In reality, this rarely happens; policy decisions are generally focused on group needs or wants.

Much attention has recently been paid to nurses and the importance of the nursing profession and how nurses impact health-care delivery. This has been especially true in the areas of patient safety and staff shortages.

In addition to active participation in national nursing organizations, nurses can influence legislation and health policy in many other ways. Nurses who want to be directly involved can lobby legislators either in person or by letter. This process may seem intimidating to the new nurse; however, there are many books and workshops available that deal with the subject and a common format is used. In addition to nurse-leaders and individual nurses, there is a need for collective influence to impact health-care policy. The need for organized group efforts by nurses to influence legislative policy has long been recognized in this country. In fact, the first state associations were organized expressly for unifying nurses to influence the passage of state licensure laws.

Nurses must exert their collective influence and make their concerns known to policy makers before they can have a major impact on political and legislative outcomes.

Political action committees (PACs) of the Congress of Industrial Organizations attempt to persuade legislators to vote in a particular way. Lobbyists of the PAC may be members of a group interested in a particular law or paid agents of the group that wants a specific bill passed or defeated. Nursing must become more actively involved with PACs to influence health-care legislation, and PACs provide one opportunity for small donors to feel like they are making a difference.

In addition, professional organizations generally espouse standards of care that are higher than those required by law. Voluntary controls often are forerunners of legal controls. What nursing is and should be depends on nurses taking an active part in their professional organizations. Currently, nursing lobbyists in our nation's capital are influencing legislation on quality of care, access to care issues, patient and health worker safety, health-care restructuring, direct reimbursement for advanced practice nurses, and funding for nursing education. Representatives of the ANA regularly attend and provide testimony for meetings of the U.S. Department of Health and Human Services, the Department of Health, the National Institutes of Health, the OSHA, and the White House to be sure that the "nursing perspective" is heard in health policy issues (Huston, 2014c).

As a whole, the nursing profession has not yet recognized the full potential of collective political activity. Nurses must exert their collective influence and make their concerns known to policy makers before they can have a major impact on political and legislative outcomes. Because they have been reluctant to become politically involved, nurses have failed to have a strong legislative voice in the past. Legislators and policy makers are more willing to deal with nurses as a group rather than as individuals; thus, joining and supporting professional organizations allow nurses to become active in lobbying for a stronger nurse practice act or for the creation or expansion of advanced nursing roles.

Personal letters are more influential than form letters, and the tone should be formal but polite. The letter should also be concise (not more than one page). Be sure to address the legislator properly by title. Establish your credibility early in the letter as both a constituent and a health-care expert. State your reason for writing the letter in the first paragraph, and refer to the specific bill that you are writing about. Then, state your position on the issue and give personal examples as necessary to support your position. Offer your assistance as a resource person for additional information. Sign the letter, including your name and contact information. Remember to be persistent, and write legislators repeatedly who are undecided on an issue. Display 6.5 displays a format common to letters written to legislators.

DISPLAY 6.5   Sample: A Letter to a Legislator

March 15, 2014
The Honorable John Doe
Member of the Senate
State Capitol, Room _____
City, State, Zip Code

Dear Senator Doe,
   I am a registered nurse and member of the American Nurses Association (ANA). I am also a constituent in your district. I am writing in support of SB XXX, which requires the establishment of minimum RN staffing ratios in acute care facilities. As a staff nurse on an oncology unit in our local hospital, I see firsthand the problems that occur when staffing is inadequate to meet the complex needs of acutely ill patients: medical errors, patient and nurse dissatisfaction, workplace injuries, and perhaps most importantly, the inability to spend adequate time with and comfort patients who are dying.
   I have enclosed a copy of a recent study conducted by John Smith and will be published in the January 2014 edition of *Nurses Today*. This article details the positive impact of legislative staffing ratio implementation on patient outcomes as measured by medication errors, patient falls, and nosocomial infection rates.
   I strongly encourage you to vote for SB XXX when it is heard by the Senate Business and Professions Committee next week. Thank you for your ongoing concern with nursing and health-care issues and for your past support of legislation to improve health-care staffing. Please feel free to contact me if you have any questions or would like additional information.

   Respectfully,
Nancy Thompson, RN, BSN
Street
City, State, Zip Code
Phone number including area code
E-mail address

Other nurses may choose to monitor the progress of legislation, count congressional votes, and track a specific legislator's voting intents as well as past voting records. Still other nurses may choose to join *network groups*, where colleagues meet to discuss professional issues and pending legislation.

For nurses interested in a more indirect approach to professional advocacy, their role may be to influence and educate the public about nursing and the nursing agenda to reform health care. This may be done by speaking with professional and community groups about health-care and nursing issues and by interacting directly with the media. Never underestimate the influence that a single nurse may have even in writing letters to the editor of local newspapers or by talking about nursing and health-care issues with friends, family, neighbors, teachers, clergy, and civic leaders.

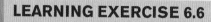

LEARNING EXERCISE 6.6

Realistic Advocacy for the Nursing Profession

Do you belong to your state nursing organization or student nursing organization? Why or why not? Make a list of six other things that you could do to advocate for the profession. Be specific. Is your list realistic in terms of your energy and commitment to nursing?

Nursing and the Media

"Although registered nurses are among the most knowledgeable, educated, frontline healthcare providers in the country, their voices are rarely ever heard or consulted by mainstream media organizations" (Taking Media into Our Own Hands, 2011, p. 10). This is because too few nurses are willing to interact with the media about vital nursing and health-care issues. Often, this is because they believe that they lack the expertise to do so or because they lack self-confidence. This is especially unfortunate because both the media and the public place a high trust in nurses and want to hear about health-care issues from a nursing perspective.

The reality is that the responsibility for nursing's image as perceived by the public lies solely upon the shoulders of those who claim nursing as their profession. Until such time as nurses are able to agree upon the desired collective image and are willing to do what is necessary to both tell and show the public what that image is, little will change (Huston, 2014d). Nurses should take every opportunity to appear in the media—in newspapers, radio, and television. Nurses should also complete special training programs to increase their self-confidence in working with journalists and other media representatives. Regardless, the first few media interactions will likely be stressful, just like any new task or learning. The following tips may be helpful to nurses learning to navigate media waters (Display 6.6):

- Remember that reporters often have short deadlines. A delay in responding to a reporter's request for an interview usually results in the reporter looking elsewhere for a source.

- Do not be unduly paranoid that the reporter "is out to get you" by inaccurately representing what you have to say. The reporter has a job to do and most reporters do their best to be fair and accurate in their reporting.

- Come to the interview prepared with any statistics, important dates and times, anecdotes, or other information you want to share.

- Limit your key points to two or three and frame them as bullet points to reduce the likelihood that you will be misheard or misinterpreted. Brief, but concise sound bites are much more quotable than rambling arguments.

- Avoid technical or academic jargon.

- Speak with credibility and confidence, but do not be afraid to say that you do not know if asked a question beyond your expertise or which would be better answered by someone else. If you choose not to answer a question, give a brief reason for not wanting to do so, rather than simply saying "no comment."

- Avoid being pulled into inflammatory arguments or blame setting. If you feel that you have been baited or that you are being pulled off on tangents, simply repeat the key points you intended to make and refocus the conversation if possible. Remember that you cannot control the questions you are asked, but you can control your responses.

- Provide contact information so that the reporter can contact you if additional information or clarifications are needed. Be aware, however, that most reporters will not allow you to preview their story prior to publication.

DISPLAY 6.6 | **Tips for Interacting with the Media**

1. Respect and meet the reporter's deadlines.
2. Assume, until proven otherwise, that the reporter will be fair and accurate in his/her reporting.
3. Have key facts and figures ready for the interview.
4. Limit your key points to two or three and frame them as bullet points.
5. Avoid technical or academic jargon.
6. Speak confidently but do not be afraid to say when you do not have the expertise to answer a question or when a question is better directed to someone else.
7. Avoid being pulled into inflammatory arguments or blame setting and repeat key points if you are pulled off into tangents.
8. Provide the reporter with contact information for follow-up and needed clarifications.

LEARNING EXERCISE 6.7

Preparing for a Media Interview

You are the staffing coordinator for a medium-sized community hospital in California. Minimum staffing ratios were implemented in January 2004. While this has represented an even greater challenge in terms of meeting your organization's daily staffing needs, you believe that the impetus behind the legislative mandate was sound. You also are a member of the state nursing association that sponsored this legislation and wrote letters of support for its passage. The hospital that employs you and the state hospital association fought unsuccessfully against the passage of minimum staffing ratios.

The local newspaper contacted you this morning and wants to interview you about staffing ratios in general as well as how these ratios are impacting the local hospital. You approach your Chief Nursing Officer, and she tells you to go ahead and do the interview if you want but to remember that you are a representative of the hospital.

Assignment: Assume that you have agreed to participate in the interview.

1. How might you go about preparing for the interview?
2. Identify three factual points that you can state during the interview as your sound bites. What would be your primary points of emphasis?
3. Is there a way to reconcile the conflict between your personal feelings about staffing ratios and those of your employer? How would you respond if asked directly by the reporter to comment about whether staffing ratios are a good idea?

INTEGRATING LEADERSHIP ROLES AND MANAGEMENT FUNCTIONS IN ADVOCACY

Nursing leaders and managers recognize that they have an obligation not only to advocate for the needs of their patients, subordinates, and themselves at a particular time but also to be active in furthering the goals of the profession. To accomplish all of these types of advocacy, nurses must value autonomy and empowerment.

However, the leadership roles and management functions to achieve advocacy with patients and subordinates and for the profession differ greatly. Advocating for patients requires that the manager create a work environment that recognizes patient's needs and goals as paramount. This means creating a work culture where patients are respected, well informed, and empowered. The leadership role required to advocate for patients is often one of risk taking, particularly when advocating for a client may be in direct conflict with a provider or institutional goal. Leaders must also be willing to accept and support patient choices that may be different from their own.

Advocating for subordinates requires that the manager create a safe and equitable work environment where employees feel valued and appreciated. When working conditions are less than favorable, the manager is responsible for relaying these concerns to higher levels of management and advocating for needed changes. The same risk taking that is required in patient advocacy is a leadership role in subordinate advocacy, since subordinate needs and wants may be in conflict with the organization. There is always a risk that the organization will view the advocate as a troublemaker, but this does not provide an excuse for managers to be complacent in this role. Managers also must advocate for subordinates in creating an environment where ethical concerns, needs, and dilemmas can be openly discussed and resolved.

Advocating for the profession requires that the nurse-manager be informed and involved in all legislation affecting the unit, organization, and the profession. The manager also must be an astute handler of public relations and demonstrate skill in working with the media. It is the leader, however, who proactively steps forth to be a role model and active participant in educating the public and improving health care through the political process.

KEY CONCEPTS

- Advocacy is helping others to grow and self-actualize and is a leadership role.

- Managers, by virtue of their many roles, must be advocates for patients, subordinates, and the profession.

- It is important for the patient advocate to be able to differentiate between controlling patient choices (domination and dependence) and in assisting patient choices (allowing freedom).

- Since the 1960s, some advocacy groups, professional associations, and states have passed Bills of Rights for patients. Although these are not legally binding, they can be used to guide professional practice.

- In workplace advocacy, the manager works to see that the work environment is both safe and conducive to professional and personal growth for subordinates.

- While much of the public wants wrongdoing or corruption to be reported, such behavior is often looked upon with distrust, and whistleblowers are often considered disloyal and experience negative repercussions for their actions.

- Leader-managers must be willing to advocate for whistleblowers, who speak out about organizational practices that they believe may be harmful or inappropriate.

- Professional issues are ethical issues. When nurses find a discrepancy between their perceived role and society's expectations, they have a responsibility to advocate for the profession.

- If nursing is to advance as a profession, practitioners and managers must broaden their sociopolitical knowledge base to better understand the bureaucracies in which they live.

- Because legislators and policy makers are more willing to deal with nurses as a group rather than as individuals, joining and actively supporting professional organizations allow nurses to have a greater voice in health-care and professional issues.

- Nurses need to exert their collective influence and make their concerns known to policy makers before they can have a major impact on political and legislative outcomes.

- Nurses have great potential to educate the public and influence policy through the media as a result of the public's high trust in nurses and because the public wants to hear about health-care issues from a nursing perspective.

ADDITIONAL LEARNING EXERCISES AND APPLICATIONS

LEARNING EXERCISE 6.8

Ethics and Advocacy

You are a new graduate staff nurse in a home health agency. One of your clients is a 23-year-old man with acute schizophrenia who was just released from the local county, acute care, behavioral health-care facility, following a 72-hour hold. He has no insurance. His family no longer has contact with him, and he is unable to hold a permanent job. He is noncompliant in taking his prescription drugs for schizophrenia. He is homeless and has been sleeping and eating intermittently at the local homeless shelter; however, he was recently asked not to return because he is increasingly agitated and, at times, violent. He calls you today and asks you "to help him with the voices in his head."

You approach the senior RN case manager in the facility for help in identifying options for this individual to get the behavioral health-care services that he needs. She suggests that you tell the patient to go to Maxwell's Mini Mart, a local convenience store, at 3 PM today and wait by the counter. Then, she tells you that you should contact the police at 2:55 PM and tell them that Maxwell's Mini Mart is being robbed by your patient so that he will be arrested. She states, "I do this with all of my uninsured mental health patients, since the state Medicaid program offers only limited mental health services and the state penal system provides full mental health services for the incarcerated." She goes on to say that the store owner and the police are aware of what she is doing and support the idea, since it is the only way "patients really have a chance of getting better." She ends the conversation by saying, "I know you are a new nurse and don't understand how the real world works, but the reality is that this is the only way I can advocate for patients like this, and you need to do the same for your patients."

Assignment:

1. Will you follow the advice of the senior RN case manager?
2. If not, how else can you advocate for this patient?

LEARNING EXERCISE 6.9

Letter Writing in Advocacy

Identify three legislative bills affecting nursing that are currently being considered in committee, the House of Representatives, or the Senate. Select one and draft a letter to your state assembly person, representative, or senator regarding your position on the bill.

LEARNING EXERCISE 6.10

Determining Nursing's Entry Level

Grandfathering is the term used to grant certain people working within the profession for a given period of time or prior to a deadline date the privilege of applying for a license without having to take the licensing examination. Grandfathering clauses have been used to allow licensure for wartime nurses—those with on-the-job training and expertise—even though they did not graduate from an approved school of nursing.

(Continued)

Some professional nursing organizations are once again proposing that the BSN become the entry-level requirement for professional nursing. Some have suggested that as a concession to current Associate Degree (ADN) and diploma-prepared nurses, all nurses who have passed the registered nursing licensure examination before the new legislation, regardless of educational preparation or experience, would retain the title of professional nurse. Non-baccalaureate nurses after that time would be unable to use the title of professional nurse.

Assignment: Do you believe that the "BSN as entry level" proposal advocates the advancement of the nursing profession? Is grandfathering conducive to meeting this goal? Would you personally support both of these proposals? Does the long-standing internal dissension about making the BSN the entry level into professional nursing reduce nursing's status as a profession? Do lawmakers or the public understand this dilemma or care about it?

LEARNING EXERCISE 6.11

How Would You Proceed?

You are an RN case manager for a large insurance company. Sheila Johannsen is a 34-year-old mother of two small children. She was diagnosed with advanced, metastatic breast cancer 6 months ago. Traditional chemotherapy and radiation seem to have slowed the spread of the cancer, but the prognosis is not good.

Sheila contacted you this morning to report that she has been in contact with a physician at one of the most innovative medical centers in the country. He told her that she might benefit from an experimental gene therapy treatment; however, she is ineligible for participation in the free clinical trials since her cancer is so advanced. The cost for the treatment is approximately $250,000. Sheila states that she does not have the financial resources to pay for the treatment and begs you "to do whatever you can to get the insurance company to pay. Otherwise, she will die."

You know that the cost of experimental treatments is almost always disallowed by your insurance company. You also know that even with the experimental treatment, Sheila's probability of a cure is very small.

Assignment: Decide how you will proceed. How can you best advocate for this patient?

LEARNING EXERCISE 6.12

Conflict of Values

You are a case manager in a disease management program, assigned to coordinate the care needs of Sam, a 72-year-old man with multiple chronic health problems. His medical history includes myocardial infarctions, implantation of a pacemaker, open-heart surgery, an inoperable abdominal aneurysm, and repeated episodes of congestive heart failure. Because of his poor health, he cannot operate the small business he owns or work for any length of time at his gardening or other hobbies.

Although Joe has told you that death would be a relief to his nearly constant discomfort and depression, his wife dismisses such talk as "nonsense" and tells Sam that "she still needs him and will always do everything in her power to keep him here with her." In deference to his wife's wishes, Joe has not completed any of the legal paperwork necessary to create a durable power of attorney

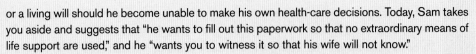

or a living will should he become unable to make his own health-care decisions. Today, Sam takes you aside and suggests that "he wants to fill out this paperwork so that no extraordinary means of life support are used," and he "wants you to witness it so that his wife will not know."

Assignment: Decide what you will do. What is your obligation to Sam? To his wife? To yourself? Whose needs are paramount? How do the ethical principles of autonomy, duty, and veracity intersect or compete in this case?

LEARNING EXERCISE 6.13

Peer Advocacy

You are a nursing student. Like many of the students in your nursing program, sometimes you feel you study too much and therefore miss out on partying with friends; something many of your college friends do on a regular basis. Today, after a particularly grueling exam, three of your nursing school peers approach you and ask you to go out with them to a party tonight, off campus, which is being co-hosted by Matt, another nursing student. Alcohol will be readily available although not everyone at the party is of legal drinking age, including you and one of your nursing peers (Jenny). Because you really do not want to drink anyway, you agree to be the designated driver.

Almost immediately after you arrive at the party, all three of your nursing peers begin drinking. At first it seems pretty harmless, but after several hours, you decide the tenor of the party is changing and becoming less controlled, and that it is time to take your friends home. Two of your peers agree, but you cannot find Jenny. As you begin searching for her, several partygoers tell you that she has been drinking "kamikazes" all night and that she "looked pretty wasted" the last time they saw her. They suggest that you check the bathroom since Jenny said she wasn't feeling very well.

When you enter the bathroom, you see Jenny slumped in the corner by the toilet. She has vomited all over the floor as well as her clothing and she reeks of alcohol. When you attempt to rouse her, her eyelids flutter but she is unable to wake up or answer any questions. Her breathing seems regular and unlabored, but she is continuing to vomit in her "blacked-out" state. Her skin feels somewhat clammy to the touch and she cannot stand or walk on her own. You are not sure how much Jenny actually had to drink or how long it has been since she "passed out."

You are worried that Jenny is experiencing acute alcohol poisoning but are not very experienced with this sort of thing. The other two nursing students you brought to the party feel you are overreacting, although they agree that Jenny has had too much to drink and needs to be watched. One of your peers suggests calling the new young, clinical instructor in the nursing program, who offered just the other day to provide rides to students who have been drinking. You think she might be able to provide some guidance. Another one tells you that she feels Jenny just needs to "sleep it off" and that she will stay with Jenny tonight to make sure she is OK, although she has had a fair amount to drink herself.

You think Jenny should be seen in the local emergency department (ED) for treatment and are contemplating calling for an ambulance. One partygoer agrees with you that Jenny should be seen at the hospital but suggests you drop Jenny off anonymously at the front door of the ED so "you won't get in any trouble." Matt encourages you not to take her to the ED at all, because he is afraid the incident will be reported to the local police since Jenny is a minor and that he could be in "real trouble" for furnishing alcohol to a minor. He argues that this could threaten

(Continued)

both his progression and Jenny's in the nursing program. He says that she can just stay at the house tonight and that he will check in on her on a regular basis.

To complicate things, you, Jenny, and the other two students you brought to the party live in the college dormitories and they lock down for the evening in another 30 minutes. It will take you at least 20 minutes to gather the manpower you need to get Jenny down to your car and up to her dormitory room by lockdown, if that is what you decide to do. If you are not inside the dormitories by lockdown, you will need to find another place to spend the evening. In addition, there will likely be someone at the door to the dormitory assigned to turn away students who are clearly intoxicated.

Assignment: Decide what you will do. How do you best advocate for a peer when they are unable to advocate for themselves? Does it matter if the risk is self-inducted? How do you weigh the benefits of advocating for one person when it can result in potential harm or risk to another person?

REFERENCES

American Cancer Society. (2013). *Patient's bill of rights.* Retrieved April 18, 2013, from http://www.cancer .org/treatment/findingandpayingfortreatment/ understandingfinancialandlegalmatters/patients-bill -of-rights

American Nurses Association. (2009). *Nursing administration. Scope & standards of practice.* Silver Springs, MD: Nursesbooks.org

American Nurses Association. (2010). *Scope and standards of practice* (2nd ed.). Silver Spring, MD: American Nurses Association. BHE/MONE, 2006.

Becze, E. (2011). Know your patients' rights under the Genetic Information Nondiscrimination Act. *ONS Connect, 26*(8), 14–15.

Consumer Watchdog. (n.d.) *The California patient's guide. Your health care rights and remedies.* Retrieved May 15, 2014, from http://www.calpatientguide.org/index.html

Gallagher, C., Hernandez, C., & Walker, M. (2012). A progressive step toward healthcare equality. *Healthcare Executive, 27*(5), 54–56.

Goodall, S. (2012). Safeguarding adults: Practical tips for training. *Nursing & Residential Care, 14*(11), 600–603.

Huston, C. (2014a). Whistle-blowing in nursing. In C. Huston (Ed.), *Professional issues in nursing* (3rd ed.). Philadelphia, PA: Lippincott Williams & Wilkins 250–265.

Huston, C. (2014b). Nursing's professional associations by Marjorie Beyers. In C. Huston (Ed.), *Professional issues in nursing* (3rd ed.). Philadelphia, PA: Lippincott Williams & Wilkins 387–406.

Huston, C. (2014c). The Nursing Profession's Historic Struggle to Increase Its Power Base. In C. Huston (Ed.), *Professional issues in nursing* (3rd ed.). Philadelphia, PA: Lippincott Williams & Wilkins 310–326.

Huston, C. (2014d). Professional identity and image. In C. Huston (Ed.), *Professional issues in nursing* (3rd ed.). Philadelphia, PA: Lippincott Williams & Wilkins 327–342.

Illinois General Assembly. (n.d.). PUBLIC HEALTH (410 ILCS 50/) Medical Patient Rights Act. Retrieved May 14, 2013, from http://www.ilga.gov/legislation/ ilcs/ilcs3.asp?ActID=1525&ChapterID=35

Jenkins, R. (2012). Using advocacy to safeguard older people with learning disabilities. *Nursing Older People, 24*(6), 31–36.

Lavelle, S., & Tusaie, K. R. (2011). Reflecting on forced medication. *Issues in Mental Health Nursing, 32*(5), 274–278.

Medline Plus (2013). *Patient rights.* Retrieved April 20, 2013, from http://www.nlm.nih.gov/medlineplus/ patientrights.html

O'Mahony Paquin, S. (2011). Social justice advocacy in nursing: What is it? How do we get there? *Creative Nursing, 17*(2), 63–67.

Orr, F. (2013). Protecting patient rights: Nursing jurisprudence in action. *Alberta RN, 68*(4), 14–15.

Papa, A., & Venella, J. (2013, January 31). Workplace violence in healthcare: Strategies for advocacy. *Online Journal of Issues in Nursing, 18*(1), 1.

Taking Media Into Our Own Hands. (2011). *National Nurse, 107*(1), 10–13. Retrieved Sept. 29, 2013, from http:// nurses.3cdn.net/37eb9af628395bf916_0im6b0snw.pdf

The Free Dictionary. (2013). *Definition of advocacy.* Accessed April 18, 2013, from http://www. thefreedictionary.com/advocacy

Thomas, M., & Willmann, J. (2012). Why nurses need whistleblower protection. *Journal of Nursing Regulation, 3*(3), 19–23.

UNIT III

Roles and Functions in Planning

7

Strategic and Operational Planning

... in the absence of clearly defined goals, we are forced to concentrate on activity and ultimately become enslaved by it.
–Chuck Conradt

... he who fails to plan, plans to fail.
–Anonymous

CROSSWALK THIS CHAPTER ADDRESSES:

BSN Essential II: Basic organizational and systems leadership for quality care and patient safety
BSN Essential III: Scholarship for evidence-based practice
BSN Essential V: Health-care policy, finance, and regulatory environments
BSN Essential VIII: Professionalism and professional values
MSN Essential II: Organizational and systems leadership
MSN Essential IV: Translating and integrating scholarship into practice
MSN Essential VI: Health policy and advocacy
AONE Nurse Executive Competency II: A knowledge of the health-care environment
AONE Nurse Executive Competency III: Leadership
AONE Nurse Executive Competency V: Business skills
QSEN Competency: Teamwork and collaboration
QSEN Competency: Evidence-based practice

LEARNING OBJECTIVES *The learner will:*

- identify contemporary paradigm shifts and trends impacting health-care organizations
- analyze social, political, and cultural forces that may affect the ability of 21st-century health-care organizations to forecast accurately in strategic planning
- describe the steps necessary for successful strategic planning
- identify barriers to planning as well as actions the leader-manager can take to reduce or eliminate these barriers
- include evaluation checkpoints in strategic planning to allow for midcourse corrections as needed
- discuss the relationship between an organizational mission statement, philosophy, goals, objectives, policies, procedures, and rules
- write an appropriate mission statement, organization philosophy, nursing service philosophy, goals, and objectives for a known or fictitious organization
- compare the societal values regarding access to and payment of health care in the United States and at least one other country
- discuss appropriate actions that may be taken when personal values are found to be in conflict with those of an employing organization
- recognize the need for periodic value clarification to promote self-awareness
- describe personal planning style

Planning is critically important to and precedes all other management functions. Without adequate planning, the management process fails and organizational needs and objectives cannot be met. *Planning* may be defined as deciding in advance what to do; who is to do it; and how, when, and where it is to be done. Therefore, all planning involves choosing among alternatives.

All planning involves choice: A necessity to choose from among alternatives.

This implies that planning is a proactive and deliberate process that reduces risk and uncertainty. It also encourages unity of goals and continuity of energy expenditure (human and fiscal resources) and directs attention to the objectives of the organization. Adequate planning also provides the manager with some means of control and encourages the most appropriate use of resources.

In effective planning, the manager must identify short- and long-term goals and changes needed to ensure that the unit will continue to meet its goals. Identifying such short- and long-term goals requires leadership skills such as vision and creativity, since it is impossible to plan what cannot be dreamed or envisioned.

Likewise, planning requires flexibility and energy—two other leadership characteristics. Yet, planning also requires management skills such as data gathering, forecasting, and transforming ideas into action.

Unit III focuses on several aspects of planning, including strategic and operational planning, planned change, time management, fiscal planning, and career planning. This chapter deals with skills needed by the leader-manager to implement strategic and operational planning. In addition, the leadership roles and management functions involved in developing, implementing, and evaluating the planning hierarchy are discussed (Display 7.1).

DISPLAY 7.1	Leadership Roles and Management Functions Associated with Operational and Strategic Planning

LEADERSHIP ROLES

1. Translates knowledge regarding contemporary paradigm shifts and trends impacting health care into vision and insights which foster goal attainment.
2. Assesses the organization's internal and external environment in forecasting and identifying driving forces and barriers to strategic planning.
3. Demonstrates visionary, innovative, and creative thinking in organizational and unit planning, thus inspiring proactive rather than reactive planning.
4. Influences and inspires group members to be actively involved in both short- and long-term planning.
5. Periodically completes value clarification to increase self-awareness.
6. Encourages subordinates toward value clarification by actively listening and providing feedback.
7. Communicates and clarifies organizational goals and values to subordinates.
8. Encourages subordinates to be involved in policy formation, including developing, implementing, and reviewing unit philosophy, goals, objectives, policies, procedures, and rules.
9. Is receptive to new and varied ideas.
10. Role models proactive planning methods to followers.

MANAGEMENT FUNCTIONS

1. Is knowledgeable regarding legal, political, economic, and social factors affecting health-care planning.
2. Demonstrates knowledge of and uses appropriate techniques in both personal and organizational planning.

(Continued)

3. Provides opportunities for subordinates, peers, competitors, regulatory agencies, and the general public to participate in planning.
4. Coordinates unit-level planning to be congruent with organizational goals.
5. Periodically assesses unit constraints and assets to determine available resources for planning.
6. Develops and articulates a unit philosophy that is congruent with the organization's philosophy.
7. Develops and articulates unit goals and objectives that reflect unit philosophy.
8. Develops and articulates unit policies, procedures, and rules that put unit objectives into operation.
9. Periodically reviews unit philosophy, goals, policies, procedures, and rules and revises them to meet the unit's changing needs.
10. Actively participates in organizational strategic planning, defining and operationalizing such strategic plans at the unit level.

LOOKING TO THE FUTURE

Because of health-care reform, rapidly changing technology, increasing government involvement in regulating health care, and scientific advances, health-care organizations are finding it increasingly difficult to identify long-term needs appropriately and plan accordingly. In fact, most long-term planners find it difficult to plan more than a few years ahead.

Unlike the 20-year strategic plans of the 1960s and 1970s, most long-term planners today find it difficult to look even 5 years in the future.

The health-care system is in chaos, as is much of the business world. Traditional management solutions no longer apply, and a lack of strong leadership in the health-care system has limited the innovation needed to create solutions to the new and complex problems that the future will bring. Because change is occurring so rapidly, managers can easily become focused on short-range plans and miss changes that can drastically alter specific long-term plans.

Health-care facilities are particularly vulnerable to external social, economic, and political forces; long-range planning, then, must address these changing dynamics. It is imperative, therefore, that long-range plans be flexible, permitting change as external forces assert their impact on health-care facilities. In as far as it is possible, a picture of the future should be used to formulate long-range planning. One reason for envisioning the future is to study developments that may have an impact on the organization. This process of learning about the future allows us to determine what we want to happen. Identifying what may or could happen allows us to avert, encourage, or direct the course of events.

There are many factors emerging in the rapidly changing health-care system that must be incorporated in planning for a health-care organization's future. Some emerging paradigms include the following:

• The tension between *"value"* and *"volume"* has reached a tipping point. With growing linkages between expected quality outcomes and reimbursement, health-care organizations must increasingly determine whether value drives volume or whether volume is necessary to achieve value. The end result in both cases is continued escalation of health-care costs.

• The transformation from *revenue management* to *cost management* will continue as declining reimbursement forces providers to focus on how to maximize limited resources and provide care at less cost.

• *Physician integration* (an interdependence between physicians and health-care organizations (typically hospitals) that may involve employment, as well as shared decision making and mutual goal setting, is changing practice patterns and reimbursement patterns as hospitals increasingly assume more of the financial and liability risks for what was historically private physician practice.

- There is a need to build different work relationships because the way we manage systems is changing. For example, health-care continues to move toward managing populations rather than individuals.

- The health-care industry continues to move away from illness care to wellness care to reduce the demand for expensive, acute care services.

- The use of *complementary and alternative medicine* is increasing as public acceptance and demand for these services increases.

- A movement is underway for interdependence of professionals and *interprofessional collaboration* rather than professional autonomy. With the movement toward managed care, autonomy has decreased for all health-care professionals, including managers.

- There continues to be a shift in framework to the patient as a consumer of cost and quality information. Historically, many providers assumed that consumers, both payers and patients, had minimal interest in or knowledge about the services that they received. Currently, a change in the balance of power among payers, patients, and providers has occurred, and providers are increasingly being held accountable for the quality of outcomes that their patients experience.

- A transition from continuity of provider to continuity of information is occurring. Historically, continuity of care was maintained by continuity of provider. In the future, however, the meaning and operationalizing of continuity will become predicated on having complete, accurate, and timely information that moves with the patient. For example, *electronic health records* (EHRs) provide such real-time, point-of-care information as well as a longitudinal medical record with full information about each patient.

- Technology, which facilitates mobility and portability of relationships, interactions, and operational processes, will increasingly be a part of high functioning organizations. EHRs and clinical decision support are examples of such technology, since both impact not only what health-care data is collected, but how it is used, communicated, and stored.

- Commercially purchased *expert networks* (communities of top thinkers, managers, and scientists) will increasingly be used to address "*wicked problems*" (problems with innumerable causes that are tough to describe, and for which there is no right answer) and improve the quality of their decision making (Saint-Amand, 2008; Camillus, 2008). Such network panels are typically made up of researchers, health-care professionals, attorneys, and industry executives.

- The health-care team will be characterized by highly educated, multidisciplinary experts. While this would appear to ease the leadership challenges of managing such a team, it is far easier to build teams of experts than to build expert teams.

In addition, Huston (2014) suggests the following factors will further influence the future of health care:

- Robotic technology and the use of prototype nurse robots called *nursebots* will serve as an adjunct to scarce human resources in the provision of health care.

- *Biomechatronics*, which creates machines that replicate or mimic how the body works, will increase in prominence in the future. This interdisciplinary field encompasses biology, neurosciences, mechanics, electronics, and robotics to create devices that interact with human muscle, skeleton, and nervous systems to establish or restore human motor or nervous system function.

- *Biometrics*, the science of identifying people through physical characteristics such as fingerprints, handprints, retinal scans, voice recognition, and facial structure, will be used to assure targeted and appropriate access to client records.

- Health-care organizations will integrate biometrics with *"smart cards"* (credit card–sized devices with a chip, stored memory, and an operating system) to ensure that an individual presenting a secure ID credential really has the right to use that credential.

- *Point-of-care testing* will improve bedside care and promote more positive outcomes, as a result of more timely decision making and treatment.

- Given declining reimbursement, the current nursing shortage, and an increasing shift in care to outpatient settings, home care agencies will increasingly explore technology-aided options such as telehealth that allow them to avoid the traditional 1:1 nurse–patient ratio with face-to-face contact.

- The Internet will continue to improve Americans' health by enhancing communications and improving access to information for care providers, patients, health plan administrators, public health officials, biomedical researchers, and other health professionals. It will also change how providers interact with patients with consumers increasingly adopting the role of *expert patient.*

- A growing elderly population, medical advances that increase the need for well-educated nurses, consumerism, the increased acuity of hospitalized patients, and a ballooning health-care system will continue to increase the demand for RNs.

- An aging workforce, improving economy, inadequate enrollment in nursing schools to meet projected demand, increased employment of nurses in outpatient or ambulatory care settings, and inadequate long-term pay incentives will lead to a nursing shortage in acute care hospitals.

Such paradigm shifts and trends change almost constantly. Successful leader-managers stay abreast of the dynamic environments in which health care are provided so that this can be reflected in their planning. The end result is proactive or visionary planning that allows health-care agencies to function successfully in the 21st century.

LEARNING EXERCISE 7.1

Forces Affecting Health Care

In small groups, identify six additional forces, beyond those identified in this chapter, affecting today's health-care system. You may include legal, political, economic, social, or ethical forces. Try to prioritize these forces in terms of how they will affect you as a manager or RN. For at least one of the six forces you have identified, brainstorm how that force would affect your strategic planning as a unit manager or director of a health-care agency.

PROACTIVE PLANNING

Planning has a specific purpose and is one approach to developing strategy. In addition, planning represents specific activities that help achieve objectives; therefore, planning should be purposeful and proactive. Although there is always some crossover between types of planning within organizations, there is generally an orientation toward one of four planning modes: reactive planning, inactivism, preactivism, or proactive planning.

Reactive planning occurs *after* a problem exists. Because there is dissatisfaction with the current situation, planning efforts are directed at returning the organization to a previous, more comfortable state. Frequently, in reactive planning, problems are dealt with separately without integration with the whole organization. In addition, because it is done in response to a crisis, this type of planning can lead to hasty decisions and mistakes.

Inactivism is another type of conventional planning. Inactivists seek the status quo, and they spend their energy preventing change and maintaining conformity. When changes do occur, they occur slowly and incrementally.

A third planning mode is *preactivism*. Preactive planners utilize technology to accelerate change and are future oriented. Unsatisfied with the past or present, preactivists do not value experience and believe that the future is always preferable to the present.

The last planning mode is *interactive* or *proactive planning*. Planners who fall into this category consider the past, present, and future and attempt to plan the future of their organization rather than react to it. Because the organizational setting changes often, adaptability is a key requirement for proactive planning. Proactive planning occurs, then, in anticipation of changing needs or to promote growth within an organization and is required of all leader-managers so that personal as well as organizational needs and objectives are met.

 Proactive planning is dynamic, and adaptation is considered to be a key requirement since the environment changes so frequently.

LEARNING EXERCISE 7.2

What Is Your Planning Style?

Individually write a plan for the current year. How would you describe your planning? Which type of planner are you? Write a brief essay that describes your planning style. Use specific examples and then share your insights in a group.

Forecasting

A mistake common to novice managers is a failure to complete adequate proactive planning. Instead, many managers operate in a crisis mode and fail to use available historical patterns to assist them in planning. Nor do they examine present clues and projected statistics to determine future needs. In other words, they fail to forecast. *Forecasting* involves trying to estimate how a condition will be in the future. Forecasting takes advantage of input from others, gives sequence in activity, and protects an organization against undesirable changes.

With changes in technology, payment structures, and resource availability, the manager who is unwilling or unable to forecast accurately impedes the organization's efficiency and the unit's effectiveness. Increased competition, changes in government reimbursement, and decreased hospital revenues have reduced intuitive managerial decision making. To avoid disastrous outcomes when making future professional and financial plans, managers need to stay well informed about the legal, political, and socioeconomic factors affecting health care.

 Managers who are uninformed about the legal, political, economic, and social factors affecting health care make planning errors that may have disastrous implications for their professional development and the financial viability of the organization.

STRATEGIC PLANNING

Planning also has many dimensions. Two of these dimensions are time span and complexity or comprehensiveness. Generally, complex organizational plans that involve a long period (usually 3 to 10 years) are referred to as *long-range* or *strategic* plans. However, strategic planning may be done once or twice a year in an organization that changes rapidly. At the unit level, any planning that is at least 6 months in the future may be considered long-range planning.

Strategic planning forecasts the future success of an organization by matching and aligning an organization's capabilities with its external opportunities. For instance, an organization could develop a strategic plan for dealing with a nursing shortage, preparing succession managers in the organization, developing a marketing plan, redesigning workload, developing partnerships, or simply planning for organizational success.

Strategic planning typically examines an organization's purpose, mission, philosophy, and goals in the context of its external environment.

Some experts suggest, however, that value-based payment, an increased need for cost cutting, quality mandates, and the need for increased operational efficiencies will require a reconfiguration of how strategic planning is done in most health-care organizations (Operational Assessment in Strategic Planning, 2012). Instead of focusing on the external environment and the marketplace, health-care organizations will need to look closely at their competencies and weaknesses, examine their readiness for change, and identify those factors critical to achieving future goals and objectives.

This operational assessment should begin with gathering data related to financial performance, human resources, strategy, and service offerings as well as outcomes and results. Feedback from senior leadership, the medical staff, and the Board is then needed so that consensus can be obtained from stakeholders regarding the organization's strengths and weaknesses. Then an action plan can be created that strengthens the organization's infrastructure. The operational assessment concludes with an evaluation of how well the organization is achieving its goals and objectives and the process begins once again (Operational Assessment in Strategic Planning, 2012).

SWOT Analysis

There are many effective tools that assist in strategic planning. One of the most commonly used in health-care organizations is *SWOT analysis* (identification of strengths, weaknesses, opportunities, and threats) (see Display 7.2). SWOT analysis, also known as *TOWS analysis*, was developed by Albert Humphrey at Stanford University in the 1960s and 1970s.

The first step in SWOT analysis is to define the desired end state or objective. After the desired objective is defined, the SWOTs are discovered and listed. Decision makers must then decide if the objective can be achieved in view of the SWOTs. If the decision is no, a different objective is selected and the process repeats.

DISPLAY 7.2	SWOT Definitions

Strengths are those *internal* attributes that help an organization to achieve its objectives.
Weaknesses are those *internal* attributes that challenge an organization in achieving its objectives.
Opportunities are *external* conditions that promote achievement of organizational objectives.
Threats are *external* conditions that challenge or threaten the achievement of organizational objectives.

Performed correctly, SWOT allows strategic planners to identify those issues most likely to impact a particular organization or situation in the future and then to develop an appropriate plan for action. Marketing Teacher Ltd. (2000–2013), however, warns that several simple rules must be followed for SWOT analysis to be successful and these are shown in Display 7.3. In essence, they suggest that honesty, specificity, simplicity, and self-awareness are integral to successful SWOT analysis.

DISPLAY 7.3	Simple Rules for SWOT Analysis

- Be realistic about the strengths and weaknesses of your organization.
- Be clear about how the present organization differs from what might be possible in the future.
- Be specific about what you want to accomplish.
- Always apply SWOT in relation to your competitors.
- Keep SWOT short and simple.
- Remember that SWOT is subjective.

Source: Adapted from Marketing Teacher Ltd. (2000–2013). SWOT analysis: Lesson. Retrieved April 22, 2013, from http://www.marketingteacher.com/wordpress/swot-analysis/

Balanced Scorecard

Balanced Scorecard, developed by Robert Kaplan and David Norton in the early 1990s, is another tool that is highly assistive in strategic planning. Indeed, JaxWorks (2012, para 2) notes that the *Harvard Business Review* calls Balanced Scorecard "one of the most significant ideas of the last 75 years."

Strategic planners using a Balanced Scorecard develop *metrics* (performance measurement indicators), collect data, and analyze that data from four organizational perspectives: financial, customers, internal business processes (or simply processes), and learning and growth. These measures "align individual, departmental, and organizational goals and identify entirely new processes for meeting customer and shareholder objectives" (JaxWorks, para 7). Since all of the measures are considered to be related, and since all of the measures are assumed to eventually lead to outcomes, an overemphasis on financial measures is avoided. The scorecard then is "balanced" in that outcomes are in balance.

Balanced Scorecards also allow organizations to align their strategic activities with the strategic plan. The best Balanced Scorecards are not a static set of measurements, but instead reflect the dynamic nature of the organizational environment. Because the Balanced Scorecard is able to translate strategy into action, it is an effective tool for translating an organization's strategic vision into clear and realistic objectives.

Strategic Planning as a Management Process

Although SWOT and Balanced Scorecard are different, they are also similar in that they can help organizations assess what they do well and what they need to do to continue to be effective and financially sound. Many other strategic planning tools exist as well, although they are not discussed in this text. Regardless of the tool(s) used, strategic planning as a management process generally includes the following steps:

1. Clearly define the purpose of the organization.
2. Establish realistic goals and objectives consistent with the mission of the organization.
3. Identify the organization's external constituencies or stakeholders and then determine their assessment of the organization's purposes and operations.
4. Clearly communicate the goals and objectives to the organization's constituents.

5. Develop a sense of ownership of the plan.
6. Develop strategies to achieve the goals.
7. Ensure that the most effective use is made of the organization's resources.
8. Provide a base from which progress can be measured.
9. Provide a mechanism for informed change as needed.
10. Build a consensus about where the organization is going.

It should be noted, though, that some critics argue that strategic planning is rarely this linear. Nor is it static. Strategic planning instead involves various actions and reactions that are partially planned and partially unplanned.

Who Should Be Involved in Strategic Planning?

Long-range planning for health-care organizations historically has been accomplished by top-level managers and the board of directors, with limited input from middle-level managers. To give the strategic plan meaning and to implement it successfully, input from subordinates from all organizational levels may be solicited. There is increasing recognition, however, of the importance of subordinate input from all levels of the organization to give the strategic plan meaning and to increase the likelihood of its successful implementation.

The first-level manager is generally more involved in long-range planning at the unit level. However, because the organization's strategic plans affect unit planning, managers at all levels must be informed of organizational long-range plans so that all planning is coordinated.

All organizations should establish annual strategic planning conferences, involving all departments and levels of the hierarchy; this action should promote increased effectiveness of nursing staff, better communication between all levels of personnel, a cooperative spirit relative to solving problems, and a pervasive feeling that the departments are unified, goal directed, and doing their part to help the organization accomplish its mission.

LEARNING EXERCISE 7.3

Making a Long-Term Plan

The human resource manager in the facility where you are a supervisor has just completed a survey of the potential retirement plans of the nursing staff and found that within 5 years, 45% of the staff will probably be retiring. You know that past and present available statistics show that you normally replace 10% to 15% of your staff each year with new hires. You are concerned, as you do not know how you will be able to handle this new increase in your need for staff.

Assignment: Make a 5-year, long-term plan that will increase the likelihood of you being able to meet this new demand. Remember that other units within your facility and other health-care organizations in your region may also be facing the same problem.

 ## ORGANIZATIONAL PLANNING: THE PLANNING HIERARCHY

There are many types of planning; in most organizations, these plans form a hierarchy, with the plans at the top influencing all the plans that follow. As depicted in the pyramid in Figure 7.1, the hierarchy broadens at lower levels, representing an increase in the number of planning components. In addition, planning components at the top of the hierarchy are more general, and lower components are more specific.

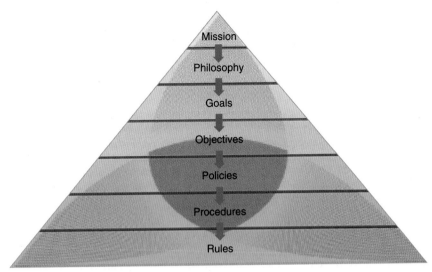

FIGURE 7.1 • The planning hierarchy.

 VISION AND MISSION STATEMENTS

Vision statements are used to describe future goals or aims of an organization. It is a description in words that conjures up a picture for all group members of what they want to accomplish together. It is critical, then, that organization leaders recognize that the organization will never be greater than the vision that guides it. An appropriate vision statement for a hospital is shown in Display 7.4.

 | DISPLAY 7.4 | **Sample Vision Statement**

County Hospital will be the leading center for trauma care in the region.

 An organization will never be greater than the vision that guides it.

The *purpose* or *mission statement* is a brief statement (typically no more than three or four sentences) identifying the reason that an organization exists. The mission statement identifies the organization's constituency and addresses its position regarding ethics, principles, and standards of practice.

A well-written mission statement will identify what is unique about the organization. For example, Brozovich and Totten (2012) suggest that all hospitals want to have high-quality, cost-effective care, but mission statements that include only this verbiage do not differentiate between organizations. In addition, the mission statement should have the capacity to drive action that reflects the mission over time. In other words, mission statements can become powerful decision-making tools when they become a template of purpose for the organization's activities (Brozovich and Totten).

Voges (2012) notes, however, that many contemporary health-care administrators find the challenges of meeting their stated mission in an era of cost cutting to be a challenge; hence the often stated adage, "no margin, no mission." Voges concludes that balance between margin and mission is key but warns that sustaining a health-care organization's mission in the face of increasing economic challenges will be difficult.

An example of a mission statement for County Hospital, a teaching hospital, is shown in Display 7.5.

DISPLAY 7.5   Sample Mission Statement

County Hospital is a tertiary care facility that provides comprehensive, holistic care to all state residents who seek treatment. The purpose of County Hospital is to combine high-quality, holistic health care with the provision of learning opportunities for students in medicine, nursing, and allied health sciences. Research is encouraged to identify new treatment regimens and to promote high-quality health care for generations to come.

The mission statement is of highest priority in the planning hierarchy because it influences the development of an organization's philosophy, goals, objectives, policies, procedures, and rules. Managers employed by County Hospital would have two primary goals to guide their planning: (a) to provide high-quality, holistic care and (b) to provide learning opportunities for students in medicine, nursing, and other allied health sciences. To meet these goals, adequate fiscal and human resources would have to be allocated for preceptorships and clinical research. In addition, an employee's performance appraisal would examine the worker's performance in terms of organizational and unit goals.

Mission statements then have value, only if they provide more than lip service. Indeed, actions taken at all levels of the organization should be congruent with the stated organization mission. This is why involving individuals from all levels of the organization in crafting mission statements is so important.

Curran and Totten (2010) suggest that in seeking employment, nurses should review the mission statement of a potential employer and ask themselves what it tells them about the organization's stakeholders, what beliefs and values are espoused, and how the organization intends to meet the needs of its stakeholders. Only then can the potential employee determine whether this is an organization they want to work for.

An organization must truly believe and act upon its mission statement; otherwise, the statement has no value.

THE ORGANIZATION'S PHILOSOPHY STATEMENT

The *philosophy* flows from the purpose or mission statement and delineates the set of values and beliefs that guide all actions of the organization. It is the basic foundation that directs all further planning toward that mission. A statement of philosophy can usually be found in policy manuals at the institution or is available on request. A philosophy that might be generated from County Hospital's mission statement is shown in Display 7.6.

The *organizational philosophy* provides the basis for developing nursing philosophies at the unit level and for nursing service as a whole. Written in conjunction with the organizational philosophy, the *nursing service philosophy* should address fundamental beliefs about nursing and nursing care; the quality, quantity, and scope of nursing services; and how nursing specifically will meet organizational goals. Frequently, the nursing service philosophy draws on the concepts of holistic care, education, and research. The nursing service philosophy in Display 7.7 builds on County Hospital's mission statement and organizational philosophy.

DISPLAY 7.6 Sample Philosophy Statement

The board of directors, medical and nursing staff, and administrators of County Hospital believe that human beings are unique, due to different genetic endowments, personal experiences in social and physical environments, and the ability to adapt to biophysical, psychosocial, and spiritual stressors. Thus, each patient is considered a unique individual with unique needs. Identifying outcomes and goals, setting priorities, prescribing strategy options, and selecting an optimal strategy will be negotiated by the patient, physician, and health-care team.

As unique individuals, patients provide medical, nursing, and allied health students invaluable diverse learning opportunities. Because the Board of Directors, medical and nursing staff, and administrators believe that the quality of health care provided directly reflects the quality of the education of its future health-care providers, students are welcomed and encouraged to seek out as many learning opportunities as possible. Because high-quality health care is defined by and depends on technological advances and scientific discovery, County Hospital encourages research as a means of scientific inquiry.

DISPLAY 7.7 Sample Nursing Service Philosophy

The philosophy of nursing at County Hospital is based on respect for the individual's dignity and worth. We believe that all patients have the right to receive effective nursing care. This care is a personal service that is based on patients' needs and their clinical disease or condition.

Recognizing the obligation of nursing to help restore patients to the best possible state of physical, mental, and emotional health and to maintain patients' sense of spiritual and social well-being, we pledge intelligent cooperation in coordinating nursing service with the medical and allied professional practitioners. Understanding the importance of research and teaching for improving patient care, the nursing department will support, promote, and participate in these activities. Using knowledge of human behavior, we shall strive for mutual trust and understanding between nursing service and nursing employees to provide an atmosphere for developing the fullest possible potential of each member of the nursing team. We believe that nursing personnel are individually accountable to patients and their families for the quality and compassion of the patient care rendered and for upholding the standards of care as delineated by the nursing staff.

The *unit philosophy*, adapted from the nursing service philosophy, specifies how nursing care provided on the unit will correspond with nursing service and organizational goals. This congruence in philosophy, goals, and objectives among the organization, nursing service, and unit is shown in Figure 7.2.

Although unit-level managers have limited opportunity to help develop the organizational philosophy, they are active in determining, implementing, and evaluating the unit philosophy. In formulating this philosophy, the unit manager incorporates knowledge of the unit's internal and external environments and an understanding of the unit's role in meeting organizational goals. The manager must understand the planning hierarchy and be able to articulate ideas both verbally and in writing. Leader-managers also must be visionary, innovative, and creative in identifying unit purposes or goals so that the philosophy not only reflects current practice but also incorporates a view of the future.

Like the mission statement, statements of philosophy in general can be helpful only if they truly direct the work of the organization toward a specific purpose. A department's decisions, priorities, and accomplishments reflect its working philosophy.

 A working philosophy is evident in a department's decisions, in its priorities, and in its accomplishments.

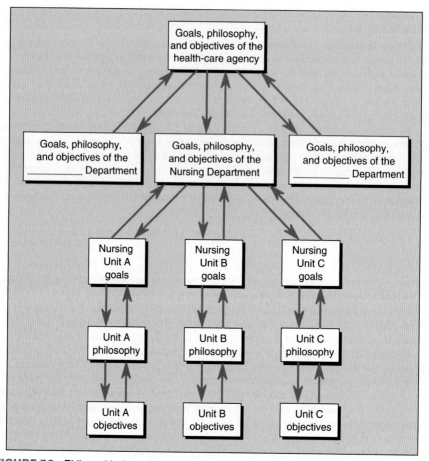

FIGURE 7.2 • Philosophical congruence in the planning hierarchy.

A person should be able to identify exactly how the organization is implementing its stated philosophy by observing members of the staff, reviewing the budgetary priorities, and talking to consumers of health care. The decisions made in an organization make the philosophy visible to all—no matter what is espoused on paper. A philosophy that is not or cannot be implemented is useless.

LEARNING EXERCISE 7.4

Developing a Philosophy Statement

Recover Inc., a fictitious for-profit home health agency, provides complete nursing and supportive services for in-home care. Services include skilled nursing, bathing, shopping, physical therapy, occupational therapy, meal preparation, housekeeping, speech therapy, and social work. The agency provides round-the-clock care, 7 days a week, to a primarily underserved rural area in northern California. The brochure the company publishes says that it is committed to satisfying the needs of the rural community and that it is dedicated to excellence.

Assignment: Based on this limited information, develop a brief philosophy statement that might be appropriate for Recover Inc. Be creative and embellish information if appropriate.

SOCIETAL PHILOSOPHIES AND VALUES

Societies and organizations have philosophies or sets of beliefs that guide their behavior. These beliefs that guide behavior are called *values*. Values have an intrinsic worth for a society or an individual. Some strongly held American values are individualism, capitalism, and competition. These values have profoundly affected health-care policy formation and implementation. The result is a health-care system that has historically promoted structured inequalities. Despite spending trillions of dollars on health care annually, tens of millions of American citizens have no health insurance and millions of others are underinsured.

Although values seem to be of central importance for health-care policy development and analysis, public discussion of this crucial variable is often neglected. Instead, health-care policy makers tend to focus on technology, cost–benefit analysis, and cost-effectiveness. Although this type of evaluation is important, it does not address the underlying values in this country that have led to unequal access to health care.

LEARNING EXERCISE 7.5

Health Care at What Cost?

Both Canada and Germany have been held up as models in health-care reform because they provide health care for all citizens. Although the United States spends more per capita than either Germany or Canada, many citizens do not have access to comprehensive, quality health care. Canadians receive hospitalization, doctor visits, and most dental care free of charge. Germany spends even less and provides a level of service similar to Canada but with a very small copayment for hospitalization. Unlike the emphasis on specialized care in the United States with limited choice of physicians, health-care systems in Canada and Germany emphasize primary care, unlimited choice of physicians, free physician visits, and an emphasis on health promotion. With little financial incentive for physician specialization and a nationwide focus on health promotion, there are many more general practitioners per capita in Germany and Canada than in the United States.

At what cost is this health care offered? Canadians and Germans experience longer waits for some high-tech procedures, and the governments of those countries have limitations on the proliferation of technology. However, the United States continues to have a higher incidence of infant mortality and low birth weight than either country and the lowest life expectancy at birth. Despite the highest spending as a percentage of gross domestic product, American consumers had the least number of physician visits and the shortest average hospital stay.

Assignment: In small groups, discuss the following: Do you agree or disagree that the US health-care system represents societal values of individualism, capitalism, and competition? Do you believe that the American people are willing to pay the costs required to pursue collectivism, cooperation, and equality in health care? Would you be willing to have fewer choices about your health care if access could be guaranteed to all? Do you believe that the cost of universal coverage should be picked up by the consumer or by the employer? Recognize that both societal and individual values will affect your feelings.

INDIVIDUAL PHILOSOPHIES AND VALUES

As discussed in Chapter 1, values have a tremendous impact on the decisions that people make. For the individual, personal beliefs and values are shaped by that person's experiences. All people should carefully examine their value system and recognize the role that it plays in how they make decisions and resolve conflicts and even how they perceive things. Therefore, the nurse-leader must be self-aware and provide subordinates with learning opportunities or experiences that foster increased self-awareness.

At times, it is difficult to assess whether something is a *true value*. McNally's (1980) classic work identified the following four characteristics that determine a true value:

1. It must be freely chosen from among alternatives only after due reflection.
2. It must be prized and cherished.
3. It is consciously and consistently repeated (part of a pattern).
4. It is positively affirmed and enacted.

If a value does not meet all four criteria, it is a *value indicator*. Most people have many value indicators but few true values. For example, many nurses assert that they value their national nursing organization, yet they do not pay dues or participate in the organization. True values require that the person take action, whereas value indicators do not. Thus, the value ascribed to the national nursing organization is a value indicator for these nurses and not a true value.

In addition, because our values change with time, periodic clarification is necessary to determine how our values may have changed. Values clarification includes examining values, assigning priorities to those values, and determining how they influence behavior so that one's lifestyle is consistent with prioritized values. Sometimes, values change as a result of life experiences or newly acquired knowledge. Most of the values we have as children reflect our parents' values. Later, our values are modified by peers and role models. Although they are learned, values cannot be forced on a person because they must be internalized. However, restricted exposure to other viewpoints also limits the number of value choices a person is able to generate. Therefore, becoming more worldly increases our awareness of alternatives from which we select our values.

LEARNING EXERCISE 7.6

Reflecting on Your Values

Using what you have learned about values, value indicators, and value clarifications, answer the following questions. Take time to reflect on your values before answering. This may be used as a writing exercise.

1. List three or four of your basic beliefs about nursing.

2. Knowing what you know now, ask yourself, "Do I value nursing? Was it freely chosen from among alternatives after appropriate reflection? Do I prize and cherish nursing? If I had a choice to do it over, would I still choose nursing as a career?"

3. Are your personal and professional values congruent? Are there any values espoused by the nursing profession that are inconsistent with your personal values? How will you resolve resultant conflicts?

Occasionally, individual values are in conflict with those of the organization. Because the philosophy of an organization determines its priorities in goal selection and distribution of resources, nurses need to understand the organization's philosophy. For example, assume that a nurse is employed by County Hospital, which clearly states in its philosophy that teaching is a primary purpose for the hospital's existence. Consequently, medical students are allowed to practice endotracheal intubation on all people who die in the hospital, allowing the students to gain needed experience in emergency medicine. This practice disturbs the nurse a great deal; it is not consistent with his or her own set of values and thus creates great personal conflict.

Nurses who frequently make decisions that conflict with their personal values may experience confusion and anxiety. This intrapersonal struggle ultimately will lead to job stress and dissatisfaction, especially for the novice nurse who comes to the organization with inadequate values clarification. The choices that nurses make about client care are not merely strategic options; they are moral choices. Internal conflict and burnout may result when personal and organizational values do not mesh.

When a nurse experiences cognitive dissonance between personal and organizational values, the result may be intrapersonal conflict and burnout.

As part of the leadership role, the manager should encourage all potential employees to read and think about the organization's mission statement or philosophy before accepting the job. The manager should give a copy of the philosophy to the prospective applicant before the hiring interview. The applicant also should be encouraged to speak to employees in various positions within the organization regarding how the philosophy is implemented at their job level. For example, a potential employee may want to determine how the organization feels about cultural diversity and what policies they have in place to ensure that patients from diverse cultures and languages have a mechanism for translation as needed. Finally, new employees should be encouraged to speak to community members about the institution's reputation for care. New employees who understand the organizational philosophy will not only have clearer expectations about the institution's purposes and goals but will also have a better understanding of how they fit into the organization.

Although all nurses should have a philosophy comparable with that of their employer, it is especially important for the new manager to have a value system consistent with that of the organization. Institutional changes that closely align with the value system of the nurse-manager will receive more effort and higher priority than those that are not true values or that conflict with the nurse-manager's value system. Managers who take a position with the idea that they can change the organization's philosophy to more closely agree with their own philosophy are likely to be disappointed.

It is unrealistic for managers to accept a position under the assumption that they can change the organization's philosophy to more closely match their personal philosophy.

Such a change will require extraordinary energy and precipitate inevitable conflict because the organization's philosophy reflects the institution's historical development and the beliefs of those people who were vital in the institution's development. Nursing managers must recognize that closely held values may be challenged by current social and economic constraints and that philosophy statements must be continually reviewed and revised to ensure ongoing accuracy of beliefs.

GOALS AND OBJECTIVES

Goals and objectives are the ends toward which the organization is working. All philosophies must be translated into specific goals and objectives if they are to result in action. Thus, goals and objectives "operationalize" the philosophy.

A *goal* may be defined as the desired result toward which effort is directed; it is the aim of the philosophy. Although institutional goals are usually determined by the organization's highest administrative levels, there is increasing emphasis on including workers in setting organizational goals. Goals, much like philosophies and values, change with time and require periodic reevaluation and prioritization.

Goals, although somewhat global in nature, should be measurable and ambitious but realistic. Goals also should clearly delineate the desired end product. When goals are not clear, simple misunderstandings may compound, and communication may break down. Organizations usually set long- and short-term goals for services rendered; economics; use of resources, including people, funds, and facilities; innovations; and social responsibilities. Display 7.8 lists sample goal statements.

> **DISPLAY 7.8   Sample Goal Statements**
>
> - All nursing staff will recognize the patient's need for independence and right to privacy and will assess the patient's level of readiness to learn in relation to his or her illness.
> - The nursing staff will provide effective patient care relative to patient needs insofar as the hospital and community facilities permit through the use of care plans, individual patient care, and discharge planning, including follow-up contact.
> - An ongoing effort will be made to create an atmosphere that is conducive to favorable patient and employee morale and that fosters personal growth.
> - The performance of all employees in the nursing department will be evaluated in a manner that produces growth in the employee and upgrades nursing standards.
> - All nursing units within County Hospital will work cooperatively with other departments within the hospital to further the mission, philosophy, and goals of the institution.

Although goals may direct and maintain the behavior of an organization, there are several dangers in using goal evaluation as the primary means of assessing organizational effectiveness. The first danger is that goals may be in conflict with each other, creating confusion for employees and consumers. For example, the need for profit maximization in health-care facilities today may conflict with some stated patient goals or quality goals. The second danger with the goal approach is that publicly stated goals may not truly reflect organizational goals. In addition, some organizational goals may be developed simply as a conduit for individual or personal goals. The final danger is that because goals are global, it is often difficult to determine whether they have been obtained.

Although goals may direct and maintain the behavior of an organization, there are several dangers in using goal evaluation as the primary means of assessing organizational effectiveness.

Objectives are similar to goals in that they motivate people to a specific end and are explicit, measurable, observable or retrievable, and obtainable. Objectives, however, are more specific and measurable than goals because they identify how and when the goal is to be accomplished.

Goals usually have multiple objectives that are each accompanied by a targeted completion date. The more specific the objectives for a goal can be, the easier for all involved in goal attainment to understand and carry out specific role behaviors. This is especially important for the nurse-manager to remember when writing job descriptions; if there is little ambiguity in the job description, there will be little role confusion or distortion. Clearly written goals and objectives must be communicated to all those in the organization responsible for their attainment. This is a critical leadership role for the nurse-manager.

Objectives can focus on either the desired process or the desired result. *Process objectives* are written in terms of the method to be used, whereas *result-focused objectives* specify the desired outcome. An example of a process objective might be "100% of staff nurses will orient new patients to the call-light system, within 30 minutes of their admission, by first demonstrating its appropriate use and then asking the patient to repeat said demonstration." An example of a result-focused objective might be "All postoperative patients will perceive a decrease in their pain levels following the administration of parenteral pain medication." Writing good objectives requires time and practice.

For the objectives to be measurable, they should have certain criteria. There should be a specific time frame in which the objectives are to be completed, and the objectives should be stated in behavioral terms, be objectively evaluated, and identify positive outcomes rather than negative outcomes.

As a sample objective, one of the goals at Mercy Hospital is that "all RNs will be proficient in the administration of intravenous fluids." Objectives for Mercy Hospital might include the following:

- All RNs will complete Mercy Hospital's course "IV Therapy Certification" within 1 month of beginning employment. The hospital will bear the cost of this program.

- RNs who score less than 90% on a comprehensive examination in "IV Therapy Certification" must attend the remedial 4-hour course "Review of Basic IV Principles" not more than 2 weeks after the completion of "IV Therapy Certification."

- RNs who achieve a score of 90% or better on the comprehensive examination for "IV Therapy Certification" after completing "Review of Basic IV Principles" will be allowed to perform IV therapy on patients. The unit manager will establish individualized plans of remediation for employees who fail to achieve this score on the examination.

The leader-manager clearly must be skilled in determining and documenting goals and objectives. Prudent managers assess the unit's constraints and assets and determine available resources before developing goals and objectives. The leader must then be creative and futuristic in identifying how goals might best be translated into objectives and thus implemented. The willingness to be receptive to new and varied ideas is a critical leadership skill. In addition, well-developed interpersonal skills allow the leader to involve and inspire subordinates in goal setting. The final step in the process involves clearly writing the identified goals and objectives, communicating changes to subordinates, and periodically evaluating and revising goals and objectives as needed.

LEARNING EXERCISE 7.7

Writing Goals and Objectives

Practice writing goals and objectives for County Hospital based on the mission and philosophy statements in this chapter. Identify three goals and three objectives to operationalize each of these goals.

POLICIES AND PROCEDURES

Policies are plans reduced to statements or instructions that direct organizations in their decision making. These comprehensive statements, derived from the organization's philosophy, goals, and objectives, explain how goals will be met and guide the general course and scope of organizational activities. Thus, policies direct individual behavior toward the organization's mission and define broad limits and desired outcomes of commonly recurring situations while leaving some discretion and initiative to those who must carry out that policy. Although some policies are required by accrediting agencies, many policies are specific to the individual institution, thus providing management with a means of internal control.

Policies also can be implied or expressed. *Implied policies*, neither written nor expressed verbally, have usually developed over time and follow a precedent. For example, a hospital may have an implied policy that employees should be encouraged and supported in their activity in community, regional, and national health-care organizations. Another example might be that nurses who limit their maternity leave to 3 months can return to their former jobs and shifts with no status change.

Expressed policies are delineated verbally or in writing. Most organizations have many written policies that are readily available to all people and promote consistency of action. Expressed policies may include a formal dress code, policy for sick leave or vacation time, and disciplinary procedures.

All organizations need to develop facility-wide policies and procedures to guide workers in their actions. These policies and procedures are ideally developed with input from all levels of the organization. Unfortunately, in many health-care organizations, this function falls to isolated *policy and procedure committees*. Involving more individuals in the process, as in a shared governance approach, should increase the quality of the end product and the likelihood that procedures will be implemented as desired.

Although top-level management is more involved in setting organizational policies (usually by policy committees), unit managers must determine how those policies will be implemented on their units. Input from subordinates in forming, implementing, and reviewing policy allows the leader-manager to develop guidelines that all employees will support and follow. Even if unit-level employees are not directly involved in policy setting, their feedback is crucial to its successful implementation. Having uniform policies and procedures developed through collaboration is critical.

In addition, policies and procedures should be evidence based. The addition of evidence to policies and procedures, however, requires the development of a process that ensures consistency, rigor, and safe nursing practice. Unfortunately, many policies continue to be driven by tradition or regulatory requirements and inadequate evidence exists to guide best practices in policy development (Examining the Evidence 7.1).

After policy has been formulated, the leadership role of managers includes the responsibility for communicating that policy to all who may be affected by it. This information should be transmitted in writing and verbally. A policy's perceived value often depends on how it is communicated.

Examining the Evidence 7.1

Source: Coursey, J., Rodriguez, R., Dieckmann, L., & Austin, P. (2013). Successful implementation of policies addressing lateral violence. AORN Journal, 97(1), 101–109.

The authors completed an online literature search (1990 to present), an ancestry approach, and informal networking to locate and appraise evidence about effectively implementing lateral violence policies. They found that most evidence was from low-level sources and that no consistent, effective means was presented to implement lateral violence policies. In addition, the evidence suggested that lateral violence policies exist in most facilities only to comply with the standards of accrediting agencies and their existence does not indicate effective implementation of those policies. The appraised evidence did, however, suggest the importance of collaboratively prepared (administrative and staff) implementation strategies.

The authors concluded that minimal evidence-based information exists that addresses effective implementation strategies for lateral violence policies and they noted that this void in the research leaves managers at a loss for best practice techniques to manage lateral violence behavior and prevent the proliferation of toxic work environments.

Procedures are plans that establish customary or acceptable ways of accomplishing a specific task and delineate a sequence of steps of required action. Established procedures save staff time, facilitate delegation, reduce cost, increase productivity, and provide a means of control. Procedures identify the process or steps needed to implement a policy and are generally found in manuals at the unit level of the organization.

The manager also has a responsibility to review and revise policies and procedure statements to ensure currency and applicability. Given the current explosion of evidence-based research as well as new regulations, technology, and drugs, keeping policies and procedures current and relevant is a tremendous management challenge. In addition, because most units are in constant flux, the needs of the unit and the most appropriate means of meeting those needs constantly change. For example, the unit manager is responsible for seeing that a clearly written policy regarding holiday and vacation time exists and that it is communicated to all those it affects. The unit manager must also provide a clearly written procedural statement regarding how to request vacation or holiday time on that specific unit. The unit manager would assess any long-term change in patient census or availability of human resources and revise the policy and procedural statements accordingly.

Because procedural instructions involve elements of organizing, some textbooks place the development of procedures in the organizing phase of the management process. Regardless of where procedural development is formulated, there must be a close relationship with planning—the foundation for all procedures.

RULES

Rules and regulations are plans that define specific action or nonaction. Generally included as part of policy and procedure statements, *rules* describe situations that allow only one choice of action. Rules are fairly inflexible, so the fewer rules, the better. Existing rules, however, should be enforced to keep morale from breaking down and to allow organizational structure. Chapter 25, on discipline, includes a more detailed discussion of rules and regulations.

OVERCOMING BARRIERS TO PLANNING

Benefits of effective planning include timely accomplishment of higher quality work and the best possible use of capital and human resources. Because planning is essential, managers must be able to overcome barriers that impede planning. For successful organizational planning, the manager must remember several points:

- The organization can be more effective if movement within it is directed at specified goals and objectives. Unfortunately, the novice manager frequently omits establishing a goal or objective. Setting a goal for a plan keeps managers focused on the bigger picture and saves them from getting lost in the minute details of planning. Just as the nursing care plan establishes patient care goals before delineating problems and interventions, managers must establish goals for their planning strategies that are congruent with goals established at higher levels.

- Because a plan is a guide to reach a goal, it must be flexible and allow for readjustment as unexpected events occur. This flexibility is a necessary attribute for the manager in all planning phases and the management process.

- The manager should include in the planning process all people and units that could be affected by a plan. Although time-consuming, employee involvement is how things are done and by whom increases commitment to goal achievement. Although not everyone will want to contribute to unit or organizational planning, all should be invited. The manager also needs to communicate clearly the goals and specific individual responsibilities to all those responsible for carrying out the plans so that work is coordinated.

- Plans should be specific, simple, and realistic. A vague plan is impossible to implement. A plan that is too global or unrealistic discourages rather than motivates employees. If a plan is unclear, the nurse-leader must restate the plan in another manner or use group process to clarify common goals.

- Know when to plan and when not to plan. It is possible to overplan and underplan. For example, one who overplans may devote excessive time to arranging details that might be better left to those who will carry out the plan. Underplanning occurs when the manager erroneously assumes that people and events will naturally fall into some desired and efficient method of production.

- Good plans have built-in evaluation checkpoints so that there can be a midcourse correction if unexpected events occur. A final evaluation should always occur at the end of the plan. If goals were not met, the plan should be examined to determine why it failed. This evaluation process assists the manager in future planning.

INTEGRATING LEADERSHIP ROLES AND MANAGEMENT FUNCTIONS IN PLANNING

Planning requires managerial expertise in health-care economics, human resource management, political and legislative issues affecting health care, and planning theory. Planning also requires the leadership skills of being sensitive to the environment, being able to appraise accurately the social and political climate, and being willing to take risks.

Clearly, the leader-manager must be skilled in determining, implementing, documenting, and evaluating all types of planning in the hierarchy because an organization's leaders are integral to realizing the mission of the organization. Managers then must draw on the philosophy and goals established at the organizational and nursing service levels in implementing planning at the unit level. Initially, managers must assess the unit's constraints and assets and determine its resources available for planning. The manager then draws on his or her leadership skills in creativity, innovation, and futuristic thinking to problem solve how philosophies can be translated into goals, goals into objectives, and so on down the planning hierarchy. The wise manager will develop the interpersonal leadership skills needed to inspire and involve subordinates in this planning hierarchy. The manager also must demonstrate the leadership skill of being receptive to new and varied ideas.

The final step in the process involves articulating identified goals and objectives clearly; this learned management skill is critical to the success of the planning. If the unit manager lacks management or leadership skills, the planning hierarchy fails.

KEY CONCEPTS

- The planning phase of the management process is critical and precedes all other functions.
- Planning is a proactive function required of all nurses.
- A plan is a guide for action in reaching a goal and must be flexible.
- Plans should be specific, simple, and realistic.
- All planning must include an evaluation step and requires periodic reevaluation and prioritization.

- All people and organizational units affected by a plan should be included in the planning.

- Plans have a time for evaluation built into them so that there can be a midcourse correction if necessary.

- New paradigms and trends emerge continuously, requiring leader-managers to be observant and proactive in organizational strategic planning.

- Because of the rapidly changing technology, increasing government regulatory involvement in health care, changing population demographics, and reduced provider autonomy, health-care organizations are finding it increasingly difficult to appropriately identify long-term needs and plan accordingly.

- Organizations and planners tend to use one of the four planning modes: reactive, inactivism, preactivism, or proactive. A proactive planning style is always the goal.

- Strategic planning tools such as SWOT and Balanced Scorecard help planners to identify those issues most likely to impact a particular organization or situation in the future and then to develop an appropriate plan for action.

- All planning in the organizational hierarchy must flow from and be congruent with planning done at higher levels in the hierarchy.

- Planning in the organizational hierarchy typically includes the development of organizational vision and mission statements, philosophies, goals, objectives, policies, procedures, and rules.

- An organizational philosophy that is not or cannot be implemented is useless.

- To avoid ongoing intrapersonal values conflicts, employees should have a philosophy compatible with that of their employer.

- Policies and procedures should be evidence based.

- Rules are fairly inflexible, so the fewer rules, the better. Existing rules, however, should be enforced to keep morale from breaking down and to allow organizational structure.

ADDITIONAL LEARNING EXERCISES AND APPLICATIONS

LEARNING EXERCISE 7.8

Exploring the Impact of Philosophy on Management Action

Susan is the supervisor of the 22-bed oncology unit at Memorial Hospital, a 150-bed hospital. Unit morale and job satisfaction are high, despite a unit occupancy rate of less than 50% in the last 6 months. Patient satisfaction on this unit is as high as or higher than that of any other unit in the hospital.

Susan's personal philosophy is that oncology patients have physical, social, and spiritual needs that are different from other patients. Both the unit and nursing service philosophy reflect this belief. Thus, nurses working in the oncology unit receive additional education, orientation, and socialization regarding their unique roles and responsibilities in working with oncology patients.

At this morning's regularly scheduled department head meeting, the Chief Nursing Officer suggests that because of extreme budget shortfalls and continuing low census, the oncology unit should be closed and its patients merged with the general medical–surgical patient population. The oncology nursing staff would be reassigned to the medical–surgical unit, with Susan as the unit's cosupervisor.

(Continued)

The idea receives immediate support from the medical–surgical supervisor because of the current staffing shortage on her unit. Susan, startled by the proposal, immediately voices her disapproval and asks for 2 weeks to prepare her argument. Her request is granted.

Assignment: What values or beliefs are guiding Susan, the Chief Nursing Officer, and the medical–surgical unit supervisor? Determine an appropriate plan of action for Susan. What impact does a unit or nursing service philosophy have on the actions of management and employees?

LEARNING EXERCISE 7.9

Incremental Goal Setting

Assume that your career goal is to become a nurse-lawyer. You are currently an RN in an acute care facility in a large, metropolitan city. You have your BSN degree but will need to take at least 12 units of prerequisite classes for acceptance into law school. A law school within commuting distance of your home offers evening classes that would allow you to continue your current day job at least part-time. Quitting your job entirely would be financially unfeasible.

Assignment: Identify at least four objectives that you need to set to achieve your career goal. Be sure that these objectives are explicit, measurable, observable or retrievable, and obtainable. Then identify at least three actions for each objective that delineate how you will achieve them.

LEARNING EXERCISE 7.10

Current Events and Planning

You are a manager in a public health agency. In reading the morning paper before going to work today, you peruse an article about the influx of Hispanic families in your county. There has been an increase of 10% in this population in the last year, and it is expected to continue to rise. You ponder how this will affect your client population and your agency.

You decide to gather your staff together and develop a strategic plan for dealing with the problems and opportunities that this change in client demographics presents.

Assignment: In examining the 10 steps listed in development of strategic plans, what are the things that you can personally influence, and what other individuals in the organization should be involved with the strategic plan? Make a list of 10 to 12 strategies that will assist you in planning for this new client population. What other statistics will you need to help you plan? What are some other future developments in your county that could have a positive or negative influence on your plan?

REFERENCES

Brozovich, J., & Totten, M. (2012). Mission-based decision-making for boards. *Trustee, 65*(4), 15–18.

Camillus, J. C. (2008, May). Strategy as a wicked problem. *Harvard Business Review,* 99–106.

Coursey, J., Rodriguez, R., Dieckmann, L., & Austin, P. (2013). Successful implementation of policies addressing lateral violence. *AORN Journal, 97*(1), 101–109.

Curran, C., & Totten, M. (2010). Mission, strategy, and stakeholders. *Nursing Economics, 28*(2), 116–118.

Huston, C. (2014). Technology in the health care workplace: Benefits, limitations, and challenges. In C. J. Huston (Ed.), *Professional issues in nursing* (3rd ed.). Philadelphia, PA: Lippincott Williams & Wilkins 214–227.

JaxWorks. (2012). *The balanced scorecard concept.* Retrieved April 22, 2013, from http://www.jaxworks .com/thebalancedscorecardconcept.htm

Marketing Teacher. (2000–2013). *SWOT analysis: Lesson.* Retrieved April 22, 2013, from http://www .marketingteacher.com/wordpress/swot-analysis/

McNally, M. (1980). Values. As individual experience broadens, realistic value systems must be flexible enough to grow... part 1. *Supervisor Nurse, 11,* 27–30.

Operational Assessment in Strategic Planning. (2012). *H&HN: Hospitals & Health Networks, 86*(11), 39–41.

Saint-Amand, A. (2008, February 6). *Building an expert exchange. Networks in decision-making.* O'Reilly Media, Inc. Retrieved April 22, 2013, from http:// en.oreilly.com/money2008/public/schedule/ detail/2187

Voges, N. (2012). The ethics of mission and margin. *Healthcare Executive, 27*(5), 30–32, 34, 36.

8

Planned Change

... managing and innovation did not always fit comfortably together. That's not surprising. Managers are people who like order. They like forecasts to come out as planned. In fact, managers are often judged on how much order they produce. Innovation, on the other hand, is often a disorderly process. Many times, perhaps most times, innovation does not turn out as planned. As a result, there is tension between managers and innovation.

—Lewis Lehro (about the first years at Minnesota Mining and Manufacturing)

... I can't understand why people are frightened of new ideas. I'm frightened of old ones.
—John Cage

CROSSWALK THIS CHAPTER ADDRESSES:

BSN Essential II: Basic organizational and systems leadership for quality care and patient safety

BSN Essential III: Scholarship for evidence-based practice

BSN Essential VI: Interprofessional communication and collaboration for improving patient health outcomes

MSN Essential II: Organizational and systems leadership

MSN Essential IV: Translating and integrating scholarship into practice

MSN Essential VII: Interprofessional collaboration for improving patient and population health outcomes

MSN Essential IX: Advanced generalist nursing practice

AONE Nurse Executive Competency I: Communication and relationship building

AONE Nurse Executive Competency II: A knowledge of the health-care environment

AONE Nurse Executive Competency III: Leadership

AONE Nurse Executive Competency V: Business skills

QSEN Competency: Teamwork and collaboration

LEARNING OBJECTIVES *The learner will:*

- differentiate between planned change and change by drift
- identify the responsibilities of a change agent
- develop strategies for unfreezing, movement, and refreezing a specific planned change
- assess driving and restraining forces for change in given situations
- apply rational–empirical, normative–reeducative, and power–coercive strategies for effecting change
- describe resistance as a natural and expected response to change
- identify and implement strategies to manage resistance to change
- involve all those who may be affected by a change in planning for that change whenever possible
- identify characteristics of aged organizations as well as strategies to keep them ever-renewing
- identify critical features of complex adaptive systems change theory
- describe the impact of chaos and the butterfly effect on both short- and long-term planning
- plan at least one desired personal change

Many forces are driving change in contemporary health care, including rising health-care costs, declining reimbursement, workforce shortages, increasing technology, the dynamic nature of knowledge, and a growing elderly population. Contemporary health-care agencies then must continually institute change to upgrade their structure, promote greater quality, and keep their workers. In fact, most health-care organizations find themselves undergoing continual change directed at organizational restructuring, quality improvement, and employee retention.

In most cases, these changes are planned. *Planned change*, in contrast to accidental change or *change by drift*, results from a well thought-out and deliberate effort to make something happen. Planned change is the deliberate application of knowledge and skills by a leader to bring about a change. Successful leader-managers must be well grounded in change theories and be able to apply such theories appropriately.

 Today, most health-care organizations find themselves undergoing continual change directed at organizational restructuring, quality improvement, and employee retention.

Many change attempts fail because the individual undertaking the change uses an unstructured approach to implementation (Mitchell, 2013). Indeed, what often differentiates a successful change effort from an unsuccessful one is the ability of the *change agent*—a person skilled in the theory and implementation of planned change—to deal appropriately with conflicted human emotions and to connect and balance all aspects of the organization that will be affected by that change. In organizational planned change, the manager is often the change agent.

In some large organizations today, however, multidisciplinary teams of individuals, representing all key stakeholders in the organization, are assigned the responsibility for managing the change process. In such organizations, this team manages the communication between the people leading the change effort and those who are expected to implement the new strategies. In addition, this team manages the organizational context in which change occurs and the emotional connections essential for any transformation.

But having a skilled change agent alone is not enough. Change is never easy, and regardless of the type of change, all major change brings feelings of achievement and pride as well as loss and stress. The leader then must use developmental, political, and relational expertise to ensure that needed change is not sabotaged.

In addition, many good ideas are never realized because of poor timing or a lack of power on the part of the change agent. For example, both organizations and individuals tend to reject outsiders as change agents because they are perceived as having inadequate knowledge or expertise about the current status, and their motives often are not trusted. Therefore, there is more widespread resistance if the change agent is an outsider. The outside change agent, however, tends to be more objective in his or her assessment, whereas the inside change agent is often influenced by a personal bias regarding how the organization functions.

Likewise, some greatly needed changes are never implemented because the change agent lacks sensitivity to timing. If the organization or the people within that organization have recently undergone a great deal of change or stress, any other change should wait until group resistance decreases.

It becomes clear that initiating and coordinating change requires well-developed leadership and management skills. It also requires vision and expert planning skills because a vision is not the same as a plan. The failure to reassess goals proactively and to initiate these changes results in misdirected and poorly used fiscal and human resources. Leader-managers must be visionary in identifying where change is needed in the organization and they must be flexible in adapting to change they directly initiated as well as change that has indirectly affected them. Display 8.1 delineates selected leadership roles and management functions necessary for leader-managers acting either in the change agent role or as a coordinator of the planned change team.

DISPLAY 8.1 Leadership Roles and Management Functions in Planned Change

LEADERSHIP ROLES

1. Is visionary in identifying areas of needed change in the organization and the health-care system.
2. Demonstrates risk taking in assuming the role of change agent.
3. Demonstrates flexibility in goal setting in a rapidly changing health-care system.
4. Anticipates, recognizes, and creatively problem solves resistance to change.
5. Serves as a role model to followers during planned change by viewing change as a challenge and opportunity for growth.
6. Role models high-level interpersonal communication skills in providing support for followers undergoing rapid or difficult change.
7. Demonstrates creativity in identifying alternatives to problems.
8. Demonstrates sensitivity to timing in proposing planned change.
9. Takes steps to prevent aging in the organization and to keep current with the new realities of nursing practice.
10. Supports and reinforces the individual adaptive efforts of those affected by change.

MANAGEMENT FUNCTIONS

1. Forecasts unit needs with an understanding of the organization's and unit's legal, political, economic, social, and legislative climate.
2. Recognizes the need for planned change and identifies the options and resources available to implement that change.
3. Appropriately assesses and responds to the driving and restraining forces when planning for change.
4. Identifies and implements appropriate strategies to minimize or overcome resistance to change.
5. Seeks subordinates' input in planned change and provides them with adequate information during the change process to give them some feeling of control.
6. Supports and reinforces the individual efforts of subordinates during the change process.
7. Identifies and uses appropriate change strategies to modify the behavior of subordinates as needed.
8. Periodically assesses the unit/department for signs of organizational aging and plans renewal strategies.
9. Continues to be actively involved in the refreezing process until the change becomes part of the new status quo.

THE DEVELOPMENT OF CHANGE THEORY: KURT LEWIN

Most of the current research on change builds on the classic change theories developed by Kurt Lewin in the mid-20th century. Lewin (1951) identified three phases through which the change agent must proceed before a planned change becomes part of the system: unfreezing, movement, and refreezing.

Unfreezing occurs when the change agent convinces members of the group to change or when guilt, anxiety, or concern can be elicited. Thus, people become discontented and aware of a need to change. For effective change to occur, the change agent needs to have made a thorough and accurate assessment of the extent of and interest in change, the nature and depth of motivation, and the environment in which the change will occur.

Because human beings have little control over many changes in their lives, the change agent must remember that people need a balance between stability and change in the workplace. Change for change's sake subjects employees to unnecessary stress and manipulation.

Change should be implemented only for good reasons.

The second phase of planned change is *movement*. In movement, the change agent identifies, plans, and implements appropriate strategies, ensuring that driving forces exceed restraining forces. Because change is such a complex process, it requires a great deal of planning and intricate timing. Recognizing, addressing, and overcoming resistance may be a lengthy process, and whenever possible, change should be implemented gradually. Any change of human behavior, or the perceptions, attitudes, and values underlying that behavior, takes time.

LEARNING EXERCISE 8.1

Unnecessary Change

Try to remember a situation in your own life that involved unnecessary change. Why do you think that the change was unnecessary? What types of turmoil did it cause? Were there things a change agent could have done that would have increased unfreezing in this situation?

The last phase is *refreezing*. During the refreezing phase, the change agent assists in stabilizing the system change so that it becomes integrated into the status quo. If refreezing is incomplete, the change will be ineffective and the prechange behaviors will be resumed. For refreezing to occur, the change agent must be supportive and reinforce the individual adaptive efforts of those affected by the change. Because change needs at least 3 to 6 months before it will be accepted as part of the system, the change agent must be sure that he or she will remain involved until the change is completed.

 Change agents must be patient and open to new opportunities during refreezing, as complex change takes time and several different attempts may be needed before desired outcomes are achieved.

It is important to remember though that refreezing does not eliminate the possibility of further improvements to the change. Indeed, measuring the impact of change should always be a part of refreezing. Display 8.2 illustrates the change agent's responsibilities during the various stages of planned change.

DISPLAY 8.2   Stages of Change and Responsibilities of the Change Agent

STAGE 1—UNFREEZING
1. Gather data.
2. Accurately diagnose the problem.
3. Decide if change is needed.
4. Make others aware of the need for change; often involves deliberate tactics to raise the group's discontent level; do not proceed to Stage 2 until the status quo has been disrupted and the need for change is perceived by the others.

STAGE 2—MOVEMENT
1. Develop a plan.
2. Set goals and objectives.
3. Identify areas of support and resistance.
4. Include everyone who will be affected by the change in its planning.
5. Set target dates.
6. Develop appropriate strategies.
7. Implement the change.

(Continued)

8. Be available to support others and offer encouragement through the change.
9. Use strategies for overcoming resistance to change.
10. Evaluate the change.
11. Modify the change, if necessary.

STAGE 3—REFREEZING
Support others so that the change continues.

LEWIN'S DRIVING AND RESTRAINING FORCES

Lewin also theorized that people maintain a state of status quo or equilibrium by the simultaneous occurrence of both *driving forces* (facilitators) and *restraining forces* (barriers) operating within any field. Driving forces advance a system toward change; restraining forces impede change.

The forces that push the system toward change are *driving forces*, whereas the forces that pull the system away from change are called *restraining forces*.

Examples of driving forces might include a desire to please one's boss, to eliminate a problem that is undermining productivity, to get a pay raise, or to receive recognition. Restraining forces include conformity to norms, an unwillingness to take risks, and a fear of the unknown.

Lewin's model suggested that people like feeling safe, comfortable, and in control of their environment. For change to occur then, the balance of driving and restraining forces must be altered. The driving forces must be increased or the restraining forces decreased.

In Figure 8.1, the person wishing to return to school must reduce the restraining forces or increase the driving forces to alter the present state of equilibrium. There will be no change or action until this occurs. Therefore, creating an imbalance within the system by increasing the driving forces or decreasing the restraining forces is one of the tasks required of a change agent.

GOAL: RETURN TO SCHOOL	
Forces driving to reach goal	**Forces restraining from reaching goal**
Opportunity for advancement	Low energy level
Status—Social gratification	Limited financial resources
Enhanced self-esteem	Unreliable transportation
Family supportive of efforts	Time with family already limited

FIGURE 8.1 • Driving and restraining forces.

LEARNING EXERCISE 8.2

Making Change Possible

Identify a change that you would like to make in your personal life (such as losing weight, exercising daily, and stopping smoking). List the restraining forces keeping you from making this change. List the driving forces that make you want to change. Determine how you might be able to change the status quo and make the change possible.

A CONTEMPORARY ADAPTATION OF LEWIN'S MODEL

Burrowes and Needs (2009) shared a more contemporary adaptation of Lewin's model in their discussion of a five-step *Stages of Change Model* (SCM). In this model, the first stage is *precontemplation*. During this stage, the individual "has no intention to change his or her behavior in the foreseeable future" (p. 41). Next comes the *contemplation* stage, at which point the individual considers making a change, but has not yet made a commitment to take action. This would be the phase in which unfreezing would occur, according to Lewin.

A transition from unfreezing to movement begins in the *preparation* stage, as the individual intends to take action in the short-term future. The *action* stage then occurs (movement) in which the individual actively modifies his or her behavior. Finally, the process ends with the *maintenance* stage at which point the individual works to maintain changes made during the action stage and prevent relapse. This stage would be synonymous with refreezing. Display 8.3 illustrates the steps of the SCM.

DISPLAY 8.3   Stages of Change Model (Burrowes & Needs, 2009)

Stage 1: Precontemplation	No current intention to change.
Stage 2: Contemplation	Individual considers making a change.
Stage 3: Preparation	There is intent to make a change in the near future.
Stage 4: Action	Individual modifies his or her behavior.
Stage 5: Maintenance	Change is maintained and relapse is avoided.

Burrowes and Needs (2009) suggest that breaking the process of change down into steps makes it easier to assess an individual's readiness to change. For example, change agents might need to consider using motivation enhancement strategies if individuals are in the contemplation stage, whereas more action-based interventions would be appropriate for individuals who have already made a commitment to change. The actions taken by change agents in the action stage would be the same as those identified by Lewin for movement and in maintenance for refreezing.

CLASSIC CHANGE STRATEGIES

In addition to being aware of the stages of change, the change agent must be highly skilled in the use of behavioral strategies to prompt change in others. Three such classic strategies for effecting change were described by Bennis, Benne, and Chinn (1969), with the most appropriate strategy for any situation depending on the power of the change agent and the amount of resistance expected from the subordinates.

One of these strategies is to give current research as evidence to support the change. This group of strategies is often referred to as *rational–empirical* strategies. The change agent using this set of strategies assumes that resistance to change comes from a lack of knowledge and that humans are rational beings who will change when given factual information documenting the need for change. This type of strategy is used when there is little anticipated resistance to the change or when the change is perceived as reasonable.

Because peer pressure is often used to effect change, another group of strategies exists, which use group process and these are called *normative–reeducative* strategies. These strategies use group norms and peer pressure to socialize and influence people so that change will occur. The change agent assumes that humans are social creatures, more easily influenced by others than by facts. This strategy does not require the change agent to have a legitimate power base. Instead, the change agent gains power by skill in interpersonal relationships. He or she focuses on noncognitive determinants of behavior, such as people's roles and relationships, perceptual orientations, attitudes, and feelings, to increase acceptance of change.

The third group of strategies, *power–coercive* strategies, features the application of power by legitimate authority, economic sanctions, or political clout of the change agent. These strategies include influencing the enactment of new laws and using group power for strikes or sit-ins. Using authority inherent in an individual position to effect change is another example of a power–coercive strategy. These strategies assume that people often are set in their ways and will change only when rewarded for the change or when they are forced by some other power–coercive method. Resistance is handled by authority measures; the individual must accept it or leave.

Often, the change agent uses strategies from each of these three groups. An example may be reflected in the change agent who wants someone to stop smoking. The change agent might present the person with the latest research on cancer and smoking (the rational–empirical approach); at the same time, the change agent might have friends and family encourage the person socially (normative–reeducative approach). The change agent also might refuse to ride in the smoker's car if the person smokes while driving (power–coercive approach). By selecting from each set of strategies, the change agent increases the chance of successful change.

LEARNING EXERCISE 8.3

Using Change Strategies to Increase Sam's Compliance

You are a staff nurse in a home health agency. One of your patients, Sam Little, is a 38-year-old man with type 1 diabetes. He has developed some loss of vision and had to have two toes amputated as consequences of his disease process. Sam's compliance with four-times-daily blood glucose monitoring and sliding-scale insulin administration has never been particularly good, but he has been worse than usual lately. Sam refuses to use an insulin pump; however, he has been willing to follow a prescribed diabetic diet and has kept his weight to a desired level.

Sam's wife called you at the agency yesterday and asked you to work with her in developing a plan to increase Sam's compliance with his blood glucose monitoring and insulin administration. She said that Sam, while believing it "probably won't help," has agreed to meet with you to discuss such a plan. He does not want, however, "to feel pressured into doing something he doesn't want to do."

Assignment: What change strategy or combination thereof (rational–empirical, normative–reeducative, and power–coercive) do you believe has the greatest likelihood of increasing Sam's compliance? How could you use this strategy? Who would be involved in this change effort? What efforts might you undertake to increase the unfreezing so that Sam is more willing to actively participate in such a planned change effort?

RESISTANCE: THE EXPECTED RESPONSE TO CHANGE

Even though change is inevitable, it creates instability in our lives and some conflict should always be expected between those supporting the status quo and those advocating for change (Amos, Johns, Hines, Skov, & Kloosterman, 2012). Indeed, conflict and resistance almost always accompany change because change alters the balance of a group.

The level of resistance, however, generally depends on the type of change proposed. Technological changes encounter less resistance than changes that are perceived as social or that are contrary to established customs or norms. For example, nursing staff are more willing to accept a change in the type of IV pump to be used than a change regarding who is able to administer certain types of IV therapy. Nursing leaders also must recognize that subordinates' values, educational levels, cultural and social backgrounds, and experiences with change (positive or negative) will have a tremendous impact on the degree of resistance. It is also much easier to change a person's behavior than it is to change an entire group's behavior. Likewise, it is easier to change knowledge levels than attitudes.

Similarly, Amos et al. (2012) suggest that straightforward change, learning to do something a different way, and responding to something that obviously needs to be changed are often relatively easy to accomplish. However, changing something that involves a challenge to the beliefs that underpin our lives threatens the security of the individuals involved and these types of changes are much more apt to result in resistance.

In an effort to eliminate resistance to change in the workplace, managers historically used an autocratic leadership style with specific guidelines for work, an excessive number of rules, and a coercive approach to discipline. The resistance, which occurred anyway, was both covert (such as delaying tactics and passive–aggressive behavior) and overt (openly refusing to follow a direct command). The result was wasted managerial energy and time and a high level of frustration.

Because change disrupts the homeostasis or balance of the group, resistance should always be expected.

Today, resistance is recognized as a natural and expected response to change and leader-managers must resist the impulse to focus on blaming others when resistance to planned change occurs. Instead, they should immerse themselves in identifying and implementing strategies to minimize or manage this resistance to change. One such strategy is to encourage subordinates to speak openly so that options can be identified to overcome objections.

In addition, it is the role of the leader to see the vision of what the future state will be like after the change has taken place and to share that vision with their followers. If people cannot see the benefit to themselves, their working practices or to patient care, then they will continue to be resistant (Stonehouse, 2012).

Likewise, workers should be encouraged to talk about their perceptions of the forces driving the planned change so that the leader can accurately assess change support and resources. It takes a strong leader to step up and engage when a change effort meets with pushback.

Still, there are individual variations in terms of risk taking and willingness to accept change. Some individuals, even at very early ages, demonstrate more risk taking than others. Certainly temperament and personality play at least some role in this. Change agents then should be aware of life history variables as well as risk-taking propensity when assessing the likelihood of an individual or group being willing to change.

Early in a planned change then, leader-managers should assess which workers will promote or resist a specific change, by both observation and direct communication. Then, the manager can collaborate with change promoters on how best to convert those individuals more resistant to change.

LEARNING EXERCISE 8.4

What Is Your Attitude Toward Change?

How do you typically respond to change? Do you embrace it? Seek it out? Accept it reluctantly? Avoid it at all cost? Is this behavioral pattern similar to your friends and that of your family? Has your behavior always fit this pattern, or has the pattern changed throughout your life? If so, what life events have altered how you view and respond to change?

Perhaps the greatest factor contributing to the resistance encountered with change is a lack of trust between the employee and the manager or the employee and the organization. Workers want security and predictability. That is why trust erodes when the ground rules change, as the assumed "contract" between the worker and the organization is altered. Subordinates' confidence in the change agent's ability to manage change depends on whether they believe that they have sufficient resources to cope with it. In addition, the leader-manager must remember that subordinates in an organization will generally focus more on how a specific change will affect their personal lives and status than on how it will affect the organization.

Perhaps that is why research by Spetz, Burgess, and Phibbs (2012) suggested that organizational stability, team leadership skills, and flexibility in implementation were key factors influencing successful implementation of a computerized patient record system (CPRS) and Bar Code Medication Administration (BCMA) in the VA health-care system over the past decade. Staff and managers faced numerous challenges since these information technology (IT) systems changed how care was organized, documented, and communicated. Most staff reported being frightened or nervous about the change and found it difficult to see the opportunities the change would bring in the future. Having an experienced change agent or project champion to help staff work through this resistance as well as to oversee implementation of training, support, workflow changes, and communication was critical to the system-wide change effort's success (Examining the Evidence 8.1).

Examining the Evidence 8.1

Source: Spetz, J., Burgess, J. F., & Phibbs, C. S. (2012). What determines successful implementation of inpatient information technology systems? American Journal of Managed Care, 18(3), 157–162.

The US Department of Veterans Affairs (VA), the nation's largest integrated health-care system, has made one of the largest investments in hospital-based information technology (HIT) in the United States, implementing a fully integrated system nationwide. Their CPRS was phased in over a decade in the early 1990s and BCMA was implemented over a much shorter time period, with implementation required 1 year after the software became available.

This qualitative study (118 interviews at 7 VA hospitals over a 15-month time) examined the factors and strategies associated with successful implementation of these HIT interventions in VA inpatient settings. Five broad themes were identified as factors affecting the process and success of implementation: (1) organizational stability and implementation team leadership, (2) implementation timelines, (3) equipment availability and reliability, (4) staff training, and (5) changes in workflow.

Overall IT implementation success depended on (1) whether there was support for change from both leaders and staff; (2) development of a gradual and flexible implementation approach; (3) allocation of adequate resources for equipment and infrastructure, hands-on support, and deployment of additional staff; and (4) how the implementation team planned for setbacks, and continued the process to achieve success. Problems that developed in the early stages of implementation tended to become persistent, and poor implementation was noted to be related to an increased risk of patient harm.

PLANNED CHANGE AS A COLLABORATIVE PROCESS

Often, the change process begins with a few people who meet to discuss their dissatisfaction with the status quo, and an inadequate effort is made to talk with anyone else in the organization. This approach virtually guarantees that the change effort will fail. People abhor "information vacuums," and when there is no ongoing conversation about the change process, gossip usually fills the void. These rumors are generally much more negative than anything that is actually happening.

As a rule, anyone who will be affected by a change should be included in planning it. When information and decision making are shared, subordinates feel that they have played a valuable role in the change. Change agents and the elements of the system—the people or groups within it—must openly develop goals and strategies together. All must have the opportunity to define their interest in the change, their expectation of its outcome, and their ideas on strategies for achieving change.

It is not always easy, however, to attain grassroots involvement in planning efforts. Even when managers communicate that change is needed and subordinate feedback is wanted, the message often goes unheeded. Some people in the organization may need to hear a message repeatedly before they listen, understand, and believe the message. If the message is one that they do not want to hear, it may take even longer for them to come to terms with the anticipated change.

Whenever possible, all those who may be affected by a change should be involved in planning for that change.

When change agents fail to communicate with the rest of the organization, they prevent people from understanding the principles that guided the change, what has been learned from prior experience, and why compromises have been made. Likewise, subordinates affected by the change should thoroughly understand the change and the impacts that will likely result. Good, open communication throughout the process can reduce resistance. Leaders must ensure that group members share perceptions about what change is to be undertaken, who is to be involved and in what role, and how the change will directly and indirectly affect each person in the organization.

THE LEADER-MANAGER AS A ROLE MODEL DURING PLANNED CHANGE

Leader-managers must act as role models to subordinates during the change process. The leader-manager must attempt to view change positively and to impart this view to subordinates. Rather than viewing change as a threat, managers should embrace it as a challenge and the chance or opportunity to do something new and innovative. Indeed, the leader has two responsibilities in facilitating change in nursing practice. First, leader-managers must be actively engaged in change in their own work and model this behavior to staff. Second, leaders must be able to assist staff members in making the needed change requirements in their work.

It is critical that managers not view change as a threat.

Managers must also believe that they can make a difference. This feeling of control is probably the most important trait for thriving in a changing environment. Unfortunately, many leader-managers lack confidence in their ability to serve as an effective change agent as noted in research conducted by Salmela, Eriksson, and Fagerström (2013) (Examining the Evidence 8.2). The end result, when this occurs, is a lack of engagement in the change process and a role modeling to followers that the change may not be worth the time and energy necessary to bring it to fruition.

Examining the Evidence 8.2

Source: Salmela, S., Eriksson, K., & Fagerström, L. (2013). Nurse leaders' perceptions of an approaching organizational change. Qualitative Health Research, 23*(5), 689–699.*

The aim of this study was to better understand nurse-leaders' perceptions of approaching organizational change. Using a three-dimensional hermeneutical method of interpretation to analyze text from 17 interviews, the researchers found that nurse-leaders' were positive toward and actively engaged in continual change on their units, but perceived themselves as mere spectators of the change process. While they believed that change might yield positive benefits, their adaptation lacked deeper engagement. This occurred in part because many felt uneasiness and anxiety with regard to their leadership role, the future of nursing care, and their mandate to be a patient advocate. The researchers concluded that while nurse-leaders' are in a critical position to influence the success of organizational change, the organizations covered in this study did not incorporate their knowledge and experience in approaching change.

"As healthcare organizations continue to change and develop to meet new political agendas, meeting the needs of patients and associated improvements to service will be shaped by those who are willing to take ideas forward" (Norman, 2012, p. 162).

ORGANIZATIONAL CHANGE ASSOCIATED WITH NONLINEAR DYNAMICS

Most 21st-century organizations experience fairly brief periods of stability followed by intense transformation. In fact, some later organizational theorists feel that Lewin's refreezing to establish equilibrium should not be the focus of contemporary organizational change since change is unforeseeable and ever present. This is particularly true in health-care organizations, where long-term outcomes are almost always unpredictable.

In the past, organizations looked at change and organizational dynamics as linear, occurring both in steps and sequentially. More contemporary theorists maintain that the world is so unpredictable that such dynamics are truly nonlinear. As a result, nonlinear change theories such as *complex adaptive systems (CAS) theory* and *chaos theory* now influence the thinking of many organizational leaders.

Complexity and Complex Adaptive Systems Change Theory

Complexity science has emerged from the exploration of the subatomic world and quantum physics and suggests that the world is complex as are the individuals who operate within it. Thus, control and order are emergent rather than predetermined, and mechanistic formulas do not provide the flexibility needed to predict what actions will result in what outcomes.

CAS theory, an outgrowth of complexity theory, suggests that the relationship between elements and agents within any system is nonlinear and that these elements are the key players in changing settings or outcomes.

CAS theory suggests that the relationship between elements and agents within any system is nonlinear and that these elements are constantly in play to change the environment or outcome.

For example, while an individual may have behaved one way in the past, CAS theory suggests that future behavior may not always be the same (not always predictable). This is because that individual's prior experience and past learning may change her or his future choices. In addition, the rules or parameters of each situation are different, even if these differences are subtle; even small variations can dramatically alter choice of action. CAS theory also suggests that the actions of any agent within the system affect all other agents in the system; that is, that context and action are interconnected. Finally, CAS theory suggests that there are always hidden or unanticipated elements in systems that make linear thinking almost impossible.

In their classic work on CAS, Olson and Eoyang (2001) suggest that the self-organizing nature of human interactions in a complex organization leads to surprising effects. Rather than focusing on the macro-level of the organization system, complexity theory suggests that most powerful change processes occur at the micro-level, where relationships, interactions, and simple rules shape emerging patterns. The main features of the CAS approach are shown in Display 8.4.

DISPLAY 8.4	Main Features of Olson and Eoyang's (2001) Complex Adaptive Systems Approach to Change

- Change should be achieved through connections among change agents instead of from the top-down.
- There should be adaptation to uncertainty during the change instead of trying to predict stages of development.
- Goals, plans, and structures should be allowed to emerge instead of depending on clear, detailed plans and goals.
- Value differences should be amplified and explored instead of focusing on consensus in change efforts.
- Patterns in one part of the organization are often repeated in another part. Thus, change does not need to begin at the top of an organization to be successful. The goal instead is self-similarity rather than differences in how change is implemented in different parts of the organization.
- Successful change fits with the current organizational environment instead of with an ideal. This is what makes it sustainable.

In applying CAS theory to planned change, it becomes clear that the multidimensionality of health-care organizations, and the individuals who work within them, results in significant challenges for the change agent. Change agents then must carefully examine and focus on the relationships between the elements and be careful not to look at any one element in isolation from the others. It also suggests that time and attention must be given to trying to understand these relationships and interactions even before unfreezing is attempted and that continual monitoring and adaptation will likely be needed for movement and refreezing to be successful.

Chaos Theory

The roots of *chaos theory*, considered by some to be a subset of complexity science, likely emerged from the early work of meteorologist Edward Lorenz in the 1960s to improve weather forecasting techniques (Massachusetts Institute of Technology [MIT] News, 2008). Lorenz discovered that even tiny changes in variables often dramatically affected outcomes.

Lorenz also discovered that even though these chaotic changes appeared to be random, they were not. Instead, he found that there were deterministic sequences and physical laws, which prevail in nature, even if this does not appear to be the case. This is why Rae (n.d.) argues that chaos theory is really about finding order in what appears to be random data.

 Chaos theory is really about finding the underlying order in apparently random data.

Determining this underlying order, however, is challenging, and the order itself is constantly changing. This chaos makes it difficult to predict the future. In addition, chaos theory suggests that even small changes in conditions can drastically alter a system's long-term behavior (commonly known as the *butterfly effect*). Thus, changes in outcomes are not proportional to the degree of change in the initial condition. As a result of this sensitivity, the behavior of a system exhibiting chaos appears to be random, even though the system is deterministic in the sense that it is well defined and contains no random parameters.

Chaos and complexity theories have great application within the health-care arena. For example, despite putting a great time of energy and time into planning, many plans with sharply delivered strategies and targets are often not effective. This is because hidden variables are not explored and general goals and boundaries are not developed. For example, a single individual or unit can undermine a planned organizational change, particularly if the actions of that individual or unit to undermine the change are covert. The change agent might inadvertently focus on the aftermath of the subversive action without ever realizing the root cause of the problem.

It is imperative that change agents have an understanding of complexity theory and chaos theory since the use of nonlinear theories to explain organizational functioning and change are expected to increase in the 21st century. Rae (n.d.) agrees, arguing that

> Chaos has already had a lasting effect on science, yet there is much … to be discovered. Many scientists believe that twentieth century science will be known for only three theories: relativity, quantum mechanics, and chaos. Aspects of chaos show up everywhere around the world, from the currents of the ocean and the flow of blood through fractal blood vessels to the branches of trees and the effects of turbulence. Chaos has inescapably become part of modern science. As chaos changed from a little-known theory to a full science of its own, it has received widespread publicity. Chaos theory has changed the direction of science: in the eyes of the general public, physics is no longer simply the study of subatomic particles in a billion-dollar particle accelerator, but the study of chaotic systems and how they work (para 33).

ORGANIZATIONAL AGING: CHANGE AS A MEANS OF RENEWAL

Organizations progress through developmental stages, just as people do—birth, youth, maturity, and aging. As organizations age, structure increases to provide greater control and coordination. The young organization is characterized by high energy, movement, and virtually constant change and adaptation. Aged organizations have established "turf boundaries," function in an orderly and predictable fashion, and are focused on rules and regulations. Change is limited.

It is clear that organizations must find a balance between stagnation and chaos, between birth and death. In the process of maturing, workers within the organization can become prisoners of procedures, forget their original purposes, and allow means to become the ends. Without change, the organization may stagnate and die. Organizations need to keep foremost what they are going to do, not what they have done.

For example, Bayan (2012), Gordon (2012), and Owarish (2013) shared insights regarding Kodak, founded in 1880 by George Eastman, and one of America's most notable companies, helping establish the market for camera film and then dominating the field. But it suffered from a variety of problems over the last four decades—almost all related to being an aged organization. Kodak's top management never fully grasped how the world around them was changing and they hung on to obsolete assumptions (such as digital prints will never replace film prints) long after they were no longer the case.

In addition, Kodak followed a pattern seen by a number of aged organizations who face technological change. First, they tried to ignore a new technology hoping it would go away by itself. Then they openly put it down by using various justifications such as it is too expensive, too slow, and too complicated. Then they tried to prolong the life of the existing technology by attempting to create synergies between the new technology and the old (like photo CD). This further delayed any serious commitment to the new order of things.

In the end, Kodak failed to realize its limitations, ignored the data, and spent an additional 15 years in avoidance mode until it became virtually irrelevant in the market. With only one full year of profit after 2004, Kodak ended up filing for bankruptcy in 2012, after 131 years of being the pioneer in the film industry.

Philpot (2013) provides another example in her accounting of Blackberry's market plunge from having 40% of the smartphone market in North America in 2010 to only 2% by the end of 2012. Philpot suggests this death spiral occurred as the result of accelerated obsolescence and notes that the "shelf life" of any business model is shorter now than ever before. She concludes that leaders today have to know how to "keep one foot in today and the other in tomorrow. In other words, their responsibility is to successfully execute their current business model while also re-inventing their company to compete in a market that they have not yet seen" (para 4).

LEARNING EXERCISE 8.5

Young or Old Organization?

Reflect on the organization in which you work or the nursing school you attend. Do you believe that this organization has more characteristics of a young or aged organization? Diagram on a continuum from birth to death where you feel that this organization would fall. What efforts has this organization taken to be dynamic and innovative? What further efforts could be made? Do you agree or disagree that most organizations change unpredictably? Can you support your conclusions with examples?

INTEGRATING LEADERSHIP ROLES AND MANAGEMENT FUNCTIONS IN PLANNED CHANGE

It should be clear that leadership and management skills are necessary for successful planned change to occur. The manager must understand the planning process and planning standards and be able to apply both to the work situation. The manager is also cognizant of the specific driving and restraining forces within a particular environment for change and is able to provide the tools or resources necessary to implement that change. The manager, then, is the mechanic who implements the planned change.

The leader, however, is the inventor or creator. Leaders today are forced to plan in a chaotic health-care system that is changing at a frenetic pace. Out of this chaos, leaders must identify trends and changes that may affect their organizations and units and proactively prepare for these changes. Thus, the leader must retain a big-picture focus while dealing with each part of the system. In the inventor or creator role, the leader displays such traits as flexibility, confidence, tenacity, and the ability to articulate vision through insights and versatile thinking. The leader also must constantly look for and attempt to adapt to the changing and unpredictable interactions between agents and environmental factors as outlined by the complexity science theorists.

Both leadership and management skills are necessary in planned change. The change agent fulfills a management function when identifying situations where change is necessary and appropriate and when assessing the driving and restraining forces affecting the plan for change. The leader is the role model in planned change. He or she is open and receptive to change and views change as a challenge and an opportunity for growth. Other critical elements in successful planned change are the change agent's leadership skills—interpersonal communication, group management, and problem-solving abilities.

Perhaps, there is no greater need for the leader than to be the catalyst for professional change as well as organizational change. Many people attracted to nursing now find that their values and traditional expectations no longer fit as they once did. It is the leader's role to help their followers turn around and confront the opportunities and challenges of the realities of emerging nursing practice; to create enthusiasm and passion for renewing the profession; to embrace the change of locus of control, which now belongs to the health-care consumer; and to engage a new social context for nursing practice.

KEY CONCEPTS

- Change should not be viewed as a threat but as a challenge and a chance to do something new and innovative.

- Change should be implemented only for good reason.

- Because change disrupts the homeostasis or balance of the group, resistance should be expected as a natural part of the change process.

- The level of resistance to change generally depends on the type of change proposed. Technological changes encounter less resistance than changes that are perceived as social or that are contrary to established customs or norms.

- Perhaps the greatest factor contributing to the resistance encountered with change is a lack of trust between the employee and the manager or the employee and the organization.

- It is much easier to change a person's behavior than it is to change an entire group's behavior. It is also easier to change knowledge levels than attitudes.

- Change should be planned and thus implemented gradually, not sporadically or suddenly.

- Those who may be affected by a change should be involved in planning for it. Likewise, workers should thoroughly understand the change and its effect on them.

- The feeling of control is critical to thriving in a changing environment.

- Friends, family, and colleagues should be used as a network of support during change.

- The successful change agent has the leadership skills of problem solving and decision making and has good interpersonal skills.

- In contrast to planned change, change by drift is unplanned or accidental.

- Historically, many of the changes that have occurred in nursing or have affected the profession are the results of change by drift.

- People maintain status quo or equilibrium when both driving and restraining forces operating within any field simultaneously occur. For change to happen, this balance of driving and restraining forces must be altered.

- Emerging theories such as complexity science suggest that change is unpredictable, occurs at random, and is dependent upon rapidly changing relationships between agents and factors in the system and that even small changes can affect an entire organization.

- Organizations are preserved by change and constant renewal. Without change, the organization may stagnate and die.

ADDITIONAL LEARNING EXERCISES AND APPLICATIONS

LEARNING EXERCISE 8.6

Implementing Planned Change in a Family Planning Clinic

You are a Hispanic RN who has recently received a 2-year grant to establish a family planning clinic in an impoverished, primarily Hispanic area of a large city. The project will be evaluated at the end of the grant to determine whether continued funding is warranted. As project director, you have the funds to choose and hire three health-care workers. You will essentially be able to manage the clinic as you see fit.

The average age of your patients will be 14 years, and many come from single-parent homes. In addition, the population with which you will be working has high unemployment, high crime and truancy levels, and great suspicion and mistrust of authority figures. You are aware that many restraining forces exist that will challenge you, but you feel strongly committed to the cause. You believe that the high teenage pregnancy rate and maternal and infant morbidity can be reduced.

Assignment:

1. Identify the restraining and driving forces in this situation.

2. Identify realistic short- and long-term goals for implementing such a change. What can realistically be accomplished in 2 years?

3. How might the project director use hiring authority to increase the driving forces in this situation?

4. Is refreezing of the planned change possible so that changes will continue if the grant is not funded again in 2 years?

LEARNING EXERCISE 8.7

Retain the Status Quo or Implement Change?

Assume that morale and productivity are low on the unit where you are the new manager. In an effort to identify the root of the problem, you have been meeting informally with staff to discuss their perceptions of unit functioning and to identify sources of unrest on the unit. You believe that one of the greatest factors leading to unrest is the limited advancement opportunity for your staff nurses. You have a fixed charge nurse on each shift. This is how the unit has been managed for as long as everyone can remember. You would like to rotate the charge nurse position but are unsure of your staff's feelings about the change.

Assignment: Using the phases of change identified by Lewin (1951), identify the actions you could take in unfreezing, movement, and refreezing. What are the greatest barriers to this change? What are the strongest driving forces?

LEARNING EXERCISE 8.8

How Would You Handle This Response to Change?

You are the unit manager of a cardiovascular surgical unit. The workstation on the unit is small, dated, and disorganized. The unit clerks have complained for some time that the chart racks on the counter above their desk are difficult to reach, that staff frequently impinge on the clerks' work

(Continued)

space to discuss patients or to chart, that the call-light system is antiquated, and that supplies and forms need to be relocated. You ask all eight of your shift unit clerks to make a "wish list" of how they would like the workstation to be redesigned for optimum efficiency and effectiveness.

Construction is completed several months later. You are pleased that the new workstation incorporates what each unit clerk included in his or her top three priorities for change. There is a new revolving chart rack in the center of the workstation, with enhanced accessibility to both staff and unit clerks. A new state-of-the-art, call-light system has been installed. A small, quiet room has been created for nurses to chart and conference, and new cubbyholes and filing drawers now put forms within arm's reach of the charge nurse and unit clerk.

Almost immediately, you begin to be barraged with complaints about the changes. Several of the unit clerks find the new call-light system's computerized response system overwhelming and complain that patient lights are now going unanswered. Others complain that with the chart rack out of their immediate work area, charts can no longer be monitored and are being removed from the unit by physicians or left in the charting room by nurses. One unit clerk has filed a complaint that she was injured by a staff member who carelessly and rapidly turned the chart rack. She refuses to work again until the old chart racks are returned. The regular day-shift unit clerk complains that all the forms are filed backward for left-handed people and that after 20 years, she should have the right to put them the way that she likes it. Several of the nurses are complaining that the workstation is "now the domain of the unit clerk" and that access to the telephones and desk supplies is limited by the unit clerks. There have been some rumblings that several staff members believe that you favored the requests of some employees over others.

Today, when you make rounds at change of shift, you find the day-shift unit clerk and charge nurse involved in a heated conversation with the evening-shift unit clerk and charge nurse. Each evening, the charge nurse and unit clerk reorganize the workstation in the manner that they believe is most effective, and each morning, the charge nurse and unit clerk put things back the way they had been the prior day. Both believe that the other shift is undermining their efforts to "fix" the workstation organization and that their method of organization is the best. Both groups of workers turn to you and demand that you "make the other shift stop sabotaging our efforts to change things for the better."

Assignment: Despite your intent to include subordinate input into this planned change, resistance is high and worker morale is decreasing. Is the level of resistance a normal and anticipated response to planned change? If so, would you intervene in this conflict? How? Was it possible to have reduced the likelihood of such a high degree of resistance?

LEARNING EXERCISE 8.9

The Nursing Profession and Change

Assignment: If professions were classified in a manner similar to organizations, do you believe that the nursing profession would be classified as (a) an aging organization, (b) in constant motion and ever renewing, or (c) a closed system that does not respond well to change?

LEARNING EXERCISE 8.10

Overcoming Resistance to a Needed Change

You are the charge nurse of a medical/surgical unit. Recently, your hospital spent millions of dollars to implement BCMA to reduce medication errors and to promote a culture of patient safety. In this system, the nurse, using a handheld device, scans the drug he or she is planning to give against the patient's medication record to make sure that the right drug, at the right dose, is being given at the right time to the right patient. The nurse then scans the patient's name band/arm band to assure the right patient is receiving the drug and finally scans his or her own name badge to document who is administering the drug to the patient. If any of the codes do not match, a signal goes off, alerting the nurse of the discrepancy.

It has come to your attention, however, that some nurses are overriding the safety features built into the bar-coding system. For example, some nurses are reluctant to wake sleeping patients to scan their bar code before they administer an IV push medication, and instead simply scan the chart label. Some nurses have overridden the bar code warning, assuming it was some kind of technological glitch. Some nurses have administered drugs to patients despite having name bands that have become smudged or torn and no longer scan well. Still other nurses are carrying multiple prescanned pills on one tray or charting that drugs have been given, even though they were left at the bedside. Finally, you learned that one nurse even affixed extra copies of her patient's bar codes to her clipboard, so that they could be scanned more quickly.

Assignment: Despite thorough orientation and training regarding bar coding, it is clear that some staff have developed "work-arounds" to the bar-coding system, increasing the risk of medication errors and patient harm. Your staff suggest that while they understand BCMA reduces risks to patients, that the equipment does not always work, and that performing the additional safety checks inherent in BCMA often takes them more time than how they did it in the past, ultimately delaying medications to patients who need them. The staff states they will try to be more careful in implementing the BCMA procedures, but you continue to sense resistance on their part. What strategies could you employ now to foster refreezing of the new BCMA system? Would rational–empirical, power–coercive, or normative–reeducative strategies be more effective? Provide a rationale for your choice.

REFERENCES

Amos, A., Johns, C., Hines, N., Skov, T., & Kloosterman, L. (2012). The handwriting on the wall: Program transformations utilizing effective change management strategies. *CANNT Journal*, 22(2), 31–35.

Bayan, R. (2012, January 20). *Elegy for Kodak: An American icon goes bankrupt.* Retrieved May 15, 2013, from http://www.forbes.com/sites/ericsavitz/2013/02/25/lessons-from-blackberrys-accelerated-obsolesence/

Bennis, W., Benne, K., & Chinn, R. (1969). *The planning of change* (2nd ed.). New York, NY: Holt, Rinehart, & Winston.

Burrowes, N., & Needs, A. (2009, January/February). Time to contemplate change? A framework for assessing readiness to change with offenders. *Aggression & Violent Behavior, 14*(1), 39–49.

Gordon, M. (2012). *The fall of Kodak: 5 lessons for small business.* Biznik. Retrieved May 13, 2014, from http://biznik.com/articles/the-fall-of-kodak-5-lessons-for-small-business

Lewin, K. (1951). *Field theory in social sciences.* New York, NY: Harper & Row.

Massachusetts Institute of Technology (MIT) News. (2008, April 30). *Edward Lorenz, father of chaos theory and butterfly effect, dies at 90.* Retrieved May 12, 2013, from http://web.mit.edu/newsoffice/2008/obit-lorenz-0416.html

Mitchell, G. (2013). Selecting the best theory to implement planned change. *Nursing Management—UK, 20*(1), 32–37.

Norman, K. (2012). Leading service improvement in changing times. *British Journal of Community Nursing, 17*(4), 162–167.

Olson, E. E., & Eoyang, G. H. (2001). *Facilitating organization change: Lessons from complexity science.* San Francisco, CA: Jossey-Boss/Pfeiffer.

Owarish, F. (2013). *Strategic leadership of technology: Lessons learned.* E-Leader Singapore. Retrieved May 14, 2013, from http://www.g-casa.com/conferences/singapore12/papers/Owarish-2.pdf

Philpot, S. (2013, February 25). *Lessons from BlackBerry's accelerated obsolescence.* Forbes. Retrieved May 14, 2014, from http://www.forbes.com/sites/ericsavitz/2013/02/25/lessons-from-blackberrys-accelerated-obsolesence/

Rae, G. (n.d.). *Chaos theory: A brief introduction.* Retrieved September 13, 2006, from http://www.imho.com/grae/chaos/chaos.html

Salmela, S., Eriksson, K., & Fagerström, L. (2013). Nurse leaders' perceptions of an approaching organizational change. *Qualitative Health Research, 23*(5), 689–699.

Spetz, J., Burgess, J. F., & Phibbs, C. S. (2012). What determines successful implementation of inpatient information technology systems? *American Journal of Managed Care, 18*(3), 157–162.

Stonehouse, D. (2012). Resistance to change: The human dimension. *British Journal of Healthcare Assistants, 6*(9), 456–457.

Time Management

9

... nothing is particularly hard if you divide it into small jobs.
–Henry Ford

... things which matter most must never be at the mercy of things that matter least.
–Johann Wolfgang von Goethe

CROSSWALK THIS CHAPTER ADDRESSES:

BSN Essential II: Basic organizational and systems leadership for quality care and patient safety
BSN Essential VI: Interprofessional communication and collaboration for improving patient health outcomes
MSN Essential II: Organizational and systems leadership
AONE Nurse Executive Competency I: Communication and relationship building
AONE Nurse Executive Competency II: A knowledge of the health-care environment
QSEN Competency: Safety
QSEN Competency: Teamwork and collaboration

LEARNING OBJECTIVES *The learner will:*

- analyze how time is managed both personally and at the unit level of the organization
- describe the importance of allowing adequate time for daily planning and priority setting
- describe how planning fallacies influence the perception of the time needed to complete a task
- complete tasks according to the priority level they have been assigned whenever possible
- build evaluation steps into planning so that reprioritization can occur
- identify common internal and external time wasters as well as interventions that can be taken to reduce their impact
- complete a time inventory to increase self-awareness regarding personal priority setting and time management
- identify how technology applications such as e-mail, the Internet, telecommunications, and social networking can both facilitate and hinder personal time management
- involve subordinates and followers in maximizing time use, and guiding work to its successful implementation and conclusion

Another part of the planning process is short-term planning. This operational planning focuses on achieving specific tasks. Short-term plans involve a period of 1 hour to 3 years and are usually less complex than strategic or long-range plans. Short-term planning may be done annually, quarterly, monthly, weekly, daily, or even hourly.

Previous chapters examined the need for prudent planning of resources, such as money, equipment, supplies, and labor. Time is an equally important resource. Being overwhelmed by work and time constraints leads to increased errors, the omission of important tasks, and general feelings of stress and ineffectiveness. If leaders are to empower others to achieve personal and shared goals, they need to become experts in the planning and implementation of goal attainment. If managers are to direct employees effectively and maximize other resources, they must first be able to find the time to do so. In other words, both must become experts at time management.

Time management can be defined as making optimal use of available time. Homisak (2012) notes that many people with poor time management skills spend inordinate amounts of time burning the candle at both ends, blaming others for their time inefficiencies, and getting others to work harder. The reality is that each person is given 86,400 seconds every day to use as they please and when they are wasted, they can never be retrieved. Homisak (p. 41) goes on to suggest that "we invite all the activities in our lives and unless we choose differently, nothing will change."

Good time management skills allow an individual to spend time on things that matter.

The keys then to optimizing time management must include prioritizing duties, managing and controlling crises, reducing stress, and balancing work and personal time (Homisak, 2012). All of these activities require some degree of both leadership skills and management functions. Leadership roles and management functions needed for effective time management are included in Display 9.1.

DISPLAY 9.1	Leadership Roles and Management Functions in Time Management

LEADERSHIP ROLES

1. Is self-aware regarding personal blocks and barriers to efficient time management.
2. Recognizes how one's own value system influences his or her use of time and the expectations of followers.
3. Functions as a role model, supporter, and resource person to others in setting priorities for goal attainment.
4. Assists followers in working cooperatively to maximize time use.
5. Prevents and/or filters interruptions that prevent effective time management.
6. Role models flexibility in working cooperatively with other people whose primary time management style is different.
7. Presents a calm and reassuring demeanor during periods of high unit activity.
8. Prioritizes conflicting and overlapping requests for time.
9. Appropriately determines the quality of work needed in tasks to be completed.

MANAGEMENT FUNCTIONS

1. Appropriately prioritizes day-to-day planning to meet short-term and long-term unit goals.
2. Builds time for planning into the work schedule.
3. Analyzes how time is managed on the unit level by using job analysis and time-and-motion studies.
4. Eliminates environmental barriers to effective time management for workers.
5. Handles paperwork promptly and efficiently and maintains a neat work area.
6. Breaks down large tasks into smaller ones that can more easily be accomplished by unit members.
7. Utilizes appropriate technology to facilitate timely communication and documentation.
8. Discriminates between inadequate staffing and inefficient use of time when time resources are inadequate to complete assigned tasks.

THREE BASIC STEPS TO TIME MANAGEMENT

There are three basic steps to time management (Fig. 9.1). The first step requires that time be set aside for planning and establishing priorities. The second step entails completing the highest priority task (as determined in step 1) whenever possible and finishing one task before beginning another. In the final step, the person must reprioritize what tasks will be accomplished based on new information received. Because this is a cyclic process, all three steps must be accomplished sequentially.

Taking Time to Plan and Establishing Priorities

Planning is essential if an individual is to manage by efficiency rather than by crisis and the old adage "fail to plan—plan to fail" is timeless. Managers who are new to time management may underestimate the importance of regular planning and fail to allot enough time for it.

In addition, many individuals fail to allow enough time for their plans to be carried out. Baiyun and Quanquan (2012) agree, noting that while many individuals make plans, often that plan is not completed in the time predicted. And despite the fact that the time allowed to carry out their plan is shown over and over again to be inadequate, most individuals continue to be optimistic that their new forecasts, which are no different, will be realistic. This phenomenon is known as *planning fallacies*. For example, the student who carries home a full backpack every night with the expectation that every assignment or task contained within the backpack will be completed is generally aware that they rarely get more than one or two significant items done in that time span. Yet, they continue to be hopeful that this will be different the next time and their behavior continues unchanged.

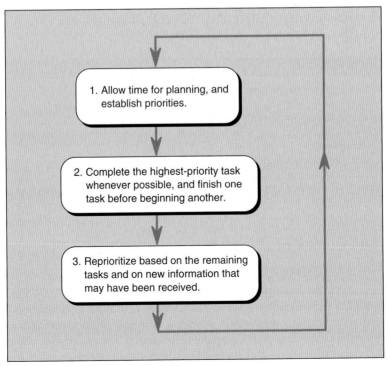

FIGURE 9.1 • The three basic steps in time management.

Researchers suggest this occurs because many individuals forget that in the past, they were interrupted unexpectedly or because individuals may not consider all the subcomponents of a task when planning (Baiyun & Quanquan, 2012). In addition, individuals may have been overly narrow in their focus on the task or subconsciously disregarded memories of how long similar tasks have taken in the past. Most people simply want to believe that tasks will always go well and that no problems will arise. This unrealistic assumption leads to serious planning errors and poor time management.

Planning occurs first in the management process because the ability to be organized develops from good planning. During planning, there should be time to think about how plans will be translated into action. The planner must pause and decide how people, activities, and materials are going to be put together to carry out the objectives.

Many individuals believe that they are unproductive if they take time out early in their day to design a plan for action, rather than immediately beginning work on tasks. Without adequate planning, however, the individual finds it difficult to get started and begins to manage by crisis. In addition, there can be no sense of achievement at day's end if the goals for the day are not clearly delineated.

Unfortunately, two mistakes common in planning are underestimating the importance of a daily plan and not allowing adequate time for planning.

Similarly, Pugsley (2009) suggests that many students fail to establish a plan for completing their learning activities. Sometimes this is because they are unclear about what the finished product must look like. Other times, they are unsure when assignments are due or how to break large assignments down into workable subcomponents. In all of these cases, the end result is that the student's ability to achieve the desired outcome, within the required timeline, is threatened. To counter this, Pugsley suggests students adopt a "SMART" approach to planning that allows learners to make effective use of every study period, whether the learning activities are formal or informal (Display 9.2).

Whether you are a student, a manager, or a staff nurse, planning takes time; it requires the ability to think, analyze data, envision alternatives, and make decisions. Examples

DISPLAY 9.2   The SMART Approach to Studying

1. Set specific, clear goals to be accomplished.
2. Record your progress as measurable progress maintains your interest.
3. Identify the steps needed to accomplish your goals.
4. Be realistic about your time constraints and set goals that can be accomplished within these constraints.
5. Set a time frame and plan for this.

Adapted from: Pugsley, L. (2009, May). How to … study effectively. Education for Primary Care, 20(3), 195–197.

LEARNING EXERCISE 9.1

Making Big Projects Manageable

Think of the last major paper you wrote for a class. Did you set short-term and intermediate deadlines? Did you break the task down into smaller tasks to eliminate a last-minute crisis? What short-term and intermediate deadlines have you set to accomplish major projects that have been assigned to you this quarter or semester? Are you realistic about the time that will be required to complete the task or are you likely to experience planning fallacies?

of the types of plans a charge nurse might make in day-to-day planning include staffing schedules, patient care assignments, coordination of lunch- and work-break schedules, and interdisciplinary coordination of patient care. Examples of an acute care staff nurse's day-to-day planning might include determining how handoff reports will be given and received; the timing and method used for initial patient assessments; the coordination of medication administration, treatments, and procedures; and the organization of documentation of the day's activities.

The Time-Efficient Work Environment

Some staff nurses appear disorganized in their efforts to care for patients. This may be the result of poor planning or it may be a symptom of a work environment that is not conducive to efficient time management. The following suggestions, using industrial engineering principles, may assist the staff nurse in planning work activities, especially when the environment poses obstacles to time efficiency:

- *Gather all the supplies and equipment that will be needed before starting an activity.* Breaking a job down mentally into parts before beginning the activity may help the staff nurse identify what supplies and equipment will be needed to complete the activity.

- *Group activities that are in the same location.* If you have walked a long distance down a hallway, attempt to do several things there before going back to the nurses station. If you are a home health nurse, group patient visits geographically when possible to minimize travel time and maximize time with patients.

- *Use time estimates.* For example, if you know an intermittent intravenous medication (IV piggyback) will take 30 minutes to complete, then use that time estimate for planning some other activity that can be completed in that 30-minute window of time.

- *Document your nursing interventions as soon as possible after an activity is completed.* Waiting until the end of the workday to complete necessary documentation increases the risk of inaccuracies and incomplete documentation.

- *Always strive to end the workday on time.* Although this is not always possible, delegating appropriately to others and making sure that the workload goal for any given day is reasonable are two strategies that will accomplish this goal.

Like staff nurses, unit managers need to coordinate how their duties will be carried out and devise methods to make work simpler and more efficient. Often, this includes simple tasks such as organizing how supplies are stored or determining the most efficient lunch and break schedules for staff. In addition, it is the manager's responsibility to see that units are appropriately stocked with the equipment nurses need to do their work. This reduces the time spent in trying to locate needed supplies.

This was certainly the case at Neepawa Health Center in Manitoba, which implemented a nursing strategy in 2010 called *Releasing Time to Care: The Productive Ward* (RTC) (Examining the Evidence 9.1). Ultimately, the goal in planning work and activities is to facilitate greater productivity and satisfaction.

Examining the Evidence 9.1

Source: Fortier, J. (2012). More time for care. Canadian Nurse, 108(8), 22–27.

Fortier shared the story of the disorganization and disjointedness she discovered when she joined the nursing staff of Neepawa Health Center in Manitoba in 2008. Fortier noted that staff spent so much time searching for supplies that patient care was not getting done; that wards and

(Continued)

supply areas were chaotic; that turnover report took upward of 40 minutes; and that communication between staff members and departments was poor.

To combat the problem, Neepawa Health Center implemented a nursing strategy in 2010 called *Releasing Time to Care: The Productive Ward* (RTC). One of the many goals of this program was to increase the efficiency of care so that less time would be spent searching for supplies so that more time could be spent at the patient bedside. In addition, experts provided training as well as support materials for staff on time management and an analysis was completed of work design so that environmental factors causing staff to waste time could be identified and addressed. "Lean" manufacturing processes, like those used by Toyota to eliminate all tasks workers do, that are not directly related to the building of vehicles, were applied to the nursing workunits with the goal being to eliminate unnecessary paperwork and searching for supplies. Work modules were also decluttered and reorganized.

Fortier noted that while the process took some time and hard work, the outcomes were clearly worth the effort. The time available for direct care increased significantly and staff turnover became almost nonexistent.

Daily planning actions that may help the unit manager identify and utilize time as a resource most efficiently might include the following:

- At the start of each workday, identify key priorities to be accomplished that day. Identify what specific actions need to be taken to accomplish those priorities and in what order they should be done. Also, identify specific actions that should be taken to meet ongoing, long-term goals.

- Determine the level of achievement that you expect for each prioritized task. Is a maximizing or "satisficing" approach more appropriate or more reasonable for each of the goals you have identified?

- Assess the staff assigned to work with you. Assign work that must be delegated to staff members who are both capable and willing to accomplish the priority task that you have identified. Be sure that you have clearly expressed any expectations you may have about how and when a delegated task must be completed. (Delegation is discussed further in Chapter 20.)

- Review the short- and long-term plans of the unit regularly. Include colleagues and subordinates in identifying unit problems or concerns so that they can be fully involved in planning for needed change.

- Plan ahead for meetings. Prepare and distribute agendas in advance.

- Allow time at several points throughout the day and at the end of the day to assess progress in meeting established daily goals and to determine if unanticipated events have occurred or if new information has been received that may have altered your original plan. Ongoing realities for the unit manager include work situations that are constantly changing, and with them, setting new priorities and adjusting older ones.

 Setting new priorities or adjusting priorities to reflect ever-changing work situations is an ongoing reality for the unit manager.

- Take regularly scheduled breaks. Planning for periodic breaks from work during the workday is an integral part of an individual's time and task management. These work breaks allow both managers and staff to refresh physically and mentally.

- Using an electronic calendar to organize your day can help make a day feel less chaotic. It can also help you identify pockets of spare time that you could use for breaks.

LEARNING EXERCISE 9.2

Setting Daily Priorities

Assume that you are the registered nurse (RN) leader of a team with one licensed vocational nurse and one nursing assistant on the 7 AM to 3 PM shift at an acute care hospital. The three of you are responsible for providing total care to 10 patients. Prioritize the following list of 10 things that you need to accomplish this morning. Use a "1" for the first thing you will do and a "10" for the last. Be prepared to provide rationale for your priorities.

___ Check medication cards/sheets against the patient medication record.

___ Listen to night shift report 11:00 PM to 7:00 AM.

___ Take brief walking rounds to assess the night shift report and to introduce yourself to patients.

___ Hang four 9:00 AM IV medications.

___ Set up the schedule for breaks and lunch among your team members.

___ Give 8:45 AM preop on patient going to surgery at 9:00 AM.

___ Pass 8:30 AM breakfast trays.

___ Meet with team members to plan the schedule for the day and to clarify roles.

___ Read charts of patients who are new to you.

___ Check 6:00 AM blood glucose laboratory results for 7:30 AM insulin administration.

Priority Setting and Procrastination

Because most individuals are inundated with requests for their time and energy, the next step in time management is prioritizing, which may well be the key to good time management. Unfortunately, some individuals lack self-awareness about what is important and therefore how to spend their time.

Priority setting is perhaps the most critical skill in good time management, because all actions we take have some type of relative importance.

One simple means of prioritizing what needs to be accomplished is to divide all requests into three categories: "don't do," "do later," and "do now" (Display 9.3). The "don't do" items probably reflect problems that will take care of themselves, are already outdated, or are better accomplished by someone else. The individual either throws away the unnecessary information or passes it on to the appropriate person in a timely fashion. In either case, the individual removes unneeded clutter from his or her work area.

DISPLAY 9.3	Three Categories of Prioritization

1. "Don't do"
2. "Do later"
3. "Do now"

Some "do later" items reflect trivial problems or those that do not have immediate deadlines; thus, they may be procrastinated. To *procrastinate* means to put off something until a future time, to postpone, or to delay needlessly. Although procrastination may be appropriate in some cases, the reality is that more often than not, it is a barrier to effective time management.

Procrastination is a difficult problem to solve because it rarely results from a single cause and can involve a combination of dysfunctional attitudes, rationalizations, and resentment. The key in procrastination is to use it appropriately and selectively. Procrastination is rarely appropriate when it is done to avoid a task because it is overwhelming or unpleasant.

Before setting "do later" items aside, the leader-manager must be sure that large projects have been broken down into smaller projects and that a specific timeline and plan for implementation are in place. The plan should include short-term, intermediate, and final deadlines. Likewise, one cannot ignore items without immediate time limits forever and must make a definite time commitment in the near future to address these requests.

The "do now" requests most commonly reflect a unit's day-to-day operational needs. These requests may include daily staffing needs, dealing with equipment shortages, meeting schedules, conducting hiring interviews, and giving performance appraisals. "Do now" requests also may represent items that had been put off earlier.

LEARNING EXERCISE 9.3

Targeting Personal Procrastination

Spend a few moments reflecting on the last 2 weeks of your life. What are the things you put off doing? Do these things form a pattern? For instance, do you always put off writing a school paper until the last minute? Do you wait to do certain tasks at work until you cannot avoid the task any longer? What things do you do when you really do not want to do something? Do you eat? Play video games? Watch TV? Read?

Assignment: Write a one-page essay on at least two things that you procrastinate and then develop two strategies for breaking each of these habits.

Making Lists

In prioritizing all the "do now" items, the leader-manager may find preparing a written list helpful. Remember, however, that a list is a plan, not a product, and that the creation of the list is not the final goal. The list is a planning tool.

Although the individual may use monthly or weekly lists, a list also can assist in coordinating daily operations. This daily list, however, should not be longer than what can be realistically accomplished in 1 day; otherwise, it demotivates instead of assists.

In addition, although the leader-manager must be cognizant of and plan for routine tasks, it is not always necessary to place them on the list because they may only distract attention from other priority tasks. Lists should allow adequate time for each task and have blocks of time built in for the unexpected. In addition, individuals who use lists to help them organize their day must be careful not to confuse importance and urgency. Not all important things are urgent, and not all urgent things are important. This is especially true when the urgency is coming from an external source.

 Not all important things are urgent, and not all urgent things are important.

In addition, the individual should periodically review lists from previous days to see what was not accomplished or completed. If a task appears on a list for several successive days, the manager must reexamine it and assess why it was not accomplished. Sometimes, tasks just need to be removed from the list. This occurs when a task has low priority, or when it is better done by someone else. Other times, undone tasks on the list should be discarded because they are no longer relevant or they represent a need that no longer exists.

Sometimes, however, items on the list remain unaccomplished because they are not divided into steps or tasks that can be completed. Breaking a big job down into smaller parts can make the task seem more manageable. For example, many well-meaning people begin thinking about completing their tax returns in early January but feel overwhelmed by a project that cannot be accomplished in 1 day. If preparing a tax return is not broken down into several smaller tasks with intermediate deadlines, it may be almost perpetually procrastinated.

 Some projects are not accomplished because they are not broken down into manageable tasks.

Reprioritizing

The last step in time management is reprioritizing. Often, one's priorities or list will change during a day, week, or longer because new information is received. If the individual does not take time to reprioritize after each major task is accomplished, other priorities set earlier may no longer be accurate. In addition, despite outstanding planning, an occasional crisis may erupt.

 No amount of planning can prevent an occasional crisis.

If a crisis does occur, the individual may need to set aside the original priorities for the day and reorganize, communicate, and delegate a new plan reflecting the new priorities associated with the unexpected event causing the crisis.

LEARNING EXERCISE 9.4

Creating Planning Lists

Do you make a daily plan to organize what needs to be done? Mentally or on paper, develop a list of five items that must be accomplished today. Prioritize that list. Now make a list of five items that must be done this week. Prioritize that list as well.

Dealing with Interruptions

All managers experience interruptions, but lower-level managers typically experience the most. This occurs in part because first- and middle-level managers are more involved in daily planning than higher-level managers and thus directly interact with a greater number of subordinates. In addition, many lower-level managers do not have a quiet workspace or clerical help to filter interruptions. Frequent work interruptions result in situational stress and lowered job satisfaction. Managers need to develop skill in preventing interruptions that threaten effective time management.

 Lower-level managers experience more interruptions than higher-level managers.

Dealing with interruptions also requires leadership skills. Leaders role model flexibility and the ability to regroup when new information or tasks emerge as priorities. Followers often look to see how their leaders are coping with change and even crisis and their reactions often mirror those of their leaders. That is often why a staff nurse who feels harried or out of control typically finds these same feelings reflected in the individuals he or she is assigned to work with.

Time Wasters

There are many time wasters, and the time wasters that are used most often vary by the individual. Four time wasters warrant special attention here (see Display 9.4). The first of these surprisingly is technology, which generally has been promoted as a time saver for most people. Indeed, technology can and does save time. E-mail now makes instantaneous, asynchronous communication to multiple parties possible simultaneously and the Internet provides virtually unlimited access to emerging, state of the science knowledge globally. In addition, social networks such as *Facebook*, *MySpace*, *Pinterest*, and *Twitter* have created new opportunities for communicating in real time to vast networks of users.

DISPLAY 9.4   **Time Wasters**

1. Technology (Internet, gaming, e-mail, and social media sites)
2. Socializing
3. Paperwork overload
4. A poor filing system
5. Interruptions

Yet, this same technology increasingly consumes more and more of our time. Many individuals find themselves randomly searching the Internet or playing online games to distract themselves from the tasks at hand. In addition, the need to check and respond to so many different communication mediums (e-mail, blackberries, voice mail, pagers, and social networking sites) is time consuming in and of itself.

Svehaug (2013, para 17) suggests that "many of us have fallen into the social media black hole, and it can be tricky to find a balance with no parameters in place." She suggests using an egg timer or some other timing device to limit the time you spent on social networking sites when you have important tasks that must be accomplished. Time Management Ninja (2013, para 10) agrees, suggesting "You don't need to check email 100 times a day. Email is not intended to be instant communication. Rather, check it morning, noon, and close of day."

You do not need to check e-mail 100 times a day.

Finally, all this technology can make it difficult to find an appropriate balance between the need for virtual and face-to-face interaction and between work and personal life. Time Management Ninja (2013) suggests that "not unplugging" is a huge risk to time management since no one can be "on" all the time. Individuals who do not unplug from their work and devices will burn out and the boundaries between work and personal life will blur.

A second time waster is socializing. Socializing with colleagues during the workday can waste significant amounts of time in a workday. Although socializing can help workers meet relationship needs or build power, it can tremendously deter productivity. This is especially true for managers with an open-door policy. Subordinates can be discouraged from taking up a manager's time with idle chatter in several ways:

- *Do not make yourself overly accessible.* Make it easy for people to ignore you. Try not to "work" at the nursing station, if this is possible. If charting is to be done, sit with your back to others. If you have an office, close the door. Have people make appointments to see you. All these behaviors will discourage casual socializers.

- *Interrupt.* When someone is rambling on without getting to the point, break in and say gently, "Excuse me. Somehow I' not getting your message. What exactly are you saying?"

- *Avoid promoting socialization.* Having several comfortable chairs in your office, a full candy dish, and posters on your walls that invite comments encourage socializing in your office.

- *Be brief.* Watch your own long-winded comments, and stand up when you are finished. This will signal an end to the conversation.

- *Schedule long-winded pests.* If someone has a pattern of lengthy chatter and manages to corner you on rounds or at the nurse' station, say, "I can' speak with you now, but I'm going to have some free time at 11 AM. Why don't you see me then?" Unless the meeting is important, the person who just wishes to chat will not bother to make a formal appointment. If you would like to chat and have the time to do so, use coffee breaks and lunch hours for socializing.

Other external time wasters that a manager must conquer are paperwork overload and a poor filing system. Managers are generally inundated with paper clutter, including organizational memos, staffing requests, quality assurance reports, incident reports, and patient evaluations. Because paperwork is often redundant or unnecessary, the manager needs to become an expert at handling it. Whenever possible, incoming correspondence should be handled the day it arrives; it should either be thrown away or filed according to the date to be completed. Try to address each piece of correspondence only once.

An adequate filing system also is invaluable to handling paper overload. Keeping correspondence organized in easily retrievable files rather than disorganized stacks saves time when the manager needs to find specific information. The manager also may want to consider increased use of computerization and e-mail to reduce the paper use and to increase response time in time-sensitive communication.

Finally, interruptions can cause a great deal of time wasting as attention is continually diverted from the task at hand. All managers need protected time to respond to time-sensitive phone calls or e-mails and it is important not to be disturbed during these times unless there is an urgent request for an answer or guidance on dealing with an emergency situation. "Once staff recognize that the manager is serious about keeping protected time and not accepting all types of interruptions, then it will become standard practice" (Ashurst, 2013, p. 51).

 ## PERSONAL TIME MANAGEMENT

Personal time management refers in part to self-knowledge. Self-awareness is a leadership skill. For people who are not certain of their own short- to long-term goals, time management, in general, poses difficulties. Svehaug (2013) suggests that to most appropriately manage time, each individual should step back and think about what they truly want to accomplish and the time they are willing and able to dedicate to achieving that goal. Honesty should be the key in performing this exercise because there is no right or wrong answer.

 Managing time is difficult if a person is unsure of his or her priorities for time management, including personal short-term, intermediate, and long-term goals.

These goals give structure to what should be accomplished today, tomorrow, and in the future. However, goals alone are not enough; a concrete plan with timelines is needed. Plans outlined in manageable steps are clearer, more realistic, and attainable. By being self-aware and setting goals accordingly, people determine how their time will be spent. If goals are not set, others often end up deciding how a person should spend his or her time.

Think for a moment about last week. Did you accomplish all that you wanted to accomplish? How much time did you or others waste? In your clinical practice, did you spend your time hunting for supplies and medicines instead of teaching your patient about his or her diabetes? Too often, irrelevant decisions and insignificant activities take priority over real purposes. Clearly, work redesign, clarification of job descriptions, or a change in the type of care delivery system may alleviate some of these problems. However, the same general principle holds: professional nurses who are self-aware and have clearly identified personal goals and priorities have greater control over how they expend their energy and what they accomplish.

When individuals lack this self-awareness, they may find it difficult to find a balance between time spent on personal and professional priorities. Indeed, a study of more than 50,000 employees from a variety of manufacturing and service organizations found that two out of every five employees were dissatisfied with the balance between their work and their personal lives (Hansen, n.d.). Effective time management then is an essential part of finding that balance between work life and personal life.

Brans (2013), building on thinking done by Benjamin Franklin more than 300 years ago, suggests that there are 12 habits that should be nurtured for optimum personal time management. These are shown in Display 9.5. All 12 habits are directed at being

---

DISPLAY 9.5   Bran's 12 Habits to Master for Personal Time Management

Habit 1: Strive to be authentic. Be honest with yourself about what you want and why you do what you do.

Habit 2: Favor trusting relationships. Build relationships with people you can trust and count on, and make sure those same people can trust and count on you.

Habit 3: Maintain a lifestyle that will give you maximum energy. Exercise, eat well, and get enough sleep.

Habit 4: Listen to your biorhythms and organize your day accordingly. Pay attention to regular fluctuations in your physical and mental energy levels throughout the day and schedule tasks accordingly.

Habit 5: Set very few priorities and stick to them. Select a maximum of two things that are your highest priority and work on them.

Habit 6: Turn down things that are inconsistent with your priorities. Say no to other people when their request is not a priority for you and you do not have the time to help.

Habit 7: Set aside time for focused effort. Schedule time every day to work on just one thing.

Habit 8: Always look for ways of doing things better and faster. Watch for tasks you do over and over again and look for ways of improving how you do them.

Habit 9: Build solid processes. Set up processes that last and that run without your attention.

Habit 10: Spot trouble ahead and solve problems immediately. Set aside time to think about what lies ahead and face all problems as soon as you can.

Habit 11: Break your goals into small units of work, and think only about one unit at a time. Spend most of your time working on the task in front of you, and avoid dreaming too much about the big goal.

Habit 12: Finish what is important and stop doing what is no longer worthwhile. Do not stop doing what you considered worth starting unless there is a good reason to give it up.

Source: Adapted from Brans, P. (2013, January 1). Twelve time management habits to master in 2013. *Forbes*, Retrieved May 20, 2014, from http://www.forbes.com/sites/patbrans/2013/01/01/twelve-time-management-habits-to-master-in-2013

self-aware regarding what is important to accomplish in one's life, staying focused on the things that matter, taking care of oneself, and following through in a timely and consistent manner.

In addition to being self-aware regarding the values that influence how people prioritize the use of their time, people must be self-aware regarding their general tendency to complete tasks in isolation or in combination. Some people prefer to do one thing at a time, whereas others typically do two or more things simultaneously. Some individuals begin and finish projects on time, have clean and organized desks because of handling each piece of paperwork only once, and are highly structured. Others tend to change plans, borrow and lend things frequently, emphasize relationships rather than tasks, and build longer-term relationships. It is important to recognize one's own preferred time management style and to be self-aware about how this orientation may affect your interaction with others in the workplace. A significant part of personal time management depends on self-awareness about how and when a person is most productive. Everyone has ways to waste time or steer clear of certain activities.

Everyone avoids certain types of work or has methods of wasting time.

Likewise, each person works better at certain times of the day or for certain lengths of time. Svehaug (2013) calls this finding your *productivity sweet spot*. Self-aware people schedule complex or difficult tasks during the periods when they are most productive and simpler or routine tasks during less productive times. Finally, each individual should be cognizant of how he or she values the time of others. For example, being punctual goes beyond common courtesy. Tardiness reflects some disregard for the value of other people's time.

A lack of punctuality suggests that you do not value other people's time.

Using a Time Inventory

Because most people have an inaccurate perception of the time they spend on a particular task or the total amount of time they are productive during the day, a time inventory may provide insight. A time inventory is shown in Display 9.6. A time inventory allows you to compare what you planned to do, as outlined by your appointments and "to do" entries, with what you actually did.

Mattison (2013) notes that one of the biggest mistakes students make when they attempt to get organized is to try and squeeze all responsibilities into their week without taking into consideration that there are only 24 hours in a day. "Going without sleep, relationship time, food or exercise is not a good option" (para 6).

When using a time inventory, Mattison suggests plotting in sleep first and then the time that is immovable, including classes and clinicals. Once that is done, students should plug in the things that are important to them, such as family time or church. Next, study time and planned break times should be included in the time inventory.

Because the greatest benefit from a time inventory is being able to objectively identify patterns of behavior, it may be necessary to maintain the time inventory for several days or even several weeks. It may also be helpful to repeat the time inventory annually to see if long-term behavior changes have been noted. Remember, there is no way to beg, borrow, or steal more hours in the day. If time is habitually used ineffectively, managing time will be very stressful.

LEARNING EXERCISE 9.5

Writing a Personal Time Inventory

Use the time inventory shown in Display 9.6 to identify your activities for a 24-hour period. Record your activities on the time inventory on a regular basis. Be specific. Do not trust your memory. Star the periods of time when you were most productive. Circle periods of time when you were least productive. Do not include sleep time. Was this a typical day for you? Could you have modified your activity during your least productive time periods? If so, how?

DISPLAY 9.6　Time Inventory

5:00 AM	
6:00 AM	
6:30 AM	
7:00 AM	
7:30 AM	
8:00 AM	
8:30 AM	
9:00 AM	
9:30 AM	
10:00 AM	
10:30 AM	
11:00 AM	
11:30 AM	
12:00 PM	
12:30 PM	
1:00 PM	
1:30 PM	
2:00 PM	
2:30 PM	
3:00 PM	
3:30 PM	
4:00 PM	
4:30 PM	
5:00 PM	
5:30 PM	
6:00 PM	
6:30 PM	
7:00 PM	
7:30 PM	
8:00 PM	
8:30 PM	
9:00 PM	
9:30 PM	
10:00 PM	
11:00 PM	
12:00 PM	
1:00 AM	
2:00 AM	
3:00 AM	
4:00 AM	

INTEGRATING LEADERSHIP ROLES AND MANAGEMENT FUNCTIONS IN TIME MANAGEMENT

There is a close relationship between time management and stress. Managing time appropriately reduces stress and increases productivity. The current status of health care, the nursing shortage, and decreasing reimbursements have resulted in many health-care organizations trying to do more with less. The effective use of time management tools, therefore, becomes even more important to enable leader-managers to meet personal and professional goals.

The leadership skills needed to manage time resources draw heavily on interpersonal communication skills. The leader is a resource and role model to subordinates in how to manage time. As has been stressed in other phases of the management process, the leadership skill of self-awareness is also necessary in time management. Leaders must understand their own value system, which influences how they use time and how they expect subordinates to use time.

The management functions inherent in using time resources wisely are more related to productivity. The manager must be able to prioritize activities of unit functioning to meet short- and long-term unit needs. To do this, the leader-manager must initiate an analysis of time management on the unit level, involve team members and gain their cooperation in maximizing time use, and guide work to its conclusion and successful implementation.

Successful leader-managers are able to integrate leadership skills and management functions; they accomplish unit goals in a timely and efficient manner in a concerted effort with subordinates. They also recognize time as a valuable unit resource and share responsibility for the use of that resource with subordinates. Perhaps most importantly, the integrated leader-manager with well-developed, time management skills can maintain greater control over time and energy constraints in his or her personal and professional life.

KEY CONCEPTS

- Because time is a finite and valuable resource, learning to use it wisely is essential for effective management.

- Time management can be reduced to three cyclic steps: (a) allow time for planning and establish priorities; (b) complete the highest priority task, and whenever possible, finish one task before beginning another; and (c) reprioritize based on remaining tasks and new information that may have been received.

- Setting aside time at the beginning of each day to plan the day allows the manager to spend appropriate time on high-priority tasks.

- Many individuals fall prey to planning fallacies, where they are overly optimistic about the time it will take to complete a task.

- Making lists is an appropriate tool to manage daily tasks. This list should not be any longer than what can realistically be accomplished in a day and must include adequate time to accomplish each item on the list and time for the unexpected.

- A common cause of procrastination is failure to break large tasks down into smaller ones so that the manager can set short-term, intermediate, and long-term goals.

- Lower-level managers have more interruptions in their work than do higher-level managers. This results in situational stress and lowered job satisfaction.

- Managers must learn strategies to cope with interruptions from socializing.

(Continued)

- Because so much paperwork is redundant or unnecessary, the manager needs to develop expertise at prioritizing it and eliminating unnecessary clutter at the work site.

- An efficient filing system is invaluable to handling paper overload.

- Personal time management refers to "the knowing of self." Managing time is difficult if a person is unsure of his or her priorities, including personal short-term, intermediate, and long-term goals.

- Being punctual implies that you value other people's time and creates an imperative for them to value your time as well.

- Effective time management is an essential part of finding that balance between work life and personal life.

- Using a time inventory is one way to gain insight into how and when a person is most productive. It also assists in identifying internal time wasters.

 ## ADDITIONAL LEARNING EXERCISES AND APPLICATIONS

LEARNING EXERCISE 9.6

A Busy Day at the Public Health Agency

You work in a public health agency. It is the agency's policy that at least one public health nurse is available in the office every day. Today is your turn to remain in the office. From 1 PM to 5 PM, you will be the public health nurse at the scheduled immunization clinic; you hope to be able to spend some time finishing your end-of-month reports, which are due at 5 PM. The office stays open during lunch; you have a luncheon meeting with a Cancer Society group from noon to 1 PM today. The RN in the office is to serve as a resource to the receptionist and handle patient phone calls and drop-ins. In addition to the receptionist, you may delegate appropriately to a clerical worker. However, the clerical worker also serves the other clinic nurses and is usually fairly busy. While you are in the office today trying to finish your reports, the following interruptions occur:

8:30 AM: Your supervisor, Anne, comes in and requests a count of the diabetic and hypertensive patients seen in the last month.

9:00 AM: An upset patient is waiting to see you about her daughter who just found out that she is pregnant.

9:00 AM: Three drop-in patients are waiting to be interviewed for possible referral to the chest clinic.

9:30 AM: The public health physician calls you and needs someone to contact a family about a child's immunization.

9:30 AM: The dental department drops off 20 referrals and needs you to pull charts of these patients.

10:00 AM: A confused patient calls to find out what to do about the bills that he has received.

10:45 AM: Six families have been waiting since 8:30 AM to sign up for food vouchers.

11:45 AM: A patient calls about her drug use; she does not know what to do. She has heard about Narcotics Anonymous and wants more information now.

Assignment: How would you handle each interruption? Justify your decisions. Do not forget lunch for yourself and the two office workers. *Note:* Attempt your own solution before reading the possible solution presented in the back of this book.

LEARNING EXERCISE 9.7

Realistic Prioritizing

You are an RN providing total patient care to four patients on an orthopedic unit during the 7 AM to 3 PM shift. Given the following patient information, prioritize your activities for the shift in eight 1-hour blocks of time. Be sure to include time for reports, planning your day's activities, breaks, and lunch. Be realistic about what you can accomplish. What activities will you delegate to the next shift? What overall goals have guided your time management? What personal values or priorities were factors in setting your goals?

Room 101 A   Ms. Jones   84 years old. Fractured left hip, secondary to fall at home. Disoriented since admission, especially at night. Fall precautions ordered. Moans frequently. Being given IV pain medication every 2 hours prn. Vital signs and checks for circulation, feeling, and movement in toes ordered every 2 hours. Scheduled for surgery at 10:30 AM. Preoperative medications scheduled for 9:30 AM and 10:00 AM. Consent yet to be signed. Family members will be here at 8:00 AM and have expressed questions about the surgery and recovery period. Patient to return from surgery at approximately 2:30 PM. Will require postoperative vital signs every 15 minutes.

Room 101 B   Ms. Wilkins   26 years old. Compound fracture of the femur with postoperative fat emboli, now resolved. Ten pound Buck's traction. Has been in the hospital 3 weeks. Very bored and frustrated with prolonged hospitalization. Upset about roommate who calls out all night and keeps her from sleeping. Wants to be moved to new room. Has also requested to have hair washed during bath today. Has IV medication running at 100 mL/h. IV antibiotic piggybacks at 8:00 AM and 12:00 PM. Oral medications at 8:00 AM, 9:00 AM, and 12:00 PM.

Room 102 A   Mr. Jenkins   47 years old. T-6 quadriplegic due to diving accident 14 years ago. Two days postoperative above-knee amputation due to osteomyelitis. Cultures show methicillin-resistant *Staphylococcus aureus* (MRSA). Strict wound isolation. Has been hospitalized for 2 weeks. Expressing great deal of anger and frustration to anyone who enters room. IV site red and puffy. IV needs to be restarted. Dressing change of operative site ordered daily. Heat lamp treatments ordered b.i.d. to small pressure sores on coccyx. IV antibiotic piggybacks at 8:00 AM, 10:00 AM, 12:00 PM, and 2:00 PM. Main IV bag to run out at 10:00 AM. 6:00 AM laboratory results to be called to physician this morning. Needs total assistance in performing activities of daily living, such as bathing and feeding self.

(Continued)

Room 103 A	Mr. Novak	19 years old. Severe tear of rotator cuff in left shoulder while playing football. One-day postoperative rotator cuff repair. Very quiet and withdrawn. Refusing pain medication, which has been ordered every 2 hours prn. Says he can handle pain and does not want to "mess up his body with drugs." He wants to be recruited into professional football after this semester. Nonverbal signs of grimacing, moaning, and inability to sleep suggest that moderate pain is present. Physician states that likelihood of Mr. Novak ever playing football again is very low but has not yet told the patient. Girlfriend frequently in room at patient's bedside. IV infusing at 150 mL/h. IV antibiotics at 8:00 AM and 2:00 PM. Has not had a bath since admission 2 days ago.

LEARNING EXERCISE 9.8

Creating a Shift Time Inventory

You are a 3 PM to 11 PM shift coordinator for a skilled nursing facility. You are the only RN on your unit this shift. All the other personnel assigned to work with you this evening are unlicensed. The unit census is 21. As the shift coordinator, your responsibility is to make shift assignments, provide needed patient treatments, administer IV medications, and coordinate the work of team members. This evening, you will need to administer treatments and/or medications to the following patients:

Room 101 A	Gina Adams	88 years old. Senile dementia. Resident for 6 years. Confused—strikes out at staff. Soft wrist restraints bilaterally. Has small grade 2 pressure ulcer on coccyx, which requires evaluation and dressing change each shift.
Room 102 B	Gus Taylor	64 years old. Diabetes. New resident. Bilateral AK amputee. Right amputation 2 weeks ago. Left amputation performed 8 years ago. Needs stump dressing on right amputation site this shift. Has developed MRSA in wound site. Wound isolation ordered. IV antibiotics due at 4:00 PM and 10:00 PM tonight. Blood glucose monitoring due at 4:30 PM and 9:00 PM with sliding-scale coverage.
Room 106 A	Marvin Young	26 years old. Closed head injury 5 years ago. Resident since that time. Decerebrate posturing only. Does not follow commands. PEG feeding tube site red and inflamed; MD has not yet been notified. Needs feeding solution bag change this PM.
Room 107 A	Sheila Abood	93 years old. Functional decline. Refusing to eat. Physician has written an order not to resuscitate in the event of cardiac or respiratory failure but wants an IV line begun this PM to minimize patient dehydration. Family will also be here this PM and wants to talk about their mother's status.
Room 109 C	Tina Crowden	89 years old. Admit from local hospital, 2 weeks post-op left hip replacement. Anticipated length of stay—2 weeks. Arrives by ambulance at 3:30 PM. Needs to have admission assessment and paperwork completed and care plan started.

Oral Medications Schedule

Room 101 A–4 PM, 8 PM

Room 101 B–4 PM, 8 PM

Room 102 A–5 PM, 9 PM

Room 103 B–4 PM, 10 PM

Room 104 C–5 PM, 6 PM, 9 PM

Room 106 B–6 PM, 9 PM

Room 108 C–9 PM

Room 109 C–5 PM, 6 PM, 8 PM, 9 PM

Assignment: Create a time inventory from 3:00 PM to 11:30 PM by using 1-hour blocks of time. Plan what activities you will do during each 1-hour block. Be sure that you start with the activities you have prioritized for the shift. Also, remember that you will be in shift report from 3:00 PM to 3:30 PM and from 11:00 PM to 11:30 PM and that you need to schedule a dinner break for yourself. Allow adequate time for planning and dealing with the unexpected. Compare the inventory that you created with other students in your class. Did you identify the same priorities? Were you more focused on professional, technical, or amenity care? Will your plan require multitasking? Was the time inventory that you created realistic? Is this a workload that you believe you could handle?

LEARNING EXERCISE 9.9

Plan Your Day

It is October of your second year as Nursing Coordinator for the surgical department. A copy of your appointment calendar for Monday, October 27, follows.

You will review your unfinished business from the preceding Friday and look at the new items of business that have arrived on your desk this morning. (The new items follow the appointment calendar.) The unit ward clerk is usually free in the afternoon to provide you with 1 hour of clerical assistance, and you have a charge nurse on each shift to whom you may delegate.

1. Assign a priority to each item, with 1 being the most important and 5 being the least important.

2. Decide when you will deal with each item, being careful not to use more time than you have open on your calendar.

3. If the problem is to be handled immediately, explain how you will do this (e.g., delegated, phone call).

4. Explain the rationale for your decisions.

Monday, October 27

8:00 AM   Arrive at work

8:15 AM   Daily rounds with each head nurse in your area

8:30 AM   Continuation of daily rounds with head nurses

9:00 AM   Open

9:30 AM   Open

(Continued)

10:00 AM	Department Head meeting
10:30 AM	United Givers committee
11:00 AM	United Givers committee continued
11:30 AM	Open
Noon	Lunch
12:30 PM	Lunch
1:00 PM	Weekly meeting with administrator—budget and annual report due
1:30 PM	Open
2:00 PM	Infection control meeting
2:30 PM	Infection control meeting continued
3:00 PM	Fire drill and critique of drill
3:30 PM	Fire drill and critique of drill continued
4:00 PM	Open
4:30 PM	Open
5:00 PM	Off duty

Correspondence

Item 1

From the desk of M. Jones, personnel manager

October 24

Dear Joan:

I am sending you the names of two new graduate nurses who are interested in working in your area. I have processed their applications; they seem well qualified. Could you manage to see them as early as possible in the week? I would hate to lose these prospective employees, and they are anxious to obtain definite confirmation of employment.

Item 2

From the desk of John Brown, purchasing agent

October 23

Joan:

We really must get together this week and devise a method to control supplies. Your area has used three times the amount of thermometer covers as any other area. Are you taking that many more temperatures? This is just one of the supplies your area uses excessively. I'm open to suggestions.

Item 3

Roger Johnson, MD, chief of surgical department

October 24

Ms. Kerr:

I know you have your budget ready to submit, but I just remembered this week that I forgot to include an arterial pressure monitor. Is there another item that we can leave out? I'll drop by Monday morning, and we'll figure something out.

Item 4

October 23

Ms. Kerr:

The following personnel are due for merit raises, and I must have their completed and signed evaluations by Tuesday afternoon: Mary Rocas, Jim Newman, Marge Newfield.

M. Jones, personnel manager

Item 5

Roger Johnson, MD, chief of surgical department

October 23

Ms Kerr:

The physicians are complaining about the availability of nurses to accompany them on rounds. I believe you and I need to sit down with the doctors and head nurses to discuss this recurring problem. I have some free time Monday afternoon.

Item 6

5 AM

Joan:

Sally Knight (your regular night RN) requested a leave of absence due to her mother's illness. I told her it would be OK to take the next three nights off. She is flying out of town on the 9 AM commuter flight to San Francisco, so phone her right away if you don't want her to go. I felt I had no choice but to say yes.

Nancy Peters, night supervisor

P.S. You'll need to find a replacement for her for the next three nights.

Item 7

To: Ms Kerr

From: Administrator

Re: Patient complaint

Date: October 23

Please investigate the following patient complaint. I would like a report on this matter this afternoon.

Dear Sir:

My mother, Gertrude Boswich, was a patient in your hospital, and I just want to tell you that no member of my family will ever go there again.

She had an operation on Monday, and no one gave her a bath for 3 days. Besides that, she didn't get anything to eat for 2 days, not even water. What kind of a hospital do you run anyway?

Elmo Boswich

Item 8

To: Joan Kerr

From: Nancy Newton, RN, head nurse

Re: Problems with X-ray department

Date: October 23

We have been having problems getting diagnostic x-ray procedures scheduled for patients. Many times, patients have had to stay an extra day to get x-ray tests done. I have

(*Continued*)

talked to the radiology chief several times, but the situation hasn't improved. Can you do something about this?

Item 9

To: All department heads

From: Storeroom

Re: Supplies

Date: October 23

The storeroom is out of the following items: Toilet tissue, paper clips, disposable diapers, and pencils. We are expecting a shipment next week.

Telephone Messages

Item 10

Sam Surefoot, Superior Surgical Supplies, Inc., returned your call at 7:50 AM on October 27. He will be at the hospital this afternoon to talk about problems with defective equipment received.

Item 11

Donald Drinkley, Channel 32-TV, called at 8:10 AM on October 27 to say he will be here at 11:30 AM to do a feature story on the open-heart unit.

Item 12

Lila Green, director of nurses at St. Joan's Hospital, called at 8:05 AM on October 24 about a phone reference on Jane Jones, RN. Ms. Jones has applied for a job there. Isn't that the one we fired last year?

Item 13

Betty Brownie, Bluebird Troop 35, called at 8 AM on October 27 about the Bluebird troop visit to patients on Halloween with trick-or-treat candy. She will call again.

LEARNING EXERCISE 9.10

Avoiding Crises

Some people always seem to manage by crisis. The following scenarios depict situations that likely could have been avoided with better planning. Write down what could have been done to prevent the crisis. Then outline at least three alternatives to deal with the problem, as it already exists.

- It is the end of your 8-hour shift. Your team members are ready to go home. You have not yet begun to chart on any of your six patients. Neither have you completed your intake/output totals or given patients the medications that were due 1 hour ago. The arriving shift asks you to give your handoff report now.

- You need to use the home computer to write your midterm essay, which is due tomorrow, but your mother is online doing the family's taxes, which must be mailed by midnight. The taxes will likely take several additional hours.

- Your computer hard drive crashes when you try to print your term paper, which is due tomorrow.

- An elderly, frail patient pulls out her IV line. You make six attempts, over a 1-hour period, to restart the line but are unsuccessful. You have missed your lunch break and now must choose between taking time for lunch and finishing your shift on time.

REFERENCES

Ashurst, A. (2013). Time is of the essence: Working to a deadline. *Nursing & Residential Care, 15*(1), 50–52.

Baiyun, Q., & Quanquan, Z. (2012). An issue of public affairs management: The effect of time slack and need for cognition on prediction of task completion. *Public Personnel Management, 41*(5), 1–8.

Brans, P. (2013, January 1). *Twelve time management habits to master in 2013.* Forbes, Retrieved May 20, 2014, from http://www.forbes.com/sites/patbrans/2013/01/01/twelve-time-management-habits-to-master-in-2013

Fortier, J. (2012). More time for care. *Canadian Nurse, 108*(8), 22–27.

Hansen, R. S. (n.d.). *Is your life in balance? Work/life balance quiz. A quintessential careers quiz.* Retrieved May 20, 2013, from http://www.quintcareers.com/work-life_balance_quiz.html

Homisak, L. (2012). Time and efficiency redux: How do you take better control of your time? *Podiatry Management, 31*(3), 41–44.

Mattison, M. (2013, Feb. 8). *Time management tips for nursing school.* Chamberlain School of Nursing. Retrieved May 21, 2013, from http://blog.chamberlain.edu/2013/02/08/time-management-tips-for-nursing-school/

Pugsley, L. (2009, May). How to … study effectively. *Education for Primary Care, 20*(3), 195–197.

Svehaug, K. (2013, May 9). *3 easy steps for managing time and reaching your goals.* The Etsy Blog. Retrieved May 21, 2013, from http://www.etsy.com/blog/en/2013/time-management/

Time Management Ninja (2013, March 8). *Beware: 10 time management rules that you are breaking.* Retrieved May 21, 2014, from http://timemanagementninja.com/2013/03/beware-10-time-management-rules-that-you-are-breaking/

10

Fiscal Planning

... nurses are practicing caring in an environment where the economics and costs of health care permeate discussions and impact decisions.
—Marian C. Turkel

... the trouble with a budget is that it's hard to fill up one hole without digging another.
—Dan Bennett

CROSSWALK THIS CHAPTER ADDRESSES:

BSN Essential II: Basic organizational and systems leadership for quality care and patient safety
BSN Essential V: Health-care policy, finance, and regulatory environments
MSN Essential II: Organizational and systems leadership
MSN Essential III: Quality improvement and safety
MSN Essential VI: Health policy and advocacy
QSEN Competency: Quality improvement
QSEN Competency: Safety
AONE Nurse Executive Competency II: A knowledge of the health-care environment
AONE Nurse Executive Competency V: Business skills

LEARNING OBJECTIVES *The learner will:*

- anticipate, recognize, and creatively problem solve budgetary constraints
- accurately compute the standard formula for calculating nursing care hours per patient day (NCH/PPD)
- demonstrate cost consciousness in identifying personal and organizational needs
- define basic fiscal terminology appropriately
- differentiate among the three major types of budgets (personnel, operating, and capital) and the two most common budgeting methods (incremental and zero based)
- identify the strengths and weaknesses of flexible budgets
- recognize the need to involve subordinates and followers in fiscal planning whenever possible
- design a decision package to aid in fiscal priority setting
- describe the impetus for the development of diagnosis-related groups (DRGs), the prospective payment system (PPS), and other managed care initiatives
- describe the resulting impact on cost and quality when healthcare reimbursement shifted from a health-care system dominated by third-party, fee-for-service plans to capitated, managed care programs
- describe the impact of the increasing shift in government and private insurer reimbursement from volume to value based
- discuss how spiraling health-care costs that had little relationship to health-care outcomes led to comprehensive health-care reform in the United States in 2010
- describe key components of the *Patient Protection and Affordable Care Act* (PPACA) as well as its implementation plan between 2010 and 2014

- recognize that rapidly changing federal and state reimbursement policies make long-range budgeting and planning very difficult for health-care organizations
- describe why nurses need to understand and actively be involved in fiscal planning and healthcare reform

For at least 30 years, health-care organizations have faced unprecedented financial challenges as a result of shrinking reimbursement and rising costs. Regulatory controls have tightened, quality expectations continue to rise, and the public is increasingly demanding more and higher quality services at little to no out-of-pocket cost. Comprehensive, systematic efforts to reform this clearly broken health-care system achieved no real momentum, however, until late in the first decade of the 21st century. Even then, convergence on proposals for reform was limited so the relatively swift passage of controversial national health-care reform in the United States in March 2010 came as a surprise to many. This legislation *The Patient Protection and Affordable Care Act* (PPACA) provided the first real hope for Americans of significant reductions in numbers of uninsured, greater access to coverage for those with preexisting conditions, and mandated health-care insurance provision by employers.

In addition, the shifting in reimbursement from *volume* to *value* has accelerated with health-care reform, with the PPACA mentioning "value" 214 times (Keckley, 2013). Value can be broadly defined as a function of quality, efficiency, safety, and cost. The idea behind changing the current payment system to one which focuses on value rather than volume, was to remove incentives for redundant and inappropriate care, now estimated to account for as much as a quarter of the nation's $2.8 trillion in annual health spending (Mitchell, 2013). The PPACA's payment reform provisions include *value-based purchasing (VBP)*, *accountable care organizations* (ACOs), *bundled payments*, the *medical home*, and the *health insurance marketplace*, all of which are based on value and discussed later in this chapter. Mitchell (2013) notes, though, that for all the talk about this shift from volume to value, only 10.9% of health-care spending in 2012 by employer-sponsored plans was based on "value," as opposed to "volume," or the number of services performed.

In addition, critics suggest that while the PPACA begins to address health-care spending run amok as well as numerous health-care quality issues, that funding challenges remain. Indeed, many proposed cuts are simply reductions in projected increases and even with these cuts, stability of organizations involved in the US health care infrastructure will be at risk (Examining the Evidence 10.1).

Examining the Evidence 10.1

Source: Goozner, M. (2013). Dissecting the president's budget. Modern Healthcare, 43*(15), 25.*

Goozner critiques the 2013 federal budget related to health care, noting that the President has called for an additional $401 billion in cuts to health-care programs over the next decade, with 75% of those cuts coming from Medicare. The biggest reductions are in the drug industry and to post–acute-care providers although other programs facing sizable cuts include graduate medical education and reimbursement for clinical laboratory services.

Goozner notes, however, that these cuts are actually reductions in projected increases. Medicare is slated in the President's plan to grow from $524 billion in 2014 to $867 billion in 2023, the end of the 10-year budget window used in Washington. That's a 65% increase over the period, or an average of better than 6% a year, a figure that reflects faster growth than the rest of the economy, even when inflation is taken into account.

(Continued)

Goozner concludes that the reforms now underway through the PPACA will not harm seniors or undermine the financial viability of providers but cautions that other health-care agencies will struggle. For example, the National Institutes of Health will receive only about a 2% a year increase over the next decade to its current $31 billion budget—barely enough to keep pace with inflation. The Centers for Disease Control and Prevention will grow from $5.5 billion in 2013 to $6.1 billion in 2023—a cumulative increase of 11% or barely a percentage point increase each year on average; The Health Resources and Services Administration budget will increase by 21.8%, or about 2% a year on average, to $6.7 billion—again barely keeping pace with inflation.

Great change has also occurred in fiscal planning at the organizational level over the past three decades in terms of scope of responsibility and accountability for cost and outcomes. Prior to the 1980s, nursing management often played only a limited role in fiscal planning in health-care organizations. Nurse-managers were frequently given budgets with little rationale and were allowed only limited input in fiscal decision making. Because nursing was generally classified as a "non-income-producing service," nursing input was undervalued. Since that time, however, health-care organizations have come to recognize the importance of nursing input in fiscal planning, and nurse-leader-managers in the 21st century are expected to be expert financial managers. The reality is that nursing budgets generally account for the greatest share of the total expenses in health-care institutions, and participation in fiscal planning has become a fundamental and powerful tool for nursing.

Many nurses, however, perceive fiscal planning to be the most difficult type of planning. This is often the result of inadequate formal education or training on budget preparation as well as forecasting. It is important to remember that fiscal planning is an acquired skill that improves with use.

Fiscal planning is not intuitive; it is a learned skill that improves with practice.

Fiscal planning also requires vision, creativity, and a thorough knowledge of the political, social, and economic forces that shape health care. Fiscal planning, then, must be included in nursing program curricula and in management preparation programs. This chapter discusses the leader-manager's role in fiscal planning, identifies types of budgets, and delineates the budgetary process. Learners will also examine health-care reimbursement concepts with specific attention given to the recent change from volume-based reimbursement to value-based reimbursement. The leadership roles and management functions involved in fiscal planning are outlined in Display 10.1.

DISPLAY 10.1   Leadership Roles and Management Functions in Fiscal Planning

LEADERSHIP ROLES

1. Is visionary in identifying or forecasting short- and long-term unit needs, thus inspiring proactive rather than reactive fiscal planning.
2. Is knowledgeable about political, social, and economic factors that shape fiscal planning and reimbursement in health care today.
3. Demonstrates flexibility in fiscal goal setting in a rapidly changing system.
4. Anticipates, recognizes, and creatively solves budgetary constraints.
5. Influences and inspires group members to become active in short- and long-range fiscal planning.
6. Recognizes when fiscal constraints have resulted in an inability to meet organizational or unit goals and communicates this insight effectively, following the chain of command.
7. Ensures that patient safety is not jeopardized by cost containment.

8. Role models leadership in needed health-care reform efforts.
9. Proactively prepares followers for the plethora of changes in health care associated with health-care reform and implementation of the *Patient Protection and Affordable Cart Act.*

MANAGEMENT FUNCTIONS

1. Identifies the importance of and develops short- and long-range fiscal plans that reflect unit needs.
2. Articulates and documents unit needs effectively to higher administrative levels.
3. Assesses the internal and external environment of the organization in forecasting to identify driving forces and barriers to fiscal planning.
4. Demonstrates knowledge of budgeting and uses appropriate techniques to budget effectively.
5. Provides opportunities for subordinates to participate in relevant fiscal planning.
6. Coordinates unit-level fiscal planning to be congruent with organizational goals and objectives.
7. Accurately assesses personnel needs by using predetermined standards or an established patient classification system.
8. Coordinates the monitoring aspects of budget control.
9. Ensures that documentation of patient's need for services and services rendered is clear and complete to facilitate organizational reimbursement.
10. Collaborates with other health-care administrators to proactively determine how health-care reform initiatives such as VBP, ACOs, bundled payments, the medical home, and the health insurance marketplace may impact organizational viability and the provision of services.

BALANCING COST AND QUALITY

Complicating fiscal planning in health-care organizations today are the dual goals of cost containment and quality care, which do not always have a linear relationship. *Cost containment* refers to effective and efficient delivery of services while generating needed revenues for continued organizational productivity. Cost containment is the responsibility of every health-care provider, and the viability of most health-care organizations today depends on their ability to use their fiscal resources wisely.

Being *cost-effective*, however, is not the same as being inexpensive; *cost-effective* means producing good results for the amount of money spent; in other words, the product is worth the price (Your Dictionary, 2013). Expensive items can be cost-effective and inexpensive items may not. Cost-effectiveness then must take into account factors such as anticipated length of service, need for such a service, and availability of other alternatives.

In addition, in terms of health care, cost and quality do not have a linear relationship. Higher spending does not necessarily result in higher quality care. Sometimes, high spending represents a duplication of services, an overutilization of services, and the use of technology that exceeds a particular patient's needs. In fact, numerous studies over the past decade have examined the relationship between higher spending and the quality and outcomes of care and found that higher spending does not necessarily result in better quality care.

Spending more does not always equate to higher quality health outcomes.

These findings are true on the macro-level as well. The United States spends more per capita on health care than does any other industrialized country, and yet our outcomes in terms of teenage pregnancy rates, low–birth-weight infants, and access to care are worse than many countries that spend significantly less. The problem then is not a scarcity of resources. The problem is that we do not use the resources we have available, in a cost-effective manner.

RESPONSIBILITY ACCOUNTING AND FORECASTING

An essential feature of fiscal planning is *responsibility accounting*, which means that each of an organization's revenues, expenses, assets, and liabilities is someone's responsibility. As a corollary, the person with the most direct control or influence on any of these financial elements should be held accountable for them. At the unit level, this accountability generally falls to the manager. The leader-manager, then, should be an active participant in unit budgeting, have a high degree of control over what is included in the unit budget, receive regular data reports that compare actual expenses with budgeted expenses, and be held accountable for the financial results of the operating unit.

Because unit managers are involved in daily operations and see firsthand their unit's functioning, they often have expertise in forecasting patient census trends as well as supply and equipment needs for their units. *Forecasting* involves making an educated budget estimate by using historical data.

The unit manager also can best monitor and evaluate all aspects of a unit's budget control. Like other types of planning, the unit manager has a responsibility to communicate budgetary planning goals to the staff. The more the staff understands the budgetary goals and the plans to carry out those goals, the more likely the goal attainment is. Sadly, many nurses have little knowledge of the nursing budget model used by their hospital system.

BASICS OF BUDGETS

A *budget* is a financial plan that includes estimated expenses as well as income for a period of time. Accuracy dictates the worth of a budget; the more accurate the budget blueprint, the better the institution can plan the most efficient use of its resources.

The budget's value is directly related to its accuracy.

Because a budget is at best a prediction, a plan, and not a rule, fiscal planning requires flexibility, ongoing evaluation, and revision. In the budget, expenses are classified as fixed or variable and either controllable or noncontrollable. *Fixed* expenses do not vary with volume, whereas *variable* expenses do. Examples of fixed expenses might be a building's mortgage payment or a manager's salary; variable expenses might include the payroll of hourly wage employees and the cost of supplies.

Controllable expenses can be controlled or varied by the manager, whereas *noncontrollable* expenses cannot. For example, the unit manager can control the number of personnel working on a certain shift and the staffing mix; he or she cannot, however, control equipment depreciation, the number and type of supplies needed by patients, or overtime that occurs in response to an emergency. A list of the fiscal terminology that a manager needs to know is shown in Display 10.2.

STEPS IN THE BUDGETARY PROCESS

The nursing process provides a model for the steps in budget planning:

1. The first step is to *assess* what needs to be covered in the budget. Generally, this determination should reflect input from all levels of the organizational hierarchy, since budgeting is most effective when all personnel using the resources are involved in the process. A composite of unit needs in terms of labor, equipment, and operating expenses can then be compiled to determine the organizational budget.
2. The second step is *diagnosis*. In the case of budget planning, the diagnosis would be the goal or what needs to be accomplished, which is to create a cost-effective budget that maximizes the use of available resources.

LEARNING EXERCISE 10.1

Would You Accept This Gift?

One of the oncologists on your unit (Dr. Sam Jones) has offered to give you his old photocopier because his office is purchasing a new one. As a condition of acceptance, he requires that all the oncologists and radiologists be allowed to use the copier free of charge.

Assignment:

1. Justify acceptance or rejection of the gift. What influenced your choice?

2. What are the fixed and variable costs?

3. What are the controllable and noncontrollable costs?

4. What factors determine whether the use of Dr. Jones gift is cost effective?

4. How much control will you, as a unit manager, have over the use of the copier?

DISPLAY 10.2 **Fiscal Terminology**

Accountable Care Organizations (ACOs)—Groups of providers and suppliers of service who work together to better coordinate care for Medicare patients (does not include Medicare Advantage) across care settings.

Acuity index—Weighted statistical measurement that refers to severity of illness of patients for a given time. Patients are classified according to acuity of illness, usually in one of four categories. The acuity index is determined by taking a total of acuities and then dividing by the number of patients.

Affordable Care Act—Officially known as the *Patient Protection and Affordable Care Act*, this act passed in March 2010 to assure that all Americans have access to affordable health insurance by reducing the barriers to obtaining health coverage as well as accessing needed health-care services.

Assets—Financial resources that a health-care organization receives, such as accounts receivable.

Baseline data—Historical information on dollars spent, acuity level, patient census, resources needed, hours of care, and so forth. This information is used as basis on which future needs can be projected.

Break-even point—Point at which revenue covers costs. Most health-care facilities have high fixed costs. Because per-unit fixed costs in a noncapitated model decrease with volume, health-care facilities under this model need to maintain a high volume to decrease unit costs.

Bundled payment—A payment structure in which different health-care providers who are treating a patient for the same or related conditions are paid an overall sum for taking care of that condition rather than being paid for each individual treatment, test, or procedure. In doing so, providers are rewarded for coordinating care, preventing complications and errors, and reducing unnecessary or duplicative tests and treatments (Healthcare.gov, 2013b).

Capitation—A prospective payment system (PPS) that pays health plans or providers a fixed amount per enrollee per month for a defined set of health services, regardless of how many (if any) services are used.

Case mix—Type of patients served by an institution. A hospital's case mix is usually defined in such patient-related variables as acuity levels, diagnosis, personal characteristics, and patterns of treatment.

Cash flow—Rate at which dollars are received and dispersed.

Controllable costs—Costs that can be controlled or that vary. An example would be the number of personnel employed, the level of skill required, wage levels, and quality of materials.

Cost–benefit ratio—Numerical relationship between the value of an activity or procedure in terms of benefits and the value of the activity's or procedure's cost. The cost–benefit ratio is expressed as a fraction.

Cost center—Smallest functional unit for which cost control and accountability can be assigned. A nursing unit is usually considered a cost center, but there may be other cost centers within a

(Continued)

unit (orthopedics is a cost center, but often the cast room is considered a separate cost center within orthopedics).

Diagnosis-related groups (DRGs)—Rate-setting PPS used by Medicare to determine payment rates for an inpatient hospital stay based on admission diagnosis. Each DRG represents a particular case type for which Medicare provides a flat dollar amount of reimbursement. This set rate may, in actuality, be higher or lower than the cost of treating the patient in a particular hospital.

Direct costs—Costs that can be attributed to a specific source, such as medications and treatments. Costs that are clearly identifiable with goods or service.

Fee-for-service (FFS) system—A reimbursement system under which insurance companies reimburse health-care providers after the needed services are delivered.

Fixed budget—Style of budgeting that is based on a fixed, annual level of volume, such as number of patient-days or tests performed, to arrive at an annual budget total. These totals are then divided by 12 to arrive at the monthly average. The fixed budget does not make provisions for monthly or seasonal variations.

Fixed costs—Costs that do not vary according to volume. Examples of fixed costs are mortgage or loan payments.

For-profit organization—Organization in which the providers of funds have an ownership interest in the organization. These providers own stocks in the for-profit organization and earn dividends based on what is left when the cost of goods and of carrying on the business is subtracted from the amount of money taken in.

Full costs—Total of all direct and indirect costs.

Full-time equivalent (FTE)—Number of hours of work for which a full-time employee is scheduled for a weekly period. For example, 1.0 FTE = five 8-hour days of staffing, which equals 40 hours of staffing per week. One FTE can be divided in different ways. For example, two part-time employees, each working 20 hours per week, would equal 1 FTE. If a position requires coverage for more than 5 days or 40 hours per week, the FTE will be greater than 1.0 for that position. Assume a position requires 7-day coverage, or 56 hours, then the position requires 1.4 FTE coverage (56/40 = 1.4). This means that more than one person is needed to fill the FTE positions for a 7-day period.

Health maintenance organization (HMO)—Historically, a prepaid organization that provided health care to voluntarily enrolled members in return for a preset amount of money on a per-person, per-month basis. Often referred to as a managed care organization (MCO).

Hours per patient-day (HPPD)—Hours of nursing care provided per patient per day by various levels of nursing personnel. HPPD are determined by dividing total production hours by the number of patients.

International Classification of Disease (ICD) codes—Coding used to report the severity and treatment of patient diseases, illnesses, and injuries to determine appropriate reimbursement. Currently in its 10th revision, ICD-10 will replace ICD-9 in October 2014, and hospitals will be required to make this transition to comply with Health Insurance Portability and Accountability Act of 1996 (HIPAA) requirements.

Indirect costs—Costs that cannot be directly attributed to a specific area. These are hidden costs and are usually spread among different departments. Housekeeping services are considered indirect costs.

Managed care—Term used to describe a variety of health-care plans designed to contain the cost of health-care services delivered to members while maintaining the quality of care.

Medicaid—Federally assisted and state-administered program to pay for medical services on behalf of certain groups of low-income individuals. Generally, these individuals are not covered by Social Security. Certain groups of people (e.g., the elderly, blind, disabled, members of families with dependent children, and certain other children and pregnant women) also qualify for coverage if their incomes and resources are sufficiently low.

Medicare—Nationwide health insurance program authorized under Title 18 of the Social Security Act that provides benefits to people aged 65 years or older. Medicare coverage also is available to certain groups of people with catastrophic or chronic illness, such as patients with renal failure requiring hemodialysis, regardless of age.

Noncontrollable costs—Indirect expenses that cannot usually be controlled or varied. Examples might be rent, lighting, and depreciation of equipment.

Not-for-profit organization—This type of organization is financed by funds that come from several sources, but the providers of these funds do not have an ownership interest. Profits generated in the not-for-profit organization are frequently funneled back into the organization for expansion or capital acquisition.

Operating expenses—Daily costs required to maintain a hospital or health-care institution.

Patient classification system—Method of classifying patients. Different criteria are used for different systems. In nursing, patients are usually classified according to acuity.

Pay for performance (also known as P4P) programs—Incentives are paid to providers to achieve a targeted threshold of clinical performance, typically a process or outcome measure associated with a specified patient population (Keckley, 2013).

Pay for value programs—Typically, these incentive payments are specific to a provider setting (i.e., hospital inpatient or outpatient, physician, home health, skilled nursing facility, and dialysis) and linked to both quality and efficiency improvements (Keckley, 2013).

Preferred provider organization (PPO)—Health-care financing and delivery program with a group of providers, such as physicians and hospitals, who contract to give services on an FFS basis. This provides financial incentives to consumers to use a select group of preferred providers and pay less for services. Insurance companies usually promise the PPO a certain volume of patients and prompt payment in exchange for fee discounts.

Production hours—Total amount of regular time, overtime, and temporary time. This also may be referred to as actual hours.

Prospective payment system—A hospital payment system with predetermined reimbursement ratio for services given.

Revenue—Source of income or the reward for providing a service to a patient.

Staffing mix—Ratio of registered nurses (RNs), licensed vocational nurses (LVNs)/licensed professional nurses (LPNs), and unlicensed workers (e.g., a shift on one unit might have 40% RNs, 40% LPNs/LVNs, and 20% others). Hospitals vary on their staffing mix policies.

Third-party payment system—A system of health-care financing in which providers deliver services to patients, and a third party, or intermediary, usually an insurance company or a government agency, pays the bill.

Turnover ratio—Rate at which employees leave their jobs for reasons other than death or retirement. The rate is calculated by dividing the number of employees leaving by the number of workers employed in the unit during the year and then multiplying by 100.

Value-Based Purchasing—A payment methodology that rewards quality of care through payment incentives and transparency. In VBP, value can be broadly considered to be a function of quality, efficiency, safety, and cost (Keckley, 2013).

Variable costs—Costs that vary with the volume. Payroll costs are an example.

Workload units—In nursing, workloads are usually the same as patient-days. For some areas, however, workload units might refer to the number of procedures, tests, patient visits, injections, and so forth.

3. The third step is to develop a *plan*. The budget plan may be developed in many ways. A budgeting cycle that is set for 12 months is called a *fiscal-year budget*. This fiscal year, which may or may not coincide with the calendar year, is then usually broken down into quarters or subdivided into monthly or semiannual periods. Most budgets are developed for a 1-year period, but a *perpetual budget* may be done on a continual basis each month so that 12 months of future budget data are always available.

Selecting the optimal time frame for budgeting is also important. Errors are more likely if the budget is projected too far in advance. If the budget is shortsighted, compensating for unexpected major expenses or purchasing capital equipment may be difficult.

 A budget that is predicted too far in advance has greater probability for error.

4. The fourth step is *implementation*. In this step, ongoing monitoring and analysis occur to avoid inadequate or excess funds at the end of the fiscal year. In most health-care institutions, monthly statements outline each department's projected budget and deviations from that budget. Some managers artificially inflate their department budgets as a cushion against budget cuts from a higher level of administration. If several departments partake in this unsound practice, the entire institutional budget may be ineffective. If a major change in the budget is indicated, the entire budgeting process must be repeated. Top-level managers must watch for and correct unrealistic budget projections before they are implemented.

5. The last step is *evaluation*. The budget must be reviewed periodically and modified as needed throughout the fiscal year. Each unit manager is accountable for budget deviations in his or her unit. Most units can expect some change from the anticipated budget, but large deviations must be examined for possible causes and remedial action taken if necessary.

TYPES OF BUDGETS

Three major types of budgets that the nurse-manager may be directly involved in with fiscal planning are personnel, operating, and capital budgets.

The Personnel Budget

The largest of the budget expenditures is the *workforce* or *personnel budget* because health care is *labor intensive*. To handle fluctuating patient census and acuity, managers need to use historical data about unit census fluctuations in forecasting short- and long-term personnel needs. Likewise, a manager must monitor the personnel budget closely to prevent understaffing or overstaffing. As patient-days or volume decreases, managers must decrease personnel costs in relation to the decrease in volume.

The largest of the budget expenditures is the *workforce* or *personnel budget* because health care is *labor intensive*.

In addition to numbers of staff, the manager must be cognizant of the *staffing mix*. Staffing mix refers to the mix (percentages) of licensed (RN and LVN) and unlicensed (certified nursing assistant [CNA], and unlicensed assistive personnel) staff working at a given time. The manager must also be aware of the patient acuity so that the most economical level of nursing care that will meet patient needs can be provided.

Although Unit V discusses staffing, it is necessary to briefly discuss here how staffing needs are expressed in the personnel budget. Most staffing is based on a predetermined *standard*. This standard may be addressed in HPPD (medical units), visits per month (home health agencies), or minutes per case (the operating room). Because the patient census, number of visits, or cases per day never remains constant, the manager must be ready to alter staffing when volume increases or decreases. Sometimes, the population and type of cases change so that the established standard is no longer appropriate. For example, an operating room that begins to perform open-heart surgery would involve more nursing time per case; therefore, the standard (number of nursing minutes per case) would need to be adjusted. Normally, the standard is adjusted upward or downward once a year, but staffing is adjusted daily depending on the volume.

The standard formula for calculating *nursing care hours (NCH) per patient-day (PPD)* is shown in Figure 10.1. A unit manager in an acute care facility might use this formula to calculate daily staffing needs. For example, assume that your budgeted NCH are 6 NCH/PPD.

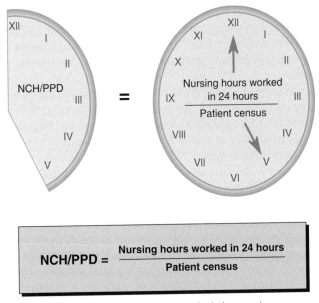

FIGURE 10.1 • Standard formula for calculating nursing care hours per patient-day. Copyright ® 2006 Lippincott Williams & Wilkins. Instructor's Resource CD-ROM to Accompany Leadership Roles and Management Functions in Nursing, by Bessie L. Marquis and Carol J. Huston.

You are calculating the NCH/PPD for today, January 31; at midnight, it will be February 1. The patient census at midnight is 25 patients. In checking staffing, you find the following information:

Shift	Staff on Duty	Hours Worked
11 PM (1/30) to 7 AM (1/31)	2 RNs	8 h each
	1 LVN	8 h
	1 CNA	8 h
7 AM to 3 PM	3 RNs	8 h each
	2 LVNs	8 h each
	1 CNA	8 h
	1 ward clerk	8 h
3 PM to 11 PM	2 RNs	8 h each
	2 LVNs	8 h each
	1 CNA	8 h
	1 ward clerk	8 h
11 PM (1/31) to 7 AM (2/1)	2 RNs	8 h each
	2 LVNs	8 h each
	1 CNA	8 h

Ideally, you would use 12 midnight to compute the NCH/PPD for January 31, but most staffing calculations based on traditional 8-hour shifts are made beginning at 11 PM and ending at 11 PM the following night. Therefore, in this case, it would be acceptable to figure the NCH/PPD for January 31 by using numerical data from the 11 PM to 7 AM shift last night and the 7 AM to 3 PM and 3 PM to 11 PM shifts today. The first step in this calculation requires a computation of total NCH worked in 24 hours (including the ward clerk's hours). This can be calculated by multiplying the total number of staff on duty each shift by the hours each worked in their shift. Each shift total then is added together to get the total number of nursing hours worked in all three shifts or 24 hours: The nursing hours worked in 24 hours are 136 hours.

The second step in solving NCH/PPD requires that you divide the nursing hours worked in 24 hours by the patient census. The patient census in this case is 25. Therefore, 136/25 = 5.44.

The NCH/PPD for January 31 was 5.44, which is less than your budgeted NCH/PPD of 6.0. It would be possible to add up to 14 additional hours of nursing care in the next 24 hours and still maintain the budgeted NCH standard. However, the unit manager must remember that the standard is flexible and that patient acuity and staffing mix may suggest the need for even more staff for February 1 than the budgeted NCH/PPD.

The personnel budget includes actual *worked time* (also called *productive time* or *salary expense*) and time that the organization pays the employee for not working (*nonproductive or benefit time*). Nonproductive time includes the cost of benefits, new employee orientation, employee turnover, sick and holiday time, and education time. For example, the average 8.5-hour shift includes a 30-minute lunch break and two 15-minute breaks. Thus, this employee would work 7.5 productive hours and have 1.0 hours of nonproductive time.

LEARNING EXERCISE 10.2

Calculating NCH/PPD

Calculate the NCH/PPD if the midnight census is 25, but use the following as the number of hours worked:

12 midnight to 12 noon	2 RNs	12 h each
	2 LVNs	12 h each
	1 can	12 h
	1 ward clerk	5 h
12 noon to 12 midnight	3 RNs	12 h each
	2 LVNs	12 h each
	1 can	12 h
	1 ward clerk	12 h

Now, calculate the NCH/PPD if the following staff were working:

12 midnight to 12 noon	3 RNs	12 h each
	1 LVN	12 h
12 noon to 12 midnight	2 RNs	12 h each
	1 LVN	12 h
	1 ward clerk	4 h

The Operating Budget

The *operating budget* is the second area of expenditure that involves all managers. The operating budget reflects expenses that change in response to the volume of service, such as the cost of electricity, repairs and maintenance, and supplies. While personnel costs lead the hospital budget, the cost of supplies runs a close second.

 Next to personnel costs, *supplies* are the second most significant component in the hospital budget.

Effective unit managers should be alert to the types and quantities of supplies used in their unit. They should also understand the relationship between supply use and patient mix, occupancy rate, technology requirements, and types of procedures performed on the unit. Saving unused supplies from packs or trays, reducing obsolete and slow-moving inventory, eliminating pilferage, and monitoring the uncontrolled usage of supplies and giveaways all represent potential cost savings. Other ways to cut supply costs might be in rental versus facility-owned equipment, stocking products on consignment, and just-in-time stockless inventory. *Just-in-time ordering* is a process whereby inventory is delivered to the organization by suppliers only when it is needed and immediately before it is to be used.

LEARNING EXERCISE 10.3

Missing Supplies

You are a unit manager in an acute care hospital. You are aware that staff occasionally leave at the end of the shift with forgotten hospital supplies in their pockets. You remember how often as a staff nurse you would unintentionally take home rolls of adhesive tape, syringes, penlights, and bottles of lotion. Usually, you remembered to return the items, but other times you did not.

Recently, however, your budget has shown a dramatic and unprecedented increase in missing supplies, including gauze wraps, blood pressure cuffs, stethoscopes, surgical instruments, and personal hygiene kits. Although this increase represents only a fraction of your total operating budget, you believe that it is necessary to identify the source of their use. An audit of patient charts and charges reveals that these items were not used in patient care.

When you ask your charge nurses for an explanation, they reveal that a few employees have openly expressed that taking a few small supplies is, in effect, an expected and minor fringe benefit of employment. Your charge nurses do not believe that the problem is widespread, and they cannot objectively document which employees are involved in pilfering supplies. The charge nurses suggest that you ask all employees to document in writing when they see other employees taking supplies and then turn in the information to you anonymously for follow-up.

Assignment: Because supplies are such a major part of the operating budget, you believe that some action is indicated. You must determine what that action should be. Analyze your actions in terms of the desirable and undesirable effects on the employees involved in taking the supplies and those who are not. Is the amount of the fiscal debit in this situation a critical factor? Is it worth the time and energy that would be required to truly eliminate this problem?

The Capital Budget

The third type of budget used by managers is the *capital budget.* Capital budgets plan for the purchase of buildings or major equipment, which include equipment that has a long life (usually greater than 5 to 7 years), is not used in daily operations, and is more expensive than operating supplies. Capital budgets are composed of long-term planning, or a major acquisitions component, and a short-term budgeting component. The long-term major acquisitions component outlines future replacement and organizational expansion that will exceed 1 year. Examples of these types of capital expenditures might include the acquisition of a positron emission tomography imager or the renovation of a major wing in a hospital. The short-term component of the capital budget includes equipment purchases within the annual budget cycle, such as call-light systems, hospital beds, and medication carts.

Often, the designation of capital equipment requires that the value of the equipment exceed a certain dollar amount. That dollar amount will vary from institution to institution, but $1,000 to $5,000 is common. Managers are usually required to complete specific capital equipment request forms either annually or semiannually and to justify their request. Capital *"budget busters"* are noted in Display 10.3.

DISPLAY 10.3	Budget Busters

- Going through the difficult process of completing a budget estimate for the coming year but never using it.
- Relying on the current year's budget numbers as a starting point for the next year's budget.
- Neglecting or underestimating costs related to capital expenditures.
- Ignoring declining patient volumes in the hope that the trend will be temporary.
- Failing to set aside enough money for unexpected capital expenses.

Source: Adapted from Barr, P. (2005). Flexing your budget: Experts urge hospitals, systems to trade in their traditional budgeting process for a more dynamic and versatile model. Modern Healthcare, 35(37), 24, 26.

BUDGETING METHODS

Budgeting is frequently classified according to how often it occurs and the base on which budgeting takes place. Four of the most common budgeting methods are incremental budgeting (also called flat-percentage increase budgeting), zero-based budgeting, flexible budgeting, and new performance budgeting.

Incremental Budgeting

Incremental or the *flat-percentage increase method* is the simplest method for budgeting. By multiplying current-year expenses by a certain figure, usually the inflation rate or consumer price index, the budget for the coming year may be projected. Although this method is simple and quick and requires little budgeting expertise on the part of the manager, it is generally inefficient fiscally because there is no motivation to contain costs and no need to prioritize programs and services. Hospitals have historically used incremental budgeting in fiscal planning.

Zero-Based Budgeting

In comparison, managers who use *zero-based budgeting* must rejustify their program or needs every budgeting cycle. This method does not automatically assume that because a program has been funded in the past, it should continue to be funded. Thus, this budgeting process is labor intensive for nurse-managers. The use of a *decision package* to set funding priorities is a key feature of zero-based budgeting. Key components of decision packages are shown in Display 10.4.

DISPLAY 10.4	Key Components of Decision Packages in Zero-Based Budgeting

1. Listing of all current and proposed objectives or activities in the department.
2. Alternative plans for carrying out these activities.
3. Costs for each alternative.
4. Advantages and disadvantages of continuing or discontinuing an activity.

The following is an *example* of a decision package for implementing a mandatory hepatitis B vaccination program at a nursing school.

Objective: All nursing students will complete a hepatitis B vaccination series.

Driving forces: Hepatitis B is a severely disabling disease that carries significant mortality. The Occupational Safety and Health Association (OSHA) requires that hepatitis B vaccine be offered to health-care workers (which includes student nurses) who have a reasonable expectation of being exposed to blood on the job. Vaccination greatly reduces the risk of contracting this disease. The current vaccination series has proven to have few serious side effects. The nursing school risks liability if it does not follow recommendations to have all high-risk groups vaccinated.

Restraining forces: The vaccination series costs $300 per student. Some students do not want to have the vaccinations and believe that requiring them to do so is a violation of free choice. It is unclear whether the school is liable if a student experiences a side effect from the vaccinations.

Alternative 1: Require the vaccinations. Because the school of nursing cannot afford to pay for the cost of the series, require that the students pay for it.

Advantage: No cost to the school. All students receive the vaccinations.

Disadvantage: Many students cannot afford the cost of the vaccination and believe that requiring it infringes on their right to control choices about their bodies.

Alternative 2: Do not require the vaccination series.

Advantage: No cost to anyone. Students have choice regarding whether to have the vaccinations and assume the responsibility of protecting their health themselves.

Disadvantage: Some nursing students will be unprotected against hepatitis B while working in a high-risk clinical setting.

Alternative 3: Require the vaccination series but share the cost between the student and the school.

Advantage: Decreased cost to students. All students would be vaccinated.

Disadvantage: Costs and limited choice.

Decision packages and zero-based budgeting are advantageous because they force managers to set priorities and to use resources most efficiently. This rather lengthy and complex method also encourages participative management because information from peers and subordinates is needed to analyze adequately and prioritize the activities of each unit.

LEARNING EXERCISE 10.4

Developing a Decision Package

Given the following objective, develop a decision package to aid you in fiscal priority setting.

Objective: To have reliable, economic, and convenient transportation when you enter nursing school in 3 months.

Additional information: You currently have no car and rely on public transportation, which is inexpensive and reliable but not very convenient. Your current financial resources are limited, although you could probably qualify for a car loan if your parents were willing to cosign the loan. Your nursing school's policy states that you must have a car available to commute to clinical agencies outside the immediate area. You know that this policy is not enforced and that some students do carpool to clinical assignments.

Assignment: Identify at least three alternatives that will meet your objective. Choose the best alternative based on the advantages and disadvantages that you identify. You may embellish information presented in the case to help your problem solving.

Flexible Budgeting

Flexible budgets are budgets that flex up and down over the year depending on volume. A flexible budget automatically calculates what the expenses should be, given the volume that is occurring. This works well in many health-care organizations as a result of changing census and manpower needs that are difficult to predict, despite historical forecasting tools.

Performance Budgeting

The fourth method of budgeting, *performance budgeting*, emphasizes outcomes and results instead of activities or outputs. Thus, the manager would budget as needed to achieve specific outcomes and would evaluate budgetary success accordingly. For example, a home health agency would set and then measure a specific outcome in a group, such as diabetic patients, as a means of establishing and justifying a budget.

CRITICAL PATHWAYS

Critical pathways (also called *clinical pathways* and *care pathways*) are a strategy for assessing, implementing, and evaluating the cost-effectiveness of patient care. These pathways reflect relatively standardized predictions of patients' progress for a specific diagnosis or procedure. For example, a critical pathway for a specific diagnosis might suggest an average length of stay of 4 days, with certain interventions completed by certain points on the pathway (much like a PERT diagram; see page 23). Patient progress that differs from the critical pathway prompts a *variance analysis*.

Critical pathways are predetermined courses of progress that patients should make after admission for a specific diagnosis or after a specific surgery.

First developed in the 1980s as a tool to reduce length of stay, critical pathways also provide a useful tool for monitoring quality of care. Once the cost of a pathway is known, analyzing the cost-effectiveness of the pathway as well as the associated cost variances is possible. By using clinical and cost variance data, decisions on changing the pathway can be made with both clinical and financial outcome projections.

The advantage of critical pathways is that they do provide some means of standardizing care for patients with similar diagnoses. Their weakness, however, is the difficulties they pose in accounting for and accepting what are often justifiable differentiations between unique patients who have deviated from their pathway. Critical pathway documentation also poses one more paperwork and utilization review function in a system already burdened with administrative costs. Despite these challenges, research suggests that critical pathways can standardize care according to evidence-based best practices, leading to improved patient outcomes.

HEALTH-CARE REIMBURSEMENT

Historically, health-care institutions used incremental budgeting and placed little or no emphasis on budgeting. Because insurance carriers reimbursed fully on virtually a limitless basis, there was little motivation to save costs and organizations found it unnecessary to justify charges. Reimbursement was based on costs incurred to provide the service plus profit (*FFS*), with no ceiling placed on the total amount that could be charged. Indeed, under FFS, the more services provided, the greater the amount that could be billed, encouraging the overtreatment of clients.

The end result of uncontrolled FFS reimbursement was skyrocketing health-care costs with health care increasingly assuming a greater percentage of gross domestic product (GDP) each year. Currently, the United States spends more of its GDP on medical care than any other nation, almost 18%. "After gobbling up a rapidly increasing share of our national economy over the past three decades, health-care spending has flattened out over the past few years. It grew from $2.5 trillion in 2009 to $2.7 trillion in 2011, but as a share of GDP it stayed flat over this 3 year period" (Rosenberg, 2013, para 3). Much of the recent stabilization in overall health-care spending, however, was not due to increased efficiencies in health-care delivery; it was due to the effects of the recession, as people who lost their jobs—and the health benefits that came with them, with enrollment in private insurance plans dropping by 11.2 million from 2007 to 2010.

 The United States spends more of its GDP on medical care than any other nation in the world.

MEDICARE AND MEDICAID

The US federal government became a major insurer of health care with the advent of Medicare and Medicaid in the mid-1960s. *Medicare* is a federally sponsored health insurance program for the elderly (older than 65 years) and for certain groups of people with catastrophic or chronic illness, regardless of age. Medicare currently provides coverage for items and services for more than 49 million beneficiaries, approximately 16% of the US population (Kaiser Family Foundation, 2013). Just over 83% of enrollees are elderly, more than 16% are disabled, and 0.9% have end-stage renal disease.

Between 2000 and 2010, Medicare spending grew as fast as or faster than increases in private expenditures (Urban Institute, 2012). But Medicare enrollment increased while private health insurance coverage fell and participation in Medicare is expected to increase dramatically in the coming years as the result of the aging population. Indeed, Sahadi (2013) suggests that the number of Medicare beneficiaries who will enroll in the program will grow by 36%, or an estimated 18 million people, between 2012 and 2023. That trend is likely to continue, given that the number of Baby Boomers turning 65 is projected to grow from an average of about 7,600 per day in 2011 to more than 11,000 per day in 2029 (Sahadi).

Part A Medicare is the hospital insurance program. *Part B Medicare* is the supplementary medical insurance program that pays for outpatient care (including laboratory and X-ray services) and physician (or other primary care provider) services. *Part C Medicare* (now called *Medicare Advantage*) allows patients more choices for participating in managed care plans. And the newest, *Medicare Part D*, which became effective January 1, 2006, allows Medicare patients to purchase at least limited prescription drug coverage. Approximately 12.6 million beneficiaries participate in Medicare Advantage and 39.33% participate in Medicare Part D (Kaiser Family Foundation). Out-of-pocket costs for Medicare beneficiaries as of 2013 are shown in Table 10.1.

TABLE 10.1   Medicare Costs Per Beneficiary in 2013

MEDICARE INSURANCE PLAN	Cost
Part B premium	Typically $104.90 each month
Part B deductible	$147 per year
Part A premium	Most people do not pay a monthly premium for Part A. The cost for Part A is up to $441 each month
Part A hospital inpatient deductible	Beneficiaries pay: • Days 1–60: $1,184 for each benefit period • Days 61–90: $296 coinsurance per day of each benefit period • Days 91 and beyond: $592 coinsurance per each "lifetime reserve day" after day 90 for each benefit period (up to 60 d over your lifetime) • Beyond lifetime reserve days: all costs
Part C	Monthly premium varies by plan
Part D	Monthly premium varies by plan (higher income consumers may pay more, up to $66.60 plus plan premium)

Source: Medicare.Gov. (2013). Medicare 2013 Costs at a Glance. Retrieved May 26, 2013 from http://www .medicare.gov/your-medicare-costs/costs-at-a-glance/costs-at-glance.html

Medicaid is a federal–state cooperative health insurance plan created primarily for the financially indigent (low-income children and adults) although it also provides medical and long-term care coverage for people with disabilities, and assistance with health and long-term care expenses for low-income seniors. Between 2011 and 2020, overall Medicaid expenditures are projected to grow between 8.1% and 8.7% (Urban Institute, 2012). Increases in overall Medicaid spending will continue to be driven by enrollment growth largely because of the *Affordable Care Act*. Both Medicare and Medicaid are coordinated by the *Centers for Medicare and Medicaid Services* (CMS).

THE PROSPECTIVE PAYMENT SYSTEM

With the advent of Medicare and Medicaid and FFS reimbursement, health-care costs skyrocketed as large segments of the population that previously had no or limited coverage began accessing services. In addition, health-care providers saw the government as having "deep pockets," which suggested almost limitless reimbursement and began providing services accordingly. As a result of rapidly escalating costs, the government began establishing regulations requiring organizations to justify the need for services and to monitor the quality of services. Health-care providers were forced for the first time to submit budgets and justify costs. This new surveillance and existence of external controls had a tremendous effect on the health-care industry.

The advent of DRGs in the early 1980s added to the need for monitoring cost containment. DRGs were predetermined payment schedules that reflected historical costs for treatment of specific patient conditions. *Medicare Severity* DRGs were implemented in 2007 and have been updated annually since.

In addition, hospitals use the ICD to code diseases, signs and symptoms, and abnormal findings. Currently in its 10th revision, ICD-10 will replace ICD-9 in October 2014, and hospitals will be required to make this transition to comply with HIPAA requirements. ICD-10 will provide significantly more coding options for treatment, reporting, and payment processes, including more than 68,000 clinical modification codes as compared with 15,000 in ICD-9 (Centers for Medicare & Medicaid Services, 2013).

With DRGs, hospitals joined the PPS, whereby they receive a specified amount for each Medicare patient's admission, regardless of the actual cost of care. Exceptions to this occur when providers can demonstrate that a patient's case is an *outlier*, meaning that the cost of providing care for that patient justifies extra payment. PPS and consequent cost-containment efforts lead to decreased length of stays for most patients.

As a result of the PPS and the need to contain costs, the length of stay for most hospital admissions has decreased greatly.

Many argue that quality standards have been lowered as a result of the PPS and that patients are being discharged before they are ready. It is the nurse-leader's responsibility to recognize when cost containment is impinging on patient safety and to take appropriate action to guarantee at least a minimum standard of care. Chapter 23 further discusses the PPS and its impact on quality control.

The government again deeply affected health-care administration in the United States in 1997 with the passage of the *Balanced Budget Act* (BBA). This act contained numerous cost-containment measures, including reductions in provider payments for traditional FFS Medicare program participants. The bulk of the savings resulted from limiting the growth rates for hospital and physician payments. A second major source of savings derived from restructuring the payment methods for rehabilitation hospitals, home health agencies, skilled nursing facilities, and outpatient services. The BBA also, for the first time, authorized payments to nurse practitioners for Medicare-provided services at 85% of the physician-fee schedule.

The ever-increasing impact of the federal government on how health care is delivered in the United States must be recognized. Accompanying this funding is an increase in regulations for facilities treating these patients and a system that rewards cost containment. Health-care providers are encountering financial crises as they attempt to meet unlimited health-care needs and services with limited fiscal reimbursement. Competition has intensified, reimbursement levels have declined, and utilization controls have increased. In addition, rapidly changing federal and state reimbursement policies make long-range budgeting and planning very difficult for health-care facilities.

THE MANAGED CARE MOVEMENT

Managed care has been a significant factor affecting health-care delivery and reimbursement since the early 1990s. Broadly defined, *managed care* is a system that attempts to integrate efficiency of care, access, and cost of care. Common denominators in managed care include the use of primary care providers as "*gatekeepers*," a focus on prevention, a decreased emphasis on inpatient hospital care, the use of clinical practice guidelines for providers, and *selective contracting* (whereby providers agree to lower reimbursement levels in exchange for patient population contracts). Managed care typically uses formularies to manage pharmacy care and focuses on continuous quality monitoring and improvement.

Utilization review is another common component of managed care. *Utilization review* is a process used by insurance companies to assess the need for medical care and to assure that payment will be provided for the care. Utilization review typically includes precertification or preauthorization for elective treatments, concurrent review, and, if necessary, retrospective review for emergency cases.

Another frequent hallmark of managed care is *capitation*, whereby providers receive a fixed monthly payment regardless of services used by that patient during the month. If the cost to provide care to someone is less than the capitated amount, the provider profits. If the cost is greater than the capitated amount, the provider suffers a loss. The goal, then, for capitated providers is to see that patients receive the essential services to stay healthy or to keep from becoming ill but to eliminate unnecessary use of health-care services. Critics of capitation argue that this reimbursement strategy leads to undertreatment of patients. A summary of managed care characteristics is found in Display 10.5.

Types of Managed Care Organizations

One of the most common types of MCOs is the HMO. An HMO is a corporate body funded by insurance premiums. The HMO's physicians and other professionals practice medicine within certain financial, geographic, and professional limits to individuals and families who have enrolled in the HMO. The *Health Maintenance Organization Act of 1973* authorized spending $375 million over 5 years to set up and evaluate HMOs in communities across the country. Although HMOs originated as an alternative to traditional health insurance plans, some of the largest private insurers, including Blue Cross and Blue Shield and Aetna, have created HMOs within their organization while maintaining their traditional indemnity plans.

In discussing HMOs, it is important to remember that there are different types of HMOs as well as different types of plans within HMOs to which members may subscribe. Several types of HMOs include (a) *staff*, (b) *independent practice association* (IPA), (c) *group*, and (d) *network*. In *staff HMOs*, physician providers are salaried by the HMO and under direct control of the HMO. In *IPA HMOs*, the HMO contracts with a group of physicians through an intermediary to provide services for members of the HMO. In a *group HMO*, the HMO

DISPLAY 10.5 Managed Care at a Glance

- Represents a wide range of financing alternatives that focus on managing the cost and quality of health care by:
    Using panels of selectively contracted providers
    Limiting benefits to subscribers who use noncontracted providers
    Implementing some type of authorization system
    Focusing on primary care rather than specialists and inpatient services
    Emphasizing preventive health care
    Relying on clinical practice guidelines for providers
    Regularly reviewing the use of health-care resources
    Continuously monitoring and improving the quality of health services
- Patients have less choice about the providers they can see and services they can access, in exchange for small copayments and no deductibles.
- MCOs often use primary care *gatekeepers* to:

    Be sure that the provider-ordered services are needed and appropriate
    See that patients are cared for in outpatient settings whenever possible
    Ration care by queuing and wait times for authorizations
    Encourage providers to follow more standardized care pathways and clinical guidelines for treatment
- Managed care is based on the concept of *capitation*, whereby providers prospectively receive a fixed monthly payment, regardless of what services are used by that patient during the month. This encourages providers to treat less, because their potential profits decline as treatment increases.

contracts directly with one independent physician group. In *network HMOs*, the HMO contracts with multiple independent physician group practices.

The types of plans available within HMOs typically vary according to the degree of provider choice available to enrollees. Two such plans include *point-of-service* (POS) and *exclusive provider organization* (EPO) options. In POS plans, the patient has the option, at the time of service, to select a provider outside the network but pays a higher premium as well as a *copayment* (amount of money enrollees pay out of their pocket at the time a service is provided) for the flexibility to do so. In the EPO option, enrollees must seek care from the designated HMO provider or pay all of the cost out of pocket.

Another common type of MCO is the PPO. PPOs render services on an FFS basis but provide financial incentives to consumers (they pay less) when the preferred provider is used. Providers are motivated to become part of a PPO because it ensures them an adequate population of patients.

More than 70 million Americans have enrolled in HMOs and almost 90 million have become a part of PPOs since their inception (National Conference of State Legislatures [NCSL], 2011). As of 2010, the breakdown of enrollment by plan type in the United States was 19% in HMOs, 58% in PPOs, and 8% in POS plans (NCSL). It should be noted that "enrollment numbers in HMOs peaked in 2001 and are declining substantially in almost every area, although managed care generally remains a dominant type of health care and coverage" (NCSL, para 2).

Medicare and Medicaid Managed Care

Although Medicare and Medicaid patients historically were excluded from managed care under the *free choice of physician rule*, these restrictions were lifted in the 1970s and 1980s. As a result, these patients could participate in private HMOs and other types of managed care programs through *Medicare Part C* (formerly the Medicare + Choice program, and now known as Medicare Advantage). To join a Medicare Advantage Plan, patients must have both

Medicare Part A and Part B. The payment system for these programs (effective 1982) was to be prospective, and the HMO was at risk for providing all benefits in return for the capitated payment.

MCOs receive reimbursement for Medicare-eligible patients based on a formula established by the CMS, which looks at age, gender, geographic region, and the average cost per patient at a given age. Then, the government gives itself a 5% discount and gives the rest to the MCO. The *BBA of 1997* expanded the role of private plans under Medicare + Choice to include PPOs, *provider-sponsored organizations*, *private* FFS plans, and *medical savings accounts* (MSAs), coupled with high-deductible insurance plans.

The CMS is now the largest managed care buyer in the United States. Of the total Medicaid enrollment in the United States in 2009, approximately 72% of participants are receiving Medicaid benefits through managed care (NCSL, 2011). In addition, all states except Alaska and Wyoming have all or a portion of their Medicaid population enrolled in an MCO (NCSL).

The Centers for Medicare and Medicaid Services is now the largest purchaser of managed care in the country.

PROPONENTS AND CRITICS OF MANAGED CARE SPEAK UP

Proponents of managed care argue that prepaid health-care plans, such as those offered by HMOs, decrease health-care costs, provide broader benefits for patients than under the traditional FFS model, appropriately shift care from inpatient to outpatient settings, result in higher physician productivity, and have high enrollee satisfaction levels.

Critics, however, suggest that participation in MCOs may result in a loss of existing physician–patient relationships, a limited choice of physicians for consumers, a lower level of continuity of care, reduced physician autonomy, longer wait times for care, and consumer confusion about the many rules to be followed. A common complaint heard from managed care subscribers is that services must be preapproved or preauthorized by a gatekeeper or that second opinions must be obtained before surgery. Although this loss of autonomy is difficult for consumers accustomed to an FFS system with few limits on choice and access, such utilization constraints are necessary due to *moral hazard*, which is the risk that the insured will overuse services just because the insurance will pay the costs. Because the copayment is typically small for patients in managed care programs, the risk of moral hazard rises.

***Moral hazard* refers to the propensity of insured patients to use more medical services than necessary because their insurance covers so much of the cost.**

Another aspect complicating health-care reimbursement through the PPS, an HMO, or a PPO is that clear and comprehensive documentation of the need for services and actual services provided is mandatory. Provision of service no longer guarantees reimbursement. Thus, the fiscal accountability of nurses goes beyond planning and implementing; it includes responsible recording and communication of activities.

Provision of service no longer guarantees reimbursement.

Perhaps the most serious concern about the advancement of managed care in this country is the change in relationships among insurers, physicians, nurses, and patients. The full impact on clinical judgment of tying physician and nursing salaries to bonuses, incentives, and penalties designed to reduce utilization of services and resources and increase profit is unknown. As a result, a need for self-awareness regarding the values that guide individual professional nursing practice has never been greater.

LEARNING EXERCISE 10.5

Providing Care with Limited Reimbursement

You are the manager at a home health agency. One of your elderly patients has insulin-dependent diabetes. He has no family support. He speaks limited English and has little understanding of his disease. He lives alone. Your reimbursement from a government agency pays $90 per visit. Because this gentleman needs so much care, you find that the actual cost to your agency is $130 for each visit to him. What will be the impact to your agency if this patient is seen twice a week for 3 months? How can you recover the lost revenue? How can you make each visit less costly and still meet the needs of the patient?

THE FUTURE OF MANAGED CARE

Managed care continues to change the face of health care in the United States. The contractual complexity and the use of prospective payment in managed care make it much more difficult for providers to anticipate potential revenues and then to bill for and collect reimbursement for services provided. Indeed, some critics of managed care suggest that health-care practitioners and institutions now bear much more of the financial risk for the cost of care than insurers.

Some declines in managed care participation have occurred in part because these plans are no longer significantly less expensive for consumers to purchase or for insurers to provide. In addition, providers have grown increasingly frustrated with limited and delayed reimbursement for services provided as well as the need to justify need for services ordered. Indeed, some providers have filed lawsuits against managed care insurers for delay of payment or nonpayment for services provided. This phenomenon, referred to as *managed care backlash*, resulted in some managed care programs beginning "to say 'yes' to more treatments although they have passed the cost along to customers in the form of higher premiums, co-pays and deductibles" (Freundlich, 2009, para 1). In addition, they began offering consumers more choice and flexibility in their plans and removing barriers like gatekeepers and capitation agreements (Freundlich).

Even with this backlash, managed care is not going to go away—at least not any time soon. It will, however, continue to change. Certainly, in reviewing the health-care reimbursement milestones of the past 75 years (Display 10.6), one can see that health-care reimbursement has changed dramatically in a relatively short time and that managed care is just one more reimbursement schema that has changed the face of health care in the United States.

DISPLAY 10.6   US Health-Care Milestones: 75 Years of Reimbursement

1929 First HMO, the Ross-Loos Clinic, established in Los Angeles.

1929 Origins of Blue Cross, when Baylor University Hospital agreed to provide 1,500 school teachers up to 21 days of hospital care for $6.00 per year.

1935 Passage of *Social Security Act.* This act originally included compulsory health insurance for states that voluntarily chose to participate, but the American Medical Association fought it and the health insurance provisions were omitted from the act.

1942 First nationwide hospital insurance bill introduced into Congress, but it failed to pass.

1946 Hill Burton Act promoted hospital development and renovation after World War II. Authorized $75 million yearly for 5 years to aid in hospital construction.

1965 Passage of Medicare and Medicaid as part of Lyndon B. Johnson's Great Society. Resulted in 50% increase in the number of medical schools in the United States.

1972 *Professional Standards Review Organizations* (PSROs) established by Congress to prevent excess hospitalization and utilization by Medicare and Medicaid patients.

1973 The *Health Maintenance Act* authorized the spending of $375 million over 5 years to set up and evaluate HMOs in communities across the country.

1974 The National Planning Act created a system of state and local health planning agencies largely supported by federal funds. This created *Health Systems Agencies* (HSAs) to inventory each community's health-care resources and to issue *Certificates of Need*.

1974 The *Employment Retirement Income and Security Act* (ERISA) passed, generally preempting state regulation of self-insuring employee benefit plans.

1983 *Diagnosis-Related Groups* (*DRGs*) established, which changed the structure of Medicare payments from a retrospectively adjusted cost-reimbursement system to a prospective, risk-based one.

1986 Act of 1986 passed. Allowed terminated employees or those who lose coverage because of reduced work hours to buy group coverage for themselves and their families for limited periods of time (up to 60 days to decide).

1988 *Medicare Catastrophic Coverage Act* (MCCA) enacted, which expanded Medicare benefits greatly to include a portion of out-of-pocket drug and physician expenses.

1989 Medicare system of paying physician charges was changed to a *resource-based relative value scale* (RBRVS) to be phased in starting in 1992.

1993 President William J. Clinton introduced the *Health Security Act*, legislation assuring universal access to all Americans. The act failed to pass.

1996 *Health Insurance Portability and Accountability Act* passed. Created *Medical Savings Accounts* (MSAs) and required the Department of Health and Human Services to establish national standards for electronic health-care transactions and national identifiers for providers, health plans, and employers. It also addressed the security and privacy of health data.

1997 Approximately one-quarter of Americans enrolled in HMOs. Almost 6 million Medicare beneficiaries enrolled in HMOs. *Balanced Budget Act* gives states the authority to implement managed care programs without federal waivers.

1999 Health-care spending comprises approximately 15% of the GDP of the United States, exceeding $1 trillion in annual health-care expenditures. Approximately 37 million Americans are uninsured and between 50 and 70 million are inadequately insured.

2001 More than 1.5 million elderly Medicare HMO patients forced to find new insurance arrangements as their HMOs pulled out of the Medicare program after losing money on Medicare enrollees. Increasing disenchantment noted with managed care.

2003 The *Medicare Prescription Drug, Improvement, and Modernization Act of 2003* passes, providing a voluntary program for prescription drug coverage under the Medicare program.

2003 The Medicare Modernization Act (MMA) of 2003 passes and commissions the IOM to "identify and prioritize options to align performance to payment in Medicare." The IOM reports provided the rationale to reconfigure the U.S. health care payment system, supporting a "pay for performance" (P4P) approach (Keckley, 2013, p. 3).

2009 Congressional committees begin active debate of a comprehensive health-care reform package. President Barack Obama announces the release of nearly $600 million in funding to strengthen community health centers that will serve 500,000 additional patients and use health information technology (HealthReform.GOV, 2013).

2010 President Barack Obama's Health Care Reform bill *Patient Protection and Affordable Care Act* (PPACA) passes, resulting in sweeping overhauls of the US health-care system and the introduction of a new Patient Bill of Rights related to insurance coverage. Provisions related to eliminating lifetime limits on insurance coverage, extending coverage to young adults, and providing new coverage to individuals who have been uninsured for at least 6 months due to a preexisting condition are implemented.

2011 The Obama Administration launches the *Partnership for Patients: Better Care, Lower Costs*, a new public–private partnership (major hospitals, employers, health plans, physicians, nurses, and patient advocates along with state and federal governments) to help improve the quality, safety, and affordability of health care for all Americans.

2011 PPACA provisions related to providing free preventive care to seniors, the establishment of a *Community Care Transitions Program*, and the creation of a new *Center for Medicare & Medicaid Innovation* are put into place.

(Continued)

2012 The PPACA establishes hospital *Value-Based Purchasing programs (VBP)* in traditional Medicare, provides incentives for physicians to join together to form Accountable Care Organizations, and provides new, voluntary options for long-term care insurance.

2013 The PPACA provides new funding to state Medicaid programs that choose to cover preventive services for patients at little or no cost, expands the authority to bundle payments, increases medical payments for primary care doctors, and begins open enrollment in the Healthcare Insurance Marketplace.

2014 The final provisions of the PPACA are phased in, including the implementation of the Healthcare Insurance Marketplace, prohibition of discrimination due to preexisting conditions or gender, the elimination of annual limits on insurance coverage, and ensuring coverage for individuals participating in clinical trials.

To provide care and appropriately advocate for patients in the 21st century, all nurses need at least a basic understanding of health-care costs. They also need to know how reimbursement strategies directly and indirectly affect their practice. Only then can nurses be active participants in the proactive and visionary fiscal planning required to survive in the current health-care marketplace.

All nurses need at least a basic understanding of health-care costs as well as how reimbursement strategies directly and indirectly affect their practice.

HEALTH-CARE REFORM AND THE PATIENT PROTECTION AND AFFORDABLE CARE ACT

In March, 2010, President Barack Obama signed the *PPACA* (often shortened to the *Affordable Care Act*) that put in place comprehensive insurance reforms that were to be phased in over a 4-year period. The act included a new *Patient Bill of Rights* (see Chapter 6) implemented in 2010; a provision for Medicare beneficiaries to get preventive services for free and discounts on brand name drugs for some patients using Medicare Part D beginning in 2011 as well as the introduction of "bundled payments"; the addition of ACOs and other programs help doctors and health-care providers work together to deliver better care in 2012; hospital VBP and open enrollment in the *Health Insurance Marketplace* beginning in October 2013; and greater access for most Americans to affordable health insurance options in 2014 (Healthcare.gov, 2013a).

Bundled Payments

Passed in October 2011 and implemented in 2013, the *Bundled Payments Initiative* gave providers flexibility to work together to coordinate care for patients over the course of a single episode of an illness. There are four broadly defined models of *bundled care*: three of these models involve retrospective payment and one is prospective. In the retrospective payment models, CMS and providers set a target payment amount for a defined episode of care. This target amount would reflect a discount to total costs for a similar episode of care as determined from historical data. Participants then would be paid for their services under the Original Medicare FFS system, but at a negotiated discount. Models 2 and 3 may include clinical laboratory services and durable medical equipment (Healthcare.gov, 2013c).

The prospective payment model differs in that CMS makes a single, prospectively determined bundled payment to a hospital that would encompass all services furnished during the inpatient stay by the hospital, physicians, and other practitioners. "Physicians and other practitioners would submit 'no-pay' claims to Medicare and would be paid by the hospital out of the bundled payment"(Healthcare.gov, 2013c, para 9).

Accountable Care Organizations

ACOs are groups of providers and suppliers of service who work together to better coordinate care for Medicare patients (does not include Medicare Advantage) across care settings. The goal of an ACO is to deliver seamless, high quality care in an environment that is truly patient centered and where patients and providers are partners in decision making.

While patient and provider participation in ACOs are voluntary at this time, the *Medicare Shared Savings Program* will reward ACOs that lower growth in health-care costs while meeting performance standards on quality of care and putting patients first (Healthcare. gov, 2013a). ACOs would only be entitled to these shared savings when savings exceed the minimum sharing rate and if the ACO meets or exceeds the quality performance standards. Additional shared savings can be earned by ACOs that include beneficiaries who receive services from a Federally Qualified Health Center or Rural Health Clinic during the performance year (Healthcare.gov, 2013a).

Hospital Value-Based Purchasing

Beginning in 2013, for the first time, the hospital VBP program paid inpatient acute care services partially on care quality, not just on the quantity of the services they provide (Healthcare.gov, 2013c). In VBP, providers are held accountable for the quality and cost of the health-care services they provide by a system of rewards and consequences, conditional upon achieving prespecified performance measures. Incentives are structured to discourage inappropriate, unnecessary, and costly care (Keckley, 2013). Critical to VBP are standardized, comparative, and transparent information on patient outcomes; health-care status; patient experience (satisfaction); and costs (direct and indirect) of services provided (Keckley, 2013). VBP payment reform is expected to reduce Medicare spending by almost $214 billion over the first 10 years of its implementation.

The Medical Home

The *medical home*, also known as the *patient-centered medical home* (PCMH), "is designed around patient needs and aims to improve access to care (e.g. through extended office hours and increased communication between providers and patients via email and telephone), increase care coordination and enhance overall quality, while simultaneously reducing costs" (NCSL, 2012, para 2). The medical home relies on a team of providers—such as physicians, nurses, nutritionists, pharmacists, and social workers—to integrate all aspects of health care, including physical health, behavioral health, access to community-based social services, and the management of chronic conditions. Communication occurs through well-developed health information technology including electronic health records.

Payment reform is also a critical part of the medical home initiative as financial incentives are offered to providers to focus on the quality of patient outcomes rather than the volume of services they provide. While the model is still evolving, national and state medical home accreditation is available, facilitating payment from both public and private payers (NCSL, 2012).

Health Insurance Marketplaces

As of October 2103, new *health insurance marketplaces*, also called *exchanges*, were created for individuals without access to health insurance through a job, for implementation in January 2014. Small businesses were also eligible to buy affordable and qualified health benefit plans in this competitive insurance marketplace. In essence, health insurance marketplaces are online insurance supermalls that cannot turn down prospective clients as a result of preexisting conditions (Zamosky, 2013). Every health insurance plan in the marketplace offers comprehensive coverage from doctors to medications to hospital visits and options can be compared based on price, benefits, and quality (Healthcare.gov, 2013d). Tax credits are provided to lower insurance costs for individuals and families earning below certain levels.

INTEGRATING LEADERSHIP ROLES AND MANAGEMENT FUNCTIONS IN FISCAL PLANNING

Managers must understand fiscal planning and health-care reimbursement, be aware of their budgetary responsibilities, and be cost-effective in meeting organizational goals. The ability to forecast unit fiscal needs with sensitivity to the organization's political, economic, social, and legislative climate is a high-level management function. Managers also must be able to articulate unit needs through budgeting to ensure adequate nursing staff, supplies, and equipment. Finally, managers must be skillful in the monitoring aspects of budget control.

Leadership skills allow the manager to involve all appropriate stakeholders in developing the budget and implementing needed reforms. This has likely never been as important as it currently is, given the current climate of health-care reform with almost countless initiatives and phased-in implementation. Other leadership skills required in fiscal planning include flexibility, creativity, and vision regarding future needs. The skilled leader is able to anticipate budget constraints and act proactively. In contrast, many managers allow budget constraints to dictate alternatives. In an age of inadequate fiscal resources, the leader is creative in identifying alternatives to meet patient needs.

The skilled leader, however, also ensures that cost containment does not jeopardize patient safety. As well, leaders are assertive, articulate people who ensure that their department's budgeting receives a fair hearing. Because leaders can delineate unit budgetary needs in an assertive, professional, and proactive manner, they generally obtain a fair distribution of resources for their unit.

KEY CONCEPTS

- Fiscal planning, as in all types of planning, is a learned skill that improves with practice.

- Historically, nursing management played a limited role in determining resource allocation in health-care institutions.

- The personnel–workforce budget often accounts for the majority of health-care organization's expenses because health care is labor intensive.

- Personnel budgets include actual worked time (productive time or salary expense) and time that the organization pays the employee for not working (nonproductive or benefit time).

- A budget is at best a forecast or prediction; it is a plan and not a rule. Therefore, a budget must be flexible and open to ongoing evaluation and revision.

- A budget that is predicted too far in advance is open to greater error. If the budget is shortsighted, compensating for unexpected major expenses or capital equipment purchases may be difficult.

- The desired outcome of budgeting is maximal use of resources to meet organizational short- and long-term needs. Its value to the institution is directly related to its accuracy.

- The operating budget reflects expenses that flex up or down in a predetermined manner to reflect variation in volume of service provided.

- Capital budgets plan for the purchase of buildings or major equipment. This includes equipment that has a long life (usually greater than 5 years), is not used daily, and is more expensive than operating supplies.

- Managers must rejustify their program or needs every budgeting cycle in zero-based budgeting. Using a decision package to set funding priorities is a key feature of zero-based budgeting.

- With the advent of state and federal reimbursement for health care in the 1960s, providers were forced to submit budgets and costs to payers that more accurately reflected their actual cost to provide these services.

- With DRGs, hospitals join the PPS, whereby they receive a specified amount for each Medicare patient's admission, regardless of the actual cost of care. Exceptions occur when the provider can demonstrate that a patient's case is an outlier, meaning that the cost of providing care for that patient justifies extra payment.

- Key principles of managed care include the use of primary care providers as gatekeepers, a focus on prevention, a decreased emphasis on inpatient hospital care, the use of clinical practice guidelines for providers, selective contracting, capitation, utilization review, the use of formularies to manage pharmacy care, and continuous quality monitoring and improvement.

- The types of plans available within HMOs typically vary according to the degree of provider choice available to enrollees.

- Managed care has altered the relationships among insurers, physicians, nurses, and patients, with providers today often having to assume a role as an agent for the patient as well as an agent of resource allocation for an insurance carrier, hospital, or particular practice plan.

- Provision of service no longer guarantees reimbursement. Clear and comprehensive documentation of the need for services and actual services provided is needed for reimbursement.

- The 2010 *PPACA* (often shortened to the *Affordable Care Act*) put in place comprehensive insurance reforms, which were to be phased in over a 4-year period.

- With bundled payments, providers agree to accept a discounted payment either retrospectively or prospectively, which represents a coordinated plan of care for patients over the course of a single episode of an illness.

- Accountable Care Organizations (ACOs) are groups of providers and suppliers of service who work together to better coordinate care for Medicare patients (does not include Medicare Advantage) across care settings with the expectation that efficiency as well as quality of care will result in shared savings.

- In VBP, providers are held accountable for the quality and cost of the health-care services they provide by a system of rewards and consequences, conditional upon achieving prespecified performance measures.

- The medical home, or PCMH, relies on a team of providers to integrate all aspects of health care through well-developed health information technology, including electronic health records.

- Health insurance marketplaces, also called exchanges, are online insurance supermalls, created for individuals without access to health insurance through a job or for small businesses who wish to buy affordable and qualified health benefit plans in a competitive insurance marketplace.

ADDITIONAL LEARNING EXERCISES AND APPLICATIONS

LEARNING EXERCISE 10.6

How Does Policy Influence Your Decision?

You are the evening house supervisor of a small, private, rural hospital. In your role as house supervisor, you are responsible for staffing the upcoming shift and for troubleshooting any and all problems that cannot be handled at the unit level.

Tonight, you receive a call to come to the emergency department (ED) to handle a "patient complaint." When you arrive, you find a Hispanic woman in her mid-20s arguing vehemently

(Continued)

with the ED charge nurse and physician. When you intercede, the patient introduces herself as Teresa Garcia and states, "There is something wrong with my father, and they won't help him because we only have Medicaid insurance. If we had private insurance, you would be willing to do something." The charge nurse intercedes by saying, "Teresa's father began vomiting about 2 hours ago and blacked out approximately 45 minutes ago, following a 14-hour drinking binge." The ED physician added, "Mr. Garcia's blood alcohol level is 0.25 (two and one-half times the level required to be declared legally intoxicated), and my baseline physical examination would indicate nothing other than he is drunk and needs to sleep it off. Besides, I have seen Mr. Garcia in the ED before, and it's always for the same thing. He does not need further treatment."

Teresa persists in her pleas to you that "there is something different this time" and that she believes this hospital should evaluate her father further. She intuitively feels that something terrible will happen to her father if he is not cared for immediately. The ED physician becomes even angrier after this comment and states to you, "I am not going to waste my time and energy on someone who is just drunk, and I refuse to order any more expensive lab tests or x-rays on this patient. If you want something else done, you will have to find someone else to order it." With that, he walks off and returns to the examination room, where other patients are waiting to be seen. The ED nurse turns to look at you and is waiting for further directions.

Assignment: How will you handle this situation? Would your decision be any easier if there were no limitations in resource allocation? Are your values to act as an agent for the patient or for the agency more strongly developed?

LEARNING EXERCISE 10.7

Weighing Choices in Budget Spending

One of your goals as the unit manager of a critical care unit is to prepare all your nurses to be certified in advanced cardiac life support. You currently have five staff nurses who need this certification. You can hire someone to teach this class locally and rent a facility for $800; however, the cost will be taken out of the travel and education budget for the unit, and this will leave you short for the rest of the fiscal year. It also will be a time-consuming effort because you must coordinate the preparation and reproduction of educational materials needed for the course and make arrangements for the rental facility. A certification class also will be provided in the near future in a large city approximately 150 miles from the hospital. The cost per participant will be $200. In addition, there would be travel and lodging expenses.

Assignment: You have several decisions to make. Should the class be held locally? If so, how will you organize it? Are you going to require your staff to have this certification or merely highly recommend that they do so? If it is required, will the unit pay the costs of the certification? Will you pay the staff nurses their regular hourly wage for attending the class on regularly scheduled work hours? Can this certification be cost-effective? Use group process in some way to make your decision.

LEARNING EXERCISE 10.8

How Will You Meet New Budget Restrictions?

You are the director of the local agency that cares for ill and well elderly patients. You are funded by a private corporation grant, which requires matching of city and state funds. You received a letter in the mail today from the state that says state funding will be cut by $35,000, effective in 2 weeks, when the state's budget year begins. This means that your private funding also will be cut $35,000, for a total revenue loss of $70,000. It is impossible at this time to seek alternative funding sources.

In reviewing your agency budget, you note that, as in many health-care agencies, your budget is labor intensive. More than 80% of your budget is attributable to personnel costs, and you believe that the cuts must come from within the personnel budget. You may reduce the patient population that you serve, although you do not really want to do so. You briefly discuss this communication with your staff; no one is willing to reduce his or her hours voluntarily, and no one is planning to terminate his or her employment at any time in the near future.

Assignment: Given the following brief description of your position and each of your five employees, decide how you will meet the new budget restrictions. What is the rationale for your choice? Which decision do you believe will result in the least disruption of the agency and of the employees in the agency? Should group decision making be involved in fiscal decisions such as this one? Can fiscal decisions such as this be made without value judgments?

Your position is project director. As the project director, you coordinate all the day-to-day activities in the agency. You also are involved in long-term planning, and a major portion of your time is allotted to securing future funding for the agency to continue. As the project director, you have the authority to hire and fire employees. You are in your early 30s and have a master's degree in nursing and health administration. You enjoy your job and believe that you have done well in this position since you started 4 years ago. Your yearly salary as a full-time employee is $80,000.

Employee #1 is Mrs. Potter. Mrs. Potter has worked at the agency since it started 7 years ago. She is an RN with 30 years of experience working with the geriatric population in public health nursing, care facilities, and private duty. She plans to retire in 7 years and travel with her independently wealthy husband. Mrs. Potter has a great deal of expertise that she can share with your staff, although at times you believe she overshadows your authority because of her experience and your young age. Her yearly salary as a full-time employee is $65,000.

Employee #2 is Mr. Boone. Mr. Boone has BS degrees in both nursing and dietetics and food management. As an RN and registered dietician, he brings a unique expertise to your staff, which is highly needed when dealing with a chronically ill and improperly nourished elderly population. In the 6 months since he joined your agency, he has proven to be a dependable, well-liked, and highly respected member of your staff. His yearly salary as a full-time employee is $55,000.

Employee #3 is Miss Barns. Miss Barns is the receptionist-secretary in the agency. In addition to all the traditional secretarial duties, such as typing, filing, and transcription of dictation, she screens incoming telephone calls and directs people who come to the agency for information. Her efficiency is a tremendous attribute to the agency. Her full-time yearly salary is $26,000.

Employee #4 is Ms. Lake. Ms. Lake is an LPN/LVN with 15 years of work experience in a variety of health-care agencies. She is especially attuned to patient needs. Although her technical nursing skills are also good, her caseload frequently is more focused around elderly patients who need companionship and emotional support. She does well at patient teaching because of her outstanding listening and communication skills. Many of your patients request her by name. She is a single mother, supporting six children, and you are aware that she has great difficulty in meeting her personal financial obligations. Her full-time yearly salary is $48,000.

Employee #5 is Mrs. Long. Mrs. Long is an "elderly help aide." She has completed nurse aide training, although her primary role in the agency is to assist well elderly with bathing, meal preparation, driving, and shopping. The time that Mrs. Long spends in performing basic care has decreased the average visit time for each member of your staff by 30%. She is widowed and uses this job to meet her social and self-esteem needs. Financially, her resources are adequate, and the money she earns is not a motivator for working. Mrs. Long works 3 days a week, and her yearly salary is $23,000.

LEARNING EXERCISE 10.9

Identifying, Prioritizing, and Choosing Program Goals

Jane is the supervisor of a small cardiac rehabilitation program. The program includes inpatient cardiac teaching and an outpatient exercise rehabilitation program. Because of limited reimbursement by third-party insurance payers for patient education, there has been no direct charge for inpatient education. Outpatient program participants pay $240 per month to attend three 1-hour sessions per week, although the revenue generated from the outpatient program still leaves an overall budget deficit for the program of approximately $6,800 per month.

Today, Jane is summoned to the associate administrator's office to discuss her budget for the upcoming year. At this meeting, the administrator states that the hospital is experiencing extreme financial difficulties due to declining reimbursements. He states that the program must become self-supporting in the next fiscal year; otherwise, services must be cut. On returning to her office, Jane decided to make a list of several alternatives for problem solving and to analyze each for driving and restraining factors. These alternatives include the following:

1. *Implement a charge for inpatient education.* This would eliminate the budget deficit, but the cost would probably have to be borne by the patient. (*Implication:* Only patients with adequate fiscal resources would elect to receive vital education.)

2. *Reduce department staffing.* There are currently three staff members in the department, and it would be impossible to maintain the same level or quality of services if staffing were reduced.

3. *Reduce or limit services.* The inpatient education program or educational programs associated with the outpatient program could be eliminated. These are both considered to be valuable aspects of the program.

4. The fee for the outpatient program could be increased. This could easily result in a decrease in program participation, because many outpatient program participants do not have insurance coverage for their participation.

Assignment: Identify at least five program goals, and prioritize them as you would if you were Jane. Based on the priorities that you have established, which alternative would you select? Explain your choice.

LEARNING EXERCISE 10.10

Addressing Conflicting Values

You are a single parent of two children younger than 5 years and are currently employed as a pediatric office nurse. You enjoy your job, but your long-term career goal is to become a pediatric nurse practitioner, and you have been taking courses part-time preparing to enter graduate school in the fall. Your application for admission has been accepted, and the next cycle for admissions will not be for another 3 years. Your recent divorce and assignment of sole custody of the children have resulted in a need for you to reconsider your plan.

Restraining Forces: You had originally planned to reduce your work hours to part time to allow time for classes and studying, but this will be fiscally impossible now. You also recognize that tuition and educational expenses will place a strain on your budget even if you continue to work full time. You have not looked into the availability of scholarships or loans and have missed the deadline for the upcoming fall. In addition, you have not yet overcome your anxiety and guilt about leaving your small children for even more time than you do now.

Driving Forces: You also recognize, however, that gaining certification as a pediatric nurse practitioner should result in a large salary increase over what you are able to make as an office nurse and that it would allow you to provide resources for your children in the future that you otherwise may be unable to do. As well, you recognize that although you are not dissatisfied with your current job, you have a great deal of ability that has gone untapped and that your potential for long-term job satisfaction is low.

Assignment: Fiscal planning always requires priority setting, and often this priority setting is determined by personal values. Priority setting is made even more difficult when there are conflicting values. Identify the values involved in this case. Develop a plan that addresses these value conflicts and has the most desirable outcomes.

LEARNING EXERCISE 10.11

How Would You Change This Budget?

Today is April 1, and you have received the following budget printout. Your charge nurses are requesting an additional RN on each shift since the acuity has increased dramatically over the last 2 years. Dr. Robb has requested two new continuous limb movement machines for the postoperative orthopedic patients on your unit at a cost of $3,000 each. In addition, you would like to attend a national orthopedics conference in New York in August at a projected cost of $1,500. The registration fee is $350 and is due now.

	Annual Budget	Expended in March	Expended Year to Date[a]	Amount Remaining
Personnel	300,000	25,000	175,000	125,000
Overtime	50,000	3,800	50,000	0
Supplies	18,000	1,500	13,500	4,500
Travel (personal)	2,200	0	1,700	500
Equipment	5,000	0	5,000	0
Staff development	1,000	200	800	200

[a]Fiscal year begins July 1.

Assignment: How will you deal with these requests based on the budget printout? What expenses can and should be deferred to the new fiscal year? In what budgeting area were your previous projections most accurate? Most inaccurate? What factors may have contributed to these inaccuracies? Were they controllable or predictable?

REFERENCES

Barr, P. (2005). Flexing your budget: Experts urge hospitals, systems to trade in their traditional budgeting process for a more dynamic and versatile model. *Modern Healthcare, 35*(37), 24, 26.

Centers for Medicare & Medicaid Services (2013). *ICD-10.* Retrieved May 27, 2013, from http://www.cms.gov/Medicare/Coding/ICD10/index.html?redirect=/icd10

Freundlich, N. (2009, May 7). *Taking note: Provider backlash.* A Century Foundation Group Blog. Retrieved May 25, 2013, from http://takingnote.tcf.org/2009/05/provider-backlash.html

Goozner, M. (2013). Dissecting the president's budget. *Modern Healthcare, 43*(15), 25.

Healthcare.gov (2013a). *Key features of the Affordable Care Act, by year.* Retrieved May 27, 2013, from http://www.healthcare.gov/law/timeline/full.html

Healthcare.gov (2013b). *Payment bundling. Definition.* Retrieved May 27, 2013, from http://www.healthcare.gov/glossary/p/payment-bundling.html

Healthcare.gov (2013c). *Improving care coordination and lowering costs by bundling payments.* Retrieved May 27, 2013, from http://www.healthcare.gov/news/factsheets/2011/08/bundling08232011a.html

Healthcare.gov. (2013d). *About the health insurance marketplace.* Retrieved May 27, 2013, from http://www.healthcare.gov/marketplace/about/index.html

HealthReform.GOV. (2013). *Strengthening community health centers*. HealthReform.GOV-a U.S. Government Web site managed by the U.S. Department of Health & Human Services. Retrieved May 25, from http://www.healthreform.gov/

Kaiser Family Foundation (2013). *Medicare beneficiaries as a percent of total population*. Retrieved May 24, 2013, from http://kff.org/medicare/state-indicator/medicare-beneficiaries-as-of-total-pop/

Keckley, P. H. (2013). *Value-based purchasing: A strategic overview for health care industry stakeholders*. Deloitte. Retrieved May 26, 2013, from http://www.deloitte.com/assets/Dcom-UnitedStates/Local%20Assets/Documents/Health%20Reform%20Issues%20Briefs/US_CHS_ValueBasedPurchasing_031811.pdf

Medicare.Gov. (2013). *Medicare 2013 Costs at a Glance*. Retrieved May 26, 2013, from http://www.medicare.gov/your-medicare-costs/costs-at-a-glance/costs-at-glance.html

Mitchell, R. (2013, March 26). Slow progress on efforts to pay docs, hospitals for 'value,' not volume. *Kaiser Health News*. Retrieved May 26, 2013, from http://www.kaiserhealthnews.org/stories/2013/march/26/employers-value-volume-purchasing.aspx

National Conference of State Legislatures. (2011, May). *Managed care and the states*. Retrieved May 25, 2013, from http://www.ncsl.org/Default.aspx?TabId=14470

National Conference of State Legislatures (2012, September). *The medical home model of care*. Retrieved May 27, 2013, from http://www.ncsl.org/issues-research/health/the-medical-home-model-of-care.aspx

Rosenberg (2013, January 13). *The real reason Medicare costs will explode*. The Fiscal Times. Retrieved My 26, 2013, from http://www.thefiscaltimes.com/Articles/2013/01/13/The-Real-Reason-Medicare-Costs-Will-Explode.aspx#page1

Sahadi. J. (2013, February 7). *The real Medicare spending problem*. CNN Money. Retrieved May 25, 2013, from http://money.cnn.com/2013/02/07/news/economy/medicare-spending/index.html

Urban Institute (2012, April). *Medicare, Medicaid and the deficit debate*. Retrieved May 26, 2013, from http://www.urban.org/UploadedPDF/412544-Medicare-Medicaid-and-the-Deficit-Debate.pdf

Your Dictionary. (2013). *Cost effectiveness-definition*. LoveToKnow Corp. Retrieved May 25, 2013, from http://www.yourdictionary.com/cost-effective

Zamosky, L. (2013, March 22). *What's ahead for the Affordable Care Act in 2013?* WEB MD. Retrieved May 27, 2013 from http://www.webmd.com/health-insurance/news/20130322/affordable-care-act-whats-next

11

Career Development: From New Graduate to Retirement

... every individual you hire for a leadership role should have the capability to grow into that role.
—Carolyn Hope Smeltzer

... career plans are about where you are today and, more importantly, where you're going tomorrow.
—Phil McPeck

CROSSWALK THIS CHAPTER ADDRESSES:

BSN Essential I: Liberal education for baccalaureate generalist nursing practice
BSN Essential II: Basic organizational and systems leadership for quality care and patient safety
BSN Essential VIII: Professionalism and professional values
BSN Essential IX: Baccalaureate generalist nursing practice
MSN Essential I: Background for practice from sciences and humanities
MSN Essential II: Organizational and systems leadership
MSN Essential IX: Advanced generalist nursing practice
AONE Nurse Executive Competency III: Leadership
AONE Nurse Executive Competency IV: Professionalism
AONE Nurse Executive Competency V: Business skills

LEARNING OBJECTIVES *The learner will:*

- describe the impact of a career development program on employee attrition, future employment opportunities, quality of work life, and competitiveness of the organization
- differentiate among stages of a career
- differentiate between the employer's and employee's responsibilities for career development
- describe three phases of long-term coaching for career development
- identify support by top management, systematic planning and implementation, and inclusion of social learning activities as integral components of management development programs
- recognize lifelong learning as a professional expectation and responsibility
- define competency and identify strategies for assuring and measuring it
- identify driving and restraining forces for specialty certification in professional nursing
- identify factors creating the current, pressing need for transition-to-practice programs to retain new graduate nurses and prepare them for employment
- develop a personal career plan
- create and/or critique a resumé for content, format, grammar, punctuation, sentence structure, and appropriate use of language

To be a fully engaged professional requires commitment to career development. *Career development* is intentional career planning and should be viewed as a critical and deliberate life process involving both the individual and the employer. It provides individuals with choices about career outcomes rather than leaving it to chance. Thus, career development is about career exploration, opportunities, and change. Before the 1970s, organizations did little to help employees plan and develop their careers. Now, subordinate career development is essential to organizational success, and most organizations accept at least some responsibility for assisting employees with this function.

For the most part, however, organizational career development efforts have centered on management development rather than activities that promote growth in nonmanagement employees. Given that more than 80% of an organization's employees are typically nonmanagement, this is often a neglected part of career development.

Career development in an organization must include more than management employees.

This chapter examines organizational justifications for employee career development, suggests the existence of career stages, and emphasizes the need for career coaching. The use of competency assessment, professional certification, and transition-to-practice programs are identified as strategies for career management with the ultimate goal of lifelong learning. Finally, professional resumés, reflection, and portfolios are discussed as career-planning tools. The leadership roles and management functions for career development are shown in Display 11.1.

DISPLAY 11.1 Leadership Roles and Management Functions Associated with Career Development

LEADERSHIP ROLES

1. Is self-aware of personal values influencing career development.
2. Encourages employees to take responsibility for their own career planning.
3. Identifies, encourages, and develops future leaders.
4. Shows a genuine interest in the career planning and career development of all employees.
5. Encourages and supports the development of career paths within and outside the organization.
6. Supports employees' personal career decisions based on each employee's needs and values.
7. Is a role model for continued professional development via specialty certification, continuing education (CE), and portfolio development.
8. Emphasizes the need for employees to develop the skill set necessary for evidence-based practice.
9. Supports new graduate nurses in their transition to practice through positive role modeling as well as the creation of nurse residencies, internships, and externships.
10. Role models lifelong learning as a professional expectation and responsibility.
11. Encourages others to continue their formal education as part of their career ladder and professional journey.

MANAGEMENT FUNCTIONS

1. Develops fair policies related to career development opportunities and communicates them clearly to subordinates.
2. Provides fiscal resources and release time for subordinate training and education.
3. Uses a planned system of short- and long-term coaching for career development and documents all coaching efforts.
4. Disseminates career and job information.
5. Works with employees to establish career goals that meet both employee and organizational needs.
6. Works cooperatively with other departments in arranging for the release of employees to take other positions within the organization.
7. Views transition-to-practice programs as an investment strategy to mitigate nurse turnover and promote employee satisfaction.

8. Coaches employees to create professional portfolios that demonstrate reflection as well as the maintenance of continued competence.
9. Attempts to match position openings with capable employees who seek new learning opportunities.
10. Creates possibilities for career progression.
11. Provides opportunities for "*legacy*" clinicians to "reinvent" themselves to renew their potential value to the organization and their coworkers.

CAREER STAGES

Before individuals can plan a successful career development program, they need to understand the normal career stages of individuals. Shirey (2009) suggests that there are three different career phases or stages among nurses: promise, momentum, and harvest. *Promise* is the earliest of the career phases and typically reflects the first 10 years of nursing employment. Individuals in this stage are less experienced and tend to experience reality overload as a result. Making wise early career choices is critical in this phase. Milestones to be attained include socialization to the nursing role (becoming an insider); building knowledge, skills, abilities, credentials, and an education base; gaining exposure to a variety of experiences; identifying strengths and building confidence; and positioning for the future.

Momentum is the middle career phase and typically reflects the nurse with 11 to 29 years of experience. Nurses in this phase are experienced clinicians with expert knowledge, skills, abilities, credentials, and education base. This is a time of accomplishment, challenge, and a sense of purpose, and the individual often achieves a high enough level of expertise to be a role model to others. Milestones to be surpassed include further building confidence in one's competence; developing experience, gaining mastery, and establishing a professional track record; and finding a voice through aligning strengths with passion. The most significant challenge to nurses in this phase, however, is likely creating possibilities for career progression, rather than stagnation. A commitment to lifelong learning and being willing to seize unexpected opportunities that may present themselves over time are often key to career divergence at this point in life.

The last stage, *harvest*, commences in late career. Shirey labels nurses with 30 to 40 years as having "*prime*" experience and nurses with more than 40 years of experience as being "*legacy*" clinicians. Although viewed as expert clinicians, the experiential value of nurses in the harvest phase may begin to decline if others perceive them as obsolescent. These prime or legacy nurse-leaders then must actively strive for ongoing "reinvention" to renew their potential value to their coworkers. Success then is defined not only by being knowledgeable but also by being savvy and adaptable. The potential for career divergence in this phase is mixed, depending upon choices made in the momentum phase. Milestones to be conquered include elevating their mastery to sage practice for advancing the profession and positioning as a professional statesperson and establishing a legacy.

Finally, an argument might be made that another career stage exists in nursing—that of *reentry*. Concurrent with nursing shortages, many nurses who were no longer working in the profession, but who possess the necessary training and experience to do so, may reenter the work setting.

LEARNING EXERCISE 11.1

Exploring Career Stages

In a group, discuss the job stages described by Shirey (2009). What stage most closely reflects your present situation? In what stages of their careers are nurses who you know (colleagues, managers, your nursing instructors)? Do you believe that male and female nurses have similar or dissimilar career stages?

JUSTIFICATIONS FOR CAREER DEVELOPMENT

The following, summarized in Display 11.2, is a list of justifications for career development programs:

DISPLAY 11.2 **Justifications for Career Development**

1. Reduces employee attrition
2. Provides equal employment opportunity
3. Improves use of personnel
4. Improves quality of work life
5. Improves competitiveness of the organization
6. Avoids obsolescence and builds new skills
7. Promotes evidence-based practice

- *Reduced employee attrition.* Career development can reduce the turnover of ambitious employees who would otherwise be frustrated and seek other jobs because of a lack of job advancement.

- *Equal employment opportunity.* Minorities and other underserved groups will have a better opportunity to move up in an organization if they are identified and developed early in their careers.

- *Improved use of personnel.* When employees are kept in jobs that they have outgrown, their productivity is often reduced. People perform better when they are placed in jobs that fit them and provide new challenges.

- *Improved quality of work life.* Nurses increasingly desire to control their own careers. They are less willing to settle for just any role or position that comes their way. They want greater job satisfaction and more career options.

- *Improved competitiveness of the organization.* Highly educated professionals often prefer organizations that have a good track record of career development. During nursing shortages, a recognized program of career development can be the deciding factor for professionals selecting a position.

- *Obsolescence avoided and new skills acquired.* Because of the rapid changes in health care, especially in the areas of consumer demands and technology, employees may find that their skills have become obsolete. A successful career development program begins to retrain employees proactively, providing them with the necessary skills to remain current in their field and, therefore, valuable to the organization. Some of the most basic career development programs, such as financial planning and general equivalency diploma programs, can be the most rewarding programs for the staff.

- *Evidence-based practice promoted.* Evidence-based practice is now the gold standard for nursing practice, yet many nurses still lack both skill and confidence in knowing how to use research and best practices to inform their practice. The astute leader-manager recognizes this knowledge deficit and uses career planning and goal setting to allow these nurses the time and resources needed to acquire these skills.

INDIVIDUAL RESPONSIBILITY FOR CAREER DEVELOPMENT

Despite the many obvious benefits of career development programs, some nurses never create a personal career plan or set goals they wish to accomplish during their career. Instead, nursing becomes just a job and not a career. This viewpoint limits opportunities for professional advancement and personal growth, since what cannot be imagined, rarely becomes a reality. Indeed, Shirey (2009, p. 400) suggests that "extraordinary careers do not just happen; they are cultivated and planned." The impact of positive role modeling by nurse-leaders in influencing this perception cannot be understated.

Career development should begin with an assessment of self as well as one's work environment, job analysis, education, training, job search and acquisition, and work experience. This is known as *career planning*. Career planning includes evaluating one's strengths and weaknesses, setting goals, examining career opportunities, preparing for potential opportunities, and using appropriate developmental activities.

Career planning in nursing should begin with an individual's decision about educational entry level for practice and quickly expand to developing advanced skills in an area of nursing practice. Even for the entry-level nurse, career planning should include, at minimum, a commitment to the use of evidence-based practice, learning new skills or bettering practice by using role models and mentors, staying aware of and being involved in professional issues, and furthering one's education. At best, it should include long-term career goals as well as a specific plan to achieve lifelong learning.

Every nurse should proactively develop a career plan that provides opportunities for new learning, challenges, and opportunities for career divergence.

THE ORGANIZATION'S RESPONSIBILITY FOR CAREER DEVELOPMENT

Organizations also have responsibilities for career development. One of the organization's responsibilities for career development is the creation of career paths and advancement/ *career ladders* ("a structured sequence of job positions through which a person can progress in an organization") (BusinessDictionary.com, 2013a) for employees. It must also attempt to match position openings with appropriate people. This includes accurately assessing employees' performance and potential in order to offer the most appropriate career guidance, education, and training. Other organizational responsibilities include the following:

- *Integrating needs.* The human resources department, nursing division, nursing units, and education department must work and plan together to match job openings with the skills and talents of present employees.

- *Establishing career paths.* Career paths must not only be developed but also be communicated to the staff and implemented consistently. When designing career paths, each successive job in each path should contain additional responsibilities and duties that are greater than the previous jobs in that path. Each successive job also must be related to and use previous skills.

  Once career paths are established, they must be communicated effectively to all concerned staff. What employees must do to advance in a particular path should be very clear. Although various forms of *career ladders* have existed for some time, they are still not widely used. This problem is not unique to nursing. Even when health-care organizations design and use a career structure, the system often breaks down once the nurse leaves that organization. For example, nurses at the level of Clinical Nurse 3 in one hospital will usually lose that status when they leave the organization for another position.

- *Disseminating career information.* The education department, human resources department, and unit manager are all responsible for sharing career information; however, employees should not be encouraged to pursue unrealistic goals.

- *Posting job openings.* Although this is usually the responsibility of the human resources department, the manager should communicate this information, even when it means that one of the unit staff may transfer to another area. Effective managers know who needs to be encouraged to apply for openings and who is ready for more responsibility and challenges.

- *Assessing employees.* One of the benefits of a good appraisal system is the important information that it gives the manager on the performance, potential, and abilities of all staff members. The use of short- and long-term coaching will give managers insight into their employees' needs and wants so that appropriate career counseling can proceed.

- *Providing challenging assignments.* Planned work experience is one of the most powerful career development tools. This includes jobs that temporarily stretch employees to their maximum skill, temporary projects, assignment to committees, shift rotation, assignment to different units, and shift charge duties.

- *Giving support and encouragement.* Because excellent subordinates make managers' jobs easier, managers are often reluctant to encourage these subordinates to move up the corporate ladder or to seek more challenging experiences outside the manager's span of control. Thus, many managers hoard their talent. A leadership role requires that managers look beyond their immediate unit or department and consider the needs of the entire organization. Leaders recognize and share talent.

- *Developing personnel policies.* An active career development program often results in the recognition that certain personnel policies and procedures are impeding the success of the program. When this occurs, the organization should reexamine these policies and make necessary changes.

- *Providing education and training.* The impact of education and training on career development and retention of subordinate staff is discussed more fully in Chapter 16. The need for organizations to develop leaders and managers is presented later in this chapter.

A comparison of individual and organizational responsibilities for career development is shown in Display 11.3.

DISPLAY 11.3   Responsibilities for Career Development

Career Planning (Individual)	Career Management (Organizational)
• Self-assess interests, skills, strengths, with weaknesses, and values	• Integrate individual employee needs and organizational needs
• Determine goals	• Establish, design, communicate, and implement career paths
• Assess the organization for opportunities	• Disseminate career information
• Assess opportunities outside	• Post and communicate all jobs for the organization openings
• Develop strategies	• Assess employees' career needs
• Implement plans	• Provide work experience for development
• Evaluate plans	• Give support and encouragement
• Reassess and make new plans as necessary, at least biannually	• Develop new personnel policies as necessary, at least biannually
	• Provide training and education

CAREER COACHING

Organizations also have some responsibility to assist employees with career coaching. Unit managers sometimes take on this role but it may also be provided by informal organization leaders who are willing to act in a mentoring capacity. *Career coaching* involves helping others to identify professional goals and career options and then designing a career plan to achieve those goals. The Executive Coaching Network (n.d.) suggests that career coaches serve as "facilitators, motivators, consultants and sounding boards dealing with business goals, people interaction and self-management issues. While behavior change will often be a key focus, the coach's role is not that of a therapist. It is not about unraveling personalities, but often involves people doing things differently in the workplace" (para 4). Raffals (n.d.) suggests that career coaching involves "enabling others to see fresh perspectives, make new decisions, take new actions, and move forward 'growthfully' and productively from these freshly exposed perspectives and choices" (para 14).

LEARNING EXERCISE 11.2

Encouragement and Coaching for Goal Achievement

In your employment, has someone ever coached you, either formally or informally, to develop your career? For example, has an employer told you about career or educational opportunities? Have they offered tuition reimbursement? If so, how did you find out about such policies? Have you ever coached (something more than just encouraging) someone to pursue educational or career goals? Share the answers to these questions in class.

Career coaching typically has three steps:

1. *Gathering data.* One of the best ways to gather data about employees is to observe their behavior. When managers spend time observing employees, they are able to determine who has good communication skills, who is well organized, who uses effective negotiating skills, and who works collaboratively. Managers also should seek information about the employee's past work experience, performance appraisals, and educational experiences. Data also should include academic qualifications and credentials. Most of this information is retrievable in the employee's personnel file. Finally, employees themselves are an excellent source of information about career needs and wants.

2. *Asking what is possible.* As part of career planning, the manager should assess the department for possible changes in the future, openings or transfers, and potential challenges and opportunities. The manager should anticipate what type of needs lie ahead, what projects are planned, and what staffing and budget changes will occur. After carefully assessing the employee's profile and future opportunities, managers should consider each staff member and ask the following questions: How can this employee be helped so that he or she is better prepared to take advantage of the future? Who needs to be encouraged to return to school, to become credentialed, or to take a special course? Which employees need to be encouraged to transfer to a more challenging position, given more responsibility on their present unit, or moved to another shift? Managers can create a stimulating environment for career development by being aware of the uniqueness of their employees.

3. *Conducting the coaching session.* The goals of career coaching include helping employees increase their effectiveness; identifying potential opportunities in the organization; and advancing their knowledge, skills, and experience. It is important not to intimidate employees when questioning them about their future and their goals. Although there is no standard procedure for career coaching, the main emphasis should be on employee growth and development. The manager can assist the employee in exploring future options. Coaching sessions give the manager a chance to discover potential future managers—employees who should then begin to be groomed for a future managerial role in subsequent coaching sessions.

Career coaching, then, can be either short or long term. In *short-term career coaching*, the manager regularly asks the employees questions to develop and motivate them. Thus, short-term coaching is a spontaneous part of the experienced manager's repertoire.

Long-term career coaching, on the other hand, is a planned management action that occurs over the duration of employment. Because this type of coaching may cover a long time, it is frequently neglected unless the manager uses a systematic scheduling plan and a form for documentation. Because employees and managers move frequently within an organization, the lack of record keeping regarding employees' career needs has deterred nursing career development. In the present climate of organizational restructuring and downsizing, a manager's staff is even more in need of career coaching, and documentation of the career coaching takes on an even more important role. Display 11.4 is an example of a long-term coaching form.

DISPLAY 11.4   Sample Long-Term Coaching Form

Name of employee _____

Name of supervisor _____

Date _____ Date of last coaching interview_____

1.   What new challenges and responsibilities could be given to this employee that would utilize his or her special talents?

    _____

    _____

2.   What events happening in the organization do you foresee affecting this employee? (Examples would be plans to go to an all-RN staff, changing the mode of patient care delivery, increasing emphasis on credentialing by the new CEO of the nursing division, changing the medication system, and changing the ratio of nonprofessionals to professionals for nurse staffing.)

    _____

    _____

3.   How should the employee be preparing to meet new or changing expectations?

    _____

    _____

4.   What specific suggestions and guidance for the future can you give this employee? (Examples would be taking specific courses to prepare for change, urging them to pursue an advanced degree, considering changing shifts, urging them to seek challenges outside of your unit, and suggesting that they apply for the next management opening.)

    _____

    _____

5.   What specific organizational resources can you offer the employee?

    _____

    _____

6.   What new information regarding this employee's long-term plans, aspirations, and potential have your review of the personnel record, your observations, and this interview given?

    _____

    _____

7.   Do the organizational and professional career plans held by the individual match your vision of his or her future? If not, how do they differ?

_____

_____

8.   What developmental and professional growth has taken place since the last coaching?

_____

_____

9.   Date of next coaching interview _____

Long-term coaching, however, is a major step in building an effective team and an excellent strategy to increase productivity and retention. The effective manager should have at least one coaching session with each employee annually, in addition to any coaching that may occur during the appraisal interview. Although some coaching should occur during the performance appraisal interview, additional coaching should be planned at a less stressful time. Coaching provides opportunities to assist employees in the growth and development necessary for expanded roles and responsibilities. A major leadership role is the development of subordinate staff. This interest in the future of individual employees plays a vital role in retention and productivity.

LEARNING EXERCISE 11.3

Career Coaching a Bored Employee

You are the registered nurse (RN) team leader on a busy step-down critical care unit. One of the certified nursing assistants (CNAs) assigned to your team is technically very competent, always completes her work on time, but frequently appears to be bored. The only time she seems to be excited about work is when she is assisting you or the other RNs with more complex skills such as central line dressing changes, peripherally inserted central catheters (PICC), and complex wound packings. She has shared at times, her long-term career goal to become an RN but has never verbalized any specific plan to achieve this. Although she is highly capable, her formal education to date is limited to a high school diploma she earned 3 years ago. She currently provides full-time financial support for herself and her 3-year-old daughter.

Assignment:

1. Identify questions you might ask the CNA that could be a part of both short- and long-term career coaching for this employee.

2. What resources might be explored to support this employee in attaining higher education?

3. What leadership role modeling could be made available to this employee to encourage her in furthering her career goals?

MANAGEMENT DEVELOPMENT

Management development is a planned system of training and developing people so that they acquire the skills, insights, and attitudes needed to manage people and their work effectively within the organization. Management development is often referred to as _succession planning_.

Many nurses feel uncertain that they have the skills needed to be effective managers, and they lack confidence that the decision making, interpersonal, and organizational skills they learned as staff nurses can translate to the management role.

Many nurses feel that they lack the knowledge and experience necessary to become a manager.

While many of these skills do transfer, becoming an effective manager is generally not intuitive. With the flattening of organizational hierarchies, an expected increase in nursing management vacancies due to retirement, and a continued increase in managerial responsibilities, new leader-managers will likely need the formal education and training that are a part of a management development program. The program must include a means of developing appropriate attitudes through social learning theory as well as adequate content on management theory.

Huston (2008) suggests that the skill sets needed by leader-managers in the year 2020 will be even more complex than they are today and that contemporary nursing and health-care organizations must begin now to create the educational models and management development programs necessary to prepare the next generation of leader-managers. Essential nurse-leader competencies for 2020 identified by Huston include having a global perspective or mindset regarding health-care and professional nursing issues; technology skills that facilitate mobility and portability of relationships, interactions, and operational processes; expert decision-making skills rooted in empirical science; the ability to create organization cultures that permeate quality health care and patient/worker safety; understanding and appropriately intervening in political processes; highly developed collaborative and team building skills; the ability to balance authenticity and performance expectations; and being able to envision and proactively adapt to a health-care system characterized by rapid change and chaos.

Support for such management development programs by the organization should occur in two ways. First, top-level management must do more than bear the cost of management development classes. They must create an organizational structure that allows managers to apply their new knowledge. Therefore, for such programs to be effective, the organization must be willing to practice a management style that incorporates sound management principles.

Second, training outcomes improve if nursing executives are active in planning and developing a systematic and integrated program. Whenever possible, nursing administrators should teach some of the classes and, at the very least, make sure that the program supports top management philosophy. Just as nurses are required to be certified in critical care before they accept a position in a CCU, so too should nurses be required to take part in a management development program before their appointment to a management position. This requires early identification and grooming of potential management candidates.

The first step in the process would be an appraisal of the present management team and an analysis of possible future needs. The second step would be the establishment of a training and development program. This would require decisions such as the following: How often should the formal management course be offered? Should outside educators be involved, or should in-house staff teach it? Who should be involved in teaching the didactic portion? Should there be two levels of classes, one for first-level and one for middle-level managers? Should the management development courses be open to all, or should people be recommended by someone from management? In addition to formal course content, what other methods should be used to develop managers? Should other methods be used, such as job rotation through an understudy system of pairing selected people with a manager and management coaching?

The inclusion of *social learning activities* also is a valuable part of management development. Management development will not be successful unless learners have ample chance to try out new skills. Providing potential managers with didactic management theory alone inadequately prepares them for the attitudes, skills, and insights necessary for effective management. Case studies, management games, transactional analysis, and sensitivity training are also effective in changing attitudes and increasing self-awareness. All of these techniques appropriately use social learning theory strategies.

COMPETENCY ASSESSMENT AS PART OF CAREER DEVELOPMENT

Competency assessment and professional specialty certification are also a part of career management. BusinessDictionary.com (2013b) suggests that the definition of a *professional* is "a person formally certified by a professional body or belonging to a specific profession by virtue of having completed a required course of studies and/or practice, and whose competence can usually be measured against an established set of standards" (para 1).

Huston (2014) notes that unfortunately, in many states, a practitioner is determined to be competent when initially licensed and thereafter, unless proven otherwise. Yet, clearly, passing a licensing exam and continuing to work as a clinician does not assure competence throughout a career. Competence requires continual updates to knowledge and practice, and this is difficult in a health-care environment characterized by rapidly emerging new technologies, chaotic change, and perpetual clinical advancements.

The Institute of Medicine (IOM) (2010) report *The Future of Nursing* agrees, suggesting that nursing graduates now need competency in a variety of areas, including continuous improvement of the quality and safety of health-care systems; informatics; evidence-based practice; a knowledge of complex systems; skills and methods for leadership and management of continual improvement; population health and population-based care management; and health policy knowledge, skills, and attitudes (Cronenwett, 2011). One must at least question how many nurses currently in practice would be able to demonstrate competency in these areas.

Assessing, maintaining, and supporting maintaining *continued competence* is also a challenge in professional nursing. For example, Huston (2014) notes that some nurses develop high levels of competence in specific areas of nursing practice as a result of work experience and specialization at the expense of staying current in other areas of practice. In addition, employers often ask nurses to provide care in areas of practice outside their area of expertise because a nursing shortage encourages them to do so. In addition, many current competence assessments focus more on skills than they do on knowledge (Huston). The issue is also complicated by the fact that there are no national standards for defining, measuring, or requiring continuing competence in nursing.

Current competence assessments often focus more on skills than they do on knowledge.

Managers should appraise each employee's competency level not only as part of performance appraisal but also as part of career development. This appraisal should lead to the development of a plan that outlines what the employee must do to achieve desired competencies in both current and future positions. Often, however, competency assessment focuses only on whether the employee has achieved required minimal competency levels to meet current federal, state, or organizational standards and not on how to exceed these competency levels. Thus, competency assessment and goal setting in career planning is proactive, with the employee identifying areas of potential future growth and the manager assisting in identifying strategies that can help the employee achieve that goal.

Competency assessment and goal setting in career planning should help the employee identify how to exceed these levels of competency.

Certainly, some individual responsibility for maintaining competence and pursuing lifelong learning is suggested by the American Nurses Association *(ANA) Code of Ethics for Nurses with Interpretive Statements* in its assertion that nurses are obligated to provide adequate and competent nursing care (ANA, 2001). State Nurse Practice Acts also hold nurses accountable for being reasonable and prudent in their practice. Both standards require the nurse to have at least some personal responsibility for continually assessing his or her professional competence through reflective practice (Huston, 2014).

In addition, the Institute of Medicine (2010) report *The Future of Nursing* calls for nursing schools and nurses to pursue learning. Foster (2012, p. 115) notes that health-care organizations must provide an environment that promotes lifelong learning, with the resources to make this a reality for practicing nurses. "This will help to ensure nurses are capable and qualified to manage the diverse patient populations that are recipients of nursing care."

The individual RN has a professional obligation to seek lifelong learning and maintain competence.

LEARNING EXERCISE 11.4

Does Mandatory Continuing Education (CE) Assure Competence in Nursing?

A majority of the states in the United States have some kind of requirements for CE for professional nurse license renewal. These requirements typically vary from a few hours to 30 hours every 2 years. Huston (2014) notes that use of mandatory CE to document continuing competence in nursing continues to be very controversial because there is limited research demonstrating correlation among CE, continuing competence, and improved patient outcomes. In addition, many professional organizations have expressed concern about the quality of mandated CE courses and the lack of courses for experts and specialists. Likewise, there is no agreement on the optimal number of annual credits needed to ensure competence.

Assignment: In small groups, debate the use of CE as a valid and reliable measure of continuing competence in nursing.

PROFESSIONAL SPECIALTY CERTIFICATION

Professional specialty certification is one way an employee can demonstrate advanced achievement of competencies. To achieve professional certification, nurses must meet eligibility criteria that may include years and types of work experience, as well as minimum educational levels, active nursing licenses, and successful completion of a nationally administered examination (Huston, 2014). Certifications normally last 5 years.

Professional associations grant specialty certification as a formal but voluntary process of demonstrating expertise in a particular area of nursing. For example, the ANA established the ANA Certification Program in 1973 to provide tangible recognition of professional achievement in a defined functional or clinical area of nursing. The American Nurses Credentialing Center (ANCC), a subsidiary of ANA, became its own corporation in 1991 and since then has certified hundreds of thousands of nurses throughout the United States and its territories in more than 40 specialty and advanced practice areas of nursing. In 2012 alone, 16,575 individuals applied for their initial certification (ANCC, 2012). A few of the other organizations offering specialty certifications for nurses are the American Association of Critical Care Nursing, the American Association of Nurse Anesthetists, the American College of Nurse Midwives, the Board of Certification for Emergency Nursing, and the Rehabilitation Nursing Certification Board.

Huston (2014) notes that it is middle- and top-level nurse-managers who play the most significant role in creating work environments that value and reward certification. For example, nurse-managers can grant tuition reimbursement or salary incentives to workers who seek certification. This is critical since the greatest barrier to nurses obtaining specialty certification in a recent study was the cost of the examination and the greatest barrier to recertification was the fee for renewal (Haskins, Hnatiuk, & Yoder, 2011). Managers can also show their support for professional certification by giving employees paid time off to take the certification exam and by publicly recognizing employees who have achieved specialty certification.

Managers should also encourage certified nurses to promote their achievements by introducing themselves as certified nurses to patients, wearing their certification pins, and publicly displaying their credentials (Haskins et al., 2011). In doing so, the certified nurse acts as a leader and role model to other nurses considering specialty certification. In addition, Altman (2011) suggests that many nurses do not seek certification due to a fear of test taking or failure and she suggests that nurse-leaders can play a pivotal role in supporting employees to overcome these fears. It may be as simple as providing study resources, granting time off to study, supporting nurses verbally during their certification journey, and rewarding and recognizing staff who do become certified.

Personal Benefits of Specialty Certification

The certified nurse often finds many personal benefits related to the attainment of such status, including more rapid promotions on career ladders, advancement opportunities into management, and personal or professional feelings of accomplishment (Knudson, 2013). In addition, they often earn more than their noncertified counterparts. Specialty-certified critical care nurses in the United States make an average of $18,000 more per year than their noncertified counterparts (Certification: Promoting Excellence in Nursing, 2013). The difference is especially pronounced in the West, where the difference is $51,000 per year between certified and noncertified critical care nurses. Some of the personal benefits associated with professional certification are shown in Display 11.5.

DISPLAY 11.5   Personal Benefits of Professional Certification

- Provides a sense of accomplishment and achievement
- Validation of specialty knowledge and competence to peers and patients
- Increased credibility
- Increased self-confidence
- Promotes greater autonomy of practice
- Provides for increased career opportunities and greater competitiveness in the job market
- May result in salary incentives

Source: Huston, C. (2014). Assuring provider competence through licensure, continuing education, and certification. In C. Huston (Ed.), Professional issues in nursing (3rd ed.). Philadelphia, PA: Lippincott Williams & Wilkins 292–307.

Patient Outcomes and Specialty Certification

Boltz, Capezuti, Wagner, Rosenberg, and Secic (2013) suggest that while many positive professional and process outcomes associated with certification exist, the relationship between specialty certification and patient outcomes is less clear. Research done by Krapohl, Manojlovich, Redman, and Zhang (2010) found no correlation between the proportion of certified nurses on an intensive care unit and three nursing-sensitive patient outcomes, although educational levels of the nurses were not considered. The association between nurses' perception of overall workplace empowerment and certification, however, was positive. Boltz et al. (2013) showed an inverse relationship between certification and patient falls, but no relationship with injurious falls, unit-acquired pressure ulcer prevalence, and restraint prevalence.

A study by Kendall-Gallagher, Aiken, Sloane, and Cimiotti (2011), however, found that nurse specialty certification was associated with better patient outcomes; however, certification had no impact on mortality and failure to rescue when the nurse did not have a baccalaureate degree. The researchers suggested then that since certification was not a substitute for education, employers might want to invest in improving nursing education levels for staff without BSN degrees, rather than investing in specialty certification for these nurses.

REFLECTIVE PRACTICE AND THE PROFESSIONAL PORTFOLIO

Kinsella (2010) suggests that "reflective practice," a term coined by Donald Schon, is one of the most popular theories of professional knowledge in the last 20 years. *Reflective practice* is defined by the North Carolina Board of Nursing (NCBN) (2011, para 7) as "a process for the assessment of one's own practice to identify and seek learning opportunities to promote continued competence." Inherent in the process is the evaluation and incorporation of this learning into one's practice. Such self-assessment is gaining popularity as a way to promote professional practice and maintain competence, which has paved the way for the creation of reflective practice/professional portfolio model for competence assessment.

A *professional portfolio*, which all nurses should maintain, can be described as a collection of materials that document a nurse's competencies and illustrate the expertise of the nurse. The professional portfolio typically contains a number of core components; biographical information, educational background, certifications achieved and employment history; a one- to two-page resumé; a competency record or checklist; personal and professional goals; professional development experiences, presentations, consultations, and publications; professional activities; community activities; honors and awards; and letters of thanks from patients, families, peers, organizations, and others (Sherrod, 2007). The individual needs to be selective in collecting best-work documentation and only include those materials that illustrate competency and highlight achievement.

All nurses should maintain a portfolio to reflect their professional growth throughout their career.

Maintaining a professional portfolio avoids lost opportunities to save documents since professional nurses should always have documentation readily available to pursue a promotion, to consider a new position, or to apply for another position in their present employment. Sinclair, Bowen, and Donkin (2013) note, however, that for the professional portfolio to truly have value, it must be more than just a collection of evidence of accomplishments; it must include reflection and be actively used as a tool to promote professional growth throughout one's career. Only then will it promote a continuous cyclic process of professional development that supports the maintenance of continued competence.

LEARNING EXERCISE 11.5

Creating a Professional Portfolio

Assignment:

1. Identify the categories of evidence you would use to organize a professional portfolio if you were to create one today.

2. Identify specific evidence you could include in each of these categories. What evidence currently exists and what would need to be created?

3. How would you incorporate reflection in creating a personal professional portfolio?

CAREER PLANNING AND THE NEW GRADUATE NURSE

During the current economic downturn, many new graduates have rushed to find a "job"—any job—in nursing, forgetting that even early employment decisions are critical to the achievement of their long-term career plans. Shirey (2009) suggests new graduates must select their first employment wisely and seek work in a facility with a strong reputation for supportive work environments and a reputation of excellence in multiple arenas.

Finding work in a facility with orientation programs, internships, residencies, and fellowships is also important to the new graduate since it takes time to gain the expertise and self-confidence that is a part of being an expert nurse. Mentors and preceptors should also be available to support the new graduate nurse and to role model high-quality, evidence-based decision making and clinical practice. If the new graduate has a positive, nurturing first employment experience, he or she is much more likely to take future career risks, to pursue lifelong learning, and to have the energy and commitment to become involved in the bigger issues of their profession.

New graduates also have responsibility during the crucial first few years of employment to gain the expertise they need to have more opportunities for career divergence in the future. This includes becoming an expert in one or more areas of practice, gaining professional certifications, and being well informed about professional nursing and health-care issues. This is also a time where participation in professional associations has great value as a result of the opportunities for mentoring and networking. Finally, all new graduates should consider at what point, continued formal education will be a part of their career ladder and professional journey.

TRANSITION-TO-PRACTICE PROGRAMS/RESIDENCIES FOR NEW GRADUATE NURSES

Arguments have grown over the last decade regarding the need for *transition-to-practice programs* (also known as *residences, externships,* or *internships*) for new graduates of nursing programs. Jones and West (2014) note that new graduate nurses often begin working with little more than a few weeks of orientation, in contrast to most other professions, which require formal and often standardized internships or residencies. This is largely a residual outcome of the traditional nursing educational system that was grounded in apprenticeship and hospital-based training programs which led to the student receiving a diploma in nursing.

Jones and West (2014) suggest the ever-changing health-care delivery care system, with its increasing complexity of patient care, evolving technology, and focus on patient safety, has raised the bar in terms of expectations for new graduate nurses. New graduates must now hit the ground running with well-developed critical thinking and problem-solving skills; the ability to exercise clinical judgment with know-how to practice from an evidence-based and outcome-driven perspective; and the ability to develop effectively from a novice to an expert in competency.

Such high expectations accompanied by inadequate advanced apprenticeship training often leads to high turnover rates for new graduate nurses. In addition, patient safety and quality of care are at risk if new graduates do not have the critical thinking skills or competencies needed to apply critical judgments to patient situations. Jones and West (2014) suggest that transition-to-practice programs bridge the gap by providing the new graduate opportunities to take the learning from nursing school and apply it in an expanded, intensive, and integrated clinical learning situation while providing direct patient care—much in the same way that the internship of physicians is based upon applying academic learning to actual care of patients and transition into the professional role.

A well-designed transition-to-practice program strengthens new graduates' skills and competencies and prepares the new nurse for the demands of caring for patients. Furthermore, a systematic approach to transition not only facilitates "*on-boarding*" (integration into staffing on the nursing unit to provide direct patient care), it reduces turnover by decreasing the toll associated with insufficient preparation for the work environment (Examining the Evidence, 11.1).

Examining the Evidence 11.1

Source: Trepanier, S., Early, S., Ulrich, B., & Cherry, B. (2012). New graduate nurse residency program: A cost-benefit analysis based on turnover and contract labor usage. Nursing Economics, 30(4), 207–214.

The purpose of this study, which included data from 15 hospitals in California, Florida, Georgia, Nebraska, Missouri, Tennessee, and Texas, was to conduct a cost–benefit analysis of new graduate nursing residency programs utilizing turnover rates and contract labor usage. Secondary data analysis of 524 new graduate RNs was conducted including descriptive and step-wise regression analyses. Findings indicated new graduate residency programs were associated with a decrease in the 12-month turnover rate from 36.08% to 6.41% ($p<0.05$) and reduction in contract labor usage from $19,099 to $5,490 per average daily census ($p<0.05$). These cost–benefit analyses suggest net savings between $10 and $50 per patient day when compared with traditional methods of orientation. The researchers concluded that new graduate nurse residency programs offer a cost-effective innovative approach and should be valued as an investment as opposed to an expense.

Jones and West (2014) suggest that employers and academe share the obligation to provide bridges from student to practicing nurse and that the inclusion of transition-to-practice programs is increasingly considered an expectation of the nursing education process and career development. Indeed, the Institute of Medicine (IOM) (2010) report on *The Future of Nursing* identified transition-to-practice programs/residencies as one of the eight key recommendations to actualize nursing contributions to the demands of health-care reform. The IOM suggests "state Boards of Nursing, accrediting bodies, the federal government, and health care organizations should take action to support nurses' completion of a transition-to-practice program (nurse residency) after they have completed a pre-licensure or advanced practice degree program or when they are transitioning into new clinical practice areas" (IOM, 2010, p. 280).

Multiple types of transition-to-practice programs exist (Jones & West, 2014). There are programs that begin in the final year of nursing school and continue through licensure, although these programs are generally not intended to take the place of employer-based residencies, which often extend to 1 year and have a planned structured, mentored experience. Most transition-to-practice programs are employer-based "new graduate classes" within a hospital or employer (hospital) based programs that take up to a year to complete. Still others are for new graduates who have yet to be hired, so they may gain skills in order to become more employable.

Traditional transition-to-practice programs (residencies) are funded and provided by employers (usually hospitals). The hospital hires a group of new graduate RNs and provides a curriculum over the first 6 months to 1 year of their employment. The new graduate hires receive full pay, though they do not have a full patient load for some time into their residency. Transition-to-practice programs are also found, however, in nonacute settings, such as primary care clinics, behavior health clinics, long-term care, home health, corrections, school nursing, and public health, and they provide exposure to career paths that new graduates may not have previously considered, and also provide an opportunity for nonacute employers to consider hiring new graduate nurses (Jones & West, 2014).

LEARNING EXERCISE 11.6

Addressing Nurse Residency Concerns

Jones and West (2014) note that while many groups are actively working to assure that nurse residences exist to provide a solid foundation for successful career development in nursing, many questions continue to exist about resource allocation (human and fiscal).

Assignment: Select any two of the following four questions and write a one-page essay defending your answers.

1. Schools have voiced concerns that transition-to-practice programs are taking preceptorship slots that have been historically allocated to pre-licensure students. Do you support this reallocation of resources?

2. Should transition-to-practice programs/residencies be a requirement for completion of nursing education?

3. Residencies have historically been a cost hospitals or employers have assumed. Should this cost be shared and why?

4. Would you participate in a school-based transition-to-practice program without an associated stipend, if it could help you gain experience? Would you pay to participate?

RESUMÉ PREPARATION

Despite the best efforts of organizations to help subordinates identify career needs, wants, and opportunities, it is how employees represent themselves that often determines whether desired career opportunities become a reality. Creating a positive image often depends on having well-developed interviewing skills (Chapter 15) and a well-prepared resumé. The resumé is an important career-planning tool. It is also a screening tool used by employers to select applicants and make promotion decisions; therefore, maintaining a current, professional resumé is a career-planning necessity for health-care professionals and should not be undertaken lightly.

Resumé Structure

Various acceptable styles and formats of resumés exist. However, because the resumé represents the professionalism of the applicant and recruiters use it to summarize an applicant's qualifications, it must be professionally prepared, make an impression, and quickly capture the reader's attention. The following are the general guidelines for resumé preparation:

- Keep your writing concise and clear.
- Type the document in a single-font format that is easy to read (12-point font or larger is recommended).
- Use bulleted points or sentences.
- Include educational background, work history, awards or honors received, scholarly achievements such as publications and presentations, and community service activities.
- Do not include personal information such as marital status, age, whether you have children, ethnicity, or religious affiliations.
- Maximize your strong points and minimize your weaknesses.

- Never lie or overstretch your accomplishments because doing so places your credibility at great risk.

- Use good grammar, correct punctuation, and proper sentence structure. Typographic errors suggest you may not be serious about the job application or that the quality of your work will be substandard.

- Use high-quality, heavy white, or off-white paper to print the resumé.

- Include a cover letter (whether by mail or e-mail), addressed to a specific individual when possible, to introduce yourself, briefly highlight key points of the resumé, and make a positive first impression.

Additional strategies for resumé preparation were identified by GE Healthcare (2009):

- Know what you want to do so that you can tailor your resumé accordingly. In other words, identify the job you really want to have and then create a resumé around the qualifications you have to perform that job. GE Healthcare suggests that when resumés are not tailored, "you come across as someone who has sent out a hundred resumés, willing to take any job at all" (p. 79). Do include a professional objective or goal statement specific to your desired job.

- Know what recruiters are looking for. Look at sample job descriptions online and note their preferred hiring criteria. Then create a resumé that highlights those qualifications and the work experience you have that have given you that expertise.

- Highlight your accomplishments. The average resumé receives less than 10 seconds of attention from recruiters so you need to make important points stand out.

A sample resumé is shown in Figure 11.1.

SUSAN CARMEL GUEVARA
628 Normal Street
Chico, CA 95928
Home phone: (530) 555-3718
sguevara©emailaccount.com

CAREER GOAL: To practice professional nursing within a progressive environment that provides challenges and opportunities for professional and personal growth.

EDUCATION
- Bachelor of Science in Nursing, California State University, Chico (CSUC), May 2009. California Public Health Certificate. Cumulative GPA 3.48; Nursing GPA 3.54.

HONORS
- Sigma Theta Tau International Society of Nursing, Kappa Omicron Chapter.
- CSUC School of Nursing Scholarship Award 2007 and 2008.
- Publication of "An Expression of Nursing, A Journal of Student Writing" in The CSUC School of Nursing Alumni newsletter, spring 2007.

WORK EXPERIENCE
- June 2006–Present:
  Nurse Attendant. Memorial Hospital, Chico, CA. Performed direct patient care under the supervision and guidance of a registered nurse. (Job description available on request.)

- July 2004–May 2006
  Home Health Aide/Respite Worker. Sommers Elder Services, Chico, CA. Performed custodial care and light housekeeping duties for home-bound elderly and the disabled.

REFERENCES: Available on request.

FIGURE 11.1 • Sample nursing resumé.

INTEGRATING LEADERSHIP ROLES AND MANAGEMENT FUNCTIONS IN CAREER DEVELOPMENT

It is clear that appropriate career management should foster positive career development, alleviate burnout, reduce attrition, and promote productivity. Management functions in career development include disseminating career information and posting job openings. The manager should have a well-developed, planned system for career development for all employees; this system should include long-term coaching, the appropriate use of transfers, and how promotions are to be handled. These policies should be fair and communicated effectively to all employees.

With the integration of leadership, managers become more aware of how their own values shape personal career decisions. In addition, the leader-manager shows genuine interest in the career development of all employees. Career planning is encouraged, and potential leaders are identified and developed. Present leaders are rewarded when they see those, whom they have helped to develop, advance in their careers and in turn develop leadership and management skills in others.

Effective managers recognize that in all career decisions, the employee must decide when he or she is ready to pursue promotions, return to school, or take on greater responsibility. Leaders are aware that every person perceives success differently. Although career development programs benefit all employees and the organization, there is an added bonus for the professional nurse. When professional nurses have the opportunity to experience a well-planned career development program, a greater viability for and increased commitment to the profession are often evident.

KEY CONCEPTS

- There are many outcomes of a career development program that justify its implementation.
- Career job sequencing should assist the manager in career management.
- Career development programs consist of a set of personal responsibilities called career planning and a set of management responsibilities called career management.
- Employees often need to be encouraged to make more formalized long-term career plans.
- Career planning should include, at minimum, a commitment to the use of evidence-based practice, learning new skills or bettering practice through the use of role models and mentors, staying aware of and being involved in professional issues, and furthering one's education.
- Designing career paths is an important part of organizational career management.
- Managers should plan specific interventions that promote growth and development in each of their subordinates.
- Most individuals progress through normal and predictable career stages.
- Career coaching involves helping others to identify professional goals and career options and designing a career plan to achieve those goals. This coaching should be both short and long terms.
- Competency assessment and goal setting in career planning should help the employee identify how to exceed the minimum levels of competency required by federal, state, or organizational standards.
- Professional specialty certification is one way that an employee can demonstrate advanced achievement of competencies.

(Continued)

- To be successful, management development must be planned and supported by top-level management. This type of planned program is called succession management.

- If appropriate management attitudes and insight are goals of a management development program, social learning techniques need to be part of the teaching strategies used.

- Multiple types of transition-to-practice programs exist, but all are focused on helping nursing students bridge from school into employment.

- Maintaining a current, professional resumé is a career-planning necessity for the health-care professional and should not be undertaken lightly.

- Cover letters (whether by mail or e-mail) should always be used when submitting a resumé. Their purpose is to introduce the applicant, briefly highlight key points of the resumé, and make a positive first impression.

- All nurses should maintain a professional portfolio (a collection of materials that document a nurse's competencies and illustrate the expertise of the nurse) to reflect their professional growth over their career.

ADDITIONAL LEARNING EXERCISES AND APPLICATIONS

LEARNING EXERCISE 11.7

Developing a Realistic 20-Year Career Plan

Develop a 20-year career plan, taking into account the constraints of family responsibilities such as marriage, children, and aging parents. Have your career plan critiqued to determine whether it is feasible and whether the timelines and goals are realistic.

LEARNING EXERCISE 11.8

Listing Policies Relating to Reimbursement of Educational Expenses for Career Advancement

You have been appointed to a committee of staff nurses in your home health agency to assist in developing a set of policies regarding the reimbursement of employee expenses for educational or career advancement. Employees have suggested that support for educational advancement is not appropriated uniformly and no criteria exist to determine who should be eligible.

Assignment: Develop a list of five to seven policies regarding who and what should be eligible for educational expenses for career advancement. Be able to justify your criteria and policies.

LEARNING EXERCISE 11.9

Preparing a Resumé

The medical center where you have applied for a position has requested that you submit a resumé along with your application. Prepare a professional resumé, using your actual experience and education. You may use any style and format that you desire. The resumé will be critiqued on its professional appearance and appropriateness of included content.

LEARNING EXERCISE 11.10

Constructing a Management Development Program

You are serving on an ad hoc committee to construct a management development program. Your organization has requested that the charge nurses work with staff development and plan a 1-week training and education program that would be required of all new charge nurses before their appointment. Because the organization will be bearing the cost of the program (i.e., paying for the educators and employee time), you are required to select appropriate content and educational methods that will not exceed 40 hours, including actual orientation time by a charge nurse.

Assignment: Develop and write up such a plan, and share it with the class. Your plan should depict hours, content, and educational methods.

LEARNING EXERCISE 11.11

Career Mapping

Career planning is often made easier when a career map is created to assist in developing a long-term master plan. Use the career guide shown in Figure 11.2, along with the individual responsibilities for career development outlined in Display 11.3, to assist with developing the personal plan described in Learning Exercise 11.7.

(*Continued*)

The informal structure even has its own communication network, known as the *grapevine*. Education Portal (2003–2013) suggests that grapevine communication is at the heart of the informal organization; it is the conversations that occur in the break room, down the halls, during the carpool, and in between work that allows the relationships of informal groups to develop. In addition, social media sites and electronic communication such as e-mail and text messages are also used to facilitate communication among informal group members.

While grapevine communication is fast and can facilitate information upward, downward, and horizontally, it is difficult to control or to stop. With little accountability for the message, grapevine communication often becomes a source for rumor or gossip.

The informal structure also has its own leaders. In addition, it also has its own communication channels, often referred to as the *grapevine*.

People need to be aware that informal authority and lines of communication exist in every group, even when they are never formally acknowledged. The primary emphasis of this chapter, however, is the identification of components of organizational structure, the leadership roles and management functions associated with formal organizational structure, and the proper utilization of committees to accomplish organizational objectives (Display 12.1).

DISPLAY 12.1	Leadership Roles and Management Functions Associated with Organizational Structure

LEADERSHIP ROLES

1. Evaluates the organizational structure frequently to determine if management positions should be eliminated to shorten the chain of command.
2. Encourages and guides employees to follow the chain of command and counsels employees who do not do so.
3. Supports personnel in advisory (staff) positions.
4. Models responsibility and accountability for subordinates.
5. Assists staff to see how their roles are congruent with and complement the organization's mission, vision, and goals.
6. Facilitates constructive informal group structure.
7. Encourages upward communication.
8. Fosters a positive organizational culture between work groups and subcultures that facilitates shared values and goals.
9. Promotes participatory decision making and shared governance to empower subordinates.
10. Uses committees to facilitate group goals, not to delay decisions.

MANAGEMENT FUNCTIONS

1. Is knowledgeable about the organization's internal structure, including personal and department authority and responsibilities within that structure.
2. Facilitates constructive formal group structure.
3. Provides the staff with an accurate unit organization chart and assists with interpretation.
4. When possible, maintains unity of command.
5. Clarifies unity of command when there is confusion.
6. Follows appropriate subordinate complaints upward through chain of command.
7. Establishes an appropriate span of control.
8. Strives to create a constructive organizational culture and positive organizational climate.
9. Uses the informal organization to meet organizational goals.
10. Uses committee structure to increase the quality and quantity of work accomplished.
11. Works, as appropriate, to achieve a level of operational excellence befitting an organization that would be eligible for magnet status or some other recognition of excellence.
12. Continually identifies, analyzes, and promotes stakeholder interests in the organization.

ORGANIZATIONAL THEORY AND BUREAUCRACY

Max Weber, a German social scientist, is known as the father of organizational theory. Generally acknowledged to have developed the most comprehensive classic formulation on the characteristics of *bureaucracy*, Weber wrote from the vantage point of a manager instead of that of a scholar. During the 1920s, Weber saw the growth of the large-scale organization and correctly predicted that this growth required a more formalized set of procedures for administrators. His statement on bureaucracy, published after his death, is still the most influential statement on the subject.

Weber postulated three "ideal types" of authority or reasons why people throughout history have obeyed their rulers. One of these, *legal-rational authority*, was based on a belief in the legitimacy of the pattern of normative rules and the rights of those elevated to authority under such rules to issue commands. Obedience, then, was owed to the legally established impersonal set of rules rather than to a personal ruler. It is this type of authority that is the basis for Weber's concept of bureaucracy.

Weber argued that the great virtue of bureaucracy—indeed, perhaps its defining characteristic—was that it was an institutional method for applying general rules to specific cases, thereby making the actions of management fair and predictable. Other characteristics of bureaucracies as identified by Weber include the following:

- There must be a clear *division of labor* (i.e., all work must be divided into units that can be undertaken by individuals or groups of individuals competent to perform those tasks).
- A well-defined *hierarchy of authority* must exist in which superiors are separated from subordinates; on the basis of this hierarchy, remuneration for work is dispensed, authority is recognized, privileges are allotted, and promotions are awarded.
- There must be impersonal rules and *impersonality of interpersonal relationships*. In other words, bureaucrats are not free to act in any way they please. Bureaucratic rules provide superiors systematic control over subordinates, thus limiting the opportunities for arbitrary behavior and personal favoritism.
- A system of procedures for dealing with work situations (i.e., regular activities to get a job done) must exist.
- A system of rules covering the rights and duties of each position must be in place.
- Selection for employment and promotion is based on technical competence.

Bureaucracy was the ideal tool to harness and routinize the energy and prolific production of the Industrial Revolution. Weber's work did not, however, consider the complexity of managing organizations in the 21st century. Weber wrote during an era when worker motivation was taken for granted, and his simplification of management and employee roles did not examine the bilateral relationships between employee and management prevalent in most organizations today.

Since Weber's research, management theorists have learned much about human behavior, and most organizations have modified their structures and created alternative organizational designs that reduce rigidity and impersonality. Yet, almost 100 years after Weber's findings, components of bureaucratic structure continue to be found in the design of most large organizations.

Current research suggests that changing an organization's structure in a manner that increases autonomy and work empowerment for nurses will lead to more effective patient care.

COMPONENTS OF ORGANIZATIONAL STRUCTURE

Weber is also credited with the development of the organization chart to depict an organization's structure. Because the organization chart (Fig. 12.1) is a picture of an organization, the knowledgeable manager can derive much information from reading the chart. For example, an organization chart can help identify roles and their expectations.

In addition, by observing elements, such as which departments report directly to the chief executive officer (CEO), the novice manager can make some inferences about the organization. For instance, reporting to a middle level manager rather than an executive officer suggests that person has less status and influence than someone who reports to an individual higher on the organization chart. Managers who understand an organization's structure and relationships will be able to expedite decisions and have a greater understanding of the organizational environment.

Relationships and Chain of Command

The organization chart defines formal relationships within the institution. Formal relationships, lines of communication, and authority are depicted on a chart by unbroken (solid) lines. These *line* positions can be shown by solid horizontal or vertical lines. Solid horizontal lines represent communication between people with similar spheres of responsibility and power but different functions. Solid vertical lines between positions denote the official *chain of command*, the formal paths of communication and authority. Those having the greatest decision-making authority are located at the top; those with the least are at the bottom. The level of position on the chart also signifies status and power.

Dotted or broken lines on the organization chart represent *staff* positions. Because these positions are advisory, a staff member provides information and assistance to the manager but has limited organizational authority. Used to increase his or her sphere of influence, staff positions enable a manager to handle more activities and interactions than would otherwise be

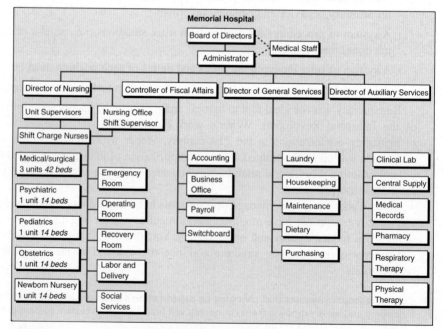

FIGURE 12.1 • Sample organizational chart. Copyright ® 2006 Lippincott Williams & Wilkins. Instructor's Resource CD-ROM to Accompany Leadership Roles and Management Functions in Nursing, by Bessie L. Marquis and Carol J. Huston.

possible. These positions also provide for specialization that would be impossible for any one manager to achieve alone. Although staff positions can make line personnel more effective, organizations can function without them.

Advisory (staff) positions do not have inherent legitimate authority. Clinical specialists and in-service directors in staff positions often lack the authority that accompanies a line relationship. Accomplishing the role expectations in a staff position may therefore be more difficult because formal authority is limited. Because only line positions have authority for decision making, staff positions may result in an ineffective use of support services unless job descriptions and responsibilities for these positions are clearly spelled out.

Unity of command is indicated by the vertical solid line between positions on the organizational chart. This concept is best described as one person/one boss in which employees have one manager to whom they report and to whom they are responsible. This greatly simplifies the manager–employee relationship because the employee needs to maintain only a minimum number of relationships and accept the influence of only one person as his or her immediate supervisor.

 Unity of command is difficult to maintain in some large health-care organizations because the nature of health care requires an interprofessional approach.

Nurses frequently feel as though they have many individuals to account to because health care often involves an interprofessional approach. Additional individuals the nurse may need to be accountable to include the immediate supervisor, the patient, the patient's family, central administration, and the physician. All have some input in directing a nurse's work. Weber was correct when he determined that a lack of unity of command results in some conflict and lost productivity. This is demonstrated frequently when health-care workers become confused about unity of command.

LEARNING EXERCISE 12.1

Who Is the Boss?

In groups or individually, analyze the following and give an oral or written report.

1. Have you ever worked in an organization in which the lines of authority were unclear? Have you been a member of a social organization in which this happened? How did this interfere with the organization's functioning?

2. Do you believe that the "one boss/one person" rule is a good idea? Do hospital clerical workers frequently have many bosses? If you have worked in a situation in which you had more than one boss, what was the result?

Span of Control

Span of control also can be determined from the organization chart. The number of people directly reporting to any one manager represents that manager's span of control and determines the number of interactions expected of him or her. Thus, there is an inverse relation between the span of control and the number of levels in hierarchy in an organization, i.e., narrower the span, the greater is the number of levels in an organization (Juneja, 2013).

Theorists are divided regarding the optimal span of control for any one manager. Quantitative formulas for determining the optimal span of control have been attempted, with suggested ranges from 3 to 50 employees. In reality, the ideal span of control in an organization depends upon various factors, such as the nature of the job, the manager's abilities, the employees' maturity, the task complexity, and the level in the organization at which the work occurs. The number of people directly reporting to any one supervisor must be the number that maximizes productivity and worker satisfaction.

Too many people reporting to a single manager delays decision making, whereas too few results in an inefficient, top-heavy organization.

Until the last decade, the principle of narrow spans of control at top levels of management, with slightly wider spans at other levels, was widely accepted. Indeed, Juneja (2013) suggests that most modern management theorists would suggest an ideal span of control as 15 to 20 subordinates per manager, as compared with the 6 subordinates per manager touted in the past. With increased financial pressures on health-care organizations to remain fiscally solvent and electronic communication technology advances, many have increased their spans of control and reduced the number of administrative levels in the organization. This is often termed *flattening the organization.*

Managerial Levels

In large organizations, several levels of managers often exist. *Top-level managers* look at the organization as a whole, coordinating internal and external influences, and generally make decisions with few guidelines or structures. Examples of top-level managers include the organization's chief operating officer or CEO and the highest level nursing administrator. Current nomenclature for top-level nurse-managers varies; they might be called vice president of nursing or patient care services, nurse administrator, director of nursing, chief nurse, assistant administrator of patient care services, or chief nurse officer (CNO).

Some top-level nurse-managers may be responsible for non-nursing departments. For example, a top-level nurse-manager might oversee the respiratory, physical, and occupational therapy departments in addition to all nursing departments. Likewise, the CEO might have various titles, such as president and director. It is necessary to remember only that the CEO is the organization's highest ranking person, and the top-level nurse-manager is its highest ranking nurse. Responsibilities common to top-level managers include determining the organizational philosophy, setting policy, and creating goals and priorities for resource allocation. Top-level managers have a greater need for leadership skills and are not as involved in routine daily operations as are lower level managers.

Middle-level managers coordinate the efforts of lower levels of the hierarchy and are the conduit between lower and top-level managers. Middle-level managers carry out day-to-day operations but are still involved in some long-term planning and in establishing unit policies. Examples of middle-level managers include nursing supervisors, nurse-managers, head nurses, and unit managers.

Currently, there are many health facility mergers and acquisitions, and reduced levels of administration are frequently apparent within these consolidated organizations. Consequently, many health-care facilities have expanded the scope of responsibility for middle-level managers and given them the title of "director" as a way to indicate new roles. The old term *director of nursing,* still used in some small facilities to denote the CNO, is now used in many health-care organizations to denote a middle-level manager. The proliferation of titles among health-care administrators has made it imperative that individuals understand what roles and responsibilities go with each position.

First-level managers are concerned with their specific unit's work flow. They deal with immediate problems in the unit's daily operations, with organizational needs, and with personal needs of employees. The effectiveness of first-level managers tremendously affects the organization. First-level managers need good management skills. Because they work so closely with patients and health-care teams, first-level managers also have an excellent opportunity to practice leadership roles that will greatly influence productivity and subordinates' satisfaction. Examples of first-level managers include primary care nurses, team leaders, case managers, and charge nurses. In many organizations, every registered nurse (RN) is considered a first-level manager. All nurses in every situation must manage themselves and those under their care. A composite look at top-, middle-, and first-level managers is shown in Table 12.1.

One of the leadership responsibilities of organizing is to periodically examine the number of people in the chain of command. Organizations frequently add levels until there are too many managers. Therefore, the leader-manager should carefully weigh the advantages and disadvantages of adding a management level. For example, does having a charge nurse on each shift aid or hinder decision making? Does having this position solve or create problems?

Centrality

Centrality, or where a position falls on the organizational chart, is determined by organizational distance. Employees with relatively small organizational distance can receive more information than those who are more peripherally located. This is why the middle manager often has a broader view of the organization than other levels of management. A middle manager has a large degree of centrality because this manager receives information upward, downward, and horizontally.

 Centrality refers to the location of a position on an organization chart where frequent and various types of communication occur.

Because all communication involves a sender and a receiver, messages may not be received clearly because of the sender's hierarchical position. Similarly, status and power often influence the receiver's ability to hear information accurately. An example of the effect of status on communication is found in the "principal syndrome." Most people can recall panic, when they were school age, at being summoned to the principal's office. Thoughts of "what did I do?" travel through one's mind. Even adults find discomfort in communicating with certain people who hold high status. This may be fear or awe, but both interfere with clear communication. The difficulties with upward and downward communication are discussed in more detail in Chapter 19.

TABLE 12.1	**Levels of Managers**		
	Top Level	*Middle Level*	*First Level*
Examples	Chief nursing officer Chief executive officer Chief financial officer	Unit supervisor Department head Director	Charge nurse Team leader Primary nurse
Scope of responsibility	Look at organization as a whole as well as external influences	Focus is on integrating unit-level day-to-day needs with organizational needs	Focus primarily on day-to-day needs at unit level
Primary planning focus	Strategic planning	Combination of long- and short-range planning	Short-range, operational planning
Communication flow	More often top-down but receives subordinate feedback both directly and via middle-level managers	Upward and downward with great centrality	More often upward; generally relies on middle-level managers to transmit communication to top-level managers

LEARNING EXERCISE 12.2

Change Is Coming

This learning exercise refers to the organization chart in Figure 12.1. Because Memorial Hospital is expanding, the Board of Directors has made several changes that require modification of the organization chart. The directors have just announced the following changes:

- The name of the hospital has been changed to Memorial General Hospital and Medical Center.
- State approval has been granted for open-heart surgery.
- One of the existing medical–surgical units will be remodeled and will become two critical care units (one six-bed coronary and open-heart unit and one six-bed trauma and surgical unit).
- A part-time medical director will be responsible for medical care on each critical care unit.
- The hospital administrator's title has been changed to executive director.
- An associate hospital administrator has been hired.
- A new hospital-wide educational department has been created.
- The old pediatric unit will be remodeled into a seven-bed pediatric wing and a seven-bed rehabilitation unit.
- The director of nursing's new title is vice president of patient care services.

Assignment: If the hospital is viewed as a large, open system, it is possible to visualize areas where problems might occur. In particular, it is necessary to identify changes anticipated in the nursing department and how these changes will affect the organization as a whole. Depict all of these changes on the old organization chart, delineating both staff and line positions. Give the rationale for your decisions. Why did you place the education department where you did? What was the reasoning in your division of authority? Where do you believe there might be potential conflict in the new organization chart? Why?

It is important, then, to be aware of how the formal structure affects overall relationships and communication. This is especially true because organizations change their structure frequently, resulting in new communication lines and reporting relationships. Unless one understands how to interpret a formal organization chart, confusion and anxiety will result when organizations are restructured.

LEARNING EXERCISE 12.3

Cultures and Hierarchies

Having been with the county health department for 6 months, you are very impressed with the physician who is the county health administrator. She seems to have a genuine concern for patient welfare. She has a tea for new employees each month to discuss the department's philosophy and her own management style. She says that she has an open-door policy, so employees are always welcome to visit her.

Since you have been assigned to the evening immunization clinic as charge nurse, you have become concerned with a persistent problem. The housekeeping staff often spends part of the evening sleeping on duty or socializing for long periods. You have reported your concerns to your health department supervisor twice. Last evening, you found the housekeeping staff having another get together. This mainly upsets you because the clinic is chronically in need of cleaning. Sometimes, the public bathrooms get so untidy that they embarrass you and your staff. You frequently remind the housekeepers to empty overflowing wastepaper baskets. You believe that this environment is demeaning to patients. This also upsets you because you and your staff work hard all evening and rarely have a chance to sit down. You believe it is unfair to everyone that the housekeeping staff is not doing its share.

On your way to the parking lot this evening, the health administrator stops to chat and asks you how things are going. Should you tell her about the problem with the housekeeping staff? Is this following an appropriate chain of command? Do you believe that there is a conflict between the housekeeping unit's culture and the nursing unit's culture? What should you do? List choices and alternatives. Decide what you should do, and explain your rationale.

Note: Attempt to solve this problem before referring to a possible solution posted in the Appendix.

Is it ever appropriate to go outside the chain of command? Of course, there are isolated circumstances when the chain of command must be breached. However, those rare conditions usually involve a question of ethics. In most instances, those being bypassed in a chain of command should be forewarned. Remember that unity of command provides the organization with a workable system for procedural directives and orders so that productivity is increased and conflict is minimized.

LIMITATIONS OF ORGANIZATION CHARTS

Because organization charts show only formal relationships, what they can reveal about an institution is limited. The chart does not show the informal structure of the organization. Every institution has in place a dynamic informal structure that can be powerful and motivating. Knowledgeable leaders never underestimate its importance because the informal structure includes employees' interpersonal relationships, the formation of primary and secondary groups, and the identification of group leaders without formal authority.

These groups are important in organizations because they provide workers with a feeling of belonging. They also have a great deal of power in an organization; they can either facilitate or sabotage planned change. Their ability to determine a unit's norms and acceptable behavior has a great deal to do with the socialization of new employees. Informal leaders are frequently found among long-term employees or people in select *gatekeeping positions*, such as the CNO's secretary. Frequently, the informal organization evolves from social activities or from relationships that develop outside the work environment.

Organization charts are also limited in their ability to depict each line position's degree of authority. *Authority* is defined as the official power to act. It is power given by the organization to direct the work of others. A manager may have the authority to hire, fire, or discipline others.

Equating status with authority, however, frequently causes confusion. The distance from the top of the organizational hierarchy usually determines the degree of status: the closer to the top, the higher the status. Status also is influenced by skill, education, specialization, level of responsibility, autonomy, and salary accorded a position. People frequently have status with little accompanying authority.

Because organizations are dynamic environments, an organization chart becomes obsolete very quickly. Grover (1999–2013) suggests that most organizations are constantly changing, with people taking on new jobs, getting hired, and getting fired, so trying to keep an organization chart current is almost impossible.

It is also possible that the organization chart may depict how things are supposed to be, when in reality, the organization is still functioning under an old structure because employees have not yet accepted new lines of authority.

In addition, organization charts may too rigidly define the jobs of people working in that organization (Grover, 1999–2013). Some employees may look at the organization chart and determine that the responsibilities there are their only responsibilities, when the reality is that most employees will on occasion, have to assist with work that is not a formal part of their job description.

Another limitation of the organization chart is that although it defines authority, it does not define responsibility and accountability. A *responsibility* is a duty or an assignment. It is the implementation of a job. For example, a responsibility common to many charge nurses is establishing the unit's daily patient care assignment. Individuals should always be assigned responsibilities with concomitant authority. If authority is not commensurate to the responsibility, role confusion occurs for everyone involved. For example, supervisors may have the responsibility of maintaining high professional care standards among their staff. If the manager is not given the authority to discipline employees as needed, however, this responsibility is virtually impossible to implement.

Accountability is similar to responsibility, but it is internalized. Thus, to be accountable means that individuals agree to be morally responsible for the consequences of their actions. Therefore, one individual cannot be accountable for another. Society holds us accountable for our assigned responsibilities, and people are expected to accept the consequences of their actions. A nurse who reports a medication error is being accountable for the responsibilities inherent in the position. Display 12.2 discusses the advantages and limitations of an organization chart.

The leader-manager should understand the interrelationships and differences among these three terms. Because the use of authority, power building, and political awareness are so important to functioning effectively in any structure, Chapter 13 discusses these organizational components in depth.

DISPLAY 12.2 **Advantages and Limitations of the Organization Chart**

ADVANTAGES
1. Maps lines of decision-making authority.
2. Helps people understand their assignments and those of their coworkers.
3. Reveals to managers and new personnel how they fit into the organization.
4. Contributes to sound organizational structure.
5. Shows formal lines of communication.

LIMITATIONS
1. Shows only formal relationships.
2. Does not indicate degree of authority.
3. Are difficult to keep current.
4. May show things as they are supposed to be or used to be rather than as they are.
5. May define roles too narrowly.
6. Possibility exists of confusing authority with status.

TYPES OF ORGANIZATIONAL STRUCTURES

Traditionally, nursing departments have used one of the following structural patterns: bureaucratic, ad hoc, matrix, flat, or various combinations of these. The type of structure used in any health-care facility affects communication patterns, relationships, and authority.

Line Structures

Bureaucratic organizational designs are commonly called line *structures* or *line organizations*. Those with staff authority may be referred to as *staff organizations*. Both of these types of organizational structures are found frequently in large health-care facilities and usually resemble Weber's original design for effective organizations. Because of most people's familiarity with these structures, there is little stress associated with orienting people to these organizations. In these structures, authority and responsibility are clearly defined, which leads to efficiency and simplicity of relationships. The organization chart in Figure 12.1 is a line-and-staff structure.

These formal designs have some disadvantages. They often produce monotony, alienate workers, and make adjusting rapidly to altered circumstances difficult. Another problem with line and line-and-staff structures is their adherence to chain of command communication, which restricts upward communication. Good leaders encourage upward communication to compensate for this disadvantage. However, when line positions are clearly defined, going outside the chain of command for upward communication is usually inappropriate.

Ad Hoc Design

The *ad hoc design* is a modification of the bureaucratic structure and is sometimes used on a temporary basis to facilitate completion of a project within a formal line organization. The ad hoc structure is a means of overcoming the inflexibility of line structure and serves as a way for professionals to handle the increasingly large amounts of available information. Ad hoc structures use a project team or task approach and are usually disbanded after a project is completed. This structure's disadvantages are decreased strength in the formal chain of command and decreased employee loyalty to the parent organization.

Matrix Structure

A *matrix organization* structure is designed to focus on both product and function. Function is described as all the tasks required to produce the product, and the product is the end result of the function. For example, good patient outcomes are the product, and staff education and adequate staffing may be the functions necessary to produce the outcome.

The matrix organization structure has a formal vertical and horizontal chain of command. Figure 12.2 depicts a matrix organizational structure and shows that the Manager of Nursing Women's Services care could report both to a Vice President for Maternal and Women's Services (Product Manager) and a Vice President for Nursing Services (Functional Manager). Although there are less formal rules and fewer levels of the hierarchy, a matrix structure is not without disadvantages. For example, in this structure, decision making can be slow because of the necessity of information sharing, and it can produce confusion and frustration for workers because of its dual-authority hierarchical design. The primary advantage of centralizing expertise is frequently outweighed by the complexity of the communication required in the design.

Service Line Organization

Similar to the matrix design is service line organization, which can be used in some large institutions to address the shortcomings that are endemic to traditional large bureaucratic organizations. *Service lines*, sometimes called *care-centered organizations*, are smaller in scale than a large bureaucratic system. For example, in this organizational design, the overall goals would be determined by the larger organization, but the service line would decide on the processes to be used to achieve the goals.

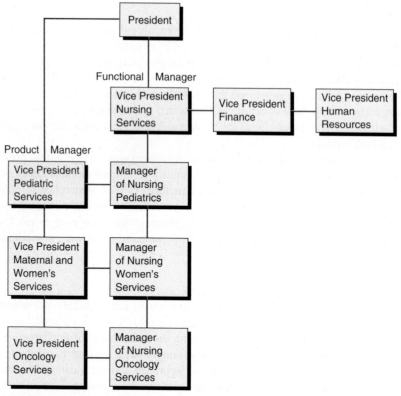

FIGURE 12.2 • Matrix organizational structure. Copyright ® 2006 Lippincott Williams & Wilkins. Instructor's Resource CD-ROM to Accompany Leadership Roles and Management Functions in Nursing, by Bessie L. Marquis and Carol J. Huston.

Flat Designs

Flat organizational designs are an effort to remove hierarchical layers by flattening the chain of command and decentralizing the organization. Thus, a single manager or supervisor would oversee a large number of subordinates and have a wide span of control (Juneja, 2013). In good times, when organizations are financially well off, it is easy to add layers to the organization in order to get the work done, but when the organization begins to feel a financial pinch, they often look at their hierarchy to see where they can cut positions.

In *flattened organizations*, there continues to be line authority, but because the organizational structure is flattened, more authority and decision making can occur where the work is being carried out. Figure 12.3 shows a flattened organizational structure. Many managers have difficulty letting go of control, and even very flattened types of structure organizations often retain many characteristics of a bureaucracy.

 ## DECISION MAKING WITHIN THE ORGANIZATIONAL HIERARCHY

The decision-making hierarchy, or pyramid, is often referred to as a *scalar chain*. By reviewing the organization chart in Figure 12.1, it is possible to determine where decisions are made within the organizational hierarchy. Although every manager has some decision-making authority, its type and level are determined by the manager's position on the chart.

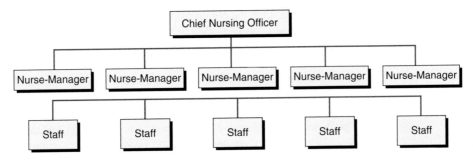

FIGURE 12.3 • Flattened organizational structure. Copyright ® 2006 Lippincott Williams & Wilkins. Instructor's Resource CD-ROM to Accompany Leadership Roles and Management Functions in Nursing, by Bessie L. Marquis and Carol J. Huston.

In organizations with *centralized decision making*, a few managers at the top of the hierarchy make the decisions and the emphasis is on top-down control. In other words, the vision or thinking of one or a few individuals in the organization guides the organization's goals and how those goals are accomplished. Execution of decision making in centralized organizations is fairly rapid.

Decentralized decision making diffuses decision making throughout the organization and allows problems to be solved by the lowest practical managerial level. Often, this means that problems can be solved at the level at which they occur, although some delays may occur in decision making if the problem must be transmitted through several levels to reach the appropriate individual to solve the problem. As a rule, however, larger organizations benefit from decentralized decision making.

This occurs because the complex questions that must be answered can best be addressed by a variety of people with distinct areas of expertise. Leaving such decisions in a large organization to a few managers burdens those managers tremendously and could result in devastating delays in decision making.

In general, the larger the organization, the greater the need to decentralize decision making.

Rai (2013) suggests, however, that centralized decision making can and does work well in organizations where staff want more direction, guidance, and coordination of activities from upper management. Rai notes that the use of bureaucratic rules and procedures can actually be healthy for an organization since it minimizes role conflict and clarified role expectations.

STAKEHOLDERS

Stakeholders are those entities in an organization's environment that play a role in the organization's health and performance or that are affected by the organization. Stakeholders may be both internal and external, they may include individuals and large groups, and they may have shared goals or diverse goals. *Internal stakeholders*, for example, may include the nurse in a hospital or the dietitian in a nursing home. Examples of *external stakeholders* for an acute care hospital might be the local school of nursing, home health agencies, and managed care providers who contract with consumers in the area. Even the Chamber of Commerce in a city could be considered a stakeholder for a health-care organization.

Every organization should be viewed as being part of a greater community of stakeholders.

Stakeholders have interests in what the organization does but may or may not have the power to influence the organization to protect their interests. Stakeholders' interests are varied, however, and their interests may coincide on some issues and not others. Organizations do not generally choose their own stakeholders; rather, the stakeholders choose to have a stake in the organizations' decisions. Stakeholders may have a supportive or threatening influence on organizational decision making. For many decisions an organization makes, it may face a diverse set of stakeholders with varied and conflicting interest and goals.

As a part of planned change, discussed in Chapter 8, and decision making, discussed in Chapter 1, a *stakeholder analysis* is an important aspect of the management process. Such an analysis should be performed when there is a need to clarify the consequences of decisions and changes. In addition to identifying stakeholders who will be impacted by a change, it is necessary to prioritize them and determine their influence. Astute leaders must always be cognizant of who their stakeholders are and the impact they may have on an organization. A depiction of some possible stakeholders for a local community hospital appears in Display 12.3.

DISPLAY 12.3   **Examples of Stakeholders in a Community Hospital**

External Stakeholders	Internal Stakeholders
Local businesses	Hospital employees
Area colleges and universities	Physicians
Insurance companies and HMOs	Patients
Community leaders	Patients' families
Unions	Union shop stewards
Professional organizations	Board of directors

ORGANIZATIONAL CULTURE

Organizational culture is the total of an organization's values, language, traditions, customs, and sacred cows—those few things present in an institution that are not open to discussion or change. For example, the hospital logo that had been designed by the original board of trustees is an item that may not be considered for updating or change.

Similarly, BusinessDictionary.com (2013) defines organizational culture as "the values and behaviors that contribute to the unique social and psychological environment of an organization. The organizational culture includes an organization's expectations, experiences, philosophy, and values that hold it together, and is expressed in its self-image, inner workings, interactions with the outside world, and future expectations. It is based on shared attitudes, beliefs, customs, and written and unwritten rules that have been developed over time and are considered valid" (para 1). Both of these definitions impart a sense of the complexity and importance of organizational culture.

Organizational culture is a system of symbols and interactions unique to each organization. It is the ways of thinking, behaving, and believing that members of a unit have in common.

Organizational culture should not, however, be confused with *organizational climate*—how employees perceive an organization. For example, an employee might perceive an organization as fair, friendly, and informal or as formal and very structured. The perception may be accurate or inaccurate, and people in the same organization may have different perceptions about the same organization. Therefore, since the organizational climate is the view of the organization by individuals, the organization's climate and its culture may differ.

Although assessing unit culture is a management function, building a constructive culture, particularly if a negative culture is in place, requires the interpersonal and communication skills of a leader. The leader must take an active role in creating the kind of organizational culture that will ensure success. The more entrenched the culture and pattern of actions, the more challenging the change process is for the leader. Given such entrenchment of culture, success in building a new culture may require new leadership and/or assistance by the use of outside analysis.

For example, many health-care organizations continue to report challenges in establishing a culture where evidence-based practice (EBP) is the norm. Often this is because senior management or organization leaders have not taken an active role in emphasizing the importance of this culture change or have not provided adequate resources (fiscal or human) to support the culture change. Examining the Evidence 12.1 details a case study where the leadership skills of vision, change agent, and team building were critical requisites to a successful organizational culture effort to incorporate EBP into the existing culture.

Examining the Evidence 12.1

Source: Plath, D. (2013). Organizational processes supporting evidence-based practice. Administration in Social Work, 37(2), 171–188.

This research examined organizational processes that supported and facilitated an EBP approach in a large, nongovernmental Australian human service organization. A case study methodology was employed, incorporating multiple sources of data to inform understanding of the organizational context and processes. Based on their understanding of what had and could be done within the organization, participants discussed strategies for engaging staff across the organization in EBP implementation. While there were differing views on the degree to which these strategies were already evident in the organization, participants spoke about the need for an organizational culture where staff understand, appreciate, and feel a part of EBP implementation. Strong leadership, targeted management, and marketing of EBP were identified as strategies to achieve such a culture.

Fundamentally, these strategies aim to better engage frontline staff with the EBP process, promoting a culture within the organization where research evidence is valued and used to inform practice. These strategies rely on strong leadership that entails communicating a vision for EBP through a range of forums throughout the organization. This vision for EBP is aligned with both effective client outcomes and practitioner satisfaction grounded in a solid evidence base. Such statements of organizational vision need to be backed up with the allocation of resources to support dissemination of research evidence and the production of practice frameworks and tools for frontline staff. The researcher concluded that considerable responsibility for EBP implementation lies with senior management in human service organizations, where leadership and resource commitment are required in culture change.

Organizations, if large enough, also have many different and competing value systems that create *subcultures*. These subcultures shape perceptions, attitudes, and beliefs and influence how their members approach and execute their particular roles and responsibilities. A critical challenge then for the nurse-leader is to recognize these subcultures and to do whatever is necessary to create shared norms and priorities. Managers must be able to assess their unit's culture and choose management strategies that encourage a shared culture. Such transformation requires both management assessment and leadership direction.

In addition, much of an organization's culture is not available to staff in a retrievable source and must be related by others. For example, feelings about collective bargaining, nursing education levels, nursing autonomy, and nurse–physician relationships differ from one organization to another. These beliefs and values, however, are rarely written down or appear in a philosophy. Therefore, in addition to creating a constructive culture, a major leadership role is to assist subordinates in understanding the organization's culture. Display 12.4 identifies questions that leaders and followers should ask when assessing organizational culture.

DISPLAY 12.4   Assessing the Organizational Culture

WHAT IS THE ORGANIZATION'S PHYSICAL ENVIRONMENT?

1. Is the environment attractive?
2. Does it appear that there is adequate maintenance?
3. Are nursing stations crowded or noisy?
4. Is there an appropriate-sized lobby? Are there quiet areas?
5. Is there sufficient seating for families in the dining room?
6. Are there enough conference rooms? A library? A chapel or place of worship?

WHAT IS THE ORGANIZATION'S SOCIAL ENVIRONMENT?

1. Are many friendships maintained beyond the workplace?
2. Is there an annual picnic or holiday party that is well attended by the employees?
3. Do employees seem to generally like each other?
4. Do all shifts and all departments get along fairly well?
5. Are certain departments disliked or resented?
6. Are employees on a first-name basis with coworkers, doctors, charge nurses, and supervisors?
7. How do employees treat patients and visitors?

HOW SUPPORTIVE IS THE ORGANIZATION?

1. Is educational reimbursement available?
2. Are good, low-cost meals available to employees?
3. Are there adequate employee lounges?
4. Are funds available to send employees to workshops?
5. Are employees recognized for extra effort?
6. Does the organization help pay for the holiday party or other social functions?

WHAT IS THE ORGANIZATIONAL POWER STRUCTURE?

1. Who holds the most power in the organization?
2. Which departments are viewed as powerful? Which are viewed as powerless?
3. Who gets free meals? Who gets special parking places?
4. Who carries beepers? Who wears laboratory coats? Who has overhead pages?
5. Who has the biggest office?
6. Who is never called by his or her first name?

HOW SAFE IS THE ORGANIZATION?

1. Is there a well-lighted parking place for employees arriving or departing when it is dark?
2. Is there an active and involved safety committee?
3. Are security guards needed?

WHAT IS THE COMMUNICATION ENVIRONMENT?

1. Is upward communication usually written or verbal?
2. Is there much informal communication?
3. Is there an active grapevine? Is it reliable?
4. Where is important information exchanged—in the parking lot? the doctors' surgical dressing room? the nurses' station? the coffee shop? during surgery or during the delivery room?

WHAT ARE THE ORGANIZATIONAL TABOOS? WHO ARE THE HEROES?

1. Are there special rules and policies that can never be broken?
2. Are certain subjects or ideas forbidden?
3. Are there relationships that cannot be threatened?

SHARED GOVERNANCE: ORGANIZATIONAL DESIGN FOR THE 21ST CENTURY?

Shared governance, one of the most innovative and empowering organization structures, was developed in the mid-1980s as an alternative to the traditional bureaucratic organizational structure. A flat type of organizational structure is often used to describe shared governance but differs somewhat, as shown in Figure 12.4. In shared governance, the organization's governance is shared among board members, nurses, physicians, and management. Thus, decision making and communication channels are altered. Group structures, in the form of *joint practice committees*, are developed to assume the power and accountability for decision making, and professional communication takes on an egalitarian structure.

In health-care organizations, shared governance empowers decision makers, and this empowerment is directed at increasing nurses' authority and control over nursing practice. Shared governance thus gives nurses more control over their nursing practice by being an accountability-based governance system for professional workers. This staff empowerment is fundamental to shared governance, as is collaborative decision making (Bennett, Ockerby, Begbie, Chalmers & O'Connell, 2012).

The stated aim of shared governance is the empowerment of employees within the decision-making system.

Although participatory management lays the foundation for shared governance, they are not the same. *Participatory management* implies that others are allowed to participate in decision making over which someone has control. Thus, the act of "allowing" participation identifies the real and final authority for the participant.

There is no single model of shared governance, although all models emphasize the empowerment of staff nurses. Generally, issues related to nursing practice are the responsibility of nurses, not managers, and nursing councils are used to organize governance.

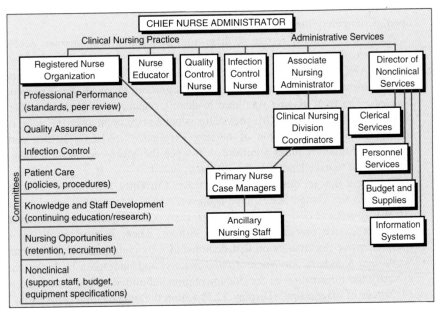

FIGURE 12.4 • Shared governance model. Copyright ® 2006 Lippincott Williams & Wilkins. Instructor's Resource CD-ROM to Accompany Leadership Roles and Management Functions in Nursing, by Bessie L. Marquis and Carol J. Huston.

These nursing councils, elected at the organization and unit levels, use a congressional format organized like a representative form of government, with a president and cabinet.

Typical governance councils include a nursing practice council, a research council, and professional development and/or education council, a nursing performance improvement or quality council, and a leadership council. Sometimes, organizations will have a retention council as well. The councils participate in decision making and coordination of the department of nursing and provide input through the shared governance process in all other areas where nursing care is delivered.

The number of health-care organizations using shared governance models is continuing to increase. However, a major impediment to the implementation of shared governance has been the reluctance of managers to change their roles. The nurse-manager's role becomes one of consulting, teaching, collaborating, and creating an environment with the structures and resources needed for the practice of nursing and shared decision making between nurses and the organization. This new role is foreign to many managers and difficult to accept. In addition, consensus decision making takes more time than autocratic decision making, and not all nurses want to share decisions and accountability. Although many positive outcomes have been attributed to implementation of shared governance, the expense of introducing and maintaining this model also must be considered because it calls for a conscientious commitment both on the part of the workers and the organization.

Shared governance requires a substantial and long-term commitment on the part of the workers and the organization.

MAGNET DESIGNATION AND PATHWAY TO EXCELLENCE

During the early 1980s, the American Academy of Nursing (AAN) began conducting research to identify the characteristics of hospitals that were able to successfully recruit and retain nurses. What they found were high-performing hospitals with well-qualified nurse executives in a decentralized environment, with organizational structures that emphasized open, participatory management.

A desire to formally recognize these high-performing hospitals was accomplished when the *American Nurses Association* (ANA) established the *American Nurses Credentialing Center* (ANCC) in 1990. Later the same year, the ANA Board of Directors approved the establishment of the *Magnet Hospital Recognition Program for Excellence in Nursing Services*. The term *magnet* was used to denote organizations that were able to attract and retain professional nurses. "Magnet status is not a prize or an award. Rather, it is a credential of organizational recognition of nursing excellence" (ANCC, 2013b, para 2). Being a magnet institution requires a culture shift since the entire organization must demonstrate a commitment to excellence (Budin, 2012).

Earning a magnet designation is not easy. Currently, only about 6.9% of all registered hospitals in the United States have achieved ANCC Magnet Recognition® status (ANCC, 2013b). To achieve designation as an organization, the organization must create and promote a comprehensive professional practice culture. Then, it must apply to ANCC, submit comprehensive documentation that demonstrates its compliance with standards in the *ANA Scope and Standards for Nurse Administrators*, and undergo a multiday onsite evaluation to verify the information in the documentation submitted and to assess the presence of the 14 "forces of magnetism" (Display 12.5) within the organization (Pinkerton, 2008). Magnet status is awarded for a 4-year period, after which the organization must reapply.

Currently, magnet recognition is awarded to both individual organizations (not just hospitals) and systems (Pinkerton, 2008). To achieve designation as a system, the system must not only retain the 14 forces of magnetism required for individual organizations, they must also demonstrate empirical modeling of five key components: transformational leadership; structural empowerment; exemplary professional practice; new knowledge innovation and improvements; and empirical quality results (Pinkerton). In addition, all parts of the system are judged as one when seeking system designation, so if one entity within the system fails, the entire system application will be denied (Pinkerton).

DISPLAY 12.5 **The 14 Forces of Magnetism for Magnet Hospital Status**

1. Quality of nursing leadership
2. Organizational structure
3. Management style
4. Personnel policies and programs
5. Professional models of care
6. Quality of care
7. Quality improvement
8. Consultation and resources
9. Autonomy
10. Community and the hospital
11. Nurses as teachers
12. Image of nursing
13. Interdisciplinary relationships
14. Professional development

A driving force to achieve magnet status is the clear link between this designation and improved outcomes. *US News & World Report* utilizes Magnet designation as a primary competence indicator in its assessment of almost 5,000 hospitals to rank and report the best medical centers in 16 specialties. Twelve of the 17 medical centers on the exclusive *US News Best Hospitals in America Honor Roll*, and all 12 of the *US News Best Children's Hospital Honor Roll*, were ANCC Magnet-recognized organizations (ANCC, 2013a).

In addition, ANCC established the *Pathway to Excellence* program in 2003, based on findings from the Texas Nurse-Friendly™ Program for Small/Rural Hospitals. The Pathway to Excellence designation recognizes health-care organizations and long-term care institutions for positive practice environments where nurses excel (ANCC, 2013c). To earn the Pathway to Excellence designation, organizations must undergo a thorough review process that meet 12 practice standards essential to an ideal nursing practice environment. "Applicants conduct a review process to fully document the integration of those standards in the organization's practices, policies and culture. Pathway designation can only be achieved if an organization's nurses validate the data and other evidence submitted, via an independent, confidential survey. This critical element exemplifies the theme of empowering and giving nurses a voice" (ANCC, 2013c, para 2).

LEARNING EXERCISE 12.4

Why Work for Them?

A list of current magnet-recognized organizations and their contact information can be found at the ANCC web site: http://www.nursecredentialing.org/Magnet/FindAMagnetFacility

Assignment: Select one of the current organizations and prepare a one-page written report about how that particular organization demonstrates the excellence exemplified by magnet status. Speak to at least five of the "forces of magnetism." Would you want to work for this particular organization?

COMMITTEE STRUCTURE IN AN ORGANIZATION

Managers are also responsible for designing and implementing appropriate committee structures. Poorly structured committees can be nonproductive for the organization and frustrating for committee members. However, there are many benefits to and justifications for well-structured committees. To compensate for some of the difficulty in organizational communication created by line and line-and-staff structures, committees are used widely to facilitate upward communication. The nature of formal organizations dictates a need for committees in assisting with management functions. In addition, as organizations seek new ways to revamp old bureaucratic structures, committees may pave the road to increased staff participation in organization governance. Committees may be advisory or may have a coordinating or informal function. They generate ideas and creative thinking to solve operational problems or improve services and often improve the quality and quantity of work accomplished. Committees also can pool specific skills and expertise and help reduce resistance to change.

Because committees communicate upward and downward and encourage the participation of interested or affected employees, they assist the organization in receiving valuable feedback and important information.

However, all of these positive benefits can be achieved only if committees are appropriately organized and led. If not properly used, the committee becomes a liability to the organizing process because it wastes energy, time, and money and can defer decisions and action. One of the leadership roles inherent in organizing work is to ensure that committees are not used to avoid or delay decisions but to facilitate organizational goals. Display 12.6 lists factors to consider when organizing committees.

DISPLAY 12.6	Factors to Consider When Organizing Committees and Making Appointments

- The committee should be composed of people who want to contribute in terms of commitment, energy, and time.
- The members should have a variety of work experience and educational backgrounds. Composition should, however, ensure expertise sufficient to complete the task.
- Committees should have enough members to accomplish assigned tasks but not so many that discussion cannot occur. Six to eight members in a committee are usually ideal.
- The tasks and responsibilities, including reporting mechanisms, should be clearly outlined.
- Assignments should be given ahead of time, with clear expectations that assigned work will be discussed at the next meeting.
- All committees should have written agendas and effective committee chairpersons.

RESPONSIBILITIES AND OPPORTUNITIES OF COMMITTEE WORK

Committees present the leader-manager with many opportunities and responsibilities. Managers need to be well grounded in group dynamics because meetings represent a major time commitment. Managers serve as members of committees and as leaders or chairpersons of committees. Because committees make major decisions, managers should use the opportunities available at meetings to become more visible in the larger organization. The manager has a responsibility to select appropriate power strategies, such as coming to meetings well prepared, and to use skill in the group process to generate influence and gain power at meetings.

Another responsibility is to create an environment at unit committee meetings that leads to shared decision making. Encouraging an interaction free of status and power is important. Likewise, an appropriate seating arrangement, such as a circle, will increase motivation for committee members to speak up. The responsible manager is also aware that staff from different cultures may have different needs in groups, which is why multicultural committees should be the norm. In addition, because gender differences are increasingly being recognized as playing a role in problem solving, communication, and power, efforts should be made to include both men and women on committees.

When assigning members to committees, cultural and gender diversity should always be a goal.

The manager must not rely too heavily on committees or use them as a method to delay decision making. Numerous committee assignments exhaust staff, and committees then become poor tools for accomplishing work. An alternative that will decrease the time commitment for committee work is to make individual assignments and gather the entire committee only to report progress.

In the leadership role, an opportunity exists for important influence on committee and group effectiveness. A dynamic leader inspires people to put spirit into working for a shared goal. Leaders demonstrate their commitment to participatory management by how they work with committees. Leaders keep the committee on course. Committees may be chaired by an elected member of the group, appointed by the manager, or led by the department or unit manager. Informal leaders may also emerge from the group process.

It is important for the manager to be aware of the possibility for groupthink to occur in any group or committee structure. *Groupthink* occurs when group members fail to take adequate risks by disagreeing, being challenged, or assessing discussion carefully. If the manager is actively involved in the work group or on the committee, groupthink is less likely to occur. The leadership role includes teaching members to avoid groupthink by demonstrating critical thinking and being a role model who allows his or her own ideas to be challenged.

ORGANIZATIONAL EFFECTIVENESS

There is no one "best" way to structure an organization. Variables such as the size of the organization, the capability of its human resources, and the commitment level of its workers should always be considered. Regardless of what type of organizational structure is used, certain minimal requirements can be identified:

- The structure should be clearly defined so that employees know where they belong and where to go for assistance.
- The goal should be to build the fewest possible management levels and have the shortest possible chain of command. This eliminates friction, stress, and inertia.
- The unit staff need to be able to see where their tasks fit into common tasks of the organization.
- The organizational structure should enhance, not impede communication.
- The organizational structure should facilitate decision making that results in the greatest work performance.
- Staff should be organized in a manner that encourages informal groups to develop a sense of community and belonging.
- Nursing services should be organized to facilitate the development of future leaders.

Despite the known difficulties of bureaucracies, it has been difficult for some organizations to move away from the bureaucratic model. However, perhaps as a result of magnet hospital research demonstrating both improved patient outcomes and improved recruitment and retention of staff, there has been an increasing effort to redesign and restructure organizations to make them more flexible and decentralized. Still, progress toward these goals continues to be slow.

INTEGRATING LEADERSHIP ROLES AND MANAGEMENT FUNCTIONS ASSOCIATED WITH ORGANIZATIONAL STRUCTURE

Integrated leader-managers need to look at organizational structure as the road map that tells them how organizations operate. Without organizational structure, people would work in a chaotic environment. Structure becomes an important tool, then, to facilitate order and enhance productivity.

Astute leader-managers understand both the structure of the organization in which they work and external stakeholders. The integrated leader-manager, however, goes beyond personal understanding of the larger organizational design. The leader-manager takes responsibility for ensuring that subordinates also understand the overall organizational structure and the structure at the unit level. This can be done by being a resource and a role model to subordinates. The role modeling includes demonstrating accountability and the appropriate use of authority.

The effective manager recognizes the difficulties inherent in advisory positions and uses leadership skills to support staff in these positions. This is accomplished by granting sufficient authority to enable advisory staff to carry out the functions of their role.

Leadership requires that problems are pursued through appropriate channels, that upward communication is encouraged, and that unit structure is periodically evaluated to determine if it can be redesigned to enable increased lower level decision making. The integrated leader-manager also facilitates constructive informal group structure. It is important for the manager to be knowledgeable about the organization's culture and subcultures. It is just as important for the leader to promote the development of a shared constructive culture with subordinates.

It is a management role to evaluate the types of organizational structure and governance and to implement those that will have the most positive impact in the department. It is a leadership skill to role model the shared authority necessary to make newer models of organizational structure and governance possible.

When serving on committees, the opportunity should be used to gain influence to present the needs of patients and staff appropriately. The integrated leader-manager comes to meetings well prepared and contributes thoughtful comments and ideas. The leader's critical thinking and role-modeling behavior discourages groupthink among work groups or in committees.

Integrated leader-managers also refrain from judging and encourage all members of a committee to participate and contribute. An important management function is to see that appropriate work is accomplished in committees, that they remain productive, and that they are not used to delay decision making. A leadership role is the involvement of staff in organizational decision making, either informally or through more formal models of organizational design, such as shared governance. The integrated leader-manager understands the organization and recognizes what can be molded or shaped and what is constant. Thus, the interaction between the manager and the organization is dynamic.

KEY CONCEPTS

- Many modern health-care organizations continue to be organized around a line or line-and-staff design and have many attributes of a bureaucracy; however, there is a movement toward less bureaucratic designs, such as ad hoc, matrix, and care-centered systems.

- A bureaucracy, as proposed by Max Weber, is characterized by a clear chain of command, rules and regulations, specialization of work, division of labor, and impersonality of relationships.

- An organization chart depicts formal relationships, channels of communication, and authority through line-and-staff positions, scalar chains, and span of control.

- Unity of command means that each person should have only one boss so that there is less confusion and greater productivity.

- Centrality refers to the degree of communication of a particular management position.

- In centralized decision making, decisions are made by a few managers at the top of the hierarchy. In decentralized decision making, decision making is diffused throughout the organization, and problems are solved at the lowest practical managerial level.

- Organizational structure affects how people perceive their roles and the status given to them by other people in the organization.

- Organizational structure is effective when the design is clearly communicated, there are as few managers as possible to accomplish goals, communication is facilitated, decisions are made at the lowest possible level, informal groups are encouraged, and future leaders are developed.

- The entities in an organization's environment that play a role in the organization's health and performance, or which are affected by the organization, are called stakeholders.

- Authority, responsibility, and accountability differ in terms of official sanctions, self-directedness, and moral integration.

- Organizational culture is the total of an organization's beliefs, history, taboos, formal and informal relationships, and communication patterns.

- Subunits of large organizations also have a culture. These subcultures may support or be in conflict with other cultures in the organization.

- Informal groups are present in every organization. They are often powerful, although they have no formal authority. Informal groups determine norms and assist members in the socialization process.

- Shared governance refers to an organizational design that empowers staff nurses by making them an integral part of patient care decision making and providing accountability and responsibility in nursing practice.

- Magnet designation is conferred by the ANCC to health-care organizations exemplifying well-qualified nurse executives in a decentralized environment, with organizational structures that emphasize open, participatory management. Magnet-designated organizations demonstrate improved patient outcomes and higher staff nurse satisfaction than organizations that do not have magnet status.

- The Pathway to Excellence designation, also conferred by the ANCC, recognizes health-care organizations with foundational quality initiatives in creating a positive work environment, as defined by nurses and supported by research.

- Too many committees in an organization is a sign of a poorly designed organizational structure.

- Committees should have an appropriate number of members, prepared agendas, clearly outlined tasks, and effective leadership if they are to be productive.

- Groupthink occurs when there is too much conformity to group norms.

ADDITIONAL LEARNING EXERCISES AND APPLICATIONS

LEARNING EXERCISE 12.5

Restructuring—In Depth

You are the supervisor at a home health agency. There are 22 RNs in your span of control. In a meeting today, John Dao, the CNO, tells you that your span of control needs adjustment to be effective. Therefore, the CNO has decided to flatten the organization and decentralize the department. To accomplish this, he plans to designate three of your staff as shift coordinators. These shift coordinators will "schedule patient visits for all the staff on their shift and be accountable for the staff that they supervise." The CNO believes that this restructuring will give you more time for implementing a continuous quality improvement program and promoting staff development.

Although you are glad to have the opportunity to begin these new projects, you are somewhat unclear about the role expectations of the new shift coordinators and how this will change your job description. In fact, you worry that this is just a precursor to the elimination of your position. Will these shift coordinators report to you? If so, will you have direct line authority or staff authority? Who should be responsible for evaluating the performance of the staff nurses now? Who will handle employee disciplinary problems? How involved should the shift coordinators be in strategic planning or determining next year's budget? What types of management training will be needed by the shift coordinators to prepare for their new role? Are you the most appropriate person to train them?

Assignment: There is great potential for conflict here. In small groups, make a list of 10 questions (not including the ones listed in the learning exercise) that you would want to ask the CNO at your next meeting to clarify role expectations. Discuss tools and skills that you have learned in the preceding units that could make this role change less traumatic for all involved.

LEARNING EXERCISE 12.6

Problem Solving: Working Toward Shared Governance

You are the supervisor of a surgical services department in a nonunion hospital. The staff on your unit have become increasingly frustrated with hospital policies regarding staffing ratios, on-call pay, and verbal medical orders but feel that they have limited opportunities for providing feedback to change the current system. You would like to explore the possibility of moving toward a shared governance model of decision making to resolve this issue and others like it but are not quite sure where to start.

Assignment: Assume that you are the supervisor in this case. Answer the following questions.

1. Who do I need to involve in this discussion and at what point?

2. How might I determine if the overarching organizational structure supports shared governance? How would I determine if external stakeholders would be impacted? How would I determine if organizational culture and subculture would support a shared governance model?

3. What types of nursing councils might be created to provide a framework for operation?

4. Who would be the members on these nursing councils?

5. What support mechanisms would need to be in place to ensure success of this project?

6. What would be my role as a supervisor in identifying and resolving employee concerns in a shared governance model?

LEARNING EXERCISE 12.7

Finding Direction

You are a new graduate working in the 3 to 11 PM shift in a large, metropolitan hospital on the pediatrics unit. You feel frustrated because you had many preceptors while you were being oriented, and each told you slightly different variations of the unit routine. In addition, the regular charge nurse has just been promoted and moved to another unit, and the charge nurse position on your unit is being filled by two part-time nurses.

You feel inadequately prepared for the job and do not know where to turn or to whom you should direct your questions. Assuming that your organization chart resembles the one in Figure 12.1, outline a plan of action that would be appropriate to take. Share your plan with a larger group.

LEARNING EXERCISE 12.8

Thinking About Committee Work

As a writing exercise, choose one of the following to examine in depth:

1. What has contributed to the productivity of the committees on which you have served?

2. Have you ever served on a committee that made recommendations on which higher authority never acted? What was the effect on the group?

LEARNING EXERCISE 12.9

Participation and Productivity

You are a 3 to 11 PM charge nurse on a surgical unit. You have been selected to chair the unit's safety committee. Each month, you have a short committee meeting with the other committee members. Your committee's main responsibility is to report upward any safety issues that have been identified. Lately, you have found an increase in needle-stick incidents, and the committee has been addressing this problem.

The committee is made up of two nursing assistants, one unit clerk, two staff RNs, and two licensed professional nurses/licensed vocational nurses. All shifts and staff cultures are represented. Lately, you have found that the meetings are not going well because one member of the group, Mary, has begun to monopolize the meeting time. She is especially outspoken about the danger of HIV and seems more interested in pointing blame regarding the needle sticks than in finding a solution to the problem.

You have privately spoken to Mary about her frequent disruption of the committee business; although she apologized, the behavior has continued. You feel that some members of the committee are becoming bored and restless, and you believe that the committee is making little progress.

Assignment: Using your knowledge of committee structure and effectiveness, outline steps that you would take to facilitate more group participation and make the committee more productive. Be specific and explain exactly what you would do at the next meeting to prevent Mary from taking over the meeting.

LEARNING EXERCISE 12.10

Finding an Organizational Culture That Fits

Joanie Smith is a 32-year-old single mother of two who will graduate in 3 months from a local associate degree nursing program. Joanie has accrued some debts in completing her nursing education. She has been offered two jobs upon graduation: one is at (Community Center Hospital) a local medium-sized hospital and one is in a larger city some distance away (Metropolitan City Hospital). Both job offers are in the obstetrical unit, which is Joanie's desired place of work as some day she hopes to return to school to become a nurse midwife.

Research on the two hospitals shows that both are accredited and have good medical staffs and Joanie has received positive feedback on both from people whose judgment she trusts.

Assignment: Pretend you are this nurse. Knowing what little you also know about Joanie and the hospitals, what additional type of information should you gather to be able to decide which of these organizations is a better fit? What particular assessment of organizational culture can you do that would help you make a better decision?

REFERENCES

American Nurses Credentialing Center. (2013a). *ANCC Magnet recognition program overview*. Retrieved May 29, 2013, from http://www.nursecredentialing .org/Magnet/ProgramOverview.aspx

American Nurses Credentialing Center. (2013b). *Growth of the program*. Retrieved May 28, 2013, from http://www.nursecredentialing.org/MagnetGrowth.aspx

American Nurses Credentialing Center. (2013c). *Pathway program overview*. Retrieved May 29, 2013, from http://www.nursecredentialing.org/Pathway/ AboutPathway

Bennett, P. N., Ockerby, C., Begbie, J., Chalmers, C., G., & O'Connell, B. (2012). Professional nursing governance in a large Australian health service. *Contemporary Nurse: A Journal for the Australian Nursing Profession, 43*(1), 99–106.

Budin, W. C. (2012). A commitment to excellence. *Journal of Perinatal Education, 21*(1), 3–5.

BusinessDictionary.com (2013). *Organizational culture. Definition*. Retrieved May 29, 2013, from http://www.businessdictionary.com/definition/ organizational-culture.html

Education Portal (2003–2013). *Characteristics of informal organizations: The grapevine & informal groups*. Retrieved May 30, 2013, from http://education-portal .com/academy/lesson/characteristics-of-informal -organizations-the-grapevine-informal-groups.html

Fayol, H. (1949). *General and industrial management* (C. Storrs, Trans.). London: Isaac Pittman and Sons.

Grover, S. (1999–2013). *What are limitations to using an organizational chart?* eHow money. Retrieved May 30, 2013, from http://www. ehow.com/info_8484657_limitations-using -organizaional-chart.html

Juneja, H. (2013). *Span of control in an organization*. Selfgrowth.com. Retrieved May 30, 2013, from http://www.selfgrowth.com/articles/Span_of _Control_in_an_Organization.html

Pinkerton, S. (2008, September–October). The MAGNET view: Pursuing ANCC magnet recognition as a system or individual organization... American Nurses Credentialing Center. *Nursing Economics, 26* (5), 323–324.

Plath, D. (2013). Organizational processes supporting evidence-based practice. *Administration in Social Work, 37*(2), 171–188.

Rai, G. S. (2013). Job satisfaction among long-term care staff: Bureaucracy iIsn't always bad. *Administration in Social Work, 37*(1), 90–99.

Schatz, T. (2013). *Basic types of organizational structure: Formal & informal*. Chron. Retrieved May 30, 2013, from http://smallbusiness.chron.com/ basic-types-organizational-structure-formal -informal-982.html

13

Organizational, Political, and Personal Power

... nearly all men can stand adversity, but if you want to test a man's character, give him power.
—Abraham Lincoln

... "Being powerful is like being a lady. If you have to tell people you are, you aren't."
—M. Thatcher

CROSSWALK THIS CHAPTER ADDRESSES:

BSN Essential II: Basic organizational and systems leadership for quality care and patient safety

BSN Essential V: Health-care policy, finance, and regulatory environments

BSN Essential VI: Interprofessional communication and collaboration for improving patient health outcomes

BSN Essential VIII: Professionalism and professional values

MSN Essential II: Organizational and systems leadership

MSN Essential VI: Health policy and advocacy

MSN Essential VII: Interprofessional collaboration for improving patient and population health outcomes

QSEN Competency: Teamwork and collaboration

AONE Nurse Executive Competency I: Communication and relationship building

AONE Nurse Executive Competency II: A knowledge of the health-care environment

AONE Nurse Executive Competency III: Leadership

AONE Nurse Executive Competency IV: Professionalism

AONE Nurse Executive Competency V: Business skills

LEARNING OBJECTIVES *The learner will:*

- assess how power dynamics in the family unit as a child, may affect an adult's perception of power, as well as the ability to use it appropriately
- explore the influence of gender in how an individual may view power and politics
- differentiate among legitimate, reward, coercive, expert, referent, charismatic, self, and information power
- recognize the need to create and maintain a small authority–power gap
- identify and use appropriate strategies to increase his or her personal power base
- use power on behalf of other people rather than over them
- empower subordinates and followers by providing them with opportunities for success
- describe how to access and build political alliances and coalitions through networking
- use appropriate political strategies in resolving unit problems
- use cooperation rather than competition and avoid overt displays of power and authority whenever possible
- explore factors that historically led to nursing's limited power as a profession

- identify driving forces in place as well as specific strategies to increase the nursing profession's power base
- identify political strategies the novice manager could use to negate the negative effects of organizational politics
- serve as a role model of an empowered nurse

Chapter 12 reviewed organizational structure and introduced status, authority, and responsibility at different levels of the organizational hierarchy. In this chapter, the organization is examined further, with emphasis on the management functions and leadership roles inherent in effective use of authority, establishment of a personal power base, empowerment of staff, and the impact of organizational politics on power. In addition, factors that have historically contributed to nursing's limited power as a profession are presented as well as the driving forces in place to change this phenomenon. Finally, this chapter introduces strategies both the individual and the nursing profession could use to increase their power base.

The word *power* is derived from the Latin verb *potere* (to be able); thus, power may be appropriately defined as that which enables one to accomplish goals. Power can also be defined as the capacity to act or the strength and potency to accomplish something. Huston (2008, p. 58) suggests that "it is almost impossible to achieve organizational or personal goals without an adequate power base. It is even more difficult to help subordinates, patients, or clients achieve their goals when powerless, since having access to and control over resources is often related to the degree of power one holds."

Having power gives one the potential to change the attitudes and behaviors of individual people and groups.

Authority, or the right to command, accompanies any management position and is a source of legitimate power, although components of management, authority, and power are also necessary, to a degree, for successful leadership. The manager who is knowledgeable about the wise use of authority, power, and political strategy is more effective at meeting personal, unit, and organizational goals. Likewise, powerful leaders are able to raise morale because they delegate more and build with a team effort. Thus, their followers become part of the growth and excitement of the organization as their own status is enhanced. The leadership roles and management functions inherent in the use of authority and power are shown in Display 13.1.

DISPLAY 13.1 Leadership Roles and Management Functions Associated with Organizational, Political, and Personal Power

LEADERSHIP ROLES

1. Creates a climate that promotes followership in response to authority.
2. Recognizes the dual pyramid of power that exists between the organization and its employees.
3. Uses a powerful persona and referent power to increase respect and decrease fear in subordinates
4. Recognizes when it is appropriate to have authority questioned or to question authority.
5. Is personally comfortable with power in the political arena.
6. Empowers others whenever possible.
7. Assists others in using appropriate political strategies.
8. Serves as a role model of the empowered nurse.
9. Strives to eliminate a perception of powerlessness among others.
10. Is vigilant in using power judiciously and mindfully.
11. Role models political skill in developing consensus, inclusion, and follower involvement.
12. Builds alliances and coalitions inside and outside of nursing.

MANAGEMENT FUNCTIONS

1. Uses authority to ensure that organizational goals are met.
2. Uses political strategies that are complementary to the unit and organization's functioning.
3. Builds a power base appropriate for the assigned management role.
4. Creates and maintains a small authority–power gap.
5. Is knowledgeable about the essence and appropriate use of power.
6. Maintains personal credibility with subordinates.
7. Avoids using power over others rather than on behalf of others whenever possible.
8. Demonstrates reasoned risk taking in decision making with political implications.
9. Uses reward power, coercive power, legitimate power, and expert power when appropriate to positively influence the achievement of organizational goals.
10. Avoids visible displays of legitimate power and overusing commands.
11. Understands the organizational structure in which he/she works, functions effectively within that structure, and deals effectively with the institution's inherent politics.
12. Promotes subordinate identification and recognition.

 ## UNDERSTANDING POWER

Power may be feared, worshipped, or mistrusted. It is frequently misunderstood. Our first experience with power usually occurs in the family unit. Because children's roles are likened to later subordinate roles and the parental power position is similar to management, adult views of the management–subordinate relationship are often influenced by how power was used in the family unit and the often unacknowledged impact of gender upon power in family dynamics. A positive or negative familial power experience may greatly affect a person's ability to deal with power systems in adulthood.

Gender and Power

Successful leaders are attentive to the influence of gender on power. Knudson-Martin (2013) suggests that an underlying assumption of couples therapy is that intimate relationships should mutually support each partner, and while virtually no couples disagree with this assumption at the time of counseling, few couples attain this ideal with most power imbalances being related to gender. Knudson-Martin suggests that male power typically does not come from outright acts of domination but from an unacknowledged preeminence of men's priorities, needs, and desires in ways that seem ordinary or natural. In addition, women often contribute to this power imbalance by being far more accommodating and submissive than their male partners.

Some of the reluctance of women to embrace power in relationships can be explained by their socialization to the female role. Some women, in particular, may hold negative connotations of power and never learn to use power constructively. Indeed, women traditionally were expected to demonstrate, at best, ambivalence toward the concept of power, and often times, to openly eschew the pursuit of power. This occurred because many women were socialized to view power differently than men.

As a result, some women view power as dominance versus submission; associated with personal qualities, not accomplishment; and dependent on personal or physical attributes, not skill. Also, some women believe that they do not inherently possess power but instead must rely on others to acquire it. Thus, rather than feeling capable of achieving and managing power, some women feel that power manages them (Huston, 2014). The end result has been that far too many women have remained unskilled in the art of the political process.

However, this historical view of women as less powerful than men is changing. In contemporary society, people are finding new ways for leaders, regardless of gender, to acquire and manage power. These changes are taking place within women, in women's view of other women holding power, in organizational hierarchies, and among male subordinates and male colleagues (Huston, 2014). Indeed, skills that have often been linked to female characteristics such as political skill in developing consensus, inclusion, and involvement are now viewed as strengths in the corporate world. These attributes are certainly not limited to women, but it is notable that the same attributes that once closed corporate doors and created the barrier popularly called the *glass ceiling* are now generally welcomed in the boardroom.

Today, gender differences regarding power are fading, and the corporate world is beginning to look at new ways for all leaders, regardless of gender, to obtain and handle power.

LEARNING EXERCISE 13.1

Is Power Different for Men and Women?

Research studies differ on how men and women view power and how others view men and women in positions of authority. Do you think that there are gender differences in how people are viewed as being powerful? Who did you feel was most powerful in your family while growing up? Why do you think that person was powerful? If you are using group work, how many in your group named powerful male figures; how many named powerful female figures? Discuss this in a group, and then go to the library or use Internet sources to see if you can find recent studies that support your views.

Power and Powerlessness

In determining whether power is desirable, it may be helpful to look at its opposite: *powerlessness*. Most people agree that they dislike being powerless and there is growing recognition that the consequences of powerless may even include poor health outcomes and morbidity. For example, stress combined with little decision-making power is linked to heart attack risk in older men (Stress Combined with Little Decision Making, 2013).

Everyone needs to have some control in their life and when that is not the case, the end result is typically a bossy and rules-oriented individual, desperate to have some degree of power or control. The leader-manager who feels powerless often creates an ineffective, petty, dictatorial, and rule-minded management style. They may become oppressive leaders, punitive and rigid in decision making, or withhold information from others, and they become difficult to work with. This suggests that while the adage that power corrupts might be true for some, it is also likely correct to say that powerlessness holds at least as much potential for corruption.

Power is likely to bring more power in an ascending cycle, whereas powerlessness will only generate more powerlessness.

In contrast, the truly powerful individual knows he/she is powerful and does not need to display this overtly. Instead, their power is evident in the respect and cooperation of their followers. Because the powerful have credibility to support their actions, they have greater capacity to get things accomplished and can enhance their base.

Apparently, then, power has a negative and a positive face. The negative face of power is the "I win, you lose" aspect of dominance versus submission. The positive face of power occurs when someone exerts influence on behalf of—rather than over—someone or something. Power, therefore, is not good or evil; it is how it is used and for what purpose that matters.

Types of Power

For leadership to be effective, some measure of power must often support it. This is true for the informal social group and the formal work group. Mindtools (1996-2013), in their classic work, postulate that several bases, or sources, exist for the exercise of power: reward power, punishment or coercive power, legitimate power, expert power, and referent power.

Reward power is obtained by the ability to grant favors or reward others with whatever they value. The arsenal of rewards that a manager can dispense to get employees to work toward meeting organizational goals is very broad. Positive leadership through rewards tends to develop a great deal of loyalty and devotion toward leaders.

Punishment or *coercive power*, the opposite of reward power, is based on fear of punishment if the manager's expectations are not met. The manager may obtain compliance through threats (often implied) of transfer, layoff, demotion, or dismissal. The manager who shuns or ignores an employee is exercising power through punishment, as is the manager who berates or belittles an employee.

Legitimate power is position power. Authority is also called legitimate power. It is the power gained by a title or official position within an organization. Legitimate power has inherent in it the ability to create feelings of obligation or responsibility. The socialization and culture of subordinate employees will influence to some degree how much power a manager has due to his or her position.

Expert power is gained through knowledge, expertise, or experience. Having critical knowledge allows a manager to gain power over others who need that knowledge. This type of power is limited to a specialized area. For example, someone with vast expertise in music would be powerful only in that area, not in another specialization. When Florence Nightingale used research to quantify the need for nurses in the Crimea (by showing that when nurses were present, fewer soldiers died), she was using her research to demonstrate expertise in the health needs of the wounded.

Referent power is power that a person has because others identify with that leader or with what that leader symbolizes. Referent power also occurs when one gives another person, feelings of personal acceptance or approval. It may be obtained through association with the powerful. People may also develop referent power because others perceive them as powerful. This perception could be based on personal charisma, the way the leader talks or acts, the organizations to which he or she belongs, or the people with whom he or she associates. People who others accept as role models or leaders enjoy referent power. Physicians use referent power very effectively; society, as a whole, views physicians as powerful, and physicians carefully maintain this image.

Although correlated with referent power, *charismatic power* is distinguished by some from referent power. Referent power is gained only through association with powerful others, whereas charisma is a more personal type of power.

Another type of power, which is often added to the French and Raven power source is *informational power*. This source of power is obtained when people have information that others must have to accomplish their goals. The various sources of power are summarized in Table 13.1.

TABLE 13.1   Sources of Power

Type	Source
Referent	Association with others
Legitimate	Position
Coercive	Fear
Reward	Ability to grant favors
Expert	Knowledge and skill
Charismatic	Personal
Informational	The need for information

THE AUTHORITY–POWER GAP

If authority is the right to command, then a logical question is, "Why do workers sometimes not follow orders?" Galinski, Magee, Ena Inesi, and Gruenfeld (2009) suggest that this may occur because people in power are prone to dismiss or, at the very least, misunderstand the viewpoints of those who lack authority. For example, "dictators often exhibit extreme behavior in ways patently detrimental to their nations; managers are often accused of not understanding their subordinates' points of view; and the dominant partner in a relationship is often accused of being insensitive to the other's needs" (Galinski et al., 2009, para 1). When followers feel that their needs and wants are immaterial and that the person in charge focuses only on his or her own perspective, their innate motivation to be a good follower declines.

Clearly then, the right to command does not ensure that employees will follow orders. The gap that sometimes exists between a position of authority and subordinate response is called the *authority–power gap*. The term *manager power* may explain subordinates' response to the manager's authority. The more power subordinates perceive a manager to have, the smaller the gap between the right to expect certain things and the resulting fulfillment of those expectations by others.

The negative effect of a wide authority–power gap is that organizational chaos may develop. There would be little productivity if every order were questioned. The organization should rightfully expect that its goals would be accomplished. One of the core dynamics of civilization is that there will always be a few authority figures pushing the many for a certain standard of performance.

People in the United States are socialized very early to respond to authority figures. In many cases, children are conditioned to accept the directives of their parents, teachers, and community leaders. The traditional nurse-educator has been portrayed as an authoritarian who demands unconditional obedience. Educators who maintain a very narrow authority–power gap reinforce dependency and obedience by emphasizing the ultimate calamity—the death of the patient. Thus, nursing students may be socialized to be overly cautious and to hesitate when making independent nursing judgments.

Because of these types of early socialization, the gap between the manager's authority and the worker's response to that authority tends to be relatively small. In other countries, it may be larger or smaller, depending on how people are socialized to respond to authority. This authority dependence that begins with our parents and is later transferred to our employers may be an important resource to managers.

Although the authority–power gap continues to be narrow, it has grown in the last 30 years. Both the women's movement and the student unrest of the 1960s have contributed to the widening of the authority–power gap. This widening gap was evident when a 1970s college student asked her mother why she did not protest as a college student; the mother replied, "I didn't know I could."

At times, however, authority should be questioned by either the leader or the subordinates. This is demonstrated in health care by the increased questioning of the authority of physicians—many of whom feel they have the authority to command—by nurses and consumers. Figure 13.1 shows the dynamics of the relationships in the organizational authority–power response.

Bridging the Authority–Power Gap

Sometimes subordinates feel badgered by very visible exercises of authority (which should be used sparingly). Because overusing commands can stifle cooperation, outright naked commands should be used only infrequently.

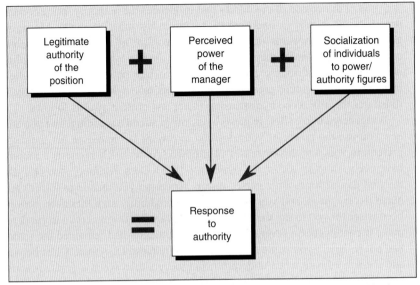

FIGURE 13.1 • Interdependency of response to authority. Copyright ® 2006 Lippincott Williams & Wilkins. Instructor's Resource CD-ROM to Accompany Leadership Roles and Management Functions in Nursing, by Bessie L. Marquis and Carol J. Huston.

LEARNING EXERCISE 13.2

Power and Authority

Think back to your childhood. Did you grow up with a very narrow authority–power gap? Have your views regarding authority and power changed since you were a child? Do you believe that children today have an authority–power gap similar to what you had as a child? Support your answers with examples.

 Overt displays of authority should be used as a last resort.

One way for the leader to bridge the gap is to make a genuine effort to know and care about each subordinate as a unique individual. This is especially important because each person has a limited tolerance of authority, and subordinates are better able to tolerate authority if they believe that the leader cares about them as individuals.

In addition, the manager needs to provide enough information about organizational and unit goals to subordinates so that they understand how their efforts and those of their manager are contributing to goal attainment. The manager will have bridged the authority–power gap if followers (a) perceive that the manager is doing a good job, (b) believe that the organization has their best interests in mind, and (c) do not feel controlled by authority.

Finally, the manager must be seen as credible for the authority–power gap not to widen. All managers begin their appointment with subordinates ready to believe them. This, again, is due to the socialization process that causes people to believe that those in power say what is true. However, the deference to authority will erode if managers handle employees carelessly, are dishonest, or seem incapable of carrying out their duties. When a manager loses credibility, the power inherent in his or her authority decreases.

Fry (2013) agrees, suggesting that truth telling is critical for the leader. "When trust in the organization is low, staff turn to their managers to find out what is happening. If you do not know the answer, tell them so. If you *do* know, share as much information as you can" (Fry, p. 33).

Another dimension of credibility that influences the authority–power relationship is *future promising*. It is best to *underpromise* if promises must be made. Managers should never guarantee future rewards unless they have control of all possible variables. If managers revoke future rewards, they lose credibility in the eyes of their subordinates. However, managers should dispense present rewards to buy patronage, making the manager more believable and building greater power into his or her legitimate authority. A scenario that illustrates the difference in dispensing future and present awards follows.

A registered nurse (RN) requests a day off to attend a wedding, and you are able to replace her. You use the power of your position to reward her and give her the day off. The RN is grateful to you, and this increases your power. Another RN requests 3 months in advance to have every Thursday off in the summer to take a class. Although you promise this to her, on the first day of June, three nurses resign, rendering you unable to fulfill your promise. This nurse is very upset, and you have lost much credibility and, therefore, power. It would have been wiser for you to say that you could not grant her original request (underpromising) or to make it contingent on several factors. If the situation had remained the same and the nurses had not resigned, you could have granted the request. Less trust is lost between the manager and the subordinate when underpromising occurs than when a granted request is rescinded, as long as the subordinate believes that the manager will make a genuine effort to meet his or her request.

LEARNING EXERCISE 13.3

Authority–Power Gap in the Student Role

You are a senior nursing student completing your final leadership practicum. Your assignment today is to assume leadership of a small team composed of the RN, one licensed vocational nurse (LVN/LPN), and one certified nursing assistant (CNA). The RN preceptor has agreed to let you take on this leadership role in her place, although she will shadow your efforts and provide support throughout the day.

Almost immediately after handoff report, a patient puts on the call light and tells you that she needs to have her sheets changed as she was incontinent in the bed. Because you are just beginning your 0800 med pass and are already behind, you ask the CNA if she has time to do this task. She immediately responds, "I'm busy and you're the student.... do it yourself. It would be a good learning experience for you." When you try to explain your leadership role for the day, she walks away, saying that she does not have time anyway.

A few minutes after that, a physician enters the unit. He wants to talk to the nurse about his patient. When you inform him that you are the student nurse caring for his patient that day, he responds... "no—I want to talk to the real nurse."

You feel frustrated with this emerging authority–power gap and seek out the RN to formulate a plan to make this gap smaller.

Assignment: Identify at least four strategies you might use to reduce the size of this authority–power. Would you involve the RN in your plan? Do you anticipate having similar authority–power gaps in the new graduate role?

Empowering Subordinates

The empowerment of staff is a hallmark of transformational leadership. To empower means to enable, develop, or allow. *Empowerment*, as discussed in Chapter 2, can be defined as decentralization of power. Empowerment occurs when leaders communicate their vision;

employees are given the opportunity to make the most of their talents; and learning, creativity, and exploration are encouraged. Empowerment plants seeds of leadership, collegiality, self-respect, and professionalism.

Individuals may be born average, but staying average is a choice.

Empowerment can also be as simple as assuring that all individuals in the organization are treated with dignity. Fry (2013, p. 33) suggests that leader-managers should "never turn a blind eye to free-range bullying, negativity, gossip, tardiness and failure to share the workload in the workplace. Instead, they should point staff to the standards of practice, the code of ethics and the mission, vision and values (the organization's and the leader-manager's practice setting's)."

Empowerment, however, is not an easy one-step process. Instead, it is a complex process that consists of responsibility for the individual desiring empowerment as well as the organization and its leadership. Individually, all practitioners must have professional traits, including responsibility for continuing education, participation in professional organizations, political activism, and most importantly, a sense of value about their work. In addition, the nurse must work in an environment that encourages empowerment, and the empowerment process must include an effective leadership style.

Rao (2012) agrees, noting that while the language of empowerment is commonly referenced, it is much more difficult to achieve in real life. He argues that most of nursing's efforts to enhance professional practice occur through structural empowerment, instead of the equally important psychological and critical social empowerment. Rao suggests for nurses to practice as professionals, they must be empowered to take action and respond to challenges using professional skill and knowledge. Unless nurses feel empowered to act, they will rely too heavily on rigid bureaucratic structures rather than their own professional power to guide practice (Examining the Evidence 13.1).

Examining the Evidence 13.1

Source: Rao, A. (2012). The contemporary construction of nurse empowerment. Journal of Nursing Scholarship, *44(4), 396–402.*

The purpose of this article was to describe how nursing's construction of empowerment has selectively shaped the manner in which the concept is applied to nursing practice and to highlight the complex interactions that shape nurse empowerment. The literature reviewed was selected from works published in the English language in the fields of nursing, management, and women's studies from 1960 to 2010.

The research findings suggest that nurse empowerment is critically important to nursing practice and that nurses working within health-care organizations must feel empowered to act, or they will rely too heavily on rigid bureaucratic structures rather than their own professional power to guide practice. Limiting nurses in this way denies the professional power their role affords them and constrains their ability to achieve extraordinary outcomes through positive deviance.

Rao notes, however, that this does not imply that nurses are powerless until they become empowered by someone else. When nurse empowerment is tied to images of nurse oppression, Rao argues that it validates the construction of nursing as a powerless profession and diminishes nurses' existent professional power. Instead, Rao suggests that nursing's efforts to enhance professional practice through empowerment must extend beyond structural empowerment and consider psychological and critical social empowerment as well. For example, nurse-leaders should focus on mobilizing power to promote nurses' professional practice and highlight the essential contribution nurses make to their organizations and communities.

One way that leaders empower subordinates is when they delegate assignments to provide learning opportunities and allow employees to share in the satisfaction derived from achievement. Empowerment is not the relinquishing of rightful power inherent in a position, nor is it a delegation of authority or its commensurate responsibility and accountability. Instead, the actions of empowered staff are freely chosen, owned, and committed to on behalf of the organization without any requests or requirements to do so.

Empowerment creates and sustains a work environment that speaks to values, such as facilitating the employee's choice to invest in and own personal actions and behaviors that result in positive contributions to the organization's mission.

Not having a commitment to empowerment is a barrier to creating an environment for empowerment in an organization. Other barriers would include a rigid organizational belief about authority and status. A manager's personal feelings regarding empowerment's potential effect on the manager's own power can also impede the empowering process.

Once organizational barriers have been minimized or eliminated, the leader should develop strategies at the unit level to empower staff. The easiest strategy is to be a role model of an empowered nurse. Another strategy would be to assist staff in building their own personal power base. This can be accomplished by showing subordinates how their personal, expert, and referent power can be expanded. Empowerment also occurs when workers are involved in planning and implementing change and when workers believe that they have some input in what is about to happen to them and some control over the environment in which they will work in the future.

LEARNING EXERCISE 13.4

Cultural Diversity

Do you think that cultural diversity might be a challenge when empowering nurses? Think of ways that various cultures may view power and empowerment differently. If you know people from other cultures, ask them how powerful people or those in authority positions are viewed in their culture and compare that with your own culture.

MOBILIZING THE POWER OF NURSING

Until the nursing profession has a seat at the health-care policy-making table, individual nurses and leader-managers will be limited in how much personal power they will hold. Huston (2014) suggests that nursing has not been the force it could be in the policy arena, stating that nurses have often been reactive rather than proactive in addressing policy decisions and legislation after the fact rather than taking part in drafting and sponsoring legislation. However, she cites several driving forces that should increase nursing's power base (Display 13.2).

DISPLAY 13.2   **Six Driving Forces to Increase Nursing's Power Base**

1. The timing is right
2. The size of the nursing profession
3. Nursing's referent power
4. Increasing knowledge base and education for nurses
5. Nursing's unique perspective
6. Desire of consumers and providers for change

Source: Huston, C. (2014). *The nursing profession's historic struggle to increase its power base. In C. Huston (Ed.), Professional issues in nursing (3rd ed.).* Philadelphia, PA: Lippincott Williams & Wilkins. Used with permission 310–326.

- *Right timing.* The errors reported in our medical system, the numbers of uninsured, and the shortcomings of our current health-care system are all reasons that consumers and legislators are willing to listen to nurses as an attempt is made to fix the health-care crisis. "Clearly the public wants a better health care system and nurses want to be able to provide high quality nursing care. Both are powerful elements for change and new nurses are entering the profession at a time when their energy and expertise will be more valued than ever" (Huston, 2014, p. 317).

- *Size of the nursing profession.* Numbers are very important in politics, and the nursing profession's size is its greatest asset. The United States has approximately 3 million RNs, which represents an impressive voting block.

- *Nursing's referent power.* The nursing profession has a great deal of referent power as a result of the high degree of trust and credibility the public places in them. Indeed, nurses have placed #1 almost every year in the Gallup Organization's annual poll on professional honesty and ethical standards since nurses were first included in the survey in 1999.

- *Increasing knowledge base and education for nurses.* There are more nurses being awarded master's and doctoral degrees than ever before. In addition, more nurses are stepping into advanced practice roles as nurse practitioners, clinical nurse specialists, certified nurse midwives, RN anesthetists, or clinical nurse-leaders. If knowledge is power, then those having knowledge can influence others, gain credibility, and gain power.

"Furthermore, leadership, management and political theory are increasingly a part of baccalaureate nursing education, although the majority of nurses still do not hold baccalaureate degrees. These are learned skills and collectively, the nursing profession's knowledge of leadership, politics, negotiation, and finance is increasing. This can only increase the nursing profession's influence outside the field" (Huston, 2014, p. 318).

- *Nursing's unique perspective.* Nursing has long been recognized as having a strong caring component. Combine that with nursing's recent surge in scientific knowledge and critical thinking, and there is a blend of art and science that brings a unique perspective to the health-care arena.

- *Desire of consumers and providers for change.* Health-care restructuring and downsizing have sparked increasing concern among consumers. The public cares about who is taking care of them. The public wants quality care.

Huston (2014) also developed an action plan for the nursing profession to build its power base (Display 13.3 shows a summary of these actions). This action plan includes the following strategies:

DISPLAY 13.3   **Action Plan for Increasing the Power of the Nursing Profession**

1. Place more nurses in positions that influence public policy.
2. Stop nurses from acting like victims.
3. Increase level of nurses' understanding regarding all health-care policy efforts.
4. Build coalitions within and outside of nursing.
5. Promote greater research to strengthen evidence-based practice.
6. Support nursing leaders.
7. Pay attention to mentoring future nurse-leaders and leadership succession.

Source: Huston, C. (2014). The nursing profession's historic struggle to increase its power base. In C. Huston (Ed.), Professional issues in nursing (3rd ed.). Philadelphia, PA: Lippincott Williams & Wilkins. Used with permission 310–326.

- *Place more nurses in positions that influence public policy.* Holding office is the ultimate in political activism. Huston (2014, p. 319) argues that "nurses are uniquely qualified to hold public office because they have the greatest firsthand experience of problems faced by patients in today's healthcare system as well as an uncanny ability to translate the healthcare experience to the general public. As a result, more nurses need to seek out this role. In addition, because the public respects and trusts nurses, nurses who choose to run for public office are often elected. The problem then is not that nurses are not elected ... the problem is that not enough nurses are running for office."

- *Stop acting like victims.* Unhappy nurses tend to look like victims. That is not to say that nurses have not been victimized in the past, but nurses need to address the cause of their unhappiness and attempt to alleviate the problem. They can confront situations, change jobs, or move into a different career path. Motivated people who care about their profession will help bring power to nursing.

- *Become better informed about all health-care policy efforts.* This means becoming involved with grassroots knowledge building and becoming better-informed consumers and providers of health care with a commitment to collective strength. Breslin (2012) agrees, noting that being politically active is part of our responsibility as nurses.

Changing nurse's view of both power and politics is perhaps the most significant key to proactive rather than reactive participation in policy setting.

- *Build coalitions inside and outside of nursing.* Health policy takes place in a virtual network of participants, professions, and organizations, both locally and nationally. Nurses have not always done well in building political coalitions with other interdisciplinary professionals with similar challenges. In addition to belonging to nursing professional organizations, nurses need to reach out to other non-nursing groups with the same concerns and goals. This interdependence and strength in numbers is what will ultimately help the profession achieve its goals.

Success comes not only with whom you know, but also, with who knows you! (Collins, 2012)

- *Conduct more research to strengthen evidence-based practice.* Great strides have been made in researching what it is that nurses do that makes a difference in patient outcomes (research on *nursing sensitivity*), but more needs to be done. Nurses must use research to present the case that nursing skills are vital to competent health care. In addition, "building and sustaining evidence-based practice in nursing will require far greater numbers of master's and doctorally prepared nurses, as well as entry into practice at an educational level similar to other professions" (Huston, 2014, p. 323).

- *Support nursing leaders.* Rather than supporting their leaders' efforts to lead, nurses have often viewed their leaders as deviants and this has occurred at a high personal cost to the innovator. In addition, nurses often resist change from their leaders and instead look to leaders in medicine or other health-related disciplines. Thus, the division in nursing often comes from within the profession itself (Huston, 2014).

- *Mentor future nurse-leaders and plan for leadership succession.* Female-dominated professions such as nursing often exemplify the *queen bee syndrome*. The queen bee is a woman who has struggled to become successful, but once successful, she refuses to help other women reach the same success. This leads to inadequate empowering of new leaders by the older, more established leaders. Increased and adequate empowering of others, mentoring the young, and ensuring leadership succession is clearly needed to advance nursing leadership. Remember that "it is the young who hold, not only the keys to the present, but also the hope for the future. The nursing profession is responsible for ensuring leadership succession and is morally bound to do it with the brightest, most highly qualified individuals " (Huston, 2014, p. 323).

STRATEGIES FOR BUILDING A PERSONAL POWER BASE

In addition to assisting with empowering the profession, nurse-leaders and nurse-managers must build a personal power base to further organizational goals, fulfill the leadership role, carry out management functions, and meet personal goals. Even a novice manager or newly graduated nurse can begin to build a power base in many ways. Habitual behaviors resulting from early lessons, passivity, and focusing on wrong targets can be replaced with new power-gaining behaviors. The following are suggested strategies for enhancing power.

Maintain Personal Energy

Power and energy go hand in hand. "To take care of others you must first take care of you. Self-care is probably one of the most important practices a nurse must cultivate to stay grounded, avoid burnout, and cope with the stress of nursing" (Creative RN, 2013, para 1). Effective leaders take sufficient time to unwind, reflect, rest, and have fun when they feel tired. Leader-managers who do not take care of themselves begin to make mistakes in judgment that may result in terrible political consequences. Taking time for significant relationships and developing outside interests are important so that other resources are available for sustenance when political forces in the organization drain energy.

You must take care of yourself before you can take care of others.

Present a Powerful Picture to Others

How people look, act, and talk influence whether others view them as powerful or powerless. Fry (2013) suggests that leader-managers choose their attitude and behaviors wisely since staff are always listening and watching their every move. The nurse who stands tall and is poised, assertive, articulate, and well groomed presents a picture of personal control and power. The manager who looks like a victim will undoubtedly become one. When individuals take the time for self-care, they exude confidence. This is apparent in not only how they dress and act but also in how they interact with others (Huston, 2008).

Pay the Entry Fee

Newcomers who stand out and appear powerful are those who do more, work harder, and contribute to the organization. They are not clock watchers or "nine-to-fivers." They attend meetings and in-service opportunities; they do committee work and take their share of night shifts and weekend and holiday assignments without complaining. A power base is not achieved by slick, easy, or quick maneuvers but through hard work. In addition, Huston (2008) suggests that it is important to be a team player. "Showing a genuine interest in others, being considerate of other people's needs and wants, and offering others support whenever possible, are all a part of successful team building. These interpersonal skills are part of emotional intelligence" (p. 61).

Determine the Powerful in the Organization

Understanding and working successfully within both formal and informal power structures are important strategies for building a personal power base. Individuals must be cognizant of their limitations and seek counsel appropriately. One should know the names and faces of those with both formal power and informal power. The powerful people in the informal structure are often more difficult to identify than those in the formal structure. When working with powerful people, look for similarities and shared values and avoid focusing on differences.

Learn the Language and Symbols of the Organization

Each organization has its own culture and value system. Watkins (2013) notes that organizational culture is "the story" in which people in the organization are embedded, and the values and rituals that reinforce that narrative. It also focuses attention on the importance of symbols and the need to understand them—including the idiosyncratic languages used in organizations. New members must understand this culture and be socialized into the organization if they are to build a power base. Being unaware of institutional taboos often results in embarrassment for the newcomer.

Learn How to Use the Organization's Priorities

Every group has its own goals and priorities for achieving those goals. Those seeking to build a power base must be cognizant of organizational goals and use those priorities and goals to meet management needs. For example, a need for a new manager in a community health service might be to develop educational programs on chemotherapy because some of the new patient caseload includes this nursing function. If fiscal management is a high priority, the manager needs to show superiors how the cost of these educational programs will be offset by additional revenues. If public relations with physicians and patients are a priority, the manager would justify the same request in terms of additional services to patients and physicians.

Increase Professional Skills and Knowledge

Because employees are expected to perform their jobs well, one's performance must be extraordinary to enhance power. One method of being extraordinary is to increase professional skills and knowledge to an expert level. Having knowledge and skill that others lack greatly augments a person's power base. Excellence that reflects knowledge and demonstrates skill enhances a nurse's credibility and determines how others view him or her.

Maintain a Broad Vision

Vision is one of the most powerful tools that a leader has in his/her toolbox. When communicated effectively, it serves as the driving force for goal attainment (The Importance of Vision, 2013). Because workers are assigned to a unit or department, they often develop a narrow view of the total organization. Power builders always look upward and outward. The successful leader recognizes not only how the individual unit fits within the larger organization but also how the institution as a whole fits into the scheme of the total community. People without vision rarely become very powerful.

Use Experts and Seek Counsel

Newcomers should seek out role models. *Role models* are experienced, competent individuals an individual wishes to emulate (Huston, 2008). Even though there may be no significant interpersonal relationship, one can learn a great deal about successful leadership, management, and decision making by observing and imitating positive role models. By looking to others for advice and counsel, people demonstrate that they are willing to be team players, that they are cautious and want expert opinion before proceeding, and that they are not rash newcomers who think they have all the answers. Aligning oneself with appropriate veterans in the organization is excellent for building power.

Be Flexible

Bossong (2013) suggests that one of the greatest assets a football quarterback has is his ability to determine at the line of scrimmage, an instant backup plan based on immediate feedback he sees or feels. The same is true for leadership. Great leaders understand the power of flexibility. Anyone wishing to acquire power should develop a reputation as someone who can compromise. The rigid, uncompromising newcomer is viewed as being insensitive to the organization's needs.

Develop Visibility and a Voice in the Organization

Newcomers to an organization must become active in committees or groups that are recognized by the organization as having clout. When working in groups, the newcomer must not monopolize committee time. In addition, novice leaders and managers must develop observational, listening, and verbal skills. Their spoken contributions to the committee should be valuable and articulated well.

Experienced leader-managers must strive for visibility and voice as well. Bossong (2013) suggests that managers should spend time with all of the staff, not just direct reports. Managers who are too far removed from workers in the organization hierarchy can have a view that is cloudy or distorted. Bossong suggests that managers at all levels of the hierarchy should get out of their offices and attempt to interact with everyone in the organization. If workers do not know their managers, they will not trust them.

Learn to Toot Your Own Horn

Accepting compliments is an art. One should be gracious but certainly not passive when praised for extraordinary effort. In addition, people should let others know when some special professional recognition has been achieved. This should be done in a manner that is not bragging but reflects the self-respect of one who is talented and unique.

Maintain a Sense of Humor

Appropriate humor is very effective. The ability to laugh at oneself and not take oneself too seriously is a most important power builder. Brody (2011) notes that humor often relieves stress or tension, especially the inherent stress that accompanies leadership. Humor allows the leader to relax so that he/she can step away from the challenge, and look at the circumstance in a different perspective.

Empower Others

Leaders need to empower others, and followers must empower their leaders. When nurses empower each other, they gain referent power. Individual nurses and the profession as a whole do not gain their share of power because they allow others to divide them and weaken them. Nurses can empower other nurses by sharing knowledge, maintaining cohesiveness, valuing the profession, and supporting each other.

Power-building and political strategies are summarized in Display 13.4.

DISPLAY 13.4   Leadership Strategies: Developing Power and Political Savvy

Power-Building Strategies	Political Strategies
Maintain personal energy	Develop information acquisition skills
Present a powerful persona	Communicate astutely
Pay the entry fee	Become proactive
Determine the powerful	Assume authority
Learn the organizational culture	Network

(Continued)

Use organizational priorities	Expand personal resources
Increase skills and knowledge	Maintain maneuverability
Have a broad vision	Remain sensitive to people, timing, and situations
Use experts and seek counsel	
Be flexible	Promote subordinates' identities
Be visible and have a voice	Meet organizational needs
Toot your own horn	
Maintain a sense of humor	
Empower others	

LEARNING EXERCISE 13.5

Building Power as the New Nurse

You have been an RN for 3 years. Six months ago, you left your position as a day charge nurse at one of the local hospitals to accept a position at the public health agency. You really miss your friends at the hospital and find most of the public health nurses older and aloof. However, you love working with your patients and have decided that this is where you want to build a lifetime career. Although you believe that you have some good ideas, you are aware that because you are new, you will probably not be able to act as change agent yet. Eventually, you would like to be promoted to agency supervisor and become a powerful force for stimulating growth within the agency. You decide that you can do a few things to build a power base. You spend a weekend designing a personal power-building plan.

Assignment: Make a power-building plan. Give six to ten specific examples of things you would do to build a power base in the new organization. Provide rationale for each selection. (Do not merely select from the general lists in the text. Outline specific actions that you would take.) It might be helpful to consider your own community and personal strengths when solving this learning exercise.

THE POLITICS OF POWER

Politics is the art of using legitimate power wisely. It requires clear decision making, assertiveness, accountability, and the willingness to express one's own views. It also requires being proactive rather than reactive and demands decisiveness. Leader-managers in power positions in today's health-care settings are more likely to recognize their innate abilities that support the effective use of power.

It is important for managers to understand politics within the context of their employing organization. After the employee has built a power base through hard work, increased personal power, and knowledge of the organization, developing skills in the politics of power is necessary. After all, power may not be gained indefinitely; it may be fleeting. For example, people often lose hard-earned power in an organization because they make political mistakes. Even seasoned leaders occasionally blunder in this arena.

Although power is a universally available resource, it does not have a finite quality and can be lost as well as gained.

It is useless to argue the ethics or value of politics in an organization, because politics exists in every organization. Thus, nurses waste energy and remain powerless when they refuse to learn the art and skill of political maneuvers. Politics becomes divisive only whenever gossip, rumor, or unethical strategies occur.

Much attention is given to improving competence, but little time is spent in learning the intricacies of political behavior. The most important strategy is to learn to "read the environment" (e.g., understand relationships within the organization) through observation, listening, reading, detachment, and analysis.

Because power implies interdependence, nurses must not only understand the organizational structure in which they work but also be able to function effectively within that structure, including dealing effectively with the institution's inherent politics. Only when managers understand power and politics will they be capable of recognizing limitations and potential for change.

Understanding one's own power can be frightening, especially when one considers that "attacks" (or opposition) from various fronts may reduce that power. When these attacks occur, people who hold powerful positions may undermine themselves by regressing rather than progressing and by being reactive rather than proactive. The following political strategies will help the novice manager to negate the negative effects of organizational politics:

- *Become an expert handler of information and communication.* Beware that facts can be presented seductively and out of context. Be cautious in accepting facts as presented, because information is often changed to fit others' needs. Managers must become artful at acquiring information and questioning others. Delay decisions until adequate and accurate information has been gathered and reviewed. Failing to do the necessary homework may lead to decisions with damaging political consequences.

  Managers must not trap themselves by discussing something about which they know very little. Political astuteness in communication is a skill to be mastered, and the politically astute manager says, "I don't know" when adequate information is unavailable. Grave consequences can result from sharing the wrong information with the wrong people at the wrong time. Determining who should know, how much they should know, and when they should know requires great finesse.

  One of the most politically serious errors that one can make is lying to others within the organization. Unlike withholding and refusing to divulge information, which may be good political strategies, lying destroys trust, and leaders must never underestimate the power of trust.

- *Be a proactive decision maker.* Nurses have had such a long history of being reactive that they have had little time to learn how to be proactive. Although being reactive is better than being passive, being proactive means getting the job done better, faster, and more efficiently. Proactive leaders prepare for the future instead of waiting for it. Seeing changes approaching in the health-care system, they prepare to meet them, not fight them.

  Assuming authority is one way that nurses can become proactive. Part of power is the image of power; a powerful political strategy also involves image. Instead of asking, "May I?" leaders assume that they may. When people ask permission, they are really asking someone to take responsibility for them. If something is not expressly prohibited in an organization or a job description, the powerful leader assumes that it may be done. Politically astute nurses have been known to create new positions or new roles within a position simply by gradually assuming that they could do things that no one else was doing. In other words, they saw a need in the organization and started meeting it. The organization, through default, allowed expansion of the role. People need to be aware, however, that if they assume authority and something goes wrong, they will be held accountable; so this strategy is not without risk.

- *Expand personal resources.* Because organizations are dynamic and the future is impossible to predict, the proactive nurse prepares for the future by expanding personal resources. Personal resources include economic stability, higher education, and a broadened skill base. Some call this the political strategy of "having maneuverability," that is, the person avoids having limited options. People with "money in the bank and gas in the tank" have a political freedom of maneuverability that others do not. People lose power if others within the organization know that they cannot afford to make a job change or lack the necessary skills to do so. Those who become economically dependent on a position lose political clout. Likewise, the nurse who has not developed additional skills or sought further education loses the political strength that comes from being able to find quality employment elsewhere.

- *Develop political alliances and coalitions.* Nurses often can increase their power and influence by forming coalitions and alliances (networking) with other groups, be they peers, sponsors, or subordinates, especially when these alliances are with peers outside the organization. In this manner, the manager keeps abreast of current happenings and consults others for advice and counsel. Although networking works among many groups, for the nurse-manager, few groups are as valuable as local and state nursing associations. More power and political clout result from working together rather than alone. When a person faces political opposition from others in the organization, group power is very useful.

Nurses must be represented in mass, in some way, before they will be able to significantly impact the decisions that directly influence their own profession.

- *Be sensitive to timing.* Successful leaders are sensitive to the appropriateness and timing of their actions. The person who presents a request to attend an expensive nursing conference on the same afternoon that his or her supervisor just had extensive dental work typifies someone who is insensitive to timing. Besides being able to choose the right moment, the effective manager should develop skill in other areas of timing, such as knowing when it is appropriate to do nothing. For example, in the case of a problem employee who is 3 months from retirement, time itself will resolve the situation. The sensitive manager also learns when to stop requesting something. That time is before a superior issues a firm "no," at which point continuing to press the issue is politically unwise.

- *Promote subordinate identification.* A manager can promote the identification of subordinates in many ways. A simple "thank you" for a job well done works well when spoken in front of someone else. Calling attention to the extra efforts of subordinates says in effect, "Look what a good job we are capable of doing." Sending subordinates sincere notes of appreciation is another way of praising and promoting. Rewarding excellence is an effective political strategy.

- *View personal and unit goals in terms of the organization.* Even extraordinary and visible activities will not result in desired power unless those activities are used to meet organizational goals. Hard work purely for personal gain will become a political liability. Frequently, novice managers think only in terms of their needs and their problems rather than seeing the large picture. Moreover, people often look upward for solutions rather than attempting to find answers themselves. When problems are identified, it is more politically astute to take the problem and a proposed solution upward rather than just presenting the problem to the superior. Although the superior may not accept the solution, the effort to problem solve will be appreciated.

- *"Leave your ego at home in a jar."* Although political actions can be negative, you should make an effort not to take political muggings personally, because you may well be a bystander hit in a crossfire. Likewise, be careful about accepting credit for all political successes, because you may just have been in the right place at the right time. Be prepared as a manager to make political errors. The key to success is how quickly you rebound.

LEARNING EXERCISE 13.6

Turning Lemons into Lemonade

The following is based on a real event. The cast includes Sally Jones, the Chief Nursing Officer; Jane Smith, the hospital administrator and CEO; and Bob Black, the assistant hospital administrator. Sally has been in her position at Memorial Hospital for 2 years. She has made many improvements in the nursing department and is generally respected by the hospital administrator, the nursing staff, and the physicians.

The present situation involves the newly hired Bob Black. Previously too small to have an assistant administrator, the hospital has grown, and this position was created. One of the departments assigned to Bob is the personnel and payroll department. Until now, nursing, which comprises 45% of all personnel, has done its own recruiting, interviewing, and selecting. Since Bob has been hired, he has shown obvious signs that he would like to increase his power and authority. Now Bob has proposed that he hire an additional clerk who will do much of the personnel work for the nursing department, although nursing administration will be able to make the final selections in hiring. Bob proposes that his department should do the initial screening of applicants, seeking references, and so on. Sally has grown increasingly frustrated in dealing with the encroachment of Bob. Having just received Bob's latest proposal, she has requested to meet with Jane Smith and Bob to discuss the plan.

Assignment: What danger, if any, is there for Sally Jones in Bob Black's proposal? Explain two political strategies that you believe Sally could use in the upcoming meeting. Is it possible to facilitate a win–win solution to this conflict? If so, how? If there is not a win–win solution, how much can Sally win?

Note: Attempt to solve this case before reading the solution presented in the Appendix.

INTEGRATING LEADERSHIP ROLES AND MANAGEMENT FUNCTIONS WHEN USING AUTHORITY AND POWER IN ORGANIZATIONS

A manager's ability to gain and wisely use power is critical to his or her success. Nurses will never be assured of adequate resources until they gain the power to manipulate the needed resources legitimately. To do this, managers must be able to bridge the authority–power gap, build a personal power base, and minimize the negative politics of the organization.

One of the most critical leadership roles in the use of power and authority is the empowerment of subordinates. The leader recognizes the dual pyramid of power and acknowledges the power of others, including that of subordinates, peers, and higher administrators.

The key then to establishing and keeping authority and power in an organization is for the leader-manager to be able to accomplish four separate tasks:

- Maintain a small authority–power gap.
- Empower subordinates whenever possible.
- Use authority in such a manner that subordinates view what happens in the organization as necessary.
- When needed, implement political strategies to maintain power and authority.

Integrating the leadership role and the functions of management reduces the risk that power will be misused. Power and authority will be used to increase respect for the position and for nursing as a whole. The leader comfortable with power ensures that the goal of political maneuvers is cooperation, not personal gain. The successful manager who has integrated the role of leadership will not seek to have power over others but instead will empower others. It is imperative for leader-managers to become skillful in the art of politics and the use of political strategy if they are to survive in the corporate world of the health-care industry. It is with the use of such strategies that organizational resources are obtained and goals are achieved.

KEY CONCEPTS

- Power and authority are necessary components of leadership and management.
- A person's response to authority is conditioned early through authority figures, experiences in the family unit, and gender role identification.
- The gap that sometimes exists between a position of authority and subordinate response is called the authority–power gap.
- The empowerment of staff is a hallmark of transformational leadership. Empowerment means to enable, develop, or allow.
- Power has both a positive and a negative face.
- Traditionally, women have been socialized to view power differently than men do. However, recent studies show that gender differences regarding power are slowly changing.
- Reward power is obtained by the ability to grant rewards to others.
- Coercive power is based on fear and punishment.
- Legitimate power is the power inherent in one's position.
- Expert power is gained through knowledge or skill.
- Referent power is obtained through association with others.
- Charismatic power results from a dynamic and powerful persona.
- Information power is gained when someone has information that another needs.
- Female-dominated professions such as nursing often exemplify the *queen bee syndrome*. The queen bee is a woman who has struggled to become successful, but once successful, refuses to help other women reach the same success.
- Even a novice manager or newly graduated nurse can begin to build a power base by using appropriate power-building tactics.
- Power gained may be lost because one is politically naive or fails to use appropriate political strategies.
- Politics exist in every organization, and leader-managers must learn the art and skills of politics.
- The nursing profession has not been the political force it could be since historically, it has been more reactive than proactive in addressing needed policy decisions and legislation.
- Numerous driving forces are in place to increase the nursing profession's power base, including timing, the size of the profession, nursing's referent power, the increasing educational levels of nurses, nursing's unique perspective, and the desire of consumers and providers for change.

ADDITIONAL LEARNING EXERCISES AND APPLICATIONS

LEARNING EXERCISE 13.7

Empowering Your Staff

After 5 years as a public health nurse, you have just been appointed as supervisor of the western region of the county health department. There is one supervisor for each region, a nursing director, and an assistant director. You have eight nurses who report directly to you. Your organization seems to have few barriers to prevent staff empowerment, but in talking with the staff that report to you, they frequently express feelings of powerlessness in their ability to effect lasting change in their patients or in changing policies within the organization. Your first planned change, therefore, is to develop strategies to empower them.

Assignment: Devise a political strategy for successfully empowering the staff that report directly to you. Consider the three elements necessary in the empowerment process: professional traits of the staff, a supportive environment, and effective leadership. Of these things, what is in your sphere of control? Where is the danger of your plan being sabotaged? What change tactics can you use to increase the likelihood of success?

LEARNING EXERCISE 13.8

Friendships and Truth

You are a middle-level manager in a public health department. One of your closest friends, Janie, is an RN under your span of control. Today, Janie calls and tells you that she injured her back yesterday during a home visit after she slipped on a wet front porch. She said that the home owners were unaware that she fell and that no one witnessed the accident. She has just returned from visiting her doctor, who advises 6 weeks of bed rest. She requests that you initiate the paperwork for workers compensation and disability, because she has no sick days left.

Shortly after your telephone conversation with Janie, you take a brief coffee break in the lounge. You overhear a conversation between Jon and Lacey, two additional staff members in your department. Jon says that he and Janie were water skiing last night, and she took a terrible fall and hurt her back. He planned to call her to see how she was feeling.

You initially feel hurt and betrayed by Janie because you believe that she has lied to you. You want to call Janie and confront her. You plan to deny her request for workers' compensation and disability. You are angry that she has placed you in this position. You are also aware that proving Janie's injury is not work related may be difficult.

Assignment: How should you proceed? What are the political ramifications if this incident is not handled properly? How should you use your power and authority when dealing with this problem?

LEARNING EXERCISE 13.9

Decision Making: Conflict and Dilemma

You are the director of a small Native American health clinic. Other than yourself and a part-time physician, your only professional staff members are two RNs. The remaining staff members are Native Americans and have been trained by you.

(Continued)

Because nurse Bennett, a 26-year-old female BSN graduate, has had several years of experience working at a large southwestern community health agency, she is familiar with many of the patients' problems. She is hard working and extremely knowledgeable. Occasionally, her assertiveness is mistaken for bossiness among the Native American workers. However, everyone respects her judgment.

The other RN, Nurse Mikiou, is a 34-year-old male Native American. He started as a medic in the Persian Gulf War and attended several career-ladder external degree programs until he was able to take the RN examination. He does not have a baccalaureate degree. His nursing knowledge is occasionally limited, and he tends to be very casual about performing his duties. However, he is competent and has never shown unsafe judgment. His humor and good nature often reduce tension in the clinic. The Native American population is very proud of him, and he has a special relationship with them. However, he is not a particularly good role model because his health habits leave much to be desired, and he is frequently absent from work.

Nurse Bennett has come to find Nurse Mikiou intolerable. She believes that she has tried working with him, but this is difficult because she does not respect him. As the director of the clinic, you have tried many ways to solve this problem. You feel especially fortunate to have nurse Bennett on your staff. It is difficult to find many nurses of her quality willing to come and live on a Native American reservation. On the other hand, if the care is to be as culturally relevant as possible, the Native Americans themselves must be educated and placed in the agencies so that one day they can run their own clinics. It is very difficult to find educated Native Americans who want to return to this reservation. Now, you are faced with a management dilemma. Nurse Bennett has said that either Nurse Mikiou must go, or she will go. She has asked you to decide.

Assignment: List the factors bearing on this decision. What (if any) power issues are involved? Which choice will be the least damaging? Justify your decision.

LEARNING EXERCISE 13.10

Power Struggle

You are team leader on a medical unit of a small community hospital. Your shift is 3 to 11 PM. When leaving the report room, John, the day-shift team leader, tells you that Mrs. Jackson, a patient who is terminally ill with cancer, has decided to check herself out of the hospital "against medical advice." John states that he has already contacted Mrs. Jackson's doctor, who expressed his concern that the patient would have inadequate pain control at home and undependable family support. He believes that she will die within a few days if she leaves the hospital. He did, however, leave orders for home prescriptions and a follow-up appointment.

You immediately go into Mrs. Jackson's room to assess the situation. She tells you that the doctor has told her she will probably die within 6 weeks and that she wants to spend what time she has left at home with her little dog, who has been her constant companion for many years. In addition, she has many things "to put in order." She states that she is fully aware of her doctor's concerns and that she was already informed by the day-shift nurse that leaving "against medical advice" may result in the insurance company refusing to pay for her current hospitalization. She states that she will be leaving in 15 minutes when her ride home arrives.

When you go to the nurse's station to get a copy of the home prescriptions and follow-up doctor's appointment for the patient, the unit clerk states, "The hospital policy says that patients who leave against medical advice have to contact the physician directly for prescriptions and an appointment, because they are not legally discharged. The hospital has no obligation to provide this service. She made the choice—now let her live with it." She refuses to give a copy of the orders to you and places the patient's chart in her lap. Short of physically removing the chart from the clerk's lap, you clearly have no immediate access to the orders.

You confront the charge nurse, who is unsure what to do and who states that the hospital policy does give that responsibility to the patient. The unit director, who has been paged, appears to be out of the hospital temporarily.

You are outraged. You believe that the patient has the "right" to her prescriptions because the doctor ordered them, assuming she would receive them before she left. You also know that if the medications are not dispensed by the hospital, there is little likelihood that Mrs. Jackson will have the resources to have the prescriptions filled. Five minutes later, Mrs. Jackson appears at the nurse's station, accompanied by her friend. She states that she is leaving and would like her discharge prescriptions.

Assignment: The power struggle in this scenario involves you, the unit clerk, the charge nurse, and organizational politics. Does the unit clerk in this scenario have informal or formal power? What alternatives for action do you have? What are the costs or consequences of each possible alternative? What action would you take?

LEARNING EXERCISE 13.11

Ego and the Chain of Command

You are the day-shift charge nurse for the intensive care unit. One of your nurses, Carol, has just requested a week off to attend a conference. She is willing to use her accrued vacation time for this and to pay the expenses herself. The conference is in 1 month, and you are a little irritated with her for not coming to you sooner. Carol's request conflicts with a vacation that you have given another nurse. This nurse requested her vacation 3 months ago.

You deny Carol's request, explaining that you will need her to work that week. Carol protests, stating that the educational conference will benefit the intensive care unit and repeating that she will bear the cost. You are firm but polite in your refusal. Later, Carol goes to the supervisor of the unit to request the time. Although the supervisor upholds your decision, you are upset because you believe that Carol has gone over your head inappropriately in handling this matter.

Assignment: Were Carol's actions appropriate in going over your head in addressing her concerns? Does ego impact your response? How are you going to deal with Carol? Decide on your approach and support it with political rationale.

REFERENCES

Bossong, J. (2013, May 19). *6 keys to leadership flexibility.* Wordpress. Retrieved May 31, 2013, from http://johnbossong.com/2013/05/19/6-keys-to-leadership-flexibility/

Breslin, J. (2012). Democrat? Republican? I'm a nurse first. *Michigan Nurse, 85*(5), 4.

Brody, R. (2011, April 12). *Leaders need sense of humor.* EzineArticles.com. Retrieved June 1, 2013, from http://ezinearticles.com/?Leaders-Need-Sense-Of-Humor&id=6171144

Collins, B. (2012). Networking and the power of being connected. *Journal of Environmental Health, 75*(3), 4–5.

Creative RN (2013, March 27). *3 Easy self-care practices for nurses.* Retrieved June 1, 2013, from http://www.creativern.com/2013/03/27/3-easy-self-care-practices/

Fry, B. (2013). Power up your leadership: Straight talk for nurse managers. *Canadian Nurse, 109*(5), 32–33.

Galinski, A. D., Magee, J. C., Ena Inesi, M., & Gruenfeld, D. H. (2009). Losing touch. Power diminishes perception and perspective. *Kellogg insight: focus on research.* Retrieved December 19, 2009, from http://insight.kellogg.northwestern.edu/index.php/Kellogg/article/losing_touch

Huston, C. (2008, April). Eleven strategies for building a personal power base. *Nursing Management, 39*(4), 58–61.

Huston, C. (2014). The nursing profession's historic struggle to increase its power base. In C. Huston (Ed.), *Professional issues in nursing* (3rd ed.). Philadelphia, PA: Lippincott Williams & Wilkins 310–326.

Knudson-Martin, C. (2013). Why power matters: Creating a foundation of mutual support in couple relationships. *Family Process, 52*(1), 5–18.

Mindtools (1996-2013). French and Raven's Five Forms of Power. Understanding Where Power Comes From in the Workplace. Retrieved Oct. 27, 2013 from http://www.mindtools.com/pages/article/newLDR_56.htm

Rao, A. (2012). The contemporary construction of nurse empowerment. *Journal of Nursing Scholarship, 44*(4), 396–402.

Stress Combined with Little Decision-Making Power Linked to Heart Attack Risk in Men (2013). *Occupational Health, 65*(1), 4.

The Importance of Vision. (2013, January 13). Retrieved June 1, 2013, from http://winningleadership.wordpress.com/2013/01/13/the-importance-of-vision/

Watkins, M. (2013, May 15). What is organizational culture? And why should we care? Retrieved June 1, 2013, from http://blogs.hbr.org/cs/2013/05/what_is_organizational_culture.html

14

Organizing Patient Care

... patients now more than ever need reassurance that they are indeed the focus of the healthcare team.
—Joan Shinkus Clark

... nurses have gone beyond the role of caregivers to become key integrators, care coordinators and efficiency experts who are redesigning the patient experience through new, innovative healthcare delivery models
—Linda Beattle

CROSSWALK THIS CHAPTER ADDRESSES:

BSN Essential II: Basic organizational and systems leadership for quality care and patient safety
BSN Essential VI: Interprofessional communication and collaboration for improving patient health outcomes
BSN Essential V: Health-care policy, finance, and regulatory environments
MSN Essential II: Organizational and systems leadership
MSN Essential III: Quality improvement and safety
MSN Essential VII: Interprofessional collaboration for improving patient and population health outcomes
QSEN Competency: Teamwork and collaboration
QSEN Competency: Patient-centered care
QSEN Competency: Quality improvement
QSEN Competency: Safety
AONE Nurse Executive Competency I: Communication and relationship building
AONE Nurse Executive Competency II: A knowledge of the health-care environment

LEARNING OBJECTIVES *The learner will:*

- differentiate among various types of patient care delivery systems, including total patient care, functional nursing, team nursing, modular nursing, primary nursing, and case management
- discuss the historical events that led to the evolution of different types of patient care delivery models
- debate the driving and restraining forces for reserving the primary nurse role for the registered nurse
- differentiate between managed care and population-based health-care management
- identify desired outcomes in disease management programs and the role the case manager plays in achieving those outcomes
- differentiate between nurse case managers and nurse navigators
- discuss how work redesign may affect social relationships on a unit
- explain what effect staff mix has on work design and patient care organization

- identify factors that must be evaluated before initiating a change in a patient care delivery system
- delineate new roles that are expanding the role of nurses beyond caregivers to key integrators, care coordinators and efficiency experts such as case managers, nurse navigators, and clinical nurse-leaders
- describe the core concepts of patient- and family-centered care
- describe the role competencies expected of the clinical nurse-leader, as described by the American Association of Colleges of Nursing

Top-level managers are most likely to influence the philosophy and resources necessary for any selected care delivery system to be effective, since without a supporting philosophy and adequate resources, the most well-intentioned delivery system will fail. It is the first- and middle-level managers, however, who generally have the greatest influence on the organizing phase of the management process at the unit or department level. It is here that leader-managers organize how work is to be done, shape the organizational climate, and determine how patient care delivery is organized.

In addition, the unit leader-manager determines how best to plan work activities so that organizational goals are met effectively and efficiently. This involves using resources wisely and coordinating activities with other departments, since how activities are organized can impede or facilitate communication, flexibility, and job satisfaction.

For organizing functions to be productive and facilitate meeting the organization's needs, the leader must also know the organization and its members well. Activities will be unsuccessful if their design does not meet group needs and capabilities. The roles and functions of the leader-manager in organizing groups for patient care are shown in Display 14.1.

DISPLAY 14.1 **Leadership Roles and Management Functions Associated with Organizing Patient Care**

LEADERSHIP ROLES

1. Periodically evaluates the effectiveness of the organizational structure for the delivery of patient care.
2. Determines if adequate resources and support exist before making any changes in the organization of patient care.
3. Examines the human element in work redesign and supports personnel during adjustment to change.
4. Inspires the work group toward a team effort.
5. Inspires subordinates to achieve higher levels of education, clinical expertise, competency, and experience in differentiated practice.
6. Ensures that chosen nursing care delivery models advance the practice of professional nursing.
7. Encourages and supports the use of nursing care delivery models that maximize the abilities of each member on the health-care team.
8. Assures congruence between the organizational mission and philosophy and the patient care delivery system selected for use.
9. Assures that the patient and family are the focus of patient care delivery, regardless of which patient care delivery system is used.

MANAGEMENT FUNCTIONS

1. Makes changes in work design to facilitate meeting organizational goals.
2. Selects a patient care delivery system that is most appropriate to the needs of the patients being served as well as the expertise of the staffing mix.
3. Uses scientific research and current literature to analyze proposed changes in nursing care delivery models.
4. Uses a patient care delivery system that maximizes human and physical resources as well as time.
5. Ensures that nonprofessional staff are appropriately trained and supervised in the provision of care.

6. Organizes work activities to attain organizational goals.
7. Groups activities in a manner that facilitates communication and coordination within and between departments.
8. Organizes work so that it is as time and cost-effective as possible.
9. Appropriately identifies cost drivers in high-cost, high-resource utilization diseases and organizes patient care to address these with efficiency across care settings.
10. Explores opportunities to use case managers, nurse navigators, and clinical nurse-leaders (CNLs) to better integrate and coordinate care.

TRADITIONAL MODES OF ORGANIZING PATIENT CARE

The five most well-known means of organizing nursing care for patient care delivery are total patient care, functional nursing, team and modular nursing, primary nursing, and case management (Display 14.2). Each of these basic types has undergone many modifications, often resulting in new terminology. For example, primary nursing was once called case method nursing and is now frequently referred to as a *professional practice model*. Team nursing is sometimes called *partners in care* or *patient service partners*, and case managers assume different titles depending on the setting in which they provide care.

DISPLAY 14.2	Traditional Patient Care Delivery Methods

Total patient care
Functional nursing
Team and modular nursing
Primary nursing
Case management

When closely examined, many of the newer models of patient care delivery systems are merely recycled, modified, or retitled versions of older models. Indeed, it is sometimes difficult to find a delivery system true to its original version or one that does not have parts of others in its design. Although some of these care delivery systems were developed to organize care in hospitals, most can be adapted to other settings. The choice of an organization model involves staff skills, availability of resources, patient acuity, and the nature of the work to be performed.

Many of the newer models of patient care delivery systems are merely recycled, modified, or retitled versions of older models.

Total Patient Care Nursing or Case Method Nursing

Total patient care is the oldest mode of organizing patient care. With total patient care, nurses assume total responsibility during their time on duty for meeting all the needs of assigned patients. *Total patient care nursing* is sometimes referred to as the *case method of assignment* because patients may be assigned as cases, much like private-duty nursing was historically carried out.

Indeed, at the turn of the 19th century, total patient care was the predominant nursing care delivery model. Care was generally provided in the patient's home, and the nurse was responsible for cooking, house cleaning, and other activities specific to the patient and family in addition to traditional nursing care. During the Great Depression of the 1930s, however, people could no longer afford home care and began using hospitals for care that had been performed by private-duty nurses in the home. During that time, nurses and students were the caregivers in hospitals and in public health agencies. As hospitals grew during the 1930s and 1940s, providing total care continued to be the primary means of organizing patient care.

This method of assignment is still widely used in hospitals and home health agencies. This organizational structure provides nurses with high autonomy and responsibility. Assigning patients is simple and direct and does not require the planning that other methods of patient care delivery require. The lines of responsibility and accountability are clear. The patient theoretically receives holistic and unfragmented care during the nurse's time on duty.

Each nurse caring for the patient can, however, modify the care regimen. Therefore, if there are three shifts, the patient could receive three different approaches to care, often resulting in confusion for the patient. To maintain quality care, this method requires highly skilled personnel and thus may cost more than some other forms of patient care. This method's opponents argue that some tasks performed by the primary caregiver could be accomplished by someone with less training and therefore at a lower cost. A structural diagram of total patient care is shown in Figure 14.1.

The greatest disadvantage of total patient care delivery occurs when the nurse is inadequately prepared or too inexperienced to provide total care to the patient. In the early days of nursing, only registered nurses (RNs) provided care; now, many hospitals assign LVNs/LPNs as well as unlicensed health-care workers to provide much of the nursing care. Because the coassigned RN may have a heavy patient load, little opportunity for supervision may exist and this could result in unsafe care.

Functional Method

The *functional method* of delivering nursing care evolved primarily as a result of World War II and the rapid construction of hospitals as a result of the Hill Burton Act. Because nurses were in great demand overseas and at home, a nursing shortage developed and ancillary

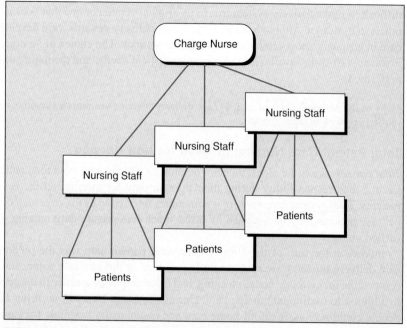

FIGURE 14.1 • Case method or total patient care structure.

personnel were needed to assist in patient care. These relatively unskilled workers were trained to do simple tasks and gained proficiency by repetition. Personnel were assigned to complete certain tasks rather than care for specific patients. Examples of functional nursing tasks were checking blood pressures, administering medication, changing linens, and bathing patients. RNs became managers of care rather than direct care providers, and *"care through others"* became the phrase used to refer to this method of nursing care. Functional nursing structure is shown in Figure 14.2.

The functional form of organizing patient care was thought to be temporary, as it was assumed that when the war ended, hospitals would not need ancillary workers. However, the baby boom and resulting population growth immediately following World War II left the country short of nurses. Thus, employment of personnel with various levels of skill and education proliferated as new categories of health-care workers were created. Currently, most health-care organizations continue to employ health-care workers of many educational backgrounds and skill levels.

Most administrators consider functional nursing to be an economical and efficient means of providing care. This is true if quality care and holistic care are not regarded as essential. A major advantage of functional nursing is its efficiency; tasks are completed quickly, with little confusion regarding responsibilities. Functional nursing does allow care to be provided with a minimal number of RNs, and in many areas, such as the operating room, the functional structure works well and is still very much in evidence. Long-term care facilities also frequently use a functional approach to nursing care.

During the past decade, however, the use of *unlicensed assistive personnel* (UAP), also known as *nursing assistive personnel*, in health-care organizations has increased. Many nurse administrators believe that assigning low-skill tasks to UAP frees the professional nurse to perform more highly skilled duties and is therefore more economical; however, others argue that the time needed to supervise the UAP negates any time savings that may have occurred. Most modern administrators would undoubtedly deny that they are using functional nursing, yet the trend of assigning tasks to workers, rather than assigning workers to the professional nurse, resembles, at least in part, functional nursing.

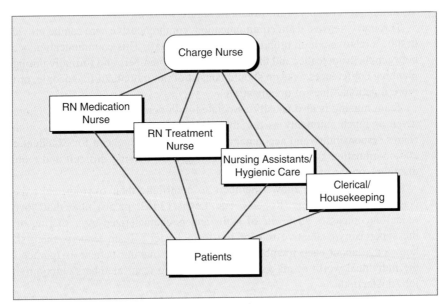

FIGURE 14.2 • Functional nursing organization structure. Copyright ® 2006 Lippincott Williams & Wilkins. Instructor's Resource CD-ROM to Accompany Leadership Roles and Management Functions in Nursing, by Bessie L. Marquis and Carol J. Huston.

Functional nursing may lead to fragmented care and the possibility of overlooking patient priority needs. In addition, because some workers feel unchallenged and understimulated in their roles, functional nursing may result in low job satisfaction. Functional nursing may also not be cost-effective due to the need for many coordinators. Employees often focus only on their own efforts, with less interest in overall results.

LEARNING EXERCISE 14.1

Transitioning to Total Patient Care

Most nursing students begin their clinical training by doing some form of functional nursing care and then advancing to total patient care for a small number of patients. Reflect back to your earliest clinical experiences as a student nurse. Which tasks were easiest for you to learn? How did you gain mastery of those tasks? Was task mastery a time-consuming process for you? Was it difficult to make the transition to total patient care? If so, why? What skills were most difficult for you to learn in providing total patient care? Do you anticipate having to learn additional skills to feel comfortable in the role of total care provider as an RN? What higher level (nonfunctional) skills do you think will be the hardest to learn and be confident with?

Team Nursing

Despite a continued shortage of professional nursing staff in the 1950s, many believed that a patient care system had to be developed that reduced the fragmented care that accompanied functional nursing. *Team nursing* was the result. In team nursing, ancillary personnel collaborate in providing care to a group of patients under the direction of a professional nurse. As the team leader, the nurse is responsible for knowing the condition and needs of all the patients assigned to the team and for planning individual care. The team leader's duties vary depending on the patient's needs and the workload. These duties may include assisting team members, giving direct personal care to patients, teaching, and coordinating patient activities. Team nursing structure is illustrated in Figure 14.3.

Through extensive team communication, comprehensive care can be provided for patients despite a relatively high proportion of ancillary staff. This communication occurs informally between the team leader and the individual team members and formally through regular team planning conferences. A team should consist of not more than five people, or it will revert to more functional lines of organization.

Team nursing is also usually associated with democratic leadership. Group members are given as much autonomy as possible when performing assigned tasks, although the team shares responsibility and accountability collectively. The need for excellent communication and coordination skills makes implementing team nursing difficult and requires great self-discipline on the part of team members.

Team nursing also allows members to contribute their own special expertise or skills. Nagi, Davies, Williams, Roberts, and Lewis (2012, p. 56) note that "overall, the team model encompasses all levels of skills and is characterized by a sharing of workload and the supervisory/evaluative role of the team leader." Team leaders, then, should use their knowledge about each member's abilities when making patient assignments. Recognizing the individual worth of all employees and giving team members autonomy results in high job satisfaction.

Disadvantages to team nursing are associated primarily with improper implementation rather than with the philosophy itself. Frequently, insufficient time is allowed for team care planning and communication. This can lead to blurred lines of responsibility, errors, and

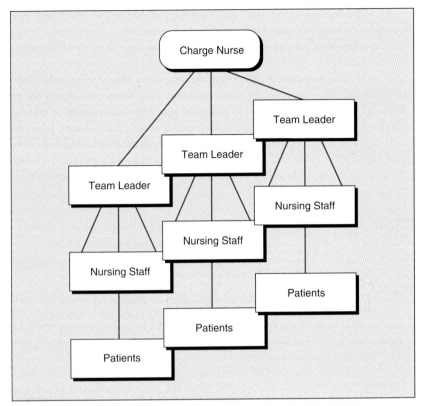

FIGURE 14.3 • Team nursing organization structure. Copyright ® 2006 Lippincott Williams & Wilkins. Instructor's Resource CD-ROM to Accompany Leadership Roles and Management Functions in Nursing, by Bessie L. Marquis and Carol J. Huston.

fragmented patient care. For team nursing to be effective then, the team leader must be an excellent practitioner and have good communication, organizational, management, and leadership skills.

The Multidisciplinary Team Leader Role

One of the recommendations of the 2010 Institute of Medicine Report, *The Future of Nursing*, was to expand the opportunities for nurses to lead and diffuse collaborative improvement efforts with physicians and other members of the health-care team to improve practice environments (Robert Wood Johnson Foundation, 2011). Some health-care organizations currently incorporate pharmacists, social workers, occupational therapists, speech therapists, and other health-care workers as part of the multidisciplinary team to assure that comprehensive and holistic health care can be provided to each patient, although the responsibility for team leadership still typically falls to the RN.

Nagi et al. (2012) note, however, that implementation problems are common in multidisciplinary or multiprofessional teams since; mutual respect and collaboration is not a given; not all workers like working in teams; and role clarification issues surrounding clinical accountability, leadership, and understanding between professionals are common. Carlyle, Crowe, and Deering (2012) concur, noting that in both the inpatient and outpatient mental health setting, nursing is usually delivered by multidisciplinary teams with an assumption that all disciplines are working within a common model of care. Carlyle et al. (2012) suggest, however, that this often is not the case.

In addition, like traditional team nursing, multidisciplinary teams require an efficient means of communication about patient goals, progress, and problems. It is not often easy to find opportunities for the whole team to meet because of work shift patterns or other work commitments.

In addition, sometimes, there are challenges in determining who the members of the team should be. For example, teamwork has long been considered an expectation in the field of trauma care since the initial assessment and resuscitation of trauma victims is most successfully carried out by an organized trauma team (Speck, Jones, Barg, & McCunn, 2012). Yet, as detailed in Examining the Evidence 14.1, general agreement about who holds critical positions on this team and what roles they hold varies between team members; in particular, the relative value of the RN as a member of the team may not be recognized.

 Examining the Evidence 14.1

Source: Speck, R. M., Jones, G., Barg, F. K., & McCunn, M. (2012). *Team composition and perceived roles of team members in the trauma bay.* Journal of Trauma Nursing, 19(3), 133–138.

The researchers used two qualitative data collection strategies in this study: participant observation and semistructured interviews. Trauma team members were observed in the trauma bay of an academic level 1 trauma center for more than 300 hours. In addition, 32 semistructured interviews were conducted with practitioners on trauma teams (attending physicians, nurses, fellows, residents, and medical students).

The researchers found that team leaders (attending physicians and fellows) viewed nurses as vital, irreplaceable members of the team. Yet, medical students and junior residents did not even consider nurses to be part of the team. This finding was further complicated by the nurses' descriptions of how they often instructed or guided junior trauma team members during cases. These researchers suggested this disconnect may be attributable to a system where medical students and residents are constantly rotating from specialties and are without a consistent model of how team leaders view nurses. Another explanation may relate to the long-standing inconsistency between nurses and physicians with regard to status, authority, gender, training, and patient care responsibilities, and discrepant attitudes regarding collaboration between physicians and nurses.

Modular Nursing

Team nursing, as originally designed, has undergone much modification in the last 30 years. Most team nursing was never practiced in its purest form but was instead a combination of team and functional structure. More recent attempts to refine and improve team nursing have resulted in many models including modular nursing.

 Most team nursing was never practiced in its purest form but was instead a combination of team and functional structure.

Modular nursing uses a mini-team (two or three members with at least one member being an RN), with members of the modular nursing team sometimes being called *care pairs*. In modular nursing, patient care units are typically divided into modules or districts and assignments are based on the geographical location of patients.

Keeping the team small in modular nursing and attempting to assign personnel to the same team as often as possible should allow the professional nurse more time for planning and coordinating team members. In addition, a small team requires less communication, allowing members better use of their time for direct patient care activities.

Primary Nursing and Interprofessional Primary Health-Care Teams

Primary Nursing

Primary nursing, also known as *relationship-based nursing*, was developed in the late 1960s, uses some of the concepts of total patient care and brings the RN back to the bedside to provide clinical care. According to Manthey (2009), "the foundational principles of primary nursing were revolutionary: For the first time in hospital nursing, explicit responsibility and authority for specific patients were clearly allocated to a specific registered nurse (whose license by law permits independent decision making about nursing care). At no time in the history of hospital nursing, had that degree of professional control over nursing practice been organizationally sanctioned at the staff nurse level" (p. 36). This required a major redesign of unit organizations, administrative structures, and managerial philosophy, as well as a challenging transformation of roles and relationships at the point of patient care (Manthey, 2009).

In primary nursing, the *primary nurse* assumes 24-hour responsibility for planning the care of one or more patients from admission or the start of treatment to discharge or the treatment's end. During work hours, the primary nurse provides total direct care for that patient. When the primary nurse is not on duty, *associate nurses*, who follow the care plan established by the primary nurse, provide care. Many experts have suggested that the role of the primary nurse should be limited to RNs; however, Manthey (2009) argues that primary nursing can succeed with a diverse skill mix just as team nursing or any other model can succeed with an all-RN staff. Primary nursing structure is shown in Figure 14.4.

Primary nursing can succeed with a diverse skill mix just as team nursing or any other model can succeed with an all-RN staff.

Although originally designed for use in hospitals, primary nursing lends itself well to home health nursing, hospice nursing, and other health-care delivery enterprises as well.

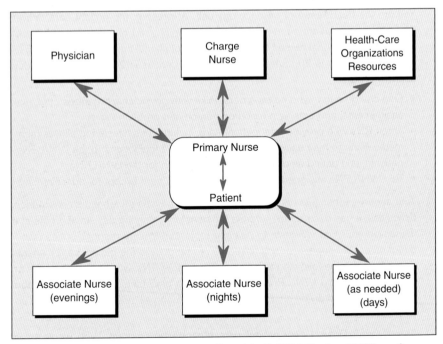

FIGURE 14.4 • Primary nursing structure. Copyright ® 2006 Lippincott Williams & Wilkins. Instructor's Resource CD-ROM to Accompany Leadership Roles and Management Functions in Nursing, by Bessie L. Marquis and Carol J. Huston.

An integral responsibility of the primary nurse is to establish clear communication among the patient, the physician, the associate nurses, and other team members. Although the primary nurse establishes the care plan, feedback is sought from others in coordinating the patient's care. The combination of clear interdisciplinary group communication and consistent, direct patient care by relatively few nursing staff allows for holistic, high-quality patient care.

Although job satisfaction is high in primary nursing, this method is difficult to implement because of the degree of responsibility and autonomy required of the primary nurse. However, for these same reasons, once nurses develop skill in primary nursing care delivery, they often feel challenged and rewarded.

Disadvantages to this method, as in team nursing, lie primarily in improper implementation. An inadequately prepared or incompetent primary nurse may be incapable of coordinating a multidisciplinary team or identifying complex patient needs and condition changes. Many nurses may be uncomfortable in this role or initially lack the experience and skills necessary for the role. In addition, although an all-RN nursing staff has not been proved to be more costly than other modes of nursing, it sometimes has been difficult to recruit and retain enough RNs to be primary nurses, especially in times of nursing shortages. Other challenges in implementing primary nursing include "shorter lengths of stay, increasing numbers of part-time positions, and variable shift lengths, combined with the ongoing pragmatic need to provide holistic, coordinated care to human beings" (Manthey, 2009, p. 37). These logistical issues can best be managed by unit-based decisions arrived at through the consensus of a unified and cohesive staff (Manthey, 2009).

LEARNING EXERCISE 14.2

Reorganizing to Accommodate a Change in Staffing Mix

You are the head nurse of an oncology unit. At present, the patient care delivery method on the unit is total patient care. You have a staff composed of 60% RNs, 35% practical nurses (licensed professional nurses [LPNs]/licensed vocational nurses [LVNs]), and 5% clerical staff. Your bed capacity is 28, but your average daily census is 24. An example of day-shift staffing follows:

- One charge nurse who notes orders, talks with physicians, organizes care, makes assignments, and acts as a resource person and problem solver
- Three RNs who provide total patient care, including administering all treatments and medications to their assigned patients, giving IV medications to the LVN/LPNs' assigned patients, and acting as a clinical resource person for the LVN/LPNs
- Two LVN/LPNs assigned to provide total patient care except for administering IV medications

Your supervisor has just told all head nurses that because the hospital is experiencing financial difficulties, it has decided to increase the number of nursing assistants in the staffing mix. The nurses on your unit will have to assume more supervisory responsibilities and focus less on direct care. Your supervisor has asked you to reorganize the patient care management on your unit to best use the following day-shift staffing: three RNs, which will include the present charge nurse position; two LVN/LPNs and two nursing assistants. You may delete the past charge nurse position and divide charge responsibility among all three nurses or divide up the work any way you choose.

Assignment: Draw a new patient care organization diagram. Who would be most affected by the reorganization? Evaluate your rationale, for both the selection of your choice and the rejection of others. Explain how you would go about implementing this planned change.

Interprofessional Primary Health-Care Teams

Like team nursing, primary care has expanded to interdisciplinary teams. Sibbald, Wathen, Kothari, and Day (2013) note *primary health-care teams* (PHCTs) are interprofessional teams that include, but are not limited to, physicians, nurse practitioners, nurses, physical therapists, occupational therapists, and social workers, who work collaboratively to deliver coordinated patient care. "Team-based models of PHCT delivery have been created to achieve (or work toward) several benefits to the health system, health care providers, and patients, including better coordination of care, increased focus on collaborative problem solving and decision making, and a commitment to patient-centered care" (Sibbald et al., p. 129). The desired outcomes for PHCTs are reduced mortality and improved quality of life for patients, a reduction in health-care costs, and a more rewarding professional experience for the health-care worker.

The challenges to implementing primary health care on the PHCT mirror many of the challenges seen in more traditional primary care, including hurdles in their formation; overcoming the traditional physician-dominated hierarchy in determining who should lead the team; role confusion; and determination of structure and function of the team. In addition, because the interprofessional team brings together differing viewpoints, life experiences, and knowledge of evidence-based practices, determining what knowledge is most important in caring for the patient can be confusing. Research by Sibbald et al. (2013) found that in most PHCTs, only a few individuals (residents, senior physicians, and nurse practitioners) actively brought research findings and knowledge to the team and allied health professionals. Sibbald et al. suggested that those with cross-team responsibilities might be better utilized as information resources.

Case Management

Case management is another work design proposed to meet patient needs. Case management is defined by the Case Management Society of America (CMSA) as "a collaborative process of assessment, planning, facilitation and advocacy for options and services to meet an individual's health needs through communication and available resources to promote quality cost-effective outcomes" (CMSA, 2008–2012, para 58).

In case management, nurses address each patient individually, identifying the most cost-effective providers, treatments, and care settings possible. This requires the case manager to drill down and identify any barriers to adherence that other providers may miss (Primary Care—the New Frontier for Case Managers, 2013). In addition, the case manager helps patients access community resources, learn about their medication regimen and treatment plan, and ensures that they have recommended tests and procedures.

While case management referrals often begin in the hospital inpatient setting, with length of stay (LOS) and profit margin per confinement used as measures of efficiency, case management now frequently extends to outpatient settings as well. Indeed, the new medical homes suggested as part of the *Patient Care Protection and Affordable Care Act* are likely to use case managers extensively.

Historically, however, the focus of case management has been episodic or component style orientation to the treatment of disease in inpatient settings and post acute care settings for insured individuals. *Acute care case management* integrates utilization management and discharge planning functions and may be unit based, assigned by patient, disease based, or primary nurse case managed.

Case managers often manage care using *critical pathways* (Chapter 10) and *multidisciplinary action plans* (MAPs) to plan patient care. The care MAP is a combination of a *critical pathway* and a *nursing care plan*. In addition, the care MAP indicates times when nursing interventions should occur. All health-care providers follow the care MAP to facilitate expected outcomes. If a patient deviates from the normal plan, a *variance* is indicated. A variance is anything that occurs to alter the patient's progress through the normal critical path.

Because the role expectations and scope of knowledge required to be a case manager are extensive, some experts have argued that this role should be reserved for the advance practice nurse or RN with advanced training, although this is not usually the case in the practice setting today. In fact, board certification as a case manager is available to any individual with a four-year degree in a health or human service area, with completed supervised field experience in case management, health, or behavioral health as part of their degree requirements (Commission for Case Management Certification, 2013).

Some feel that the role of case manager should be reserved for the advance practice nurse or RN with advanced training.

Other implementation challenges associated with case management nursing revolve around confusion related to the specific job of the case manager since case management entails different roles and functions in different settings (Gray & White, 2012). For example, in some settings, case managers participate in direct care or have direct communication with patients. In others, the case manager is an advocate for patients although the patient may have no direct knowledge or interaction with that individual.

Smith (2011) suggests that most nurses will experience role ambiguity and role conflict when they first take on the case manager role, primarily because of inadequate role definition, unexpected ethical challenges, and lack of prior insight into the case manager role. Gray and White (2012) suggest that the role of the nurse case manager must be clear and concise before care can be delivered efficiently, at the right level, and in a way that produces improved patient outcomes.

LEARNING EXERCISE 14.3

Developing a Case Management Plan

Jimmy Jansen is a 44-year-old man with type 1 diabetes mellitus. He was recently referred to your home health agency for case management follow-up at home. He is experiencing multiple complications from his diabetes, including the recent onset of blindness and peripheral neuropathy. His left leg was amputated below the knee last year as a result of a gangrenous infection of his foot. He is unable to wear his prosthesis at present because he has a small ulcer at the stump site. His chart states that he has been only "intermittently compliant" with blood glucose testing or insulin administration in the past despite the visit of a community health nurse on a weekly basis over the past year. His renal function has become progressively worse over the past 6 months, and it is anticipated that he will need to begin hemodialysis soon.

His social history reveals that he recently separated from his wife and has no contact with an adult son who lives in another state. He has not worked for more than 10 years and has no insurance other than Medicaid. The home he lives in is small, and he says that he has not been able to keep it up with his wife gone. No formal safety assessment of his home has been conducted. He also acknowledges that he is not eating right because he now must do his own cooking. He cannot drive and states, "I don't know how I'm going to get to the clinic to have my blood cleaned by the kidney machine."

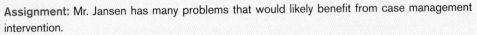
Assignment: Mr. Jansen has many problems that would likely benefit from case management intervention.

1. Make a list of five nursing diagnoses for Mr. Jansen that you would use to prioritize your interventions.

2. Then make a list of at least five goals that you would like to accomplish in planning Mr. Jansen's care. Make sure that these goals reflect realistic patient outcomes.

3. What referrals would you make? What interventions would you implement yourself? Would you involve other disciplines in his plan of care?

4. What is your plan for follow-up and evaluation?

DISEASE MANAGEMENT

One role that is increasingly assumed by case managers is coordinating disease management (DM) programs. DM, also known as *population-based health-care* and *continuous health improvement*, is a comprehensive, integrated approach to the care and reimbursement of high-cost, chronic illnesses.

The goal of DM is to address such illnesses or conditions with maximum efficiency across treatment settings regardless of typical reimbursement patterns. Thus, a continuum of chronic illness care is established that includes early detection and early intervention. This prevents or reduces exacerbation of the disease, acute episodes (known as *cost drivers*), and the use of expensive resources such as hospital inpatient care, making prevention and proactive case management two important areas of emphasis. In addition, DM programs include comprehensive tracking of patient outcomes. Thus, the goals for DM are focused on integrating components and improving long-term outcomes.

In DM programs, common high-cost, high-resource utilization diseases are identified, and population groups are targeted for implementation. This is one of the most important differences between case management and DM. In *population-based health care*, the focus is on "covered lives" or populations of patients, rather than on the individual patient. The goal in DM is to service the optimal number of covered lives required to reach operational and economic efficiency. In other words, DM is effective when cost drivers are reduced at the same time that patient needs are met.

Providing optimum, cost-effective care to individual patients is critical to the success of a DM program; however, the focus for planning, implementation, and evaluation is population based.

Other primary features of DM programs include the use of a multidisciplinary health-care team, including specialists in the area, the selection of large population groups to reduce adverse selection, the use of standardized clinical guidelines—clinical pathways reflecting best practice research to guide provider practice, and the use of integrated data management systems to track patient progress across care settings and allow continuous and ongoing improvement of treatment algorithms. Common features of DM programs are shown in Display 14.3.

One thing is clear—DM continues to grow as a means of organizing patient care. This is particularly true in the government sector, which did not really begin embracing DM demonstration projects until early in the 21st century, many of which are now mainstream initiatives, in an effort to deliver better outcomes at better prices. In addition, DM continues to hold significant promise as a strategy for promoting cost-effective, quality health care in

DISPLAY 14.3   Common Features of Disease Management Programs

1. Provide a comprehensive, integrated approach to the care and reimbursement of common, high-cost, chronic illnesses.
2. Focus on prevention as well as early disease detection and intervention to avoid costly acute episodes but provide comprehensive care and reimbursement.
3. Target population groups (population based) rather than individuals.
4. Employ a multidisciplinary health-care team, including specialists.
5. Use standardized clinical guidelines–clinical pathways reflecting best practice research to guide providers.
6. Use integrated data management systems to track patient progress across care settings and allow continuous and ongoing improvement of treatment algorithms.
7. Frequently employ professional nurses in the role of case manager or program coordinator.

the future, and DM programs can only be expected to expand in scope and quantity. Similarly, RNs, in their roles as case managers, will continue to experience new and expanded roles as key players in the development, coordination, and evaluation of DM programs.

LEARNING EXERCISE 14.4

Researching Disease Management Programs

Search the Internet for DM (disease management, not diabetes mellitus) programs. What chronic diseases were most commonly represented in the DM programs that you identified? What entities (private insurance companies, managed care insurers, government, pharmaceutical companies, private companies, etc.) sponsored these programs? What is the process for referral? Are the programs accredited? Are RNs used as case managers or program coordinators? What standardized clinical guidelines are used in the program, and are they evidence based?

Assignment: Select one of the programs that you found, and write a one-page summary regarding your findings.

SELECTING THE OPTIMUM MODE OF ORGANIZING PATIENT CARE

Most health-care organizations use one or more modes to organize patient care. While not all care must be provided by RNs, the care delivery system chosen should be based on patient acuity and not on economics alone. In addition, the knowledge and skill required for particular activities with specific populations should always be the true driver in determining appropriate care delivery models. Nursing departments need to organize delivery of patient care based on the best method for their particular situation.

Many nursing units have a history of selecting methods of organizing patient care based upon the most current popular mode rather than objectively determining the best method for a particular unit or department.

If evaluation of the present system reveals deficiencies, the manager needs to examine available resources and compare those with resources needed for the change. Nursing managers often elect to change to a system that requires a high percentage of RNs, only to discover resources are inadequate, resulting in a failed planned change. One of the leadership responsibilities in organizing patient care is to determine the availability of resources and support for proposed changes. There must be a commitment on the part of top-level administration and a majority of the nursing staff for a change to be successful. Because health care is multidisciplinary, the care delivery system used will have a heavy impact on many others outside the nursing unit; therefore, those affected by a system change must be involved in its planning. Change affects other departments, the medical staff, and the health-care consumer. Perhaps, most importantly, the philosophy of the nursing services division must support the delivery model selected.

Another mistake frequently made when changing modes of patient care delivery is to not fully understand how the new system should function or be implemented. Managers must carry out adequate research and be well versed in the system's proper implementation if the change is to be successful. It is important also to remember that not every nurse desires a challenging job with the autonomy of personal decision making. Many forces interact simultaneously in employee job design situations. Satisfaction does not occur only because of role fulfillment but also because of social and interpersonal relations. Therefore, the nurse-leader-manager needs to be aware that redesigning work that disrupts group cohesiveness may result in increased levels of job dissatisfaction.

Not every nurse desires a challenging job, with the autonomy of personal decision making.

Such change should not be taken lightly. The leader-manager should consider the following when evaluating the current system and considering a change:

- Is the method of patient care delivery providing the level of care that is stated in the organizational philosophy? Does the method facilitate or hinder other organizational goals?
- Is the delivery of nursing care organized in a cost-effective manner?
- Does the care delivery system satisfy patients and their families? (Satisfaction and quality care differ; either may be provided without the other being present.)
- Does the organization of patient care delivery provide some degree of fulfillment and role satisfaction to nursing personnel?
- Does the system allow implementation of the nursing process?
- Does the system promote and support the profession of nursing as both independent and interdependent?
- Does the method facilitate adequate communication among all members of the health-care team?
- How will a change in the patient care delivery system alter individual and group decision making? Who will be affected? Will autonomy decrease or increase?
- How will social interactions and interpersonal relationships change?
- Will employees view their unit of work differently? Will there be a change from a partial unit of work to a whole unit? (For example, total patient care would be a whole unit of work, whereas team nursing would be a partial unit.)
- Will the change require a wider or more restricted range of skills and abilities on the part of the caregiver?
- Will the redesign change how employees receive feedback on their performance, either by self-evaluation or by others?
- Will communication patterns change?

The most appropriate organizational model to deliver patient care for each unit or organization depends on the skill and expertise of the staff, the availability of registered professional nurses, the economic resources of the organization, the acuity of the patients, and the complexity of the tasks to be completed.

Newer Health-Care Delivery Models and Nursing Roles

Beattie (2009) suggests that health-care delivery models have emerged that are expanding the role of nurses beyond caregivers to be key integrators, care coordinators, and efficiency experts who are redesigning the patient experience. A white paper, entitled *Innovative Care Delivery Models: Identifying New Models That Effectively Leverage Nurses*, was published by Health Workforce Solutions in 2009. This white paper suggested that nurses form the backbone of almost all these new models and that eight common themes could be identified among the most successful care delivery models. These are shown in Display 14.4.

In addition, three emerging roles are detailed in this chapter: nurse navigators, Clinical Nurse Leaders (CNLs), and nurses working in settings that embrace patient- and family-centered care.

DISPLAY 14.4   Common Themes Found Among Emerging Care Delivery Models

1. Elevating the role of nurses and transitioning from caregivers to "care integrators."
2. Taking a team approach to interdisciplinary care.
3. Bridging the continuum of care outside of the primary care facility.
4. Defining the home as a setting of care.
5. Targeting high users of health care, especially older adults.
6. Sharpening focus on the patient, including an active engagement of the patient and her or his family in care planning and delivery, and a greater responsiveness to the patient's wants and needs.
7. Leveraging technology.
8. Improving satisfaction, quality, and cost.

Nurse Navigators

The *nurse navigator* role is a relatively new role for professional nurses. Nurse navigators help patients and families navigate the complex health-care system by providing information and support as they traverse their illness (Llewellyn, 2013). Nurse navigation commonly occurs in targeted clinical settings such as oncology, whereby a breast cancer nurse navigator might work with a woman from the time she is first diagnosed and then follow her throughout the course of her illness.

Nurse navigators are also expected to be increasingly visible with the new Insurance Exchanges (Healthcare Marketplace) that will roll out with health-care reform (Llewellyn, 2013). In this case, consumers are expected to go to nurse navigators to learn about and purchase an insurance plan from the Exchanges. Critics suggest, however, that further role definition is needed to differentiate between the role case managers and nurse navigators will play in the coming decade.

The Clinical Nurse-Leader

Many of the newer patient care delivery models include the nurse as a clinical expert leading other members of a team of partners. For example, the American Association of Colleges of Nursing (AACN) identified a new nursing role in the early 1990s, that of the CNL, that is more responsive to the realities of the modern health-care system. The CNL, as an advanced generalist with a master's degree in nursing, is expected to provide clinical leadership at the point of care in all health-care settings, implement outcomes-based practice and quality improvement strategies, engage in clinical practice, and create and manage microsystems of care that are responsive to the health-care needs of individuals and families (AACN, 2007).

The CNL role, however, is not one of administration or management. Instead, the CNL "assumes accountability for healthcare outcomes for a specific group of clients within a unit or setting through the assimilation and application of research-based information to design, implement, and evaluate client plans of care" (AACN, 2007, p. 6). The CNL then is a provider and a manager at the point of care to individuals and cohorts, and as such, designs, implements, and evaluates client care by coordinating, delegating, and supervising the care provided by the health-care team (AACN).

The CNL also plays a key role in collaborating with interdisciplinary teams. Susan B. Hasmiller, a Robert Wood Johnson Senior Advisor for Nursing, suggested that the CNL as a leader of these teams identifies risk-analysis strategies and resources needed to ensure the safe delivery of care and then relies on patient-centered, evidence-based practice and performance data to make needed decisions (Robert Wood Johnson Foundation [RWJ], 2009). As such, the CNL shows "enormous promise" in redesigning the way healthcare is delivered (RWJ, para 1).

In addition, the Veterans Health Administration became an early adopter of the CNL role, implementing the CNL initiative across all VA settings. At the VA, CNLs serve as the point person on patient care teams and are leaders in the health-care delivery system. "This revolutionary role is providing an increasingly positive impact on patient care outcomes, and professional career satisfaction for many staff nurses" (US Department of Veterans Affairs, 2013, para 2).

Patient- and Family-Centered Care

While not specifically a patient care delivery model, patient- and family-centered care does represent a change in the paradigm of care and does strongly influence how care must be delivered. Abraham and Moretz (2012) suggest that patient- and family-centered care is an innovative approach to the planning, delivery, and evaluation of health care grounded in mutually beneficial partnerships between patients, families, and health-care providers.

The philosophy of patient-centered care is based on the premise that care should be organized first and foremost around the needs of patients (Planetree, 2013). The Institute for Patient- and Family-Centered Care (IPFCC) (2013) agrees, suggesting that patient- and family-centered care is an approach to the planning, delivery, and evaluation of health care that is grounded in mutually beneficial partnerships among health-care providers, patients, and families, thus redefining the relationships in health care.

The Institute of Medicine identified patient-centered care as one of six points for health-care redesign and one way to provide care "that is respectful of and responsive to individual patient preferences, needs, and values, and ensuring that patient values guide all clinical decisions" (Warren, 2012). Core concepts of patient- and family-centered care are shown in Display 14.5.

DISPLAY 14.5   Core Concepts of Patient- and Family-Centered Care

- Patient care is organized first and foremost around the needs of patients.
- Patient and family perspectives are sought out and their choices are honored.
- Health-care providers communicate openly and honestly with patients and families to empower them to be effective partners in their health-care decision making.
- Patients, families, and health-care providers collaborate regarding facility design and the implementation of care.
- The voice of the patient and family are represented at both the organizational and policy levels as well as in the health system's strategic planning.

Source: Planetree (2013); Moretz and Abraham (2012); Abraham and Moretz (2012); Institute for Patient- and Family-Centered Care (IPFCC) (2013).

Warren (2012) notes that *Planetree,* and the IPFCC have been two of the most prominent pioneers in developing and promoting patient- and family-centered care. According to its mission statement, "Planetree is a non-profit organization that provides education and information in a collaborative community of healthcare organizations, facilitating efforts to create patient-centered care in healing environments" (Planetree, 2013, para 15). The Planetree model encourages the use of soft colors, lighting, home-like fabrics, and music for patient rooms and common areas as well as opportunities for patients and families to learn about their illness in order to foster participation in their care.

Founded in 1992, the IPFCC is a not-for-profit organization offering health-care providers and institutions information and core guiding concepts related to patient- and family-centered care. These concepts include open visitation; family presence during all procedures; patient, family, and staff communication and collaboration in care plan development, multidisciplinary rounds, and bedside handoffs between nurses; information availability in patient and family resource centers; and the use of patient and family advisors in performance and safety improvement efforts (IPFCC, 2013).

Abraham and Moretz (2012) suggest that while nurses do not bear the sole responsibility for advancing patient- and family-centered care, nurses must act as catalysts for initiating and integrating the health-care provider, patient, and family partnership practices in daily care. Moretz and Abraham (2012, p. 106) agree, suggesting that "no matter what one's nursing role – clinical, educational, administrative – it is possible to champion patient- and family-centered change so true collaboration with patients and families becomes embedded in the organizational culture." This requires the leadership skills of vision, planned change, team building, and collaboration.

LEARNING EXERCISE 14.5

Changing Organization Cultures to Be Patient- and Family-Centered

Assignment: Adoption of patient- and family-centered care often requires changing an organization culture so that patients and families are truly recognized as partners in care, whether at the bedside or at the institutional level in strategic planning. It also requires a reconsideration of many of the rules and barriers often in place that pose obstacles for patients and families to be active participants in care decisions.

Assignment: Select any one of the following rules/procedures/situations common to many hospitals and write a one-page essay outlining why it would not be consistent with a patient- and family-centered care approach. Include in the discussion how the rule/procedure/situation could be changed to better reflect the core concepts shown in Learning Exercise 14.4.

1. Visiting hours end at 9 PM unless someone is willing to "bend the rules."
2. Only one visitor is allowed at a time in the critical care units and then for only 20 minutes every hour.
3. Flat, comfortable sleeping surfaces are not readily available for family members who wish to spend the night in patient rooms.
4. Physicians typically make patient care rounds between 0700 and 0800, before family members have arrived.
5. Handoff report occurs behind closed doors and family members do not participate.
6. Family lounges are too small to accommodate all visitors during peak visiting hours.
7. Staff complain in handoff report that patients are unwilling to follow the plan of care, rather than asking if the patients themselves were involved in determining the plan of care.
8. Dining halls are open only to staff in the middle of the night.

INTEGRATING LEADERSHIP ROLES AND MANAGEMENT FUNCTIONS IN ORGANIZING PATIENT CARE

Organizing is an all-important management function. The work must be organized so that organizational goals are sustained. Activities must be grouped so that resources, people, materials, and time are used fully. The integrated leader-manager understands that the organization and unit's nursing philosophy and the availability of resources greatly influence the type of patient care delivery system that should be chosen and the potential success of future work redesign.

The integrated leader-manager, then, is responsible for selecting and implementing a patient care delivery system that facilitates the accomplishment of unit goals. All members of the work group should be assisted with role clarification, especially when work is redesigned or new systems of patient care delivery are implemented. This team effort in work activity increases productivity and worker satisfaction. The emphasis is on seeking solutions to poor organization of work rather than finding fault.

There is no one "best" mode for organizing patient care. Integrating leadership roles and management functions ensures that the type of patient care delivery model selected will provide quality care and staff satisfaction. It also ensures that change in the mode of delivery will not be attempted without adequate resources, appropriate justification, and attention to how it will affect group cohesiveness. Historically, nursing has frequently adopted models of patient care delivery based on societal events (e.g., a nursing shortage and a proliferation of types of health-care workers) rather than upon well-researched models with proven effectiveness that promote professional practice. The leadership role demands that the primary focus of patient care delivery be on promoting a professional model of practice that also reduces costs and improves patient outcomes.

Given projected health-care worker shortages, many health-care organizations are concerned there will be too few health-care workers to deliver care using the same models presently used. Health-care agencies must begin now to explore how newer nursing roles such as case managers, nurse navigators, and CNLs might be used to better integrate and coordinate care—before, not after, all answers and solutions are established. As many forces come together to change the future of health care, it behooves all healthcare profession to think smarter, to think outside the box, and to discover innovative ways to organize and deliver care that is patient- and family-centered to clients both inside and outside the acute care setting.

KEY CONCEPTS

- Total patient care, utilizing the case method of assignment, is the oldest form of patient care organization and is still widely used today.

- Functional nursing organization requires the completion of specific tasks by different nursing personnel.

- Team nursing typically uses a nurse-leader who coordinates team members of varying educational preparation and skill sets in the care of a group of patients.

- The use of multidisciplinary team increases the likelihood that care will be comprehensive and holistic, although the responsibility for team leadership still typically falls to the nurse.

- Modular nursing uses mini-teams, typically an RN and unlicensed health-care worker(s), to provide care to a small group of patients, usually centralized geographically.

- Primary care nursing is organized so that the patient is at the center of the structure. One health-care provider (typically the RN) has 24-hour responsibility for care planning and coordination.

(Continued)

- Interprofessional teams now also provide primary care in the form of PHCTs. These teams typically include, but are not limited to, physicians, nurse practitioners, nurses, physical therapists, occupational therapists, and social workers working collaboratively to deliver coordinated patient care.

- Case management is a collaborative process that assesses, plans, implements, coordinates, monitors, and evaluates options and services to meet an individual's health needs through communication and available resources to promote quality and cost-effective outcomes.

- Although the focus historically for case management has been the individual patient, the case manager employed in a DM program plans the care for populations or groups of patients with the same chronic illness.

- The care MAP is a combination of a critical path and a nursing care plan, except that it shows times when nursing interventions should occur as well as variances.

- Delivery systems may have elements of the various designs present in the system in use in any organization.

- Each unit's care delivery structure should facilitate meeting the goals of the organization, be cost-effective, satisfy the patient, provide role satisfaction to nurses, allow implementation of the nursing process, and provide for adequate communication among health-care providers.

- When work is redesigned, it frequently has personal consequences for employees that must be considered. Social interactions, the degree of autonomy, the abilities and skills necessary, employee evaluation, and communication patterns are often affected by work redesign.

- The *nurse navigator* assists patients and families to navigate the complex health-care system by providing information and support as they traverse their illness.

- The CNL, is an experienced, nurse possessing a graduate degree, who provides clinical leadership in all health-care settings, implements outcomes-based practice and quality improvement strategies, engages in clinical practice, and creates and manages microsystems of care that are responsive to the health-care needs of individuals and families.

- The philosophy of patient- and family-centered care is based on the premise that care should be organized first and foremost around the needs of patients and family members.

 ADDITIONAL LEARNING EXERCISES AND APPLICATIONS

LEARNING EXERCISE 14.6

Creating a Plan to Reduce Resistance

You work in an intensive care unit where there is an all-RN staff. The staff work 12-hour shifts, and each nurse is assigned one or two patients, depending on the nursing needs of the patient. The unit has always used total patient care delivery assignments. Recently, your unit manager informed the staff that all patients in the unit would be assigned a case manager in an effort to maximize the use of resources and to reduce LOS in the unit. Many of the unit staff resent the case manager and believe that this has reduced the RN's autonomy and control of patient care. They are resistant to the need to document variances to the care MAPs and are generally uncooperative but not to the point that they are insubordinate.

Although you feel some loss of autonomy, you also think that the case manager has been effective in coordinating care to speed patient discharge. You believe that at present, the atmosphere in the unit is very stressful. The unit manager and case manager have come to you and requested that you assist them in convincing the other staff to go along with this change.

Assignment: Using your knowledge of planned change and case management, outline a plan for reducing resistance.

LEARNING EXERCISE 14.7

Types of Patient Care Delivery Models Used in Your Area

In a group, investigate the types of patient care delivery models used in your area. Do not limit your investigation to hospitals. If possible, conduct interviews with nurses from a variety of delivery systems. Share the report of your findings with your classmates. How many different models of patient care delivery did you find? What is the most widely used method in health-care facilities in your area? Does this vary from models identified most frequently in current nursing literature?

LEARNING EXERCISE 14.8

Implementing a Managed Care System

You are the director of a home health agency that has recently become part of a managed care system. In the past, only a physician's order was necessary for authorization from the Medicare system, but now approval must come from the managed care organization (MCO). In the past, public health certified nurses (all BSNs) have acted as case managers for their assigned caseload. Now the MCO case manager has taken over this role, creating much conflict among the staff. In addition, there is pressure from your board to cut costs by using more nonprofessionals who are less skilled for some of the home care. You realize that unless you do so, your agency will not survive financially.

You have visited other home health agencies and researched your options carefully. You have decided that you must use some type of team approach.

Assignment: Develop a plan, objectives, and a time frame for implementation. In your plan, discuss who will be most affected by your changes. As a change agent, what will be your most important role?

LEARNING EXERCISE 14.9

The Clinical Nurse-Leader Application

You are the unit coordinator of a medical/surgical unit in a small acute care hospital. One of your greatest management challenges has been implementing evidence-based practice at the unit level. Your staff nurses have access to many health-care resources via their computer workstations. In addition, computerized provider order entry is used in your hospital, which includes links to best practices and standardized clinical guidelines. Yet, you are aware that some of your staff continue to do things as they have always been done, despite repeated workshops on how best to integrate new evidence into their clinical practice. You hope to address this problem by hiring someone with the leadership skills needed to champion the change effort and the management skills necessary to direct staff in their new roles.

When you return to your office today, you find an application for employment from a CNL. She recently completed her CNL program as part of a master's entry program so her clinical experience is limited to what she received in nursing school. You are aware though that her educational background will have prepared her to lead a change effort on the unit to foster evidence-based decision making and outcomes-focused practice.

(Continued)

You also have an employment application from a master's prepared nurse with many years of clinical experience as a staff and charge nurse although she is just returning from a 5-year leave of absence to care for a sick family member. She completed a master's thesis as part of her graduate nursing education 20 years ago, so you know she has at least some expertise in nursing research and its translation to practice. Given your budget constraints, you can hire only one of these individuals.

Assignment: Identify the driving and restraining forces for hiring the CNL or for hiring the experienced nurse with clinical and research expertise. Do you believe that the limited clinical experience of the CNL would impact her ability to serve as a leader and change agent on the floor? Would the CNL have the management skill set you also want in your new hire? Do you believe that the CNL would be better prepared as a leader in this change effort? Justify which employee you would choose to hire and suggest strategies you might use to help this individual acquire the leadership, management, and change skill sets they may be lacking to achieve your desired outcomes.

REFERENCES

Abraham, M., & Moretz, J. (2012). Implementing patient- and family-centered care: Part I—Understanding the challenges. *Pediatric Nursing, 38*(1), 44–47.

American Association of Colleges of Nursing. (2007, February). *White paper on the education and role of the clinical nurse leader.* Retrieved December 22, 2009, from http://www.aacn.nche.edu/Publications/WhitePapers/CNL2-07.pdf

Beattie, L. (2009). *New health care delivery models are redefining the role of nurses.* Nursezone.com. Retrieved June 2, 2013, from http://www.nursezone.com/nursing-news-events/more-features/New-Health-Care-Delivery-Models-are-Redefining-the-Role-of-Nurses_29442.aspx

Carlyle, D. D., Crowe, M. M., & Deering, D. D. (2012). Models of care delivery in mental health nursing practice: A mixed method study. *Journal of Psychiatric & Mental Health Nursing, 19*(3), 221–230.

Case Management Society of America. (2008–2012). *Glossary/FAQs. Case management—Definition.* Retrieved June 2, 2013, from http://www.cmsa.org/Consumer/GlossaryFAQs/tabid/102/Default.aspx

Commission for Case Management Certification. (2013). *Certification & renewal.* Retrieved June 3, 2013, from http://ccmcertification.org/node/428

Gray, F. C., & White, A. (2012). Concept analysis: Case management role confusion. *Nursing Forum, 47*(1), 3–8.

Institute for Patient- and Family-Centered Care (IPFCC). (2013). *Institute for patient- and family-centered care.* Retrieved June 3, 2013, from http://www.ipfcc.org/

Llewellyn, A. (2013, April 15). *Nurse navigators: How do they differ from case managers?* Dorland Health. Retrieved June 3, 2013, from http://www.dorlandhealth.com/cip_weekly/Nurse-Navigators-How-Do-They-Differ-From-Case-Managers_2734.html

Manthey, M. (2009). The 40th anniversary of primary nursing: Setting the record straight. *Creative Nursing, 15*(1), 36–38.

Moretz, J., & Abraham, M. (2012). Implementing patient- and family-centered care: Part II—Strategies and resources for success. *Pediatric Nursing, 38*(2), 106–171.

Nagi, C., Davies, J., Williams, M., Roberts, C., & Lewis, R. (2012). A multidisciplinary approach to team nursing within a low secure service: The team leader role. *Perspectives in Psychiatric Care, 48*(1), 56–61.

Planetree (2013). *About us.* Retrieved June 3, 2013, from http://planetree.org/?page_id=510

Primary Care—The New Frontier for Case Managers? (2013). *Case Management Advisor, 24*(5), 49–51.

Robert Wood Johnson Foundation. (2009). *Clinical nurse leaders as agents of change.* Retrieved June 2, 2013, from http://www.rwjf.org/en/about-rwjf/newsroom/newsroom-content/2009/02/clinical-nurse-leaders-as-agents-of-change.html

Robert Wood Johnson Foundation. (2011). *Initiative on the future of nursing. IOM recommendations.* Retrieved June 2, 2013, from http://thefutureofnursing.org/recommendations

Sibbald, S. L., Wathen, C., Kothari, A., & Day, B. (2013). Knowledge flow and exchange in interdisciplinary primary health care teams (PHCTs): An exploratory study. *Journal of the Medical Library Association, 101*(2), 128–137.

Smith, A. C. (2011, August). Role ambiguity and role conflict in nurse case managers: An integrative review. *Professional Case Management, 16*(4), 182–196.

Speck, R. M., Jones, G., Barg, F. K., & McCunn, M. (2012). Team composition and perceived roles of team members in the trauma bay. *Journal of Trauma Nursing, 19*(3), 133–138.

US Department of Veterans Affairs. (2013). *VA partners with you for career success.* Retrieved June 3, 2013, from https://www.vacareers.va.gov/careers/nurses/quality-initiatives.asp

Warren, N. (2012). Involving patient and family advisors in the patient and family-centered care model. *MEDSURG Nursing, 21*(4), 233–239.

UNIT V

Roles and Functions in Staffing

15

Employee Recruitment, Selection, Placement, and Indoctrination

… Employee selection is so crucial that nothing else—not leadership, not team building, not training, not pay incentives, not total quality management—can overcome poor hiring decisions …
–Gerald Graham

… I have always surrounded myself with the best people to do their jobs, because I do not want to learn what they already know better than I do.
–Shirley Sears Chater

CROSSWALK THIS CHAPTER ADDRESSES:

BSN Essential II: Basic organizational and systems leadership for quality care and patient safety
BSN Essential VI: Interprofessional communication and collaboration for improving patient health outcomes
BSN Essential V: Health-care policy, finance, and regulatory environments
BSN Essential VIII: Professionalism and professional values
MSN Essential II: Organizational and systems leadership
MSN Essential VII: Interprofessional collaboration for improving patient and population health outcomes
QSEN Competency: Teamwork and collaboration
QSEN Competency: Safety
AONE Nurse Executive Competency I: Communication and relationship building
AONE Nurse Executive Competency II: A knowledge of the health-care environment
AONE Nurse Executive Competency V: Business skills

LEARNING OBJECTIVES *The learner will:*

- describe demand and supply factors leading to nursing shortages
- determine the number and types of personnel needed to fulfill an organizational philosophy, meet fiscal planning responsibilities, and carry out a chosen patient care delivery system
- identify variables that impact an organization's ability to recruit candidates successfully for job openings
- delineate the relationship between recruitment and retention
- describe interview techniques that reduce subjectivity and increase reliability and validity during the interview process
- develop appropriate interview questions to determine whether an applicant is qualified and willing to meet the requirements of a position
- differentiate between legal and illegal interview inquiries
- analyze how personal values and biases affect employment selection decisions

- consider organizational needs and employee strengths in making placement decisions
- select appropriate activities to be included in the induction and orientation of employees

After planning and organizing, staffing is the third phase of the management process. In staffing, the leader-manager recruits, selects, places, and indoctrinates personnel to accomplish the goals of the organization. These steps, which are depicted in Display 15.1, are typically sequential, although each step has some interdependence with all staffing activities.

DISPLAY 15.1   Sequential Steps in Staffing

1. Determine the number and types of personnel needed to fulfill the philosophy, meet fiscal planning responsibilities, and carry out the chosen patient care delivery system selected by the organization.
2. Recruit, interview, select, and assign personnel based on established job description performance standards.
3. Use organizational resources for induction and orientation.
4. Ascertain that each employee is adequately socialized to organization values and unit norms.
5. Use creative and flexible scheduling based on patient care needs to increase productivity and retention.

Staffing is an especially important phase of the management process in health-care organizations because such organizations are usually *labor intensive* (i.e., numerous employees are required for an organization to accomplish its goals). In addition, many health-care organizations are open 24 hours a day, 365 days a year, and client demands and needs are often variable. This large workforce must reflect an appropriate balance of highly skilled, competent professionals and ancillary support workers.

The workforce should also reflect the gender, culture, ethnicity, age, and language diversity of the communities that the organization serves. The lack of ethnic, gender, and generational diversity in the workforce has been linked to *health disparities* in the populations served (Huston, 2014b). The importance of this goal cannot be overstated.

This chapter examines national and regional trends for professional nurse staffing. It also addresses preliminary staffing functions, namely determining staffing needs and recruiting, interviewing, selecting, and placing personnel. It also reviews two employee indoctrination functions: induction and orientation. The management functions and leadership roles inherent in these staffing responsibilities are shown in Display 15.2.

DISPLAY 15.2   Leadership Roles and Management Functions Associated with Preliminary Staffing Functions

LEADERSHIP ROLES

1. Plans for future staffing needs proactively by being knowledgeable regarding current and historical staffing variables.
2. Identifies and recruits talented people to the organization.
3. Encourages and seeks diversity in staffing.
4. Is self-aware regarding personal biases during the preemployment process.
5. Seeks to find the best possible fit between employees' unique talents and organizational staffing needs.
6. Periodically reviews induction and orientation programs to ascertain they are meeting unit needs.
7. Ensures that each new employee understands appropriate organizational policies.
8. Continually aspires to create a work environment that promotes retention and worker satisfaction.
9. Promotes hiring based on preferred criteria rather than minimum criteria.

(Continued)

MANAGEMENT FUNCTIONS

1. Ensures that there is an adequate skilled workforce to meet the goals of the organization.
2. Shares responsibility for the recruitment of staff with organization recruiters.
3. Plans and structures appropriate interview activities.
4. Uses techniques that increase the validity and reliability of the interview process.
5. Applies knowledge of the legal requirements of interviewing and selection to ensure that the organization is not unfair in its hiring practices.
6. Develops established criteria for employment selection purposes.
7. Uses knowledge of organizational needs and employee strengths to make placement decisions.
8. Interprets information in employee handbook and provides input for handbook revisions.
9. Participates actively in employee orientation.

PREDICTING STAFFING NEEDS

Accurately predicting staffing needs is a crucial management skill because it enables the manager to avoid staffing crises. Managers should know the source of their nursing pool, the number of students enrolled in local nursing schools, the usual length of employment of newly hired staff, peak staff resignation periods, and times when the patient census is highest. In addition, managers must consider the patient care delivery system in place, the education and knowledge level of needed staff, budget constraints, historical staffing needs and availability, and the diversity of the patient population to be served.

Managers also need to have a fairly sophisticated understanding of third-party insurer reimbursement since this has a significant impact on staffing in contemporary health-care organizations. For example, as government and private insurer reimbursements declined in the 1990s, many health-care organizations—hospitals in particular—began downsizing by replacing registered nurse (RN) positions with unlicensed assistive personnel. Even hospitals that did not downsize during this period often did little to recruit qualified RNs. This downsizing and shortsightedness regarding recruitment and retention contributed to an acute shortage of RNs in many health-care settings in the late 1990s.

Hospital downsizing and shortsightedness regarding recruitment and retention contributed to the beginning of an acute shortage of RNs in many health-care settings by the late 1990s.

The manager also should be aware of the role that national and local economics play in staffing. Historically, nursing shortages occur when the economy is on the upswing and decline when the economy recedes, because many unemployed nurses return to the workforce and part-time employees return to full-time employment. This is only a guideline, however, as some workforce shortages have occurred regardless of the economic climate. There is little doubt, however, that the current projected shortages would be even worse, had the economic downturn not occurred, since the recession caused many part-time nurses to return to full-time employment and others to delay their retirement.

Historically, when the economy improves, nursing shortages occur. When the economy declines, nursing vacancy rates decline as well.

IS THERE A CURRENT NURSING SHORTAGE?

Health-care managers have long been sensitive to the importance of physical (technology and space) and financial resources to the success of service delivery. It is the shortage of human resources, however, that likely poses the greatest challenge to most health-care organizations today. Indeed, the world is experiencing an international nursing shortage although it has been obscured by a number of factors, most noteworthy is the global recession.

Economists suggest that as a result of that recession, many nurses who had planned to retire have put off their retirements; many nurses who were working part time increased their employment to full time; and some nurses who had been out of the profession for 5 years or more returned to the workforce. Economists call this situation a *nursing employment bubble* and warn that all "bubbles eventually burst" (Schaeffer, 2013, p. 3). This certainly could be the case if the economy were to dramatically improve and these nurses were to suddenly retire or reduce their workhours. A significant nursing shortage could emerge literally overnight.

Schaeffer (2013) notes that an additional 712,000 nursing jobs will be created between 2010 and 2020 and that 495,500 jobs will be vacated by retired nurses between 2010 and 2020. Both of these predictions suggest a shortage of approximately 285,000 nurses between 2015 and 2020. This projection is significantly less than the early 21st-century projections of shortfalls of close to 1 million nurses by 2020, but it is still substantial enough to warrant concern.

One could reasonably assume then that each and every nurse as well as potential nurse would be valued and treated as a scarce commodity today. Yet, we know this is not the case. Many new RN graduates currently report difficulty finding jobs. Why is this occurring? In some cases, it reflects skittishness on the part of health-care organizations to take on new staff during an economic downturn, particularly inexperienced ones who may need prolonged orientation and training. Instead, health-care organizations are seeking to hire experienced nurses, with specialty certifications in hand, who can assume full patient loads upon hire. One must at least question, however, whether this is shortsighted, since it is likely that these organizations will be desperate to hire these same graduates in a few short years when the economy improves and large groups of nurses once again exit the workforce or reduce their working hours.

Supply and Demand Factors Leading to the Shortage

Resolving projected shortages will be difficult since the shortage will be compounded by both supply and demand factors. The *Bureau of Labor Statistics' Employment Projections 2010 to 2020* released in February 2012 suggest the Registered Nursing workforce will be the top occupation in terms of job growth through 2020, accounting for one out of every five new jobs created in 2012 (AACN, 2012). This demand is expected to continue or accelerate. In addition, demand will be driven by technological advances in patient care and by the increasing emphasis on preventive health care. Also, the growing elderly population will require more nursing care.

Supply factors contributing to the nursing shortage will include an aging workforce with imminent retirements expected and inadequate nursing education enrollments. Too few students are being enrolled in nursing education programs to replace the nurses who are retiring. Ironically, the inadequate number of new nurses is not caused by a lack of nursing school applicants. The problem is that there are inadequate resources to provide nursing education to those interested in pursuing nursing as a career.

Indeed, the American Association of Colleges of Nursing (AACN) (2012) reports that in 2011, US nursing schools turned away 75,587 qualified applicants from baccalaureate and graduate nursing programs due to insufficient numbers of faculty, clinical sites, classroom space, clinical preceptors, and budget constraints. Indeed, almost two-thirds of nursing schools responding to the survey pointed to faculty shortages as a reason for not accepting all qualified applicants into their programs (AACN, September, 2012).

The "graying" of the nursing faculty also contributes to the projected shortage. The average age of nursing faculty members continues to increase, narrowing the number of productive years nurse-educators can teach. McNeal (2012) notes that of the 32,000 nurse-educators nationwide, on average they are 55 years of age or older. This finding is in sharp contrast to other academic disciplines in which only 35% are above the age of 54; and, in the health sciences, only 29% of faculty are above 54 years of age (McNeal).

One must question where the faculty will come from to teach the new nurses that will be needed to solve the current shortage. Nursing faculty salaries have also failed to keep pace with that of nurses employed in clinical settings, making it even more difficult to attract and keep graduate and doctorally prepared nurses in academic settings. Clearly then, given the lag time required to educate master's- or doctorally prepared faculty, the faculty shortage may end up being the greatest obstacle to solving the nursing shortage (Huston, 2014a). Long-term planning and aggressive intervention will be needed for some time to ensure that an adequate, highly qualified nursing workforce will be available to meet the health-care needs of US citizens.

> The nursing faculty shortage will likely be the greatest obstacle to solving the projected nursing shortage.

RECRUITMENT

Recruitment is the process of actively seeking out or attracting applicants for existing positions and should be an ongoing process. In complex organizations, work must be accomplished by groups of people; therefore, the organization's ability to meet its goals and objectives relates directly to the quality of its employees. Unfortunately, some managers feel threatened by bright and talented people and surround themselves with mediocrity. Wise leader-managers surround themselves with people of ability, motivation, and promise.

In addition, organizations must remember that nonmonetary factors are just as important, if not more so, in recruiting new employees. Before recruiting begins, organizations must identify reasons a prospective employee would choose to work for them over a competitor. Organizations considered best places to work generally have two characteristics: They're "financially fit" organizations whose leadership is "keeping the ball rolling to keep revenue and patient satisfaction going upward" (Best Places, 2012, para 3).

The Nurse-Recruiter

The manager may be greatly or minimally involved with recruiting, interviewing, and selecting personnel depending on (a) the size of the institution, (b) the existence of a separate personnel department, (c) the presence of a nurse-recruiter within the organization, and (d) the use of centralized or decentralized nursing management.

Generally speaking, the more decentralized nursing management and the less complex the personnel department is, the greater the involvement of lower level managers in selecting personnel for individual units or departments. When deciding whether to hire a nurse-recruiter or decentralize the responsibility for recruitment, the organization needs to weigh benefits against costs. Costs include more than financial considerations. For example, an additional cost to an organization employing a nurse-recruiter might be the eventual loss of interest by managers in the recruiting process. The organization loses if managers relegate their collective and individual responsibilities to the nurse-recruiter.

When organizations use nurse-recruiters, a collaborative relationship must exist between managers and recruiters. Managers must be aware of recruitment constraints and the recruiter must be aware of individual department needs and culture. Both parties must understand the organization's philosophy, benefit programs, salary scale, and other factors that influence employee retention.

Recruitment and Retention

Recruiting adequate numbers of nurses is less difficult if the organization is located in a progressive community with several schools of nursing and if the organization has a good reputation for quality patient care and fair employment practices. It will likely be much more difficult to recruit nurses to rural areas that historically have experienced less appropriation of health-care professionals per capita than urban areas. In addition, some health-care organizations find it necessary to do external recruitment, partly because of their lack of attention to retention.

Because most recruitment is expensive, health-care organizations often seek less costly means to achieve this goal. One of the best ways to maintain an adequate employee pool is by word of mouth; the recommendation of the organization's own satisfied and happy staff. Recruitment, however, is not the key to adequate staffing in the long term. Retention is and it only occurs when the organization is able to create a work environment that makes staff want to stay.

Some turnover, however, is normal and, in fact, desirable. *Turnover* infuses the organization with fresh ideas. It also reduces the probability of *groupthink*, in which everyone shares similar thought processes, values, and goals. However, excessive or unnecessary turnover reduces the ability of the organization to produce its end product and is expensive. Such costs generally include human resource expenses for advertising and interviewing; recruitment fees such as sign-on bonuses; increased use of traveling nurses, overtime, and temporary replacements for the lost worker; lost productivity; and the costs of training time to bring the new employee up to desired efficiency.

The leader-manager recognizes the link between retention and recruitment. The middle-level manager often has the greatest impact in creating a positive social climate to promote retention. In addition, the closer the fit between what the nurse is seeking in employment and what the organization can offer, the greater the chance that the nurse will be retained.

LEARNING EXERCISE 15.1

Examining Recruitment Advertisements

Select one of the following:

1. In small groups, examine several nursing journals that carry job advertisements. Select three advertisements that particularly appeal to you. What do these advertisements say or what makes them stand out? Are similar key words used in all three advertisements? What bonuses or incentives are being offered to attract qualified professional nurses?

2. Select a health-care agency in your area. Write an advertisement or recruitment poster that accurately depicts the agency and the community. Compare your completed advertisement or recruitment flyer with those created by others in your group.

INTERVIEWING AS A SELECTION TOOL

An *interview* may be defined as a verbal interaction between individuals for a particular purpose. Although other tools such as testing and reference checks may be used, the interview is frequently accepted as the foundation for hiring, despite its well-known limitations in terms of reliability and validity.

The purposes or goals of the selection interview are threefold: (a) the interviewer seeks to obtain enough information to determine the applicant's suitability for the available position;

(b) the applicant obtains adequate information to make an intelligent decision about accepting the job, should it be offered; and (c) the interviewer seeks to conduct the interview in such a manner that regardless of the interview's result, the applicant will continue to have respect for and goodwill toward the organization.

There are many types of interviews and formats for conducting them. For example, interviews may be unstructured, semistructured, or structured. The *unstructured interview* requires little planning because the goals for hiring may be unclear, questions are not prepared in advance, and often the interviewer does more talking than the applicant. The unstructured interview continues to be the most common selection tool in use today (McKay, 2009).

Semistructured *interviews* require some planning since the flow is focused and directed at major topic areas although there is flexibility in the approach. The *structured interview* requires greater planning time yet because questions must be developed in advance that address the specific job requirements, information must be offered about the skills and qualities being sought, examples of the applicant's experience must be received, and the willingness or motivation of the applicant to do the job must be determined. The interviewer who uses a structured format would ask the same essential questions of all applicants.

Limitations of Interviews

The major defect of the hiring interview is subjectivity. Most interviewers feel confident that they can overcome this subjectivity and view the interview as a reliable selection tool, despite the element of subjectivity. In fact, McKay (2009) warns that interviewing is a lot more difficult than people think, and many people think they are better interviewers than they really are. "There is also a belief that interviewing is all about talking to people, and interviewing is just about good conversation. The selection interview is much more than a conversation, and good conversationalists aren't necessarily good interviewers" (McKay, para 3).

 Many people think they are better interviewers than they really are.

Research findings regarding the validity and reliability of interviews vary; however, the following findings are generally accepted:

- The same interviewer will consistently rate the interviewee the same. Therefore, the *intrarater reliability* is said to be high.
- If two different interviewers conduct unstructured interviews of the same applicant, their ratings will not be consistent. Therefore, *interrater reliability* is extremely low in unstructured interviews.
- Interrater reliability is better if the interview is *structured* and the same format is used by both interviewers.
- Even if the interview has *reliability* (i.e., it measures the same thing consistently), it still may not be valid. *Validity* occurs when the interview measures what it is supposed to measure, which in this case, is the potential for productivity as an employee. Structured interviews have greater validity than unstructured interviews and thus should be better predictor of job performance and overall effectiveness than unstructured interviews.

O'Brien and Rothstein (2011) note, however, that even with a structured interview and established validity, inter-rater reliability can be poor. This is especially true if interviewers must complete rating scales, since variation is commonplace in terms of either the leniency or stringency of rankings by different reviewers. This then obscures true differences in validity (see Examining the Evidence 15.1).

Examining the Evidence 15.1

Source: O'Brien, J., & Rothstein, M. G. (2011). Leniency: Hidden threat to large-scale, interview-based selection systems. Military Psychology (Taylor & Francis Ltd), 23(6), 601–615.

The researchers noted the challenges in making hiring selection decisions when individual interviews from different locations are pooled, and selection occurs on a top-down basis, even when structured interview formats are used. These challenges are compounded when ratings from individual interviewers are not comparable, for example, because interviewers vary in the validity of their judgments or tend to use the rating scales in different ways.

In this study, the researchers investigated variability in individual interviewer performance, including both validity and rater error. Data sources included the interview ratings and basic training performance outcomes of 2,552 applicants as well as the survey responses of 59 interviewers who evaluated applicants in interviews held in multiple settings across Canada.

An interview guide was provided in reference materials used by interviewers. The guide included interviewer questions and content areas to address as part of the interview process. Interviewers were trained, used anchored rating scales, and took notes as part of the process. Then, validity and rater error were evaluated using multilevel logistic regression models.

This study found no evidence that interviewers varied in the validity of their judgments. This was consistent with previous evidence on the possible effects of structure-related interventions like training on interviewer performance. Interviewers did, however, vary, in their use of rating scales. This finding suggests that interview structure may be limited in its effect on interviewer judgment.

The researchers concluded that exclusive concern with interview validity may contribute to neglect of other important interview outcomes and properties, to the detriment of the selection system overall. For example, when individual interviewer validity is estimated, those who are lenient or stringent are not evaluated on equivalent, comparable sets of interviewees, obscuring true differences in validity. This suggests that those managing large-scale selection systems should pay particular attention to the consistent and accurate use of rating scales by interviewers, or selection decisions may be negatively affected.

- High interview assessments are not related to subsequent high-level job performance.
- Validity increases when there is a team approach to the interview.
- The attitudes and biases of interviewers greatly influence how candidates are rated. Although steps can be taken to reduce subjectivity, it cannot be eliminated entirely.
- The interviewer is more influenced by unfavorable information than by favorable information. Negative information is weighed more heavily than positive information about the applicant.
- Interviewers tend to make up their minds about hiring applicants very early in the job interview. Decisions are often formed in the first few minutes of the interview.
- In unstructured interviews, the interviewer tends to do most of the talking, whereas in structured interviews, the interviewer talks less. The goal should always be to have the interviewee do most of the talking.

In addition, Sutherland (2012) suggests that interviews do not allow candidates to demonstrate their clinical skills, and interviewers run the risk of biasing their decisions on "first impressions." In addition, interviewers may be overly impressed with superficial signs such as composure, manner of speech, and physical appearance (Sutherland).

Regardless of these inherent defects, interviewing continues to be widely used as a selection tool. By knowing the limitations of interviews and using findings from current research evidence, interviewers should be able to conduct interviews so that they will have an increased predictive value.

As a predictor of job performance and overall effectiveness, the structured interview is much more reliable than the unstructured interview.

Overcoming Interview Limitations

Interview research has helped managers to develop strategies for overcoming its limitations. The following strategies will assist the manager in developing an interview process with greater reliability and validity.

Use a Team Approach

Having more than one person interview the job applicant reduces individual bias. Staff involvement in hiring can be viewed on a continuum from no involvement to a team approach, using unit staff for the hiring decisions. When hiring a manager, using a staff nurse as part of the interview team is effective, especially if the staff nurse is mature enough to represent the interests and needs of the unit rather than his or her own self-interests.

Develop a Structured Interview Format for Each Job Classification

Managers should obtain a copy of the job description and know the educational and experiential requirements for each position prior to the interview. In addition, because each job has different position requirements, interviews must be structured to fit the position. The same structured interview should be used for all employees applying for the same job classification. A well-developed structured interview uses open-ended questions and provides ample opportunity for the interviewee to talk. The structured interview is advantageous because it allows the interviewer to be consistent and prevents the interview from becoming sidetracked. O'Brien and Rothstein (2011) warn, however, that although structured interviews are often considered a panacea, individual differences in interviewer performance persist in the face of even the most rigorous structure. Display 15.3 is an example of a structured interview.

DISPLAY 15.3   Sample Structured Interview

MOTIVATION
Why did you apply for employment with this organization?

PHYSICAL
Do you have any physical limitations that would prohibit you from accomplishing the job?
How many days have you been absent from work during the last year of employment?

EDUCATION
What was your grade point average in nursing school?
What were your extracurricular activities, offices held, awards conferred?
For verification purposes, are your school records listed under the name on your application?

PROFESSIONAL
In what states are you licensed to practice?
Do you have your license with you?
What certifications do you hold?
What professional organizations do you currently participate in that would be of value in the job for which you are applying?

MILITARY EXPERIENCE
What are your current military obligations?
Which military assignments do you think have prepared you for this position?

PRESENT EMPLOYER

How did you secure your present position?

What is your current job title? What was your title when you began your present position?

What supervisory responsibilities do you currently have?

How would you describe your immediate supervisor?

What are some examples of success at your present job?

How do you get along with your present employer?

How do you get along with your present colleagues?

What do you like most about your present job?

What do you like least about your present job?

May we contact your present employer?

Why do you want to change jobs?

For verification purposes only, is your name the same as it was while employed with your current employer?

PREVIOUS POSITION(S)

Ask similar questions about recent past employment. Depending on the time span and type of other positions held, the interviewer does not usually review employment history that took place beyond the position just previous to the current one.

SPECIFIC QUESTIONS FOR REGISTERED NURSES

What do you like most about nursing?

What do you like least about nursing?

What is your philosophy of nursing?

PERSONAL CHARACTERISTICS

Which personal characteristics are your greatest assets?

Which personal characteristics cause you the most difficulty?

PROFESSIONAL GOALS

What are your career goals?

Where do you see yourself 10 years from now?

CONTRIBUTIONS TO ORGANIZATION

What can you offer this organization? This unit or department?

GENERAL QUESTIONS

What questions do you have about the organization?

What questions do you have about the position?

What other questions do you have?

LEARNING EXERCISE 15.2

Creating Additional Interview Criteria

You are a home health nurse with a large caseload of low-income, inner-city families. Because of your spouse's job transfer, you have just resigned from your position of 3 years to take a similar position in another public health district. Your agency supervisor has asked you to assist her with interviewing and selecting your replacement. Five applicants meet the minimum criteria. They each have at least 2 years of acute care experience, a baccalaureate nursing degree, and a state public health credential. Because you know the job requirements better than anyone, your supervisor has asked that you develop additional criteria and a set of questions to ask each applicant.

Assignment:

1. Use a decision grid (see Fig. 1.3 on page 21) to develop additional criteria. Weight the criteria so that the applicants will have a final score.

2. Develop an interview guide of six appropriate questions to ask the applicants.

Use Scenarios to Determine Decision-Making Ability

Use scenarios to determine decision-making ability. In addition to obtaining answers to a particular set of questions, the interview also should be used to determine the applicant's decision-making ability. This can be accomplished by designing scenarios that require problem-solving and decision-making skills. The same set of scenarios should be used with each category of employee. For example, a set could be developed for new graduates, critical care nurses, unit secretaries, and licensed practical nurses. Patient care situations, as shown in Display 15.4, require clinical judgment and are very useful for this purpose.

DISPLAY 15.4 Sample Interview Questions Using Case Situations

Each recent graduate applying for a position at Country Hospital will be asked to respond to the following:

CASE 1

You are working on the evening shift of a surgical unit. Mr. Jones returned from the postanesthesia care unit following a hip replacement 2 hours ago. While in the recovery room, he received 10 mg of morphine sulfate intravenously for incisional pain. Thirty minutes ago, he complained of mild incisional pain but then drifted off to sleep. He is now awake and complaining of moderate to severe incisional pain. His orders include the following pain relief order: morphine sulfate 8 to 10 mg, IV push every 3 hours for pain. It has been 2½ hours since Mr. Jones' last pain medication. What would you do?

CASE 2

One of the licensed professional nurses (LPNs)/licensed vocational nurses (LVNs) on your team seems especially tired today. She later tells you that her new baby kept her up all night. When you ask her about the noon finger-stick blood glucose level on Mrs. White (82 years old), she looks at you blankly and then says quickly that it was 150. Later, when you are in Mrs. White's room, she tells you that she does not remember anyone checking her blood glucose level at noon. What do you do?

Conduct Multiple Interviews

Candidates should be interviewed more than once on separate days. This prevents applicants from being accepted or rejected merely because they were having a good or bad day. Regardless of the number of interviews held, the person should be interviewed until all the interviewers' questions have been answered, and they feel confident that they have enough information to make the right decision.

Provide Training in Effective Interviewing Techniques

Training should focus on communication skills and advice on planning, conducting, and controlling the interview. It is unfair to expect a manager to make appropriate hiring decisions if he or she has never had adequate training in interview techniques. Unskilled interviewers often allow subjective data rather than objective data affect their hiring evaluation. In addition, unskilled interviewers may ask questions that could be viewed as discriminatory or that are illegal.

Planning, Conducting, and Controlling the Interview

Planning the interview in advance is vital to its subsequent success as a selection tool. If other interviewers are to be present, they should be available at the appointed time. The plan also should include adequate time for the interview. Before the interview, all interviewers should review the application, noting questions concerning information supplied by the applicant. Although it takes considerable practice, consistently using a planned sequence in the interview format will eventually yield a relaxed and spontaneous process. The following is a suggested interview format:

1. Introduce yourself and greet the applicant.
2. Make a brief statement about the organization and the available positions.
3. Clarify the position for which the person is applying.
4. Discuss the information on the application and seek clarification or amplification as necessary.
5. Discuss employee qualifications and proceed with the structured interview format.
6. If the applicant appears qualified, discuss the organization and the position further.
7. Explain the subsequent procedures for hiring, such as employment physicals, and hiring date. If the applicant is not hired at this time, discuss how and when he or she will be notified of the interview results.
8. Terminate the interview.

Try to create and maintain a comfortable environment throughout the interview, but do not forget that the interviewer is in charge of the interview. If the interview has begun well and the applicant is at ease, the interview will usually proceed smoothly. During the meeting, the manager should pause frequently to allow the applicant to ask questions. The format should always encourage and include ample time for questions from the applicant. Often, interviewers are able to infer much about applicants by the types of questions that they ask.

 Remember that the interviewer should have control of the interview and set the tone.

Moving the conversation along, covering questions on a structured interview guide, and keeping the interview pertinent but friendly becomes easier with experience. Methods that help reach the goals of the interview follow:

- Ask only job-related questions.
- Use open-ended questions that require more than a "yes" or "no" answer.
- Pause a few seconds after the applicant has seemingly finished before asking the next question. This gives the applicant a chance to talk further.
- Return to topics later in the interview on which the applicant offered little information initially.
- Ask only one question at a time.
- Restate part of the applicant's answer if you need elaboration.
- Ask questions clearly, but do not verbally or nonverbally indicate the correct answer. Otherwise, by watching the interviewer's eyes and observing other body language, the astute applicant may learn which answers are desired.
- Always appear interested in what the applicant has to say. The applicant should never be interrupted, nor should the interviewer's words ever imply criticism of or impatience with the applicant.
- Use language that is appropriate for the applicant. Terminology or language that makes applicants feel the interviewer is either talking down to them or talking over their heads is inappropriate.
- Keep a written record of all interviews. Note taking ensures accuracy and serves as a written record to recall the applicant. Keep note taking or use of a checklist, however, to a minimum so that you do not create an uncomfortable climate.

In addition, McNamara (n.d.) suggests that

- Applicants should be involved in the interview as soon as possible.
- Factual data should be elicited before asking about controversial matters (such as feelings and conclusions).
- Fact-based questions should be interspersed throughout the interview to avoid having respondents disengage.
- The interviewer should ask questions about the present before questions about the past or future.
- Applicant should be allowed to close the interview with information they want to add or to comment regarding their impressions of the interview.

As the interview draws to a close, the interviewer should make sure that all questions have been answered and that all pertinent information has been obtained. Usually, applicants are not offered a job at the end of a first interview unless they are clearly qualified and the labor market is such that another applicant would be difficult to find. In most cases, interviewers need to analyze their impressions of the applicant, compare these perceptions with members of the selection team, and incorporate those impressions with other available data about the applicant. It is important, however, to let applicants know if they are being seriously considered for the position and how soon they can expect to hear a final outcome.

When the applicant is obviously not qualified, the interviewer should not give false hope and instead should tactfully advise the person as soon as possible that he or she does not have the proper qualifications for the position. Such applicants should believe that they have been treated fairly. The interviewer should, however, maintain records of the exact reasons for rejection in case of later questions.

Evaluation of the Interview

Interviewers should plan post-interview time to evaluate the applicant's interview performance. Interview notes should be reviewed as soon as possible and necessary points clarified or amplified. Using a form to record the interview evaluation is a good idea. The final question on the interview report form is a recommendation for or against hiring. In answering this question, two aspects must carry the most weight:

- *The requirements for the job*. Regardless of how interesting or friendly people are, unless they have the basic skills for the job, they will not be successful at meeting the expectations of the position. Likewise, those overqualified for a position will usually be unhappy in the job.
- *Personal bias*. Because completely eliminating the personal biases inherent in the interview is impossible, it is important for the interviewer to examine any negative feelings that occurred during the interview. Often, the interviewer discovers that the negative feelings have no relation to the criteria necessary for success in the position.

Legal Aspects of Interviewing

The organization must be sure that the application form does not contain questions that violate various employment acts. Likewise, managers must avoid unlawful inquiries during the interview. Inquiries cannot be made regarding age, marital status, children, race, sexual preference, financial or credit status, national origin, or religion.

 Interview inquiries regarding age, marital status, children, race, sexual preference, financial or credit status, national origin, or religion are illegal because they are deemed discriminatory.

In addition to federal legislation, many states have specific laws pertaining to information that can and cannot be obtained during the process. For example, some states prohibit asking

TABLE 15.1   **Acceptable and Unacceptable Interview Inquiries**

Subject	Acceptable Inquiries	Unacceptable Inquiries
Name	If applicant has worked for the organization under a different name. If school records are under another name. If applicant has another name.	Inquiries about name that would indicate lineage, national origin, or marital or criminal status.
Marital and family status	Whether applicant can meet specified work schedules or has commitments that may hinder attendance requirements. Inquiries as to anticipated stay in the position.	Any question about applicant's marital status or number or age of children. Information about child care arrangements. Any questions concerning pregnancy.
Address or residence	Place of residence and length resided in city or state.	Former addresses, names or relationships of people with whom applicant resides, or if owns or rents home.
Age	If older than 18 or statement that hire is subject to age requirement. Can ask if the applicant is between 18 and 70.	Inquiry of specific age or date of birth.
Birthplace	Can ask for proof of US citizenship.	Birthplace of the applicant or spouse or any relative.
Religion	No inquiries allowed.	
Race or color	Can be requested for affirmative action but not as employment criteria.	All questions about race are prohibited.
Character	Inquiry into actual convictions that relate to fitness to perform job.	Questions relating to arrests or conviction of a crime.
Relatives	Relatives employed in organization. Names and addresses of parents if the applicant is a minor.	Questions about who the applicant lives with or the number of dependents.
Notify in case of emergency	Name and address of a *person* to be notified.	Name and address of a *relative* to be notified.
Organizations	Professional organizations.	Requesting a list of all memberships.
References	Professional or character reference.	Religious references.
Physical condition	All applicants can be asked if they are able to carry out the physical demands of the job.	Employers must be prepared to justify any mental or physical requirements. Specific questions regarding handicaps are forbidden.
Photographs	Statement that a photograph may be required *after* employment.	Requirement that a photograph be taken *before* interview or hiring.
National origin	If necessary to perform job, languages applicant speaks, reads, or writes.	Inquiries about birthplace, native language, ancestry, date of arrival in the United States, or native language.
Education	Academic, vocational, or professional education. Schools attended. Ability to read, speak, and write foreign languages.	Inquiries about racial or religious affiliation of a school. Inquiry about dates of schooling.
Sex	Inquiry or restriction of employment is only for bona fide occupational qualification, which is interpreted very narrowly by the courts.	Cannot ask sex on application. Sex cannot be used as a factor for hiring decisions.
Credit rating	No inquiries.	Questions about car or home ownership are also prohibited.
Other	Notice may be given that misstatements or omissions of facts may be cause for dismissal.	

about a woman's ability to reproduce or her attitudes toward family planning. Table 15.1 lists subjects that are most frequently part of the interview process or applicant form, with examples of acceptable and unacceptable inquiries.

Managers who maintain interview records and receive applicants with an open and unbiased attitude have little to fear regarding charges of discrimination. Remember that each applicant should feel good about the organization when the interview concludes and be able to recall the experience as a positive one. It is a leadership responsibility to see that this goal is accomplished.

TIPS FOR THE INTERVIEWEE

Just as there are things that the interviewer should do to prepare and conduct the interview, there are things interviewees should do to increase the likelihood that the interview will be a mutually satisfying and enlightening experience (Display 15.5). The interviewee must also prepare in advance for the interview. Obtaining copies of the philosophy and organization chart of the organization to which you are applying should give you some insight as to the organization's priorities and help you to identify questions to ask the interviewer. Speaking to individuals who already work at the organization should be helpful in determining whether the organization philosophy is implemented in practice.

DISPLAY 15.5 Interviewing Tips for Applicants

1. Prepare in advance for the interview.
2. Obtain copies of the philosophy and organization chart of the organization to which you are applying.
3. Schedule an appointment for the interview.
4. Dress professionally and conservatively.
5. Practice responses to potential interview questions in advance.
6. Arrive early on the day of the interview.
7. Greet the interviewer formally and do not sit down before he or she does unless given permission to do so.
8. Shake the interviewer's hand upon entering the room and smile.
9. During the interview, sit quietly, be attentive, and take notes only if absolutely necessary.
10. Do not chew gum, fidget, slouch, or play with your hair, keys, or writing pen.
11. Ask appropriate questions about the organization or the specific job for which you are applying.
12. Avoid a "what can you do for me?" approach and focus instead on whether your unique talents and interests are a fit with the organization.
13. Answer interview questions as honestly and confidently as possible.
14. Shake the interviewer's hand at the close of the interview, and thank him or her for his or her time.
15. Send a brief, typed thank you note to the interviewer within 24 hours of the interview.

Schedule an appointment for the interview. Do not allow yourself to be drawn into an impromptu interview when you are dropping off an application or seeking information from the human resource department. You will want to be professionally dressed and will likely need time to reflect and prepare for the interview.

Practice responses to potential interview questions. It is difficult to spontaneously answer interview questions about your personal philosophy of nursing, your individual strengths and weaknesses, and your career goals if you have not given them advance thought.

On the day of the interview, arrive about 10 minutes early to allow time for you to collect your thoughts and be mentally ready. Anticipate some nervousness (this is perfectly normal). Greet the interviewer formally (not by first name) and do not sit down before the interviewer does unless given permission to do so. Be sure to shake the interviewer's hand upon entering the room and to smile. Smiling will reduce both your anxiety and that of the interviewer. Remember that many interviewers make up their mind early in the interview process, so first impressions count a lot.

During the interview, sit quietly, be attentive, and take notes only if absolutely necessary. Do not chew gum, fidget, slouch, or play with your hair, keys, or writing pen. Dress conservatively and make sure that you are neatly groomed. Ask appropriate questions about the organization or the specific job for which you are applying. Questions about wages, benefits, and advancement opportunities should likely come later in the interview. Avoid a "what can you do for me?" approach, and focus instead on whether your unique talents and interests are a fit with the organization. Answer interview questions as honestly and confidently as possible. Avoid rambling and never lie. If you do not know the answer to a question, say so. Also, if you need a few moments to reflect on a complex question before answering, state that as well.

At the close of the interview, shake the interviewer's hand and thank him or her for taking time to talk with you. It is always appropriate to clarify at that point when hiring decisions will be made and how you will be notified about the interview's outcome. You may want to send a brief thank you note to the interviewer as well, so be sure to note their correct title and the spelling of their name before you leave.

The Connecticut Department of Labor (2002–2012) also suggests that candidates should assess the interview itself as soon as it is completed. This assessment should include reactions to the interview, including what went well and what went poorly. In addition, candidates should assess what they learned from the experience and what they might do differently in future interviews.

SELECTION

After applicants have been recruited, completed their applications, and been interviewed, the next step in the preemployment staffing process is selection. *Selection* is the process of choosing from among applicants the best-qualified individual or individuals for a particular job or position. This process involves verifying the applicant's qualifications, checking his or her work history, and deciding if a good match exists between the applicant's qualifications and the organization's expectations. Determining whether a "fit" exists between an employee and an organization is seldom easy.

Educational and Credential Requirements

Consideration should be given to educational requirements and credentials for each job category as long as a relationship exists between these requirements and success on the job. If requirements for a position are too rigid, the job may remain unfilled for some time. In addition, people who might be able to complete educational or credential requirements for a position are sometimes denied the opportunity to compete for the job. Therefore, many organizations have a list of *preferred criteria* for a position and a second list of *minimal criteria*. In addition, frequently, organizations will accept *substitution criteria* in lieu of preferred criteria. For example, a position might require a bachelor's degree, but a master's degree is preferred. However, 5 years of nursing experience could be substituted for the master's degree.

Clearly, there is a movement among health-care employers to hire more nurses with at least a BSN degree and to urge staff to pursue higher degrees (Trossman, 2012). Nurse executives value what all nurses bring to patient care, but they want to ensure staff can meet the challenges that continue to come their way and that patient care is optimized. With research supporting that educational entry level matters and that improvements in patient outcomes correlate with the number of baccalaureate or higher educated nurses, it is difficult to support not having higher education levels as preferred criteria, if not required criteria for nursing hires (Trossman).

In addition, the American Nurses Credentialing Center's (ANCC) Magnet Recognition Program® requires nurse-managers and leaders to have a degree in nursing at either the baccalaureate or graduate level (Trossman, 2012). Also, as of June 2013, Magnet applicants will be required to provide an action plan and set a target demonstrating their progress toward having 80% of direct care RNs having a baccalaureate or higher degree in nursing by 2020 (Trossman).

Reference Checks and Background Screening

All applications should be examined to see if they are complete and to ascertain that the applicant is qualified for the position. It is very important to check the academic and professional credentials of all job applicants. In a competitive job market, candidates may succumb to the pressure of "embroidering" their qualifications. Once a determination is made that an applicant is qualified, references are requested, and employment history is verified. In addition, a background check is often required.

Clearly, a strong application and excellent references do not necessarily guarantee excellent job performance; however, carefully reviewing applications and checking references may help prevent a bad hiring decision. Ideally, whenever possible, these actions as well as verifying work experience and credentials should be done before the interview. Some managers prefer to interview first so that time is not wasted in processing the application if the interview results in a decision not to hire, and this is a personal choice. A position should never be offered until applications have been verified and references obtained.

Positions should never be offered until information on the application has been verified and references have been checked.

Occasionally, reference calls will reveal unsolicited information about the applicant. Information obtained by any method may not be used to reject an applicant unless a justifiable reason for disqualification exists. For example, if the applicant volunteers information about his or her driving record or if this information is discovered by other means, it cannot be used to reject a potential employee unless the position requires driving.

Mandatory background checks have also become commonplace in health-care settings. This has occurred because health-care providers have access to vulnerable patients or protected health and financial information (Avoiding Bad Hires, 2013). Some concerns exist, however, as to who may be overseeing this screening and whether they are truly qualified to assess the risk. In some cases, the individuals responsible for screening background checks are administrative recruiters with no previous experience in health care, who may not understand the dynamic of what is involved in hiring health-care providers (Avoiding Bad Hires).

Complicating the issue are guidelines issued in 2012 by the Equal Employment Opportunity Commission (EEOC) that stopped short of banning criminal background checks but said that refusing to hire someone with a criminal record could constitute illegal discrimination if such decisions disproportionately affected minority groups (Avoiding Bad Hires, 2013). The EEOC went on to suggest that any decision not to hire must be "job related and consistent with business necessity" and must take into account factors such as the nature and gravity of the criminal offense, the amount of time since the conviction, and the relevance of the offense to the job being sought.

Preemployment Testing

Preemployment testing is generally used only when such testing is directly related to the ability to perform a specific job, although the use of personality tests is becoming much more common in health-care organizations. Curry (2011) suggests that assessing an applicant's baseline personality traits and compatibility with an organization's culture makes all the difference in his/her success as an employee. "Employees who fit in well with a staff and clinic culture have greater longevity than do new hires with higher skill levels but less compatible personalities" (Curry 2011, p. 141). That is because applicants who cannot align with coworkers typically do not emotionally commit to the organization and thus have higher turnover rates.

Although testing is not a stand-alone selection tool, it can, when coupled with excellent interviewing and reference checking, provide additional information about candidates to make the best selection. Lawsuits, however, have resulted from allegedly improper implementation and interpretation of preemployment testing and this makes some employers shy away from doing it.

Physical Examination as a Selection Tool

A medical examination is often a requirement for hiring. This examination determines if the applicant can meet the requirements for a specific job and provides a record of the physical condition of the applicant at the time of hiring. The physical examination also may be used to identify applicants who will potentially have unfavorable attendance records or may file excessive future claims against the organization's health insurance.

Only those selected for hire can be required to have a physical examination, which is nearly always conducted at the employer's expense. If the physical examination reveals information that disqualifies the applicant, he or she is not hired. Most employers make job offers contingent on meeting certain health or physical requirements.

Making the Selection

When determining the most appropriate person to hire, the leader must be sure that the same standards are used to evaluate all candidates. Final selection should be based on established criteria, not on value judgments and personal preferences.

Frequently, positions are filled with internal applicants. These positions might be entry level or management. Internal candidates should be interviewed in the same manner as newcomers to the organization; however, some organizations give special consideration and preference to their own employees. Every organization should have guidelines and policies regarding how transfers and promotions are to be handled.

Finalizing the Selection

Once a final selection has been made, the manager is responsible for closure of the preemployment process as follows:

1. Follow up with applicants as soon as possible, thanking them for applying and informing them when they will be notified about a decision.
2. Candidates not offered a position should be notified of this as soon as possible. Reasons should be provided when appropriate (e.g., insufficient education and work experience), and candidates should be told whether their application will be considered for future employment or if they should reapply.
3. Applicants offered a position should be informed in writing of the benefits, salary, and placement. This avoids misunderstandings later regarding what employees think they were promised by the nurse-recruiter or the interviewer.
4. Applicants who accept job offers should be informed as to preemployment procedures such as physical examinations and supplied with the date to report to work.
5. Applicants who are offered positions should be requested to confirm in writing their intention to accept the position.

Because selection involves a process of reduction (i.e., diminishing the number of candidates for a particular position), the person making the final selection has a great deal of responsibility. These decisions have far-reaching consequences, both for the organization and for the people involved. For these reasons, the selection process should be as objective as possible. The selection process is shown in Figure 15.1.

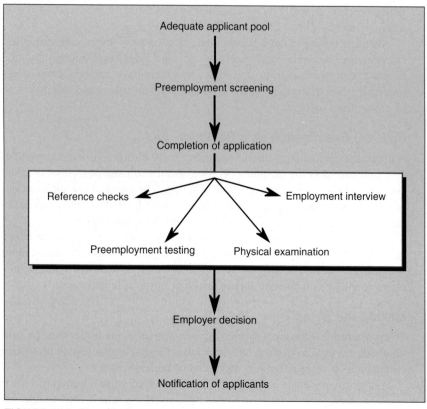

FIGURE 15.1 • The selection process.

LEARNING EXERCISE 15.3

Making a Hiring Selection and Assessing Its Impact

You are the head nurse of a surgical unit, a position that you have held for 6 years. You are comfortable with your role and know your staff well. Recently, the day charge nurse resigned. Two of your staff, Nancy and Sally, have applied for the position.

Nancy, an older nurse, has been with the organization for 8 years but has been assigned to your department for only 5 years. She has 12 years of experience in acute care nursing. She performs her job competently and has good interpersonal relationships with the other staff and with patients and physicians. Although her motivation level is adequate for her current job, she has demonstrated little creativity or initiative in helping the surgical unit to establish a reputation for excellence. Nor has she demonstrated specific skills in predicting or planning for the future.

Sally, a nurse in her mid-30s, has been with the organization and the unit for 3 years. She has been a positive driving force behind many of the changes that have occurred. She is an excellent clinician and is highly respected by physicians and staff. The older staff, however, appear to resent her because they feel she attempted too much change before "paying her dues."

Both nurses have baccalaureate degrees and meet all the position qualifications for the job. Both nurses can be expected to work at least another 5 years in the new position. There is no precedent for your decision.

You must make a selection. If you do not use seniority as a primary selection criterion, many of the long-term employees may resent both Sally and you, and they may become demotivated. You are aware that Nancy is limited in her futuristic thinking and that the unit may not grow and develop under her leadership as it could under that of Sally.

Assignment: Identify how your own values will affect your decision. Rank your selection criteria and make a decision about what you will do. Determine the personal, interpersonal, and organizational impact of your decision.

PLACEMENT

The astute leader is able to assign a new employee to a position within his or her sphere of authority, where the employee will have a reasonable chance for success. Nursing units and departments develop subcultures that have their own norms, values, and methods of accomplishing work. It is possible for one person to fit in well with an established group, whereas another equally qualified person would never become part of that group.

In addition, many positions within a unit or department require different skills. For example, in a hospital, decision-making skills might be more important on a shift where leadership is less strong; communication skills might be the most highly desired skill on a shift where there is a great deal of interaction among a variety of nursing personnel.

Frequently, newcomers suffer feelings of failure because of inappropriate placement within the organization. This can be as true for the newly hired experienced employee as for the novice nurse. Appropriate placement is as important to the organization's functioning as it is to the new employee's success. Faulty placement can result in reduced organizational efficiency, increased attrition, threats to organizational integrity, and frustration of personal and professional ambitions.

Conversely, proper placement fosters personal growth, provides a motivating climate for the employee, maximizes productivity, and increases the probability that organizational goals will be met. Leaders who are able to match employee strengths to job requirements facilitate unit functioning, accomplish organizational goals, and meet employee needs.

LEARNING EXERCISE 15.4

Which Two Graduates Would You Choose—and Why?

You are the supervisor of a critical care surgical unit. For the past several years, you have been experimenting with placing four newly graduated nurses directly into the unit, two from each spring and fall graduating class. These nurses are from the local BSN program. You consult closely with the nursing faculty and their former employers before making a selection.

Overall, this experiment has worked well. Only two new graduates were unable to develop into critical care nurses. Both of these nurses later transferred back into the unit after 2 years in a less intensive medical–surgical area.

Because of the new graduates' motivation and enthusiasm, they have complemented your experienced critical care staff nicely. You believe that your success with this program has been due to your well-planned and structured 4-month orientation and education program, careful selection, and appropriate shift placement.

(Continued)

This spring, you have narrowed the selection down to four acceptable and well-qualified candidates. You plan to place one on the 3 PM to 11 PM shift and one on the 11 PM to 7 PM shift. You sit in your office and review the culture of each shift and your notes on the four candidates. You have the following information:

3 PM to 11 PM shift: A very assertive, all-female staff; 85% RNs and 15% LPNs/LVNs. This is your most clinically competent group. They are highly respected by everyone, and although the physicians often have confrontations with them, the physicians also tell you frequently how good they are. The nurses are known as a group that lacks humor and does not welcome newcomers. However, once the new employee earns their trust, they are very supportive. They are intolerant of anyone not living up to their exceptionally high standards. Your two unsuccessful new graduate placements were assigned to this shift.

11 PM to 7 AM shift: A very cohesive and supportive group. Although overall these nurses are competent, this shift has some of your more clinically weak staff. However, it is also the shift that rates the highest with families and patients. They are caring and compassionate. Every new graduate that you have placed on this shift has been successful. Of the nurses on this shift, 30% are men. The group tends to be very close and has a number of outside social activities.

Your four applicants consist of the following:

- *John:* A 30-year-old married man without children. He has had a great deal of emergency department experience as a medical emergency technician. He appears somewhat aloof. His definite career goals are 2 years in critical care, 3 years in emergency department, and then flight crew. Instructors praise his independent judgment but believe that he was somewhat of a loner in school. Former employers have rated him as an independent thinker and very capable.
- *Sally:* A 22-year-old unmarried woman. She is at the top of her class clinically and academically. She has not had much work experience other than the last 2 years as a summer nursing intern at a medical center, where her performance appraisal was very good. Instructors believe that she lacks some maturity and interpersonal skills but praise her clinical judgment. She does not want to work in a regular medical–surgical unit. She believes that she can adapt to critical care.
- *Joan:* A mature, divorced 38-year-old woman. She has no children. She has had a great deal of health-related work experience in counseling and has had limited clinical work experience (only nursing school). Former employers praise her attention to detail and her general competence. Instructors praise her interpersonal skills, maturity, and intelligence. She is quite willing to work elsewhere if not selected. She has a long-term commitment to nursing.
- *Mary:* A dynamic, 28-year-old married mother of two. She was previously an LPN/LVN and returned to school to get her degree. She did not do as well academically due to working and family commitments. Former employers and instructors speak of her energy, organization, and interpersonal skills. She appears to have fewer independent decision-making skills than the others do. She previously worked in a critical care unit.

Assignment: Select the two new graduates and place them on the appropriate shift. Support your decisions with rationale.

INDOCTRINATION

As a management function, *indoctrination* refers to the planned, guided adjustment of an employee to the organization and the work environment. Although the words "induction" and "orientation" are frequently used to describe this function, the indoctrination process includes three separate phases: induction, orientation, and socialization. Because socialization is part of the staff development and team-building process, it will be covered in the next chapter.

Indoctrination denotes a much broader approach to the process of employment adjustment than either induction or orientation. It seeks to (a) establish favorable employee attitudes toward the organization, unit, and department; (b) provide the necessary information and education for success in the position; and (c) instill a feeling of belonging and acceptance. Effective indoctrination programs result in higher productivity, fewer rule violations, reduced attrition, and greater employee satisfaction. The employee indoctrination process begins as soon as a person has been selected for a position and continues until the employee has been socialized to the norms and values of the work group. An example of employee indoctrination content is shown in Display 15.6. Effective indoctrination programs assist employees in having successful employment tenure.

DISPLAY 15.6	Employee Indoctrination Content

1. Organization history, mission, and philosophy
2. Organization service and service area
3. Organizational structure, including department heads, with an explanation of the functions of the various departments
4. Employee responsibilities to the organization
5. Organizational responsibilities to the employee
6. Payroll information, including how increases in pay are earned and when they are given (progressive or unionized companies publish pay scales for all employees)
7. Rules of conduct
8. Tour of the facility and of the assigned department
9. Work schedules, staffing, and scheduling policies
10. When applicable, a discussion of the collective bargaining agreement
11. Benefit plans, including life insurance, health insurance, pension, and unemployment
12. Safety and fire programs
13. Staff development programs, including in-service, and continuing education for relicensure
14. Promotion and transfer policies
15. Employee appraisal system
16. Workload assignments
17. Introduction to paperwork/forms used in the organization
18. Review of selection in policies and procedures
19. Specific legal requirements, such as maintaining a current license and reporting of accidents
20. Introduction to fellow employees
21. Establishment of a feeling of belonging and acceptance, showing genuine interest in the new employee

Note: Much of this content could be provided in an employee handbook, and the fire and safety regulations could be handled by a media presentation. Appropriate use of videotapes or film strips can be very helpful in the design of a good orientation program. All indoctrination programs should be monitored to see if they are achieving their goals. Most programs need to be revised at least annually.

Induction

Induction, the first phase of indoctrination, takes place after the employee has been selected but before performing the job role. The induction process includes all activities that educate the new employee about the organization and employment and personnel policies and procedures.

Induction activities are often performed during the placement and preemployment functions of staffing or may be included with orientation activities. However, induction and orientation are often separate entities, and new employees suffer if content from either program is omitted. The most important factor is to provide the employee with adequate information.

Employee handbooks, an important part of induction, are usually developed by the personnel department. Managers, however, should know what information the employee handbooks contain and should have input into their development. Most employee handbooks contain a form that must be signed by the employee, verifying that he or she has received and read it. The signed form is then placed in the employee's personnel file.

The handbook is important because employees cannot assimilate all the induction information at one time, so they need a reference for later. However, providing an employee with a personnel handbook is not sufficient for real understanding. The information must be followed with discussion by various people during the employment process, such as the personnel manager and staff development personnel during orientation. The most important link in promoting real understanding of personnel polices is the first-level manager.

Orientation

Induction provides the employee with general information about the organization, whereas *orientation* activities are more specific for the position. A sample 2-week orientation schedule is shown in Display 15.7. Organizations may use a wide variety of orientation programs. For example, a first-day orientation could be conducted by the hospital's personnel department, which could include a tour of the hospital and all of the induction items listed in Display 15.6.

DISPLAY 15.7	Sample Two-Week Orientation Schedule for Experienced Nurses

WEEK 1

Day 1, Monday:

8:00 AM–10:00 AM	Welcome by personnel department; employee handbooks distributed and discussed
10:00 AM–10:30 AM	Coffee and fruit served; welcome by staff development department
10:30 AM–12:00 PM	General orientation by staff development
12:00 PM–12:30 PM	Tour of the organization
12:30 PM–1:30 PM	Lunch
1:30 PM–3:00 PM	Fire and safety films; HIPAA training
3:00 PM–4:00 PM	Afternoon tea and introduction to each unit supervisor

Day 2, Tuesday:

8:00 AM–10:00 AM	Report to individual units Time with unit supervisor; introduction to assigned preceptor
10:00 AM–10:30 AM	Coffee with preceptor
10:30 AM–12:00 PM	General orientation of policies and procedures
12:00 PM–12:30 PM	Lunch
12:30 PM–4:30 PM	electronic health record orientation

Day 3, Wednesday:	Assigned all day to unit with preceptor
Day 4, Thursday:	Assigned all day to unit with preceptor
Day 5, Friday:	Morning with preceptor, afternoon with supervisor and staff development for wrap-up

WEEK 2

Monday to Wednesday:	Work with preceptor on shift and unit assigned, gradually assuming greater responsibilities
Thursday:	Assign 80% of normal assignment with assistance and supervision from preceptor
Friday:	Carry normal workload. Have at least a 30-minute meeting with immediate supervisor to discuss progress

The next phase of the orientation program could take place in the staff development department, where aspects of concern to all employees such as fire safety, accident prevention, and health promotion would be presented The third phase would be the individual orientation for each department. At this point, specific departments such as dietary, pharmacy, and nursing would each be responsible for developing their own programs. A sample distribution of responsibilities for orientation activities is shown in Display 15.8.

DISPLAY 15.8   Responsibilities for Orientation

1. Personnel or Human Resources Department: Performs salary and payroll functions, insurance forms, physical examinations, income withholding forms, tour of the organization, employee responsibilities to the organization and vice versa, additional labor–management relationships, and benefit plan.
2. Staff Development Department: Hands out and reviews employee handbook; discusses organizational philosophy and mission; reviews history of the organization; shows media presentation of various departments and how they function (if a media presentation is not available, introduces various department heads, and shares how departments function); discusses organizational structure, fire and safety programs, HIPAA certification and EHR training, and verifications; discusses available educational and training programs; and reviews selected policies and procedures, including medication, treatment, and charting policies.
3. The Individual Unit: Tour of the department, introductions, review of specific unit policies that differ in any way from general policies, review of unit scheduling and staffing policies and procedures, work assignments, promotion and transfer policies, and establishment of a feeling of belonging, acceptance, and socialization.

Because induction and orientation involve many different people from a variety of departments, they must be carefully coordinated and planned to achieve preset goals. The overall goals of induction and orientation include helping employees by providing them with information that will smooth their transition into the new work setting and health-care team.

The purpose of the orientation process is to make the employee feel like a part of the team. This will reduce burnout and help new employees become independent more quickly in their new roles.

It is important to look at productivity and retention as the orientation program is planned, structured, and evaluated. Organizations should periodically assess their induction and orientation program in light of organizational goals; programs that are not meeting organizational goals should be restructured. For example, if employees consistently have questions about the benefit program, this part of the induction process should be evaluated.

Too often, various people having partial responsibility for induction and orientation "pass the buck" regarding failure of or weaknesses in the program. It is the joint responsibility of the personnel/human resources department, the staff development department, and each nursing service unit to work together to provide an indoctrination program that meets the needs of employees and the organization.

For some time, managers in health-care organizations, especially hospitals, did not fulfill their proper role in the orientation of new employees. Managers assumed that between the personnel/human resources and staff development, or in-service, departments, the new employee would become completely oriented. This often frustrated new employees because although they received an overview of the organization, they received little orientation to the specific unit. Because each unit has many idiosyncrasies, the new employee was left feeling inadequate and incompetent. The latest trend in orientation is for the nursing unit to take a greater responsibility for individualizing orientation.

The unit leader-manager must play a key role in the orientation of the new employee. An adequate orientation program minimizes the likelihood of rule violations, grievances, and misunderstandings; fosters feelings of belonging and acceptance; and promotes enthusiasm and morale.

INTEGRATING LEADERSHIP ROLES AND MANAGEMENT FUNCTIONS IN EMPLOYEE RECRUITMENT, SELECTION, PLACEMENT, AND INDOCTRINATION

Productivity is directly related to the quality of an organization's personnel. Active recruitment allows institutions to bring in the most qualified personnel for a position. After those applicants have been recruited, managers—using specified criteria—have a critical responsibility to see that the best applicant is hired. To ensure that all applicants are evaluated by using the same standards and that personal bias is minimized, the nurse-manager must be skilled in interviewing and other selection processes.

Leadership roles in preliminary staffing functions include planning for future staffing needs and keeping abreast of changes in the health-care field. Predicted nursing shortages will pose staffing challenges for some time to come. Leadership is also necessary in the preemployment interview process to ensure that all applicants are treated fairly and that the interview terminates with applicants having positive attitudes about the organization. Because leaders are fully aware of nuances, strengths, and weaknesses within their sphere of authority, they are able to assign newcomers to areas that offer the greatest potential for success.

The integration of leadership roles and management functions in the organization ensures positive public relations because applicants know that they will be treated fairly. In addition, there is greater likelihood that the pool of applicants will be sufficient because future needs are planned for proactively. The leader-manager uses the selection and placement process as a means to increase productivity and retention, accomplish the goals of the organization, and meet the needs of new employees.

The integrated leader-manager also knows that a well-planned and implemented induction and orientation program is a wise investment of organizational resources. It provides the opportunity to mold a team effort and infuse employees with enthusiasm for the organization. New employees' impressions of an organization during this period will stay with them for a long time. If the impressions are positive, they will be remembered in the difficult times that will ultimately occur during any long tenure of employment.

KEY CONCEPTS

- The first step in the staffing process is to determine the type and number of personnel needed.

- A number of factors are contributing to a projected, severe nursing shortage, including the aging of the nursing workforce, accelerating demand for professional nurses, inadequate enrollment in nursing programs of study, and the aging of nursing faculty.

- Successfully recruiting an adequate workforce depends on many variables, including financial resources, an adequate nursing pool, competitive salaries, the organization's reputation, the location's desirability, and the status of the national and local economy.

- Effective recruiting methods include advertisements, career days, literature, and the informal use of members of the organization as examples of satisfied employees.

- Despite their limitations in terms of reliability and validity, interviews continue to be widely used as a method of selecting employees for hire.

- The limitations of interviews are reduced when a structured approach is used in asking questions of applicants.
- The interview should meet the goals of both the applicant and the manager.
- Managers must be skilled in planning, conducting, and controlling interviews.
- Because of numerous federal acts that protect the rights of job seekers, interviewers must be cognizant of the legal constraints on interviews.
- Selection should be based on the requirements necessary for the job; these criteria should be developed before beginning the selection process.
- Leaders should seek to proactively recruit and hire staff with age, gender, cultural, ethnic, and language diversity to better mirror the rapidly increasing diversity of the communities they serve.
- New employees should be placed on units, departments, and shifts where they have the best chance of succeeding.
- Indoctrination consists of induction, orientation, and socialization of employees.
- A well-prepared and executed orientation program educates the new employee about the desired behaviors and expected goals of the organization and actively involves the new employee's immediate supervisor.

ADDITIONAL LEARNING EXERCISES AND APPLICATIONS

LEARNING EXERCISE 15.5

Assessing Personal Bias in Interviewing

You are a new evening charge nurse on a medical floor in an acute care hospital. This is your first management position. You graduated 18 months ago from the local university with a bachelor's degree in nursing. Your immediate supervisor has asked you to interview two applicants who will be graduating from nursing school in 3 months. Your supervisor believes that they both are qualified. Because the available position is on your shift, she wants you to make the final hiring decision.

Both applicants seem equally qualified in academic standing and work experience. Last evening, you interviewed Lisa and were very impressed. Tonight, you interviewed John. During the meeting, you kept thinking that you knew John from somewhere but could not recall where. The interview went well, however, and you were equally impressed with John.

After John left, you suddenly remembered that one of your classmates used to date him and that he had attended some of your class parties. You recall that on several occasions, he appeared to abuse alcohol. This recollection bothers you, and you are not sure what to do. You know that tomorrow your supervisor wants to inform the applicants of your decision.

Assignment: Decide what you are going to do. Support your decision with appropriate rationale. Explain how you would determine which applicant to hire. How great a role did your personal values play in your decision?

LEARNING EXERCISE 15.6

How Would You Strengthen This Orientation Process?

As a new head nurse, one of your goals is to reduce attrition. You plan to do this by increasing retention, thus reducing costs for orienting new employees. In addition, you believe that the increased retention will provide you with a more stable staff.

In studying your notes from exit interviews, it appears that new employees seldom develop a loyalty to the unit but instead use the unit to gain experience for other positions. You believe that one difficulty with socializing new employees might be your unit's orientation program. The agency allows 2 weeks of orientation time (80 hours) when the new employee is not counted in the nursing care hours. These are referred to as *nonproductive hours* and are charged to the education department. Your unit has the following 2-week schedule for new employees:

Week 1

Monday, Tuesday	9 AM to 5 PM	Classroom
Wednesday, Thursday, Friday	7 AM to 11 AM	Assigned to work with someone on the unit

Week 2

Monday, Tuesday	7 AM to 3:30 PM	Assigned to unit with an employee
Wednesday, Thursday, Friday		Assigned to shift they will be working for orientation to shift

Following this 2-week orientation, the new employee is expected to function at 75% productivity for 2 or 3 weeks and then perform at full productivity. The exception to this is the new graduate (RN) orientation. These employees spend one extra week on 7 AM to 3 PM and one extra week assigned to their particular shift before being counted as staff.

Your nursing administrator has stated that you may alter the orientation program in any way you wish as long as you do not increase the nonproductive time and you ensure that the employee receives information necessary to meet legal requirements and to function safely.

Assignment: Is there any way for you to strengthen the new employee orientation to your unit? Outline your plans (if any), and state the rationale for your decision.

LEARNING EXERCISE 15.7

Choosing Your Place in the Workforce

You are a nursing student who will graduate in 3 months. You are aware that most of the acute care hospitals in the immediate area are not hiring new graduates although there are a few openings in a small, rural hospital about 40 miles from where you live. There are some openings in home health, public health, community health, telehealth, and case management in the local community as well. You need to get a job as soon as possible as you are a single parent and have accrued significant debt in your educational degree quest.

Your career goal is to work in a high-paced, skill-intensive, acute care hospital environment like the ED, ICU, or trauma, but you have not yet achieved the specialty certifications you need to do so and there are no openings in these units for new graduates at present anyway. You enjoyed the autonomy and patient interaction that you experienced in your public health practicum as part of school, and the Monday to Friday work schedule of the public health nurses appeals to you since you have small children. The salary, however, would be significantly lower than if you worked in an acute care setting and you are not sure that this would be enough to make ends meet. Moreover, the orientation period at the public health facility would be fairly brief.

Finally, you also have an interest in pediatric oncology, a specialty not available to you unless you relocate to a regional medical center almost 200 miles from where you currently live.

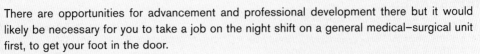

There are opportunities for advancement and professional development there but it would likely be necessary for you to take a job on the night shift on a general medical–surgical unit first, to get your foot in the door.

Assignment:

1. Determine how you will move forward in making a decision about where you will seek employment.

2. Make a list of 10 factors that you need to consider in weighting conflicting wants, needs, and obligations.

3. What evaluation criteria can you generate to look at both the process you used to make your decision and the decision itself?

LEARNING EXERCISE 15.8

Ethical Issues in Hiring

You are the head nurse of an intensive care unit and are interviewing Sam, a prospective charge nurse for your evening shift. Sam is currently the unit supervisor at Memorial Hospital, which is the other local hospital and your organization's primary competitor. He is leaving Memorial Hospital for personal reasons.

Sam, well qualified for the position, has strong management and clinical skills. Your evening shift needs a strong manager with the excellent clinical skills, which Sam also has. You feel fortunate that Sam is applying for the position.

Just before the close of the interview, however, Sam shuts the door, lowers his voice secretively, and tells you that he has vital information regarding Memorial's plans to expand and reorganize its critical care unit. He states that he will share this information with you if you hire him.

Assignment: How would you respond to Sam? Should you hire him? Identify the major issues in this situation. Support your hiring decision with rationale from this chapter and other readings.

LEARNING EXERCISE 15.9

Reducing Your Anxiety About Possible Hiring Interview Questions

Assignment: Make a list of three or four interview questions you may face in your new graduate interview, which you feel most insecure about answering. Then, share your questions with a small group of your peers. Work together to identify strong and weak responses to those interview questions. Make sure that every individual in the group has a chance to get feedback about the interview questions they are most anxious about.

LEARNING EXERCISE 15.10

Your Best Interview

Assignment: Do you remember your first interview for a job? How would you evaluate your abilities as someone being interviewed? Have you ever had the responsibility to interview someone for an employment position? What would you identify as your strengths and weaknesses in the interview process as both interviewer and interviewee? If you hired someone in the past how would you rate their performance as an employee? Were they more competent or less competent than they seemed at the time you interviewed them?

REFERENCES

American Association of Colleges of Nursing (AACN). (2012, August). *Nursing shortage*. Retrieved June 7, 2013, from http://www.aacn.nche.edu/Media/FactSheets/NursingShortage.htm

Avoiding Bad Hires Requires Healthcare Insight, Auditing. (2013). *Healthcare Risk Management, 35*(2), 19.

'Best Places': Financially Fit, Employee-Oriented, Reform-Ready. (2012). *Modern Healthcare*, 8–14.

Connecticut Department of Labor, Project Management Office. (2002–2012). *Tips for job seekers. Employment interviewing*. Retrieved June 7, 2013, from http://www.ctdol.state.ct.us/progsupt/jobsrvce/intervie.htm

Curry, I. (2011). Getting the right employees, getting rid of the wrong ones. *Podiatry Management, 30*(1), 141–143.

Huston, C. (2014a). The current nursing shortage. In *Professional issues in nursing: Challenges and opportunities* (3rd ed.). Philadelphia, PA: Lippincott Williams & Wilkins 68–85.

Huston, C. (2014b). Diversity in the nursing workforce. In *Professional issues in nursing: Challenges and opportunities* (3rd ed.). Philadelphia, PA: Lippincott Williams & Wilkins 136–155.

McKay, R. A. (2009, February 21). *The hiring interview is not a conversation*. Retrieved December 29, 2009, from http://www.e-bizarticles.com/the-hiring-interview-is-not-a-conversation.html

McNamara, C. (n.d.). *General guidelines for conducting interviews*. Free Management Library. Retrieved June 6, 2013, from http://managementhelp.org/evaluatn/intrview.htm

McNeal, G. J. (2012, spring). The nurse faculty shortage. *The ABNF Journal, 23*(2), 23.

O'Brien, J., & Rothstein, M. G. (2011). Leniency: Hidden threat to large-scale, interview-based selection systems. *Military Psychology (Taylor & Francis Ltd), 23*(6), 601–615.

Schaeffer, R. (2013, May–July). The Nursing Shortage....Fact or Fiction?. (2013). *Arizona Nurse, 66*(2), 3.

Sutherland, C. (2012). How clinical observation enhances recruitment and selection. *Nursing Management—UK, 19*(7), 34–37.

Trossman, S. (2012). Have BSN? Will hire. *American Nurse, 44*(4), 1–6.

16

Socializing and Educating Staff for Team Building in a Learning Organization

... environments rich in continuing education ripen staff development, morale and retention.
—Diane Postlen-Slattery and Kathryn Foley

... as part of the lifelong learning process, nurse leaders will increasingly use mentors and personal coaches to help them refine their tools and skills and to identify new lenses through which to view current concerns or issues.
—Karen S. Haase-Herrick

CROSSWALK THIS CHAPTER ADDRESSES:

BSN Essential I: Liberal education for baccalaureate generalist nursing practice

BSN Essential II: Basic organizational and systems leadership for quality care and patient safety

BSN Essential III: Scholarship for evidence-based practice

BSN Essential VI: Interprofessional communication and collaboration for improving patient health outcomes

BSN Essential VIII: Professionalism and professional values

MSN Essential I: Background for practice from sciences and humanities

MSN Essential II: Organizational and systems leadership

MSN Essential IV: Translating and integrating scholarship into practice

MSN Essential VII: Interprofessional collaboration for improving patient and population health outcomes

QSEN Competency: Evidence-based practice

QSEN Competency: Teamwork and collaboration

AONE Nurse Executive Competency I: Communication and relationship building

AONE Nurse Executive Competency III: Leadership

AONE Nurse Executive Competency IV: Professionalism

LEARNING OBJECTIVES *The learner will:*

- describe characteristics of learning organizations
- differentiate between education and training
- select an appropriate sequence of events for educational planning
- identify problems that may occur when the responsibility for staff development is shared
- select appropriate educational strategies that facilitate learning in a variety of situations
- discuss criteria that should be used to evaluate staff development activities
- demonstrate knowledge of the needs of the adult learner versus the needs of the child learner and describe teaching strategies that best meet the needs of both groups of learners
- explain the difference between motivation to learn and readiness to learn

- apply principles of social learning theory
- identify strategies that could be used to help staff deal successfully with role transitions
- select strategies to assist the new graduate nurse with socialization to the nursing role
- explain why experienced nurses may have difficulty in role transition
- compare and contrast the roles of mentor, preceptor, and role model
- choose criteria for the selection of preceptors that would likely result in effective role transition for the protégé
- develop coaching techniques that enhance learning
- address the unique challenges of building a cohesive team through education and socialization, when a diverse workforce exists

Health-care organizations face major challenges in upgrading the skills of their workforce and in maintaining a competent staff. This is especially true in times of exponential knowledge growth and limitless new technology applications. Educating staff and assuring continuing competency then is a critical and difficult task for most 21st-century organizations.

This chapter begins by introducing the concept of the *learning organization* (LO) and the various components of staff development. Education and training are differentiated as are role models, preceptors, and mentors. The needs of the adult learner are explored, and the concept of coaching as a staff development tool is introduced. The role of the organization, leader-managers, and staff development departments in creating a culture that supports and promotes evidence-based practice is emphasized. Finally, the need to build a cohesive team, including the needs of a culturally diverse workforce, is explored. The leadership roles and management functions associated with socializing and educating staff for team building are shown in Display 16.1.

DISPLAY 16.1   Leadership Roles and Management Functions Associated with Socializing and Educating Staff for Team Building in a Learning Organization

LEADERSHIP ROLES

1. Clarifies unit norms and values to all new employees.
2. Infuses a team spirit among employees.
3. Serves as a role model to all employees and a mentor to select employees.
4. Encourages mentorship between senior staff and junior employees.
5. Observes carefully for signs of knowledge or skill deficit in new employees and intervenes appropriately.
6. Assists employees in developing personal strategies to cope with role transition.
7. Applies adult learning principles when helping employees learn new skills or information.
8. Coaches employees spontaneously regarding knowledge and skill deficits.
9. Is sensitive to the unique socialization and education needs of a culturally and ethnically diverse staff.
10. Continually promotes aspects of the LO to employees.
11. Assists nursing staff in overcoming organization barriers to effective evidence-based practice.
12. Encourages and supports workers as they pursue lifelong learning individually and collectively.

MANAGEMENT FUNCTIONS

1. Is aware of and clarifies organizational and unit goals for all employees.
2. Clarifies role expectations for all employees.
3. Uses positive and negative sanctions appropriately to socialize new employees.
4. Carefully selects preceptors and encourages positive role modeling by experienced staff.
5. Provides methods of meeting the special orientation needs of new graduates, international nurses, and experienced nurses changing roles.

6. Works with the education department to delineate shared and individual responsibility for staff development.
7. Ensures that there are adequate resources for staff development and makes appropriate decisions regarding resource allocation during periods of fiscal restraint.
8. Assumes responsibility for quality and fiscal control of staff development activities.
9. Ensures that all staff are competent for roles assigned.
10. Provides input in formulating staff development policies.
11. Ensures that the organization provides resources to promote evidence-based nursing practice.

THE LEARNING ORGANIZATION

A growing body of literature supports the concept that learning should go beyond the boundaries of individual learning and that organizations that incorporate learning as a major part of their philosophy will be more successful. This concept was first introduced by Senge (1994), who called such organizations *LOs*. Since learning is viewed as an important part of quality, LOs view learning as the key to the future for individuals, as well as for organizations. In addition, the LO promotes a shared vision and collective learning in order to create positive and needed organizational change.

 The LO promotes a shared vision and collective learning in order to create positive and needed organizational change.

The key characteristics of Senge's model of LOs (five disciplines) include the following:

- *Systems thinking.* The organization encourages staff to see themselves as connected to the whole organization and work activities are seen as having an impact beyond the individual. This creates a sense of community and builds a commitment on the part of individual workers not only to the organization but also to each other.
- *Personal mastery.* Each member of the staff has a commitment to improve his or her personal abilities. This personal and professional learning is then integrated into the team and organization.
- *Team learning.* It is through the collaboration of team members that LOs achieve their goals.
- *Mental models.* The goal in the LO is to foster organizational development through diverse thinking. Assumptions held by individuals then are challenged since this releases individuals from traditional thinking and promotes the full potential of individuals to learn.
- *Shared vision.* When all the employees of the LO share a common vision, they are more willing to put their personal goals and needs aside and instead focus on teamwork and collaboration.

Since Senge, many theorists have furthered our understanding of LOs. For example, Green, Reid, and Larson (2012) suggest that the conceptual foundation of a rapid learning health system has both human and technological aspects. The human factors include stakeholders motivated by a desire to continuously improve the system for patients. The technological aspects include a search for and use of current, robust data to guide clinical and administrative decision making, based on evidence and reporting systems that are accessible system-wide, allowing learning to permeate throughout the organization.

Glaser and Overhage (2013) agree, suggesting that the foundation for an LO in health care is continuous knowledge development—the formation of a closed "learning loop," in which information generated by clinical research is methodically captured and translated into evidence that can provide the basis for improving patient care. Glaser and Overhage suggest that while some individuals still view the LO as an ideal, it should be viewed as an imperative and note that "many organizations are already engaged in constantly revamping and retooling themselves, perhaps unknowingly reaching for that ideal goal of becoming a learning organization" (Glaser & Overhage, 2012, p. 62).

In addition, in September 2012, the Institute of Medicine (2012) released a 4,000 page report, *Best Care at Lower Cost: The Path to Continuously Learning Health Care in America.* In this report, the IOM outlined a series of recommendations to improve the nation's health-care system. One of the key recommendations was to reward providers for continuous learning and quality. This quest for continuous learning and quality creates a health-care delivery system that learns from and evolves with every patient interaction (Glaser & Overhage, 2013).

STAFF DEVELOPMENT

This recognition by LOs that learning is never ending and that the organization has at least some responsibility for developing their employees is responsible in part for the growth in staff development programs. An LO does not just meet licensure requirements for education and training but encourages individual growth and supports staff development activities both financially and philosophically.

This fostering of growth and learning in employees is not, however, solely the result of altruistic motives by the organization. The staff's knowledge level and capabilities often determine the number of staff required to carry out unit goals. Therefore, the better trained and more competent the staff, the fewer the number of staff required, which in turn saves the organization money and increases productivity.

Staff development is a cost-effective method of increasing productivity.

Training Versus Education

Education and training are two components of staff development. Managers historically had a greater responsibility for seeing that staff were properly trained than they did for meeting educational needs. A more equal balance has been achieved in the past two decades.

Training may be defined as an organized method of ensuring that people have knowledge and skills for a specific purpose and that they have acquired the necessary knowledge to perform the duties of the job. The knowledge may require increased affective, motor, or cognitive skills.

To assist employees with their training needs, the manager must first determine what those needs are. This requires more than just asking employees about their knowledge deficits or giving employees a skills checklist or test; it requires careful observation so that deficiencies are identified and corrected before they handicap the employee's socialization. This is a leadership role. When such deficiencies are not corrected early, other employees often create a climate of nonacceptance that prevents assimilation of the new employee.

Education is more formal and broader in scope than training. Whereas training has an immediate use, education is designed to develop individuals in a broader sense. Recognizing educational needs and encouraging educational pursuits are roles and responsibilities of the leader. Managers may appropriately be requested to teach classes or courses; however, unless they have specific expertise, they would not normally be responsible for an employee's formal education.

Responsibilities of the Education Department

Staff development is a broad area of responsibility and is borne by many people in the organization. Its official functions are often housed, however, within an education department. Since most education departments have staff or advisory authority rather than line authority on the organization chart, education personnel generally have little or no formal authority over those for whom they are providing educational programs. Likewise, the unit manager may have little authority over personnel in the education department. Because of the ambiguity of overlapping roles and difficulties inherent in line and staff positions, it is important that those responsible for educating and training be identified and given the authority to carry out the programs.

 If staff development activities are to be successful, it is necessary to delineate and communicate the authority and responsibility for all components of education and training.

In some organizations, the responsibility for staff development is decentralized. This has occurred as a result of fiscal concerns, the awareness of the need to socialize new employees at the unit level, and recognition of the relationship between employee competence and productivity. Some difficulties associated with decentralized staff development include the conflict created by *role ambiguity* whenever two people share responsibility. Role ambiguity is sometimes reduced when staff development personnel and managers delineate the difference between training and education.

Other difficulties arising from the shared responsibility among managers, personnel department staff, and educators for the indoctrination, education, and training of personnel may include a lack of cost-effectiveness evaluation and limited accountability for the quality and outcomes of the educational activities. The following suggestions can help overcome the difficulties inherent in a staff development system in which there is shared authority:

- The education department must ensure that all parties involved in the indoctrination, education, and training of nursing staff understand and carry out their responsibilities in that process.
- If a non-nursing administrator is responsible for the staff development department, there must be input from the nursing department in formulating staff development policies and delineating duties.
- An education advisory committee should be formed with representatives from top-, middle-, and first-level management; staff development; and the human resource department. Representatives from all classifications of employees receiving training or education should be part of this committee.
- Accountability for various parts of the staff development program must be clearly communicated.
- Some method of determining the cost and benefits of various programs should be used.

 ## LEARNING THEORIES

All managers have a responsibility to improve employee performance through teaching. Therefore, they must be familiar with basic learning theories. Understanding teaching–learning theories allows managers to structure training and use teaching techniques to change employee behavior and improve competence, which is the goal for all staff development.

TABLE 16.1	Characteristics and Learning Environment of Pedagogy and Andragogy
Pedagogy	*Andragogy*
	Characteristics
Learner is dependent	Learner is self-directed
Learner needs external rewards and punishment	Learner is internally motivated
Learner's experience is inconsequential or limited	Learner's experiences are valued and varied
Subject centered	Task or problem centered
Teacher directed	Self-directed
	Learning Environment
The climate is authoritative	The climate is relaxed and informal
Competition is encouraged	Collaboration is encouraged
Teacher sets goals	Teacher and class set goals
Decisions are made by teacher	Decisions are made by teacher and students
Teacher lectures	Students process activities and inquire about projects
Teacher evaluates	Teacher, self, and peers evaluate

Adult Learning Theory

Many managers attempt to teach adults with pedagogical or child-learning strategies. This type of teaching is usually ineffective for mature learners because adults have special needs. Knowles (1970) developed the concept of *andragogy*, or *adult learning*, to separate adult learner strategies from *pedagogy*, or *child learning*. Knowles suggested that the point at which an individual achieves a self-concept of essential self-direction is the point at which he or she psychologically becomes an adult (Atherton, 2011).

Adult learners then are mature, self-directed people who have learned a great deal from life experiences and are focused toward solving problems that exist in their immediate environments. This is because adult learners need to know why they need to learn something before they are willing to learn it. In addition, Knowles believed that adults need to be responsible for their own decisions and to be treated as capable of self-direction (Atherton, 2011).

Adult learning theory has contributed a great deal to the manner in which adults are currently taught in staff development programs. Table 16.1 shows how child and adult (pedagogical and andragogical) learning environments typically differ. Display 16.2 identifies the implications of Knowles' work for trainers and educators.

DISPLAY 16.2   Implications of Knowles' Work for Trainers and Educators

- A climate of openness and respect will assist in the identification of what the adult learner wants and needs to learn.
- Adults enjoy taking part in and planning their learning experiences.
- Adults should be involved in the evaluation of their progress.
- Experiential techniques work best with adults.
- Mistakes are opportunities for adult learning.
- If the value of the adult's experience is rejected, the adult will feel rejected.
- Adults' readiness to learn is greatest when they recognize that there is a need to know (such as in response to a problem).
- Adults need the opportunity to apply what they have learned very quickly after the learning.
- Assessment of need is imperative in adult learning.

While most adults enjoy and take pride in being treated as an adult in terms of learning, there are some obstacles to learning for adults that do not exist in children. Since learning tends to become problem centered as we age, adults often miss out on opportunities to enjoy learning for the sheer sake of learning itself. Similarly, adults often experience more external obstacles to learning, including time, energy, and institutional barriers. These and other obstacles to adult learning are shown in Display 16.3 as are the assets or driving forces, which encourage learning in the adult.

DISPLAY 16.3   Obstacles and Assets to Adult Learning

OBSTACLES TO LEARNING

Institutional barriers
Time
Self-confidence
Situational obstacles
Family reaction
Special individual obstacles

ASSETS FOR LEARNING

High self-motivation
Self-directed
A proven learner
Knowledge experience reservoir
Special individual assets

Social Learning Theory

Social learning theory is also an important part of LOs since it suggests we learn from our interactions with others in a social context. (This is a part of the teamwork and mental model development in LOs.) Albert Bandura, a social psychologist, is often credited with developing social learning theory in the 1970s. Bandura (1977) believed that direct reinforcement could not account for all types of learning, and that instead, most people learn their behavior by direct experience and observation, known as *observational learning* or *modeling* (Cherry, 2013).

Indeed, Bandura felt that four separate processes were involved in social learning. First, people learn as a result of the direct experience of the effects of their actions. Second, knowledge is frequently obtained through vicarious experiences, such as by observing someone else's actions. Third, people learn by judgments voiced by others, especially when vicarious experience is limited. Fourth, people evaluate the soundness of the new information by reasoning through inductive and deductive logic. If observational learning is to become successful, individuals must be motivated to imitate the behavior that has been modeled (Cherry, 2013). Figure 16.1 depicts Bandura's social learning theory process.

Other Learning Theories

The following learning concepts may also be helpful to the leader-manager in meeting the learning needs of staff in LOs:

- *Readiness to learn.* This refers to the maturational and experiential factors in the learner background that influence learning and is not the same as motivation to learn. *Maturation* means that the learner has received the prerequisites for the next stage of learning. The prerequisites could be behaviors or prior learning. *Experiential factors* are skills previously acquired that are necessary for the next stage of learning.

- *Motivation to learn.* If learners are informed in advance about the benefits of learning specific content and adopting new behaviors, they are more likely to be motivated to attend the training sessions and learn. Telling employees why and how specific educational or training programs will benefit them personally is a vital management function in staff development.

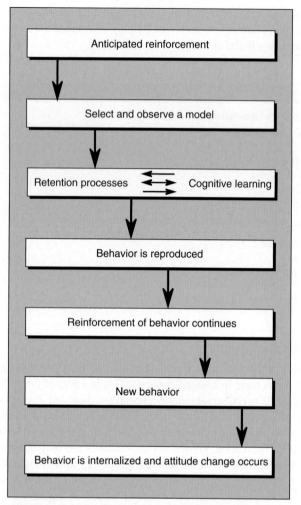

FIGURE 16.1 • The social learning theory process.

- *Reinforcement.* Because a learner's first attempts are often unsuccessful, a preceptor is essential. Good preceptors can reinforce desired behavior. Once the behavior or skill is learned, it needs continual reinforcement until it becomes internalized.

- *Task learning.* The learning of complex tasks is facilitated when tasks are broken into parts, beginning with the simplest and continuing to the most difficult. It is necessary, however, to combine *part learning* with *whole learning.* When learning motor skills, *spaced practice* is more effective than *massed practice.*

- *Transfer of learning.* The goal of training is to transfer new learning to the work setting. For this to occur, there should first be as much similarity between the training context and the job as possible. Second, adequate practice is mandatory, and *overlearning* (learning repeated to the degree that it is difficult to forget) is recommended. Third, the training should include a variety of different situations so that the knowledge is generalized. Fourth, whenever possible, important features or steps in a process should be identified. Finally, the learner must understand the basic principles underlying the tasks and how a variety of situations will modify how the task is accomplished. Learning in the classroom will not be transferred without adequate practice in a simulated or real situation and without an adequate understanding of underlying principles.

- *Span of memory.* The effectiveness of staff development activities depends to some extent on the ability of the participants to retain information. Effective strategies include the chance for repeated rehearsal, grouping items to be learned (three or four items for oral presentations and four to six visually), having the material presented in a well-organized manner, and *chunking.*
- *Chunking.* This occurs when two independent items of information are presented and then grouped together into one unit. Although the mind can remember only a limited number of chunks of data, experienced nurses can include more data in the chunks than can novice nurses.
- *Knowledge of results.* Research has demonstrated that people learn faster when they are informed of their progress. The knowledge of results must be automatic, immediate, and meaningful to the task at hand. People need to experience a feeling of progress, and they need to know how they are doing when measured against expected outcomes.

ASSESSING STAFF DEVELOPMENT NEEDS

Although managers may not be involved in implementing all educational programs, they are responsible for identifying learning needs. If educational resources are scarce, staff desires for specific educational programs may need to be sacrificed to fulfill competency and new learning needs. Because managers and staff may identify learning needs differently, an educational needs assessment should be carried out before developing programs.

Staff development activities are normally carried out for one of three reasons: to establish competence, to meet new learning needs, and to satisfy interests the staff may have in learning in specific areas.

Many staff development activities are generated to ensure that workers at each level are competent to perform the duties assigned to the position. *Competence* is defined as having the abilities to meet the requirements for a particular role. Health-care organizations use many resources to determine competency. State board licensure, national certification, and performance review are some of the methods used to satisfy competency requirements (Huston, 2014a). Other methods are self-administered checklists, record audits, and peer evaluation. Many of these methods are explained in Unit VII. For staff development purposes, it is important to remember that in the case of deficient competencies, some staff development activity must be implemented to correct the deficiencies. Another learning need that frequently affects health-care organizations is the need to meet new technological and scientific challenges. Much of a manager's educational resources will be used to meet these new learning needs.

Some organizations implement training programs because they are faddish and have been advertised and marketed well. Educational programs are expensive, however, and should not be undertaken unless a demonstrated need exists.

In addition to developing rationale for educational programs, the use of an assessment plan will be helpful in meeting learner needs. The sequence that should be used in developing an educational program is shown in Display 16.4.

DISPLAY 16.4	Sequence for Developing an Educational Program

1. Identify the desired knowledge or skills that the staff should have.
2. Identify the present level of knowledge or skill.
3. Determine the deficit of desired knowledge and skills.
4. Identify the resources available to meet needs.
5. Make maximum use of available resources.
6. Evaluate and test outcomes after use of resources.

EVALUATION OF STAFF DEVELOPMENT ACTIVITIES

Because staff development includes participation and involvement from many departments, it may be very difficult to control the evaluation of staff development activities effectively. It would be very easy for the personnel department, middle-level managers, and the education department to "pass the buck" among one another for accountability regarding these activities.

In addition, the evaluation of staff development must consist of more than merely having class participants fill out an evaluation form at the end of the class session, signing an employee handbook form, or assigning a preceptor for each new employee. Evaluation of staff development should include the following four criteria:

- *Learner's reaction.* How did the learner perceive the orientation, the class, the training, or the preceptor?

- *Behavior change.* What behavior change occurred as a result of the learning? Was the learning transferred? Testing someone at the end of a training or educational program does not confirm that the learning changed behavior. There needs to be some method of follow-up to observe if behavior change occurred.

- *Organizational impact.* Although it is often difficult to measure how staff development activities affect the organization, efforts should be made to measure this criterion. Examples of measurements are assessing quality of care, medication errors, accidents, quality of clinical judgment, turnover, and productivity.

- *Cost-effectiveness.* All staff development activities should be quantified in some manner. This is perhaps the most neglected aspect of accountability in staff development. All staff development activities should be evaluated for quality control, impact on the institution, and cost-effectiveness. This is true regardless of whether the education and training activities are carried out by the manager, the preceptor, the personnel department, or the education department.

LEARNING EXERCISE 16.1

Designing a Teaching Plan

You have been working in a home health agency for 3 years. During that time, the acuity of your caseload has increased dramatically, and you find that teaching home health aides has become more difficult, as the equipment they need to use has become more complex. The home health aides seem motivated to learn, but you believe that part of the difficulty lies with how you are presenting the material. Many of them have a limited knowledge of nursing procedures.

One of your clients is Mr. Jones, who has no family. His insurance company has approved a visit from a home health aide every other day to bathe him and help him ambulate with a walker. Because of his chronic severe respiratory disease, he must be ambulated with oxygen but does not need it when resting. Today, you have scheduled a session with Mr. Jones' home health aide for a demonstration and return demonstration on how to connect and disconnect the oxygen and how to use the walker. The aide is very competent in basic hygiene skills but has not always used good body mechanics when providing patient care, and she seems intimidated by new equipment.

Assignment: Using your knowledge of the learning theories presented in this chapter, construct a teaching plan for this aide. Support your plan with appropriate rationale.

SHARED RESPONSIBILITY FOR IMPLEMENTING EVIDENCE-BASED PRACTICE

Chapter 11 discussed the individual's responsibility for a professional practice that was evidenced based. However, the organization, as well as the individual, has a responsibility to promote best practices. One way that health-care organizations can demonstrate their commitment to becoming an LO is to promote and facilitate professional practice that is evidenced based, since nurses often find that barriers to evidence-based practices exist within organizations.

In discussing such organizational constraints, Prevost (2014) delineates various difficulties nurses face in their attempt to use best practices, including inadequate access to research findings and poor administrative support. Prevost suggests organizations employ the strategies shown in Display 16.5 to encourage the use of evidence-based decision making in establishing clinical best practices:

DISPLAY 16.5	Strategies for Promoting Evidence-Based Decision Making in Establishing Clinical Best Practices

- Develop and refine research-based policies and procedures.
- Build consensus from the interdisciplinary team through the development of protocols, decision trees, standards of care and institutional clinical practice guidelines, and other such mechanisms.
- Make research findings accessible through libraries and computer resources.
- Provide organization support such as time to do research and educational assistance in showing staff how to interpret research statistics and use findings.
- Encourage cooperation among professionals.
- When possible, hire nurse researchers or consultants to assist staff.

Although much progress has been made in developing research experts to collect and critique findings to adopt evidence-based practice, much still needs to be done by organizations and staff development departments. Organizational cultures often do not support the nurse who seeks out and uses research to change long-standing practices rooted in tradition (Prevost, 2014). It is the integrated leader-manager who must create and support an organizational culture that values and uses research to improve clinical practice.

Facilitating evidence-based practice is a shared responsibility of the professional nurse, the organization, leader-managers, and the education or staff development department.

SOCIALIZATION AND RESOCIALIZATION

In addition to training and educating staff, the leader-manager is also responsible for socializing employees to their roles and to the organization. This role is not limited, however, to the leader-manager; the education department, especially during orientation, other employees, and many members of an organization are also expected to assist with employee socialization. *Socialization* then refers to a learning of the behaviors that accompany each role by instruction, observation, and trial and error.

Socialization and the New Nurse

The first socialization to the nursing role occurs during nursing school and continues after graduation. Because nurse administrators and nursing faculty may hold different values and both assist in socializing the new nurse, there is potential for the new nurse to develop conflict and frustration, often termed *reality shock*. Indeed, the first year of employment is often cited as the most difficult time in a nurse's career (Martin & Wilson, 2011).

Several mechanisms do exist, however, to ease the role transition of new graduates. *Anticipatory socialization* carried out in educational settings helps prepare new nurses for their professional role. However, managers should not assume that such anticipatory socialization has occurred. Instead, they should build opportunities for sharing and clarifying values and attitudes about the nursing role into orientation programs. Use of the group process is an excellent mechanism to promote the sharing that provides support for new graduates and assists them in recovering from reality shock.

In addition, managers should be alert for signs and symptoms of role stress and *role overload* in new nurses; they should intervene by listening to these graduates and helping them to develop appropriate coping behaviors. In addition, managers must recognize the intensity of new nurses' practice experience, encourage them to have a balanced life, foster a work environment that has zero tolerance for disrespect, and strive to create work relationship models that promote interdependency of physicians and nursing staff.

Martin and Wilson (2011) go one step further; they suggest that managers must actively create a caring work environment that includes two things: helping the new RN adapt to the culture of nursing and helping them to develop the skills they need to function as a professional nurse. In their phenomenological study, Martin and Wilson found that all new graduates described aspects significant to their professional acculturation, including unrealistic expectations, a desire for perfectionism, and having to learn to work in a stressful environment. However, they also noted that caring relationships with colleagues played a role in how well they adapted to the culture of nursing, as well as the length and quality of the movement from novice to advanced beginner to competent nurse (see Examining the Evidence 16.1).

Examining the Evidence 16.1

Source: Martin, K., & Wilson, C. B. (2011). Newly registered nurses' experience in the first year of practice: A phenomenological study. International Journal For Human Caring, 15(2), 21–27.

A purposive convenience sample ($n = 7$) was chosen from newly licensed RNs who had been in practice in an acute care setting for at least 1 year, and who had participated in an intensive "transitions program," to ease new graduates into nursing practice. The transitions program was a dynamic, 2-week course that provided the newly graduated nurse with a variety of experiences to help ease the transition from nursing student to professional nurse. These experiences included interactive classroom activities on topics such as delegation, time management, conflict resolution, managing change, communication and personality styles, recognizing the art of nursing, the importance of self-care to transition into nursing practice and the opportunity to practice caring in a small group format, and skills lab activities.

Semistructured audio-taped individual interviews were conducted by the primary researcher until redundancy in data was achieved. The interview question guiding this study was, "Tell me your experience as a new nurse during your first year of practice." A seven-step process for data analysis using interpretive phenomenological inquiry was chosen as a framework for approaching the data.

Findings of the study suggested two themes that were congruent with the literary and theoretical context within which the study was situated; adapting to the culture of nursing and the development of professional responsibilities. Adapting to the culture of nursing for these novice nurses, was sometimes a treacherous journey, and their stories were congruent with Kramer's (1974) theoretical framework of reality shock. Adaptation was also linked to the level of caring experienced in the relationships developed with colleagues and interprofessional team members, such as physicians.

The second category, development of professional responsibilities, included surviving as a novice nurse, excitement in becoming an advanced beginner, and success in achieving competent practice. Again, adaptation was linked to the quality of the caring relationships experienced.

Managers should also ensure that the new nurse's values are supported and encouraged so that work and academic values can blend. New professionals need to understand the universal nature of role transition and know that it is not limited to nurses. Providing a class on role transition also may assist new graduates in socialization.

 It is important to remember that no one is immune to a loss of idealism and commitment in response to stress in the workplace.

In addition, some hospitals have developed prolonged orientation periods for new graduates that last from 6 weeks to 6 months. This extended orientation, or *internship*, contrasts sharply with the routine 2-week orientation that is normal for most other employees. During this time, graduate nurses are usually assigned to work with a preceptor and gradually take on a patient assignment equal to that of the preceptor. Even longer internships, known as *nurse residencies*, were discussed in Chapter 11.

LEARNING EXERCISE 16.2

Investigating Emotional Exhaustion in New Graduates

Talk with at least four nursing graduates who have been working as nurses for at least 3 months and no more than 3 years. Make sure at least two of them are recent graduates and two of them have been working at least 18 months. Ask them about their socialization to nursing after graduation. Did any of them experience difficulty transitioning from academe to clinical practice? If so, how long did it last? Did they recover? If so, how? Share your findings with other members of your group.

LEARNING EXERCISE 16.3

Great Influences

Who or what has been the greatest influence on your socialization to the nursing role? Were positive or negative sanctions used? Write a short essay (three or four paragraphs) describing this socialization. If appropriate, share this in a group.

Resocialization and the Experienced Nurse

Resocialization occurs when individuals are forced to learn new values, skills, attitudes, and social rules as a result of changes in the type of work they do, the scope of responsibility they hold, or in the work setting itself. Individuals who frequently need resocialization include experienced nurses who change work settings, either within the same organization or in a new organization; and nurses who undertake new roles.

For example, the *transition from expert to novice* is very difficult. Many nurses transfer or change jobs because they no longer find their present job challenging. However, this results in the need to assume a learning role in their new environment. The employee assigned to orient the nurse in role transition should be aware of the difficulties that this nurse will experience. Transferred employees' lack of knowledge in the new area should never be belittled; and whenever possible, the special expertise they bring from their former work area should be acknowledged and utilized.

Another transition that is difficult is from the *familiar to the unfamiliar*. In new positions, employees must not only learn new job skills, they typically must work in an unfamiliar environment. Special orientation materials should be developed and made available in departments to which nurses transfer more often than others. In addition to providing necessary staff development content, these orientation programs should focus on efforts to promote the self-esteem of these nurses as they learn the skills necessary for their new role.

The managers of departments that receive frequent transfers should prepare a special orientation for experienced nurses transferring to the department.

Transitioning into a new job would result in less role strain if programs were designed to facilitate role modification and role expansion. For example, when a nurse transfers from a medical floor to labor and delivery, the nurse does not know the group norms, is unsure of expected values and behaviors, and goes from being an expert to being a novice. All of this creates a great deal of *role strain*. This same type of *role stress* occurs when experienced nurses move from one organization to another or from an inpatient setting to a community setting. Often, nurses feel powerless during role transitions, which may culminate in anger and frustration as they seek socialization to a different role.

Programs to assist nurses with the transition to a new position should do more than just provide an orientation to the new position; they also should address specific values and behaviors necessary for the new roles. The values and attitudes expected in a hospice nursing role may be quite different from those expected of a trauma nurse. Managers should not assume that the experienced nurse is aware of the new role's expected attitudes.

In addition, employees adopting new values often experience role strain and managers need to support employees during this value resocialization. Members of the reference group may use negative sanctions, saying things like, "Well, we don't believe in doing that here." This can make new, experienced employees feel as though the values held in other nursing roles were bad or wrong. Therefore, the manager should make efforts to see that formerly held values are not belittled. Excellent companies have leaders who take responsibility for shaping the values of new employees. By instilling and clarifying organizational values, managers promote a homogeneous staff that functions as a team.

Values and attitudes may be a source of conflict as nurses learn new roles.

The Socialization and Orientation of New Managers

Probably, no other aspect of an employee's work life has as great an influence on productivity and retention as the quality of supervision exhibited by the immediate manager. Unfortunately, the orientation and socialization of new managers is often neglected by organizations. In addition, many restructured hospital organizational designs have created different and expanded roles for existing managers without ensuring that managers are adequately prepared for these new roles.

There is a growing recognition that good managers do not emerge from the workforce without a great deal of conscious planning on the part of the organization.

A management development program should be ongoing, and individuals should receive some management development instruction before their appointment to a management position. When an individual is filling a position where the previous manager is still available for orientation, the orientation period should be relatively short. The previous manager usually spends no longer than 1 week working directly with the new manager, especially when the new manager is familiar with the organization. A short orientation by the outgoing manager allows the newly appointed manager to gain control of the unit quickly and establish his or her own management style. If the new manager has been recruited from outside the organization, the orientation period may need to be extended.

Frequently, a new manager will be appointed to a vacant or newly established position. In either case, no one will be readily available to orient the new manager. In such cases, the new manager's immediate superior appoints someone to assist the new manager in learning the role. This could be a manager from another unit, the manager's supervisor, or someone from the unit who is familiar with the manager's duties and roles.

A new manager's orientation does not cease after the short introduction to the various tasks. Every new manager needs guidance, direction, and continued orientation and development during the first year in this new role. This direction comes from several sources in the organization:

- *The new manager's immediate superior.* This could be the unit supervisor if the new manager is a charge nurse, or it could be the chief nursing executive if the new manager is a unit supervisor. The immediate superior should have regularly scheduled sessions with the new manager to continue the ongoing orientation process.

- *A group of the new manager's peers.* There should be a management group in the organization with which the new manager can consult. The new manager should be encouraged to use the group as a resource.

- *A mentor.* If someone in the organization decides to mentor the new manager, it will undoubtedly benefit the organization. Although mentors cannot be assigned, the organization can encourage experienced managers to seek out individuals to mentor.

Clinical nurses who have recently assumed management roles often experience guilt when they decrease their involvement with direct patient care. When employees and physicians see a nurse-manager assuming the role of caregiver, they often make disparaging remarks such as, "Oh, you're working as a real nurse today." This tends to reinforce the nurse's value conflict in the new role.

Nurses moving into positions of increased responsibility also experience role stress created by *role ambiguity* and role overload. Role ambiguity describes the stress that occurs when job expectations are unclear. *Role overload*, often a major stress for nurse-managers, occurs when the demands of the role are excessive. In addition, as nurses move into positions with increased status, their job descriptions may become more general. Therefore, clarifying job roles becomes an important tool in the resocialization process.

Socializing International Nurses

One solution to nursing shortages has been the active recruitment of nurses from overseas. Huston (2014c) suggests that the ethical obligation to the foreign nurse does not end with his or her arrival in a new country. Instead, the sponsoring country must do whatever it can to see that the migrant nurse is assimilated into the new work environment as well as the new culture.

For example, language skills are often a significant issue for foreign nurses and this is made even more challenging by the use of American slang and the shorthand abbreviations that are a common part of nursing. Differing interpretations of nonverbal behavior may further cloud the picture. In addition, foreign-born nurses may find it difficult to fit into a unit's organization culture and thus fail to establish a sense of community life within the organization. Finally, many foreign nurses experience cultural, professional, and psychological dissonance that is associated with anxiety, homesickness, and isolation.

Newton, Pillay, and Higginbottom (2012) agree, noting that although most foreign nurses relocate for improved income and professional status, these overwhelmingly erode upon relocation. Instead the internationally educated nurse experiences cultural displacement as a consequence of communication and language differences, feelings of being an outsider, and differences in nursing programs. The end result is a deskilling process and discrimination that further hinders transition and demoralizes many of these nurses (Newton et al., 2012).

Bae (2011) notes that the challenges these foreign nurses face affect not only their adaptation experiences but also their retention and the quality of patient care. International nurses who have successfully adapted to their host cultures are more satisfied with their jobs, have a better quality of life, and stay longer in their jobs; therefore, it is important for them to have adequate support and assistance in their adaptation to the host country (Bae, 2011).

Clarifying Role Expectations Through Role Models, Preceptors, and Mentors

One additional strategy for promoting both socialization and resocialization as well as the clarification of role expectations is the use of role models, preceptors, and mentors. Webster's New World College Dictionary (2010) defines a *role model* as someone who is unusually effective or inspiring in some social role, job, etc., and thus serves as a model for others. Role models in nursing are experienced, competent employees. The relationship between the new employee and the role model, however, is a passive one (i.e., employees see that role models are skilled and attempt to emulate them, but the role model does not actively seek this emulation). One of the exciting aspects of role models is their cumulative effect. The greater the number of excellent role models available for new employees to emulate, the greater the possibilities for new employees to perform well.

A *preceptor* is an experienced nurse who provides knowledge and emotional support, as well as a clarification of role expectations, on a one-to-one basis. An effective preceptor can role model and adjust teaching to each learner as needed. Occasionally, however, the fit between a preceptor and preceptee is not good. This risk is lower if preceptors willingly seek out this responsibility and if they have attended educational courses outlining preceptor duties and responsibilities. In addition, preceptors need to have an adequate knowledge of adult learning theory.

Organizations that use preceptors to help new employees clarify their roles and improve their skill level should be careful not to overuse preceptors to the point that they become tired or demotivated. In addition, workload assignments for the preceptor should be decreased whenever possible so that adequate time can be devoted to helping the preceptee problem solve and learn. Incentive pay for preceptors reinforces that the organization values this role.

Finally, most organizations can avoid many of the potential hazards of preceptorship programs by (a) carefully selecting the preceptors, (b) selecting only preceptors who have a strong desire to be role models, (c) preparing preceptors for their role by giving formal classes in adult learning and other social learning concepts, and (d) having either experienced staff development or supervisory personnel monitor the preceptor and preceptee closely to ensure that the relationship continues to be beneficial and growth producing for both.

LEARNING EXERCISE 16.4

Criteria for Preceptorship

You have been selected to represent your unit on a committee to design a preceptor program for your department. One of the committee's first goals is to develop criteria for selecting preceptors.

Assignment: In groups, select a minimum of five and a maximum of eight criteria that would be appropriate for selecting preceptors on your unit. Would you have minimum education or experience requirements? What personality or behavioral traits would you seek? Which of the criteria that you identified are measurable?

LEARNING EXERCISE 16.5

The First-Time Preceptor

You are a new graduate nurse in your first job as a staff nurse on an oncology unit. You have been assigned to orient with Steve, an experienced RN and longtime employee on the unit. This is, however, Steve's first experience as a preceptor.

Steve is an expert clinician and you marvel at how expert his assessments are and how intuitive his nursing diagnoses seem to be. Steve is a role model for you in terms of being an expert clinical nurse.

Steve, however, seems to have difficulty teaching in the preceptor role. He accomplishes his work quickly and often, without explanation—even though you are at his side. He is also resistant to allowing you to practice many of the basic skills and tasks you are qualified to do, suggesting instead that you should just watch him do it and learn by shadowing. When you question Steve about this practice, he reassures you that he believes you are competent and that you will be a good nurse, but states that he does not yet feel comfortable in "letting you do things on your own."

You are becoming increasingly frustrated with this preceptorship and worry that you are not getting the experience you will need to autonomously function as a registered nurse when your orientation ends in 6 weeks. Yet you also value the opportunity to work so closely with such a skilled clinician and wonderful role model.

Assignment: Determine what you will do. What goals are driving your decision? What are the potential risks and benefits inherent in your plan?

Mentors take on an even greater role in using education as a means for role clarification. Madison (2014) describes mentoring as a distinctive interactive relationship between two individuals, occurring most commonly in a professional setting. Although some individuals use the terms *preceptor* and *mentor* interchangeably, this is not the case. For example, preceptors are usually assigned, but true mentors freely choose who they will mentor. The mentor makes a conscious decision to assist the protégé in attaining expert status and in furthering his or her career. Preceptors have a relatively short relationship with the person to whom they have been assigned, but the relationship between the mentor and mentee is longer and more intense.

Schira (2007) as summarized by Madison (2014) describes typical phases in mentoring relationships. The first phase includes finding and connecting with a more experienced person in the workplace. A mentoring relationship can be established when a "chemistry" is present that fosters reciprocal trust and openness. The second phase includes teaching, modeling, and insider knowledge that fosters a sense of competence and confidence. The intensity of the relationship can escalate to high levels during this learning, listening, and sharing phase. The third phase includes a sense of change and growth as the mentoring relationship begins to move to a conclusion. The intensity wanes as the mentee begins to move toward independence. The last stage finds both the mentee and the mentor achieving a different, independent relationship, hopefully based on positive, collegial characteristics. Display 16.6 depicts these stages of the mentoring relationship.

A mentor, as no other, is able to instill the values and attitudes that accompany each role. This is because mentors lead by example. A mentor's strong moral and ethical fiber encourages mentees to think critically and take a stand on ethical dilemmas in the workplace. Becoming a mentor requires committing to a personal relationship. It also requires teaching skills and a genuine interest and belief in the capabilities of others. A mentor may have

DISPLAY 16.6 **Stages of the Mentoring Relationship**

1. Finding and connecting
2. Learning and listening
3. Changing and shifting
4. Mentoring others

Source: Schira, M. (2007). Leadership: A peak and perk of professional development. Nephrology Nursing Journal: Journal of the American Nephrology Nurses' Association, 34(3), 289–294.

various roles in the mentor–mentee relationship. The mentor is often a role model and a visionary for the mentee. Mentors may also open doors in the organization, be someone who the mentee can use to bounce ideas off, or be a supporter or problem solver. The mentor is often a teacher or counselor, especially in career advice. Last, Madison (2014) states that the relationship is both intense and caring.

Not every nurse will be fortunate to have a mentor to facilitate each new career role. Most nurses will be lucky if they have one or two mentors throughout their lifetimes.

OVERCOMING MOTIVATIONAL DEFICIENCIES

Sometimes, difficulties in socialization or resocialization occur because of motivational deficiencies. A planned program should be implemented to correct the deficiencies by using positive and negative sanctions.

Positive Sanctions

Positive sanctions can be used as an interactional or educational process of socialization. If deliberately planned, they become educational. However, sanctions given informally through the group process or reference group, use the social interaction process. The reference group sets norms of behavior and then applies sanctions to ensure that new members adopt the group norms before acceptance into the group. These informal sanctions offer an extremely powerful tool for socialization and resocialization in the workplace. Managers should become aware of what role behavior they reward and what new employee behavior the senior staff is rewarding.

Negative Sanctions

Negative sanctions, like rewards, provide cues that enable people to evaluate their performance consciously and to modify behavior when needed. For positive or negative sanctions to be effective, they must result in the role learner internalizing the values of the organization.

Negative sanctions are often applied in very subtle and covert ways. Making fun of a new graduate's awkwardness with certain skills or belittling a new employee's desire to use nursing care plans is a very effective negative sanction that may be used by group members to mold individual behavior to group norms. This is not to say that negative sanctions should never be used. New employees should be told when their behavior is not an acceptable part of their role. However, the sanctions used should be constructive and not destructive.

The manager should know what the group norms are, be observant of sanctions used by the group to make newcomers conform, and intervene if group norms are not appropriate.

COACHING AS A TEACHING STRATEGY

Coaching as a means to develop and train employees is a teaching strategy rather than a learning theory. Coaching is one of the most important tools for empowering subordinates, changing behavior, and developing a cohesive team. It is perhaps the most difficult role for a manager to master. *Coaching* is one person helping the other to reach an optimum level of performance. The emphasis is always on assisting the employee to recognize greater options, to clarify statements, and to grow.

Coaching may be long term or short term. *Short-term coaching* is effective as a teaching tool, for assisting with socialization, and for dealing with short-term problems. *Long-term coaching* as a tool for career management and in dealing with disciplinary problems is different and is discussed in other chapters. Short-term coaching frequently involves spontaneous teaching opportunities. Learning Exercise 16.6 is an example of how a manager can use short-term coaching to guide an employee in a new role.

LEARNING EXERCISE 16.6

Paul's Complaint

Paul is the charge nurse on a surgical floor from 3 PM to 11 PM. One day, he comes to work a few minutes early, as he occasionally does, so that he can chat with his supervisor, Mary, before taking patient reports. Usually, Mary is in her office around this time. Paul enjoys talking over some of his work-related management problems with her because he is fairly new in the charge nurse role, having been appointed 3 months ago. Today, he asks Mary if she can spare a minute to discuss a personnel problem.

Paul: Sally is becoming a real problem to me. She is taking long break times and has not followed through on several medication order changes lately.

Mary: What do you mean by "long breaks" and not following through?

Paul: In the last 2 months, she has taken an extra 15 minutes for dinner three nights a week and has missed changes in medication orders eight times.

Mary: Have you spoken to Sally?

Paul: Yes, and she said that she had been an RN on this floor for 4 years, and no one had ever criticized her before. I checked her personnel record, and there is no mention of those particular problems, but her performance appraisals have only been mediocre.

Mary: What do you recommend doing about Sally?

Paul: I could tell her that I won't tolerate her extended dinner breaks and her poor work performance.

Mary: What are you prepared to do if her performance does not improve?

Paul: I could give her a written warning notice and eventually fire her if her work remains below standard.

Mary: Well, that is one option. What are some other options available to you? Do you think that Sally really understands your expectations? Do you feel that she might resent you?

Paul: I suppose I should sit down with Sally and explain exactly what my expectations are. Since my appointment to charge nurse, I've talked with all the new nurses as they have come on shift, but I just assumed that the old-timers knew what was expected on this unit. I've been a little anxious about my new role; I never thought about her resenting my position.

(Continued)

Mary: I think that is a good first option. Maybe Sally interpreted your not talking with her, as you did all the new nurses, as a rejection. After you have another talk with her, let me know how things are going.

Analysis: The supervisor has coached Paul toward a more appropriate option as a first choice in solving this problem. Although Mary's choice of questions and guidance assisted Paul, she never "took over" or directed Paul but instead let him find his own better solution. As a result of this conversation, Paul had a series of individual meetings with all his staff and shared with them his expectations. He also enlisted their assistance in his efforts to have the shift run smoothly. Although he began to see an improvement in Sally's performance, he realized that she was a marginal employee who would need a great deal of coaching. He reported back to Mary and outlined his plans for improving Sally's performance further. Mary reinforced Paul's handling of the problem by complimenting his actions.

MEETING THE EDUCATIONAL NEEDS OF A CULTURALLY DIVERSE STAFF

In the 21st century, nurse-leaders should expect to work with a more diverse workforce. According to Huston (2014b), there are three main types of diversity in the workforce: ethnicity, gender, and generational. Creating an organization that celebrates a diverse workforce rather than merely tolerating it is a leadership role and requires well-planned learning activities. There should also be sufficient opportunity for small groups so that personnel can begin recognizing their own biases and prejudices.

Heterogeneity of staff in a teaching–learning setting may add strength or create difficulty. Factors such as gender, age, English language proficiency, and culture may affect success and cooperative learning of groups. Although meeting the educational needs of a heterogeneous staff may be more time consuming and beset with communication challenges, the educational needs must be met. The ability of all nurses to work well with a culturally diverse staff is essential. Managers should respect cultural diversity and recognize the desirability of having nurses from numerous cultures on their staff.

Education staff should be aware that learners with diverse learning styles and cultural backgrounds may perceive both the classroom and instruction different from learners who have never experienced a culture different from that of the mainstream United States. Managers should also consider older nurses' learning styles and preceptor needs. Older nurses often learn best in a different manner than do new graduates and respond well to sharing anecdotal case histories. In addition, whether teaching in a classroom or at the bedside, there are several things that staff development personnel can do to facilitate the learning process, such as giving the learner plenty of time to respond to questions and restating information that is not understood.

LEARNING EXERCISE 16.7

Cultural Considerations in Teaching

You are the evening charge nurse for a large surgical unit. Recently, your longtime and extremely capable unit clerk retired, and the manager of the unit replaced the clerk with 23-year-old Nan, who does not have a health-care background and is a recent immigrant. She speaks English with an accent but can be easily understood. She is intelligent but is shy and unassertive.

Nan received a 2-week unit clerk orientation that consisted of actual classroom time and working directly with the retiring clerk. She has been functioning on her own for 2 weeks, and you realize that her orientation was insufficient. Last evening, after her 10th mistake, you became rather sharp with her, and she broke down in tears.

You are frustrated by this situation. Your unit is very busy in the evening with returning surgeries and surgeons making rounds and leaving a multitude of orders. On the other hand, you believe that Nan has great potential. You realize that there is much to learn in this job and, for a person without a health-care background, that learning the terminology, physicians' names, and unit routine is difficult. You spend the morning devising a training plan for Nan.

Assignment: Using your knowledge of learning theories, explain your teaching plan, and support your plan with appropriate rationale. How might Nan's lack of an American education and socialization influence her learning?

INTEGRATING LEADERSHIP AND MANAGEMENT IN TEAM BUILDING THROUGH SOCIALIZING AND EDUCATING STAFF IN A LEARNING ORGANIZATION

The new momentum in organizations is toward team building and providing a continual supportive learning environment. Health-care science and technology change so rapidly that without adequate teaching–learning skills and educational services, organizations will be left behind. Likewise, it has become obvious in the new millennium that teams, rather than individuals, function more efficiently. Learning together and for the organization makes the sum of the team more important than the individual and the workplace becomes more productive when there is team compatibility.

The integrated leader-manager knows that a well-planned and well-implemented staff development program is an important part of being an LO. The leader-manager accepts the ultimate responsibility for staff development and uses appropriate teaching theories to assist with teaching and training staff. In addition, he or she shares the responsibility for assessing educational needs, educational quality, and fiscal accountability of all staff development activities.

The integrated leader-manager is also one who encourages continuous learning from all individuals in the organization and is a role model of the lifelong learner. This is especially important in promoting evidence-based nursing practice. The nurse-leader should use evidence-based practice and make research resources available to the staff. He or she understands that by building and supporting a knowledgeable team, the collective knowledge generated will be greater than any single individual's contribution.

There is perhaps no other part of management, however, that has as great an influence on reducing burnout as successfully socializing new employees to the values of the organization. Socialization, a critical component of introducing the employee into the organization, is a complex process directed at the acquisition of appropriate attitudes, cognition, emotions, values, motivations, skills, knowledge, and social patterns necessary to cope with the social and professional environment. It differs from and has a greater impact than either induction or orientation on subsequent productivity and retention. It can also help build loyalty and team spirit. This is the time to instill the employee with pride in the organization and the unit. This type of affective learning becomes the foundation for subsequent increased satisfaction and motivation.

As part of socialization, the integrated leader-manager supports employees during difficult role transitions. Mentoring and role modeling are encouraged, and role expectations are clarified. The manager recognizes that employees who are not supported and socialized to the organization will not develop the loyalty necessary in the competitive marketplace. Leaders understand that creating a positive work environment where there is interdisciplinary respect will assist employees in their role transitions.

Finally, the manager ensures that resources for staff development are used wisely. A focus of staff development should be keeping staff updated with new knowledge and ascertaining that all personnel remain competent to perform their roles. By integrating the leadership role with the management functions of staff development, the manager is able to collaborate with education personnel and others so that the learning needs of unit employees are met.

KEY CONCEPTS

- The philosophy of LOs is the concept that collective learning goes beyond the boundaries of individual learning and releases gains for both the individual and the organization.

- The leader is a role model of the lifelong learner.

- Training and education are important parts of staff development.

- All staff development activities should be evaluated for quality control and fiscal accountability.

- There is a shared responsibility for the promotion of evidence-based nursing practice.

- Managers and education department staff have a shared responsibility for the education and training of staff.

- Theories of learning and principles of teaching must be considered if staff development activities are to be successful.

- Social learning theory suggests that people learn most behavior by direct experience and observation.

- The socialization of people into roles occurs with all professions and is a normal sociological process.

- Socialization and resocialization are often neglected areas of the indoctrination process.

- New graduates, international nurses, new managers, and experienced nurses in new roles have unique socialization needs.

- Difficulties with resocialization usually centers on unclear role expectations (role ambiguity), an inability to meet job demands, or deficiencies in motivation. Role strain and role overload contribute to the problem.

- The terms role model, preceptor, and mentor are not synonymous, and all play an important role in assisting with the socialization of employees.

- People from different cultures and age groups may have different socialization and learning needs.

ADDITIONAL LEARNING EXERCISES AND APPLICATIONS

LEARNING EXERCISE 16.8

Accepting Additional Responsibility

You are an experienced staff nurse on an inpatient specialty unit. Today, a local nursing school instructor approaches you and asks if you would be willing to become a preceptor for a nursing student as part of his 10-week leadership–management clinical rotation. The instructor relays that there will be no instructor on site and that the student has had only minimal exposure to acute care clinical skills. The student will have to work very closely with you on a one-to-one basis. The school of nursing can offer no pay for this role, but the instructor states that she would be happy to write a thank you letter for your personnel file and that she would be available at any time to address questions that might arise.

The unit does not reduce workload for preceptors, although credit for service is given on the annual performance review. The unit supervisor states that the choice is yours but warns that you may also be called upon to assist with the orientation of a nurse who will transfer to the unit in 6 weeks time. You have mixed feelings about whether to accept this role. Although you enjoy having students on the unit and being in the teaching role, you are unsure if you can do both your normal, heavy workload and give this student and the new employee the time that they will undoubtedly need to learn. You do feel a "need to give back to your profession" and personally believe that nurses need to be more supportive of each other, but you are significantly concerned about role overload.

Assignment: Decide if you will accept this role. Would you place any constraints upon the instructor, the student, the new employee, or your supervisor as a condition of accepting the role? What were the strongest driving forces for your decision? What were the greatest restraining forces? What evaluation criteria would you develop to assess whether your final decision was a good one?

LEARNING EXERCISE 16.9

Addressing Resocialization Issues

You are one of the care coordinators for a home health agency. One of your duties is to orient new employees to the agency. Recently, the chief nursing executive hired Brian, an experienced acute care nurse, to be one of your team members. Brian seemed eager and enthusiastic. He confided in you that he was tired of acute care and wanted to be more involved with long-term patient and family caseloads.

During Brian's orientation, you became aware that his clinical skills were excellent, but his therapeutic communication skills were inferior to those of the rest of your staff. You discussed this with Brian and explained how important communication is in gaining the trust of agency patients and that trust is necessary if the needs of the patients and the goals of the agency are to be met. You referred Brian to some literature that you believed might be helpful to him.

After a 3-week orientation program, Brian began working unsupervised. It is now 4 weeks later. Recently, you received a complaint from one of the other nurses and one from a patient regarding Brian's poor communication skills. Brian seems frustrated and has not gained acceptance from the other nurses in your work group. You suspect that some of the nurses resent Brian's superior clinical skills, whereas others believe that he does not understand his new role, and they are becoming impatient with him. You are genuinely concerned that Brian does not seem to be fitting in.

Assignment: Could this problem have been prevented? Decide what you should do now. Outline a plan to resocialize Brian into his new role and make him feel like a valued part of the staff.

LEARNING EXERCISE 16.10

Effective Interpersonal Problem Solving

You have been working at Memorial Hospital for 3 months and have begun to feel fairly confident in your new role. However, one of the older nurses working on your shift constantly belittles your nursing education. Whenever you request assistance in problem solving or in learning a new skill, she says, "Didn't they teach you anything in nursing school?" Your charge nurse has given you a satisfactory 3-month evaluation, but you are becoming increasingly defensive regarding the comments of the other nurse.

Assignment: Explain how you plan to evaluate the accuracy of the older nurse's comments. Might you be contributing to the problem? How will you cope with this situation? Would you involve others? What efforts can you make to improve your relationship with this coworker?

LEARNING EXERCISE 16.11

Changing Learning Needs

Learning needs and the maturity of those in a class often influence course content and teaching methods. Look back at how your learning needs and maturity level have changed since you were a beginning nursing student. When viewed as a whole, were you and the other beginning nursing students child or adult learners? Compare Knowles's (1970) pedagogy and andragogy characteristics to determine this.

Are pedagogical teaching strategies appropriate for beginning nursing students? If so, when does the nursing student make a transition from child to adult learner? What teaching modes do you believe would be most conducive to learning for a beginning nursing student? Would this change as students progressed through the nursing program? Support your beliefs with rationale.

REFERENCES

Atherton, J. S. (2011). *Learning and teaching; Knowles' andragogy: An angle on adult learning.* Retrieved 8 June 2013, from http://www.learningandteaching .info/learning/knowlesa.htm

Bae, S. H. (2011). Organizational socialization of international nurses in the New York metropolitan area. *International Nursing Review, 59*(1), 81–87.

Bandura, A. (1977). *Social learning theory.* Englewood Cliffs, NJ: Prentice-Hall.

Cherry, K. (2013). *Social learning theory. An overview of Bandura's social learning theory.* About.com: Psychology. Retrieved June 8, 2013, from http://psychology.about.com/od/ developmentalpsychology/a/sociallearning.htm

Glaser, J., & Overhage, J. M. (2013). The role of healthcare IT: Becoming a learning organization. *Healthcare Financial Management, 67*(2), 56.

Greene, S., Reid, R., & Larson, E. (2012). Implementing the learning health system: From concept to action. *Annals of Internal Medicine, 157*(3), 207–210.

Huston, C. (2014a). Assuring provider competence through licensure, continuing education and certification. In C. Huston (Ed.), *Professional issues in nursing* (3rd ed.). Philadelphia, PA: Lippincott Williams & Wilkins 292–307.

Huston, C. (2014b). Diversity in the nursing workforce. In C. Huston (Ed.), *Professional issues in nursing* (3rd ed.). Philadelphia, PA: Lippincott Williams & Wilkins 136–155.

Huston, C. (2014c). Importing foreign nurses to meet America's demand for nurses. In *Professional issues in nursing: Challenges and opportunities* (3rd ed.). Philadelphia, PA: Lippincott Williams & Wilkins 86–106.

Institute of Medicine. (2012, September). *Best care at lower cost: The path to continuously learning health care in America.* Retrieved June 8, 2013, from http://www .iom.edu/Reports/2012/Best-Care-at-Lower-Cost -The-Path-to-Continuously-Learning-Health-Care -in-America.aspx

Knowles, M. (1970). *The modern practice of adult education: Andragogy versus pedagogy.* New York, NY: Association Press.

Kramer, M. (1974). *Reality shock: Why nurses leave nursing.* St. Louis, MO: CV Mosby.

Madison, J. (2014). Socialization and mentoring. In C. Huston (Ed.), *Professional issues in nursing* (3rd ed.). Philadelphia, PA: Lippincott Williams & Wilkins 121–135.

Martin, K., & Wilson, C. B. (2011). Newly registered nurses' experience in the first year of practice: A phenomenological study. *International Journal For Human Caring, 15*(2), 21–27.

Newton, S., Pillay, J., & Higginbottom, G. (2012). The migration and transitioning experiences of internationally educated nurses: A global perspective. *Journal of Nursing Management, 20*(4), 534–550.

Prevost, S. S. (2014). Defining evidence-based best practices. In C. Huston (Ed.), *Professional issues in nursing* (3rd ed.). Philadelphia, PA: Lippincott Williams & Wilkins 18–29.

Schira, M. (2007). Leadership: A peak and perk of professional development. *Nephrology Nursing Journal: Journal of the American Nephrology Nurses' Association, 34*(3), 289–294.

Senge, P. (1994). *The fifth discipline: The art and practice of the learning organization.* New York, NY: Currency Doubleday.

Webster's New World College Dictionary. (2010). As cited in *Your Dictionary*. Wiley Publishing, Cleveland, Ohio. *Role model: Definition.* Used by arrangement with John Wiley & Sons, Inc. Retrieved June 8, 2013, from http://www .yourdictionary.com/role-model

17

Staffing Needs and Scheduling Policies

... the accurate definition and quantification of the work of nursing is critical to the identification of appropriate nursing resource requirements.

–Graf, Millar, Feilteau, Coakley, and Erickson

... for nurses, staffing is everything. It determines patient care, their own physical, emotional and mental well being, the nature of their workplace, and whether or not they'll choose to stay in the profession.

–QuadraMed Corporation (2013)

CROSSWALK THIS CHAPTER ADDRESSES:

BSN Essential II: Basic organizational and systems leadership for quality care and patient safety
BSN Essential IV: Information management and application of patient care technology
BSN Essential VI: Interprofessional communication and collaboration for improving patient health outcomes
BSN Essential V: Health-care policy, finance, and regulatory environments
MSN Essential II: Organizational and systems leadership
MSN Essential III: Quality improvement and safety
MSN Essential V: Informatics and health-care technologies
QSEN Competency: Patient-centered care
QSEN Competency: Teamwork and collaboration
QSEN Competency: Quality improvement
QSEN Competency: Safety
QSEN Competency: Informatics
AONE Nurse Executive Competency I: Communication and relationship building
AONE Nurse Executive Competency II: A knowledge of the health-care environment
AONE Nurse Executive Competency III: Leadership
AONE Nurse Executive Competency IV: Professionalism
AONE Nurse Executive Competency V: Business skills

LEARNING OBJECTIVES *The learner will:*

- use an evidence-based approach in determining staffing needs
- differentiate between centralized and decentralized staffing, citing the advantages and disadvantages of each
- identify organizational variables that impact the numbers of staff needed to carry out the goals of the organization
- use standardized patient classification formulas to determine staffing needs based on patient acuity
- calculate nursing care hours per patient-day if given total hours of care in a 24-hour period as well as the patient census
- accurately use staffing formulas to avoid over- and understaffing

- explain the relationship of flex time and self-scheduling to increased job satisfaction
- identify the driving and restraining forces for the implementation of mandatory minimum staffing ratios in acute care hospitals
- provide examples of how generational (the veteran generation, baby boomers, generation X, and generation Y) values differences may impact staffing and scheduling needs and wants
- recognize the need for workforce diversity to meet the unique cultural and linguistic needs represented in the patient populations served
- select appropriate staffing policies for a given situation
- discuss the minimum written staffing and scheduling policies an agency should have

In addition to selecting, developing, and socializing staff, managers must be certain that adequate numbers and an appropriate mix of personnel are available to meet unit needs and organizational goals. These staffing determinations should be based on existing research evidence that correlates staffing mix, numbers of staff needed, and patient outcomes.

In addition, because staffing patterns and scheduling policies directly affect the daily lives of all personnel, they must be administered fairly as well as economically. This chapter examines different methods for determining staffing needs, communicating staffing plans, and developing and communicating scheduling policies. In addition, unit fiscal responsibility for staffing is discussed, with sample formulas and instructions for calculating daily staffing needs.

The manager's responsibility for adequate and well-communicated staffing and scheduling policies is stressed, as is the need for periodic reevaluation of staffing philosophy to meet stated care delivery. There is a focus on the leadership responsibility for developing trust through fair staffing and scheduling procedures. Existing and proposed legislation regarding mandatory staffing requirements is also discussed, including the manager's role for ensuring that the organization can facilitate the changes required by law. The leadership roles and management functions inherent in staffing and scheduling are shown in Display 17.1.

| DISPLAY 17.1 | Leadership Roles and Management Functions Associated with Staffing and Scheduling |

LEADERSHIP ROLES

1. Identifies creative and flexible staffing methods to meet the needs of patients, staff, and the organization.
2. Is knowledgeable regarding contemporary methods and tools used in staffing and scheduling.
3. Assumes a responsibility toward staffing that builds trust and encourages a team approach.
4. Role models the use of evidence in making appropriate staffing and scheduling decisions.
5. Is alert to extraneous factors that have an impact on unit and organizational staffing.
6. Is ethically accountable to patients and employees for adequate and safe staffing.
7. Encourages diversity of thought, gender, age, and culture in nursing staffing.
8. Proactively plans for staffing shortages so that patient care goals will be met.
9. Communicates work schedules as well as scheduling policies clearly and effectively to staff.
10. Assesses if and how workforce intergenerational values impact staffing needs and responds accordingly.

MANAGEMENT FUNCTIONS

1. Provides adequate staffing to meet patient care needs according to the philosophy of the organization and evidence-based needs.
2. Uses organizational goals and patient classification tools to minimize understaffing and overstaffing as patient census and acuity fluctuate.
3. Schedules staff in a fiscally responsible manner.
4. Periodically examines the unit standard of productivity to determine if changes are needed.

(Continued)

5. Ascertains that scheduling policies are not in violation of state and national labor laws, organizational policies, or union contracts.
6. Assumes accountability for quality and fiscal control of staffing.
7. Evaluates scheduling and staffing procedures and policies on a regular basis.
8. Develops and implements fair and uniform scheduling policies and communicates these clearly to all staff.
9. Selects acuity-based staffing tools that reduce subjectivity and promote objectivity in patient acuity determinations.

UNIT MANAGER'S RESPONSIBILITIES IN MEETING STAFFING NEEDS

The requirement for night, evening, weekend, and holiday work that is frequently necessary in health-care organizations can be stressful and frustrating. Managers should do what they can to see that employees feel they have some control over scheduling, shift options, and staffing policies. Each organization has different expectations regarding the unit manager's responsibility in long-range human resource planning and in short-range planning for daily staffing. Although many organizations now use staffing clerks and computers to assist with staffing, the overall responsibility for scheduling continues to be an important function of first- and middle-level managers.

CENTRALIZED AND DECENTRALIZED STAFFING

Some organizations decentralize staffing by having unit managers make scheduling decisions. Other organizations use *centralized staffing*, where staffing decisions are made by personnel in a central office or staffing center. Such centers may or may not be staffed by registered nurses (RNs), although someone in authority would be a nurse even when a staffing clerk carries out the day-to-day activity.

In organizations with *decentralized staffing*, the unit manager is often responsible for covering all scheduled staff absences, reducing staff during periods of decreased patient census or acuity, adding staff during periods of high patient census or acuity, preparing monthly unit schedules, and preparing holiday and vacation schedules. Nursing management is highly decentralized in most hospitals, with considerable variation found in staffing among patient care units.

Advantages of decentralized staffing are that the unit manager understands the needs of the unit and staff intimately, which leads to the increased likelihood that sound staffing decisions will be made. In addition, the staff feels more in control of their work environment because they are able to take personal scheduling requests directly to their immediate supervisor. Decentralized scheduling and staffing also lead to increased autonomy and flexibility, thus decreasing nurse attrition.

Decentralized staffing, however, carries the risk that employees will be treated unequally or inconsistently. In addition, the unit manager may be viewed as granting rewards or punishments through the staffing schedule. Decentralized staffing also is time consuming for the manager and often promotes more "special pleading" than centralized staffing. However, undoubtedly, the major difficulty with decentralized staffing is ensuring high-quality staffing decisions throughout the organization.

In centralized staffing, the manager's role is limited to making minor adjustments and providing input. For example, the manager would communicate special staffing needs and assist with obtaining staff coverage for illness and sudden changes in patient census. Therefore, the manager in centralized staffing continues to have ultimate responsibility for seeing that adequate personnel are available to meet the needs of the organization.

Centralized staffing is generally fairer to all employees because policies tend to be employed more consistently and impartially. In addition, centralized staffing frees the middle-level manager to complete other management functions. Centralized staffing also allows for the most efficient (cost-effective) use of resources because the more units that can be considered together, the easier it is to deal with variations in patient census and staffing needs. Centralized staffing, however, does not provide as much flexibility for the worker, nor can it account as well for a worker's desires or special needs. In addition, managers may be less responsive to personnel budget control if they have limited responsibility in scheduling and staffing matters. The strengths and limitations of decentralized and centralized staffing are summarized in Display 17.2.

DISPLAY 17.2	Strengths and Limitations of Decentralized and Centralized Staffing	
	Strengths	**Limitations**
Decentralized Staffing	✓ Manager retains greater control over unit staffing ✓ Staff are able to take requests directly to their manager ✓ Provides greater autonomy and flexibility for individual staff member	✓ Can result in more special pleading and arbitrary treatment of employees ✓ May not be cost-effective for organization since staffing needs are not viewed holistically ✓ More time consuming for the unit manager
Centralized Staffing	✓ Provides organization-wide view of staffing needs, which encourages optimal utilization of staffing resources ✓ Staffing policies tend to be employed more consistently and impartially ✓ More cost-effective than decentralized staffing ✓ Frees the middle-level manager to complete other management functions	✓ Provides less flexibility for the worker and may not account for a specific worker's desires or special needs ✓ Managers may be less responsive to personnel budget control in scheduling and staffing matters

It is important, though, to remember that centralized and decentralized staffing are not synonymous with centralized and decentralized decision making. For example, a manager can work in an organization that has centralized staffing but decentralized organizational decision making. Regardless of whether the organization has centralized or decentralized staffing, all unit managers should understand scheduling options and procedures and accept fiscal responsibility for staffing.

Decentralized scheduling and staffing lead to increased autonomy and flexibility but centralized staffing is fairer to all employees because policies tend to be employed more consistently and impartially.

COMPLYING WITH STAFFING MANDATES

As the current health-care system is evaluated, nurse-managers must be cognizant of new recommendations and legislation affecting staffing. Many states in the United States, with the backing of professional nursing organizations, have moved toward imposing mandatory licensed staffing requirements, and one state (California) has enacted legislation requiring mandatory staffing ratios that affect hospitals and long-term care facilities. In fact, as of 2013, 15 states (CA, CT, IL, ME, MN, NJ, NV, NY, NC, OH, OR, RI, TX, VT, and WA) plus the District of Columbia had enacted legislation and/or adopted regulations addressing nurse staffing (American Nurses Association [ANA], 2013).

Under Assembly Bill 394, passed in 1999 and crafted by the California Nurses Association, all hospitals in California had to comply with the minimum staffing ratios shown in Display 17.2 by January 1, 2004 (National Nurses United, 2010–2013), with subsequent modifications following in the next few years (also shown in Display 17.3). These ratios, developed by the California Department of Health Services, represent the maximum number of patients an RN can be assigned to care for under any circumstance.

DISPLAY 17.3	Minimum Staffing Ratios for Hospitals in California January 2004 and January 2008	

Unit	Minimum Nurse–Patient Ratio January 2004	Minimum Nurse–Patient Ratio January 2008
Critical care/ICU	1:2	1:2
Neonatal ICU	1:2	1:2
Operating room	1:1	1:1
Labor and delivery	1:2	1:2
Antepartum	1:4	1:4
Postpartum couplets	1:4	1:4
Postpartum women only	1:6	1:6
Pediatrics	1:4	1:4
Step-down	1:4	1:3
Medical–surgical	1:6	1:5
Oncology (initial)	1:5	1:4
Psychiatry	1:6	1:6
Emergency department	1:4	1:4
Telemetry and specialty units	1:5	1:4

Source: National Nurses United (2010–2013). RN to patient ratios. Retrieved June 9, 2013, from http://www.nationalnursesunited.org/page/-/files/pdf/ratios/basics-unit-0704.pdf

Proponents of legislated minimum staffing ratios say that ratios are needed because many hospitals' current staffing levels are so low that both RNs and their patients are negatively affected (Huston, 2014a). In addition, numerous articles have appeared in the media attesting to grossly inadequate staffing in hospitals and nursing homes, and professional nursing organizations such as the American Nurses Association have expressed concern about the effect poor staffing has on nurses' health and safety and on patient outcomes. Adequate staffing, then, is needed to ensure that care provided is at least safe and hopefully more. Proponents also suggest that such ratios protect the most basic elements of the public health we take for granted and argue that the government must take on this responsibility to ensure that safe health care is provided to all Americans (Huston, 2014a).

However, there are arguments against staffing ratios. Huston (2014a) notes that the current nursing shortage makes it difficult to fill the slots when ratios exist, and the ratios may merely serve as a Band-Aid to the greater problems of quality of care. In addition, numbers alone do not ensure improved patient care, as not all RNs have equivalent clinical experience and skill levels. There is also the argument that staffing may actually decline with ratios since they might be used as the ceiling or as ironclad criteria if institutions are not willing to make adjustments for patient acuity or RN skill level.

In addition, some critics suggest that mandatory staffing ratios create significant opportunity costs that may restrict employers and payers from responding to market forces; subsequently, they may be unable to take advantage of improved technological support or respond to changes in patient acuity. In addition, mandatory staffing ratios may cause conflicts between nurses and hospitals that might otherwise not exist.

The bottom line, however, is that minimum staffing ratios would not have been proposed in the first place had staffing abuses and the resultant declines in the quality of patient care not occurred. The implementation and subsequent evaluation of mandatory staffing ratios in states having such ratios should provide greater insight into the ongoing debate about the need for mandatory staffing ratios.

Minimum staffing ratios would not have been proposed in the first place had staffing abuses and the resultant declines in the quality of patient care not occurred.

LEARNING EXERCISE 17.1

Comparing Staffing Ratios

Many states are currently considering the adoption of minimum staffing legislation, and as such are closely monitoring the outcomes in states that have already taken such action.

Assignment: Compare the current staffing ratios used at the facility in which you work or do clinical practicums with those shown in Display 17.3. How do they compare? Is there an effort to legislate minimum staffing ratios in the state in which you live? Who or what would you anticipate to be the greatest barrier to implementation of staffing ratios in your state?

STAFFING AND SCHEDULING OPTIONS

Because it is beyond the scope of this book to discuss all of the creative staffing and scheduling options available, only a few are discussed here. Some of the more frequently used creative staffing and scheduling options are shown in Display 17.4.

There are advantages and disadvantages to each type. Twelve-hour shifts have become commonplace in acute care hospitals even though there continues to be debate about whether extending the length of shifts results in increased judgment errors related to fatigue. In their review of the literature, Geiger-Brown and Trinkoff (2010) found that nurses working 12-hour

DISPLAY 17.4   Common Staffing and Scheduling Options in Health-Care Organizations

- 10- or 12-hour shifts.
- Premium pay for weekend work.
- Part-time staffing pool for weekend shifts and holidays.
- Cyclical staffing, which allows long-term knowledge of future work schedules because a set staffing pattern is repeated every few weeks. Figure 17.1 shows a master staffing pattern that repeats every 4 weeks.
- Job sharing.
- Allowing nurses to exchange hours of work among themselves.
- Flextime.
- Use of supplemental staffing from outside registries and float pools.
- Staff self-scheduling.
- Shift bidding, which allows nurses to bid for shifts rather than requiring mandatory overtime.

(Continued)

Position	Name	Week I S	M	T	W	T	F	S	Week II S	M	T	W	T	F	S	Week III S	M	T	W	T	F	S	Week IV S	M	T	W	T	F	S
Full-time	RN 1				X		X		X					X					X		X		X						X	
Full-time	RN 2	X					X				X			X		X				X					X			X		X
Full-time	RN 3			X				X	X				X			X			X			X	X				X			
Full-time	RN 4	X				X					X				X	X				X					X					X
Full-time	RN 5				X		X		X					X					X		X		X						X	
Full-time	RN 6	X				X					X				X	X				X					X					X
Full-time	RN 7		X					X	X				X			X			X			X	X				X			
Full-time	RN 8	X					X				X				X	X				X					X					X
Part-time	8 hr/wk RN 9	On												On	On														On
Part-time	8 hr/wk RN 10						On	On												On	On								
Part-time	8 hr/wk RN 11	On												On	On														On
Part-time	8 hr/wk RN 12						On	On												On	On								
Total RNs on duty each day		6	7	7	6	6	6	6	6	7	7	6	6	6	6	6	7	7	6	6	6	6	6	7	6	7	6	6	6

Elements: Every other weekend off   Number of split days off each period: 2   X: Scheduled day off
Maximum days worked: 4   Operates in multiples of 4, 8, 12 . . .
Minimum days worked: 2   Schedule repeats itself every 4 weeks

FIGURE 17.1 • Four-week cycle master time sheet. Copyright ® 2006 Lippincott Williams & Wilkins. Instructor's Resource CD-ROM to Accompany Leadership Roles and Management Functions in Nursing, by Bessie L. Marquis and Carol J. Huston.

shifts experienced an increase in patient care errors; needlestick injuries; musculoskeletal disorders, involving their neck, shoulder, and back; fatigue; and drowsy driving as a result of sleep deprivation.

The Georgia Nurses Association (2012) agrees, suggesting that 12-hour shifts may cause undue stress and fatigue in health-care workers and that this is especially true in older workers. For this reason, many organizations often limit the number of consecutive 10- or 12-hour days a nurse can work or the number of hours that can be worked in a given day.

Yet, many nurses report a higher level of satisfaction with this staffing option since they work less days each week and have more consecutive time for leisure and personal obligations. In addition, some agencies pay overtime for any shift over 8 hours while others do not. Extended work shifts also provide a solution for difficulties with child care, as they reduce the number of working days. Estryn-Béhar and Van der Heijden (2012) suggest that while these extended shifts seem to be an answer to work/family conflicts for nurses, the risk of health and quality of care has been highly underestimated with 10- and 12-hour shifts leading to higher rates of burnout, mistakes, and worse health for the nurse (Examining the Evidence 17.1).

Examining the Evidence 17.1

Source: Estryn-Béhar, M., & Van der Heijden, B. I. (2012). Effects of extended work shifts on employee fatigue, health, satisfaction, work/family balance, and patient safety. Work, 41, 4283–4290.

The objective of this study was to perform a secondary analysis of a large European data base, collected in 2003, in order to determine the effect of work schedule on these three parameters (work/family balance, health, and safety), after adjustment for various risk factors. A survey regarding work schedule was sent to 77,681 nurses in three types of health-care institutions; hospitals ($N =147$), nursing homes ($N = 185$), and home care institutions ($N = 76$). The response rate was 51.7% ($N = 39,898$). Adequate data were obtained from 25,924 to complete a multivariate analysis, including 20 explanatory variables simultaneously.

The study found that nurses working 12-hour shifts during the night reported being satisfied with working time for their private life. On the other hand, nurses working alternating shifts and 10-hour shifts at night reported more difficulties with their private and family life. Nurses working 12-hour shifts during the day and those working alternating shifts reported more interruptions and disturbances in the job, high quantitative demand, and high physical load.

Health status in nurses working 10- or 12-hour shifts was worse than nurses who worked 8-hour shifts. They also reported feeling more tired, had lower quality and quantity of sleep, were more afraid of making mistakes, and had higher burnout scores. Thus, while nurses often chose night shifts or 12-hour shifts in order to reduce their work/home conflicts, it was at the expense of their own health and safety.

In addition, the researchers noted that there are legitimate concerns about the safety of the employee and the patient in an extended work hour environment. Shifts exceeding 8 hours do carry an increased risk of accidents with the risk after 12 hours being about twice that of 8 hours.

The researchers concluded that although the implementation of 12-hour shifts seems to be an answer to work/family conflicts for nurses, and, as such, responds to recruitment problems for managers, the risk of health and quality of care has been highly underestimated. They suggest that organizations develop measures such as extended child care, allowing naps during night shifts, and reduction of changing shifts at short notice.

Another increasingly common staffing and scheduling alternative is the use of supplemental nursing staff such as *agency nurses* and *travel nurses*. These nurses are usually directly employed by an external nursing broker and work for premium pay (often two to three times that of a regularly employed staff nurse), without benefits. While such staff provide scheduling relief, especially in response to unanticipated increases in census or patient acuity, their continuous use is expensive and can result in poor continuity of nursing care.

Some hospitals have created their own internal supplemental staff by hiring per diem employees and creating *float pools*. *Per diem* staff generally have the flexibility to choose if and when they want to work. In exchange for this flexibility, they receive a higher rate of pay but usually no benefits.

Float pools are generally composed of employees who agree to cross-train on multiple units so that they can work additional hours during periods of high census or worker shortages. Float pools are adequate for filling intermittent staffing holes but, like agency or registry staff, they are not an answer to the ongoing need to alter staffing according to census since they result in a lack of staff continuity. In addition, many staff feel uncomfortable with floating if they have not been adequately oriented to the new unit. Float staff must be able to perform the core competencies of the unit they are floating to meet their legal and moral obligations as caregivers.

 Float staff must be able to perform the core competencies of the unit they are floating to meet their legal and moral obligations as caregivers.

LEARNING EXERCISE 17.2

Choosing 8- or 12-Hour Shifts

You are the manager of an intensive care unit. Many of the nurses have approached you requesting 12-hour shifts. Other nurses have approached you stating that they will transfer out of the unit if 12-hour shifts are implemented. You are exploring the feasibility and cost-effectiveness

(Continued)

of using both 8- and 12-hour shifts so that staff could select which type of scheduling they wanted.

Assignment: Would this create a scheduling nightmare? Will you limit the number of 12-hour shifts that staff could work in a week? Would you pay overtime for the last 4 hours of the 12-hour shift? Would you allow staff to choose freely between 8- and 12-hour shifts? What other problems may result from mixing 8- and 12-hour shifts?

Some organizations have made an effort to meet the needs of a diverse workforce by using flextime and self-scheduling. *Flextime* is a system that allows employees to select the time schedules that best meet their personal needs while still meeting work responsibilities. In the past, most flextime has been possible only for nurses in roles that did not require continuous coverage. However, staff nurses recently have been able to take part in a flextime system through prescheduled shift start times. Variable start times may be longer or shorter than the normal 8-hour workday. When a hospital uses flextime, units have employees coming and leaving the unit at many different times. Although flextime staffing creates greater employee choices, it may be difficult for the manager to coordinate and could easily result in overstaffing or understaffing.

Self-scheduling allows nurses in a unit to work together to construct their own schedules rather than have schedules created by management. With self-scheduling, employees typically are given 4- to 6-week schedule worksheets to fill out several weeks in advance of when the schedule is to begin. The nurse-manager then reviews the worksheet to make sure that all guidelines or requirements have been met. Although self-scheduling offers nurses greater control over their work environment, it is not easy to implement. Success depends on the leadership skills of the manager to support the staff and demonstrate patience and perseverance throughout the implementation.

One of the newer methods of reducing staff shortages and also allowing nurses some control over scheduling extra shifts and to reduce mandatory overtime is *shift bidding*. In most organizations that use shift bidding, the organization sets the opening price for a shift. For example, this may be at a higher rate of pay than the hourly wage of some nurses, and nurses may bid down the price in order to be assigned the overtime shift. Generally, organizations will choose the nurse with the lowest bid to work the shift, but some organizations may deny bids to nurses who work too much overtime (Huston, 2014b).

Obviously, all scheduling and staffing patterns, from traditional to creative, have shortcomings. Therefore, any changes in current policies should be evaluated carefully as they are implemented. Because all scheduling and staffing patterns have a heavy impact on employees' personal lives, productivity, and budgets, it is wise to have a 6-month trial of new staffing and scheduling changes, with an evaluation at the end of that time to determine the impact on financial costs, retention, productivity, risk management, and employee and patient satisfaction.

LEARNING EXERCISE 17.3

Self-Scheduling Holiday Dilemma

You graduated last year from your nursing program and were excited to obtain the job that you wanted most. The unit where you work has a very progressive supervisor who believes in empowering the nursing staff. Approximately 6 months ago, after considerable instruction, the unit began self-scheduling. You have enjoyed the freedom and control that this has given you over your work hours. There have been some minor difficulties among staff, and occasionally the unit was slightly overstaffed or understaffed. However, overall, the self-scheduling has seemed to work well.

Today (September 15), you come to work on the 3 PM to 11 PM shift after 2 days off and see that the schedule for the upcoming Thanksgiving and Christmas holiday period has been posted, and many of the staff have already scheduled their days on and their days off. When you take a close look, it appears that no one has signed up to work Christmas Eve, Thanksgiving Day, or Christmas Day. You are very concerned, because self-scheduling includes responsibility for adequate coverage. There are still a few nurses, including yourself, who have not added their days to the schedule, but even if all of the remaining nurses work all three holidays, it will provide only scant coverage.

Assignment: What leadership role (if any) should you take in solving this dilemma? Should you ignore the problem and schedule yourself for only one holiday and let your supervisor deal with the issue? Remember, you are a new nurse, both in experience and on this unit. List the options for decision making available to you and, using rationale to support your decision, plan a course of action.

WORKLOAD MEASUREMENT TOOLS

Requirements for staffing are based on whatever standard unit of measurement for productivity is used in a given unit. A formula for calculating *nursing care hours per patient-day* (NCH/ PPD) is reviewed in Figure 17.2. This is the simplest formula in use and continues to be used widely. In this formula, all nursing and ancillary staff are treated equally for determining hours of nursing care, and no differentiation is made for differing acuity levels of patients. These two factors alone may result in an incomplete or even inaccurate picture of nursing care needs, and the use of NCH/PPD as a workload measurement tool may be too restrictive, since it may not represent the reality of today's inpatient care setting, where staffing fluctuates not only among shifts but within shifts as well.

As a result, *patient classification systems* (PCSs), also known as *workload management*, or *patient acuity tools*, were developed in the 1960s. Oakes (2012) suggests that patient acuity systems provide the language nurses need to make their work visible at all levels of their organization. QuadraMed Corporation (2013) goes one step further in suggesting that achieving the optimum balance between nurse staffing and patient acuity is key to a health-care organization's financial viability.

A PCS groups patients according to specific characteristics that measure acuity of illness in an effort to determine both the number and mix of the staff needed to adequately care for those patients. Because other variables within the system have an impact on NCH, it is usually not possible to transfer a PCS from one facility to another. Instead, each basic classification system must be modified to fit a specific institution.

$$\text{NCH/PPD} = \frac{\text{Nursing Hours Worked in 24 Hours}}{\text{Patient Census}}$$

FIGURE 17.2 • Standard formula for calculating nursing care hours (NCH) per patient-day (PPD). Copyright ® 2006 Lippincott Williams & Wilkins. Instructor's Resource CD-ROM to Accompany Leadership Roles and Management Functions in Nursing, by Bessie L. Marquis and Carol J. Huston.

PCSs are institution specific and must be modified to reflect the unique staff and patient population of each health-care organization.

There are several types of PCS measurement tools. The *critical indicator* PCS uses broad indicators such as bathing, diet, intravenous fluids and medications, and positioning to categorize patient care activities. The *summative task* type requires the nurse to note the frequency of occurrence of specific activities, treatments, and procedures for each patient. For example, a summative task–type PCS might ask the nurse whether a patient required nursing time for teaching, elimination, or hygiene. Both types of PCSs are generally filled out prior to each shift, although the summative task type typically has more items to fill out than the critical incident or criterion type.

Once an appropriate PCS is adopted, hours of nursing care must be assigned for each patient classification. Although an appropriate number of hours of care for each classification is generally suggested by companies marketing PCSs, each institution is unique and must determine to what degree that classification system must be adapted for that institution. QuadraMed Corporation (2013) notes the primary purpose of the acuity system is to have subjectivity give way to objective data. With this data, organizations can staff according to documented need rather than perceived convenience, decreasing distrust, fostering collaboration, and moving finance and patient management toward a common goal.

In addition, Oakes (2012) stresses the importance of organizations correctly interpreting the acuity data. When robust data inform planning, forecasting, and decision making, organizations can better understand how nursing workloads contribute to financial efficiency and productivity. "Most importantly, nurses have the capacity, via an acuity tool, to become key informers of organizational planning and to demonstrate how much work is required, the type of work and when it will be required" (Oakes 2012, p. 11).

It is important though to remember that staffing according to a PCS does not always mean that staffing is adequate or that it will be perceived as adequate. Indeed, it is not uncommon to have staffing perceived as adequate one day and considered inadequate the next day, even if there are the same number of patients and staff.

It is not uncommon to have staffing perceived as adequate one day and considered inadequate the next day, even if there are the same number of patients and staff.

It is clear that PCSs will not solve all staffing problems, as all systems have special features and faults as well. Although such systems provide a better definition of problems, it is up to people in the organization to make judgments and use the information obtained by the system appropriately to solve staffing problems. A sample classification system is illustrated in Table 17.1.

In addition, the middle-level manager must be alert to internal or external forces affecting unit needs that may not be reflected in the organization's patient care classification system. Examples of such forces could be a sudden increase in nursing or medical students using the unit, a lower skill level of new graduates, or cultural and language difficulties of recently hired foreign nurses. The organization's classification system may prove to be inaccurate, or the hours allotted for each category or classification of patient may be inaccurate (too high or too low). This does not imply that unit managers should not be held accountable for the standard unit of measurement; rather, they must be cognizant of justifiable reasons for variations.

Some futurists have suggested that eventually *workload measurement systems* may replace acuity-based staffing systems or that the two will be used as a hybrid tool for determining staffing needs. Workload measurement is a technique that evaluates work performance as well as necessary resource levels. Therefore, it goes beyond patient diagnosis or acuity level and

TABLE 17.1	Patient Care Classification Using Four Levels of Nursing Care Intensity			
Area of Care	*Category 1*	*Category 2*	*Category 3*	*Category 4*
Eating	Feeds self or needs little food	Needs some help in preparing food tray; may need encouragement	Cannot feed self but is able to chew and swallow	Cannot feed self and may have difficulty swallowing
Grooming	Almost entirely self-sufficient	Needs some help in bathing, oral hygiene, hair combing, and so forth	Unable to do much for self	Completely dependent
Excretion	Up and to bathroom alone or almost alone	Needs some help in getting up to bathroom or using urinal	In bed, needs bedpan or urinal placed; may be able to partially turn or lift self	Completely dependent
Comfort	Self-sufficient	Needs some help with adjusting position or bed (e.g., tubes and IVs)	Cannot turn without help, get drink, adjust position of extremities, and so forth	Completely dependent
General health	Good—for diagnostic procedure, simple treatment, or surgical procedure (D&C, biopsy, and minor fracture)	Mild symptoms—more than one mild illness, mild debility, mild emotional reaction, and mild incontinence (not more than once per shift)	Acute symptoms—severe emotional reaction to illness or surgery, more than one acute illness, medical or surgical problem, severe or frequent incontinence	Critically ill—may have severe emotional reaction
Treatments	Simple—supervised ambulation, dangle, simple dressing, test procedure preparation not requiring medication, reinforcement of surgical dressing, x-pad, vital signs once per shift	Any category 1 treatment more than once per shift, Foley catheter care, I&O; bladder irrigations, sitz bath, compresses, test procedures requiring medications or follow-ups, simple enema for evacuation, vital signs every 4 hours	Any treatment more than twice per shift, medicated IVs, complicated dressings, sterile procedures, care of tracheostomy, Harris flush, suctioning, tube feeding, vital signs more than every 4 hours	Any elaborate or delicate procedure requiring two nurses, vital signs more often than every 2 hours
Medications	Simple, routine, not needing preevaluation or postevaluation; medications no more than once per shift	Diabetic, cardiac, hypotensive, hypertensive, diuretic, anticoagulant medications, prn medications, more than once per shift, medications needing preevaluation or postevaluation	High amount of category 2 medications; control of refractory diabetes (need to be monitored more than every 4 hours)	Extensive category 3 medications; IVs with frequent, close observation and regulation

(Continued)

TABLE 17.1 Patient Care Classification Using Four Levels of Nursing Care Intensity *(Continued)*

Area of Care	Category 1	Category 2	Category 3	Category 4
Teaching and emotional support	Routine follow-up teaching; patients with no unusual or adverse emotional reactions	Initial teaching of care of ostomies; new diabetics; tubes that will be in place for periods of time; conditions requiring major change in eating, living, or excretory practices; patients with mild adverse reactions to their illness (e.g., depression and overly demanding)	More intensive category 2 items; teaching of apprehensive or mildly resistive patients; care of moderately upset or apprehensive patients; confused or disoriented patients	Teaching of resistive patients, care and support of patients with severe emotional reaction

examines the specific number of care hours needed to meet a given population's care needs. Thus, workload measurement systems typically capture census data, care hours, patient acuity, and patient activities. While complicated, workload measurement systems do hold promise for more accurately predicting the nursing resources needed to staff hospitals effectively.

Regardless of the workload measurement tool used (NCH/PPD, PCS, workload measurement system, etc.), the units of workload measurement need to be reviewed periodically and adjusted as necessary. This is both a leadership role and a management responsibility.

LEARNING EXERCISE 17.4

Calculating Staffing Needs

You use a PCS to assist you with your daily staffing needs. The following are the hours of nursing care needed for each acuity level patient per shift:

	Category I Acuity Level	Category II Acuity Level	Category III Acuity Level	Category IV Acuity Level
NCH/PPD needed for day shift	2.3	2.9	3.4	4.6
NCH/PPD needed for PM shift	2.0	2.3	2.8	3.4
NCH/PPD needed for night shift	0.5	1.0	2.0	2.8

When you came on duty this morning, you had the following patients:

One patient in category I acuity level
Two patients in category II acuity level
Three patients in category III acuity level
One patient in category IV acuity level

Note that you must be overstaffed or understaffed by more than half of the hours a person is working to reduce or add staff. For example, for nurses working 8-hour shifts, the staffing must be over or under more than 4 hours to delete or add staff.

Assignment: Calculate your staffing needs for the day shift. You have on duty one RN and one licensed vocational nurse (LVN)/licensed professional nurse (LPN) working 8-hour shifts and a ward clerk for 4 hours. Are you understaffed or overstaffed?

If you had the same number of patients but the acuity levels were the following, would your staffing needs be the same?

  Two patients in category I acuity level
  Three patients in category II acuity level
  Two patients in category III acuity level
  Zero patients in category IV acuity level

THE RELATIONSHIP BETWEEN NURSING CARE HOURS, STAFFING MIX, AND QUALITY OF CARE

It is difficult to pick up a nursing journal today that does not have at least one article that speaks to the relationship between NCH, staffing mix, quality of care, and patient outcomes. This has occurred in response to the "restructuring" and "reengineering" boom that occurred in many acute care hospitals in the 1990s. Restructuring and reengineering was done to reduce costs, increase efficiency, decrease waste and duplication, and reshape the way that care was delivered (Huston, 2014c).

Given that health care is labor intensive, cost cutting under restructuring and reengineering often included staffing models that reduced RN representation in the staffing mix and increased the use of unlicensed assistive personnel (UAP). This fairly rapid and dramatic shift in both RN care hours and staffing mix provided fertile ground for comparative studies that examined the relationship between NCH, staffing mix, and patient outcomes.

Although early research on NCH, staffing mix, and patient outcomes lacked standardization in terms of tools used and measures examined, nationwide attention shifted to this issue and a plethora of better-funded and more-rigorous scientific study followed. For example, Needleman et al. (2011), Aiken et al. (2010), and McHugh (2013) suggest that as the numbers of staff increase, the number of adverse events, mortality, and readmission decrease.

The right staffing mix matters as well, as demonstrated by a year-long, multi-institution research project that examined the impact of staffing on nurse-sensitive patient outcomes. This study found that higher use of agency, float pool, or overtime nursing hours correlated with higher patient fall rates (QuadraMed Corporation, 2012). Indeed, a review of the current literature generally suggests that as RN hours decrease in NCH/PPD, adverse patient outcomes generally increase, including increased errors and patient falls as well as decreased patient satisfaction (Huston, 2014b).

However, in 2009, the California HealthCare Foundation released a report on the California ratios that found no change in the average length of patient stay or any significant reduction in certain nursing-sensitive adverse events as the result of minimum staffing ratio implementation (Domrose, 2010). While there is a great deal of speculation as to why the anticipated improvements did not occur, the study concluded there was no evidence that mandated ratios improved patient outcomes. Staffing levels then should be considered to be important—though not the only—factor in safe patient care (Domrose). In addition, it is important to remember that "it takes a lot of data and years of data to do the kind of analysis that demonstrates whether or not a policy works" (McHugh as cited in Domrose 2010, p. 27).

Staffing levels should be considered an important–though not the only–factor in safe patient care

Unit managers must understand the effect that major restructuring and redesign have on their staffing and scheduling policies as well. As new practice models are introduced, there must be a simultaneous examination of the existing staff mix and patient care assessments to ensure that appropriate changes are made in staffing and scheduling policies.

For example, decreasing licensed staff, increasing numbers of UAP, and developing new practice models have a tremendous impact on patient care assignment methods. Past practices of relying on part-time staff, responding to staff preferences for work, and providing a variety of shift lengths and shift rotations may no longer be enough. Administrative practices also have saved money in the past by sending people home when there was low census; they have also floated them to other areas to cover other unit needs, not scheduled staff for consecutive shifts because of staff preferences, and had scheduling policies that were unreasonably accommodating. Finally, patient assignments in the past were often made without attention to patient continuity and were assigned by numbers rather than workload. Some of these past practices benefited staff, and some benefited the organization, but few of them benefited the patient. Indeed, assigning a different nurse to care for a patient each day of an already reduced length of stay may contribute to negative patient outcomes.

Therefore, an honest appraisal of current staffing, scheduling, and assignment policies is needed at the same time that organizations are restructured and new practice models are engineered. Changing these policies often has far-reaching consequences, but this must be done for new models of care to be successfully implemented. For example, if primary nursing is to be effective, then nurses must work a number of successive days with a client to ensure that there is time to formulate and evaluate a plan of care. In this example, floating policies and requests for days off may need to be changed or modified to fit the philosophy of primary nursing care delivery.

Determining an appropriate skill mix depends on the patient care setting, acuity of patients, and other factors. There is no national standard to determine whether staffing decisions are suitable for a given setting. In addition, many of the tools and methods used to determine staffing have been unreliable and invalid, either in their development or their application. However, some formulas allow for adjustment for variations in the skill mix of staff. These formulas are still relatively new but may be a better tool to use when making staffing decisions. Having an adequate number of knowledgeable, trained nurses is imperative to attaining desired patient outcomes.

MANAGING A DIVERSE STAFF

Managers must also be cognizant of the need to have an ethnically and culturally diverse staff to meet the needs of an increasingly diverse patient population. Indeed, national standards for providing culturally and linguistically appropriate services in health care were released by the US Department of Health and Human Services (2013) Office of Minority Health. Of the 15 standards put forth, several directly address the need for cultural and linguistic diversity in staffing. For example, Standard 5 requires that health-care organizations offer language assistance services, including bilingual staff and interpreter services, at no cost to clients with limited English proficiency. Standard 7 ensures the competency of this language assistance by interpreters and bilingual staff and Standard 6 requires that all verbal offers and written notices regarding patients' access to these services be available to patients in their preferred languages.

Managers must clearly understand the unique cultural and linguistic needs represented in their patient population and try to address these needs through an appropriately diverse staff.

GENERATIONAL CONSIDERATIONS FOR STAFFING

In addition to ethnic and cultural diversity, managers must be alert to how generational diversity may impact staffing needs. Stokowski (2013) notes that social scientists maintain that this is the first time in history that four generations of nurses have worked together. In previous years, earlier retirement from nursing and shorter life spans kept the workforce to three generations.

Some researchers suggest that the different generations represented in nursing today have different value systems that may impact staffing (Display 17.5). For example, most experts identify four generational groups in today's workforce; the veteran generation (also called the silent generation or the traditionalist), the baby boomers, generation X, and generation Y (also called the Millennials).

DISPLAY 17.5	Generational Work Groups
Generation	**Year of Birth**
Silent generation or veteran generation	1925 to 1942
Baby boomer or boom	1943 to early 1960s
Generation X	Early 1960s to early 1980s
Generation Y	Early 80s to 2000

The *veteran generation* is typically recognized as those nurses born between 1925 and 1942. Currently, about 5% of employed nurses belong to this age group (Stokowski, 2013). Having lived through several international military conflicts (World War II, the Korean War, and Vietnam) and the Great Depression, they are often risk averse (particularly regarding personal finances), respectful of authority, supportive of hierarchy, and disciplined (Patterson, 2007). They are also called the *silent generation* because they tend to support the status quo rather than protest or push for rapid change. As a result, these nurses are less likely to question organizational practices and more likely to seek employment in structured settings. Their work values are traditional and they are often recognized for their loyalty to their employers.

The *boom generation* (born 1943 to 1960), representing 40% of the current workforce (Stokowski, 2013), also displays traditional work values; however, they tend to be more materialistic and thus are willing to work long hours at their jobs in an effort to get ahead. Indeed, this generation, which includes many of today's nursing leaders, is more apt than any other to be called "workaholics." Yet, many boomers are caring for family members from both sides. In addition, many boomers volunteer their time to advance environmental, cultural, or educational causes.

In addition, this generation of workers is often recognized as being more individualistic as a result of the "permissive parenting" many of this generation experienced growing up, and constantly being told that their future contained limitless opportunities for achievement (Patterson, 2007). This individualism often results in greater creativity and thus nurses born in this generation may be best suited for work that requires flexibility, independent thinking, and creativity. Yet, it also encourages this generation to challenge rules.

In contrast, "generation Xers" (born between 1961 and 1981), a much smaller cohort than the baby boomers who preceded them, or the generation Yers who follow them, may lack the interest in lifetime employment at one place that prior generations have valued, instead valuing greater work hour flexibility and opportunities for time off. This likely reflects the fact that many individuals born in this generation had both parents working outside their home as they were growing up and they want to put more emphasis on family and leisure time in their own family units. Thus, this generation may be less economically driven than prior generations and may define success differently than the Veteran generation or the baby boomers. They are, however, pragmatic, self-reliant, and amenable to change (Patterson, 2007). Forty percent of the RN workforce belongs to this generational cohort (Stokowski, 2013).

Generation Y, also known as the *Millennials* (born 1982 to 2000), represents the first cohort of truly global citizens. They are known for their optimism, self-confidence, relationship orientation, volunteer mindedness, and social consciousness. They are also highly sophisticated in their use of technology, which allows them to view the world as a "smaller, diverse, highly-networked environment in which to work and live" (Patterson, 2007, p. 20). This is why some people call this generation "*digital natives.*" Generation Y currently represents only 15% of the nursing workforce, but this number will increase rapidly over the coming decade (Stokowski, 2013).

Generation Y, however, may demand a different type of organizational culture to meet their needs. In fact, generation Y nurses may test the patience of their baby-boomer leaders since they may appear to be brash or inpatient and often come with a sense of entitlement that can be an affront to older workers. On the other hand, generation Y is known to work together well in teams, exhibit a high degree of altruism, have a higher ecoawareness, and far greater multicultural ease than their older coworkers.

Mensik (2007) suggests that although generational diversity poses new management challenges, it also provides a variety of perspectives and outlooks that enhance workplace balance and productivity. She suggests that the literature often focuses on differences and negative attributes between the generations, particularly for generations X and Y and that a balanced view is needed. For example, the literature repeatedly suggests that generations X and Y may have less loyalty to their employers than the generations who preceded them, but Mensik cites current research, which suggests that their commitment to employment longevity is actually greater than the boomers who precede them.

Mensik (2007) concludes that instead of focusing on generational differences, nurses should move forward and put their energies into seeking collaboration between the generations. In addition, patients should benefit from the optimal outcomes that should occur when all generations of the workforce can work together as a higher performing team. Anderson (2013) agrees, suggesting that diversity of generations leads to diversity of thought which can be very valuable to the nurse-manager, staff nurses, and ultimately patients.

Generational diversity, like cultural diversity, should be viewed as a strength in the workforce.

THE IMPACT OF NURSING STAFF SHORTAGES UPON STAFFING

As discussed in Chapter 15, shortages of nurses have always occurred periodically, whether nationally, regionally, or locally. It has been difficult for the profession as a whole to accurately predict exactly when and where there will be a short supply of professional nurses, but all nurse-managers will at some time face a short supply of staff—both RNs and others.

Health-care organizations have used many solutions to combat this problem. Such things as advanced planning and recruitment have already been discussed. Another long-term solution to a shortage of staff is *cross-training.* Cross-training involves giving personnel with varying educational backgrounds and expertise the skills necessary to take on tasks normally outside their scope of work and to move between units and function knowledgeably. These are all good solutions for long-term problem solving and show vision on the part of the leader-manager.

However, staffing shortages frequently occur on a day-to-day basis. These occur because of an increase in patient census, an unexpected increase in client needs, or an increase in staff absenteeism or illness. Health-care organizations have used many methods to deal with an unexpected short supply of staff. Chief among the solutions are closed-unit staffing, drawing from a central pool of nurses for additional staff, requesting volunteers to work extra duty, and mandatory overtime.

Closed-unit staffing occurs when the staff members on a unit make a commitment to cover all absences and needed extra help themselves in return for not being pulled from the unit in times of low census. In *mandatory overtime*, employees are forced to work additional shifts, often under threat of patient abandonment, should they refuse to do so. Some hospitals routinely use mandatory overtime in an effort to keep fewer people on the payroll.

A health-care worker who is in an exhausted state represents a risk to public health and patient safety. While mandatory overtime is neither efficient nor effective in the long term, it has an even more devastating short-term impact with regard to staff perceptions of a lack of control and its subsequent impact on mood, motivation, and productivity. Nurses who are forced to work overtime do so under the stress of competing duties—to their job, their family, their own health, and their patient's safety (Huston, 2014b). Clearly, mandatory overtime should be a last resort, not standard operating procedure because an institution does not have enough staff.

Regardless of how the manager chooses to deal with an inadequate number of staff, certain criteria must be met:

- Decisions made must meet state and federal labor laws and organizational policies.
- Staff must not be demoralized or excessively fatigued by frequent or extended overtime requests.
- Long-term as well as short-term solutions must be sought.
- Patient care must not be jeopardized.

FISCAL AND ETHICAL ACCOUNTABILITY FOR STAFFING

Regardless of inherent difficulties, PCSs and the assignment of NCH remain a method for controlling the staffing function of management. As long as managers realize that all systems have weaknesses and as long as they periodically evaluate the system, managers will be able to initiate needed change. It is crucial, however, for managers to make every effort to base unit staffing on their organization's PCS. Nursing care remains labor intensive, and the manager is fiscally accountable to the organization for appropriate staffing. Accountability for a prenegotiated budget is a management function.

Growing federal and state budget deficits has resulted in increased pressure for all health-care organizations to reduce costs. Because personnel budgets are large in health-care organizations, a small percentage cut in personnel may result in large savings. Thus, managers must increase staffing when patient acuity rises as well as decrease staffing when acuity is low; to do otherwise is demoralizing to the unit staff. It is important for managers to use staff to provide safe and effective care economically.

Fiscal accountability to the organization for staffing is not incompatible with ethical accountability to patients and staff. The manager's goal is to stay within a staffing budget *and* meet the needs of patients and staff.

Some organizations require only that managers end the fiscal year within their budgeted NCH and pay less attention to daily or weekly NCH. Shift staffing based on a patient acuity system does, however, allow for more consistent staffing and is better able to identify overstaffing and understaffing on a timelier basis. In addition, this is a fairer method of allocating staff.

The disadvantage of shift-based staffing is that it is time consuming and somewhat subjective, because acuity or classification systems leave much to be determined by the person assigning the acuity levels. The greater the degree of objectivity and accuracy in any system, the longer the time required to make staffing computations. Perhaps the greatest danger in staffing by acuity is that many organizations are unable to supply the extra staff when the system shows unit understaffing. However, the same organization may use the acuity-based staffing system to justify reducing staff on an overstaffed unit. Therefore, a staffing classification system can be demotivating if used inconsistently or incorrectly.

Employees have the right to expect a reasonable workload. Managers must ensure that adequate staffing exists to meet the needs of staff and patients. Managers who constantly expect employees to work extra shifts, stay overtime, and carry unreasonable patient assignments are not being ethically accountable.

Effective managers, however, do not focus totally on numbers of personnel but look at all components of productivity. They examine nursing duties, job descriptions, patient care organization, staffing mix, and staff competencies. Such managers also use every opportunity to build a productive and cohesive team.

Uncomplaining nursing staff have often put forth superhuman efforts during periods of short staffing simply because they believed in their supervisor and in the organization. However, just as often, the opposite has occurred: Nurses on units that were only moderately understaffed spent an inordinate amount of time and wasted energy complaining about their plight. The difference between the two examples has much to do with trust that such conditions are the exception, not the norm; that real solutions and not Band-Aid approaches to problem solving will be used to plan for the future; that management will work just as hard as the staff in meeting patient needs; and that the organization's overriding philosophy is based on patient interest and not financial gain.

DEVELOPING STAFFING AND SCHEDULING POLICIES

Nurses will be more satisfied in the workplace if staffing and scheduling policies and procedures are thoughtfully developed, fairly applied, and clearly communicated to all employees. Personnel policies represent the standard of action that is communicated in advance so that employees are not caught unaware regarding personnel matters. Written policies generally provide a means for greater consistency and fairness. In addition to being standardized, personnel policies should be written in a manner that allows some flexibility. A leadership challenge for the manager is to develop policies that focus on outcomes rather than constraints or rules that limit responsiveness to individual employee needs.

Scheduling and staffing policies should be reviewed and updated periodically. When formulating policies, management must examine its own philosophy and consider prevailing community practices. Unit-level managers will seldom have complete responsibility for formulating organizational personnel policies but should have some input as policies are reviewed. There are, however, nursing department and unit personnel policies that supervisors develop and implement.

The policies in Display 17.6 should be formalized by the manager and communicated to all personnel. To ensure that unit-level staffing policies do not conflict with higher level policies, there should be adequate input from the staff, and they should be developed in collaboration with personnel and nursing departments. For example, some states have labor laws that prohibit 12-hour shifts. Other states allow workers to sign away their rights to overtime pay for shifts greater than 8 or 12 hours. In addition, in organizations with union contracts, many staffing and scheduling policies are incorporated into the union contract. In such cases, staffing changes might need to be negotiated at the time of contract renewal.

DISPLAY 17.6 **Unit Checklist of Employee Staffing Policies**

1. Name of the person responsible for the staffing schedule and the authority of that individual if it is other than the employee's immediate supervisor
2. Type and length of staffing cycle used
3. Rotation policies, if shift rotation is used
4. Fixed shift transfer policies, if fixed shifts are used
5. Time and location of schedule posting
6. When shift begins and ends
7. Day of week schedule begins
8. Weekend off policy
9. Tardiness policy
10. Low census procedures
11. Policy for trading days off
12. Procedures for days-off requests
13. Absenteeism policies
14. Policy regarding rotating to other units
15. Procedures for vacation time requests
16. Procedures for holiday time requests
17. Procedures for resolving conflicts regarding requests for days off, holidays, or requested time off
18. Emergency request policies
19. Policies and procedures regarding requesting transfer to other units
20. Mandatory overtime policy

INTEGRATING LEADERSHIP ROLES AND MANAGEMENT FUNCTIONS IN STAFFING AND SCHEDULING

The manager is responsible for providing adequate staffing to meet patient care needs. The leader assumes an ethical accountability to patients and employees for adequate and appropriate staffing. The leader-manager then must pay attention to fluctuations in patient census and workload units to ensure that understaffing or overstaffing is minimized and to ensure fiscal accountability to the organization.

Using evidence and evidence-based tools in making these staffing decisions is critical for contemporary nurse leader-managers. Yet, Douglas (2010, p. 55) provides a reasoned counterpart in her assertion that while the call for "data driven staffing is loud and even overdue, that the approach to it must be harmonized with the human side as well." The end goal then must be the right combination of hard and soft data with the end result being "highly informed use of data and information with the understanding and wisdom necessary to achieve optimal outcomes" (Douglas 2010, p. 62).

The prudent leader-manager is also cognizant of the need to have comprehensive scheduling and staffing policies that are not only fair but also in compliance with organizational policies, union contracts, and labor laws. When possible, employees should be involved in developing these staffing and scheduling policies. This helps establish the trust needed to build team spirit when dealing with temporary staff shortages.

Unit staffing and scheduling policies should be reviewed and revised on a timely basis to reflect changes in community and national trends as well as contemporary methods of staffing and scheduling. In addition, the leader should be alert for factors that affect the standard of productivity and negotiates changes in the standard when appropriate.

The leader also looks for innovative methods to overcome staffing difficulties. Knowing that staff needs are in part related to work design, the prudent leader-manager looks for ways to redesign work to reduce staffing needs. When leadership roles are integrated with management functions, creative staffing and scheduling options can occur.

KEY CONCEPTS

- The manager has both a fiscal and an ethical duty to plan for adequate staffing to meet patient care needs.

- Innovative and creative methods of staffing and scheduling should be explored to avoid understaffing and overstaffing as patient census and acuity fluctuate.

- Staffing and scheduling policies must not violate labor laws, state or national laws, or union contracts.

- Workload measurement tools include NCH/PPD, PCS, and workload measurement systems. All workload measurement tools should be periodically reviewed to determine if they are a valid and reliable tool for measuring staffing needs in a given organization.

- Mandatory overtime should be a last resort, not standard operating procedure because an institution does not have enough staff.

- Research clearly shows that as professional nursing representation in the skill mix increases, patient outcomes generally improve and adverse incidents decline.

- Those with staffing responsibility must remain cognizant of mandatory staffing ratios and comply with such mandates.

- Managers should attempt to have a diverse staff that will meet the cultural and language needs of the patient population.

- Fair and uniform staffing and scheduling policies and procedures must be written and communicated to all staff.

- Existing staffing policies must be examined periodically to determine if they still meet the needs of the staff and the organization.

ADDITIONAL LEARNING EXERCISES AND APPLICATIONS

LEARNING EXERCISE 17.5

Implementing a New Nursing Care Delivery Model

You are serving on an ad hoc committee to examine ways to improve the continuity of patient assignments because your unit is thinking about switching from total patient care to a primary nursing care delivery model. The committee is having a difficult time formulating policies because you currently have a great number of nurses who work part-time, 2 days on and 2 days off. In addition, your unit has a census that goes up and down unexpectedly, resulting in nurses being floated out of the unit often. The committee is committed to providing continuity of care in the new patient care delivery system.

Assignment: Develop several scheduling and staffing policies that have the probability of increasing continuity of assignment and will not result in a financial liability to the unit. How will these polices be fairly executed, and do they have the potential to cause staff to leave the unit?

LEARNING EXERCISE 17.6

Making Sound Staffing Decisions

You are the staffing coordinator for a small community hospital. It is now 12:30 PM, and your staffing plan for the 3 PM to 11 PM shift must be completed no later than 1 PM. (The union contract stipulates that any "call offs" that must be done for low census must be done at least 2 hours before the shift begins; otherwise, employees will receive a minimum of 4 hours of pay.) You do, however, have the prerogative to call off staff for only half a shift (4 hours). If they are needed for the last half of the shift (7 PM to 11 PM), you must notify them by 5 PM tonight. A local outside registry is available for supplemental staff; however, their cost is two and a half times that of your regular staff, so you must use this resource sparingly. Mandatory overtime is also used but only as a last resort.

The current hospital census is 52 patients, although the ED is very busy and has 4 possible patient admissions. There are also two patients with confirmed discharge orders and three additional potential discharges on the 3 PM to 11 PM shift. All units have just submitted their PCS calculations for that shift.

You have five units to staff: the ICU, pediatrics, obstetrics (includes labor, delivery, and postpartum), medical, and surgical departments. The ICU must be staffed with a minimum of a 1:2 nurse–patient ratio. The pediatric unit is generally staffed at a 1:4 nurse–patient ratio and the medical and surgical departments at a 1:6 ratio. In obstetrics, a 1:2 ratio is used for labor and delivery, and a 1:6 ratio is used in postpartum. On reviewing the staffing, you note the following:

ICU

Census = 6. Unit capacity = 8. The PCS shows a current patient acuity level requiring 3.2 staff. One of the potential admissions in the ED is a patient who will need cardiac monitoring. One patient, however, will likely be transferred to the medical unit on 3 PM to 11 PM shift. Four RNs are assigned for that shift.

Pediatrics

Census = 8. Unit capacity = 10. The PCS shows a current acuity level requiring 2.4 staff. There are two RNs and one CNA assigned for the 3 PM to 11 PM shift. There are no anticipated discharges or transfers.

Obstetrics

Census = 6. Unit capacity = 8. Three women are in active labor, and three women are in the postpartum unit with their babies. Two RNs are assigned to the obstetrics department for the 3 PM to 11 PM shift. There are no in-house staff on that shift that have been cross-trained for this unit.

Medical Floor

Census = 19. Unit capacity = 24. The PCS shows a current acuity level requiring 4.4 staff. There are two RNs, one LVN, and two CNA assigned for the 3 PM to 11 PM shift. Three of the potential ED admissions will come to this floor. Two of the potential patient discharges are on this unit.

Surgical Floor

Census = 13. Unit capacity = 18. The PCS shows a current acuity level requiring 3.6 staff. Because of sick calls, you have only one RN and two CNAs assigned for the 3 PM to 11 PM shift. Both confirmed patient discharges as well as one of the potential discharges are from this unit.

Assignment: Answer the following questions:

1. Which units are overstaffed, and which are understaffed?

2. Of those units that are overstaffed, what will you do with the unneeded staff?

3. How will you staff units that are understaffed? Will outside registry or mandatory overtime methods be used?

4. How did staffing mix and PCS acuity levels factor into your decisions, if at all?

5. What safeguards can you build into the staffing plan for unanticipated admissions or changes in patient acuity during the shift?

LEARNING EXERCISE 17.7

Reviewing Pros and Cons of Staffing Solutions

You are serving on a committee to help resolve a chronic problem with short staffing on your unit, which is a pediatric ICU. Volunteer overtime, cross-training with the regular non–intensive care pediatric unit, and closed-unit staffing have been suggested as possible solutions.

Assignment: Make a list of the pros and cons of each of these suggestions to bring back to the committee for review. Share your list with group members.

LEARNING EXERCISE 17.8

Choosing a Delivery Care Model and Staffing Pattern

You have been hired as the unit supervisor of the new rehabilitation unit at Memorial Hospital. The hospital decentralizes the responsibility for staffing, but you must adhere to the following constraints:

1. All staff must be licensed.
2. The ratio of LVNs/LPNs to RNs is 1:1.
3. An RN must always be on duty.
4. Your budgeted NCH/PPD is 8.2.
5. You are not counted into the NCH/PPD, but ward clerks are counted.
6. Your unit capacity is seven patients, and you anticipate a daily average census of six patients.
7. You may use any mode of patient care organization.

Your patients will be chronic, not acute, but will be admitted for an active 2- to 12-week rehabilitation program. The emphasis will be in returning the patient home with adequate ability to perform activities of daily living. Many other disciplines, including occupational and physical therapy, will be part of the rehabilitation team. A waiting list for the beds is anticipated because this service is needed in your community. You anticipate that most of your patients will have had cerebrovascular accidents, spinal cord injuries, other problems with neurologic deficits, and amputations.

You have hired four full-time RNs and two part-time RNs. The part-time RNs would like to have at least 2 days of work in a 2-week pay period; in return for this work guarantee, they have agreed to cover for most sick days and vacations and some holidays for your regular RN full-time staff.

You also have hired three full-time LVNs/LPNs and two part-time LVNs/LPNs. However, the part-time LVNs/LPNs would like to work at least 3 days per week. You have decided not to hire a ward clerk but to use the pediatric ward clerk for 4 hours each day to assist with various duties. Therefore, you need to calculate the ward clerk's 4 hours into the total hours worked.

You have researched various types of patient care delivery models (Chapter 14) and staffing patterns. Your newly hired staff is willing to experiment with any type of patient care delivery model and staffing pattern that you select.

Assignment: Determine which patient care delivery model and staffing pattern you will use. Explain why and how you made your choice. Next, show a 24-hour and 7-day staffing pattern. Were you able to create a schedule that adhered to the given constraints? Was this a time-consuming process?

LEARNING EXERCISE 17.9

Floating Again

You are a new RN, having graduated just 4 months ago from nursing school. When you arrive for work tonight, you are told that because your unit is experiencing a low census, you must once again float to another unit. This is the third night in a row that you have been required to float and the last two nights were to two different units. When you question why it is your turn to float again, you are told that this is the last night you will work before having 3 days off and that it makes more sense to have you go than to have someone else who will be working the next few nights and could provide continuity of care. Another nurse says that this is the last night for her in a 7-day work stretch and that it would not be fair for her to have to float at this point. In addition, one of the nurses says she has not been cross-trained for the unit needing staff and another one says that she is there only because she swapped nights with another nurse as a personal favor and therefore should not have to float. The charge nurse recognizes your frustration but says that because the current floating policy is not clear, she had to make a decision and selected you to float. She invites you though to help her create a written floating policy that is fairer to all.

Assignment: You feel that the lack of a clearly written policy about floating resulted in arbitrary and unfair treatment and you decide to use your upcoming days off to begin work on a new policy which comprehensively covers all aspects of floating. Create such a policy. Make sure it addresses the qualifications necessary to float, as well as how floating will be determined when employee needs and arguments are conflicting. Then have your peers review your floating policy. Do they feel your policy is comprehensive? Clear? Safe? Fair?

REFERENCES

Aiken, L, Sloane, D., Cimiotti, J., Clarke, S., Flynn, L., Seago, J., … Smith, H. (2010). Implications of the California nurse staffing mandate for other states. *Health Services Research, 45*(4), 904–921.

American Nurses Association. (2013) *Safe staffing saves lives.* Retrieved June 9, 2013, from http://www .safestaffingsaveslives.org/WhatisANADoing/ StateLegislation.aspx

Anderson, L. (2013, January 31). *The nurse manager's guide to handling a multigenerational workforce.* Nurse Together. Retrieved June 11, 2013, from http://www .nursetogether.com/the-nurse-managers-guide-to -handling-a-multigenerational-workforce

Domrose, C. (2010, February 8). The sum of staffing: States consider the pros and cons of mandating RN staffing levels. *NurseWeek (West), 17*(2), 18–19.

Douglas, K. (2010, January–February). The human side of staffing. *Nursing Economic$, 28*(1), 55–57, 62.

Estryn-Béhar, M., & Van der Heijden, B. I. (2012). Effects of extended work shifts on employee fatigue, health, satisfaction, work/family balance, and patient safety. *Work, 41,* 4283–4290.

Geiger-Brown, J., & Trinkoff, A. M. (2010, March). Is it time to pull the plug on 12-hour shifts? *Journal of Nursing Administration, 40*(3), 100–102.

Georgia Nurses Association. (2012). 12-Hour Shifts and Fatigue. *Georgia Nursing, 72*(1), 7–8.

Huston, C. (2014a). Mandatory Minimum staffing ratios: Are they working? In C. Huston (Ed.), *Professional issues in nursing.* Philadelphia, PA: Lippincott Williams & Wilkins 172–187.

Huston, C. (2014b). Mandatory overtime in nursing: How much? How often? In C. Huston (Ed.), *Professional issues in nursing.* Philadelphia, PA: Lippincott Williams & Wilkins 188–200.

Huston, C. (2014c). Unlicensed assistive personnel and the registered nurse. In C. Huston (Ed.), *Professional issues in nursing.* Philadelphia, PA: Lippincott Williams & Wilkins 107–120.

McHugh, M. (2013). Hospital nursing and 30-day readmissions among medicare patients with heart failure, acute myocardial infarction, and pneumonia. *Medical Care, 51*(1), 52–59.

Mensik, J. S. (2007, November). A view on generational differences from a generation X leader. *Journal of Nursing Administration, 37*(11), 483–484.

National Nurses United. (2010–2013). *Ratio Basics.* Retrieved June 9, 2013, from http://www .nationalnursesunited.org/page/-/files/pdf/ratios/ basics-unit-0704.pdf

Needleman, J., Buerhaus, P., Pankratz, S., Leibson, C., Stevens, S., & Harris, M. (2011). Nurse staffing and inpatient hospital mortality. *The New England Journal of Medicine, 364,* 1037–1045.

Oakes, R. (2012). Matching care to patient demand. *Kai Tiaki Nursing New Zealand, 18*(11), 11.

Patterson, C. K. (2007). The impact of generational diversity in the workplace. *Diversity Factor, 15*(3), 17–22.

QuadraMed Corporation. (2012). *Nurse staffing and patient outcomes: Bridging research into evidenced-based practice.* Unpublished internal study of data from nine hospitals and 49 inpatient units.

QuadraMed Corporation. (2013). *White paper. Five reasons why CFOs should care about staffing and acuity.* Retrieved June 10, 2013, from http://www.quadramed.com/Solutions---Services/Care-Management/White-Papers/Five-Reasons-Why-CFOs-Should-Care-about-Staffing_w.aspx

Stokowski, L. A. (2013, April 11). *The 4-generation gap in nursing.* Medscape Nurses News. Retrieved June 10, 2013, from http://www.medscape.com/viewarticle/781752_2

US Department of Health and Human Services. (2013, May). *The National CLAS Standards.* Retrieved June 8, 2013, from http://minorityhealth.hhs.gov/templates/browse.aspx?lvl=2&lvlid=15

UNIT VI

Roles and Functions
in Directing

18

Creating a Motivating Climate

… how we feel about and enjoy our work is crucial to how we perceive the quality of our lives.
—Jo Manion

… whether you think you can or whether you think you can't, you're right.
—Henry Ford

CROSSWALK THIS CHAPTER ADDRESSES:

BSN Essential II: Basic organizational and systems leadership for quality care and patient safety
BSN Essential VIII: Professionalism and professional values
MSN Essential II: Organizational and systems leadership
QSEN Competency: Teamwork and collaboration
AONE Nurse Executive Competency I: Communication and relationship building
AONE Nurse Executive Competency III: Leadership
AONE Nurse Executive Competency V: Business skills

LEARNING OBJECTIVES *The learner will:*

- describe the relationship between motivation and behavior
- differentiate between intrinsic and extrinsic motivation
- recognize the need to create a work environment in which both organizational and individual needs can be met
- delineate how the work of individual motivation theorists has contributed to the understanding of what motivates individuals inside and outside the work setting
- recognize the complexity of using incentives and rewards so that they motivate rather than demotivate
- recognize the need to individualize reward systems for each subordinate
- develop strategies for creating a motivating work environment
- develop increased self-awareness about personal motivation and the need for "self-care" to remain motivated in a leadership or management role
- identify positive reinforcement techniques that may be used by a manager in an organization
- describe the constraints managers face in creating a climate that will motivate employees
- identify the organization's responsibility for effective promotions
- describe the advantages and disadvantages of promoting from within an organization versus recruiting externally for advancement opportunities

This unit reviews the fourth phase of the management process: *directing*. This phase also may be referred to as *coordinating* or *activating*. Regardless of the nomenclature, this is the "doing" phase of management, requiring the leadership and management skills necessary to accomplish the goals of the organization. Managers direct the work of their subordinates during this phase and leaders support them so they can achieve desired outcomes. Components of the directing phase discussed in this unit include creating a motivating climate, establishing organizational communication, managing conflict, facilitating collaboration, negotiating, and understanding the impact of collective bargaining and employment laws on management.

In planning and organizing, leader-managers attempt to establish an environment that is conducive to getting work done. In directing, the leader-manager sets those plans into action. This chapter focuses on creating a motivating climate as a critical element in meeting employee and organizational goals.

The amount and quality of work accomplished by managers directly reflects their motivation and that of their subordinates. Why are some managers or employees more motivated than others? How do demotivated managers affect their subordinates? What can the manager do to help the employee who is demotivated? The motivational problems frequently encountered by the manager are complex. To respond to demotivated staff, managers need an understanding of the relationship between motivation and behavior.

Motivation is the force within the individual that influences or directs behavior. Because motivation comes from within the person, managers cannot directly motivate subordinates. The leader can, however, create an environment that maximizes the development of human potential. Management support, collegial influence, and the interaction of personalities in the work group can have a synergistic effect on motivation. The leader-manager must identify those components and strengthen them in hopes of maximizing motivation at the unit level.

All human beings have needs that motivate them. The leader focuses on the needs and wants of individual workers and uses motivational strategies appropriate for each person and situation. Leaders should apply techniques, skills, and knowledge of motivational theory to help workers achieve what they want out of work. At the same time, these individual goals should complement the goals of the organization. The manager bears primary responsibility for meeting organizational goals, such as reaching acceptable levels of productivity and quality.

The leader-manager, then, must create a work environment in which both organizational and individual needs can be met. Adequate tension must be created to maintain productivity while encouraging subordinates' job satisfaction. Thus, while the worker is achieving personal goals, organizational goals are being met. This is not an easy task. The leadership roles and management functions inherent in creating such an environment are included in Display 18.1.

| DISPLAY 18.1 | Leadership Roles and Management Functions Associated with Creating a Motivating Work Climate |

LEADERSHIP ROLES

1. Recognizes each worker as a unique individual who is motivated by different things.
2. Identifies the individual and collective value system of the unit and implements a reward system that is consistent with those values.
3. Listens attentively to individual and collective work values and attitudes to identify unmet needs that can cause dissatisfaction.
4. Encourages workers to "stretch" themselves in an effort to promote self-growth and self-actualization.
5. Promotes a positive and enthusiastic image to subordinates in the clinical setting.
6. Encourages mentoring, sponsorship, and coaching with subordinates.
7. Devotes time and energy to create an environment that is supportive and encouraging to the discouraged individual.
8. Is authentic rather than automatic in giving praise and positive reinforcement.
9. Develops a unit philosophy that recognizes the unique worth of each employee and promotes reward systems that make each employee feel successful.
10. Demonstrates through actions and words a belief in subordinates that they desire to meet organizational goals.
11. Is self-aware regarding own enthusiasm for work and takes steps to remotivate self as necessary.

(Continued)

MANAGEMENT FUNCTIONS

1. Uses legitimate authority to provide formal reward systems.
2. Uses positive feedback to reward the individual employee.
3. Develops unit goals that integrate organizational and subordinate needs.
4. Maintains a unit environment that eliminates or reduces job dissatisfiers.
5. Promotes a unit environment that focuses on employee motivators.
6. Creates the tension necessary to maintain productivity while encouraging subordinate job satisfaction.
7. Clearly communicates expectations to subordinates.
8. Demonstrates and communicates sincere respect, concern, trust, and a sense of belonging to subordinates.
9. Assigns work duties commensurate with employee abilities and past performance to foster a sense of accomplishment in subordinates.
10. Identifies achievement, affiliation, or power needs of subordinates and develops appropriate motivational strategies to meet those needs.

This chapter examines motivational theories that have guided organizational efforts and resource distribution for the last 100 years. Special attention is given to the concepts of intrinsic versus extrinsic motivation and organizational motivation versus self-motivation.

INTRINSIC VERSUS EXTRINSIC MOTIVATION

Motivation involves the action people take to satisfy unmet needs. It is the willingness to put effort into achieving a goal or reward to decrease the tension caused by the need. *Intrinsic motivation* comes from within the person, driving him or her to be productive (see Display 18.2).

DISPLAY 18.2	Intrinsic and Extrinsic Motivation
Intrinsic	*Extrinsic*
Comes from within the individual	Comes from outside the individual
Often influenced by family unit and cultural values	Rewards and reinforcements are given to encourage certain behaviors and/or levels of achievement

This does not mean, however, that others cannot influence an individual's intrinsic motivation. Parents and peers, for example, often play major roles in shaping a person's values about what he or she wants to do and be. Parents who set high but attainable expectations for their children, and who constantly encourage them in a nonauthoritative environment, tend to impart strong achievement drives. Cultural background also has an impact on intrinsic motivation since some cultures value career mobility, job success, and recognition more than others.

Intrinsic motivation can be and often is impacted by others.

Rewards resulting from *extrinsic motivation* (which is motivation that is enhanced by the work environment) occur after the work has been completed. Although all people are intrinsically motivated to some degree, it is unrealistic for the organization to assume that all workers have adequate levels of intrinsic motivation to meet organizational goals. Thus, the organization must provide a climate that stimulates both extrinsic and intrinsic drives.

The intrinsic motivation to achieve is directly related to a person's level of aspiration. Extrinsic motivation is motivation enhanced by the job environment or external rewards.

LEARNING EXERCISE 18.1

Thinking About Motivation

Think back to when you were a child. What rewards did your parents use to promote good behavior? Was your behavior more intrinsically or extrinsically motivated? Were strong achievement drives encouraged and supported by your family? If you have children, what rewards do you use to influence their behavior? Are they the same rewards that your parents used? Why or why not?

Because people have constant needs and wants, they are always motivated to some extent. In addition, because all human beings are unique and have different needs, they are motivated differently. The difference in motivation can be explained in part by our large- and small-group cultures. For example, because American culture tends to value material goods and possessions more highly than many other cultures, rewards in this country are frequently tied to those values.

Because motivation is so complex, the leader faces tremendous challenges in accurately identifying individual and collective motivators.

Organizations also have cultures and values. Motivators vary among organizations as well as among units in organizations. Even in similar or nearly identical work environments, large variations in individual and group motivation often exist. Much research has been undertaken by behavioral, psychological, and social scientists to develop theories and concepts of motivation. Economists and engineers have focused on extrinsic fiscal rewards to improve performance and productivity, whereas human relations scientists have stressed intrinsic needs for recognition, self-esteem, and self-actualization. To better understand the current view that both extrinsic and intrinsic rewards are necessary for high productivity and worker satisfaction, one needs to look at how motivational theory has evolved over time.

MOTIVATIONAL THEORY

Chapter 2 introduced traditional management philosophy, which emphasizes paternalism, worker subordination, and bureaucracy as a means to predictable but moderate productivity. In this philosophy, high productivity means greater monetary incentives for the worker, and workers are viewed as being motivated primarily by economic factors. This traditional management philosophy is still in use today. Many factory and assembly line production jobs as well as jobs that use production incentive pay are based on these principles. The shift from traditional management philosophy to a greater focus on the human element and worker satisfaction as factors in productivity began during the human relations era (1930 to 1970).

Maslow

Continued focus on human motivation did not occur until Abraham Maslow's work in the 1950s. Most nurses are familiar with Maslow's *hierarchy of needs* and theory of human motivation. Maslow (1970) believed that people are motivated to satisfy certain needs, ranging from basic survival to complex psychological needs, and that people seek a higher need only when the lower needs have been predominantly met. Maslow's hierarchy of needs is depicted in Figure 18.1.

Although Maslow's work helps to explain personal motivation, his early work, unfortunately, was not applied to motivation in the workplace. His later work, however, offers much insight into motivation and worker dissatisfaction. In the workplace, Maslow's work contributed to the recognition that people are motivated by many needs other than economic security.

Because of Maslow's work, managers began to realize that people are complex beings, and rather than just being motivated by economics, their many needs motivating them at any one time.

It also became clear that motivation is internalized and that if productivity is to increase, management must help employees meet lower-level needs. The shifting focus on what motivates employees has tremendously affected how organizations value workers today.

Skinner

B.F. Skinner was another theorist in this era who contributed to the understanding of motivation, dissatisfaction, and productivity. Skinner's (1953) research on *operant conditioning* and *behavior modification* demonstrated that people could be conditioned to behave in a certain way based on a consistent reward or punishment system. Behavior that is rewarded will be repeated, and behavior that is punished or goes unrewarded is extinguished. Skinner's work continues to be reflected today in the way many managers view and use discipline and rewards in the work setting.

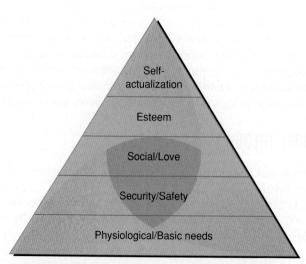

FIGURE 18.1 • Maslow's hierarchy of needs. Copyright ® 2006 Lippincott Williams & Wilkins. Instructor's Resource CD-ROM to Accompany Leadership Roles and Management Functions in Nursing, by Bessie L. Marquis and Carol J. Huston.

Herzberg

Frederick Herzberg (1977) believed that employees can be motivated by the work itself and that there is an internal or personal need to meet organizational goals. He believed that separating personal motivators from job dissatisfiers was possible. This distinction between *hygiene* or *maintenance factors* and *motivator factors* was called the motivation–hygiene theory or two-factor theory. Display 18.3 lists motivator and hygiene factors identified by Herzberg.

DISPLAY 18.3 Herzberg's Motivators and Hygiene Factors	
Motivators	*Hygiene Factors*
Achievement	Salary
Recognition	Supervision
Work	Job security
Responsibility	Positive working conditions
Advancement	Personal life
Possibility for growth	Interpersonal relationships and peers
	Company policy
	Status

Herzberg maintained that motivators or job satisfiers are present in work itself; they give people the desire to work and to do that work well. Hygiene or maintenance factors keep employees from being dissatisfied or demotivated but do not act as real motivators. It is important to remember that the opposite of dissatisfaction may not be satisfaction. When hygiene factors are met, there is a lack of dissatisfaction, not an existence of satisfaction. Likewise, the absence of motivators does not necessarily cause dissatisfaction.

For example, salary is a hygiene factor. Although it does not motivate in itself, when used with other motivators such as recognition and advancement, it can be a powerful motivator. If, however, salary is deficient, employee dissatisfaction can result. Maxfield (2013, para 5) agrees, noting that "money is much more apt to play the role of *de*-motivator than motivator, because it is difficult to stay motivated if you don't think your pay is fair. But, if you do think your pay is fair, then you stop thinking about it and its power to motivate fades. Leaders need to establish fair pay, but they shouldn't rely on fair pay to motivate."

Some argue, however, that money can truly be a motivator, as evidenced by people who work insufferable hours at jobs they truly do not enjoy. Some theorists would argue that money in this case might be taking the place of some other unconscious need. Some people in Herzberg's studies, however, did report job satisfaction solely from hygiene or maintenance factors. Herzberg asserts that these people are only temporarily satisfied when hygiene factors are improved, show little interest in the kind and quality of their work, experience little satisfaction from accomplishments, and tend to show chronic dissatisfaction with other hygiene factors such as salary, status, and job security.

Herzberg's work suggests that although the organization must build on hygiene or maintenance factors, the motivating climate must actively include the employee. The worker must be given greater responsibilities, challenges, and recognition for work well done. The reward system must meet both motivation and hygiene needs, and the emphasis given by the manager should vary with the situation and the employee involved. Although hygiene factors in themselves do not motivate, they are needed to create an environment that encourages the worker to move on to higher-level needs. Hygiene factors also combat employee dissatisfaction and are useful in recruiting an adequate personnel pool.

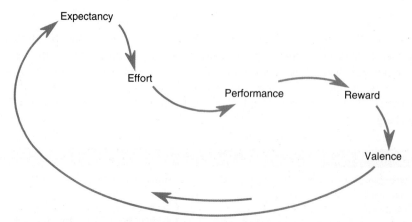

FIGURE 18.2 • Vroom's expectancy model. Copyright ® 2006 Lippincott Williams & Wilkins. Instructor's Resource CD-ROM to Accompany Leadership Roles and Management Functions in Nursing, by Bessie L. Marquis and Carol J. Huston.

Vroom

Victor Vroom (1964), another motivational theorist in the human relations era, developed an *expectancy model*, which looks at motivation in terms of the person's valence, or preferences based on social values. In contrast to *operant conditioning*, which focuses on observable behaviors, the expectancy model says that a person's expectations about his or her environment or a certain event will influence behavior. In other words, people look at all actions as having a cause and effect; the effect may be immediate or delayed, but a reward inherent in the behavior exists to motivate risk taking.

In Vroom's expectancy model (Fig. 18.2), people make conscious decisions in anticipation of reward; in operant conditioning, people react in a stimulus–response mode. Managers using the expectancy model must become personally involved with their employees to understand better the employees' values, reward systems, strengths, and willingness to take risks.

McClelland

David McClelland (1971) examined what motives guide a person to action, stating that people are motivated by three basic needs: achievement, affiliation, and power. *Achievement-oriented* people actively focus on improving what is; they transform ideas into action, judiciously and wisely, taking risks when necessary. In contrast, *affiliation-oriented* people focus their energies on families and friends; their overt productivity is less because they view their contribution to society in a different light from those who are achievement oriented. Research shows that women generally have greater affiliation needs than men and that nurses generally have high affiliation needs. *Power-oriented* people are motivated by the power that can be gained as a result of a specific action. They want to command attention, get recognition, and control others.

LEARNING EXERCISE 18.2

Identifying Goals and Motivation

List six goals that you hope to accomplish in the next 5 years. Identify which goals are most related to achievement needs, affiliation needs, and power needs. Remember that most people are motivated in part by all three needs, and no one motivational need is better than the others. However, each person must recognize and understand which basic needs motivate him or her most.

McClelland theorizes that managers can identify achievement, affiliation, or power needs of their employees and develop appropriate motivational strategies to meet those needs.

Gellerman

Saul Gellerman (1968), another humanistic motivational theorist, identified several methods to motivate people positively. One such method, *stretching*, involves assigning tasks that are more difficult than what the person is used to doing. Bednarz (2013) agrees, noting that employees must be challenged to stretch their personal and professional limits. This includes personal and professional development in areas of vocational knowledge, skills, and expertise. Stretching should not, however, be a routine or daily activity. All employees need to have time to rest and regroup after being stretched.

The challenge of "stretching" is to energize people to enjoy the beauty of pushing themselves beyond what they think they can do.

Another method, *participation*, entails actively drawing employees into decisions affecting their work. Gellerman strongly believed that motivation problems usually stem from the way the organization manages and not from the staff's unwillingness to work hard. According to Gellerman, most managers "overmanage"—they make the employee's job too narrow and fail to give the employee any decision-making power.

Bednarz (2013) agrees, suggesting that in order to stretch employees, managers must develop confidence in their abilities. This means allowing employees to experiment with new ideas and techniques while understanding that, "as people grow through their experiences, many lessons are best learned through personal mistakes and failure. Individuals who know they have the liberty to perform their jobs without fear of retribution if they falter are more motivated and empowered to stretch the limits of their capabilities" (Bednarz, para 7).

McGregor

Douglas McGregor (1960) examined the importance of a manager's assumptions about workers on the intrinsic motivation of the workers. These assumptions, which McGregor labeled *Theory X* and *Theory Y* (depicted in Display 18.4), led to the realization in management science that how the manager views, and thus treats, the worker will have an impact on how well the organization functions.

DISPLAY 18.4   McGregor's Theory X and Theory Y

Theory X Employees	Theory Y Employees
Avoid work if possible	Like and enjoy work
Dislike work	Are self-directed
Must be directed	Seek responsibility
Have little ambition	Are imaginative and creative
Avoid responsibility	Have underutilized intellectual capacity
Need threats to be motivated	Need only general supervision
Need close supervision	Are encouraged to participate in problem solving
Are motivated by rewards and punishment	

McGregor did not consider Theory X and Theory Y as opposite points on the spectrum but rather as two points on a continuum extending through all perspectives of people. McGregor believed that people should not be artificially classified as always having Theory X or Theory Y assumptions about others; instead, most people belong on some point on the continuum. Likewise, McGregor did not promote either Theory X or Theory Y as being the one superior management style, although many managers have interpreted Theory Y as being the ultimate management model. No one style is effective in all situations, at all times, and with all people. McGregor, without making value judgments, simply stated that in any situation, the manager's assumptions about people, whether grounded in fact or not, affect motivation and productivity.

> Theory Y is not a "better" management style than Theory X; the style which is "best" depends on the variables inherent in a given situation.

The work of all these theorists has added greatly to the understanding of what motivates people in and out of the work setting. Research reveals that motivation is extremely complex and that there is tremendous variation in what motivates different people. Therefore, managers must understand what can be done at the unit level to create a climate that allows the worker to grow, increases motivation and productivity, and eliminates dissatisfiers that drain energy and promote frustration.

CREATING A MOTIVATING CLIMATE

Because the organization has such an impact on extrinsic motivation, it is important to examine organizational climates or attitudes that directly influence worker morale and motivation. For example, organizations frequently overtly or covertly reinforce the image that each employee is expendable and that individual recognition is in some way detrimental to the employee and his or her productivity within the organization. Just the opposite is true, because employees are an organization's most valuable asset. Nurses who experience satisfaction stay where they are, contributing to an organization's retention.

Incentives and Rewards

Many organizations use incentives or rewards to foster a motivating climate. The use of incentives and rewards for this purpose, however, can be very challenging. Some individuals erroneously believe that if a small reward results in desired behavior, then a larger reward will result in even more of the desired behavior. This simply is not true. There appears to be a perceived threshold beyond which increasing the incentive results in no additional meaning or weight.

In addition, recent research suggests that offering rewards in defined categories, even when the categories are meaningless, can increase motivation, since the very act of segmenting these rewards motivates people to perform better and longer (Wood, 2013). This occurs because people feel they might "miss out" if they do not obtain a second reward. The researchers concluded that instead of presenting one big reward, organizations should set up more small rewards. Even if they are not all that different, people will generally work harder when different rewards are available (Wood).

Using incentives and rewards to motivate workers can also be complicated by a view of rewards as competition. When rewards lack consistency, there is greater risk that the reward itself will become a source of competition and thereby lower morale. An attitude prevails that "a limited number of awards are available, and an award received by anyone else limits the chances of my getting one; thus, I cannot support recognition for my peers." All employees should be recognized for meeting milestones.

Likewise, rewarding one person's behavior and not the behavior of another who has accomplished a similar task at a similar level promotes jealousy and can demotivate. Rewards and praise should be spontaneous and not relegated to predictable events, such as routine annual performance reviews and recognition dinners. Rewards and praise should be given whenever possible and whenever they are deserved.

If positive reinforcement and rewards are to be used as motivational strategies, then rewards must represent a genuine accomplishment on the part of the person and should be somewhat individual in nature. For example, many managers erroneously consider annual merit pay increases as rewards that motivate employees. Most employees, however, recognize annual merit pay increases as a universal "given"; thus, this reward has little meaning and little power to motivate.

Organizations must be cognizant of the need to offer incentives at a level where employees value them. This requires that the organization and its managers understand employees' collective values and devise a reward system that is consistent with that value system.

Generational Differences and Motivation

Managers also must be cognizant of an employee's individual values and attempt to reward each worker accordingly. The ability to recognize each worker as a unique person who is motivated differently and then to act upon those differences is a leadership skill.

For example, some researchers have suggested that generational differences exist in terms of motivational factors and that while relatively stable, an individual's motives can change over the life cycle in terms of rank ordering, absolute levels, and motive strength as changes in life goals and self-concept occur (Inceoglu, Segers, & Bartram, 2012).

In addition, research by Inceoglu et al. (2012) suggest that as people age, a shift in motives generally occurs. Inceoglu et al. clarify that this does not mean that motivation decreases with age; rather, that older employees tend to become less motivated by extrinsic job features and instead become more motivated by intrinsic factors.

Deal et al. (2013) cautions, however, that existing research on generational differences has rarely considered the effects of managerial level within the organization and that this seems like an obvious confounding variable since employees at higher levels are typically older than those at lower levels and since organizational level appears to impact many of the variables examined in research on generational differences including job satisfaction. In their survey of 3,440 participants, Deal et al. found that while there was some difference in work motivation by generation, more of the variance could be explained by managerial level. Individuals at lower managerial levels had higher levels of external motivation than did those at higher managerial levels, whereas individuals at higher managerial levels had higher levels of intrinsic, identified, and *introjected* (employees believe that they "should" engage in work activities but have not fully embraced the value of the activities) motivation. These findings suggest that organizations should look beyond just generational difference when attempting to understand and improve employee motivation (Examining the Evidence 18.1).

Examining the Evidence 18.1

Source: Deal, J. J., Stawiski, S., Graves, L., Gentry, W. A., Weber, T. J., & Ruderman, M. (2013). Motivation at work: Which matters more: Generation or managerial level? Consulting Psychology Journal: Practice & Research, 65(1), 1–16.

The purpose of this study was to investigate whether work motivation differed by generations or whether differences in work motivation were better explained by managerial level. The study population was 3,440 individuals (1,723 men and 1,717 women) from more than 200 different organizations, who participated voluntarily in a web-based survey between March 2008 and December 2010. The survey included a series of questions about demographic and lifestyle characteristics, motivation, work attitudes, and beliefs about leadership.

(Continued)

LEARNING EXERCISE 18.4

Write a Detailed Plan to Motivate—Quickly!

You are the manager of a medical unit in a community hospital. The hospital has faced extreme budget cuts during the last 5 years as a result of decreased reimbursement. Your unit used to be a place where nurses wanted to work, and you rarely had openings for long, even though it was necessary for the hospital to contain costs and shorten nursing care hours per patient-day. A recent hiring freeze has accelerated worker dissatisfaction in your staff.

In the last week, five of the unit nurses, all excellent long-time employees, have stopped by your office either in tears, anger, or frustration. Their various comments have included, "Working here is no longer fun," "I used to love my job," "I am tired of working with incompetent people," and "I am sick to death of calling for supplies that should be stocked on the floor." You know that funding will not increase in the near future, but you think that perhaps there are things you could do to make the situation better for your staff.

Assignment: In examining the strategies for creating a motivating climate and the atmosphere that supports finding joy in work, decide what you as an individual unit manager can do to provide a more positive work environment. Avoid taking items from the list in Display 18.4, but write a detailed plan that is feasible, that could be implemented fairly quickly, and that would have the potential to turn this situation around.

PROMOTION: A MOTIVATIONAL TOOL

Promotions are reassignments to a position of higher rank. It is normal for promotions to include a pay raise. Most promotions include increased status, title changes, more authority, and greater responsibility; therefore, they can be used as a significant motivational tool.

Because of the importance that US society places on promotions, certain guidelines must accompany promotion selection to ensure that the process is fair, equitable, and motivating. When position openings occur, they are often posted and filled quickly with little thought of long-term organizational or employee goals. This frequently results in negative personnel outcomes. To avoid this, the following elements should be determined in advance:

- *Whether recruitment will be internal or external.* There are obvious advantages and disadvantages to recruiting for promotions from both inside and outside the organization. Recruiting from within can help to develop employees to fill higher-level positions as they become vacant. It can also serve as a powerful motivation and recognition tool since all employees know that opportunities for advancement are possible, and this encourages them to perform at a higher level.

There are advantages to recruiting from outside the organization, however. When promotions are filled with people outside the organization, the organization is infused with people with new ideas. This prevents the stagnation that often occurs when all promotions are internal. External candidates, however, often cost more in terms of salary than internal ones. This is because external candidates generally need a financial incentive to leave their current positions for something else.

Regardless of what the organization decides, the policy should be consistently followed and communicated to all employees. Some companies recruit from within first and recruit from outside the organization only if they are unable to find qualified people from among their own employees.

- *What the promotion and selection criteria will be.* Employees should know in advance what the criteria for *promotion* are and what selection method is to be used. Some organizations use an interview panel as a selection method to promote all employees beyond the level of charge nurse. Decisions regarding the selection method and promotion criteria should be justified with rationale. In addition, employees need to know what place seniority will have in the selection criteria.

- *The pool of candidates that exists.* When promotions are planned, as in succession management, there will always be an adequate pool of candidates identified and prepared to seek higher-level positions. A word of caution must be given regarding the zeal with which managers urge subordinates to seek promotions. The leader's role is to identify and prepare such a pool. It is not the manager's role to urge the employee to seek a position in a manner that would lead the employee to think that he or she was guaranteed the job or to unduly influence him or her in the decision to seek such a job.

When employees actively seek promotions, they are making a commitment to do well in the new position. When they are pushed into such positions, the commitment to expend the energy to do the job well may be lacking. In addition, for many reasons, the employee may not feel ready, either due to personal commitments or because he or she feels inadequately educated or experienced. Indeed, it is possible to promote an individual beyond his or her level of capability (known as the *Peter Principle*). In this case, promotions demotivate that individual as well as everyone in the organization.

The Peter Principle suggests that individuals often rise "to the level of their incompetence."

- *Handling rejected candidates.* All promotion candidates who are rejected must be notified before the selected candidate is notified. This is common courtesy. They should be thanked for applying and, when appropriate, encouraged to apply for future position openings. Sometimes, managers should tell employees which deficiencies kept them from getting the position. For instance, employees should be told if they lack some educational component or work experience that would make them a stronger competitor for future promotions. This can be an effective way of encouraging career development.

- *How employee releases are to be handled.* Knowledge that the best candidate for the position currently holds a critical job or difficult position to fill should not influence decisions regarding promotions. Managers frequently find it difficult to release employees to another position within the organization. Policies regarding the length of time that a manager can delay releasing an employee should be written and communicated. On the other hand, some managers are so good at developing their employees that they frequently become frustrated because their success at career development results in constantly losing their staff to other departments. In such cases, higher-level management should reward such leaders and set release policies that are workable and realistic.

LEARNING EXERCISE 18.5

Why Won't Beth Apply for the Position?

You have been the evening charge nurse of a large surgical unit for the last 4 years. Each year, you perform a career development conference with all your licensed staff. These sessions are held separately from the performance appraisal interviews. You have been extremely pleased with the results of these conferences. Two of your licensed vocational nurses/licensed

(Continued)

professional nurses are now enrolled in a registered nurse (RN) program. Several of the RNs from your unit have obtained advanced clinical positions, and many have returned to school. As a result of your encouragement and support, several of the nurses have taken charge positions on other units. You are proud of your ability to recognize talent and to perform successful career counseling.

This is the last time that you will be performing career counseling, because you have resigned your position to return to graduate school. You have encouraged several of the staff to apply for your position but think that one particular nurse—Beth, a 34-year-old woman—would be exceptional. She is extremely capable clinically, very mature, well respected by everyone, and has excellent interpersonal skills. Beth only works 4 days a week but has been invaluable to you in the 4 years since you have been charge nurse. However, Beth is one of the few nurses who has never acted on any of your suggestions at previous career-coaching interviews.

Last week, you had another coaching interview with Beth and told her of your plans. You urged her to apply for your position and told her that you would recommend her to your supervisor, although you would not be making the final selection. Beth told you that she would think about it, and today she told you that she does not wish to apply for the position. You are very disappointed and believe that perhaps you have failed in some way.

Assignment: Examine this scenario carefully. Make a list of the possible reasons that Beth declined the promotion. Be creative. Were the coaching sessions valuable or a waste of your time? Compare your findings with others in the group. After comparison, determine what influence, if any, personal values had on the development of the lists.

PROMOTING SELF-CARE

Managers can also create a motivating climate by being a positive and enthusiastic role model in the clinical setting. Indeed Smith-Trudeau (2013) suggests that when managers enjoy their work and can create fun workplaces, that employee trust, communication, and productivity increase, leading to lower turnover, higher morale, and a stronger bottom line.

Managers, however, must be internally motivated before they can motivate others. Indeed, Fernet (2013) suggests that psychological health is a prerequisite for employees to achieve their full potential. Managers who frequently project unhappiness to subordinates contribute to low unit morale. A burned-out, tired manager will develop a lethargic and demotivated staff. Therefore, managers must constantly monitor their own motivational level and do whatever is necessary to restore their motivation to be role models to staff.

 The attitude and energy level of managers directly affect the attitude and productivity of their employees.

Similarly, when clinicians suffer, so too do patients, since caregivers cannot provide quality care when they themselves are depleted (Schuster, 2013). Fernet (2013) suggests that when employees engage in their job for the inherent pleasure and satisfaction they experience (intrinsic motivation) and/or because they personally endorse the importance or value of their work (identified regulation), that psychological well-being occurs. In contrast, when employees perform their job to gain a sense of self-worth or to avoid feelings of anxiety and guilt and/or because they are pressured by demands, threats, or rewards by an external agent, negative consequences such as burnout are more likely to occur.

Van Beek, Hu, Schaufeli, Taris, and Schreurs (2012) agree, noting that employees who work hard because they are mainly driven or pushed by a strong need to prove themselves and because they personally value work outcomes often experience burnout. Engaged employees who work hard because they are mainly pulled by their inherently enjoyable and satisfying work are more apt to be psychologically healthy.

It is imperative then that discouraged managers acknowledge their own feelings and seek assistance accordingly. Managers are responsible to themselves and to subordinates to remain motivated to do the best job possible. Nursing is a stressful profession, and managers must practice health-seeking behaviors and find social supports when confronted with stress or else risk burnout as a result. Burnout and other forms of work-related stress are related to negative organizational outcomes such as illness, absenteeism, turnover, performance deterioration, decreased productivity, and job dissatisfaction. These outcomes cost the organization and impede quality of care. "Finding ways to help nurses relax, reflect, refocus or re-energize then is critical in helping them to prevent or overcome burnout" (Schuster, 2013, para 3).

Perhaps the most important strategy for avoiding burnout and maintaining a high motivation level is *self-care*. For self-care, the manager should seek time off on a regular basis to meet personal needs, seek recreation, form relationships outside the work setting, and have fun.

Often, friends and colleagues are essential for emotional support, guidance, and renewal. A proper diet and exercise are important to maintain physical health as well as emotional health. Finally, the manager must be able to separate his or her work life and personal life; the manager should remember that there is life outside of work and that time should be relished and protected. Ultimately, the decision to practice self-care rests with each nurse.

INTEGRATING LEADERSHIP ROLES AND MANAGEMENT FUNCTIONS IN CREATING A MOTIVATING CLIMATE AT WORK

Most human behavior is motivated by a goal that the person wants to achieve. Identifying employee goals and fostering their attainment allow the leader to create an environment that encourages employees to reach personal and organizational goals. The motivational strategy that the leader uses should vary with the situation and the employee involved; it may be formal or informal. It may also be extrinsic, although because of a limited formal power base, the leader generally focuses on other aspects of motivation. The leader must listen, support, and encourage the discouraged employee. However, perhaps the most important role that the leader has in working with the demotivated employee is that of role model. Leaders who maintain a positive attitude and high energy levels directly and profoundly affect the attitude and productivity of their followers.

When creating a motivating climate, the manager uses formal authority to reduce dissatisfiers at the unit level and to implement a reward system that reflects individual and collective value systems. This reward system may be formalized, or it may be as informal as praise. Managers, by virtue of their position, have the ability to motivate subordinates by "stretching" them intermittently with increasing responsibility and assignments that they are capable of achieving. The manager's role, then, is to create the tension necessary to maintain productivity while encouraging subordinates' job satisfaction. Therefore, the success of the motivational strategy is measured by increased productivity and benefit to the organization and by growth in the person, which motivates him or her to accomplish again.

KEY CONCEPTS

- Because human beings have constant needs and wants, they are always motivated to some extent. However, what motivates each human being varies significantly.

- Managers cannot intrinsically motivate people, because motivation comes from within the person. The humanistic manager can, however, create an environment in which the development of human potential can be maximized.

- Maslow stated that people are motivated to satisfy certain needs, ranging from basic survival to complex psychological needs, and that people seek a higher need only when the lower needs have been predominantly met.

- Skinner's research on operant conditioning and behavior modification demonstrates that people can be conditioned to behave in a certain way based on a consistent reward or punishment system.

- Herzberg maintained that motivators, or job satisfiers, are present in the work itself and encourage people to want to work and to do that work well. Hygiene or maintenance factors keep the worker from being dissatisfied or demotivated but do not act as true motivators for the worker.

- Vroom's expectancy model says that people's expectations about their environment or a certain event will influence their behavior.

- McClelland's studies state that all people are motivated by three basic needs: achievement, affiliation, and power.

- Gellerman states that most managers in organizations overmanage, making the responsibilities too narrow and failing to give employees any decision-making power or to stretch them often enough.

- McGregor points out the importance of a manager's assumptions about workers on the intrinsic motivation of the worker.

- There appears to be a perceived threshold beyond which increasing reward incentives results in no additional meaning or weight in terms of productivity.

- Offering rewards in defined categories, even when the categories are meaningless, can increase motivation, since the very act of segmenting these rewards appears to motivate people to perform better and longer.

- Positive reinforcement is one of the most powerful motivators the manager can use and is frequently overlooked or underused.

- The supervisor or manager's personal motivation is an important factor affecting staff's commitment to duties and morale.

- The success of a motivational strategy is measured by the increased productivity and benefit to the organization and by the growth in the person, which motivates him or her to accomplish again.

- Because of the importance that American society places on promotions, certain guidelines must accompany promotion selection to ensure that the process is fair, equitable, and motivating.

- Policies regarding promotion should be in writing and communicated to all employees.

- Recruitment from within has been shown to have a positive effect on employee motivation, whereas recruitment from outside the organization allows for new ideas and prevents stagnation.

- It is possible to promote individuals beyond their level of capability. The Peter Principle, as it is known, suggests that individuals may rise "to the level of their incompetence."

- Managers must show their own positive attitude to demonstrate to employees that there is joy in work.

ADDITIONAL LEARNING EXERCISES AND APPLICATIONS

LEARNING EXERCISE 18.6

Create a Plan to Remotivate a New Employee

You are a county public health coordinator. You have grown concerned about the behavior of one of the new RNs assigned to work in the agency. This new nurse, Sally Brown, is a recent graduate of a local BSN program. She came to work for the agency immediately after her graduation 6 months ago and for the first few months appeared to be extremely hard working, knowledgeable, well liked, and highly motivated. Recently, though, several small incidents involved Sally. The agency's medical director became very angry with her over a medication error that she had made. Sally was already feeling badly about the careless error. Soon after, a patient's husband began disliking Sally for no discernible reason and refused Sally entrance to his home to care for his wife. Then, 2 weeks ago, a diabetic patient died fairly suddenly from renal failure, and although no one was to blame, Sally thought that if she had been more observant and skilled in assessment, she would have detected subtle changes in the patient's condition sooner.

Although you have been supportive of Sally, you recognize that she is in danger of becoming demotivated. Her once-flawless personal appearance now borders on being unkempt, she is frequently absent from work, and her once-pleasant personality has been exchanged for withdrawal from her coworkers.

Assignment: Using your knowledge of new role identification, assimilation, and motivational theory, develop a plan to assist this young nurse. What can you do to provide a climate that will remotivate her and decrease her job dissatisfaction? Explain what you think is happening to this nurse and the rationale behind your plan, which should be realistic in terms of the time and energy that you have to spend on one employee. Be sure to identify the responsibilities of the employee as well.

LEARNING EXERCISE 18.7

A Nursing Officer's Dilemma

You are the Chief Nursing Officer of County Hospital. Dr. Martin Jones, a cardiologist, has approached you about having an ICU/CCU nurse make rounds with him each morning on all of the patients in the hospital with a cardiac-related diagnosis. He believes that this will probably represent a 90-minute commitment of nursing time daily. He is vague about the nurse's exact role or purpose, but you believe that there is great potential for better and more consistent patient education and care planning.

Beth, one of your finest ICU/CCU nurses, agrees to assist Dr. Jones. Beth has always wanted to have an expanded teaching role. However, for various reasons, she has been unable to relocate to a larger city where there are more opportunities for teaching. You warn Beth that it might be some time before this role develops into an autonomous position, but she is eager to assist Dr. Jones. The other ICU/CCU staff agree to cover Beth's patients while she is gone, although it is obviously an extension of an already full patient load.

After 3 weeks of making rounds with Dr. Jones, Beth comes to your office. She tearfully reports that rounds frequently take 2 to 3 hours and that making rounds with Dr. Jones amounts to little

(Continued)

more than "carrying his charts, picking up his pages, and being a personal handmaiden." She has assertively stated her feelings to him and has attempted to demonstrate to Dr. Jones how their allegiance could result in improved patient care. She states that she has not been allowed any input into patient decisions and is frequently reminded of "her position" and his ability to have her removed from her job if she does not like being told what to do. She is demoralized and demotivated. In addition, she believes that her peers resent having to cover her workload because it is obvious that her role is superficial at best.

You ask Beth if she wants you to assign another nurse to work with Dr. Jones, and she says that she would really like to make it work but does not know what action to take that would improve the situation.

You call Dr. Jones, and he agrees to meet with you at your office when he completes rounds the following morning. At this visit, Dr. Jones confirms Beth's description of her role but justifies his desire for the role to continue by saying, "I bring $10 million of business to this hospital every year in cardiology procedures. The least you can do is provide the nursing assistance I am asking for. If you are unable to meet this small request, I will be forced to consider taking my practice to a competitive hospital." However, after further discussion, he does agree that eventually he would consider a slightly more expanded role for the nurse after he learns to trust her.

Assignment: Do you meet Dr. Jones's request? Does it make any difference whether Beth is the nurse, or can it be someone else? Does the revenue that Dr. Jones generates supersede the value of professional nursing practice? Should you try to talk Beth into continuing the position for a while longer? While trying to reach a goal, people must sometimes endure a difficult path, but at what point does the means not justify the end? Be realistic about what you would do in this situation. What do you perceive to be the greatest obstacles in implementing your decision?

LEARNING EXERCISE 18.8

To Work or Not to Work?

You are a nurse in a long-term care facility. The facility barely meets minimum licensing standards for professional nursing staffing. Although agency recruiters have been actively seeking to hire more licensed staff, pay at the facility for professional staff is less than at local acute care hospitals and the patient–nurse ratio is significantly higher. There appears to be little chance of improving the RN staffing mix in your agency in the near future. The nursing administrator is extremely supportive of the staff's efforts but can do little to ease the current workload for licensed staff other than to turn away patients or close the agency. As a result, all of the nurses on the unit have been working at least 48 hours per week during the last 6 months; many have been working several double shifts and putting in many overtime hours each pay period.

Morale is deteriorating, and the staff has begun to complain. Most of the licensed staff are feeling burned out and demotivated. Many have started refusing to work overtime or to take on extra shifts. You feel a responsibility to the patients, community, and organization and have continued to work the extra hours but you are exhausted as well.

Today is your first evening off in 6 days. At 2 PM, the phone rings, and you suspect that it is the agency calling you to come in to work. You delay answering while you decide what to do. The answering machine turns on, and you hear your administrator's voice. She says that they are desperate. Two new patients were admitted during the day, and the facility is full. She says that she appreciates all the hours you have been working but needs you once again, although she is unable to give you tomorrow off in compensation. You feel conflicting loyalties to the unit, patients, supervisor, and yourself.

Assignment: Decide what you will do. Will you agree to work? Will you return the administrator's telephone call or pretend that you are not at home? When do your loyalties to your patients and the organization end and your loyalties to yourself begin? Is the administrator taking advantage of you? Are the other staff being irresponsible? What values have played a part in your decision making?

LEARNING EXERCISE 18.9

Remotivating Oneself

You are a school nurse and have worked in the same school for 2 years. Before that time, you were a staff nurse at a local hospital working in pediatrics and later for a physician. You have been an RN for 6 years.

When you began your job, it was exciting. You believed that you were really making a difference in children's lives. You started several good health promotion programs and worked hard upgrading your health aides' education and training.

Several months ago, funding for the school was drastically cut, and several of your favorite programs were eliminated. You have been depressed about this and lately have been short-tempered at work. Today, one of your best health aides gave you her 2-week notice and said, "This isn't a good place to work anymore." You realize that many of the aides and several of the schoolteachers have picked up your negative attitude.

There is much that you still love about your job, and you are not sure if the budget problems are temporary or long term. You go home early today and contemplate what to do.

Assignment: Should you stay in this job or leave? If you stay, how can you get remotivated? Can you remotivate yourself if the budget cuts are long term? Make a plan about what to do.

LEARNING EXERCISE 18.10

Downsizing Panic and Anxiety

As the result of rising costs and shrinking reimbursement, many hospitals downsized their staffs in an effort to shrink costs. Because the hospital where you are the Chief Nursing Administrator is faced with mandatory staffing ratios, it is impossible to cut further staff nurse positions and meet requirements for state licensing.

Therefore, the CEO of the hospital has mandated that management positions be reduced by 30% throughout the hospital. The CEO has decided that department heads can reduce management positions by any method they choose as long as it is done in 6 months. Job duties are to be reassigned among the remaining managers.

This affects you significantly, as nursing has more managers than any other department. It does not appear that attrition or turnover rates in the next months will be adequate to eliminate the need for some reassignments, demotions, or termination of your group of 17 managers. This includes both house supervisors and unit managers.

(Continued)

The news travels rapidly through the hospital grapevine. Semi-hysteria prevails, with many managers consulting you regarding whether their position is in jeopardy and what they can do to increase the likelihood of their retention. Morale is rapidly plummeting, and relationships are becoming increasingly competitive rather than cooperative.

Assignment: Determine how you will handle this situation. What strategies might you implement to reduce the immediate anxiety level? What advice can you give to staff who may face either a layoff or a demotion? Is it possible to preserve the morale of your managers in an uncertain situation such as this?

LEARNING EXERCISE 18.11

Just Getting By

You are a senior student in an ADN nursing program. You are also a single mother of three grade-school aged children, currently living at home with your parents who are retired. Your recent divorce left you emotionally shattered as well as financially destitute. You work part time as a waitress at a local coffee shop at night to help buy groceries and pay your educational expenses, but there is never enough money and you are just trying to do what you can to get by. Your barely passing grades at school reflect the recent disorganization in your life. In addition, you feel physically exhausted and increasingly depressed.

Today, one of your nursing instructors calls you into her office, noting the drop in your grades, and expresses concern that "you are not living up to your academic potential." She encourages you to try harder because she knows that you had hoped at some point to return to school, and your current grades would not likely qualify you to do so.

You leave her office, feeling more discouraged than ever. There is already no time in your life for self-care and doing better in school would require you to either work less or spend less time with your family, neither of which seems like a plausible alternative to you.

Assignment: Decide what you will do. Make sure the expectations you set for yourself are reasonable. Are the expectations intrinsically or extrinsically determined? Also identify whether your plan of action is more driven by achievement, affiliation, or power needs.

REFERENCES

Amabile, T. M., & Kramer, S. J. (2010, January–February). What really motivates workers. *Harvard Business Review, 88,* 44–45.

Asbjörnson, K., & Brenner, M. (2010, Winter). Leadership is a performing art. *Leader to Leader, 2010*(55), 18–23.

Bednarz, T. F. (2013). *Motivation must be personal to be effective.* Leaders to Leader. Retrieved June 12, 2013, from http://blog.majoriumbusinesspress .com/2013/02/12/motivation-must-be-personal-to-be -effective/

Biro, (2013, January 13). *5 ways leaders rock employee recognition.* Forbes. Retrieved June 13, 2013, from http://www.forbes.com/sites/ meghanbiro/2013/01/13/5-ways-leaders-rock -employee-recognition/

Deal, J. J., Stawiski, S., Graves, L., Gentry, W. A., Weber, T. J., & Ruderman, M. (2013). Motivation at work: Which matters more: Generation or managerial level? *Consulting Psychology Journal: Practice & Research, 65*(1), 1–16.

Fernet, C. (2013). The role of work motivation in psychological health. *Canadian Psychology, 54*(1), 72–74

Gellerman, S. W. (1968). *Management by motivation.* New York, NY: American Management Association.

Herzberg, F. (1987, September/October). One more time: How do you motivate employees? HBR Classic. Harvard Business Review, pp. 5-16. Retrieved Oct. 6, 2013 from http://www.facilitif.eu/user_files/file/herzburg _article.pdf.

Inceoglu, I., Segers, J., & Bartram, D. (2012). Age-related differences in work motivation. *Journal of Occupational & Organizational Psychology*, *85*(2), 300–329.

Maslow, A. (1970). *Motivation and personality* (2nd ed.). New York, NY: Harper & Row.

Maxfield, D. (2013, May 14). *Motivating without money.* Crucial Skills. Retrieved June 12, 2013, from http://www.crucialskills.com/2013/05/motivating-without-money/

McClelland, D. C. (1971). *Assessing human motivation.* Morristown, NJ: General Learning Press.

McGregor, D. (1960). *The human side of enterprise.* New York, NY: McGraw-Hill.

Schuster, J. L (2013, June 10). *With nurses at risk of compassion fatigue, hospitals try to ease their stress.* The Washington Post. Retrieved October 6, 2013 from http://articles.washingtonpost.com/

2013-06-10/national/39865768_1_burnout-intensive-care-unit-nurses

Skinner, B. F. (1953). *Science and human behavior.* New York, NY: Free Press.

Smith-Trudeau, P. (2013). Nurse managers cultivating a fun culture. *Vermont Nurse Connection*, *16*(2), 3.

van Beek, I., Hu, Q., Schaufeli, W. B., Taris, T. W., & Schreurs, B. J. (2012). For fun, love, or money: What drives workaholic, engaged, and burned-out employees at work? *Applied Psychology: An International Review*, *61*(1), 30–55.

Vroom, V. (1964). *Work and motivation.* New York, NY: John Wiley and Sons.

Wood, J. (2013, June 2). *Separating rewards into categories increases motivation.* Psych Central. Retrieved June 13, 2013, from http://psychcentral.com/news/2013/06/02/separating-rewards-into-categories-increases-motivation/55490.html

19

Organizational, Interpersonal, and Group Communication

... effective communication is the lifeblood of a successful organization. It reinforces the organization's vision, connects employees to the business, fosters process improvement, facilitates change and drives business results by changing employee behavior.
—Watson Wyatt Worldwide

... the difference between the right word and the almost right word is the difference between lightning and a lightning bug.
—Mark Twain

CROSSWALK THIS CHAPTER ADDRESSES:

BSN Essential II: Basic organizational and systems leadership for quality care and patient safety

BSN Essential IV: Information management and application of patient care technology

BSN Essential VI: Interprofessional communication and collaboration for improving patient health outcomes

BSN Essential VIII: Professionalism and professional values

MSN Essential II: Organizational and systems leadership

MSN Essential V: Informatics and health-care technologies

MSN Essential VII: Interprofessional collaboration for improving patient and population health outcomes

QSEN Competency: Patient-centered care

QSEN Competency: Teamwork and collaboration

QSEN Competency: Quality improvement

QSEN Competency: Safety

QSEN Competency: Informatics

AONE Nurse Executive Competency I: Communication and relationship building

AONE Nurse Executive Competency II: A knowledge of the health-care environment

AONE Nurse Executive Competency III: Leadership

AONE Nurse Executive Competency: Professionalism

AONE Nurse Executive Competency: Business skills

LEARNING OBJECTIVES *The learner will:*

- identify the relationship between the sender, message, and receiver in any given communication
- differentiate between the internal and external climate in which communication occurs
- identify barriers to effective organizational communication
- describe strategies managers can take to increase the likelihood of clear and complete organizational communication

- choose appropriate communication modes for specific situations and messages
- differentiate among assertive, passive, aggressive, and passive–aggressive communication
- diagram upward, downward, horizontal, and diagonal communication
- recognize ISBAR (Introduction, Situation, Background, Assessment, and Recommendation) and SBAR (Situation, Background, Assessment, and Recommendation) as a structured, orderly approach in providing accurate, relevant information, in emergent patient situations as well as routine handoffs
- write in a clear and concise manner using appropriate language for the receiver of the message
- demonstrate listening skills consistent with those outlined in the GRRRR (Greeting, Respectful Listening, Review, Recommend or Request More Information, and Reward) listening model
- recognize culture and gender as significant variables impacting communication
- recognize the need for confidentiality in sensitive interpersonal, group, or organizational communication
- describe the opportunities as well as the challenges new technologies pose for communication in contemporary organizations
- recognize the potential benefits of social media as a communication tool as well as the potential risks and identify principles for social networking use that minimize those risks
- accurately assess stages of group formation (forming, storming, norming, and performing)
- identify specific group-building and maintenance roles that must be established for groups to accomplish work

Although some functions of management such as planning, organizing, and controlling can be reasonably isolated, communication impacts all management activities and cuts across all phases of the management process. The nurse-leader communicates with clients, colleagues, superiors, and subordinates. In addition, because nursing practice tends to be group oriented, interpersonal communication among group members is necessary for continuity and productivity. One must have excellent interpersonal communication skills then to be an effective leader-manager. In fact, communication is perhaps the most critical leadership skill.

Organizational communication is even more complex than interpersonal or group communication, as there are more communication channels, more individuals to communicate with, more information to transmit, and new technologies, which both complicate and ease care delivery. Thus, organizational communication is a high-level management function; it must be systematic, have continuity, and be appropriately integrated into the organizational structure, encouraging an exchange of views and ideas. Organizational communication is complex, however, and communication failure often results in a failure to meet organizational goals. In addition, there are confidentiality risks that must be addressed.

In addition, the leader is responsible for developing a cohesive team to meet organizational goals. To do this, the leader must articulate issues and concerns so that workers will not become confused about priorities. The ability to communicate effectively often determines success as a leader-manager and developing expertise in all aspects of communication is critical to managerial success. Leadership skills and management functions inherent in organizational, interpersonal, and group communication are listed in Display 19.1.

| DISPLAY 19.1 | Leadership Roles and Management Functions Associated with Organizational, Interpersonal, and Group Communication |

LEADERSHIP ROLES

1. Understands and appropriately uses both the formal and informal communication network in the organization.
2. Communicates clearly and precisely in language that others will understand.
3. Is sensitive to the internal and external climate of the sender or receiver and uses that awareness in interpreting messages.

(Continued)

4. Appropriately observes and interprets the verbal and nonverbal communication of followers.
5. Role models assertive communication and active listening.
6. Demonstrates congruency in verbal and nonverbal communication.
7. Recognizes status, power, and authority as barriers to manager–subordinate communication and uses communication strategies to overcome those barriers.
8. Role models the use of social networking principles that promote collaboration, shared decision making, and evidence-based practice, while protecting patient rights and confidentiality.
9. Seeks a balance between technological communication options and the need for human touch, caring, and one-on-one, face-to-face interaction.
10. Maximizes group functioning by keeping group members on course, encouraging the shy, controlling the garrulous, and protecting the weak.

MANAGEMENT FUNCTIONS

1. Understands and appropriately uses the organization's formal communication network.
2. Determines the appropriate communication mode or combination of modes for optimal distribution of information in the organizational hierarchy.
3. Prepares written communications that are clear and uses language that is appropriate for the message and the receiver.
4. Consults with other departments or disciplines in coordinating overlapping roles and group efforts.
5. Differentiates between "information" and "communication" and appropriately assesses the need for subordinates to have both.
6. Prioritizes and protects client and subordinate confidentiality.
7. Ensures that staff and self are trained to appropriately and fully utilize technological communication tools.
8. Establishes a technology-enabled communication infrastructure that leverages the benefits of social media while minimizing the risks.
9. Uses knowledge of group dynamics for attaining goals and maximizing organizational communication.

This chapter examines multiple forms of communication. Barriers to communication in large organizations and managerial strategies to minimize those difficulties are presented. Channels and modes of communication are compared, and guidelines are given for managerial selection of the optimum channel or mode. In addition, assertiveness, nonverbal behavior, and active listening as interpersonal communication factors are discussed. The chapter also includes a discussion of how ISBAR (Introduction, Situation, Background, Assessment, and Recommendation) and SBAR (Situation, Background, Assessment, Recommendation) can be used to provide a more structured, orderly approach in communicating client data, how technology continues to alter communication in health-care settings, and the ever-increasing challenge of maintaining confidentiality in a system where so many people have access to so much information.

 ## THE COMMUNICATION PROCESS

Answers.com (2013, para 1) provides a definition of *communication* as "the exchange of thoughts, messages, or information, by speech, signals, writing, or behavior." Communication can also occur on at least two levels: *verbal* and *nonverbal*. Thus, whenever two or more people are aware of each other, communication begins.

 Communication begins the moment that two or more people become aware of each other's presence.

What happens, however, when the thoughts, ideas, and information exchanged do not have the same meaning for both the sender and the receiver of the message? What if the verbal and nonverbal messages are incongruent? Does communication occur if an idea is transmitted but not translated into action?

Because communication is so complex, many models exist to explain how organizations and individuals communicate. Basic elements common to most models are shown in Figure 19.1. In all communication, there is at least one sender, one receiver, and one message. There is also a mode or medium through which the message is sent—for example, spoken, written, or nonverbal.

An internal and an external climate also exist in communication. The *internal climate* includes the values, feelings, temperament, and stress levels of the sender and the receiver. Weather conditions, temperature, timing, and the organizational climate itself are parts of the external climate. The *external climate* also includes status, power, and authority as barriers to manager–subordinate communication (see Display 19.2).

DISPLAY 19.2   The Internal and External Climate in Communication

Internal climate	Includes internal factors such as the values, feelings, temperament, and stress levels of the sender and the receiver
External climate	Includes external factors such as the weather, temperature, timing, status, power, authority, and the organizational climate itself

---

Both the sender and the receiver must be sensitive to the internal and external climate, because the perception of the message is altered greatly depending upon the climate that existed at the time the message was sent or received. For example, an insecure manager who is called to meet with superiors during a period of stringent layoffs will probably view the message with more trepidation than a manager who is secure in his or her role.

Because each person is different and thus makes decisions and perceives differently, assessing external climate is usually easier than assessing internal climate. In assessing internal climate, remember that the human mind perceives only what it expects to

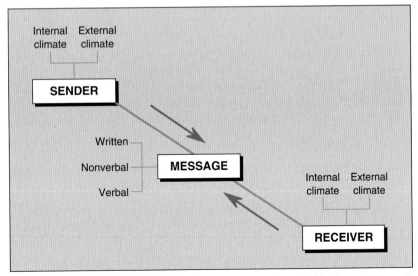

FIGURE 19.1 • The communication process. Copyright ® 2006 Lippincott Williams & Wilkins. Instructor's Resource CD-ROM to Accompany Leadership Roles and Management Functions in Nursing, by Bessie L. Marquis and Carol J. Huston.

perceive. The unexpected is generally ignored or misunderstood. In other words, receivers cannot communicate if the message is incompatible with their expectations. If senders want communication to be effective, they need to decide what the receiver will see or hear.

 Effective communication requires the sender to validate what receivers see and hear.

 # VARIABLES AFFECTING ORGANIZATIONAL COMMUNICATION

Formal organizational structure has an impact on communication. People at lower levels of the organizational hierarchy are at risk for inadequate communication from higher levels. This occurs because of the number of levels that communication must filter through in large organizations. As the number of employees increases (particularly more than 1,000 employees), the quantity of communication generally increases; however, employees may perceive it as increasingly closed. In large organizations, it is impossible for individual managers to communicate personally with each person or group involved in organizational decision making. Not only is spatial distance a factor but the presence of subgroups or subcultures also affects what messages are transmitted and how they are perceived.

LEARNING EXERCISE 19.1

Large Organization Communication

Have you ever been employed in a large organization? Was the communication within that organization clear and timely? What or who was your primary source of information? Were you a part of a subgroup or subculture? If so, how did that affect communication?

Gender is also a significant factor in organizational communication, as men and women communicate and use language differently. Women are generally perceived as being more relationship oriented than men but this is not always the case. Women are also characterized as being more collaborative in their communication, whereas men are more competitive.

Complicating the picture further is the historical need in the health-care industry for a predominantly male medical profession to closely communicate with a predominantly female nursing profession. In addition, the majority of health-care administrators continue to be male. Therefore, male physicians and administrators may feel little incentive to seek the collaborative approach in communication that female nurses may desire. The quality of organizational and unit-level communication then continues to be affected by differences in gender, power, and status.

 Differences in gender, power, and status significantly affect the types and quality of organizational and unit-level communication.

Power and status also impact organizational communication. Garon (2012) notes that communication problems are commonplace in health-care organizations when health-care workers believe they cannot speak up or be heard. This then negatively impacts worker job satisfaction, teamwork, as well as patient safety and limits the ability of organizational leaders to address the problems that are affecting the ability of the organization to function and change. The importance of the manager in setting up a culture of open communication cannot be underestimated (Examining the Evidence 19.1).

Examining the Evidence 19.1

Source: Garon, M. (2012). Speaking up, being heard: Registered nurses' perceptions of workplace communication. Journal of Nursing Management, 20(3), 361–371.

This study used a descriptive, qualitative approach, consisting of focus group interviews of 33 registered nurses (RNs), in staff or management positions from a variety of health-care settings in California, to explore the perceptions of staff RNs and managers regarding their ability to speak up and be heard in the workplace. Data were analyzed using thematic content analysis.

Study findings were organized into three categories: influences on speaking up, transmission and reception of a message, and outcomes or results. The influences on the nurses' decision to speak up fell into two broad areas: personal and organizational. Personal influences included cultural background, values, how they were raised, language and education. The organizational influences consisted of peers, managers, and administrators.

Factors in the work environment that influenced nurses speaking up included peer influences, manager and administrative influences, and environment or culture. Overall, the strongest theme in this area and in the study was references to a climate of openness. Staff and managers agree that the leaders created this climate.

Outcomes of speaking up emerged as the final category. Staff nurses wanted to know that the issues they brought up were acted upon. Several expressed feelings that—nothing ever changes—leading them to believe that it was a waste of time and energy to continue to bring up issues.

Findings supported the researcher's concerns that nurses are still not speaking up, and that the effects of this are harmful to patients, staff, and organizations. Further changes in health-care environments are needed to foster effective communication and nurse-managers are in the ideal place to advance these changes. Study participants stressed the importance of "open door policies" and listening skills and noted the importance of nurse-managers being able to listen without blame or criticism, creating environments that encourage nurses to come forward with their concerns.

ORGANIZATIONAL COMMUNICATION STRATEGIES

Although organizational communication is complex, the following strategies increase the likelihood of clear and complete communication:

- *Leader-managers must assess organizational communication.* Who communicates with whom in the organization? Is the communication timely? Does communication within the formal organization concur with formal lines of authority? Are there conflicts or disagreements about communication? What modes of communication are used?

- *Leader-managers must understand the organization's structure and recognize who will be affected by decisions.* Both formal and informal communication networks need to be considered. *Formal communication networks* follow the formal line of authority in the organization's hierarchy. *Informal communication networks* occur among people at the same or different levels of the organizational hierarchy but do not represent formal lines of authority or responsibility.

  For example, an informal communication network might occur between a hospital's CEO and her daughter, who is a clerk on a medical wing. Although there may be a significant exchange of information about unit or organizational functioning, this communication network would not be apparent on the organization chart. It is imperative, then, that managers be very careful about what they say and to whom until they have a good understanding of the formal and informal communication networks.

- *Communication is not a one-way channel.* If other departments or disciplines will be affected by a message, the leader-manager must consult with those areas for feedback before the communication occurs.

- *Communication must be clear, simple, and precise.* This requires the sender to adjust their language as necessary to the target audience.

- *Senders should seek feedback regarding whether their communication was accurately received.* One way to do this is to ask the receiver to repeat the communication or instructions. In addition, the sender should continue follow-up communication in an effort to determine if the communication is being acted upon. The sender is responsible for ensuring that the message is understood.

- *Multiple communication methods should be used, when possible, if a message is important.* Using a variety of communication methods in combination increases the likelihood that everyone in the organization who needs to hear the message actually will hear it.

- *Managers should not overwhelm subordinates with unnecessary information. Information* is formal, impersonal, and unaffected by emotions, values, expectations, and perceptions. *Communication,* on the other hand, involves perception and feeling. It does not depend on information and may represent shared experiences. In contrast to information sharing, superiors must continually communicate with subordinates.

 Although information and communication are different, they are interdependent.

Most staff need little information about ordering procedures or organizational supply vendors as long as supplies are adequate and appropriate to meet unit needs. If, however, a vendor is temporarily unable to meet unit supply needs, the use of supplies by staff becomes an issue requiring close communication between managers and subordinates. The manager must communicate with the staff about which supplies will be inadequately stocked and for how long. The manager also may choose to discuss this inadequacy of resources with the staff to identify alternative solutions.

Channels of Communication

Because large organizations are so complex, communication channels used by the manager may be upward, downward, horizontal, diagonal, or through the "grapevine." In *upward communication,* the manager is a subordinate to higher management. Needs and wants are communicated upward to the next level in the hierarchy. Those at this higher level make decisions for a greater segment of the organization than do the lower-level managers.

In *downward communication,* the manager relays information to subordinates. This is a traditional form of communication in organizations and helps to coordinate activities in various levels of the hierarchy.

In *horizontal communication,* managers interact with others on the same hierarchical level as themselves who are managing different segments of the organization. The need for horizontal communication increases as departmental interdependence increases.

In *diagonal communication,* the manager interacts with personnel and managers of other departments and groups such as physicians, who are not on the same level of the organizational hierarchy. Although these people have no formal authority over the manager, this communication is vital to the organization's functioning. Diagonal communication tends to be less formal than other types of communication.

The most informal communication network is often called the *grapevine. Grapevine communication* flows quickly and haphazardly among people at all hierarchical levels and usually involves three or four people at a time. Senders have little accountability for the message, and often the message becomes distorted as it speeds along. Given the frequency of grapevine communication in all organizations, all managers must attempt to better understand how the grapevine works in their own organization as well as who is contributing to it. The channels of communication are summarized in Display 19.3.

Grapevine communication is subject to error and distortion because of the speed at which it passes and because the sender has little formal accountability for the message.

DISPLAY 19.3	Channels of Communication
Upward	From subordinate to superior
Downward	From superior to subordinate
Horizontal	From peer to peer
Diagonal	Between individuals at differing hierarchy levels and job classifications
Grapevine	Informal, haphazard, and random, usually involving small groups

LEARNING EXERCISE 19.2

When and How Will You Tell?

Assume that you are the project director of a small family planning clinic. You have just received word that your federal and state funds have been slashed and that the clinic will probably close in 3 months. Although an additional funding source may be found, it is improbable that it will occur within that time period. The Board of Directors informed you that this knowledge is not to be made public at this time.

You have five full-time employees at the clinic. Because two of these employees are your close friends, you feel some conflict about withholding this information from them. You are aware that another clinic in town currently has job openings and that the positions are generally filled quickly.

Assignment: It is important that you staff the clinic for the next 3 months. When will you notify the staff of the clinic's intent to close? Will you communicate the closing to all staff at the same time? Will you use downward communication? Should the grapevine be used to leak news to employees? When might the grapevine be appropriate to pass on information?

COMMUNICATION MODES

A message's clarity is greatly affected by the mode of communication used. In general, the more direct the communication, the greater the probability that it will be clear. The more people involved in filtering the communication, the greater the chance of distortion. The manager must evaluate each circumstance individually to determine which mode or combination of modes is optimal for each situation. The manager uses the following modes of communication most frequently:

- *Written communication.* Written messages (including memos, reports, e-mail, and texting, which will be discussed later in this chapter) allow for documentation. They may, however, be open to various interpretations and generally consume more managerial time. Most managers are required to do a considerable amount of this type of communication and therefore need to be able to write clearly.

- *Face-to-face communication.* Oral communication is rapid but may result in fewer people receiving the information than necessary. Managers communicate verbally upward and downward and formally and informally. They also communicate verbally in formal meetings, with people in peer work groups, and when making formal presentations.
- *Telephone communication.* A telephone call is rapid and allows the receiver to clarify the message at the time it is given. It does not, however, allow the receipt of nonverbal messages for either the sender or receiver of the message. Accents may be difficult to understand as well in a multicultural workforce. Because managers today use the telephone so much, it has become an important communication tool, but it does have limits as an effective communication device.
- *Nonverbal communication.* Nonverbal communication includes facial expression, body movements, and gestures and is commonly referred to as *body language*. Nonverbal communication is considered more reliable than verbal communication because it conveys the emotional part of the message. There is significant danger, however, in misinterpreting nonverbal messages if they are not assessed in context with the verbal message. Nonverbal communication occurs any time managers are seen (e.g., messages are transmitted to subordinates every time the manager communicates verbally or just walks down a hallway).

ELEMENTS OF NONVERBAL COMMUNICATION

Much of our communication occurs through nonverbal channels that must be examined in the context of the verbal content. Generally, if verbal and nonverbal messages are incongruent, the receiver will believe the nonverbal message. Because nonverbal behavior can be and frequently is misinterpreted, receivers must validate perceptions with senders. The incongruence between verbal and nonverbal leads to many communication problems.

Because nonverbal communication indicates the emotional component of the message, it is generally considered more reliable than verbal communication.

Silence can also be used as a means of nonverbal communication. This supports the old adage that *even silence can be deafening.* The following section identifies other nonverbal clues that can occur with or without verbal communication.

Space

The study of how space and territory affect communication is called *proxemics* (Loo, n.d.). All of us have an invisible zone of psychological comfort that acts as a buffer against unwanted touching and attacks. The degree of space we require depends on who we are talking to as well as the situation we are in (Loo). It also varies according to cultural norms. Some cultures require greater space between the sender and the receiver than others. In the United States, between 0 and 18 inches of space is typically considered appropriate only for intimate relationships; between 18 inches and 4 feet is appropriate for personal interactions; between 4 and 12 feet is common for social exchanges; and more than 12 feet is a public distance (Loo). Most Americans claim a territorial personal space of about 4 feet.

Proxemics, then, may contribute to the message being sent. Distance may imply a lack of trust or warmth, whereas inadequate space, as defined by cultural norms, may make people feel threatened or intimidated. Likewise, the manager who sits beside employees during performance appraisals sends a different message than the manager who speaks to the employee from the opposite side of a large and formal desk. In this case, distance increases power and status on the part of the manager; however, the receptivity to distance and the message that it implies varies with the culture of the receiver.

Environment

The area where communication takes place is an important part of the communication process. Communication that takes place in a superior's office is generally taken more seriously than that which occurs in the cafeteria.

Appearance

Much is communicated by our clothing, hairstyle, use of cosmetics, and attractiveness. Care should be exercised, however, to be sure that organizational policies regarding desired appearance are both culturally and gender sensitive.

Eye Contact

Decker (2013) suggests that eye contact over the last 10 to 15 years has plummeted as a result of individuals looking down at their smart devices when they are supposedly communicating with other people. Decker says "if you don't have eye communication, you flat out don't have communication" (para 2). That is because this nonverbal clue is associated with sincerity.

Eye contact invites interaction and emotional connection. Likewise, breaking eye contact suggests that the interaction is about to cease. It signals to your listeners that you are not interested in them and that you are not engaged in the conversation (Decker). Blinking, staring, or looking away when speaking also makes it difficult to connect with others emotionally. However, one must always remember, that like space, the presence or absence of eye contact is strongly influenced by cultural standards.

Posture

Posture and the way that you control the other parts of your body are also extremely important as part of nonverbal communication. For example, Cherry (2013) suggests that sitting up straight may indicate that a person is focused and paying attention to what's going on. Sitting with the body hunched forward, on the other hand, can imply that the person is bored or indifferent. Crossing arms across one's chest may suggest defensiveness or aggressiveness. Moreover, the weight of a message is increased if the sender faces the receiver; stands or sits appropriately close; and, with head erect, leans toward the receiver.

Gestures

A message accented with appropriate gestures takes on added emphasis. Too much gesturing can, however, be distracting. For example, hand movement can emphasize or detract from the message. Gestures also have a cultural meaning. Some cultures are more tactile than others. Indeed, the use of touch is one gesture that often sends messages that are misinterpreted by receivers from different cultures.

Facial Expression and Timing

Effective communication requires a facial expression that agrees with your message. Staff perceive managers who present a pleasant and open expression as approachable. Likewise, a nurse's facial expression can greatly affect how and what clients are willing to relate. On the other hand, hesitation often diminishes the effect of your statement or implies untruthfulness.

Vocal Expression

Vocal clues such as tone, volume, and inflection add to the message being transmitted. Tentative statements sound more like questions than statements, leading listeners to think that you are unsure of yourself, and speaking quickly may be interpreted as being nervous. The goal, then, should always be to convey confidence and clarity.

All nurses must be sensitive to nonverbal clues and their importance in communication. This is especially true for nursing leaders. Effective leaders make sure that both verbal and nonverbal communications agree.

Effective leaders are congruent in their verbal and nonverbal communication so that followers are clear about the messages they receive.

Likewise, leaders are sensitive to nonverbal and verbal messages from followers and look for inconsistencies that may indicate unresolved problems or needs. Often, organizational difficulties can be prevented because leaders recognize the nonverbal communication of subordinates and take appropriate and timely action.

VERBAL COMMUNICATION SKILLS

Highly developed verbal communication skills are critical for the leader-manager. Ibe (2013) notes the inability to communicate needs or to challenge other people's ideas can cause tension in relationships, leading to stress, anxiety, or even depression. *Assertive communication*, on the other hand, reduces this type of stress, improves productivity, and contributes to a healthy workforce.

Assertive communication is a way of communicating that allows people to express themselves in direct, honest, and appropriate ways that do not infringe on another person's rights. A person's position is expressed clearly and firmly by using "I" statements as well as direct eye contact and a calm voice. In addition, assertive communication always requires that verbal and nonverbal messages be congruent. To be successful in the directing phase of management, the leader must have well-developed skills in assertive communication.

There are many misconceptions about assertive communication. The first is that all communication is either assertive or passive. Actually, at least four possibilities for communication exist: passive, aggressive, indirectly aggressive or passive–aggressive, or assertive. *Passive communication* occurs when a person suffers in silence although he or she may feel strongly about the issue. Thus, passive communicators avoid conflict, often at the risk of bottling up feelings which may lead to an eventual explosion (Ibe, 2013).

Aggressive communication is generally direct, threatening, and condescending. It infringes on another person's rights and intrudes into that person's personal space. This behavior is also oriented toward "winning at all costs" or demonstrating self-excellence. Thus, it is a bullying type of communication and a form of dominance (Atlanta Black Star, 2013). Thomson (2013) suggests that payoffs to being an aggressive communicator are that you often get others to do what you want because they are afraid to stand up to you. The problem, however, is that this communication style typically creates enemies, leads to unstable relationships, and the feelings of power and self-confidence it creates can erode quickly if someone does stand up to you (Thomson).

Passive–aggressive communication is an aggressive message presented in a passive way. It generally involves limited verbal exchange (often with incongruent nonverbal behavior) by a person who feels strongly about a situation. This person feigns withdrawal in an effort to manipulate the situation. For example, the passive–aggressive communication may say yes when they want to say no or be sarcastic or complain about others behind their backs (Mayo Clinic Staff, 2011). Over time, this type of behavior damages relationships and undercuts mutual respect (Mayo Clinic Staff).

The second misconception is that those who communicate or behave assertively get everything they want. This is untrue. Being assertive involves both rights and responsibilities.

The third misconception about assertiveness is that it is unfeminine. Although the role of women in society in general has undergone tremendous change in the last 100 years, some individuals continue to find great difficulty in accepting that both female and male nurses play assertive, active, decision-making role. Assertive communication involves conveying a message that insists on being heard.

An assertive communication model helps people to unlearn common self-deprecating speech patterns that signal insecurity and a lack of confidence. The nursing profession must be more assertive in its need to be heard. Eventually, a form of peer pressure can emerge that reshapes others and results in an assertive nursing voice.

 Assertive communication is not rude or insensitive behavior, rather, it is having an informed voice that insists on being heard.

A fourth misconception is that the terms *assertive* and *aggressive* are synonymous. To be assertive is to not be aggressive, although some cultures find the distinction blurred. Even when faced with someone else's aggression, the assertive communicator does not become aggressive. When under attack by an aggressive person, an assertive person can do several things:

- *Reflect.* Reflect the speaker's message back to him or her. Focus on the affective components of the aggressor's message. This helps the aggressor to evaluate whether the intensity of his or her feelings is appropriate to the specific situation or event. For example, assume that an employee enters a manager's office and begins complaining about a newly posted staff schedule. The employee is obviously angry and defensive. The manager might use reflection by stating, "I understand that you are very upset about your schedule. This is an important issue, and we need to talk about it."

- *Repeat the assertive message.* Repeated assertions focus on the message's objective content. They are especially effective when the aggressor overgeneralizes or seems fixated on a repetitive line of thinking. For example, if a manager requests that an angry employee step into his or her office to discuss a problem, and the employee continues his or her tirade in the hallway, the manager might say, "I am willing to discuss this issue with you in my office. The hallway is not the appropriate place for this discussion."

- *Point out the implicit assumptions.* This involves listening closely and letting the aggressor know that you have heard him or her. In these situations, managers might repeat major points or identify key assumptions to show that they are following the employee's line of reasoning.

- *Restate the message by using assertive language.* Rephrasing the aggressor's language will defuse the emotion. Paraphrasing helps the aggressor to focus more on the cognitive part of the message. The manager might use restating by changing a "you" message to an "I" message.

- *Question.* When the aggressor uses nonverbal clues to be aggressive, the assertive person can put this behavior in the form of a question as an effective means of helping the other person become aware of an unwarranted reaction. For example, the desperate, angry employee may imply threats about quitting or transferring to another unit. The manager could appropriately confront the employee about his or her implied threat to see if it is real or simply a reflection of the employee's frustration.

 As in nonverbal communication, the verbal communication skills of the leader-manager in a multicultural workplace require cultural sensitivity.

Even when dealing with staff from the same cultural background, assertive communication requires administrative skill to decide whether to speak face-to-face, send an electronic or paper memo, telephone, or not to communicate about a particular matter at all.

SBAR and ISBAR as Verbal Communication Tools

Accrediting bodies and organizations dedicated to improving the quality of health care have directed health-care organizations to identify and implement strategies for improving and standardizing professional communication. Indeed, the 2007 Joint Commission's *Annual Report on Quality and Safety* identified inadequate communication between care providers or between care providers and patients/families as a consistent root cause of *sentinel events* (an unexpected occurrence involving death or serious physical or psychological injury, or the risk thereof) (Jordan, 2009). *SBAR (Situation, Background, Assessment, and Recommendation)* and *ISBAR* (adds *identification* as first step) are strategies that have been developed to address this problem.

SBAR, first used in the Navy to standardize important and urgent communication in nuclear submarines and further developed by Kaiser Permanente, is an easy-to-remember tool that provides a structured, orderly approach in providing accurate, relevant information, in emergent patient situations as well as routine handoffs (Display 19.4). *Handoffs* (verbal exchange of information, which occurs between two or more health-care providers about a patient's condition, treatment plan, care needs, etc.) typically occur both at change of shift and when patients are transferred to different units. Using SBAR helps health-care providers avoid long narrative descriptions and ensures that facts, which are essential for the proper assessment of the patient's needs, are passed on (Jordan, 2009). Clearly, SBAR has great potential for reducing communication errors, thus increasing patient safety.

DISPLAY 19.4   **SBAR as a Communication Tool**

S	Situation	Introduce yourself and the patient and briefly state the issue that you want to discuss (generally the patient's condition)
B	Background	Describe the background or context (patient's diagnosis, admission date, medical diagnosis, and treatment to date)
A	Assessment	Summarize the patient's condition and state what you think the problem is
R	Recommendation	Identify any new treatments or changes ordered and provide opinions or recommendations for further action

Some health-care organizations have chosen to include an *introduction step (ISBAR)* to SBAR because they feel it is important that the clinicians start off with an introduction if they do not actively know the person they are speaking with during a patient handoff or over the phone (ISBAR, 2013). This step includes an introduction of the person doing the handoff, their role in the patient's care, and the unit they are calling from if the handoff occurs over the phone (ISBAR).

LEARNING EXERCISE 19.3

Handoff with ISBAR

Today you were assigned to provide total patient care for Mr. Dixon. He is a 73-year-old male who was admitted for a total knee replacement 2 days ago. Today, the bloody output from Mr. Dixon's Jackson Pratt drains increased dramatically and the incision site appears to be reddened, swollen, and hot. He has required IV pain medication every 3 to 4 hours, which reduces his pain from a level 6 to 8 out of 10 to a level of 2 to 3. He is refusing to use his continuous passive motion machine because he says it is too painful. He is also nauseated and refused his lunch today. His bowel sounds are diminished. Mr. Dixon's wife is at the bedside and shares with you that the patient does not normally complain, so she is worried that something might be wrong. Mr. Dixon's surgeon is not expected to see this patient until later this evening, after the close of his private practice.

Assignment: Use ISBAR to prepare your handoff report for the next shift. Then share what you have prepared with a peer. Ask them to critique whether you communicated all vital patient information and whether your assessment and recommendations were appropriate for the situation.

LISTENING SKILLS

Research shows that most people hear or actually retain only a small amount of the information given to them. In fact, communication failure is a common root cause of medical error. It is important then that the leader-manager approaches listening as an opportunity to learn.

To become better listeners, leaders must first become aware of how their own experiences, values, attitudes, and biases affect how they receive and perceive messages. Second, they must overcome the information and communication overload inherent in the middle-management role. It is easy for overwhelmed managers to stop listening actively to the many subordinates who need and demand their time simultaneously.

Finally, the leader must continually work to improve listening skills by giving time and attention to the message sender. The leader's primary purpose is to receive the message being sent rather than forming a response before the transmission of the message is complete.

The leader who actively listens gives genuine time and attention to the sender, focusing on verbal and nonverbal communication.

Boynton (2009) suggests that using a listening model such as *GRRRR (Greeting, Respectful Listening, Review, Recommend or Request More Information, and Reward)* is especially helpful in organizations where disruptive behavior, toxic environments, and power struggles interfere with listening (see Display 19.5). In the *Greeting* stage, a simple respectful greeting is offered to establish a professional dialogue. Next, participants demonstrate *Respectful Listening* by giving each other time to think and transmit critical information without interrupting. *Review* occurs when the speaker summarizes the information he has conveyed to make sure that the message was understood correctly. Once the speaker is finished conveying this summary and the other party has validated or clarified it, the listener has enough information to *Recommend or Request More Information*. The communication exchange ends when both parties *Reward* each other by recognizing and thanking each other for a collaborative exchange. GRRRR can be used regardless of the relative rank and status of the participants since maintaining structured communication is even more vital when power differences exist (Boynton, 2009).

DISPLAY 19.5	GRRR (Boynton, 2009) as a Listening Tool	
G	Greeting	Offer greetings and establish positive environment
R	Respectful listening	Listen without interrupting and pause to allow others to think
R	Review	Summarize message to make sure it was heard accurately
R	Recommend or request more information	Seek additional information as necessary
R	Reward	Recognize that a collaborative exchange has occurred by offering thanks

LEARNING EXERCISE 19.4

Practice Your Listening Skills

Assignment: Form small groups. Assign a group leader and have that person quickly read the following brief telephone transcript to group members. Group members should be told to take whatever notes they would need to report the conversation to their unit manager. Group members should not be allowed to read this exercise, only listen. The group leader should read the transcript only once and then ask group members the questions at the end of the call transcript.

Caller: Hi, my name is Joe Merlisch and I was a patient at the med center last week on 3 East.... room 211 or 213, I'm not sure. Dr Trenweth took care of me–did surgery on my left knee. My hearing aids disappeared when I was there and Lori told me that the hospital would take care of getting them replaced, but no one has ever called me. My son Seth says that Medicare won't replace them without me paying another $850 deductible and my private insurance says they won't cover it at all. I think it's a problem with that "donut hole" in Medicare–isn't that what they call it? They were the Medihearing brand and they cost me $1700 when I bought them. I need to get them replaced because I have 60% hearing loss in my right and 70% in my left. You guys don't know what it's like when you can't hear anything anyone is saying to you. My wife, Nora is mad at me all the time because she thinks I'm just ignoring her and I just don't hear her. Now you guys want me to drive the 70 miles back to the hospital to look in your lost and found and see if my hearing aids are there. Well,.... I'm not going to and I need someone to fix this. Why don't you drive out here and show me what you've got in that lost and found? I've talked to at least 10 people today and everyone just keeps shunting me from person to person. Isn't there anyone there who can fix this for me? What kind of hospital are you anyway?

The group leader should then ask group members to test their listening skills by writing down answers to the following questions:

What is the patient's name?
What is the patient's wife's name?
What is the doctor's name?
What was lost?
When was this item lost?
What room was the patient in at the hospital?
How much did the lost hearing aids cost?
What brand were the hearing aids?
How far is it from the patient's home to the hospital?
How many people have this people spoken to today already?

WRITTEN COMMUNICATION WITHIN THE ORGANIZATION

Although communication may take many forms, written communication is used most often in large organizations. The written communication issued by the manager reflects greatly on both the manager and the organization. Thus, the manager must be able to write clearly and professionally and to use understandable language. Many types of written communication are used in organizations. Organizational policy, procedures, events, and change may be announced in writing. Job descriptions, performance appraisals, and letters of reference are also forms of written communication.

Often, though, the written communication used most by managers in their daily work life is the *memo*. Perkins and Brizee (2013) suggest that business memos have a twofold purpose: They bring attention to problems and they solve problems. Thus, it is important to choose the audience of a memo wisely and to ensure that everyone on the distribution list of the memo actually needs to read it. Typically, memos should be sent to only a small-to-moderate number of people. In addition, memos should not be used for highly sensitive messages, which are better communicated face-to-face or by telephone (Perkins and Brizee).

Perkins and Brizee (2013) suggest that business memos should be comprised of the following components:

- *Header* (includes the to, from, date, and subject lines): one-eighth of the memo
- *Opening, context, and task* (includes the purpose of the memo, the context and problem, and the specific assignment or task): one-fourth of the memo
- *Summary, discussion segment* (the details that support your ideas or plan): one-half of the memo
- *Closing segment, necessary attachments* (the action that you want your reader to take and a notation about what attachments are included): one-eighth of the memo

In addition, because writing is a learned skill that improves with practice, Writing Help Central (n.d.) suggests the following in writing professional correspondence:

- Keep your message short and concise. Less than one page is always preferred. Use bullets to highlight key points.
- Use the first paragraph to express the context or purpose of the memo and to introduce the problem. In next paragraphs, address what has been done or needs to be done to address the problem at hand.
- Add a conclusion to summarize the memo, clarify what the reader is expected to do, and to address any attachments that are a part of the memo.
- Focus on the recipient's needs. Make sure that your communication addresses the recipient's expectations and what he or she needs to know.
- Use simple language so that the message is clear. Keep paragraphs to less than three or four sentences.
- Review the message and revise as needed. Almost all important communication requires several drafts. Always reread the written communication before sending it. Look for areas that might be misunderstood. Pay attention to tone. Have all of the key points been made?
- Use spelling and grammar checks to be sure that the communication looks professional. Remember that your document is a direct reflection of you, and even the most important message will likely be ignored if the communication is perceived as unprofessional.

LEARNING EXERCISE 19.5

Revising a Formal Business Letter

Read the following formal business letter and assess the quality of the writing. Rewrite the letter so that it is clearly written and professional in nature. Be prepared to read your letter to the class.

Mrs. Joan Watkins

October 19, 2013

Brownie Troop 407

Anywhere, USA 00000

Dear Mrs. Watkins:

I am the official Public Relations Coordinator for County Hospital and serve as correspondence officer for requests from public service groups. We have more than 100 requests such as yours

(Continued)

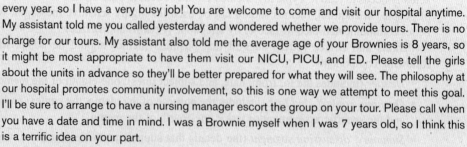

every year, so I have a very busy job! You are welcome to come and visit our hospital anytime. My assistant told me you called yesterday and wondered whether we provide tours. There is no charge for our tours. My assistant also told me the average age of your Brownies is 8 years, so it might be most appropriate to have them visit our NICU, PICU, and ED. Please tell the girls about the units in advance so they'll be better prepared for what they will see. The philosophy at our hospital promotes community involvement, so this is one way we attempt to meet this goal. I'll be sure to arrange to have a nursing manager escort the group on your tour. Please call when you have a date and time in mind. I was a Brownie myself when I was 7 years old, so I think this is a terrific idea on your part.

Sincerely,

Ima Verbose, MSN

Public Relations Coordinator

County Hospital

THE IMPACT OF TECHNOLOGY ON CONTEMPORARY ORGANIZATIONAL COMMUNICATION

Technology has dramatically changed how nurses communicate and perform their work. Younger generations of nurses, who grew up using computers, cell phones, and instant messaging, recognize that technology has given us the potential for instant information access and exchange. These nurses approach and accept technology as an adjunct to their nursing cognizance and do not question its presence or use.

The Internet

Nurses are increasingly using the *Internet* as both a communication tool and an information source. As a communication tool, the Internet provides access to e-mail, file transfer protocol, and the World Wide Web. As an information source, the Internet allows nurses to access the latest research and best practice information so that their care can be evidence based.

The growth of the Internet as an information source for all types of information, including health, is expected to continue to grow exponentially. Gobry (2011) points out the Internet as a sector now produces about 3% of the US gross domestic product, more than agriculture or energy, and representing more than 20% of the economic growth in this country for the past 5 years.

Hospital Information Systems and Intranets

The use of *hospital information system* configurations such as stand-alone systems, online interactive systems, networked systems, and integrative systems has also increased. Some organizations have created internal electronic data repositories as a way of cataloging internal reference materials, such as policy and procedure manuals. This increases the likelihood that staff will be able to find such resources when they need them and that they are as up to date as possible. In such a system, references are typically converted to the portable document format and launched electronically via an *intranet* (internal networks, not normally accessible from the Internet) that allow workers and departments to share files, use Web sites, and collaborate (Huston, 2014).

Wireless, Local Area Networking

The use of *wireless, local area networking* (WLAN) is also growing. WLAN uses spread-spectrum radio frequency modulation technology instead of hardwired systems or paper-based records and allows caregivers to access, update, and transmit critical patient and treatment information when hardwiring is impractical or impossible (Huston, 2014).

Social Media and Organizational Communication

It is clear that the telecommunication technology growth experienced in the late 20th century is continuing to proliferate even more rapidly in the 21st century. This advancing technology may help to balance the constraints being placed on other patient care resources. Technologies such as social networking, texting, e-mail, and the intranet are increasing the potential for effective and efficient communication throughout the organization.

Ferguson (2013) suggests that social media, including web and mobile-based technology platforms such as Twitter, YouTube, Facebook, and wiki platforms, will form the next technological wave in health-care communication, replacing commonly used pagers, which are limited to unidirectional communication. Indeed, social media can be used as a means of gathering, sharing, and disseminating best practices and new ideas, and it provides for instantaneous communication to virtually limitless audiences.

Yet, many health-care organizations are slow to embrace these new technologies as communication tools. For example, some organizations ban or discourage the use of smart phones, afraid that "health professionals will idle their days away on social media or breach confidentiality" (Ferguson, 2013, para 4). This limits the ability of staff to improve care delivery, and overall quality and safety through access to information and decision support. Piscotty et al. (2013) agree, suggesting that nurses often find workarounds to circumvent such restrictions anyway, such as increased use of their personal smartphones or use of Internet access designated for patients and visitors.

In addition, Ferguson (2013, para 8) notes that Google remains blocked by server administrators on many desktop PCs at nurse's stations "while the bedside nurse must hurriedly access his/her hardcopy drug handbook that is a few years out-of-date, attempting to provide the most up-to-date research-inspired, evidence-based, care." Ferguson suggests that Internet access to search tools such as Google Scholar at the point of care could prove helpful in the uptake of evidence-based care. He also suggests that if nurses can be trusted with administering controlled drugs, the day-to-day management of hospitals, and with highly confidential data, that they should be able to be trusted with the Internet at point-of-care delivery.

Ferguson (2013) goes on to note that while some nurses have been reprimanded for making comments online about patient care and posting inappropriate photos of themselves or patients, maintaining patient confidentiality and ethical practice has always been considered a foundational component of nursing professionalism. He concludes that while there are risks to the use of social media, prohibition is folly and futile. "Rather than blocking this innovative communication tool, we need to learn how to manage it, risks and all, and most importantly, leverage the benefits from increased communication, dissemination, and potential for shared decision making" (Ferguson, 2013, para 11).

Piscotty et al. (2013) agree, noting that social media can improve provider-to-provider communication and coordination of patient care, facilitating the quick transfer of information. In addition, professional networks can provide forums to share and obtain information, pose questions, and connect with others who have similar professional interests. The resulting quick dissemination and acquisition of clinical knowledge has the potential for rapid translation of up-to-date information into practice.

Piscotty et al. (2013) warn though that social media does have the potential to cause distractions and interruptions. The distraction may occur because of the device notifying the nurse via sound or vibration that a message has been received. Additionally, there may also be a mental distraction imposed by knowledge that a message is waiting and an urge to view the message. In addition, social media misuse may violate patient rights and has been implicated in boundary violations of patients by nurses and nursing students, including blogging about specific patients and posting actual pictures of patients or body parts on Facebook. These actions have led the American Nurses Association (2011) and the National Council of State Boards of Nursing (2011) to establish the *Principles for Social Networking* shown in Display 19.6.

DISPLAY 19.6	American Nurses Association/National Council of State Boards of Nursing Principles for Social Networking

1. Nurses must not transmit or place online individually identifiable patient information.
2. Nurses must observe ethically prescribed professional patient–nurse boundaries.
3. Nurses should understand that patients, colleagues, institutions, and employers may view postings.
4. Nurses should take advantage of privacy settings and seek to separate personal and professional information online.
5. Nurses should bring content that could harm a patient's privacy, rights, or welfare to the attention of appropriate authorities.
6. Nurses should participate in developing institutional policies governing online conduct.

Sources: American Nurses Association. (2011, September). Principles for social networking and the nurse. Silver Spring, MD: Author; National Council of State Boards of Nursing. (2011, August). White Paper: A nurses' guide to the use of social media. Chicago, IL: Author. Retrieved June 16, 2013, from http://www.nursingworld.org/FunctionalMenuCategories/ AboutANA/Social-Media/Social-Networking-Principles-Toolkit/6-Tips-for-Nurses-Using-Social-Media-Poster.pdf

Balancing Technology and the Human Element

However, even the most advanced communication technology cannot replace the human judgment needed by leaders and managers to use that technology appropriately. Examples of the type of communication challenges that managers face in such a rapidly evolving technological society include the following:

- Determining which technological advances can and should be used at each level of the organizational hierarchy to promote efficiency and effectiveness of communication
- Assessing the need for and providing workers with adequate training to appropriately and fully utilize the technological communication tools that may become available to them
- Balancing cost and benefits
- Aligning communication technology with the organizational mission
- Finding a balance between technological communication options and the need for human touch, caring, and one-on-one, face-to-face interaction (Huston, 2014; Huston, 2013).

Even the most advanced communication technology cannot replace the human judgment needed by leaders and managers to use that technology appropriately.

COMMUNICATION, CONFIDENTIALITY, AND HEALTH INSURANCE PORTABILITY AND ACCOUNTABILITY ACT

Nurses have a duty to maintain confidential information revealed to them by their patients. This *confidentiality* can be breached legally only when one provider must share information about a patient so that another provider can assume care. In other words, there must be a legitimate professional need to know. The same level of confidentiality that is required to protect patient rights is expected regarding sensitive personal communications between managers and subordinates.

Confidentiality can be breached legally only when one provider must share information about a patient so that another provider can assume care.

The *1996 Health Insurance Portability and Accountability Act* (HIPAA) calls for strict protections and privacy of medical information. Enactment of HIPAA requires putting in place mechanisms and accountabilities to protect patients' privacy. Violations of HIPAA can result in significant fines for a facility. There is an ethical duty to maintain confidentiality as well.

Protecting confidentiality and privacy of personal or patient information becomes even more difficult as a result of increased electronic communication because the information available by electronic communication is typically easier to access than traditional information-retrieval methods and because computerized databases are unable to distinguish whether the user has a legitimate right to such information. For example, the federal government has mandated computerized patient records, and many health-care organizations are beginning to implement this mandate. Unfortunately, the discussion and determination of who in the organization should have access to what information are often inadequate before such hardware is put in place, and great potential exists for violations of confidentiality. Clearly, any nurse-manager working with clinical information systems has a responsibility to see that confidentiality is maintained and that any breaches in confidentially are dealt with swiftly and appropriately.

LEARNING EXERCISE 19.6

When Personal and Professional Obligations Conflict

You are an RN employed by an insurance company that provides workers' compensation coverage for large companies. Your job requires that you do routine health screening on new employees to identify personal and job-related behaviors that may place these clients at risk for injury or illness and then to counsel them appropriately regarding risk reduction.

One of the areas that you assess during your patient history is high-risk sexual behavior. One of the clients you saw today expressed concern that he might be positive for HIV because a former girlfriend, with whom he had unprotected sex, recently tested positive for HIV. He tells you that he is afraid to be tested "because I don't want to know if I have it." He seems firm on his refusal to be tested. You go ahead and provide him information about HIV testing and what he can do in the future to prevent transmission of the virus to himself and others.

Later that evening, you are having dinner with your 26-year-old sister, and she reveals that she has a "new love" in her life. When she tells you his name and where he works, you immediately recognize him as the client you counseled in the office today.

Assignment: What will you do with the information you have about this client's possible HIV exposure? Will you share it with your sister? What are the legal and ethical ramifications inherent in violating this patient's confidentiality? What are the conflicting personal and professional obligations? Would your action be the same if a casual acquaintance revealed to you that this client was her new boyfriend? Be as honest as possible in your analysis.

Electronic Health Records

Even health records have changed as a result of technology. The *electronic health record* (EHR) is a digital record of a patient's health history that may be made up of records from many locations and/or sources, such as hospitals, providers, clinics, and public health agencies (Huston, 2014). For example, an EHR might include immunization status, allergies, patient demographics, laboratory test and radiology results, advanced directives, current medications taken, and current health-care appointments. The EHR is available 24 hours a day, 7 days a week, and has built in safeguards to assure patient health information confidentiality and security.

In January 2004, President George Bush set a goal that most Americans would have an EHR by 2014. This goal was endorsed by President Barack Obama and supported financially with $30 billion in stimulus funds to support hospital implementation over the next few years. As a result, this optional improvement has become a near-mandatory initiative (Haughom, Kriz, & McMillan, 2011).

Many federal programs currently exist to support EHR adoption, including those around *meaningful use* (capturing the right data that can improve patient outcomes); the implementation of electronic information exchange; consumer e-health; and workforce training (Centers for Medicare and Medicaid Services, 2010; Take 5 with a Nurse Leader, 2012). The process, however, to make such system-wide changes is not easy and resistance is high. Nor is it cheap. Many challenges continue to exist in understanding and demonstrating meaningful use, capturing the relevant data electronically as part of clinical workflows, and not having the appropriate certified technology (Miliard, 2012).

Meaningful use refers to capturing the right data to improve patient outcomes.

In addition, most hospitals and health systems continue to doubt their ability to meet new mandated EHR standards, with only 48% of health-care leaders in a recent survey feeling confident in their organization's readiness to meet Stage 1 meaningful use requirements (Miliard). Thirty-nine percent said they were somewhat confident; 3% said they were not confident at all; and 10% indicated that they did not know their level of readiness. Even with these concerns, nearly three-quarters (71%) of hospital and health system leaders said they are more than 50% of the way to completing EHR system adoption (Miliard).

GROUP COMMUNICATION

Managers must communicate with large and small groups as well as with individual employees. Because a group communicates differently than individuals do, it is essential that the manager has an understanding of group dynamics, including the sequence that each group must go through before work can be accomplished. Tuckman and Jensen (1977), building on the work of earlier management theorists, labeled these stages *forming, storming, norming,* and *performing*.

When people are introduced into work groups, they must go through a process of meeting each other: the *forming* stage. Here, interpersonal relationships are formed, expectations are defined, and directions are given. They then progress through a stage where there is much competition and attempts at the establishment of individual identities: the *storming* stage. Individuals in the storming stage begin to feel comfortable enough with each other to disagree and if managed appropriately, this discourse can lead to increased trust, positive competition, and effective bargaining (Forming, Storming, Norming, Performing, 2009). Next, the group begins to establish rules and design its work: the *norming* stage. Sometimes, norming never occurs because no one takes the time to agree on and enforce ground rules and processes (Forming, Storming, Norming, and Performing). Finally, during the *performing* stage, the work actually gets done. Table 19.1 summarizes each stage.

TABLE 19.1	Stages of Group Process	
Group Development Stage	Group Process	Task Process
Forming	Testing occurs to identify boundaries of interpersonal behaviors, establish dependency relationships with leaders and other members, and determine what is acceptable behavior	Testing occurs to identify the tasks, appropriate rules, and methods suited to the task's performance
Storming	Resistance to group influence is evident as members polarize into subgroups; conflict ensues and members rebel against demands imposed by the leader	Resistance to task requirements and the differences surface regarding demands imposed by the task
Norming	Consensus evolves as group cohesion develops; conflict and resistance are overcome	Cooperation develops as differences are expressed and resolved
Performing	Interpersonal structure focuses on task and its completion; roles become flexible and functional; energies are directed to task performance	Problems are solved as the task performance improves; constructive efforts are undertaken to complete task; more of group energies are available for the task

Some experts suggest, however, that there is another phase: *termination or closure*. In this phase, the leader guides members to summarize, express feelings, and come to closure. A celebration at the end of committee work is a good way to conclude group effort.

Because a group's work develops over time, the addition of new members to a committee typically result in a return to the forming stage, often slowing productivity. In addition, some developmental stages will be performed again or delayed if new members join a group. Therefore, it is important when assigning members to a committee to select those who can remain until the work is finished or until their appointment time is over.

GROUP DYNAMICS

In addition to forming, storming, and norming, two other functions of groups are necessary for work to be performed. One has to do with the task or the purpose of the group, and the other has to do with the maintenance of the group or support functions. Managers should understand how groups carry out their specific tasks and roles.

Group Task Roles

There are 11 tasks that each group performs. A member may perform several tasks, but for the work of the group to be accomplished, all of the necessary tasks will be carried out either by members or by the leader. These roles or tasks follow:

1. *Initiator.* Contributor who proposes or suggests group goals or redefines the problem. There may be more than one initiator during the group's lifetime.
2. *Information seeker.* Searches for a factual basis for the group's work.
3. *Information giver.* Offers an opinion of what the group's view of pertinent values should be.
4. *Opinion seeker.* Seeks opinions that clarify or reflect the value of other members' suggestions.
5. *Elaborator.* Gives examples or extends meanings of suggestions given and how they could work.

6. *Coordinator.* Clarifies and coordinates ideas, suggestions, and activities of the group.
7. *Orienter.* Summarizes decisions and actions, identifies and questions departures from predetermined goals.
8. *Evaluator.* Questions group accomplishments and compares them with a standard.
9. *Energizer.* Stimulates and prods the group to act and raises the level of its actions.
10. *Procedural technician.* Facilitates group action by arranging the environment.
11. *Recorder.* Records the group's activities and accomplishments.

B. T. Chapman suggests a different taxonomy for labeling the roles that are often held by individuals in groups, particularly in terms of having productive meetings (Urseny, 2007). Chapman suggests that there must always be someone in charge who can act as the *group facilitator.* In addition, there must be a *minutes keeper, time keeper, next agenda person,* and *action plan keeper.* These roles are further defined in Display 19.7.

| DISPLAY 19.7 | B. T. Chapman's Group Roles Taxonomy for Productive Meetings |

- Facilitator: Creates the final meeting agenda and estimates the time for each agenda item. Runs the meeting and gives notice when a decision is to be made or when future action is needed.
- Minutes keeper: Records the meeting's minutes but does not take down every word. Records directions given, decisions, or actions made and approved by the group.
- Time keeper: Keeps the group on schedule by tracking the time allotted for each issue on the agenda. Seeks agreement from the group before allowing discussion on an issue to go over the predesignated time limit.
- Next agenda person: Records issues for the next meeting and helps to create the following agenda. Includes on the next agenda who is responsible for what issue and the time that should be allowed for discussion.
- Action plan keeper: Records decisions for action in two ways; 30 days or long term. If something must be done before the next meeting, it goes on the 30-day list. More complex projects go on the long-term list, which is reviewed at each meeting.

Source: Urseny, L. (2007, January 26). Sticking to the agenda. Chico Enterprise Record, Section E, 4E.

Group Building and Maintenance Roles

Group task roles contribute to the work to be done; group-building roles provide for the care and maintenance of the group. Examples of group-building roles include the following:

- *Encourager.* Accepts and praises all contributions, viewpoints, and ideas with warmth and solidarity.

- *Harmonizer.* Mediates, harmonizes, and resolves conflict.

- *Compromiser.* Yields his or her position in a conflict situation.

- *Gatekeeper.* Promotes open communication and facilitates participation by all members.

- *Standard setter.* Expresses or evaluates standards to evaluate group process.

- *Group commentator.* Records group process and provides feedback to the group.

- *Follower.* Accepts the group's ideas and listens to discussion and decisions.

Organizations need to have a mix of members—enough people to carry out the work and also people who are good at team building. One group may perform more than one function and group-building role.

Individual Roles of Group Members

Group members also carry out roles that serve their own needs. Group leaders must be able to manage member roles so that individuals do not disrupt group productivity. The goal, however, should be management and not suppression. Not every group member has a need that results in the use of one of these roles. The eight individual roles follow:

- *Aggressor*. Expresses disapproval of others' values or feelings through jokes, verbal attacks, or envy.
- *Blocker*. Persists in expressing negative points of view and resurrects dead issues.
- *Recognition seeker*. Works to focus positive attention on himself or herself.
- *Self-confessor*. Uses the group setting as a forum for personal expression.
- *Playboy*. Remains uninvolved and demonstrates cynicism, nonchalance, or horseplay.
- *Dominator*. Attempts to control and manipulate the group.
- *Help seeker*. Uses expressions of personal insecurity, confusion, or self-deprecation to manipulate sympathy from members.
- *Special interest pleader*. Cloaks personal prejudices or biases by ostensibly speaking for others.

 Managers must be well grounded in group dynamics and group roles because of the need to facilitate group communication and productivity within the organization.

While managers must understand group dynamics and roles to facilitate communication and productivity, leaders tend to make an even greater impact on group effectiveness. Dynamic leaders inspire followers toward participative management by how they work and communicate in groups. Leaders keep group members on course, draw out the shy, politely cut off the garrulous, and protect the weak.

LEARNING EXERCISE 19.7

Identifying Group Stages and Roles

Compile a list of the various groups with which you are currently involved. Describe the stage of each one. Did it take longer for some of your groups to get to the performing stage than others? If membership in the group changed, describe what happened to the productivity level. Can you identify which individuals in the group are fulfilling group task roles? Group maintenance and building roles? Individual roles?

INTEGRATING LEADERSHIP AND MANAGEMENT IN ORGANIZATIONAL, INTERPERSONAL, AND GROUP COMMUNICATION

Communication is critical to successful leadership and management. A manager has the formal authority and responsibility to communicate with many people in the organization. Cultural diversity and rapidly flourishing communication technologies also add to the complexity of this organizational communication. Because of this complexity, the manager must understand each unique situation well enough to be able to select the most appropriate internal communication network or channel.

After selecting a communication channel, the manager faces an even greater challenge in communicating the message clearly, either verbally or in writing, in a language appropriate for the message and the receiver. To select the most appropriate communication mode for a specific message, the manager must determine what should be told, to whom, and when. Because communication is a learned skill, managers can improve their written and verbal communication with repetition.

The interpersonal communication skills are more reflective of the leadership role. Sensitivity to verbal and nonverbal communication; recognition of status, power, and authority as barriers to manager–subordinate communication; and consistent use of assertiveness techniques are all leadership skills. Nurse-leaders who are perceptive and sensitive to the environment and people around them have a keen understanding of how the unit is functioning at any time and are able to intervene appropriately when problems arise. Through consistent verbal and nonverbal communication, the nurse-leader is able to be a role model for subordinates.

The integrated leader-manager also uses groups to facilitate communication. Group work is a tool for increasing productivity. All members of work groups should be assisted with role clarification and productive group dynamics.

Organizational communication requires both management functions and leadership skills. Management functions in communication ensure productivity and continuity through appropriate sharing of information. Leadership skills ensure appraisal and intervention in meeting expressed and tacit human resource needs. Leadership skills in communication also allow the leader-manager to clarify organizational goals and direct subordinates in reaching those goals. Communication within the organization would fail if both leadership skills and management functions were not present.

KEY CONCEPTS

- Communication forms the core of management activities and cuts across all phases of the management process. It is also the core of the nurse–patient, nurse–nurse, and nurse–physician relationship.

- Depending on the manager's position in the hierarchy, the overwhelming majority of managerial time is often directed at some type of organizational communication; thus, organizational communication is a high-level management function.

- Because most managerial communication time is spent speaking and listening, managers must have excellent interpersonal communication skills.

- Communication in large organizations is particularly difficult due to their complexity and size.

- Managers must understand the structure of the organization and recognize whom their decisions will affect. Both formal and informal communication networks need to be considered.

- The clarity of the message is significantly affected by the mode of communication used. In general, the more direct the communication, the greater the probability of clear communication. The more people involved in filtering the communication, the greater the chance of distortion.

- Written communication is used most often in large organizations.

- A manager's written communication reflects greatly on both the manager and the organization. Thus, managers must be able to write clearly and professionally and use understandable language.

- The incongruence between verbal and nonverbal messages is the most significant barrier to effective interpersonal communication.

- Effective leaders are congruent in their verbal and nonverbal communication so that followers are clear about the messages they receive. Likewise, leaders are sensitive to nonverbal and verbal messages from followers and look for inconsistencies that may indicate unresolved problems or needs.

- To be successful in the directing phase of management, the leader must have well-developed skills in assertive communication.

- SBAR and ISBAR provide structured, orderly approaches to provide accurate, relevant information, in emergent patient situations as well as routine handoffs.

- Most people hear or retain only a small amount of the information given to them.

- Active listening is an interpersonal communication skill that improves with practice.

- Using a listening model such as *GRRRR* (Greeting, Respectful Listening, Review, Recommend or Request More Information, and Reward) is especially helpful in organizations where disruptive behavior, toxic environments, and power struggles interfere with listening.

- Adding new members to an established group disrupts productivity and group development.

- Group members perform certain important tasks that facilitate work.

- Group members also perform roles that assist with group-building activities.

- Some group members will perform roles to meet their individual needs.

- Rapidly flourishing communication technologies have great potential to increase the efficiency and effectiveness of organizational communication. They also, however, pose increasing challenges to patient confidentiality.

ADDITIONAL LEARNING EXERCISES AND APPLICATIONS

LEARNING EXERCISE 19.8

Writing a Memo

You are a school nurse. In the last 2 weeks, nine cases of head lice have been reported in four different classrooms. The potential for spread is high, and both the teachers and parents are growing anxious.

Assignment: Compose a memo for distribution to the teachers. Your goals are to inform, reassure, and direct future inquiries.

LEARNING EXERCISE 19.9

Identifying and Rephrasing Nonassertive Responses

Decide if the following responses are an example of assertive, aggressive, passive–aggressive, or passive behavior. Change those that you identify as aggressive, passive–aggressive, or passive into assertive responses.

Situation	Response
1. A coworker withdraws instead of saying what is on his mind. You say:	"I guess you are uncomfortable talking about what's bothering you. It would be better if you talked to me."
2. This is the third time in 2 weeks that your coworker has asked for a ride home because her car is not working. You say:	"You're taking advantage of me, and I won't stand for it. It's your responsibility to get your car fixed."
3. An attendant at a gas station neglected to replace your gas cap. You return to inquire about it. You say:	"One of the guys here forgot to put my gas cap back on! I want it found now, or you'll buy me a new one."
4. You would like to have a turn at being in charge on your shift. You say to your head nurse:	"Do you think that, ah, you could see your way clear to letting me be in charge once in a while?"

(Continued)

Situation	Response
5. A committee meeting is being established. The proposed time is convenient for other people but not for you. The time makes it impossible for you to attend meetings regularly. When you are asked about the time, you say:	"Well, I guess it's OK. I'm not going to be able to attend very much, but it fits into everyone else's schedule."
6. In a conversation, a doctor suddenly asks, "What do you women libbers want anyway?" You respond:	"Fairness and equality."
7. An employee makes a lot of mistakes in his work. You say:	"You're a lazy and sloppy worker!"
8. You are the only woman in a meeting with seven men. At the beginning of the meeting, the Chair asks you to be the secretary. You respond:	"No. I'm sick and tired of being the secretary just because I'm the only woman in the group."
9. A physician asks to borrow your stethoscope. You say:	"Well, I guess so. One of you doctors walked off with mine last week, and this new one cost me $65. Be sure you return it, OK?"
10. You are interpreting the I&O sheet for a physician, and he interrupts you. You say:	"You could understand this if you'd stop interrupting me and listen."

LEARNING EXERCISE 19.10

Memo to Chief Executive Officer Leads to Miscommunication

Carol White, the coordinator for the multidisciplinary mental health outpatient services of a 150-bed psychiatric hospital, feels frustrated because the hospital is very centralized. She believes that this keeps the hospital's therapists and nurse-managers from being as effective as they could if they had more authority. Therefore, she has worked out a plan to decentralize her department, giving the therapists and nurse-managers more control and new titles. She sent her new plan to CEO Joe Short and has just received this memo in return.

Dear Ms. White:

The Board of Directors and I met to review your plan and think it is a good one. In fact, we have been thinking along the same lines for quite some time now. I'm sure you must have heard of our plans. Because we recently contracted with a physician's group to cover our crisis center, we believe this would be a good time to decentralize in other ways. We suggest that your new substance abuse coordinator report directly to the new chief of mental health. In addition, we believe your new director of the suicide prevention center should report directly to the chief of mental health. He then will report to me.

I am pleased that we are both moving in the same direction and have the same goals. We will be setting up meetings in the future to iron out the small details.

Sincerely,

Joe Short, CEO

Assignment: How and why did Carol's plan go astray? How did her mode of communication affect the outcome? Could the outcome have been prevented? What communication mode would have been most appropriate for Carol to use in sharing her plan with Joe? What should be her plan now? Explain your rationale.

LEARNING EXERCISE 19.11

Writing a Letter of Reference

Unit managers are frequently asked to write letters of reference for employees who have been terminated. The information used in writing these letters comes from performance evaluations, personal interviews with staff and patients, evidence of continuing education, and personal observations. Assume that you are a unit manager and that you have collected the following information on Mary Doe, an RN who worked at your facility for 3 months before abruptly resigning with 48 hours' notice.

Performance Evaluation

Three-month evaluation scant.

- The following criteria were marked "competent": amount of work accomplished, relationships with patients and coworkers, work habits, and basic skills.
- The following criteria were identified as "needing improvement": quality of work, communication skills, and leadership skills.
- No criteria were marked unsatisfactory or outstanding.
- Narrative comments were limited to the following: "has a bit of a chip on her shoulder," "works independently a lot," and "assessment skills improving."

Interviews with Staff

- Coworker RN Judy: "She was OK. She was a little strange—she belonged to some kind of traveling religious cult. In fact, I think that's why she left her job."
- Coworker licensed vocational nurse (LVN)/licensed professional nurse (LPN) Lisa: "Mary was great. She got all her work done. I never had to help her with her meds or AM care. She took her turn at floating, which is more than I can say for some of the other RNs."
- Coworker RN John: "When I was the charge nurse, I found I needed to seek Mary out to find out what was going on with her patients. It made me real uncomfortable."
- Coworker LVN/LPN Joe: "Mary hated it here—she never felt like she belonged. The charge nurse was always hassling her about little things, and it really seemed unfair."

Patient Comments

- "She helped me with my bath and got all my pills on time. She was a good nurse."
- "I don't remember her."
- "She was so busy—I appreciated how efficient she was at how she did her job."
- "I remember Mary. She told me she really liked older people. I wish she had had more time to sit down and talk to me."

Notes from Personnel File

Twenty-four years old. Graduated from 3-year diploma school 2 years ago. Has worked in three jobs since that time.

(Continued)

Continuing Education

Current CPR card. No other continuing education completed at this facility.

Assignment: Mary Doe's prospective employer has requested a letter of reference to accompany Mary's application to become a hospice nurse/counselor. No form has been provided, so you must determine an appropriate format. Decide which information you should include in your letter and which should be omitted. Will you weigh some information more heavily than other information? Would you make any recommendations about Mary Doe's suitability for the hospice job? Be prepared to read your letter aloud to the class, and justify your rationale for the content that you included.

LEARNING EXERCISE 19.12

Bringing a Group Together

You are the evening charge nurse of a medical unit. The staff on your unit has voiced displeasure in how requests for days off are handled. Your manager has given you the task of forming a committee and reviewing the present policy regarding requests for days off on the unit. On your committee are four LVNs, three certified nursing assistants, and five RNs. All shifts are represented. There are three men among the group members, and there is a fairly broad range of ethnic and cultural groups.

Tomorrow will be your fourth meeting, and you are becoming a bit frustrated because the meetings do not seem to be accomplishing much to reach the objectives that the group was charged to meet. The objective was to develop a fair method to handle special requested days off that were not part of the normal rotation.

On your first meeting, you spent time getting to know the members and identified the objective. Various committee members contacted other hospitals, and others did a literature search to determine how other institutions handled this matter. During the second meeting, this material was reviewed by all members. At the last meeting, the group was very contentious. In fact, several raised their voices. Others sat quietly, and some seemed to pout. Only the three men could agree upon anything. One LVN thought that the RNs were overly represented. One RN thought that the policy for day-off requests should be separated into three different policies—one for each classification. You are not sure how to bring this committee together or what, if any, action you should take.

Assignment: Review the section in this chapter about how groups work. Write a one-page essay on what is happening in the group, and answer the following questions. Should you add members to the committee? Does your group have too many task members and not enough team-building members? What should be your role in getting the group to perform its task? What could be some strategies you could use that would perhaps bring the group together?

REFERENCES

American Nurses Association. (2011, September). *Principles for social networking and the nurse.* Silver Spring, MD: Author.

Answers.com. (2013). *Communication.* Definition. Retrieved June 14, 2013, from http://www.answers.com/topic/communication

Atlanta Black Star (2013, March 22). *Effective communication is neither too passive nor too aggressive.* Retrieved June 16, 2013, from http://atlantablackstar.com/2013/03/22/effective-communication-is-neither-too-passive-nor-too-aggressive/

Boynton, B. (2009, November–December). How to improve your listening skills. *American Nurse Today, 4*(9), 50–51.

Centers for Medicare and Medicaid Services. (2010). *Medicare & Medicaid EHR incentive program.* Retrieved May 4, 2013, from https://www.cms .gov/Regulations-and-Guidance/Legislation/ EHRIncentivePrograms/downloads/MU_Stage1 _ReqOverview.pdf

Cherry, K. (2013). *Understanding body language.* About.com Psychology. Retrieved June 16, 2013, from http:// psychology.about.com/od/nonverbalcommunication/ ss/understanding-body-language_7.htm

Decker , B. (2013, May 30). *Decline of eye contact – and how you can correct it.* Decker Communications. Retrieved June 16, 2013 from http://decker.com/blog/ tag/eye-contact/

Ferguson, K. (2013, March 14). It's time for the nursing profession to leverage social media. *Journal of Advanced Nursing, 69* (4), 745–747. Retrieved June 16, 2013, from http://onlinelibrary.wiley.com/ doi/10.1111/jan.12036/full

Forming, Storming, Norming, Performing: Four-Stage Evolution of a Top Team. (2009, December). *Clinical Trials Administrator, 7*(12), 140–141.

Garon, M. (2012). Speaking up, being heard: Registered nurses' perceptions of workplace communication. *Journal of Nursing Management, 20*(3), 361–371.

Gobry, P-E. (2011, May 24). *The internet is 20% of economic growth.* Business Insider. Retrieved June 13, 2013, from http://www.businessinsider.com/ mckinsey-report-internet-economy-2011-5

Haughom, J., Kriz, S., & McMillan, D. (2011). Overcoming barriers to EHR adoption. *Healthcare Financial Management, 65*(7), 96–100.

Huston, C. J. (2013, May 31). The impact of emerging technology on nursing care: Warp speed ahead. *The Online Journal of Issues in Nursing*, 18(2), Manuscript 1. Retrieved June 14, 2013, from http:// www.nursingworld.org/MainMenuCategories/ ANAMarketplace/ANAPeriodicals/OJIN/ TableofContents/Vol-18-2013/No2-May-2013/ Impact-of-Emerging-Technology.html.aspx

Huston, C. J. (2014). Technology in the health care workplace: Benefits, limitations, and challenges. In *Professional issues in nursing: Challenges and opportunities* (3rd ed.). Philadelphia, PA: Lippincott Williams & Wilkins 214–227.

Ibe, P. (2013, May 19). *Assertive communication for a healthy workplace.* 3 Plus International. Retrieved June 16, 2013, from http://3plusinternational .com/2013/05/assertive-communication/

ISBAR: Adding an Extra Step in Handoff Communication. (2013). *StrategiesforNurse Managers.com.* Retrieved June 16, 2013, from http://www .strategiesfornursemanagers.com/ce_detail/222773.cfm

Jordan, K. W. (2009, February 17). *SBAR: A communication formula for patient safety.* Boston.com. Retrieved February 19, 2010, from http://www.boston.com/jobs/ healthcare/oncall/articles/2009/02/17/perspective/

Loo, T. (n.d.) *How to communicate using space.* Retrieved June 13, 2013, from http://hodu.com/space.shtml

Mayo Clinic Staff (2011, June 11). *Stress management. Being assertive: Reduce stress, communicate better.* Retrieved June 16, 2013, from http://www .mayoclinic.com/health/assertive/SR00042

Miliard, M. (2012, April 24). Meaningful use still a challenge despite strides, say hospitals. *Healthcare IT News.* Retrieved May 2, 2013, from www .healthcareitnews.com/news/meaningful-use-still -challenge-despite-strides-say-hospitals

National Council of State Boards of Nursing. (2011, August). *White Paper: A nurses' guide to the use of social media.* Chicago, IL: Author. Retrieved June 16, 2013 from http://www.nursingworld.org/ FunctionalMenuCategories/AboutANA/Social-Media/ Social-Networking-Principles-Toolkit/6-Tips-for -Nurses-Using-Social-Media-Poster.pdf

Perkins, C., & Brizee, A. (2013, March 10). *Audience and purpose.* Purdue Online Writing Lab. OWL. Retrieved June 16, 2013, from http://owl.english .purdue.edu/owl/resource/590/1/

Piscotty, R., Voepel-Lewis, T, Lee, S.H., Annis-Emeott, A., Lee, E, & Kalisch, B. (2013, May). To tweet or not to tweet? Nurses, social media, and patient care. *Nursing Management, 44* (5), 52–53.

Take 5 with a Nurse Leader. (2012). *The American Nurse.* Retrieved May 1, 2013, from www.theamericannurse .org/index.php/2012/10/05/take-5-with-a-nurse-leader/

Thomson, B. (2013). *Are you an aggressive communicator?* Southeast Psych. Retrieved June 16, 2013, from http://blog.southeastpsych.com/2013/03/28/are-you -an-aggressive-communicator/

Tuckman, B. W., & Jensen, M. A. C. (1977). Stages of small group development revisited. *Group and Organization Studies, 2*(4), 419.

Urseny, L. (2007, January 26). Sticking to the agenda. *Chico Enterprise Record,* Section E, 4E.

Writing Help Central. (n.d.). *Letter writing resources.* Retrieved June 14, 2013, from http://www .writinghelp-central.com/letter-writing.html

20

Delegation

... Delegation is primarily about entrusting your authority to others.
—Raphael M. Barishansky

... at its most basic, delegation is empowering one person to act for another.
—Susanne A. Quallich

CROSSWALK THIS CHAPTER ADDRESSES:

BSN Essential II: Basic organizational and systems leadership for quality care and patient safety

BSN Essential VI: Interprofessional communication and collaboration for improving patient health outcomes

BSN Essential VIII: Professionalism and professional values

MSN Essential II: Organizational and systems leadership

MSN Essential VII: Interprofessional collaboration for improving patient and population health outcomes

QSEN Competency: Patient-centered care

QSEN Competency: Teamwork and collaboration

QSEN Competency: Safety

AONE Nurse Executive Competency I: Communication and relationship building

AONE Nurse Executive Competency II: A knowledge of the health-care environment

AONE Nurse Executive Competency III: Leadership

AONE Nurse Executive Competency IV: Professionalism

AONE Nurse Executive Competency V: Business skills

LEARNING OBJECTIVES *The learner will:*

- identify specific strategies that increase the likelihood of effective delegation
- recognize delegation as a learned skill imperative to professional nursing practice
- delegate tasks using appropriate priority setting and use of personnel in vicarious situations
- differentiate between tasks that should and should not be delegated
- identify common causes of underdelegation, overdelegation, and improper delegation as well as strategies to overcome these delegation errors
- recognize the need to give adequate information and authority to complete delegated tasks
- identify factors that must be considered when determining what tasks can be safely delegated to subordinates
- discuss how the role of the registered nurse as delegator has changed with the increased use of nursing assistive personnel and unlicensed assistive personnel
- determine whether delegation to an unlicensed worker is appropriate in a given situation, using a decision tree developed by the National Council of State Boards of Nursing (NCSBN) or a State Board of Nursing
- identify leadership strategies that can be used to reduce subordinate resistance to delegation

- describe cultural phenomena that must be considered when delegating to a multicultural staff or in encouraging multicultural staff to delegate
- describe actions the manager can take to reduce the liability of supervision, particularly when delegating tasks

Delegation has long been a function of registered nursing, although the scope of delegation and the tasks being delegated have changed dramatically the past two decades. *Delegation* can be defined simply as getting work done through others or as directing the performance of one or more people to accomplish organizational goals. Huston (2009) defines delegation as giving someone else the authority to complete a task or action on your behalf. Similarly, the North Carolina Nursing Administrative Code defines delegation as a "transfer or hand-off to a competent individual, the authority to perform a task/activity in a specific setting/situation" (Winstead, 2013, p. 9).

Even more complex definitions of delegation, supervision, and assignment have been created by the American Nurses Association (ANA) and the National Council of State Boards of Nursing (NCSBN) in response to the emerging complexity of delegation in today's health-care arena, where increasing numbers of unlicensed and relatively untrained workers provide direct patient care. Historically, the ANA and the NCSBN defined delegation differently, with the ANA defining delegation as the transfer of responsibility for the performance of a task from one person to another and the NCSBN defining delegation as transferring to a competent individual the authority to perform a selected nursing task in a selected situation (Huston, 2014).

Both groups have come together, however, to issue a *Joint Statement on Delegation*, intended to support nurses in using delegation safely and effectively (Does Your Staff Understand Delegation, 2009). In addition, both suggest that delegation is a skill that must be taught and practiced for proficiency.

Experts also agree that delegation is an essential element of the directing phase of the management process because much of the work accomplished by managers (first-, middle-, and top-level managers) occurs not only through their own efforts but also through those of their subordinates. Frequently, there is too much work to be accomplished by one person. In these situations, delegation often becomes synonymous with productivity and is not an option—but a necessity. Tredgold (2013, para 6) agrees, noting that "often people want to be great leaders, but don't want to delegate, even refuse to delegate, but this is a self defeating trait. We end up becoming occupied doing stuff, rather than getting as much stuff done as is possible."

There are many good reasons for delegating. Sometimes, managers must delegate routine tasks so they are free to handle problems that are more complex or require a higher level of expertise. Managers may delegate work if someone else is better prepared or has greater expertise or knowledge about how to solve a problem. Delegation can also be used to provide learning or "stretching" opportunities for subordinates. Subordinates who are not delegated enough responsibility may become bored, nonproductive, and ineffective. Thus, in delegating, the leader-manager contributes to employees' personal and professional development.

 The mark of a great leader is when he or she can recognize the excellent performance of someone else and allow others to shine for their accomplishments.

The leadership roles and management functions inherent in delegation are shown in Display 20.1.

DISPLAY 20.1 Leadership Roles and Management Functions Associated with Delegation

LEADERSHIP ROLES

1. Functions as a role model, supporter, and resource person in delegating tasks to subordinates.
2. Encourages followers to use delegation as a time management strategy and team-building tool.
3. Assists followers in identifying situations appropriate for delegation.
4. Communicates clearly when delegating tasks.
5. Maintains patient safety as a minimum criterion in determining the most appropriate person to carry out a delegated task.
6. Plans ahead and delegates proactively, rather than waiting until time urgency is present and crisis responses are required.
7. Conveys a feeling of confidence and encouragement to the individual who has taken on a delegated task.
8. Is an informed and active participant in the development of local, state, and national guidelines for unlicensed assistive personnel (UAP)/nursing assistive personnel (NAP) scope of practice.
9. Is sensitive to how cultural phenomena affect transcultural delegation.
10. Uses delegation as a means for stretching and empowering workers to learn new skills and be successful.
11. Works to establish a culture of mutual trust, teamwork, and open communication so that delegation becomes a strategy health-care workers feel comfortable using to achieve organizational, patient, and personal goals.

MANAGEMENT FUNCTIONS

1. Creates job descriptions and scope of practice statements for all personnel, including NAP, that conform to national, state, and professional recommendations for ensuring safe patient care.
2. Is knowledgeable regarding legal liabilities of subordinate supervision.
3. Accurately assesses subordinates' capabilities and motivation when delegating.
4. Delegates a level of authority necessary to complete delegated tasks.
5. Shares accountability for delegated tasks.
6. Consciously attempts to see the subordinate's perspective to reduce the likelihood of resistance in delegation.
7. Develops and implements a periodic review process for all delegated tasks.
8. Avoids overburdening subordinates by giving them permission to refuse delegated tasks.
9. Provides recognition or reward for the completion of delegated tasks.
10. Provides formal education and training opportunities on delegation principles for staff.

DELEGATING EFFECTIVELY

Delegation is not easy. It requires you to trust somebody else to perform a task that you believe to be important. It also takes effort: you have to explain how you do a particular task, train somebody else to do it, and then monitor that person. Yet, it is also absolutely critical to managerial productivity and efficiency. The following strategies will increase the likelihood of successful and effective delegation (Display 20.2). Each of these strategies is detailed below.

DISPLAY 20.2 Strategies for Successful Delegation

Plan ahead.
Identify necessary skill and education levels to complete the delegated task.
Select capable personnel.
Communicate goals clearly.
Empower the delegate.
Set deadlines and monitor progress.
Monitor the role and provide guidance.
Evaluate performance.
Reward accomplishment.

Plan Ahead

Plan ahead when identifying tasks to be accomplished. Always make an attempt to delegate before you become overwhelmed. In addition, always be sure to carefully assess the situation before delegating and to clearly delineate the desired outcomes.

Identify Necessary Skills and Education Levels

Identify the skill or educational level necessary to complete the job. Often, legal and licensing statutes such as the Nurse Practice Act (NPA) determine this. Anderson (2013) notes that professional nurses work with a variety of different types of caregivers but the scope of practice for the RN is typically defined by the Board of Nursing in each state. The challenge is that the RN must also understand the scope of practice of others on the nursing team who are providing patient care.

Nurses then must be aware of their state NPA essential elements regarding delegation, including the following:

- The state's NPA definition of delegation
- Items that cannot be delegated
- Items that cannot be routinely delegated
- Guidelines for RNs about tasks that can be delegated
- A description of professional nursing practice
- A description of licensed vocational nurse (LVN)/licensed professional nurse (LPN) nursing practice and unlicensed nursing roles
- The degree of supervision required to complete a task
- The guidelines for lowering delegation risks
- Warnings about inappropriate delegation
- If there is a restricted use of the word "nurse" to licensed staff

In addition, the manager should know the official job description expectations for each worker classification in the organization, as they may be more restrictive than the state NPA.

Select Capable Personnel

Identify which individuals can complete the job in terms of capability and time to do so. Remember that it is a leadership role to stretch new and capable employees who want opportunities to learn and grow. Also, look for employees who are innovative and willing to take risks. It is also important that the person to whom the task is being delegated considers the task to be important.

This does not suggest, however, that skill and expertise are not needed. Leader-managers should always ask the individuals to whom they are delegating if they are capable of completing the delegated task and validate this perception by direct observation.

Communicate Goals Clearly

The goals for delegation should always be clearly communicated. This includes identifying any limitations or qualifications that are being imposed on the delegated task. Knox (2013) notes that the delegator must communicate specifically what, how, and by when delegated tasks are to be accomplished. This communication should also include the purpose and goal of the task, any limitations for task completion, and the expectations for reporting.

Empower the Delegate

Delegate the authority and the responsibility necessary to complete the task. Nothing is more frustrating to a creative and productive employee than not having the resources or authority to carry out a well-developed plan.

Set Deadlines and Monitor Progress

Set time lines, and monitor how the task is being accomplished through informal but regularly scheduled meetings. This shows an interest on the part of the nurse-leader, provides for a periodic review of progress, and encourages ongoing communication to clarify any questions or misconceptions. Knox (2013) agrees, suggesting that the RN must monitor and evaluate both the patient and the staff's performance of delegated tasks and be prepared to intervene on behalf of the patient as necessary. In doing so, the leader-manager provides staff feedback to increase competency in task performance. In addition, this keeps the delegated task before the subordinate and the manager so that both share accountability for its completion. Although the final responsibility belongs to the delegator, the subordinate doing the task accepts responsibility for completing it appropriately and is accountable to the person who delegated the task.

 Responsibility is shared when a task is delegated.

Model the Role and Provide Guidance

The leader-manager should convey a feeling of confidence and encouragement to the individual who has taken on a delegated task. If the worker is having difficulty carrying out the delegated task, the leader-manager should be available as a role model and resource in identifying alternative solutions. Leaders should encourage employees, however, to attempt to solve problems themselves first, although they should always be willing to answer questions about the task or to clarify desired outcomes as necessary.

Finding a balance between providing guidance and allowing others to best determine how to accomplish a delegated task, however, is sometimes difficult. Although the desired end product should be specified, it is important to give the subordinate feedback and an appropriate degree of autonomy in deciding exactly how the work can be accomplished.

Reassuming the delegated task should be a manager's last resort, because this action fosters a sense of failure in the employee and demotivates rather than motivates. Delegation is useless if the manager is unwilling to allow divergence in problem solving and thus re-does all work that has been delegated. However, the manager may need to delegate work previously assigned to an employee so that the employee has time to do the newly assigned task.

Evaluate Performance

Evaluate the delegation experience after the task has been completed. Include positive and negative aspects of how the person completed the task. Were the outcomes achieved? Ask the individual you delegated to, what you could have done differently to facilitate their completion of the delegated tasks. This shared reflection encourages the development of a mutually trusting and productive relationship between delegators and subordinates.

Reward Accomplishment

Be sure to appropriately reward a successfully completed task. Leaders are often measured by the successes of those on their teams. Therefore, the more recognition team members receive, the more recognition will be given to their leader.

 The right to delegate and the ability to provide formal rewards for successful completion of delegated tasks are a reflection of the legitimate authority inherent in the management role.

LEARNING EXERCISE 20.1

Difficulty in Delegation

Is it difficult for you to delegate to others? If so, do you know why? Are you more apt to underdelegate, overdelegate, or delegate improperly? Think back to the last thing you delegated. Was this delegation successful? What safeguards can you build in to decrease this delegation error?

Delegation is a high-level skill essential to the manager that improves with practice. As managers gain the maturity and self-confidence needed to delegate wisely, they increase their impact and power both within and outside the organization. Subordinates gain self-esteem and increased job satisfaction from the responsibility and authority given to them, and the organization moves a step closer toward achieving its goals.

COMMON DELEGATION ERRORS

Delegation is not intuitive for most people; instead, it is a critical leadership skill that must be learned. Frequent mistakes made by managers in delegating include underdelegating, overdelegating, and improper delegating (Display 20.3).

DISPLAY 20.3	Common Delegating Errors

Underdelegating
Overdelegating
Improper delegating

Underdelegating

Underdelegating frequently stems from the individual's false assumption that delegation may be interpreted as a lack of ability on his or her part to do the job correctly or completely. Delegation does not need to limit the individual's control, prestige, and power; rather, delegation can extend their influence and capability by increasing what can be accomplished. In fact, delegation can be empowering, both to the person delegating and to the person being delegated to.

Another cause of underdelegating is the individual's desire to complete the whole job personally due to a lack of trust in the subordinates; some nurses believe that he or she needs the experience or that he or she can do it better and faster than anyone else, and indeed— sometimes, this is the case. Case (2013) agrees, noting that many RNs find it difficult to transfer authority. This is especially the case for individuals who are new to delegation since they often feel as though they must give up control (Delegating, n.d.). It may be frightening to allow a team member to complete a task for which you are ultimately responsible. Communicating frequently with those to whom you've delegated to check the progress of the task can help decrease this fear and should give the delegator some sense of control (Delegating, n.d).

It may be unnerving to allow a team member to complete a task for which you are ultimately responsible.

Other individuals underdelegate because there is not enough time to delegate It takes time to delegate because the delegator must adequately explain the task or teach their team member the skills necessary to complete the delegated task. The problem is paradoxical because one of the main benefits of delegation is saving time (Delegating, n.d.). Case (2013) states, however, that delegators should always remember that time spent in training another to do a job can be repaid 10-fold in the future. In addition to increased productivity, delegation can also provide the opportunity for subordinates to experience feelings of accomplishment and enrichment.

Nurses also may underdelegate because they lack experience in the job or in delegation itself. Other nurses refuse to delegate because they have an excessive need to control or be perfect. The leader-manager who accepts nothing less than perfection limits the opportunities available for subordinate growth and often wastes time redoing delegated tasks.

In addition, some individuals underdelegate because they fail to anticipate the help they will need. In an ideal situation, the best time to delegate is *before* you become overwhelmed (Huston, 2009). While crises happen that require you to reorganize your priorities, more often than not you can foresee hectic or challenging times. For example, waiting until the end of your shift to delegate the tasks you didn't have time to finish is unfair to the person you're delegating to, and that individual is likely to resent your request (Huston).

Finally, some novice managers emerging from the clinical nurse role underdelegate because they find it difficult to assume the manager role. This occurs, in part, because the nurses have been rewarded in the past for their clinical expertise and not their management skills. As managers come to understand and accept the need for the hierarchical responsibilities of delegation, they become more productive and develop more positive staff relationships.

Overdelegating

In contrast to underdelegating, which overburdens the manager, some managers *overdelegate*, burdening their subordinates. Some managers overdelegate because they are poor managers of time, spending most of it just trying to get organized. Others overdelegate because they feel insecure in their ability to perform a task.

It is critical that the manager is sensitive to the workload constraints of his or her staff. Staff should always have the right to refuse a delegated task. The servant leader always asks the person they want to delegate to, if they have time to help, instead of just assuming that their needs are greater than those of the staff member. Managers also must be careful not to overdelegate to exceptionally competent employees, because they may become overworked and tired, which can decrease their productivity.

Improper Delegating

Improper delegation includes such things as delegating at the wrong time, to the wrong person, or for the wrong reason. It also may include delegating tasks and responsibilities that are beyond the capability of the person to whom they are being delegated or that should be done by someone with greater expertise, training, or authority.

Knox (2013) emphasizes that one of the most important aspects of delegation is determining if a task should be delegated. To do this, she suggests the nurse make an assessment of the patient or a group of patients and determine what activities can be delegated to a specific member of the health-care team. In addition, Knox notes that the decision to delegate a task must match the staff's competency and level of supervision available. Finally, Knox notes that appropriate delegation must include a consideration of who is the most appropriate person is to delegate to.

Delegating decision making without providing adequate information is another example of improper delegation. If the manager requires a higher quality than *satisficing*, this must be made clear at the time of the delegation. Not everything that is delegated needs to be handled in a maximizing mode. Almost all of these delegation errors could be avoided if the five rights of delegation, identified by the American Nurses Association (ANA) and the National Council of State Boards of Nursing (NCSBN) (n.d.), were followed. These are shown in Display 20.4.

DISPLAY 20.4	The Five Rights of Delegation

- **Right task**
  One that is delegable for a specific patient
- **Right circumstances**
  Appropriate patient setting, available resources, and other relevant factors considered
- **Right person**
  Right person is delegating the right task to the right person to be performed on the right person.
- **Right direction/communication**
  Clear, concise description of the task, including its objective, limits, and expectations
- **Right level of supervision**
  Appropriate monitoring, evaluation, intervention, as needed, and feedback

Source: American Nurses Association (ANA) and the National Council of State Boards of Nursing (NCSBN) (n.d.). Joint statement on delegation. Retrieved June 17, 2013, from https://www.ncsbn.org/Delegation_joint_statement _NCSBN-ANA.pdf

DELEGATION AS A FUNCTION OF PROFESSIONAL NURSING

With the restructuring of care delivery models, RNs at all levels are increasingly being expected to make assignments for and supervise the work of different levels of employees. To increase the likelihood that the increased delegation required in today's restructured health-care organizations does not result in an unsafe work environment, organizations should take appropriate action. Huston (2014) suggests that (a) organizations must have a clearly defined structure where RNs are recognized as leaders of the health-care team, (b) job descriptions clearly define the roles and responsibilities of all, (c) educational programs are developed to help personnel learn roles and responsibilities of each other's roles, and (d) adequate programs are developed to foster leadership and delegation.

RNs asked to assume the role of supervisor and delegator need preparation to assume these leadership tasks, including instruction in personnel supervision and delegation principles. Repeated education programs on delegation principles and role clarity are necessary to demonstrate consistency in delegating appropriate role activities and to begin to feel confident in delegating because in many cases, nurses who are well prepared to provide care for patients may not be well prepared to be a delegator.

The RN, although well trained in the role of direct care provider, may not be adequately prepared for the role of delegator.

In addition, nursing schools and health-care organizations need to do a better job of preparing professional RNs for the delegator role. This includes educating them about the NPA governing the scope of practice in their state; basic principles of delegating to the right person, at the right time, and for the right reason; and actions that must be undertaken when work is delegated in an inappropriate or unsafe manner. Knox (2013, para 5) states that "knowledge of state practice acts and agency directives are essential when making decisions about what patient care tasks can be delegated."

Finally, health-care organizations need to assure that new nurses are supported in their early efforts to delegate and that these skills are not learned by trial and error. Instead, leaders must create workplace cultures where teamwork, mutual respect, and open communication are valued, and where nurses believe they can delegate without fearing they will be perceived as lazy or incompetent (Examining the Evidence 20.1).

Nurses must believe they can delegate without fearing they will be perceived as lazy or incompetent.

Examining the Evidence 20.1

Source: Kærnested, B., & Bragadóttir, H. (2012). Delegation of registered nurses revisited: Attitudes towards delegation and preparedness to delegate effectively. Nordic Journal of Nursing Research & Clinical Studies/Vård I Norden, 32(1), 10–15.

The descriptive, correlational study surveyed 71 RNs working in five medical acute care inpatient units at a university hospital in Iceland to determine the attitudes of these nurses toward delegation and their preparedness to delegate effectively. In addition, the study sought to determine whether attitude and preparedness to delegate were related to age, experience, education in delegation, workload, and job satisfaction.

Overall, participants showed a relatively positive attitude toward delegation, although there was potential for improvement. The majority of participants reported they do delegate, but noted that they still spent a large amount of time on tasks that could be done by others. One out of four participants agreed wholly or moderately that staff lacked the necessary commitment and experience to complete delegated tasks in a satisfactory manner and that it was easier for them to just do it themselves. In addition, just over 45% of participants suggested they were always, often, or sometimes worried that staff would regard them as lazy for delegating tasks. This was especially true for younger nurses (<30 years old). While novice nurses stated they understood basic delegation principles, they also felt they lacked the skills to delegate effectively and they suggested that much of what they knew about delegation had been learned through trial and error on the job. Participants with less than 5 years of experience believed they would delegate more if they were more confident about delegating.

The researchers concluded that the results signified to some extent, a lack of trust, teamwork, and communication in nursing delegation. They noted that effective delegation by registered nurses (RNs) needs constant attention within educational programs as well as in health-care settings, regardless of the time and economic situation within which health care is practiced. The researchers suggest this will not occur solely by educating RNs about who and what can be delegated; instead, it must be done by teaching, practicing, and nurturing mutual trust and effective communication within nursing teams.

LEARNING EXERCISE 20.2

Assessing Nurses' Comfort with Delegation

Informally survey nurses in the agency in which you work or do clinical practicums. How many of them have received formal education on delegation principles? How comfortable do these nurses feel in determining what should be delegated to whom? How comfortable do you feel in delegating work to other members of the health-care team?

Delegating to Unlicensed Assistive Personnel

In an effort to contain spiraling health-care costs, many health-care providers in the 1990s chose to eliminate RN positions or to replace licensed professional nurses with UAP or NAP. (In 2007, the ANA stopped using the term UAP and replaced it with NAP, suggesting that many NAPs are now licensed or formally recognized in some manner.) Both UAP and NAP include but are not limited to nurse extenders, care partners, nurse's aides, orderlies, assistants, attendants, health care assistants, and technicians (Huston, 2014).

Almost all RNs in acute care institutions and long-term care facilities are currently involved in some capacity with the assignment, delegation, and supervision of the NAP in the delivery of nursing care. The primary argument for utilizing NAP in acute care settings is cost (although nursing shortages are a contributing factor). NAP can free professional nurses from tasks and assignments (specifically, non-nursing functions) that can be completed by less extensively trained personnel at a lower cost.

Assuming the role of delegator and supervisor to NAP, however, increases the scope of liability for the RN. Although nurses are not automatically held liable for all acts of negligence on the part of those they supervise, they may be held liable if they were negligent in the supervision of those employees at the time they committed the negligent acts. Liability is based on a supervisor's failure to determine which patient needs could safely be assigned to a subordinate or for failing to closely monitor a subordinate who requires such supervision. In delegating, the RN needs to know well the skills of the person to whom work is delegated. The liability of supervision is discussed in Chapter 5.

In assigning tasks to NAP, the RN must be aware of the job description, knowledge base, and demonstrated skills of each person.

In addition, RNs should recognize that although the Omnibus Budget Reconciliation Act of 1987 established regulations for the education and certification of nurse's aides (minimum of 75 hours of theory and practice and successful completion of an examination in both areas), no federal or community standards have been established for training the more broadly defined NAP (Huston, 2014). Some standards and guidelines are now required for the preparation and use of NAP in certified home health agencies and skilled nursing facilities, but there are no required education standards or guidelines for the use of NAP in acute care hospitals that cross state lines and jurisdictions.

The UAP has no license to lose for "exceeding scope of practice" and nationally established standards for scope of practice do not exist for UAP.

This does not imply that all NAPs are uneducated and unprepared for the roles they have been asked to fill. Indeed, NAP educational levels vary from less than a high school graduate to those holding advanced degrees. It merely suggests that the RN, in delegating to NAP, must carefully assess what skills and knowledge that each NAP has or risk-increased personal liability for the failure to do so (Huston, 2014).

Unfortunately, many institutions do not have distinct job descriptions for NAP that clearly define their scope of practice. While some institutions limit the scope of practice for NAP to non-nursing functions, other organizations allow NAP to perform many skills traditionally reserved for the licensed nurse. Some NAPs have little background in health care and only rudimentary training. Yet they may be allowed to insert catheters, read electrocardiograms, suction tracheostomy tubes, change sterile dressings, and perform other traditional nursing functions (Huston, 2014). This is because some agencies interpret regulations broadly, allowing NAP a broader scope of practice than that advocated by professional nursing associations or State Boards of Nursing. Few states use the ANA or NCSBN definitions for delegation, supervision, or assignment. Most states, however, reported no standardized curriculum in place for NAP employed in acute care hospitals (Huston, 2014).

Some State Boards of Nursing, in an effort to more clearly define the scope of practice for NAP, have issued task lists. Training of the NAP is not based on the notion that such individuals will be performing activities independently. Task lists, however, suggest no need for delegation, as NAP already have a list of nursing activities that he or she may perform without waiting for the delegation process. But what happens when the condition of a client changes? Are NAP with fewer than 75 hours of training astute enough to recognize that there has been a change in the client's condition and alert the RN?

In addition, in the late 1990s, the NCSBN established a *decision tree for delegation*, which includes a step-by-step analysis nurses can use to decide whether a task should be delegated. Many State Boards of Nursing have also adopted decision trees that are posted on their Web sites. See Figure 20.1 for an example of the decision tree created by the Kentucky Board of

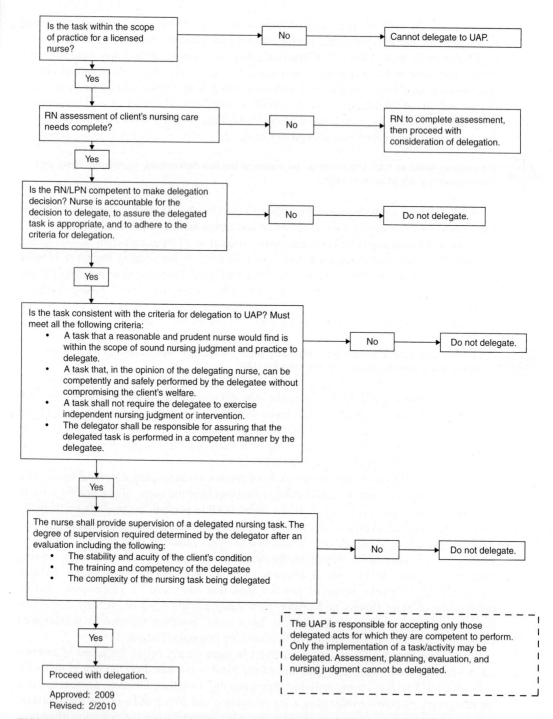

FIGURE 20.1 • KBN decision tree for delegation to unlicensed assistive personnel (UAP).
Source: Kentucky Board of Nursing. (2010). Decision tree for delegation to unlicensed assistive personnel (UAP). Retrieved June 17, 2013, from http://kbn.ky.gov/NR/rdonlyres/E1591ED0-5C3E-425C-ACE6-396268CE1774/0/DecisionTreeforDelegationtoUAP.pdf (Reprinted with permission of the Kentucky Board of Nursing).

Registered Nursing (2010) to guide nurses in delegating to unlicensed workers. In addition, Display 20.5 suggests criteria developed by the North Carolina Board of Registered Nursing (2013) that may be helpful in determining what tasks can safely be delegated to UAP.

New decision trees created by the NCSBN and State Boards of Nursing guide RNs in determining what can safely be delegated to unlicensed workers.

DISPLAY 20.5	Criteria for Delegation to an Unlicensed Assistive Personnel

The North Carolina Board of Registered Nursing (2013) suggests that tasks should be delegated to UAP only if they meet ALL of the following criteria:

1. Frequently recur in the daily care of a client or group of clients
2. Are performed according to an established (standardized) sequence of steps
3. Involve little or no modification from one client-care situation to another
4. May be performed with a predictable outcome
5. Do not inherently involve ongoing assessment, interpretation, or decision making which cannot be logically separated from the procedure(s) itself
6. Do not endanger the health or well-being of clients
7. Are allowed by agency policy/procedures

Source: North Carolina Board of Nursing (2013). Delegation: Non-nursing functions. Position Statement for RN and LPN Practice. Retrieved June 18, 2013, from http://allnurses.com/north-carolina-nursing/north-carolina -board-465130.html

It is critical that the RN never loses sight of his or her ultimate responsibility for ensuring that patients receive appropriate, high-quality care. This means that while NAP may complete non-nursing functions such as bathing, vital signs, and the measurement and recording of intake and output, it is the RN who must analyze that information and then use the nursing process to see that desired patient outcomes are achieved. This is consistent with delegation principles suggested by the ANA, which note that while RNs may delegate tasks and elements of care, they cannot delegate the nursing process (Is It OK to Delegate? 2012). Only RNs have the formal authority to practice nursing, and activities that rely on the nursing process or require specialized skill, expert knowledge, or professional judgment should never be delegated.

Case (2013, para 11) agrees, noting that "while nursing tasks may be delegated, the licensed nurse's generalist knowledge of patient care indicates that the practice-pervasive functions of assessment, evaluation and nursing judgment must not be delegated." This includes such skills as the initial and ongoing assessment of patients, administering treatments and medications ordered by a licensed prescriber, initiating and coordinating the plan of care, teaching and counseling patients, promoting and maintaining health, and teaching and supervising students (Case).

It is the RN who bears the legal liability for allowing UAP to perform tasks that should be accomplished only by a licensed health-care professional.

The outcomes associated with the increased use of NAP are not yet known. An increasing number of studies suggest a direct link between decreased RN staffing and declines in patient outcomes. Some of these declines in patient outcomes noted in the literature include an increased incidence of patient falls, nosocomial infections, and medication errors (Huston, 2014).

Certainly, at some point, given the increasing complexity of health care and the increasing acuity of patient illnesses, there is a maximum representation of NAP in the staffing mix that should not be breached. Until those levels are determined, RNs can expect a continued increase in the utilization of NAP. To protect their patients and their professional license, RNs must continue to seek current information regarding national efforts to standardize the scope of practice for NAP and professional guidelines regarding what can be safely delegated to the NAP.

Subordinate Resistance to Delegation

Resistance is a common response by subordinates to delegation. One of the most common causes of subordinate resistance to, or refusal of, delegated tasks is the failure of the delegator to see the subordinate's perspective. Workloads assigned to NAP are generally highly challenging, both physically and mentally. In addition, NAPs frequently must adapt rapidly to changing priorities, often imposed on him or her by more than one delegator. If the subordinate is truly overwhelmed, additional delegation of tasks is inappropriate, and the RN should reexamine the necessity of completing the delegated task personally or finding someone else who is able to complete the task.

 The leader-manager should always attempt to see the delegated task from the perspective of the individual being delegated to.

Some subordinates resist delegation simply because they believe that they are incapable of completing the delegated task. If the employee is capable but lacks self-confidence, the astute leader may be able to use performance coaching to empower the subordinate and build self-confidence levels. If, however, the employee is truly at high risk for failure, the appropriateness of the delegation must be questioned and a task more appropriate to that employee's ability level should be delegated.

Another cause of subordinate resistance to delegation is an inherent resistance to authority. Some subordinates simply need to "test the water" and determine what the consequences are of not completing delegated tasks. In this case, the delegator must be calm but assertive about his or her expectations and provide explicit work guidelines, if necessary, to maintain an appropriate authority power gap. It is an ongoing leadership challenge to instill a team spirit between delegators and their subordinates.

Finally, resistance to delegation may be occurring because tasks are overdelegated in terms of specificity. All subordinates need to believe that there is some room for creativity and independent thinking in delegated tasks. Failure to allow for this human need results in disinterested subordinates who fail to internalize responsibility and accountability for the delegated task. When delegating to NAP, the RN should try to mix routine and boring tasks with more challenging and rewarding assignments. An additional strategy is to provide NAP with consistent, constructive feedback, both positive and negative, to foster growth and self-esteem.

When subordinates resist delegation, the delegator may be tempted to avoid confrontation and simply do the delegated task independently. This is seldom appropriate. Instead, the delegator must ascertain why the delegated task was not accomplished and take appropriate action to eliminate these restraining forces.

LEARNING EXERCISE 20.3

Dealing with Resistance to Delegation

You are the team leader for 10 patients. An experienced LVN/LPN and nurse's aide are also assigned to the team. It is an extremely busy day, and there is a great deal of work to be done. Several times today, you have found the LVN/LPN taking long breaks in the lounge or chatting socially at the front desk, despite the unmet needs of many patients. On those occasions, you have clearly delegated work tasks and time lines to her. Several hours later, you follow up on the delegated tasks and find that they were not completed. When you seek out the LVN/LPN, you find that she went to lunch without telling you or the aide. You are furious at her apparent disregard for your authority.

Assignment: What are possible causes of the LVN/LPN's failure to follow up on delegated tasks? How will you deal with this LVN/LPN? What goal serves as the basis for your actions? Justify your choice with rationale.

DELEGATING TO A TRANSCULTURAL WORK TEAM

The increasing diversity of both the workforce and the client populations being served has ramifications for delegation. Challenges in delegation are seen for both the culturally diverse delegatee and the delegator. For example, numerous studies have shown that nurses from an Asian background may require more time to develop delegation skills since assertiveness and asking for help from others may violate values that are culturally bound (NMC Says Asian Nurses, 2012). Wong (2012) agrees, noting that assertiveness is more highly valued in American culture than many other cultures and that this can be a challenge to nurses from other cultural backgrounds who are expected to delegate work.

According to Giger and Davidhizar (2008), there are six cultural phenomena that must be considered when working with staff from a culturally diverse background: communication, space, social organization, time, environmental control, and biologic variations.

Communication, the first of the cultural phenomena, is greatly affected by cultural diversity in the workforce because dialect, volume, use of touch, context of speech, and kinesics such as gestures, stance, and eye movement all influence how messages are sent and received. For example, delegation delivered in a softer tone may be perceived as less important than delegation received in a loud tone, even if the delegated tasks have equal importance. Similarly, a manager may make an inappropriate assumption about a person's inability to carry out an important delegated task if that person represents a culture that values softer speech and more passive behavior.

Space is the second cultural phenomenon influencing delegation. Space refers to the distance and intimacy techniques that are used when relating verbally or nonverbally to others. It is important that the delegator recognizes the personal space needs of each staff member and acts accordingly. If these space needs are not recognized and respected, the likelihood that a delegated task will be heard and followed through on appropriately will be reduced.

The third cultural phenomenon, *social organization*, refers to the importance of a group or unit in providing social support in a person's life. For many cultures, the family unit is the most important social organization. In some cultures, the duty to family always takes precedence over the needs of the organization. In other cultures, this values ranking is less clear, and the employee may experience great intrapersonal conflict in prioritizing delegated work tasks and obligations to the family unit. It is important, then, that the delegator is aware that employees' values differ and is sensitive in delegating critical tasks to employees who are experiencing stress in the family unit.

Time is the fourth cultural phenomenon affecting delegation. Cultural groups can be past, present, or future oriented. *Past-oriented cultures* are interested in preserving the past and maintaining tradition. *Present-oriented cultures* focus on maintaining the status quo and on daily operations. *Future-oriented cultures* focus on goals to be achieved and are more visionary in their approach to problems. For example, strategic planning might best be delegated to a person from a future-oriented culture, although the leader-manager should always be alert for opportunities to create new insight and stretching opportunities for subordinates.

Environmental control, the fifth cultural phenomenon, refers to the person's perception of control over his or her environment (internal *locus of control*). Some cultures believe more strongly in fate, luck, or chance than other cultures, and this may affect how a person approaches and carries out a delegated task. The person who believes that he or she has an internal locus of control is more likely to be creative and autonomous in decision making.

The final phenomenon, *biological variations*, refers to the biopsychosocial differences between racial and ethnic groups, such as susceptibility to disease and physiologic differences. Display 20.6 provides a summary of considerations when delegating to a transcultural work team.

DISPLAY 20.6   **Cultural Phenomena to Consider When Delegating to a Transcultural Team**

Communication: Especially dialect, volume, use of touch, and eye contact
Space: Interpersonal space differs between cultures
Social organization: Family unit of primary importance in some cultures
Time: Cultures tend to be past, present, or future oriented
Environmental control: Cultures often have either internal or external locus of control
Biological variations: Susceptibility to diseases (e.g., Tay-Sachs) and physiologic differences (e.g., height and skin color)

LEARNING EXERCISE 20.4

Cultural Considerations in Delegation

You are a new charge nurse working on a surgical unit and have one of the recently hired Filipino travel nurses working on your unit. This is the end of her second week of orientation on the unit. She also received a month of classroom orientation and enculturation when she was first hired. Today, you assign her as one of your team leaders, responsible for a team of LVN/LPNs and certified nursing assistants. She has been working with another team leader for more than a week, but this is her first day to have the team to herself.

You check with her several times during the morning to see how things are going. She speaks shyly without making eye contact and says that "everything is okay." At about noon, one of the LVN/LPNs comes to you and says that the new nurse has not delegated tasks appropriately and is trying to do too much of the work herself. In addition, some of the other members of the team find her unsmiling behavior and lack of eye contact unsettling.

Assignment: Do you feel that you made an appropriate assignment? Since things do not seem to be going well, what should you do now? In a small group, develop a plan of action with the following goals: (a) ensure that patient care is accomplished safely, (b) build self-esteem in the Filipino nurse, and (c) be a cultural bridge to staff.

INTEGRATING LEADERSHIP ROLES AND MANAGEMENT FUNCTIONS IN DELEGATION

The right to delegate and the ability to provide formal rewards for successful completion of delegated tasks reflect the legitimate authority inherent in the management role. Delegation provides a means of increasing unit productivity. It is also a managerial tool for subordinate accomplishment and enrichment.

Delegation, however, is not easy. It requires high-level management skills since effective delegation involves selecting the right person for the right reason, and at the right time and assessing the qualifications, availability, and experience of individuals being delegated to

(Huston, 2009). Novice managers often make delegation errors such as delegating too late, not delegating enough, delegating to the wrong person or for the wrong reason, and failing to provide appropriate supervision and guidance of delegated tasks.

Delegation also requires highly developed leadership skills such as sensitivity to subordinates' capabilities and needs, the ability to communicate clearly and directly, the willingness to support and encourage subordinates in carrying out delegated tasks, and the vision to see how delegation might result in increased personal growth for subordinates as well as increased unit productivity.

With the increased use of NAP in patient care, the need for nurses to have highly developed delegation skills has never been greater. The challenge continues to be using NAP only to provide personal care needs or nursing tasks that do not require the skill and judgment of the RN. With increasing patient loads and the current nursing shortage, many health-care organizations and the RNs who work within them are tempted to allow NAP to perform tasks that should be limited to professional nursing practice. Nurses must remember, however, that the responsibility for assuring that patients are protected and that NAP do not exceed their scope of practice, ultimately falls to the RN. When UAPs are allowed to encroach into professional nursing care, patients are placed at risk (Huston, 2014).

Using delegation skills appropriately will help to reduce the personal liability associated with supervising and delegating to NAP. It will also ensure that clients' needs are met and their safety is not jeopardized.

KEY CONCEPTS

- Professional nursing organizations and regulatory bodies are actively engaged in clarifying the scope of practice for unlicensed workers and delegation parameters for RNs.

- Delegation is not an option for the manager—it is a necessity.

- Delegation should be used for assigning routine tasks and tasks for which the manager does not have time. It is also appropriate as a tool for problem solving, changes in the manager's own job emphasis, and building capability in subordinates.

- In delegation, managers must clearly communicate what they want to be done, including the purpose for doing so. Limitations or qualifications that have been imposed should be delineated. Although the manager should specify the end product desired, it is important that the subordinate has an appropriate degree of autonomy in deciding how the work is to be accomplished.

- Managers must delegate the authority and the responsibility necessary to complete the task.

- RNs who are asked to assume the role of supervisor and delegator need preparation to assume these leadership tasks.

- Assuming the role of delegator and supervisor to the NAP increases the scope of liability for the RN.

- Although the Omnibus Budget Reconciliation Act of 1987 established regulations for the education and certification of "nurse's aides" (minimum of 75 hours of theory and practice and successful completion of an examination in both areas), no federal or community standards have been established for training the more broadly defined NAP.

- The RN always bears the ultimate responsibility for ensuring that the nursing care provided by his or her team members meets or exceeds minimum safety standards.

- When subordinates resist delegation, the delegator must ascertain why the delegated task was not accomplished and take appropriate action to remove these restraining forces.

- Transcultural sensitivity in delegation is needed to create a productive multicultural work team.

ADDITIONAL LEARNING EXERCISES AND APPLICATIONS

LEARNING EXERCISE 20.5

Need for Immediate Delegation

You are the charge nurse on the 7 AM to 3 PM shift in an oncology unit. Immediately after report in the morning, you are overwhelmed by the following information:

- The nursing aide reports that Mrs. Jones has become comatose and is moribund. Although this is not unexpected, her family members are not present, and you know that they would like to be notified immediately.
- There are three patients who need 0730 insulin administration. One of these patients had a 0600 blood sugar of 400.
- Mr. Johnson inadvertently pulled out his central line catheter when he was turning over in bed. His wife just notified the ward clerk by the call-light system and states that she is applying pressure to the site.
- The public toilet is overflowing, and urine and feces are pouring out rapidly.
- Breakfast trays arrived 15 minutes ago, and patients are using their call lights to ask why they do not yet have their breakfast.
- The medical director of the unit has just discovered that one of her patients has not been started on a chemotherapeutic drug that she ordered 3 days ago. She is furious and demands to speak to you immediately.

Assignment: The other RNs are all very busy with their patients, but you have the following people to whom you may delegate: yourself, a ward clerk, and an IV-certified LVN/LPN. Decide who should do what and in what priority. Justify your decision.

LEARNING EXERCISE 20.6

Issues with Delegating Discipline

You are the supervisor of the oncology unit. One of your closest friends and colleagues is Paula, the supervisor of the medical unit. Frequently, you cover for each other in the event of absence or emergency. Today, Paula stops at your office to let you know that she will be gone for 7 days to attend a management workshop on the East Coast. She asks that you check on the unit during her absence. She also asks that you pay particularly close attention to Mary Jones, an employee on her unit. She states that Mary, who has worked at the hospital for 4 years, has been counseled repeatedly about her unexcused absences from work and has recently received a written reprimand specifying that she will be terminated if there is another unexcused absence. Paula anticipates that Mary may attempt to break the rules during her absence. She asks that you follow through on this disciplinary plan in the event that Mary again takes an unexcused absence. Her instructions to you are to terminate Mary if she fails to show up for work this week for any reason.

When you arrive at work the next day, you find that Mary called in sick 20 minutes after the shift was to begin. The hospital's policy is that employees are to notify the staffing office of illness no less than 2 hours before the beginning of their shift. When you attempt to contact Mary by telephone at home, there is no answer.

Later in the day, you finally reach Mary and ask that she come in to your office early the next morning to speak about her inadequate notice of sick time. Mary arrives 45 minutes late the next morning. You are already agitated and angry with her. You inform her that she is to be terminated for any rule broken during Paula's absence and that this action is being taken in accord with the disciplinary contract that had been established earlier.

Mary is furious. She states that you have no right to fire her because you are not her "real boss" and that Paula should face her herself. She goes on to say that "Paula told me that the disciplinary contract was just a way of formalizing that we had talked and that I shouldn't take it too seriously." Mary also says, "Besides, I didn't get sick until I was getting ready for work. The hospital rules state that I have 12 sick days each year." Although you feel certain that Paula was very clear about her position in reviewing the disciplinary contract with Mary, you begin to feel uncomfortable with being placed in the position of having to take such serious corrective action without having been involved in prior disciplinary review sessions. You are, however, also aware that this employee has been breaking rules for some time and that this is just one in a succession of absences. You also know that Paula is counting on you to provide consistency of leadership in her absence.

Assignment: Discuss how you will handle the situation. Was it appropriate for Paula to delegate this responsibility to you? Is it appropriate for one manager to carry out another manager's disciplinary plan? Does it matter that a written disciplinary contract had already been established?

LEARNING EXERCISE 20.7

How Will You Plan This Busy Morning?

You are a staff nurse who functions as a modular leader on a general medical–surgical unit. The group for which you are responsible is assigned patients in Rooms 401 through 409, with a maximum capacity of 13 patients.

In your unit, a modular type of patient care organization is employed, using a combination of licensed and unlicensed staff. Each module consists of one RN, one LVN/LPN, and one NAP. The LVN/LPN is IV certified and can maintain and start IVs but cannot hang piggybacks or give IV push medications. The LVN/LPN may give all other medications except IV medications. The RN gives all IV medications. The NAP, with the assistance of his or her modular team members, generally bathes and feeds patients and provides other care that does not require a license.

The RN, as modular leader, divides up the workload at the beginning of the shift between the three modular team members. In addition, he or she acts as a teacher and resource person for the other members of the module.

Today is Wednesday. You have one LVN/LPN and one NAP assigned to work with you—LVN Franklin and NAP Martinez. LVN Franklin is 26 years old and the mother of four preschool children. Her husband is a city bus driver. NAP Martinez is 53 years old and a grandmother with no children living at home. Her husband died 2 years ago. She says that work keeps her "happy." The patient roster this morning is as follows:

Room	Patient	Age	Diagnosis	Condition	Acuity Level
401	Mrs. Jones	33	Mastectomy for breast CA	2 days postop/fair	II
402	Mrs. Redford	55	Back pain–pelvic	Good	I

(Continued)

Room	Patient	Age	Diagnosis	Condition	Acuity Level
403	Mrs. Worley	46	Cholecystectomy	2 d postop/good	III
404–1	Mrs. Smith	83	Parkinson's, CVD, hypertension	Fair	II
404–2	Mrs. Dewey	26	PID	Good–home today	I
405–1	Mr. Arthur	71	Metastatic CA	Poor–semi-comatose/ chemotherapy	IV
405–2	Mr. Vines	34	Possible peptic ulcer	Good–UGI today	III
406–1	Vacant				
406–2	Miss Brown	24	Dilatation and curettage	To OR this AM	III
407–1	Mrs. West	41	Myocardial infarction Heparin lock from yesterday/telemetry	Fair/ICU	III
408–1	Mr. Niles	21	Open reduction femur (MVA)	Fair/3 d postop	III
408–2	Mr. Ford	44	Gastrectomy	Fair/1 d postop	III
409	Mrs. Land	42	Depression	Fair/barium enema today	III

Additional information about patients:

- Mr. Niles is depressed because he believes that his football career is over.
- There have been problems with Mr. Ford's IV and his nasogastric tube. Both will need to be replaced today.
- Mrs. Worley requires frequent changes (every 2 to 3 hours) of the dressings at the laparoscopy site owing to a high volume of serous drainage.
- Mrs. Jones will need instructions regarding her postoperative activities and has begun to talk about her prognosis.
- Mrs. Land began to talk with you yesterday about her husband's recent death.
- The preparation for the barium enema will result in Mrs. Land's having frequent toileting needs today.
- Mrs. Smith requires assistance with feeding at mealtime.
- Mr. Arthur is no longer able to turn himself in bed.
- Mr. Vines states that being in the same room with a critically ill patient upsets him, and he has asked to be moved to a new room.

Assignment: How will you make out your assignments this morning? Assign these patients to the LVN/LPN, NAP, and yourself. Be sure to include assessments, procedures, and basic care needs. What will you do if a patient is admitted to your team? Explain the rationale for all your patient assignments. Refer to the sample acuity levels provided to assist in determining patient needs and staffing.

LEARNING EXERCISE 20.8

Evaluating Staffing Safeguards

Interview a middle- or top-level manager of a local health-care agency. Determine the staffing mix at his or her agency. Are there minimum hiring criteria for the NAP? Are there written guidelines for determining tasks appropriate for NAP delegation? What educational or training opportunities on delegation are made available to staff who must delegate work assignments on a regular basis?

On the basis of your interview results, write an essay evaluating whether you believe there are adequate safeguards in place at that agency to protect the licensed staff, unlicensed staff, and clients. Would you feel comfortable working in such a facility?

LEARNING EXERCISE 20.9

Deciding Delegation Using the Nurse Practice Act

Which of the following tasks would you be willing to delegate to an NAP? Use your state's NPA or a decision tree created by the NCSBN or a state Board of Nursing, as a reference for this case. Discuss your answers in small groups. Did you all agree? If not, what factors were significant in your differences?

1. Uncomplicated wet-to-dry dressing change on a patient 3 days post-hip replacement
2. Every 2-hour checks on a patient with soft wrist restraints to assess circulation, movement, and comfort
3. Cooling measures for a patient with a temperature of 104°F
4. Calculation of IV credits, clearing IV pumps, and completing shift intake/output totals
5. Completing phlebotomy for daily drawing of blood
6. Holding pressure on the insertion site of a femoral line that has just been removed
7. Educating a patient about components of a soft diet
8. Conducting guaiac stool tests for occult blood
9. Performing electrocardiographic testing
10. Feeding a patient with swallowing precautions (high risk of choking post-cardiovascular accident
11. Oral suctioning
12. Tracheostomy care
13. Ostomy care

LEARNING EXERCISE 20.10

Reflecting on Negative Delegation Experiences

Write a one-page essay about one of the following situations you have experienced:

- A supervisor asked you to complete a task you believed was beyond your capability
- A supervisor delegated a task to you but failed to give you adequate authority to carry out the task
- A supervisor gave such explicit directions on how to complete a delegated task that you felt demoralized

REFERENCES

American Nurses Association (ANA) and the National Council of State Boards of Nursing (NCSBN). (n.d.). *Joint statement on delegation.* Retrieved June 17, 2013, from https://www.ncsbn.org/Delegation_joint _statement_NCSBN-ANA.pdf

Anderson, L. (2013, February 10). *Understanding the different scope of nursing practice.* nursetogether.com. Retrieved June 19, 2013, from http://www.nursetogether.com/ understanding-the-different-scope-of-nursin

Case, B. (2013). *Delegation skills.* Advance for Nurses. Retrieved June 20, 2013, from http://nursing .advanceweb.com/Article/Delegation-Skills.aspx

Delegating. Leadership Skills Training. (n.d.). *Park/ Scholarships.* Retrieved June 20, 2013, from http:// www.ncsu.edu/project/parkprgrd/PSTrainingModules/ delegating/del12frame.htm

Does Your Staff Understand Delegation? (2009, January). *OR Manager, 25*(1), 21–23.

Giger, J., & Davidhizar, R. (2008). *Transcultural nursing: Assessment and intervention* (5th ed.). St Louis, MO: Mosby Year Book.

Huston, C. (2009, March). 10 tips for successful delegation: Improve patient care and save time by recognizing when to delegate and learning how to do it wisely. *Nursing, 39*(3), 54–56.

Huston, C. (2014). *Professional issues in nursing: Challenges and opportunities* (3rd ed.). Unlicensed assistive personnel and the registered nurse (chapter 7). Philadelphia, PA: Lippincott Williams & Wilkins 107–120.

Is It OK to Delegate? (2012, December 3). *American Nurse.* Retrieved June 18, 2013, from http://www .theamericannurse.org/index.php/2012/12/03/is-it -ok-to-delegate/

Kærnested, B., & Bragadóttir, H. (2012). Delegation of registered nurses revisited: Attitudes towards delegation and preparedness to delegate effectively. *Nordic Journal of Nursing Research & Clinical Studies/Vård I Norden, 32*(1), 10–15.

Kentucky Board of Nursing. (2010). *Decision tree for delegation to unlicensed assistive personnel (UAP).* Retrieved June 17, 2013, from http://kbn.ky.gov/NR/rdonlyres/ E1591ED0-5C3E-425C-ACE6-396268CE1774/0/ DecisionTreeforDelegationtoUAP.pdf

Knox, C. (2013, January 3). *The five rights of delegation.* Essentials of Correctional Nursing. Retrieved June 19, 2013, from http://essentialsofcorrectionalnursing .com/2013/01/03/a-case-example-the-five-rights-of -delegation/

NMC Says Asian Nurses. (2012). NMC says Asian nurses may need support with delegating work. *Nursing Standard, 26*(26), 5.

North Carolina Board of Nursing. (2013). *Delegation: Non-nursing functions.* Position Statement for RN and LPN Practice. Retrieved June 18, 2013, from http:// allnurses.com/north-carolina-nursing/north-carolina -board-465130.html

Tredgold, G. (2013, May 30). *Why delegation is important.* Leadership Principles. Retrieved June 18, 2013, from http://www.leadership-principles.com/2013/05/30/ why-delegation-is-important/

Winstead, J. V. (2013, winter). Delegation: What are the nurse's responsibilities? *Nursing Bulletin.* Official Bulletin of the North Carolina Board of Nursing (pp. 8–16). Retrieved June 18, 2013, from http://www .ncbon.com/WorkArea/linkit.aspx?LinkIdentifier=id &ItemID=3240

Wong, M. (2012, August 2). *Do foreign nurses lack cultural competency?* Healthecareers.com. Retrieved June 20, 2013, from http://www.healthecareers .com/article/do-foreign-nurses-lack-cultural -competency/170789

21

Effective Conflict Resolution and Negotiation

... getting good players is EASY. Gettin' 'em to play together is the hard part.
–Casey Stengel

... negotiation in the classic diplomatic sense assumes parties more anxious to agree than to disagree.
–Dean Acheson

CROSSWALK THIS CHAPTER ADDRESSES:

BSN Essential II: Basic organizational and systems leadership for quality care and patient safety
BSN Essential VI: Interprofessional communication and collaboration for improving patient health outcomes
BSN Essential VIII: Professionalism and professional values
MSN Essential II: Organizational and systems leadership
MSN Essential VII: Interprofessional collaboration for improving patient and population health outcomes
QSEN Competency: Teamwork and collaboration
QSEN Competency: Safety
AONE Nurse Executive Competency I: Communication and relationship building
AONE Nurse Executive Competency III: Leadership
AONE Nurse Executive Competency IV: Professionalism
AONE Nurse Executive Competency V: Business skills

LEARNING OBJECTIVES *The learner will:*

- differentiate between qualitative and quantitative conflict and between intrapersonal and interpersonal conflict
- identify the stages of conflict
- describe manifestations of workplace violence, incivility, bullying, and mobbing as well as strategies that might be used to immediately confront and intervene
- seek win–win conflict resolution outcomes whenever possible
- identify the functional and dysfunctional results of various methods of conflict resolution
- select appropriate conflict resolution strategies to solve various conflict situations
- identify the components of effective collaboration
- describe strategies that can be used before, during, and after negotiation to increase the likelihood that desired outcomes will be achieved
- identify effective ways to counter commonly used tactics in conflict negotiation
- describe how alternative dispute resolution might be used to resolve conflicts when negotiation has not been successful
- recognize the challenges as well as rewards in seeking consensus to address group conflict

Stanton (2013) notes that health care is delivered by people working in both large and small organizations and that each worker is part of many groups, both formal and informal. Being able to work well with other people, within and across departmental and other organizational boundaries, is essential to efficiency and effectiveness in patient care. Yet, dynamic environments, characterized by interactions among many people, within a defined setting, are always conducive to conflict (Stanton, 2013).

Conflict is generally defined as the internal or external discord that results from differences in ideas, values, or feelings between two or more people. Because managers have interpersonal relationships with people having a variety of different values, beliefs, backgrounds, and goals, conflict is an expected outcome. Conflict is also created when there are differences in economic and professional values and when there is competition among professionals. Scarce resources, restructuring, and poorly defined role expectations also are frequent sources of conflict in organizations.

Openly acknowledging that conflict is a naturally occurring and expected phenomenon in organizations reflects a tremendous shift from how sociologists viewed conflict a century ago. The current sociological view is that organizational conflict should be neither avoided nor encouraged but managed. The leader's role is to create a work environment where conflict may be used as a conduit for growth, innovation, and productivity. When organizational conflict becomes dysfunctional, the manager must recognize it in its early stages and actively intervene so that subordinates' motivation and organizational productivity are not adversely affected.

Conflict is neither good nor bad, and it can produce growth or destruction, depending on how it is managed.

Conflict resolution, or problem solving, appears to be learned less frequently through developmental experiences; rather, it requires a conscious learning effort. Thus, the skills necessary to manage conflict effectively can be learned.

This chapter presents an overview of growth-producing versus dysfunctional conflict in organizations. The history of conflict management, categories of conflict, the conflict process itself, and strategies for successful conflict resolution are discussed. Incivility, workplace violence, bullying, and mobbing are presented as threats to safety as well as patient care and negotiation as a conflict resolution strategy is emphasized. Leadership skills and management functions necessary for conflict resolution at the unit level are outlined in Display 21.1.

DISPLAY 21.1	Leadership Roles and Management Functions Associated with Conflict Resolution

LEADERSHIP ROLES

1. Is self-aware and conscientiously works to resolve intrapersonal conflict.
2. Addresses conflict as soon as it is perceived and before it becomes felt or manifest.
3. Immediately confronts and intervenes when incivility, bullying, and mobbing occur.
4. Seeks a win–win solution to conflict whenever feasible.
5. Lessens the perceptual differences that exist between conflicting parties and broadens the parties' understanding about the problems.
6. Assists subordinates in identifying alternative conflict resolutions.
7. Recognizes and accepts individual differences in team members.
8. Uses assertive communication skills to increase persuasiveness and foster open communication.
9. Role models honest and collaborative negotiation efforts.
10. Encourages consensus building when group support is needed to resolve conflicts.

MANAGEMENT FUNCTIONS

1. Creates a work environment that minimizes the antecedent conditions for conflict.
2. Establishes a workplace culture that has zero tolerance for incivility, bullying, mobbing, and violence.
3. Appropriately uses legitimate authority in a competing approach when a quick or unpopular decision needs to be made.
4. When appropriate, formally facilitates conflict resolution among team members.
5. Accepts mutual responsibility for reaching predetermined supraordinate goals.
6. Obtains needed unit resources through effective negotiation strategies.
7. Compromises unit needs only when the need is not critical to unit functioning and when higher management gives up something of equal value.
8. Is adequately prepared to negotiate for unit resources, including the advance determination of a bottom line and possible trade-offs.
9. Addresses the need for closure and follow-up to negotiation.
10. Pursues alternative dispute resolution (ADR) when conflicts cannot be resolved using traditional conflict management strategies.

THE HISTORY OF CONFLICT MANAGEMENT

Early in the 20th century, conflict was considered to be an indication of poor organizational management, was deemed destructive, and was avoided at all costs. When conflict occurred, it was ignored, denied, or dealt with immediately and harshly. The theorists of this era believed that conflict could be avoided if employees were taught the one right way to do things and if expressed employee dissatisfaction was met swiftly with disapproval.

In the mid-20th century, when organizations recognized that worker satisfaction and feedback were important, conflict was accepted passively and perceived as normal and expected. Attention centered on teaching managers how to resolve conflict rather than how to prevent it. Although conflict was considered to be primarily dysfunctional, it was believed that conflict and cooperation could happen simultaneously. The interactionist theorists of the 1970s, however, recognized conflict as a necessity and actively encouraged organizations to promote conflict as a means of producing growth. From this, one can infer that some conflict is desired, although its extent is difficult to know. Perhaps more important than the quantification of conflict is the impact this conflict has on the organization.

Some level of conflict in an organization appears desirable, although the optimum level for a specific person or unit at a given time is difficult to determine.

Too little conflict results in organizational stasis. Too much conflict reduces the organization's effectiveness and eventually immobilizes its employees (Fig. 21.1). With few formal instruments to assess whether the level of conflict in an organization is too high or too low, the responsibility for determining and creating an appropriate level of conflict on the individual unit often falls to the leader-manager.

Conflict also has a qualitative nature. A person may be totally overwhelmed in one conflict situation yet can handle several simultaneous conflicts at a later time. The difference is in the quality or significance of that conflict to the person experiencing it. Although *quantitative* and *qualitative* conflicts produce distress at the time they occur, they can lead to growth, energy, and creativity by generating new ideas and solutions. If handled inappropriately, quantitative and qualitative conflicts can lead to demoralization, decreased motivation, and lowered productivity.

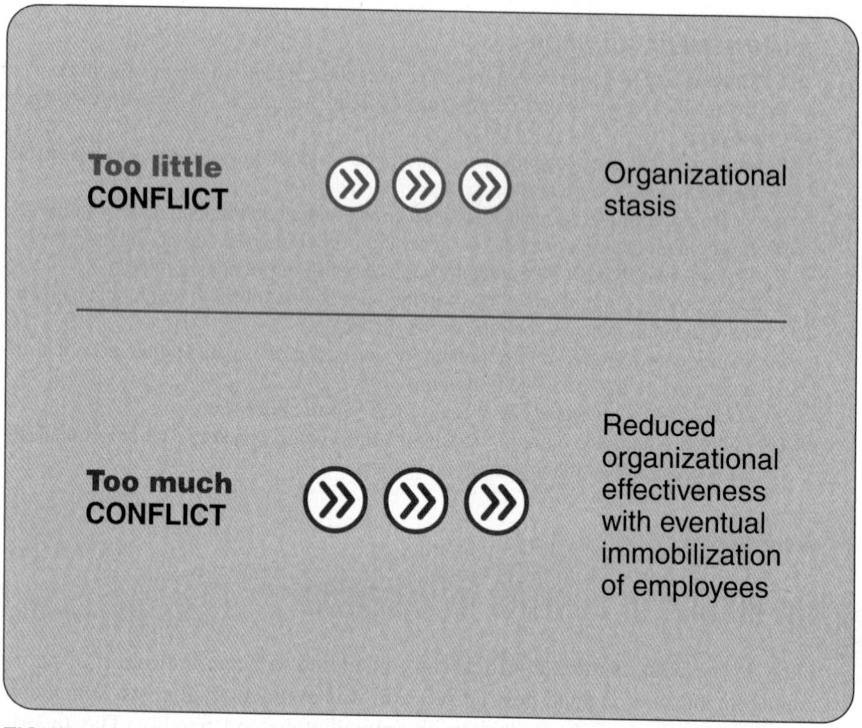

Too little CONFLICT » » »   Organizational stasis

Too much CONFLICT » » »   Reduced organizational effectiveness with eventual immobilization of employees

FIGURE 21.1 • The relationship between organizational conflict and effectiveness. Copyright ® 2006 Lippincott Williams & Wilkins. Instructor's Resource CD-ROM to Accompany Leadership Roles and Management Functions in Nursing, by Bessie L. Marquis and Carol J. Huston.

Nursing managers can no longer afford to respond to conflict traditionally (i.e., to avoid or suppress it), because this is nonproductive. In an era of shrinking health-care dollars, it has become increasingly important for managers to confront and manage conflict appropriately. The ability to understand and deal with conflict appropriately is a critical leadership skill.

LEARNING EXERCISE 21.1

Thinking and Writing About Conflict

Do you generally view conflict positively or negatively?

Does conflict affect you more cognitively, emotionally, or physically?

How was conflict expressed in the home in which you grew up?

Does the way that you handle conflict mirror that of your role models as a child?

Do you believe that you have too much or too little conflict in your life?

Do you feel like you have control over the issues that are now causing conflict in your life?

Assignment: Write a one-page essay, answering one of the questions above.

CATEGORIES OF CONFLICT: INTERGROUP, INTRAPERSONAL, AND INTERPERSONAL

There are three primary categories of conflict: intergroup, intrapersonal, and interpersonal (Fig. 21.2). *Intergroup conflict* occurs between two or more groups of people, departments, and organizations. An example of intergroup conflict might be two political affiliations with

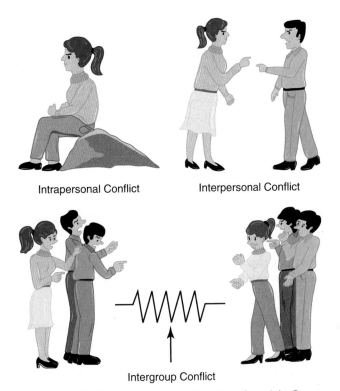

Intrapersonal Conflict   Interpersonal Conflict

Intergroup Conflict

FIGURE 21.2 • Primary categories of conflict. Copyright ®
2006 Lippincott Williams & Wilkins. Instructor's Resource
CD-ROM to Accompany Leadership Roles and Management
Functions in Nursing, by Bessie L. Marquis and Carol J. Huston.

widely differing or contradictory beliefs or nurses experiencing intergroup conflict with family and work issues.

Intrapersonal conflict occurs within the person. It involves an internal struggle to clarify contradictory values or wants. Stacey, Johnston, Stickley, and Diamond (2011) suggest that the values nurses hold when they enter the profession generally remain intact; however, workplace constraints and resistance may prevent the nurse from applying those values. This then affects the capacity of the nurse to work with people in distress and can lead to high levels of stress and job attrition.

For managers, intrapersonal conflict may result from the multiple areas of responsibility associated with the management role. Managers' responsibilities to the organization, subordinates, consumers, the profession, and themselves sometimes conflict, and that conflict may be internalized. Being self-aware and conscientiously working to resolve intrapersonal conflict as soon as it is first felt is essential to the leader's physical and mental health.

Interpersonal conflict happens between two or more people with differing values, goals, and beliefs and may be closely linked with bullying, incivility, and mobbing. *Bullying* is defined by Townsend (2012) as repeated, offensive, abusive, intimidating, or insulting behaviors; abuse of power; or unfair sanctions that make recipients feel humiliated, vulnerable, or threatened, thus creating stress and undermining their self-confidence. *Incivility* is defined by Clark (2010) as behavior that lacks authentic respect for others that requires time, presence, willingness to engage in genuine discourse and intention to seek common ground. Clark notes that it can be a short walk from incivility to aggressive behavior and violence. In addition, interpersonal conflict can be manifested by *mobbing*, when employees "gang up" on an individual. The degree of harm a nurse experiences from bullying or mobbing often depends upon the frequency, intensity, and duration of the behavior and/or tactic used (Hockley, 2014).

When bullying, incivility, and mobbing occur in the workplace, this is known as *workplace violence*. Hockley (2014) maintains that in addition to physical violence, the term describes various antisocial behaviors and incidents that lead a person to believe that he or she has been harmed by the experience. It includes but is not limited to such behaviors as engaging in favoritism, being verbally abusive, sending abusive correspondence, bullying, pranks, and setting workers up for failure. It also includes economic aggression such as denying workers promotional opportunities. Countless practice settings are hindered by maladaptive social behaviors that victimize nurses and impact patient care. Hockley maintains that the responsibility for dealing with this type of conflict should initially lie with front-line staff, but the manager must become involved if the conflict is not resolved.

Unfortunately, many nurses report having been bullied during their work life. Indeed, research by Roche, Diers, Duffield, and Catling-Pauli (2010) found that about one-third of nurses perceived emotional abuse during the last five shifts worked, 14% reported threats, and 20% reported actual violence. Hauge, Skogstad, and Einarsen (2009) suggested that this occurs because bullying thrives in stressful working environments and individuals who are bullied in the workplace often go on to bully others.

Violence and workplace aggression are increasingly being recognized as epidemic in the health-care workplace.

While nurses of all ages and experience levels report bullying, new graduate nurses seem to be victimized more often than any other group. These behaviors can, over a prolonged time, cause the individual to develop low self-esteem, to feel worthless, or to feel frustrated (Hockley, 2014). In addition, because this interpersonal conflict may not be reported or managed, it often results in consequences such as absenteeism and turnover.

Inglis, Schaper, and Swartz (2013), recognizing the problem of the bullying of new nurses, suggest that organizations can reduce this attrition and by providing new nurses with opportunities to address strong negative emotional responses to conflict (hot buttons) and to practice constructive strategies when engaging in conflict. In doing so, new graduates can begin to recognize how their own behaviors may influence the escalation or de-escalation of conflict (Examining the Evidence 21.1).

Examining the Evidence 21.1

Source: Inglis, R. L., Schaper, A.M., & Swartz, S. L. (2013, April 14). Conflict engagement skill building for nurse residents. Session presented at the Sigma Theta Tau International conference. Creating healthy work environments. Indianapolis, IN. Virginia Henderson International Nursing Library. Retrieved June 20, 2013, from http://www.nursinglibrary.org/vhl/handle/10755/290986

This presentation suggested that the experience of incivility in higher education may influence how well a newly graduated nurse deals with conflict and disruptive behaviors in the workplace. Noting that newly registered nurses frequently report acts of disrespect and destructive conflict resulting in high levels of attrition in the first year or two of employment, the researchers suggested the addition of conflict resolution training to nurse residency programs as one strategy for addressing the problem.

To test their hypothesis, a modified Conflict Engagement program, advocated by the American Nurse Association, was delivered to 45 new graduates completing a nurse residency program. The program included a 4-hour workshop followed by 1-hour monthly meetings termed "Learning Circles" for 6 months. The Learning Circles provided these new nurses with opportunities to address strong negative emotional responses to conflict (hot buttons) and to practice construc-tive strategies when engaging in conflict. The Learning Circles incorporated role modeling, role play, and case studies of conflict situations.

The trainers also provided personal consultation to help new nurses address unique conflict situations. Nurse residents easily identified previous experiences of incivility in nursing educa-tion, including incivility between nursing staff and nursing students during a clinical rotation; however, they did not expect to experience incivility as a new nurse. Personal experiences with conflict, particularly generational conflict, emerged as an influencing factor in understanding the value of conflict engagement training. Between the third and fourth Learning Circle, a majority of the nurse residents began to recognize how their own behaviors influenced the escalation or de-escalation of conflict.

It is critical that leader-managers immediately confront and intervene when workplace violence is occurring. Zero tolerance should be the expectation since bullying and incivility impact turnover, productivity, and quality of care. Townsend (2012) reported that up to 70% of nurses who were bullying victims leave their jobs; roughly 60% of new registered nurses (RNs) quit their first job within 6 months of being bullied; and one in three new graduate nurses considered quitting nursing altogether because of abusive or humiliating encounters. In addition, researchers from Georgetown University and the Thunderbird School of Global Management found that incivility and rude behavior influenced productivity and commitment from workers and that nearly half (48%) intentionally decreased their work effort as a result, while 38% intentionally decreased the quality of their work (Cheung-Larivee, 2013).

To end abusive behaviors, clear zero-tolerance policies must be communicated loudly and clearly from upper administration and a culture of safety that encourages open, respectful communication must be encouraged (Townsend, 2012). Also, the Joint Commission has issued leadership standards that include creating processes for managing bullying behaviors and adopting a code of conduct for staff (Townsend).

THE CONFLICT PROCESS

Before managers can or should attempt to intervene in conflict, they must be able to assess its five stages accurately. The first stage in the conflict process, *latent conflict*, implies the existence of antecedent conditions such as short staffing and rapid change. In this stage, conditions are ripe for conflict, although no conflict has actually occurred and none may ever occur. Much unnecessary conflict could be prevented or reduced if managers examined the organization more closely for antecedent conditions. For example, change and budget cuts almost invariably create conflict. Such events, therefore, should be well thought out so that interventions can be made before the conflicts created by these events escalate.

If the conflict progresses, it may develop into the second stage: *perceived conflict*. Perceived or substantive conflict is intellectualized and often involves issues and roles. The person recognizes it logically and impersonally as occurring. Sometimes, conflict can be resolved at this stage before it is internalized or felt. Stanton (2013) notes the importance when conflict is first perceived, to directly address whether a conflict really exists. He notes that "we often assume other people's behavior is intentional when, in fact, they may not be aware their actions are causing difficulties for someone else. In an environment characterized by open communication and mutual support, many conflicts can be resolved simply by pointing out the problem" (para 30).

The third stage, *felt conflict*, occurs when the conflict is emotionalized. Felt emotions include hostility, fear, mistrust, and anger. It is also referred to as *affective conflict*. It is possible to perceive conflict and not feel it (e.g., no emotion is attached to the conflict, and the person views it only as a problem to be solved). A person also can feel the conflict but not perceive the problem (e.g., he or she is unable to identify the cause of the felt conflict).

In the fourth stage, *manifest conflict*, also called *overt conflict*, action is taken. The action may be to withdraw, compete, debate, or seek conflict resolution. Individuals are uncomfortable with or reluctant to address conflict for many reasons. These include fear of retaliation, fear of ridicule, fear of alienating others, a sense that they do not have the right to speak up, and past negative experiences with conflict situations. Indeed, people often learn patterns of dealing with manifest conflict early in their lives, and family background and experiences often directly affect how conflict is dealt with in adulthood. Gender also may play a role in how we respond to conflict. Historically, men were socialized to respond aggressively to conflict, whereas women were more likely taught to try to avoid conflicts or to pacify them.

The final stage in the conflict process is *conflict aftermath*. There is always conflict aftermath—positive or negative. If the conflict is managed well, people involved in the conflict will believe that their position was given a fair hearing. If the conflict is managed poorly, the conflict issues frequently remain and may return later to cause more conflict. Figure 21.3 shows a schematic of this conflict process.

The aftermath of conflict may be more significant than the original conflict if the conflict has not been handled constructively.

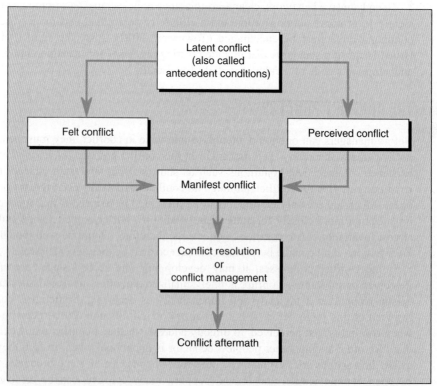

FIGURE 21.3 • The conflict process. Copyright ® 2006 Lippincott Williams & Wilkins. Instructor's Resource CD-ROM to Accompany Leadership Roles and Management Functions in Nursing, by Bessie L. Marquis and Carol J. Huston.

LEARNING EXERCISE 21.2

Personal Conflict Solving

It is important for managers to be self-aware regarding how they view and deal with conflict. In your personal life, how do you solve conflict? Is it important for you to win? When was the last time you were able to solve conflict by reaching supraordinate goals with another person? Are you able to see the other person's position in conflict situations? In conflicts with family and friends, are you least likely to compromise values, scarcities, or role expectations?

CONFLICT MANAGEMENT

The optimal goal in resolving conflict is creating a win–win solution for all involved. This outcome is not possible in every situation, and often the manager's goal is to manage the conflict in a way that lessens the perceptual differences that exist between the involved parties. A leader recognizes which conflict management or resolution strategy is most appropriate for each situation. Common conflict management strategies are identified in Display 21.2. The choice of the most appropriate strategy depends on many variables, such as the situation itself, the urgency of the decision, the power and status of the players, the importance of the issue, and the maturity of the people involved in the conflict.

The optimal goal in resolving conflict is creating a win–win solution for all involved.

DISPLAY 21.2	Common Conflict Resolution Strategies

Compromising
Competing
Cooperating/accommodating
Smoothing
Avoiding
Collaborating

Compromising

In *compromising*, each party gives up something it wants. Although many see compromise as an optimum conflict resolution strategy, antagonistic cooperation may result in a lose–lose situation because either or both parties perceive that they have given up more than the other and may therefore feel defeated. For compromising not to result in a lose–lose situation, both parties must be willing to give up something of equal value. Compromising definitely becomes a win–win when both parties perceive they have won more than the other person. It is important that parties in conflict do not adopt compromise prematurely if collaboration is both possible and feasible.

Competing

The *competing* approach is used when one party pursues what it wants at the expense of the others. Because only one party typically wins, the competing party seeks to win regardless of the cost to others. In addition, Stanton (2013) notes that it is entirely possible that both parties may lose, particularly if the outcome adversely affects the subsequent working relationship. This is because win–lose conflict resolution strategies leave the loser angry, frustrated, and wanting to get even in the future.

Managers may use competing when a quick or unpopular decision needs to be made. It is also appropriately used when one party has more information or knowledge about a situation than the other. Competing in the form of resistance is also appropriate when an individual needs to resist unsafe patient care policies or procedures, unfair treatment, abuse of power, or ethical concerns.

Cooperating/Accommodating

Cooperating is the opposite of competing. In the cooperating approach, one party sacrifices his or her beliefs and allows the other party to win. The actual problem is usually not solved in this win–lose situation. *Accommodating* is another term that may be used for this strategy. The person cooperating or accommodating often expects some type of payback or an accommodation from the winning party in the future. Cooperating and accommodating are appropriate political strategies if the item in conflict is not of high value to the person doing the accommodating.

Smoothing

Smoothing is used to manage a conflict situation. Smoothing occurs when one party in a conflict attempts to pacify the other party or to focus on agreements rather than differences. In doing so, the emotional component of the conflict is minimized. Managers often use smoothing to get someone to accommodate or cooperate with another party. Although it may be appropriate for minor disagreements, smoothing rarely results in resolution of the actual conflict.

Avoiding

In the *avoiding* approach, the parties involved are aware of a conflict but choose not to acknowledge it or attempt to resolve it. Avoidance may be indicated in trivial disagreements, when the cost of dealing with the conflict exceeds the benefits of solving it, when the problem should be solved by people other than you, when one party is more powerful than the other, or when the problem will solve itself. The greatest problem in using avoidance is that the conflict remains, often only to reemerge at a later time in an even more exaggerated fashion. Stanton (2013) agrees, noting that passive approaches like avoidance, giving up, and accommodating are likely to result in poor outcomes for one or both parties.

Unfortunately, American Sentinel (2012) notes that avoidance and withdrawal are the most common conflict resolution strategies used by nurses. This finding was similar to research conducted by Kaitelidou et al. (2012), which suggested that avoidance was the most frequent mode of conflict resolution used by health-care personnel while accommodation was the least frequently used mode (Examining the Evidence 21.2).

Examining the Evidence 21.2

Source: Kaitelidou, D., Kontogianni, A., Galanis, P., Siskou, O., Mallidou, A., Pavlakis, A., & Liaropoulos, L. (2012). *Conflict management and job satisfaction in paediatric hospitals in Greece.* Journal of Nursing Management, 20(4), 571–578.

Recognizing that conflict is inherent to hospitals as in all complex organizations, and that health-care personnel deal with internal and external conflicts daily, the researchers administered a five-part questionnaire, specific to conflicts in hospitals, to 286 health personnel (a response rate of 66%). Thirty-seven percent of the study participants were physicians, 47% were nurses, and 16% were nursing assistants.

A majority (77%) of the respondents suggested they had no training in conflict resolution and reported having conflicts with colleagues in their own ward. Physicians reported more conflicts with their colleagues (73.3%) than did nurses and nursing assistants (48.1% and 40.9%, respectively). When asked what they do to resolve a conflict, the majority of both nurses and physicians stated that they used avoidance (64% and 61%, respectively). Both physicians and nursing personnel chose collaboration as the second favorable technique to resolve their conflicts (45% and 42%, respectively), while competition was the third choice for both groups (26.4% for physicians and 20% for nursing personnel). Physicians selected the competitive style of conflict resolution more often than did nurses ($v_2 = 2$, $P = 0.1$). The least frequent mode was accepting the will (accommodating) of the opposing side (9.5% of physicians and 6.7% of nurses).

The researchers concluded that while using avoidance as a conflict resolution strategy may be appropriate as a short-term technique when a problem is emerging, it may be dysfunctional if it lasts a long time since it prevents recognition that a problem exists. One-third of participants (32.6%) agreed that detecting initial symptoms of conflict and adopting the most effective behavior in conflict resolution is essential and noted that conflict has an influence on patients' quality of care since conflict results in communication between staff being interrupted and valuable information about patients' care needs being withheld.

In contrast, research conducted by Losa Iglesias and Becerro de Bengoa Vallejo (2012) found that the most common conflict resolution strategy used by nurses to resolve workplace conflict was compromising, followed by competing, avoiding, accommodating, and collaborating. Accommodation was most common for nurses working in clinical settings, whereas nurses employed in academic settings were more competitive in their approach.

Collaborating

Collaborating is an assertive and cooperative means of conflict resolution that results in a win–win solution. In collaboration, all parties set aside their original goals and work together to establish a *supraordinate* or priority common goal. In doing so, all parties accept mutual responsibility for reaching the supraordinate goal.

Although it is very difficult for people truly to set aside original goals, collaboration cannot occur if this does not happen. For example, a married couple experiencing serious conflict over whether to have a baby may first want to identify whether they share the supraordinate goal of keeping the marriage together. A nurse who is unhappy that she did not receive requested days off might meet with her supervisor and jointly establish the supraordinate goal that staffing will be adequate to meet patient safety criteria. If the new goal is truly a jointly set goal, each party will perceive that an important goal has been achieved and that the supraordinate goal is most important. In doing so, the focus remains on problem solving and not on defeating the other party.

Collaboration is rare when there is a wide difference in power between the groups and individuals involved. Many think of collaboration as a form of cooperation, but this is not an accurate definition. In collaboration, problem solving is a joint effort with no superior–subordinate, order-giving–order-taking relationships. True collaboration requires mutual respect; open and honest communication; and equitable, shared decision-making powers.

 Although conflict is a pervasive force in health-care organizations, only a small percentage of time is spent in true collaboration.

Collaboration enhances a person's participation in decision making to accomplish mutual goals and therefore is the best method to resolve conflict to achieve long-term benefits. Because it may involve others over whom the manager has no control and because its process is often lengthy, it may not be the best approach for all situations.

In addition, it is not easy. Vaughn (2009) suggests that the most common barriers to collaboration between members of the multidisciplinary health-care team are patriarchal relationships; lack of time; gender- and generational-based differences; cultural differences; and lack of role clarification of team members. He concludes then that while collaboration evokes warm feelings in nursing leadership circles as a result of its win–win outcomes, it is difficult to truly implement and requires a high degree of self-awareness as well as conflict communication skills.

LEARNING EXERCISE 21.3

Conflicting Personal, Professional, and Organizational Obligations

You are an RN. You have been working on the oncology unit since your graduation from the state college a year ago. Your supervisor, Mary, has complimented your performance. Lately, she has allowed you to be relief charge nurse on the 3 to 11 PM shift when the regular charge nurse is not there. Occasionally, you have been asked to work on the medical–surgical units when your department has a low census. Although you dislike leaving your own unit, you have cooperated because you felt that you could handle the other clinical assignments and wanted to show your flexibility.

On arriving at work tonight, the nursing office calls and requests that you help out in the busy delivery room. You protest that you do not know anything about obstetrics and that it is impossible for you to take the assignment. Carol, the supervisor from the nursing office, insists that you are the most qualified person; she says to "just go and do the best you can." Your own unit supervisor is not on duty, and the charge nurse says that she does not feel comfortable advising you in this conflict. You feel torn between professional, personal, and organizational obligations.

Assignment: What should you do? Select the most appropriate conflict resolution strategy. Give rationale for your selection and for your rejection of the others. After you have made your choice, read the analysis found in the Appendix.

MANAGING UNIT CONFLICT

Managing conflict effectively requires an understanding of its origin. Some of the sources of organizational conflict are shown in Display 21.3. Some common causes of unit conflict are unclear expectations, poor communication, lack of clear jurisdiction, incompatibilities or disagreements based on differences of temperament or attitudes, individual or group conflicts of interest, and operational or staffing changes. In addition, not only does diversity in gender, age, and culture influence conflict resolution, it may also create conflict itself. This occurs as a result of communication difficulties, including language and literacy issues and a growing recognition that some factors are beyond assimilation.

DISPLAY 21.3	Common Causes of Organizational Conflict

- Poor communication
- Inadequately defined organizational structure
- Individual behavior (incompatibilities or disagreements based on differences of temperament or attitudes)
- Unclear expectations
- Individual or group conflicts of interest
- Operational or staffing changes
- Diversity in gender, culture, or age

Ellis and Abbott (2012) suggest that managers may be tempted to ignore organizational conflict, but should not since all these types of conflicts can disrupt working relationships and result in lower productivity. Perhaps the most important reason though for the proactive management of conflict is the impact that it has on patients (Ellis & Abbott). When a team or individuals within a team are in conflict, patient care suffers since conflict breeds poor communication and poor communication breeds poor care. It is imperative, then, that the manager can identify the origin of unit conflicts and intervene as necessary to promote cooperative, if not collaborative, conflict resolution.

At times, unit conflict requires that the manager facilitates conflict resolution between others. CRM Learning (2013) suggests that it is almost always best for the individuals involved in a conflict to work it out on their own, but sometimes they simply cannot or will not. Before beginning to help other people in a conflict situation, the leader-manager must first analyze the appropriateness of intervening. If the issue is extremely important to them or the organization, it is likely worth intervening. The manager may also want to intervene if the relationship with one or both parties is highly significant to them, even if the issue is not. Finally, CRM Learning suggests that the manager should consider what will happen if no one intervenes. If the short- or long-term results are extremely negative, whether the issue or relationships are important, it might still be advisable to intervene.

The following is a list of strategies that a manager may use to facilitate conflict resolution between members in the workplace:

- *Confrontation*. Many times, team members inappropriately expect the manager to solve their interpersonal conflicts. Managers instead can urge subordinates to attempt to handle their own problems by using face-to-face communication to resolve conflicts, as e-mails, answering machine messages, and notes are too impersonal for interpersonal conflicts that can have significant conflict aftermath.

- *Third-party consultation*. Sometimes, managers can be used as a neutral party to help others resolve conflicts constructively. This should be done only if all parties are motivated to solve the problem and if no differences exist in the status or power of the parties involved. If the conflict involves multiple parties and highly charged emotions, the manager may find outside experts helpful for facilitating communication and bringing issues to the forefront.

- *Behavior change*. This is reserved for serious cases of dysfunctional conflict. Educational modes, training development, or sensitivity training can be used to solve conflict by developing self-awareness and behavior change in the involved parties.

- *Responsibility charting*. When ambiguity results from unclear or new roles, it is often necessary to have the parties come together to delineate the function and responsibility of roles. If areas of joint responsibility exist, the manager must clearly define such areas as ultimate responsibility, approval mechanisms, support services, and responsibility for informing. This is a useful technique for elementary jurisdictional conflicts. An example of a potential jurisdictional conflict might arise between the house supervisor and unit manager in staffing or between an in-service educator and unit manager in determining and planning unit educational needs or programs.

- *Structure change*. Sometimes, managers need to intervene in unit conflict by transferring or discharging people. Other structure changes may be moving a department under another manager, adding an ombudsman, or putting a grievance procedure in place. Often, increasing the boundaries of authority for one member of the conflict will act as an effective structure change to resolve unit conflict. Changing titles and creating policies are also effective techniques.

- *Soothing one party.* This is a temporary solution that should be used in a crisis when there is no time to handle the conflict effectively or when the parties are so enraged that immediate conflict resolution is unlikely. Waiting a few days allows most individuals to deal with their intense feelings and to be more objective about the issues. Regardless of how the parties are soothed, the manager must address the underlying problem later or this technique will become ineffective.

NEGOTIATION

Negotiation in its most creative form is similar to collaboration and in its most poorly managed form may resemble a competing approach. Negotiation frequently resembles compromise when it is used as a conflict resolution strategy. During negotiation, each party gives up something, and the emphasis is on accommodating differences between the parties. Few people are able to meet all of their needs or objectives. Most day-to-day conflict is resolved with negotiation. A nurse who says to another nurse "I'll answer that call light if you'll count narcotics" is practicing the art of negotiation.

Although negotiation implies winning and losing for both parties, there is no rule that each party must lose and win the same amount. Most negotiators want to win more than they lose, but negotiation becomes destructively competitive when the emphasis is on winning at all costs. A major goal of effective negotiation is to make the other party feel satisfied with the outcome. The focus in negotiation should be to create a *win–win* situation.

Many small negotiations take place every day spontaneously and succeed without any advance preparation. However, not all nurses are expert negotiators. If managers wish to succeed in important negotiations for unit resources, they must (a) be adequately prepared, (b) be able to use appropriate negotiation strategies, and (c) apply appropriate closure and follow-up. To become more successful at negotiating, managers need to do several things before, during, and after the negotiation (Display 21.4).

DISPLAY 21.4   Before, During, and After the Negotiation

BEFORE
1. Be prepared mentally by having done your homework.
2. Determine the incentives of the person you will be negotiating with.
3. Determine your starting point, trade-offs, and bottom line.
4. Look for hidden agendas, both your own and the parties with whom you are negotiating.

DURING
1. Maintain composure.
2. Ask for what you want assertively.
3. Role model good communication skills (speaking and listening), assertiveness, and flexibility.
4. Be patient and take a break if either party becomes angry or tired during the negotiation.
5. Avoid using destructive negotiation techniques, but be prepared to counter them if they are used against you.

AFTER
1. Restate what has been agreed upon, both verbally and in writing.
2. Recognize and thank all participants for their contributions to a successful negotiation.

Before the Negotiation

For managers to be successful, they must systematically prepare for the negotiation. As the negotiator, the manager begins by gathering as much information as possible regarding the issue to be negotiated. Because knowledge is power, the more informed the negotiator is the greater is his or her bargaining power. Adequate preparation prevents others in the negotiation from catching the negotiator off guard or making him or her appear uninformed.

In addition, individuals must remember that few negotiations begin at the table. This makes it especially important to know the who, what, when, where, and how of an issue. This is the area where strategies are prepared. For example, Witzler (2010a) suggests that it is important, whenever possible, to determine the incentives of your counterpart in negotiation, especially if they are not in perfect alignment with the group he or she is representing.

However, another level of preparation is the emotional level, which is the human side of every negotiation and interaction. Remember that the "opponents" you face across the bargaining table are individuals like you. The way the other party perceives you as being fair and open to negotiate often plays a role in the decisions that will be reached in the negotiation.

It is also important for managers to decide where to start in the negotiation. Brodow (2013) notes that successful negotiators are not afraid to ask for what they want. In addition, they should be assertive (not aggressive) since they know that everything is negotiable. He calls this *negotiation consciousness* and suggests that it is what makes the difference between effective negotiators and everybody else.

Because negotiators must be willing to make compromises, they should, however, choose a starting point that is high but not ridiculous. This selected starting point should be at the upper limits of their expectations, realizing that they may need to come down to a more realistic goal. For instance, let us say that you would really like four additional full-time RN positions and a full-time clerical position budgeted for your unit. You know that you could make do with three additional full-time RN positions and a part-time clerical assistant, but you begin by asking for what would be ideal.

It is almost impossible in any type of negotiation to escalate demands; therefore, the negotiator must start at an extreme but reasonable point. It also must be decided beforehand how much can be compromised and what is an acceptable *bottom line* (or the least acceptable resolution). Can the manager accept, at a minimum, one full-time RN position or two or three?

 The very least for which a person will settle is often referred to as the bottom line.

The wise manager also has other options in mind when negotiating for important resources. An alternative option is another set of negotiating preferences that can be used so that managers do not need to use their bottom lines but still meet their overall goal. For instance, you have requested four full-time RN positions and one full-time clerical position. You could get by with three full-time RNs and one part-time clerk. However, you believe strongly that you cannot continue to provide safe patient care unless you are given two RNs and a part-time clerk—your bottom line. However, if the original negotiation is unsuccessful, reopen negotiations by saying that a second option that does not entail increasing the staff would be to float a ward clerk for 4 hours each day, implement a unit-dose system, require housekeeping to pass out linen, and have dietary pass all the patient meal trays. This way, the overall goal of providing more direct patient care by the nursing staff could still be met without adding nursing personnel.

Stanton (2013) adds that expert negotiators always prepare in advance to concede something. Knowing in advance what you can concede allows you to compromise without feeling that you are giving up and makes it easier for the other party to agree on a workable compromise. The manager also needs to consider other trade-offs that are possible in these situations. *Trade-offs* are secondary gains, often future oriented, that may be realized as a result of conflict. For example, while attending college, a parent may feel intrapersonal conflict because he or she is unable to spend as much time as desired with his or her children. The parent is able to compromise by considering the trade-off: eventually, everyone's life will be better because of the present sacrifices. The wise manager will consider trading something today for something tomorrow as a means to reach satisfactory negotiations.

The manager also must look for and acknowledge *hidden agendas*—the covert intention of the negotiation. Usually, every negotiation has a covert and an overt agenda. For example, new managers may set up a meeting with their superior with the established agenda of discussing the lack of supplies on the unit. However, the hidden agenda may be that the manager feels insecure and is really seeking performance feedback during the discussion.

Having a hidden agenda is not uncommon and is not wrong by any means. Everyone has them, and it is not necessary or even wise to share these hidden agendas. Managers, however, must be introspective enough to recognize their hidden agendas so that they are not paralyzed if the agenda is discovered and used against them during the negotiation. If the manager's hidden agenda is discovered, he or she should admit that it is a consideration but not the heart of the negotiation.

For instance, although the hidden agenda for increasing unit staff might be to build the manager's esteem in the eyes of the staff, there may exist a legitimate need for additional staff. If, during the negotiations, the fiscal controller accuses the manager of wanting to increase staff just to gain power, the manager might respond by saying, "It is always important for a successful manager to be able to gain resources for the unit, but the real issue here is an inadequate staff."

Managers who protest too strongly that they do not have a hidden agenda appear defensive and vulnerable.

During the Negotiation

Because negotiation may be a highly charged experience, the negotiator always wants to appear calm, collected, and self-assured. At least part of this self-assurance comes from having adequately prepared for the negotiation. Part of the preparation should have included learning about the people with whom the manager is negotiating. People come with a variety of personality types, and over the course of their careers, managers will come across most if not all of these personality types in various negotiations. Preparation, however, is not enough. In the end, the negotiator must have clarity in his or her communication, assertiveness, good listening skills, the ability to regroup quickly, and flexibility.

Negotiation is psychological and verbal. The effective negotiator always appears calm and self-assured.

Indeed, Brodow (2013) suggests that effective negotiators are like detectives; they ask probing questions and then become quiet. The other negotiator will tell you everything you need to know if you listen. He encourages negotiators to follow the *70/30 Rule*—listen 70% of the time, and talk only 30% of the time. In addition, you should encourage the other negotiator to talk by asking lots of *open-ended questions* that cannot be answered with a simple "yes" or "no."

In addition, the negotiator must remember that concerns about *status* pervade almost every negotiation. For example, Witzler (2010b) suggests that most people are less likely to accept a job offer, even one that would be a substantial improvement on a current job, if it is worse than an offer made to a peer. "The desire to achieve better outcomes than others—from friends and coworkers to competitors—can cause individuals to leave value on the table" (Witzler, 2010b, para 4). Witzler suggests that negotiators often make implicit comparisons with others and then fail to understand why the other side finds certain demands offensive. Strategies commonly used by leaders during negotiation to increase their persuasiveness and foster open communication are shown in Display 21.5.

DISPLAY 21.5	Strategies to Increase Persuasiveness and Foster Open Communication During the Negotiation

1. Use only factual statements that have been gathered in research.
2. Listen carefully, and watch nonverbal communication.
3. Keep an open mind, because negotiation always provides the potential for learning. It is important not to prejudge. Instead, a cooperative (not competitive) climate should be established.
4. Try to understand where the other party is coming from. It is probable that one person's perception is different from that of another. The negotiation needs to concentrate on understanding, not just on agreeing.
5. Always discuss the conflict. It is important not to personalize the conflict by discussing the parties involved in the negotiation.
6. Try not to belabor how the conflict occurred or to fix blame for the conflict. Instead, the focus must be on preventing its recurrence.
7. Be honest.
8. Start tough so that concessions are possible. It is much harder to escalate demands in the negotiation than to make concessions.
9. Delay when confronted with something totally unexpected in negotiation. In such cases, the negotiator should respond, "I'm not prepared to discuss this right now" or "I'm sorry, this was not on our agenda; we can set up another appointment to discuss that." If asked a question about something that the negotiator does not know, he or she should simply say, "I don't have that information at this time."
10. Never tell the other party what you are willing to negotiate totally. You may be giving up the ship too early.
11. Know the bottom line, but try never to use it. If the bottom line is used, the negotiator must be ready to back it up or he or she will lose all credibility. Negotiations should always result in both sides improving their positions; however, in reality, people sometimes have to walk away from the negotiating table if the situation cannot be improved because not every negotiation can result in terms that are agreeable to each party.
    Brodow (2013, para 10) says this is why someone should never negotiate without options. "If you depend too much on the positive outcome of a negotiation, you lose your ability to say NO. When you say to yourself, 'I will walk if I can't conclude a deal that is satisfactory,' the other side can tell that you mean business." If, however, the bottom line is reached, the negotiator should tell the other party that an impasse has been reached and that further negotiation is not possible at this time. Then, the other party should be encouraged to sleep on it and reconsider. The door should always be left open for further negotiation. Another appointment can be made. Both parties should be allowed to save face.
12. Take a break if either party becomes angry or tired during the negotiation. Go to the bathroom or make a telephone call. Remember that neither party can effectively negotiate if either is enraged or fatigued. Brodow (2013) notes that being patient in negotiation can be very difficult for Americans. We often are in a hurry to complete the negotiation while individuals from Asian, South American, or Middle East cultures will tell you that they look at time differently. They believe that rushing is more likely to cause mistakes and leave money on the table, so whoever can be more flexible about time generally has the advantage (Brodow).

Destructive Negotiation Tactics

Some negotiators win by using specific intimidating or manipulative tactics. People using these tactics take a competing approach to negotiation rather than a collaborative approach. These tactics might be conscious or unconscious but are used repeatedly because they have been successful for that person. Successful managers do not use these types of tactics, but because others with whom they negotiate may do so, they must be prepared to counter such tactics.

One such tactic is *ridicule*. The goal in using ridicule is to intimidate others involved in the negotiation. If you are negotiating with someone who uses ridicule, maintain a relaxed body posture, steady gaze, and patient smile. Brodow (2013) notes it is very important in negotiation not to take the issues or the other person's behavior personally. All too often, negotiations fail because one or both of the parties get sidetracked by personal issues unrelated to the negotiation at hand. Successful negotiators focus on solving the problem, which is: "How can we conclude an agreement that respects the needs of both parties? Obsessing over the other negotiator's personality, or over issues that are not directly pertinent to making a deal, can sabotage a negotiation. If someone is rude or difficult to deal with, try to understand their behavior and don't take it personally" (Brodow, para 16).

Another tactic some people use is *ambiguous* or *inappropriate questioning*. For example, in one negotiating situation, the ICU supervisor had requested additional staff to handle open heart surgery patients. During her bargaining, the CEO suddenly said, "I never did understand the heart; can you tell me about the heart?" The supervisor did not fall into this trap and instead replied that the physiology of the heart was irrelevant to the issue. Because people tend to answer an authority figure, it is necessary to be on guard for this type of diversionary tactic.

Flattery is another technique that makes true collaboration in negotiation very difficult. The person who has been flattered may be more reluctant to disagree with the other party in the negotiation, and thus his or her attention and focus are diverted. One method that managers can use to discern flattery from other honest attempts to compliment is to be aware of how they feel about the comment. If they feel unduly flattered by a gesture or comment, it is a good indication that they were being flattered. For example, asking for advice or instruction may be a subtle form of flattery, or it may be an honest request. If the request for advice is about an area in which the manager has little expertise, it is undoubtedly flattery. However, exchanging positive opening comments with each other when beginning negotiation is an acceptable and enjoyable practice performed by both parties.

Nurses are also particularly sympathetic to gestures of *helplessness*. Because nursing is a helping profession, the tendency to nurture is high, and managers must be careful not to lose sight of the original intent of the negotiation—securing adequate resources to optimize unit functioning.

Some people win in negotiation simply by rapidly and *aggressively taking over* and controlling the negotiation before other members realize what is happening. If managers believe that this may be happening, they should call a halt to the negotiations before decisions are made. Saying simply, "I need to have time to think this over" is a good method of stopping an aggressive takeover. The manager needs to be aware of destructive negotiation tactics and develop strategies to overcome them because such tactics are antithetical to collaboration.

 Destructive negotiation tactics are never a part of collaborative conflict resolution.

Leaders use an honest, straightforward approach and develop assertive skills for use in conflict negotiation. Maintaining human dignity and promoting communication require that all conflict interactions be assertive, direct, and open. Conflict must be focused on the issues and resolved through joint compromise.

Closure and Follow-Up to Negotiation

Just as it is important to start the formal negotiation with some pleasantries, it is also good to close on a friendly note. Once a compromise has been reached, restate it so that everyone is clear about what has been agreed upon. If managers win more in negotiation than they anticipated, they should try to hide their astonishment. At the end of any negotiation, whether it is a short 2-minute conflict negotiation in the hallway with another RN or an hour-long formal salary negotiation, the result should be satisfaction by all parties that each has won something. It is a good idea to follow up formal negotiation in writing by sending a letter or a memo stating what was agreed.

LEARNING EXERCISE 21.4

An Exercise in Negotiation Analysis

You are one of a group of staff nurses who believe that part of your job dissatisfaction results from being assigned different patients every day. Your unit uses a system of total patient care, and the head nurse makes assignments. Two staff nurses have gone to the head nurse and requested that each nurse be allowed to pick his or her own patients based on the previous day's assignment and the ability of the nurse. The head nurse believes that the staff nurses are being uncooperative because it is the head nurse's responsibility to see that all the patients get assigned and receive adequate care. Although continuity of care is the goal, many part-time nurses are used on the unit, and not all the nurses are able to care for every type of patient. At the end of the conference, the two nurses are angry, and the head nurse is irritated. However, the next day, the head nurse indicates willingness to meet with the staff nurses. The other nurses believe this is a sign that the head nurse is willing to negotiate a compromise. They plan to get together tonight to plan the strategy for tomorrow's meeting.

Assignment: What are the goals for each party? What could be a possible hidden agenda for each party? What could happen if the conflict escalates? Devise a workable plan that would accomplish the goals of both parties and develop strategies for implementation (see the Appendix for an analysis of these problems).

ALTERNATIVE DISPUTE RESOLUTION

Many disputes can be solved informally. Occasionally, however, parties cannot reach agreement through negotiation. In these cases, ADR may be indicated to keep some privacy in the dispute and to avoid expensive litigation. Types of ADR include mediation, fact finding, arbitration, due process hearings, and the use of ombudspersons.

Mediation, which uses a neutral third party, is a confidential, legally nonbinding process designed to help bring the parties together to devise a solution to the conflict. As such, the mediator does not take sides and has no vested interest in the outcome. Instead, the mediator asks questions to clarify the issues at hand (*fact finding*), listens to both parties, meets with parties privately as necessary, and helps to identify solutions both parties can live with.

There are times, however, when mediators are unable to help conflicted parties come to agreement. When this occurs, formal *arbitration* may be used. Unlike mediation, which seeks to help conflicted parties come together to reach a decision themselves, arbitration is a binding conflict resolution process in which the facts of the case are heard by an individual who makes a final decision for the parties in conflict.

Due process hearings are actual court hearings, which focus on evaluating and resolving conflicts through discovery, presentation of evidence, sworn testimony including that of expert witnesses, and cross-examination (Mueller, 2009). A hearing officer objectively listens to both sides of the issue and makes a decision following the letter of the law (Mueller). Case law established through precedence often determines the outcome.

Another option for individuals experiencing conflict may be guidance from *ombudspersons*. Ombudspersons generally hold an official title as such within an organization. Their function is to investigate grievances filed by one party against another and to ensure that individuals involved in conflicts understand their rights as well as the process that should be used to report and resolve the conflict.

SEEKING CONSENSUS

Consensus means that negotiating parties reach an agreement that all parties can support, even if it does not represent everyone's first priorities. Consensus decision making does not provide complete satisfaction for everyone involved in the negotiation as an initially unanimous decision would, but it does indicate willingness by all parties to accept the agreed-upon conditions.

In committees or groups working on shared goals, consensus is often used to resolve conflicts that may occur within the group. To reach consensus often requires the use of an experienced facilitator, and having consensus-building skills is a requirement of good leadership. Building consensus ensures that everyone within the group is heard but that the group will ultimately end up with one agreed-upon course of action. Consensual decisions are best used for decisions that relate to a core problem or need a deep level of group support to implement successfully.

Perhaps the greatest challenge in using consensus as a conflict resolution strategy is that like collaboration, it is time consuming. It also requires all of the parties involved in the negotiation to have good communication skills and to be open minded and flexible. It is also important for the leader to recognize when achieving consensus has become unrealistic.

INTEGRATING LEADERSHIP SKILLS AND MANAGEMENT FUNCTIONS IN MANAGING CONFLICT

There are many benefits to establishing and maintaining an appropriate amount of conflict in the workplace, including increased harmony and productivity, a pleasant working environment, reductions in stress and anxiety, and decreased victimized behavior (Hudson, 2003–2013). In addition, the manager who creates a stable work environment that minimizes the antecedent conditions for conflict has more time and energy to focus on meeting organizational and human resource needs. When conflict does occur in the unit, managers must be able to discern constructive from destructive conflict. Conflict that is constructive will result in creativity, innovation, and growth for the unit. When conflict is deemed to be destructive, managers must deal appropriately with that conflict or risk an aftermath that may be even more destructive than the original conflict. Consistently using conflict resolution strategies with win–lose or lose–lose outcomes will create disharmony within the unit. Leaders who use optimal conflict resolution strategies with a win–win outcome promote increased employee satisfaction and organizational productivity.

Negotiation also requires both management functions and leadership skills. Well-prepared managers know with whom they will be negotiating and prepare their negotiation accordingly. They are prepared with trade-offs, multiple alternatives, and a clear bottom line to ensure that their unit acquires needed resources. Successful negotiation mandates the use of the leadership components of self-confidence and risk taking. If these attributes are not present, the leader-manager has little power in negotiation and thus compromises the unit's ability to secure desired resources. Other attributes that make leaders effective in negotiation are sensitivity to others and the environment and interpersonal communication skills. The leader's use of assertive communication skills, rather than destructive tactics, results in an acceptable level of satisfaction for all parties at the close of the negotiation.

KEY CONCEPTS

- Conflict can be defined as the internal discord that results from differences in ideas, values, or feelings of two or more people.

- Because managers have a variety of interpersonal relationships with people with different values, beliefs, backgrounds, and goals, conflict is an expected outcome.

- The most common sources of organizational conflict are communication problems, organizational structure, and individual behavior within the organization.

- Conflict theory has changed dramatically during the last 100 years. Currently, conflict is viewed as neither good nor bad because it can produce growth or be destructive, depending on how it is managed.

- Too little conflict results in organizational stasis, whereas too much conflict reduces the organization's effectiveness and eventually immobilizes its employees.

- Conflict also has a qualitative component, and the impact of a conflict on any individual varies significantly in terms of how it is perceived and handled.

- The three categories of conflict are intrapersonal, interpersonal, and intergroup.

- The first stage in the conflict process is called latent conflict, which implies the existence of antecedent conditions. Latent conflict may proceed to perceived conflict or to felt conflict. Manifest conflict may also ensue. The last stage in the process is conflict aftermath.

- The optimal goal in conflict resolution is creating a win–win solution for everyone involved.

- Common conflict resolution strategies include compromise, competing, accommodating, smoothing, avoiding, and collaboration.

- As a negotiator, it is important to win as much as possible, lose as little as possible, and make the other party feel satisfied with the outcome of the negotiation.

- Because knowledge is power, the more informed the negotiator is, the greater is his or her bargaining power.

- The leader, while able to recognize and counter negotiation tactics, always strives to achieve an honest, collaborative approach to negotiation.

- The manager must know his or her bottom line but try never to use it.

- Closure and follow-up are important parts of the negotiation process.

- ADR usually involves at least one of the elements of mediation, fact finding, arbitration, and the use of ombudspersons.

- Seeking consensus, a concord of opinion, although time consuming, is an effective conflict resolution and negotiation strategy.

ADDITIONAL LEARNING EXERCISES AND APPLICATIONS

LEARNING EXERCISE 21.5

Choosing the Most Appropriate Resolution Approach

In the following situations, choose the most appropriate conflict resolution strategy (avoiding, smoothing, accommodating, competing, compromising, or collaborating). Support your decision with rationale, and explain why other methods of conflict management were not used.

(Continued)

Situation 1

You are a circulating nurse in the operating room. Usually, you are assigned to Room 3 for general surgery, but today you have been assigned to Room 4, the orthopedic room. You are unfamiliar with the orthopedic doctors' routines and attempt to brush up on them quickly by reading the doctors' preference cards before each case today. So far, you have managed to complete two cases without incident. The next case comes in the room, and you realize that everyone is especially tense; this patient is the wife of a local physician, and the doctors are performing a bone biopsy for possible malignancy. You prepare the biopsy area, and the surgeon, who has a reputation for a quick temper, enters the room. You suddenly realize that you have prepped the area with Betadine, and this surgeon prefers another solution. He sees what you have done and yells, "You are a stupid, stupid nurse."

Situation 2

You are the ICU charge nurse and have just finished an exhausting 8 hours on duty. Working with you today were two nurses who work 12-hour shifts. Each of you were assigned two patients, all with high acuity levels. You are glad that you are going out of town tonight to attend an important seminar, because you are certainly tired. You are also pleased that you scheduled yourself an 8-hour shift today and that your replacement is coming through the door. You will just have time to give report and catch your plane.

It is customary for 12-hour nurses to continue with their previous patients and for assignments not to be changed when 8- and 12-hour staff are working together. Therefore, you proceed to give report on your patients to the 8-hour nurse coming on duty. One of your patients is acutely ill with fever of unknown origin and is in the isolation room. It is suspected that he has meningitis. Your other patient is a multiple trauma victim. In the middle of your report, the oncoming nurse says that she has just learned that she is pregnant. She says, "I can't take care of a possible meningitis patient. I'll have to trade with one of the 12-hour nurses." You approach the 12-hour nurses, and they respond angrily, "We took care of all kinds of patients when we were pregnant, and we are not changing patients with just 4 hours left in our shift."

When you repeat this message to the oncoming nurse, she says, "Either they trade or I go home!" Your phone call to the nursing office reveals that because of a flu epidemic, there are absolutely no personnel to call in, and all the other units are already short staffed.

Situation 3

You are an RN graduate of a BSN nursing program. Since you graduated 6 months ago, you have been working at an outpatient emergency clinic and have just recently begun to feel more confident in your new role. However, one of the older, diploma-educated nurses working with you constantly belittles baccalaureate nursing education. Whenever you request assistance in problem solving or in learning a new skill, she says, "Didn't they teach you anything in nursing school?" The clinic supervisor has given you satisfactory 3- and 6-month evaluations, but you are becoming increasingly defensive regarding the comments of the other nurse.

Situation 4

You are the charge nurse on a step-down unit. It is your first day back from a 2-week vacation. The shift begins in 10 minutes, and you sit down to make staffing assignments. The central staffing office has noted that you must float one of your RNs to the oncology unit. When you check the floating roster, you note that Jenny, one of the RNs assigned to work on your unit today, was the last to float. (She floated yesterday.) That leaves you to choose from Mark and Lisa, your other two RNs. According to the float roster, Mark floated 10 days ago, and Lisa floated last 11 days ago. You tell Lisa that it is her turn to float.

Lisa states that she floated three times in a row while Mark was on vacation for 2 weeks last month. Mark says that vacations should not count and that he should not float because it is not his turn. Lisa says that Jenny should float, as she floated to oncology yesterday and already knows the patients. Jenny says that she agreed to come in and work today (on her day off) to help the unit, and she would not have agreed to do this if she had known that she would have to float. Mark says that it is the last day of a 6-day stretch, and he does not want to float. Jenny says that it is not her turn to float, and she does not want to float willingly.

Situation 5

You are a new nurse working on a busy medical/surgical floor. The mode of patient care delivery used on the unit is team nursing. You have grown increasingly frustrated, however, with a licensed vocational nurse (LVN)/licensed professional nurse (LPN) on your team who is unwilling to answer call lights. You have directly observed her both ignore call lights and go out of her way to avoid answering the lights. When you confront her, she always provides an excuse such as she was on her way to do something for another patient or that she did not notice the blinking call light. The end result is that you often must run from one end of the hall to the other to answer the call lights since patient safety could be at risk. Your frustration level has risen to the point that you no longer wish to work with this person.

Situation 6

You are a staff nurse on a small telemetry unit. The unit is staffed at a ratio of one nurse for every four patients and the charge nurse is counted in this staffing since there is a full-time unit secretary and monitor technician to assist at the desk. The charge nurse is responsible for making the daily staffing assignments. While you recognize that the charge nurse needs to reduce her patient care assignment to have time to perform the charge nurse duties, you have grown increasingly frustrated that she normally assigns herself only one patient, if any, and these patients always have the lowest acuity level on the floor. This has placed a disproportionate burden on the other nurses, who often feel the assignment they are being given may be unsafe. The charge nurse is your immediate supervisor. She has not generally been responsive to concerns expressed by the staff to her about this problem.

LEARNING EXERCISE 21.6

Negotiating the Graduation Ceremony

Often, one group is more powerful or has greater status and refuses to relinquish this power position, thus making collaboration impossible. Therefore, negotiating a compromise to a win–win solution, rather than a lose–lose solution, becomes imperative. In the following situation, describe if you could, and how you would, go about negotiating a win–win solution to conflict.

You are a senior member of a traditional on-campus baccalaureate nursing class. Three years ago, your university implemented an online RN-BSN program. The first students from that program graduated last year, and they held a small, private end-of-program ceremony, separate from the on-campus BSN students.

This year, as a result of ongoing state budget cuts, the school of nursing can no longer subsidize two separate end-of-program ceremonies. This means that the 21 RN-BSN students and the 33 on-campus BSN students must now work together to plan a joint ceremony.

(Continued)

Resistance is high. The two groups of students have spent no time together and do not know each other. The on-campus students have been planning their ceremony since they started the nursing program and have collected additional money each semester to fund a formal dinner and dance reception in the evening and breakfast at one of the nicest hotels in town. Money from the school of nursing would be used to subsidize the cost of a live band and the reception hall. The online students would like to limit the evening reception to cake and punch at the college to reduce the cost because most of them will incur additional travel and lodging costs to attend graduation. However, they would like to have the school of nursing use the funds available to host a "picnic in the park" the following day, to which they can bring their families. Both groups perceive that the "other group is trying to control the situation and is not being sensitive to our needs or wants." Both groups have contacted university officials to complain about the situation, and a number of students are threatening not to attend the ceremony if the two groups must be merged.

You have been appointed as the unofficial spokesperson for the RN-BSN graduates. Joan is the unofficial spokesperson for the on-campus BSN students. You live only 30 miles from campus, so coming to campus to try to resolve the conflict is not a significant hardship.

The faculty member, Alice, who is the liaison for the end-of-program ceremony has become alarmed at the situation and has contacted both you and Joan. She states that she will cancel the ceremony if the conflict is not resolved. The faculty member agrees to work with you and Joan to mediate the conflict, but time is of the essence. The semester ends soon, and the on-campus students can get no refund on their reception hall deposit after the end of the current week. She wants the conflict resolved in a win–win situation so that no parties leave angry.

Assignment: Where will you begin? How will you get input from the group that you are representing? Would you plan a face-to-face meeting with Joan to attempt to resolve this conflict? What strategies might you use to help both groups win as much as possible and lose as little as possible? Explain your rationale. Remember, you wish to negotiate a compromise, and although you desire a win–win solution, you are limited in time and may not be able to facilitate a true collaboration. How will you deal with conflicted parties who perceive that they have lost more than they have won? What is your bottom line?

LEARNING EXERCISE 21.7

Behavioral Tactics—Appropriate or Not?

You are a woman who is a unit manager with a master's degree in health administration. You are about to present your proposed budget to the CEO, who is a man. You have thoroughly researched your budget and have adequate rationale to support your requests for increased funding. Because the CEO is often moody, predicting his response is difficult.

You are also aware that the CEO has some very traditional views about women's role in the workplace, and generally this does not include a major management role. Because he is fairly paternalistic, he is charmed and flattered when asked to assist "his" nurses with their jobs. Your predecessor, also a woman, was fired because she was perceived as brash, bossy, and disrespectful by the CEO. In fact, the former unit manager was one of a series of nursing managers who had been replaced in the last several years because of these characteristics. From what you have been told, the nursing staff did not share these perceptions.

You sit down and begin to plan your strategy for this meeting. You are aware that you are more likely to have your budgetary needs met if you dress conservatively, beseech the CEO's assistance and support throughout the presentation, and are fairly passive in your approach.

In other words, you will be required to assume a traditionally feminine, helpless role. If you appear capable and articulate, you may not achieve your budgetary goals and may not even keep your job. It would probably not be necessary for you to continue to act this way, except in your interactions with the CEO.

Assignment: Are such behavioral tactics appropriate if the outcome is desirable? Are such tactics simply smart negotiation, or are they destructively manipulative? What would you do in this situation? Outline your strategy for your budget presentation, and present rationale for your choices.

LEARNING EXERCISE 21.8

Your First Budget Presentation

You are the unit manager of the new oncology unit. It is time for your first budget presentation to the administration. You have already presented your budget to the Director of Nurses, who had a few questions but expressed general agreement. However, it is the policy at Memorial Hospital that the unit manager's present budget be presented to the budget committee, consisting of the fiscal manager, the Director of Nurses, a member of the board of trustees, and the Executive Director. You know that money is scarce this year because of the new building, but you really believe that you need the increases you have requested in your budget. Basically, you have asked for the following:

- Replace the 22% aides on your unit with 10% LVNs/LPNs and 12% RNs.
- Increase educational time paid by 5% to allow for certification in chemotherapy.
- Provide a new position of clinical nurse specialist in oncology.
- Convert one room into a sitting room and mini-kitchen for patients' families.
- Add shelves and a locked medication box in each room to facilitate primary nursing.
- Provide no new equipment, but replace existing equipment that is broken or outdated.

Assignment: Outline your plan. Include your approach what is and what is not negotiable and what arguments you would use. Give a rationale for your plan.

LEARNING EXERCISE 21.9

Handling Staff–Patient Conflict

You are the supervisor of a rehabilitation unit. Two of your youngest female nursing assistants come to your office today to report that a young male paraplegic patient has been making lewd sexual comments and gestures when they provide basic care. When you question them about their response to the actions of the patient, they maintain that they normally simply look away and try to ignore him, although they are offended by his actions. They are reluctant to confront the patient directly.

Because it is anticipated that this patient may remain on your unit for at least a month, the nursing assistants have asked you to intervene in this conflict by either talking to the patient or by assigning other nurses responsibility for his care.

Assignment: How will you handle this staff–patient conflict? Is avoidance (assigning different staff to care for the patient) an appropriate conflict resolution strategy in this situation? Will you encourage the nursing assistants to confront the patient directly? What coaching or role playing might you use with them if you choose this approach? Will you confront the patient yourself? What might you say?

LEARNING EXERCISE 21.10

Handling Personal Issues in a Professional Manner

You are a male unit supervisor of a pediatric trauma unit at Children's Hospital. Three years ago, you ended a serious romantic relationship with a nurse named Susan, who was employed at a different hospital in the same city. The break up was not mutual, and Susan was hurt and angry.

Six months ago, Susan accepted a position as a unit supervisor at Children's Hospital. This has required you and Susan to interact formally at department head meetings and informally regarding staffing and personnel issues on a regular basis. Often, these interactions have been marked by either covert hostility on Susan's part, nonverbal aggression, or sniping comments. When you attempted to confront Susan about her behavior, she stated that "she didn't have a problem and that you shouldn't flatter yourself to think that she does."

The situation is becoming increasingly more difficult to "work around," and both staff and fellow unit supervisors have become aware of the ongoing tension. You love your position and do not want to leave Children's Hospital, but it is becoming increasingly apparent that the situation cannot continue as it is.

Assignment: Answer the following questions:

1. How might gender have influenced the latent conditions, perceived or felt conflict, manifest conflict, and conflict aftermath in this situation?

2. What conflict strategies might you use to try to resolve this conflict? Avoidance? Smoothing? Accommodation? Competing? Compromise? Collaboration?

3. Would the use of a mediator be helpful in this situation?

LEARNING EXERCISE 21.11

Choosing the Most Appropriate Resolution Approach

Choose one of the following situations and write a one-page essay, discussing which conflict resolution strategy is most appropriate for this situation. Explain why other conflict resolution strategies were rejected.

Situation 1

You are an RN on a surgical unit. MJ is an orthopedic surgery patient who is 2 days postop. Her physician has ordered patient-controlled analgesia (PCA) using morphine, as well as prn IM injections of Demerol every 3 to 4 hours. The patient has continued to verbalize a significant amount of pain.

Today, Dr. Jones writes an order for you to give MJ an additional 100 mg Demerol IM now, even though she had 100 mg less than 1 hour ago as well as her PCA. The dose he ordered is contraindicated in your drug handbook. You approach Dr. Jones with your concerns about the safety of such a dose as well as your questioning of the patient's pain level. Dr. Jones interrupts you shortly after you begin and says in a curt, hostile tone, "I am the doctor and I write the medication orders. You are the nurse and your responsibility is to implement my care plan. Give the medication now or I will see that you are fired."

Situation 2

Today is Wednesday. Julie, a long-time employee on your unit where you are a manager, believes she is entitled to certain privileges regarding scheduling. You have told her to review the policy concerning weekends and days off. Julie believes she deserves every other weekend off, with Friday and Monday off on the weekends she works.

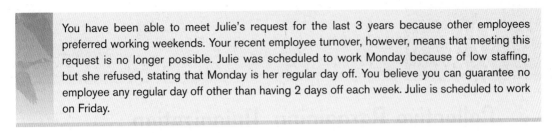

You have been able to meet Julie's request for the last 3 years because other employees preferred working weekends. Your recent employee turnover, however, means that meeting this request is no longer possible. Julie was scheduled to work Monday because of low staffing, but she refused, stating that Monday is her regular day off. You believe you can guarantee no employee any regular day off other than having 2 days off each week. Julie is scheduled to work on Friday.

REFERENCES

American Sentinel. (2012, September 24). *Nursing career strategies: Guidelines for painless conflict resolution.* Nursetogether.com. Retrieved June 21, 2013, from http://www.nursetogether.com/nursing-career -strategies-guidelines-for-painless-conflict -resolution#sthash.Y0q2bYSh.dpuf

Brodow, E. (2013). *Ten tips for negotiating in 2013.* Ed Brodow Seminars. Retrieved June 21, 2013, from http://www.brodow.com/Articles/NegotiatingTips.html

Cheung-Larivee, K. (2013, January 31). *How rude! Workplace incivility hurts bottom line.* FierceHealthcare. Retrieved June 21, 2013, from http://www.fiercehealthcare.com/story/how-rude -workplace-incivility-hurts-bottom-line/2013-01 -31#ixzz2Wss5nNiD

Clark, C. M. (2010) Why civility matters. *Reflections on Nursing Leadership, 36*(1). Retrieved June 21, 2013, from http://www.reflectionsonnursingleadership.org/ Pages/Vol36_1_Clark2_civility.aspx

CRM Learning. (2013, June 16). *The decision to get involved—4 things to consider.* Retrieved June 21, 2013, from http://www.crmlearning.com/ blog/?tag=conflict-management

Ellis, P., & Abbott, J. (2012). Strategies for managing conflict within the team. *British Journal of Cardiac Nursing, 7*(3), 138–140.

Hauge, L., Skogstad, A., & Einarsen, S. (2009, October– December). Individual and situational predictors of workplace bullying: Why do perpetrators engage in the bullying of others? *Work & Stress, 23*(4), 349–358.

Hockley, C. (2014). Violence in nursing: The expectations and the reality. In C. J. Huston (Ed.), *Professional issues in nursing: Challenges and opportunities* (3rd ed.). Philadelphia, PA: Lippincott Williams & Wilkins.

Hudson, K. (2003–2013). *Conflict resolution. Dynamic nursing education.* Retrieved June 21, 2013, from http://dynamicnursingeducation.com/class.php?class _id=70&pid=14

Inglis, R. L., Schaper, A. M., & Swartz, S. L. (2013, April 14). Conflict engagement skill building for nurse residents. Session presented at the Sigma Theta Tau International conference *Creating Healthy Work Environments*, Indianapolis, IN. Virginia

Henderson International Nursing Library. Retrieved June 20, 2013, from http://www.nursinglibrary.org/ vhl/handle/10755/290986

Kaitelidou, D., Kontogianni, A., Galanis, P., Siskou, O., Mallidou, A., Pavlakis, A., & Liaropoulos, L. (2012). Conflict management and job satisfaction in paediatric hospitals in Greece. *Journal of Nursing Management, 20*(4), 571–578.

Losa Iglesias, M. E., & Becerro de Bengoa Vallejo, R. (2012). Conflict resolution styles in the nursing profession. *Contemporary Nurse: A Journal for the Australian Nursing Profession, 43*(1), 73–80.

Mueller, T. (2009, June). Alternative dispute resolution: A new agenda for special education policy. *Journal of Disability Policy Studies, 20*(1), 4–13.

Roche, M., Diers, D., Duffield, C., & Catling-Pauli, C. (2010). Violence toward nurses, the work environment, and patient outcomes. *Journal of Nursing Scholarship, 42*(1), 13–22.

Stacey G., Johnston, K., Stickley, T. & Diamond, B. (2011) How do nurses cope with values and practice conflict? *Nursing Times,107*(5), 20–23.

Stanton, K. (2013). *Resolving workplace conflict.* Advance for Nurses. Retrieved June 20, 2013, from http://nursing.advanceweb.com/Continuing -Education/CE-Articles/Resolving-Workplace -Conflict.aspx

Townsend, T. (2012, January). Break that bullying cycle. *American Nurse Today.* Retrieved June 21, 2013, from http://www.americannursetoday.com/article .aspx?id=8648

Vaughn, P. (2009, September–November). Collaboration and conflict management: A brief review of current thought. *Oklahoma Nurse, 54*(3), 4.

Witzler, L. (2010a, March 2). *Understand your counterpart's incentives.* The President and Fellows of Harvard College. Retrieved June 20, 2013, from http:// www.pon.harvard.edu/daily/business-negotiations/ understand-your-counterparts-incentives/

Witzler, L. (2010b, February 16). *How status conscious are you?* The President and Fellows of Harvard College. Retrieved June 20, 2013, from http://www.pon .harvard.edu/daily/business-negotiations/how-status -conscious-are-you/

22

Collective Bargaining, Unionization, and Employment Laws

During the past decade, the downsizing of nursing staffs, systems redesign, and oppressive management practices have created such poor nursing practice environments that improvement in wages no longer is viewed as the primary purpose of collective bargaining.
–Karen Budd, Linda Warino, and Mary Ellen Patton

… Organizations with unfair management policies are more likely to become unionized. It is within managerial power to eliminate some of the needs that staff have for joining unions.
–Carol Huston

CROSSWALK THIS CHAPTER ADDRESSES:

BSN Essential II: Basic organizational and systems leadership for quality care and patient safety
BSN Essential V: Health-care policy, finance, and regulatory environments
BSN Essential VI: Interprofessional communication and collaboration for improving patient health outcomes
BSN Essential VII: Professionalism and professional values
MSN Essential II: Organizational and systems leadership
MSN Essential III: Quality improvement and safety
MSN Essential VI: Health policy and advocacy
MSN Essential VII: Interprofessional collaboration for improving patient and population health outcomes
QSEN Competency: Teamwork and collaboration
QSEN Competency: Quality improvement
QSEN Competency: Safety
AONE Nurse Executive Competency I: Communication and relationship building
AONE Nurse Executive Competency II: A knowledge of the health-care environment
AONE Nurse Executive Competency III: Leadership
AONE Nurse Executive Competency IV: Professionalism
AONE Nurse Executive Competency V: Business skills

LEARNING OBJECTIVES *The learner will:*

- identify factors that influence whether nurses join unions
- describe the relationship between national economic prosperity, the existence of nursing shortages and surpluses, and the unionization rates of nurses
- differentiate between the leader's and manager's roles in collective bargaining
- identify major legislation that has impacted the ability of nurses to unionize
- identify the steps necessary to start a union
- identify the largest unions representing health-care employees, and nurses in particular

- philosophically debate the potential conflicts inherent in having a professional organization also serve as a collective bargaining agent
- reflect on whether going on strike can be viewed as an ethically appropriate action for professional nurses
- differentiate between federal and state labor standards and labor contracts
- explore labor laws regarding overtime and working conditions present in the state in which he or she lives or will seek employment
- explain how equal employment legislation has affected employment and hiring practices
- identify how the Civil Rights Act, the Americans with Disabilities Act, and the Age Discrimination and Employment Act have attempted to reduce discrimination in the workplace
- identify the purpose of the Occupational Safety and Health Act (OSHA)
- identify strategies for eliminating sexual harassment in the workplace

Factors that have an impact on the directional aspects of management include collective bargaining, unionization, and employment laws. It is possible to make these factors positive rather than negative influences on management effectiveness. To accomplish this, managers must first understand the interrelationship of unionization and management, the proliferation of legislation regarding employment practices, and the impact of both on the health-care industry.

Managers must be able to see collective bargaining and employment legislation from four perspectives: the organization, the worker, general historical and societal, and personal. Managers who can gain this broad perspective will better understand how management and employees can work together cooperatively despite unionization and employment legislation. Many industrialized countries have adopted an attitude of acceptance and tolerance for the difficulties of managing under these influences. However, in the United States, many organizations view these forces with resentment and hostility.

This chapter examines the leadership roles and management functions necessary to create a climate in which unionization and legislation are compatible with organizational goals. The leadership roles and management functions inherent in dealing with collective bargaining, unionization, and employment laws are shown in Display 22.1.

| DISPLAY 22.1 | Leadership Roles and Management Functions Associated with Collective Bargaining, Unionization, and Employment Laws |

LEADERSHIP ROLES
1. Is self-aware regarding personal attitudes and values regarding collective bargaining and employment laws.
2. Recognizes and accepts reasons why people seek unionization.
3. Creates a work environment that is sensitive to employee needs, thereby reducing the need for unionization.
4. Maintains an accommodating or cooperative approach when dealing with unions and employment legislation.
5. Is a role model for fairness.
6. Is nondiscriminatory in all personal and professional actions.
7. Examines the work environment periodically to ensure that it is supportive for all members regardless of gender, race, age, disability, or sexual orientation.
8. Immediately confronts and addresses sexual harassment in adopting a zero tolerance approach to the problem.
9. Embraces the intent of laws barring discrimination and providing equal opportunity.
10. Actively seeks a culturally and ethnically diverse workforce to meet the needs of an increasingly diverse client population.

(Continued)

MANAGEMENT FUNCTIONS

1. Understands and appropriately implements union contracts.
2. Administers personnel policies fairly and consistently.
3. Works cooperatively with the personnel department and top-level administration when dealing with union activity.
4. Promotes worker identification with management.
5. Immediately and fully investigates all complaints regarding violations of the collective bargaining contract and takes appropriate action.
6. Creates opportunities for subordinates to have input into organizational decision-making to discourage unionization.
7. Is alert for discriminatory employment practices in the workplace and intervenes immediately when problems exist.
8. Ensures that the unit or department meets state licensing regulations.
9. Understands and follows labor and employment laws that relate to the manager's sphere of influence and organization responsibilities.
10. Ensures that the work environment is safe.
11. Works closely with human resource management when dealing with employment legislation issues.

UNIONS AND COLLECTIVE BARGAINING

Collective bargaining involves activities occurring between organized labor and management that concern employee relations. Such activities include the negotiation of formal labor agreements and day-to-day interactions between unions and management. Huston (2014a) maintains that the issue at the heart of the debate on collective bargaining and nursing is whether nursing—long recognized as a care-giving profession—should be a part of bargaining efforts to improve working conditions. Although this may seem to represent a dichotomy, it is also true that unions and collective bargaining are very much a part of many nurses' lived experience.

Although first- and middle-level managers usually have little to do with negotiating the labor contract, they are greatly involved with the contract's daily implementation. The middle manager has the greatest impact on the quality of the relationship that develops between labor and management. Terminology associated with unions and collective bargaining is shown in Display 22.2.

DISPLAY 22.2 Collective Bargaining Terminology

Agency shop: Also called an *open shop.* Employees are not required to join the union.

Arbitration: Terminal step in the grievance procedure, where a third party reviews the grievance, completes fact finding, and reaches a decision. Always indicates the involvement of a third party. Arbitration may be voluntary on the part of management and labor or imposed by the government in a compulsory arbitration.

Collective bargaining: Relations between employers, acting through their management representatives, and organized labor.

Conciliation and mediation: Synonymous terms that refer to the activity of a third party to help disputants reach an agreement. However, unlike an arbitrator, this person has no final power of decision-making.

Fact finding: Rarely used in the private sector but used frequently in labor–management disputes that involve government-owned companies. In the private sector, fact finding is usually performed by a board of inquiry.

Free speech: Public Law 101, Section 8, states that "the expressing of any views, argument, or dissemination thereof, whether in written, printed, graphic, or visual form, shall not constitute or be evidence of an unfair labor practice under any provisions of this Act, if such expression contains no threat of reprisal or force or promise of benefit."

Grievance: Perception on the part of a union member that management has failed in some way to meet the terms of the labor agreement.

Lockout: Closing a place of business by management in the course of a labor dispute for the purpose of forcing employees to accept management terms.

National Labor Relations Board (NLRB): Labor board formed to implement the Wagner Act. Its two major functions are to (a) determine who should be the official bargaining unit when a new unit is formed and who should be in the unit and (b) adjudicate unfair labor charges.

Professionals: Professionals have the right to be represented by a union but cannot belong to a union that represents nonprofessionals unless a majority of them vote for inclusion in the nonprofessional unit.

Strike: Concerted withholding of labor supply to bring about economic pressure on employers and cause them to grant employee demands.

Union shop: Also called a *closed shop*. All employees are required to join the union and pay dues.

HISTORICAL PERSPECTIVE OF UNIONIZATION IN AMERICA

Unions have been present in America since the 1790s. Skilled craftsmen formed early unions to protect themselves from wage cuts during the highly competitive era of industrialization. The history of unionization reveals that union membership and activity increase sharply during times of high employment and prosperity and decrease sharply during economic recessions and layoffs.

Union activity also tends to change in response to workforce excesses and shortages. For decades, employment demand for nurses has increased and decreased periodically. High demand for nurses is tied directly to a healthy national economy, and historically, this has been correlated with increased union activity. Similarly, when nursing vacancy rates are low, union membership and activity tends to decline.

Nurses' perceptions of whether they are valued by their employers have also always had an impact on unionization rates. The rapid downsizing and restructuring of the 1990s left many nurses feeling that management did not listen to them or care about their needs.

Management that is perceived to be deaf to the workers' needs provides a fertile ground for union organizers, because unions thrive in a climate that perceives the organizational philosophy to be insensitive to the worker.

For many reasons, however, collective bargaining was slow in coming to the health-care industry. Until labor laws were amended, the unionization of health-care workers was illegal. Nursing's long history as a service commodity further delayed labor organization in health-care settings. Initial collective bargaining in the profession took place in organizations that were deemed government or public. This was made possible by *Executive Order 10988*, authored in 1962. This order lifted restrictions preventing public employees from organizing. Therefore, collective bargaining by nurses at city, county, and district hospitals and health-care agencies began in the 1960s.

In 1974, Congress amended the *Wagner Act*, extending national labor laws to private, nonprofit hospitals; nursing homes; health clinics; health maintenance organizations; and other health-care institutions. These amendments opened the door to much union activity for professions and the public employee sector. Indeed, a review of union-membership figures readily shows that, since 1960, most collective bargaining activity in the United States

TABLE 22.1	Labor Legislation	
Year	Legislation	Effect
1935	National Labor Act/Wagner Act	Gave unions many rights in organizing; resulted in rapid union growth
1947	Taft-Hartley Amendment	Returned some power to management; resulted in a more equal balance of power between unions and management
1962	Kennedy *Executive Order* 10988	Amended the 1935 Wagner Act to allow public employees to join unions
1974	Amendments to Wagner Act	Allowed nonprofit organizations to join unions
1989	National Labor Relations Board ruling	Allowed nurses to form their own separate bargaining units

occurred in the public and professional sectors of industry, most notably among faculty at institutions of higher education, teachers at primary and secondary levels, and physicians. There have been gradual declines in unionization in the private and blue-collar sectors since membership peaked in the 1950s.

From 1962 through 1989, slow but steady increases occurred in the numbers of nurses represented by collective bargaining agents. In 1989, the NLRB ruled that nurses could form their own separate bargaining units, and union activity increased. However, the American Hospital Association immediately sued the American Nurses Association (ANA), and the ruling was halted until 1991 when the Supreme Court upheld the 1989 NLRB decision. Table 22.1 outlines the legislation that led to unionization in health care.

UNION REPRESENTATION OF NURSES

As of 2012, just over 18% of the nation's registered nurses (RNs) belonged to unions, down from almost 20% in 2008 (Moberg, 2013). Not only did the proportion of unionized nurses drop in those 4 years, so did the actual number, despite the total number of nurses increasing by about 70,000. Still, nurses are roughly twice as likely to be in a union as are other workers (Moberg).

 Nurses are roughly twice as likely to be in a union as are other workers.

In fact, as of 2012, the union-membership rate of wage and salary workers in the United States across all areas of employment was 11.3%, compared with 11.8% in 2011 (Warner, 2013). The 2012 figure represents a 97-year low and those who are unionized are primarily the shrinking public sector (Liu, 2013). In the private sector, unionization fell to 6.6%, down from a peak of 35% during the 1950s (Liu).

Nurses are represented by a multitude of unions. The *California Nurses Association* (CNA)/*National Nurses Organizing Committee* joined with two other nurses' unions (*United American Nurses* [UANs] and the *Massachusetts Nurses Association*) to create a new 150,000+ member advocacy association known as *National Nurses United* (NNU) in 2009. While all three unions maintained their separate identities, the merger did give these members a greater national voice with the end result being that NNU won most—if not all—of the organizing efforts it has undertaken since the merger (Commins, 2012).

The *Service Employees International Union* (SEIU) is another large union in the health-care industry, representing more than 1.1 million nurses, licensed practical nurses (LPNs), doctors, lab technicians, nursing home workers, and home care workers (SEIU, 2013).

In addition, the National Federation of Nurses (NFN) merged with the American Federation of Teachers (AFT) in February 2013, making AFT the nation's third largest nurses' union, after NNU and SEIU (Moberg, 2013).

Also in 2013, the National Union of Healthcare Workers (NUHW), which formed in 2009 when SEIU took control of California local United Healthcare Workers West, affiliated with CNA. This affiliation unites 10,000 health-care workers at NUHW with 85,000 RNs at CNA (Robertson, 2013). Like NNU, this is a strategic alliance, and not a merger. Such alliances are becoming increasingly commonplace as unions recognize that increased negotiating power comes with greater membership.

Some of the other unions that represent nurses include the ANA; the National Union of Hospital and Health Care Employees of the Retail, Wholesale and Department Store Union; the American Federation of Labor–Congress of Industrial Organizations (AFL-CIO); the United Steelworkers of America; the American Federation of Government Employees, AFL-CIO; the American Federation of State, County, and Municipal Employees, AFL-CIO; the International Brotherhood of Teamsters; the American Federation of State, County, and Municipal Employees, which operates mostly in the public sector; the "24/7 Frontline Service Alliance," and the United Auto Workers.

Union representation also varies by state. The states with the most union-organizing for all industries, including health care, are New York, California, Pennsylvania, Michigan, and Illinois (Huston, 2014a).

 ## AMERICAN NURSES ASSOCIATION AND COLLECTIVE BARGAINING

One difficult union issue faced by nurse-managers that is not typically encountered in other disciplines stems from the dual role of their professional organization—ANA. The mission of the ANA is to represent the interests of the nation's 3.1 million RNs through its constituent member nurses associations, its organizational affiliates, and its workforce advocacy affiliate—the Center for American Nurses (ANA, 2013).

The NLRB, however, recognizes the ANA, at most state levels, as a collective bargaining agent. The use of state associations as bargaining agents has been a divisive issue among American nurses. Some nurse-managers believe that they have been disenfranchised by their professional organization. Other managers recognize the conflicts inherent in attempting to sit on both sides of the bargaining table. For some members of the nursing profession, this issue presents no conflict. Regardless of individual values, however, there does appear to be some conflict in loyalty.

This conflict has manifested itself in the recent splitting away of state nurses associations from the parent ANA organization. Since California RNs broke from the ANA in 1995 over dissatisfaction with the control held by nurses in managerial positions in hospitals, other states have also disaffiliated, including Massachusetts, Maine, New York, and Pennsylvania. In addition, many nurses unions, including the just-absorbed NFN, split off from the ANA as a result (Moberg, 2013). In 1999, the ANA responded by establishing, then spinning off, the UANs as a parallel association of state collective bargaining organizations. NFN consisted of some of the UAN groups that did not want to join with NNU, but then the New York State Nurses Association left NFN. Moberg questions whether new mergers will lead to more cooperation among the sometimes rancorous nursing unions—or to more progress in organizing a field that is growing faster than its union membership.

There are no easy solutions to the dilemma created by the dual role held by the ANA. Clarifying issues begins with the manager examining the motivation of nurses to participate in collective bargaining. The manager must at least try to hear and understand the employees' points of view.

LEARNING EXERCISE 22.1

The Role of the ANA as Collective Bargaining Agent

How do you feel about the ANA's certification as a collective bargaining agent? Do you belong to the state student nurses association? Why or why not? Do you plan to join your state ANA? What are the primary driving and restraining forces for your decision? Divide into two groups to debate the pros and cons of having the ANA, rather than other unions, represent nurses.

EMPLOYEE MOTIVATION TO JOIN OR REJECT UNIONS

Knowing that human behavior is goal-oriented, it is important to examine what personal goals union membership fulfills. Nurse-managers often tell each other that health-care institutions differ from other types of industrial organizations. This is really a myth, because most nurses work in large and impersonal organizations. The nurse frequently feels powerless and vulnerable as an individual alone in a complex institution. It is this vulnerability that often encourages nurses to join unions.

The reality though is that at least six primary motivations for joining a union exist (Display 22.3). The first is to increase the power of the individual. Liu (2013) notes that unions restore demand to an economy, by raising wages for their members and putting more purchasing power to work. This enables more hiring. Wages are typically higher in health-care organizations that have been unionized.

DISPLAY 22.3   Union Membership: Pros and Cons

REASONS WHY NURSES JOIN UNIONS

1. To increase the power of the individual
2. To increase their input into organizational decision-making
3. To eliminate discrimination and favoritism
4. Because of a social need to be accepted
5. Because they are required to do so as part of employment (closed shop)
6. Because they believe it will improve patient outcomes and quality of care

REASONS WHY NURSES DO NOT WANT TO JOIN UNIONS

1. A belief that unions promote the welfare state and oppose the American system of free enterprise
2. A need to demonstrate individualism and promote social status
3. A belief that professionals should not unionize
4. An identification with management's viewpoint
5. Fear of employer reprisal
6. Fear of lost income associated with a strike or walkout

In addition, employees know that singly, they are much more dispensable. Because a large group of employees is less dispensable, nurses generally increase their bargaining power and reduce their vulnerability by joining a union. This is a particularly strong motivating force for nurses when jobs are scarce and they feel vulnerable. Indeed, during the massive downsizing and restructuring of the 1990s, collective bargaining priorities shifted from wages and benefits to job security. Moberg (2013) suggests that current health-care environment again seems ripe for unionization, noting that hospital professionals are frustrated that their control over their work has been undermined by new for-profit hospital chains and corporatized nonprofit chains.

A feeling of powerlessness or the perception that the administration does not care about the employees is a major driving force for unionization.

When there are nursing shortages, nurses feel less vulnerable, and other reasons to join unions become motivating factors. A second motivator driving nurses toward unionization is the desire to communicate their aims, feelings, complaints, and ideas to others and to have input into organizational decision-making.

Because unions emphasize equality and fairness, nurses also join them because they need to eliminate discrimination and favoritism. This might be a particularly strong motivator for members of groups that have experienced discrimination, such as women and minorities.

Many social factors also act as motivators to nurses with regard to union activity. A fourth motivation stems from the social need to be accepted. Sometimes, this social need results from family or peer pressure. Because many working-class families have a long history of strong union ties, children are frequently raised in a cultural milieu that promotes unionization.

A fifth reason why nurses sometimes join unions is because the union contract dictates that all nurses belong to the union. This has been a big driving force among blue-collar workers. However, the *closed shop*—or requirement that all employees belong to a union—has never prevailed in the health-care industry. Most health-care unions have *open shops*, allowing nurses to choose if they want to join the union.

Finally, some nurses join unions because they believe that patient outcomes are better in unionized organizations due to better staffing and supervised management practices. Johnstone (2012) suggests that seeking union membership to promote better working conditions actually supports patient safety ethics. This is because the nurse is demonstrating genuine moral concern about the risks to patient safety associated with inappropriate skill mix and nurse–patient ratios that jeopardize patient safety and quality care.

Although historically, unions focus heavily on wage negotiations, current issues deemed by nurses to be just as or more important are nonmonetary, such as guidelines for staffing, float provisions, shared decision-making, and scheduling.

Just as there are many reasons to join unions, there are also a number of reasons why nurses reject unions (Display 22.3). Perhaps the strongest reasons are societal and cultural factors. Many people distrust unions because they believe that unions promote the welfare state and undermine the American system of free enterprise. Other reasons for rejecting unions might be a need to demonstrate that nurses can get ahead on their own merits.

Professional employees have also been slow in forming unions for several reasons that deal with class and education. They argue that unions were appropriate for the blue-collar worker but not for the university professor, physician, or engineer. Nurses who reject unions on this basis usually are driven by a need to demonstrate their individualism and social status. Some employees identify with management, and thus, frequently adopt its viewpoint toward unions. Such nurses, therefore, would reject unions because their values more closely align with management than with workers. Although employees are protected under the *National Labor Relations Act* (NLRA), many reject unions because of fears of employer reprisal. Nurses who reject unions on this basis could be said to be motivated, most of all, by a need to keep their job.

In addition, some employees reject unions simply because they have a right to not belong to a union. The United States is comprised of 24 "right-to-work" states that grant workers a choice about whether or not to belong to a union. In the other 26 and Washington, D.C., employees do not have to belong to the union but must still pay a portion of the union dues that go toward collective bargaining and other nonpolitical union-related activities (Right to Work, 2013).

Finally, some nurses reject unions out of the fear of lost income associated with a *strike* or *walkout*. Strikes and walkouts are, however, closely regulated by law. The NLRA states in part that "employees shall have the right to engage in other concerted activities for the purpose of collective bargaining or other mutual aid or protection." The phrase *other concerted activities* refers to "working to rule," "blue flu" epidemics, work slowdowns, filing a barrage of grievances, participating in informational or recognition picketing, and striking. Unions must, however, give employers and the Federal Mediation and Conciliation Service 10 days notice of their intent to strike. In doing so, the facility should have a reasonable amount of time to stop admitting patients, transfer existing patients to other facilities, and reduce medical procedures that require nurse-intensive labor. Problems occur when management continues to admit new patients or attempts to maintain normal operations.

The threat of strikes though is very real to union members. Selvam (2012) notes that the NNU threatened strikes 18 times in 2011, affecting 46 hospitals. This forced hospitals to hire replacement nurses for at least 60 hours to 5 days, negatively impacting both hospital budgets and employee paychecks (Selvam). It should be noted, however, that nurses do have the option to refuse to participate in strikes or to cross picket lines when strikes occur. They risk derision by their peers in doing so, however, since strikebreakers—commonly known as "*scabs*"—are viewed as taking the management's side on the issue and may never be fully accepted by their peers after the strike action has ended (Huston, 2014a).

AVERTING THE UNION

Once managers understand the drives and needs behind joining unions, they can begin to address those needs and possibly avert some of them. One way to remain abreast of employee potential concerns that may encourage them to seek union representation is to review the current literature and research on nurse satisfaction and dissatisfaction. When managers are aware of the concerns of RNs nationwide, they are better able to assess their own staff's potential for the type of dissatisfaction that can lead to unionization.

It is within managerial power to eliminate some of the needs that staff have for joining unions.

Clearly, organizations with unfair management policies are more likely to become unionized. Managers can encourage feelings of power by allowing subordinates to have input into decisions that will affect their work. Managers can also listen to ideas, complaints, and feelings and take steps to ensure that favoritism and discrimination are not part of their management style. Additionally, the manager can strengthen the drives and needs that make nurses reject unions. By building a team effort, sharing ideas and future plans from upper management with the staff, and encouraging individualism in employees, the manager can facilitate the worker's identification with management.

When nurses begin to show signs of job dissatisfaction and when they feel frustrated, stressed, or powerless, they send a wake-up call to nursing management. Leaders must be alert to employment practices that are unfair or insensitive to employee needs and must intervene appropriately before such issues lead to unionization. However, organizations offering liberal benefit packages and fair management practices may still experience union activity if certain social and cultural factors are present. If union activity does occur, managers must be aware of specific employee and management rights so that the NLRA is not violated by managers or employees.

Display 22.4 lists practices the organization may put in place to discourage union activity. If the organization waits until the union arrives, it will be too late to perform these functions.

DISPLAY 22.4	**Before the Union Comes**

1. Know and care about your employees.
2. Establish fair and well-communicated personnel policies.
3. Use an effective upward and downward system of communication.
4. Ensure that all managers are well-trained and effective.
5. Establish a well-developed formal procedure for handling employee grievances.
6. Have a competitive compensation program of wages and benefits.
7. Have an effective performance appraisal system in place.
8. Use a fair and well-communicated system for promotions and transfers.
9. Use organizational actions to indicate that job security is based on job performance, adherence to rules and regulations, and availability of work.
10. Have an administrative policy on unionization.

LEARNING EXERCISE 22.2

Discussing the Pros and Cons of Unions

List the reasons why you would or would not join a union. Share this with others in your group and examine the following questions. Would you feel differently about unions if you were a manager? What influences you the most in your desire to join or reject unions? Have you ever felt discriminated against or powerless in the workplace?

THE NURSE AS SUPERVISOR: ELIGIBILITY FOR PROTECTION UNDER THE NATIONAL LABOR RELATIONS ACT

Mayer and Shimabukuro (2012) note that the NLRA establishes certain protections for private sector employees who want to form or join a labor union. These protections do not, however, extend to supervisors.

The NLRA defines a supervisor as "any individual having authority, in the interest of the employer, to hire, transfer, suspend, lay off, recall, promote, discharge, assign, reward, or discipline other employees, or responsibly to direct them, or to adjust their grievances, or effectively to recommend such action, if in connection with the foregoing, the exercise of such authority is not of a merely routine or clerical nature, but requires the use of independent judgment" (Matthews, 2010, para 12).

However, a 2006 NLRB ruling deemed that *charge nurses* might also be considered supervisors since they are responsible for the coordination and provision of patient care throughout a unit (Matthews, 2010). Even part-time charge nurses were so labeled. This finding has been contested legally since that time and several interpretations have occurred. Reinterpretations by the NLRB are expected in the future.

In addition, the definition of supervisor in nursing came into question with several administrative and court rulings in the early 1990s. These rulings came about as a result of a case involving four LPNs/LVNs (licensed vocational nurses) employed at Heartland Nursing Home in Urbana, Ohio. During late 1988 and early 1989, these LPNs complained to management about what they thought were disparate enforcement of the absentee policy; short staffing; low wages for nurses' aides; an unreasonable switching of prescription business from one pharmacy to another, which increased the nurses' paperwork; and management's failure to communicate with employees (NLRB, n.d.). Despite assurances from the Vice President for Operations that they would not be harassed for bringing their concerns to headquarters' attention, three of the LPNs were terminated as a result of their actions.

In response to what they perceived to be illegal termination, the LPNs filed for protection under the NLRA. The NLRB ruled that because the LPNs had responsibility to ensure adequate staffing, to make daily work assignments, to monitor the aides' work to ensure proper performance, to counsel and discipline aides, to resolve aides' problems and grievances, to evaluate aides' performances, and to report to management, they should be classified as "supervisors," thereby making them ineligible for protection under the NLRA.

On appeal, the administrative law judge (ALJ) disagreed, concluding that the nurses were not supervisors and that the nurses' supervisory work did not equate to responsibly directing the aides *in the interest of the employer*, noting that the nurses' focus is on the well-being of the residents rather than on the employer.

In another turnabout, the U.S. Court of Appeals for the Sixth Circuit then reversed the decision of the ALJ, arguing that the NLRB's test for determining the supervisory status of nurses was inconsistent with the statute and that the interest of the patient and the interest of the employer were not mutually exclusive. The court said that, in fact, the interests of the patient are the employer's business and argued that the welfare of the patient was no less the object and concern of the employer than it was of the nurses. The court also argued that the statutory dichotomy the NLRB first created was no more justified in the health-care field than it would be in any other business in which supervisory duties are necessary to the production of goods or the provision of services (*NLRB v. Health Care & Retirement Corp.*, 1994).

The court further stated that it was up to Congress to carve out an exception for the health-care field, including nurses, should Congress not wish for such nurses to be considered supervisors. The court reminded the NLRB that the courts, and not the board, bear the final responsibility for interpreting the law. After concluding that the board's test was inconsistent with the statute, the court found that the four LPNs involved in this case were indeed supervisors and ineligible for protection under the NLRA (*NLRB v. Health Care & Retirement Corp.*, 1994).

This same interpretation, at least for full-time charge nurses, was used in another landmark court case in September 2006 to determine whether charge nurses, both permanent and rotating, at Oakwood Healthcare Inc. were "supervisors" within the meaning of the NLRA, and thus could be excluded from a unit of nurses represented by a union (Mayer & Shimabukuro, 2012). Upholding the definition that supervisors "assign," and "responsibly direct" employees as well as exercise "independent judgment," the NLRB concluded that 12 permanent charge nurses employed by Oakwood Healthcare were supervisors. Rotating charge nurses were not if this role was less than 10% to 15% of their work time.

Matthews (2010) notes that the Oakwood case has set precedence and figured in approximately 35 subsequent decisions in both health-care and industrial settings, although there have been no further rulings addressing the charge nurse/supervisor status. Hence, the *Oakwood* ruling is still in effect today, specifying that nurses, on average, with less than 10% to 15% (equal to about one shift per pay period) of their time as charge nurse are considered staff nurses, while nurses working more than 15% of their professional time as charge nurses are considered supervisors.

UNION-ORGANIZING STRATEGIES

Unions use a number of strategies to organize health-care workers (Display 22.5), including one-on-one and group meetings with union representatives. Other strategies include providing literature about union benefits, writing letters, and otherwise contacting potential union members. However, Haugh (2006) suggests that unions have added additional methods of organizing—namely, community and corporate pressure. This pressure is usually directed at acute-care hospitals.

DISPLAY 22.5	Some Union-Organizing Strategies

1. Meetings (both group and one-on-one)
2. Leaflets and brochures
3. Pressure on the hospital corporation through media and community contacts
4. Political pressure of regional legislators and local lawmakers
5. Corporate campaign strategies
6. Activism of local employees
7. Using lawsuits
8. Bringing pressure from financiers
9. Technology

In corporate campaigns, the union uses public events, political connections, and the local media to bring into question a hospital's quality of care, level of charity work, its tax exempt status (if nonprofit), and nurse staffing. Haugh (2006) maintains that unions are very effective in involving influential power brokers, both financiers and lawmakers. Unions are designing corporate campaigns using allegations of discrimination, boycotts, rallies, and visits to Board members' homes. Another strategy contributing to labor union successes is activism. Central labor councils, local labor unions, and state labor federations are reaching out to community groups, faith-based organizations, and elected officials in an effort to create unrest and to change the community environment in which workers organize.

In addition, unions often file lawsuits against the employer. Labor unions maintain the goal of breaking employer resolve and demonstrate their ability to protect employees by initiating legal action on behalf of employees against targeted employers. Other corporate strategies include union organizers establishing Web sites to enable them to keep tabs on the hospital system (Haugh, 2006). The Internet has made information about how to organize a union very accessible to interested workers. E-mail has also proved to be an inexpensive and efficient means of mass communication with regard to critical union issues.

MANAGERS' ROLE DURING UNION-ORGANIZING

Because of the health-care industry's movement toward unionization, most nurses will probably be involved with unions in some manner during their careers. Managers who are not employed in a unionized health-care organization should anticipate that one or more unions will attempt to organize nurses within the next few years.

Nurse-managers, as legally defined hospital "supervisors," are legal spokespersons for the hospital. As such, the NLRB closely monitors what they may say and do. Prohibited managerial activities include threatening employees, interrogating employees, promising employee rewards for cessation of union activity, and spying on employees. However, if the astute manager picks up early clues of union activity, the organization may be able to take steps that will discourage the unionization of its employees.

Employees have a right to participate in union-organizing under the NLRA, and managers must not interfere with this right.

There have been some small gains, however, recently in terms of restoring some rights to management. The U.S. Court of Appeals for the District of Columbia Circuit ruled in May 2013 that health-care organizations do not have to display a list of workers' collective bargaining rights, including the rights of workers to join a union and bargain collectively to improve wages and working conditions (Bump, 2013). This overturned a ruling scheduled to go into effect in January. The Court said the NLRB violated employers' free speech rights in trying to force them to display the posters or face charges of committing an unfair labor practice. "Unions had hoped the posters would help them boost falling membership, but business groups argued that they were too one-sided in favor of unionization" (Hananel, 2013, para 3).

STEPS TO ESTABLISH A UNION

The first step in establishing a union is demonstrating an adequate level of desire for unionization among the employees. The NLRB requires that at least 30% of employees sign an interest card before an election for unionization can be held. Most unions, however, will require between 60% and 70% of the employees to sign interest cards before spending the time and money involved in an organizing campaign.

Union representatives have generally been careful to keep a campaign secret until they were ready to file a petition for election. They did this so that they could build momentum without interference from the employer.

After a designated number of cards have been generated, the organization is forced to have an election. At that time, all employees of the same classification, such as RNs, would vote on whether they desire unionization. A choice in every such election is *no representation*, which means that the voters do not want a union. During the election, 50% plus one of the petitioned units must vote for unionization before the union can be recognized. A process similar to that of certification can also decertify unions. *Decertification* may occur when at least 30% of the eligible employees in the bargaining unit initiate a petition asking to no longer be represented by the union.

It is important to remember that there are differences between organizing in a health-care facility and other types of organizations. Generally, the solicitation and distribution of union literature is banned entirely in "immediate patient care areas." Middle-level and first-level managers should never, however, independently attempt to deal with union-organizing activity. They should always seek assistance and guidance from upper management and the personnel department.

The entire list of rights for management and labor during the organization and establishment phases of unionization is beyond the scope of this book. Throughout the years, Congress has amended various labor acts and laws so that power is balanced between management and labor. At times, the balance of power has shifted back and forth, but Congress eventually enacts laws that restore the balance. The manager must ensure that the rights of management and employees are protected. The two most sensitive areas of any union contract, once wages have been agreed upon, are discipline and the grievance process, which are discussed in Unit VII.

EFFECTIVE LABOR–MANAGEMENT RELATIONS

Before the 1950s, labor–management relations were turbulent. History books are filled with battles, strikes, mass-picketing scenes, and brutal treatment by management and employees. Over the last 30 years, employers and unions have substantially improved their relationships. Although evidence is growing that contemporary management has come to accept the reality that unions are here to stay, businesses in the United States are still less comfortable with unions than their counterparts in many other countries. Likewise, unions have come to accept the fact that there are times when organizations are not healthy enough to survive aggressive union demands.

It is possible to create a climate in which labor and management can work together to accomplish mutual goals.

Faced with the reality of negotiations with a bargaining agent, management has several choices. It may actively oppose the union by using various union-busting techniques, or it may more subtly oppose the union by attempting to discredit it and win employee trust. *Acceptance* also may run along a continuum. Management may accept the union with reluctance and suspicion. Although managers know that the union has legitimate rights, they often believe that they must continually guard against the union encroaching further into traditional management territory.

There is also the type of union acceptance known as *accommodation*. Increasingly common, accommodation is characterized by management's full acceptance of the union, with both the union and the management showing mutual respect. When these conditions exist, labor and management can establish mutual goals, particularly in the areas of safety, cost reduction, efficiency, elimination of waste, and improved working conditions. Such cooperation represents the most mature and advanced type of labor–management relations.

The attitudes and philosophies of the leaders in management and the union determine the type of relationship that develops between the two parties in any given organization. When dealing with unions, managers must be flexible. It is critical that they do not ignore issues or try to overwhelm others with power. The rational approach to problem-solving must be used.

Unionization in the health-care industry will undoubtedly expand. It is important to learn how to deal with this potential constraint to effective management. Managers must learn to work with unions and to develop the art of using unions to assist the organization in building a team effort to meet organizational goals.

LEARNING EXERCISE 22.3

List and Support Your Reasons for or Against Striking

You are a staff nurse in the intensive care unit (ICU) at one of your city's two hospitals. You have worked at this hospital for 5 years and transferred to the ICU 2 years ago. You love nursing but are sometimes frustrated in your job due to a short supply of nurses, excessive overtime demands, and the stress of working with critically ill patients.

The hospital has a closed shop, so union dues are deducted from your pay even though you are not actively involved in the union. The present union contract is up for renegotiation, and the union and management have been unable to agree on numerous issues. When the management made its last offer, the new contract was rejected by the nurses. Now that the old contract has expired, nurses are free to strike if they vote to do so.

You had voted for accepting the management offer; you have two children to support, and it would be devastating to be without work for a long time. Last night, the nurses voted on whether to return to the bargaining table and try to renegotiate with management or to go out on strike. Again, you voted for no strike. You have just heard from your friend that the strike vote won. Now, you must decide if you are going to support your striking colleagues or cross the picket line and return to work tomorrow. Your friends are pressuring you to support their cause. You know that the union will provide some financial compensation during the strike but believe that it will not be adequate for you to support yourself and your children. You agree with union assertions that the organization has overworked and underpaid you and that it has been generally unresponsive to nursing needs. On the other hand, you believe that your first obligation is to your children.

Assignment: List all of the reasons for and against striking. Decide what you will do. Use appropriate rationale from outside readings to support your final decision. Share your thoughts with the class. Take a vote in class to determine how many would strike and how many would cross the picket line.

EMPLOYMENT LEGISLATION

Like unionization, the many legal issues involved in recruitment and employment have an impact on the directing function. These potential constraints are present regardless of union presence. The American industrial relations system is regarded as one of the most legalistic in the Western world, and it continues to grow. Few aspects of the employment relationship are free from regulation by either state or federal law. Employment laws discussed here provide a cursory examination of such laws. Many of these regulations relate to specific aspects of personnel management, such as the laws that deal with collective bargaining or the equal employment laws that regulate hiring. Some personnel regulations are discussed in previous chapters and others are discussed later. The prudent manager will always work closely with human resource management when dealing with employment legislation issues.

Some observers believe that employment and labor–management laws have become so prescriptive that they preclude experimentation and creativity on the part of management. Others believe that, like collective bargaining, the proliferation of employment laws must be viewed from a historical standpoint to understand their need. Regardless of whether one believes such laws and regulations are necessary, they are a fact of each manager's life.

The feeling that the employer is fair to all will set the stage for the type of team-building that is so important in effective management.

Being able to handle management's legal requirements effectively requires a comprehension of labor laws and their interpretation. The leader who embraces the intent of laws barring discrimination and providing equal opportunity becomes a role model for fairness. Employment laws, such as those given in Table 22.2, fall into one of five categories:

1. *Labor standards.* These laws establish minimum standards for working conditions regardless of the presence or absence of a union contract. Included in this set are minimum wage, health and safety, and equal pay laws.
2. *Labor relations.* These laws relate to the rights and duties of unions and employers in their relationship with each other.
3. *Equal employment.* The laws that deal with employment discrimination were introduced in Chapter 15.
4. *Civil and criminal laws.* These are statutory and judicial laws that proscribe certain kinds of conduct and establish penalties.
5. *Other legislation.* Nursing managers have some legal responsibilities that do not generally apply to industrial managers. For instance, licensed personnel are required to

TABLE 22.2 Employment and Labor Laws

Title of Legislation	Regulation
Fair Labor Standards Act (1938); has been amended many times since 1938	Sets minimum wage and maximum hours that can be worked before overtime is paid
Civil Rights Act of 1964	Sets equal employment practices
Executive Order 11246 (1965) and *Executive Order 11375* (1967)	Sets affirmative action guidelines
Age Discrimination Act (1967) and 1978 amendment	Protects against forced retirement
Rehabilitation Act (1973)	Protects the disabled
Vietnam Veterans Act (1973/1974)	Provides reemployment rights

have a current, valid license from the state in which they practice. Additionally, most states require that employers of nurses report certain types of substance abuse to the state licensing boards. Confidentiality laws also have a significant impact on health-care organizations.

Labor Standards

Labor standards are regulations dealing with the conditions of the employee's work, including physical conditions, financial aspects, and the number of hours worked. Regulations may be issued by state and/or federal bodies. When the regulations overlap, the more stringent regulation is likely the one that applies.

 State and federal employment legislation often overlap; as a general rule, the employer must abide by the stricter of the two regulations.

Minimum Wages and Maximum Hours

More than 85% of all nonsupervisory employees are now covered by the *Fair Labor Standards Act* (FLSA). This law was enacted by Congress in 1938 and established an hourly minimum wage at that time of 25 cents. Since then, the law has been amended numerous times.

It is often said that in addition to putting a "floor under wages," the FLSA also puts a "ceiling over hours." The latter statement, however, is not quite accurate. The FLSA sets a maximum number of hours in any week beyond which a person may be employed only if he or she is paid an overtime rate. Some states have enacted a law that makes an exception to this weekly rule on overtime. The exception is an 80-hour, 2-week pay period ceiling, after which the employee must receive overtime pay. Overtime pay can be significant, so it is imperative that managers know which standard their organization is using.

Hours worked includes all the time that the employee is required to be on duty. Therefore, mandatory classes, orientation, conferences, etc., must be recorded as duty time and are subject to the overtime rules. The FLSA does not require time clocks but does require that some record be maintained of hours worked.

The FLSA also regulates the minimum amount of overtime pay, which is at least 1.5 times the basic rate. When state and federal laws differ on when overtime pay begins, the stricter rule usually applies. Some union contracts also have stricter overtime pay agreements than the FLSA.

Federal labor laws exempt certain employees from the minimum wage and overtime pay requirements. Executive employees, administrative employees, and professional employees are the three most notable white-collar exemptions. The functions of the position, rather than the title or the fact that employees are paid a monthly wage, differentiate an exempt employee. Certain students, apprentice learners, and other special circumstances also may qualify an employee for an exemption to FLSA regulations. The personnel department in any large organization is particularly helpful to the manager in implementing these labor laws. Managers, however, should have a general understanding of how these laws restrict staffing and scheduling policies.

The *Equal Pay Act of 1963* requires that men and women performing equal work receive equal compensation. Four equal pay tests exist: *equal skill, equal effort, equal responsibility*, and *similar working conditions*. This law had a great impact on nursing management when it was enacted. Before 1963, male orderlies were routinely paid a higher wage than female aides performing identical duties. Although this fact seems incredible today, at the time, many managers condoned this widespread practice of blatant wage discrimination. Most health-care agencies now call these employees "nursing assistants," whether they are male or female, and all are paid the same wage.

LEARNING EXERCISE 22.4

Time Clocks

Until the 1950s, most health-care organizations did not require that employees use a time clock when arriving at or leaving work for meal breaks. Now, time clocks are the norm for hospitals and some other, but not all, health-care organizations.

Assignment: Survey several community hospitals, clinics, student health centers, home health-care facilities, and other organizations that employ nurses. How many of them require nurses to use time clocks? How do you feel about professionals being required to use a time clock for meal breaks? Discuss this issue in class and with the nurses you know.

Labor Relations Laws

In addition to laws regarding collective bargaining, the manager needs to be aware of one section of the *Wagner Act* (1935) and the *Taft-Hartley Amendment* (1947), which deals with unfair labor practices by employers and unions. The original *Wagner Act* listed and prohibited five unfair labor practices:

1. To interfere with, restrain, or coerce employees in a manner that interfered with their rights as outlined under the act. Examples of these activities are spying on union gatherings, threatening employees with job loss, or threatening to close down a company if the union organizes.
2. To interfere with the formation of any labor organization or to give financial assistance to a labor organization. This provision was included to prohibit "employee representation plans" that were primarily controlled by management.
3. To discriminate with regard to hiring, tenure, etc., to discourage union membership.
4. To discharge or discriminate against an employee who filed charges or testified before the NLRB.
5. To refuse to bargain in good faith.

The original *Wagner Act* gave so much power to the unions that it was necessary in 1947 to pass additional federal legislation to restore a balance of power to labor–management relations. The *Taft-Hartley Amendment* retained the provisions under the Wagner Act that guaranteed employees the right to collective bargaining. However, the Taft-Hartley Amendment added the provision that employees have the right to refrain from taking part in unions. In addition to that provision, the *Taft-Hartley Amendment* added and prohibited the following six unfair labor practices of unions:

1. Requiring a self-employed person or an employer to join a union.
2. Forcing an employer to cease doing business with another person. (This placed a ban on secondary boycotts, which were then prevalent in unions.)
3. Forcing an employer to bargain with one union when another union has already been certified as the bargaining agent.
4. Forcing the employer to assign certain work to members of one union rather than another.
5. Charging excessive or discriminatory initiation fees.
6. Causing or attempting to cause an employer to pay for unnecessary services. This prohibited *featherbedding*, a term used to describe union practices that prevented the displacement of workers due to advances in technology.

Equal Employment Opportunity Laws

Under the American free enterprise system, employers have historically been able to hire whomever they desired. Today, a transplanted employer of the 1920s might be shocked to see that racial and ethnic minorities, women, the elderly, and the disabled have acquired substantial rights in the workplace. The first legislation in the area of employment hiring practices resulted from years of discrimination against minorities. More recent legislation has been aimed at eliminating discrimination that occurs for other reasons. The US government's *Equal Employment Opportunity Commission* (USEEOC) Web site lists the following types of discrimination: age, disability, equal pay/compensation, genetic information, national origin, pregnancy, race/color, religion, retaliation, sex, and sexual harassment (USEEOC, n.d.-a).

Equal employment opportunities have fostered profound changes in the American workplace. Women, minorities, and the handicapped have had success in gaining jobs previously denied to them. However, only modest gains in achieving ethnic diversity have occurred in nursing (Huston, 2014b).

Although men are seen as a minority in nursing, there are those who feel that male minority status has led to advantages rather than discrimination, particularly in hiring and promotion. Some experts have suggested that the more rapid career trajectory and relatively higher pay for male nurses compared with female nurses likely reflect the historical trend that more men are employed full time in their career paths while women tend to have career gaps related to child bearing or rearing families and often work fewer hours (Huston, 2014b).

Discrimination involving pregnant employees particularly interests nurse-managers because nursing is such a predominately female profession and because nurses are often exposed to hazardous chemical, radiation, and infectious organisms. The *Pregnancy Discrimination Act*, which amended Title VII of the *Civil Rights Act of 1964*, requires that pregnant employees be treated the same as other employees who are temporarily disabled. Managers should use common sense as well as ethical and humane treatment when dealing with the pregnant employee.

Civil Rights Act of 1964

The *Civil Rights Act of 1964* laid the foundation for equal employment in the United States. The thrust of Title VII of the Civil Rights Act is twofold: It prohibits discrimination based on factors unrelated to job qualifications and it promotes employment based on ability and merit. The areas of discrimination specifically mentioned are race, color, religion, sex, and national origin.

This act was strengthened by President Lyndon Johnson's *Executive Order 11246* in 1965 and *Executive Order 11375* in 1967. These executive orders sought to correct past injustices. Because the government believed that some groups had a long history of being discriminated against, it wanted to build in a mechanism that would assist those groups in "catching up" with the rest of the American workforce. Therefore, it created an affirmative action component. *Affirmative action* plans are not specifically required by law but may be required by court order. In most states, affirmative action plans are voluntary unless government contracts are involved. Some states, such as California, have voted to eliminate affirmative action in the workplace, arguing that it actually resulted in reverse discrimination. Many organizations, however, have voluntarily put an affirmative action plan in place when the plan does not conflict with state regulations.

Affirmative action differs from *equal opportunity*. The United States Equal Employment Opportunity legislation is aimed at preventing discrimination. Affirmative action plans are aimed at actively seeking to fill job vacancies with members from groups who are underrepresented, such as women, ethnic minorities, and the handicapped.

The USEEOC is responsible for enforcing Title VII of the Civil Rights Act and the investigatory responsibility of the USEEOC is broad. When it finds that a charge of discrimination is justified, the agency attempts to reach an agreement through persuasion and conciliation. When the USEEOC is unable to reach an agreement, it has the power to bring civil action against the employer. When discrimination is found, the courts will order restoration of rightful economic status; this means that the court may order that the employee receives back the pay for up to 2 years. In health-care organizations, when discrimination has been found (such as unequal pay for men and women in nursing assistant jobs), financial awards in class action suits have been extraordinarily high. Managers must be alert for any such discriminatory practices. Some states have fair employment legislation that is stricter than the federal act. Again, the stricter regulations always apply.

Age Discrimination and Employment Act

Enacted by Congress in 1967, the purpose of the *Age Discrimination in Employment Act* (ADEA) was to promote the employment of older people based on their ability rather than age. In early 1978, the ADEA was amended to increase the protected age to 70. In 1987, Congress voted to remove even this age restriction except in certain job categories.

Although some people are alarmed by the removal of mandatory age retirements, trends continue toward earlier retirement. However, reversal of this trend may have serious consequences for some organizations. In particular, it could have a significant impact on organizations that are labor-intensive, particularly if those labor-intensive organizations also have demanding physical requirements such as those in nursing. For example, a 49-year-old nurse in Tennessee filed suit in mid-2013, claiming violation of the ADEA and state law when her employer began openly seeking "young rising stars" to replace older workers (Yamada, 2013).

LEARNING EXERCISE 22.5

Addressing Mary's Failing Health

You are the manager of a well-baby newborn nursery. Among your staff is 79-year-old LVN/LPN Mary Jones, who has worked for the hospital for 50 years. No mandatory retirement age exists. This has not been a problem in the past, but Mary's general health is now making this a problem for your unit. Mary has grown physically fragile. Cataracts cloud her vision, and she suffers from hypertension. Last month, she began to prepare a little girl for circumcision because she did not read the armband properly.

Your staff has become increasingly upset over Mary's inability to fulfill her job duties. The physicians, however, support Mary and found the circumcision incident humorous. Last week, you requested that Mary have a physical examination, at hospital expense, to determine her physical ability to continue working.

You were not particularly surprised when she returned with medical approval. Her physician spoke sharply with you. Admitting privately that Mary's health was rapidly failing, the physician told you that working was Mary's only reason for living and left you with these words: "Force Mary to retire and she will die within the year."

Assignment: Using your knowledge of age discrimination, patient safety, employee rights, and management responsibilities, decide on an appropriate course of action for this case. Be creative and think beyond the obvious. Be able to support your decisions.

Sexual Harassment

Although job discrimination related to gender became illegal with the *Civil Rights Act of 1964*, it was not until 1977 that the federal appeals court upheld a claim that a supervisor's verbal and physical advances constituted sexual harassment in the workplace. Since then, sexual harassment has been recognized as a form of sex discrimination that violates Title VII of the *Civil Rights Act*.

The USEEOC (n.d.-b, para 2) defines *sexual harassment* as "unwelcome sexual advances, requests for sexual favors, and other verbal or physical conduct of a sexual nature when submission to or rejection of this conduct explicitly or implicitly affects an individual's employment; unreasonably interferes with an individual's work performance; or creates an intimidating, hostile, or offensive work environment." The EEOC (n.d.-b) states that sexual harassment can occur in a variety of circumstances including but not limited to the following:

- The victim as well as the harasser may be a woman or a man. The victim does not have to be of the opposite sex.
- The harasser can be the victim's supervisor, an agent of the employer, a supervisor in another area, a coworker, or a nonemployee.
- The victim does not have to be the person harassed but could be anyone affected by the offensive conduct.
- Unlawful sexual harassment may occur without economic injury to or discharge of the victim.
- The harasser's conduct must be unwelcome.

Since the 1977 ruling, allegations of sexual harassment and lawsuits have permeated virtually every type of industry, and the health-care system is not immune. Indeed, sexual harassment as well as other types of nonphysical violence are worldwide problems for nurses, with English-speaking countries exhibiting the highest rates of both physical violence and sexual harassment in nursing (Examining the Evidence 22.1).

Examining the Evidence 22.1

Source: Spector, P. E., Shou, Z. E., & Che, X. X. (2013, February 19). Nurse exposure to physical and nonphysical violence, bullying, and sexual harassment: A quantitative review. International Journal of Nursing Studies. Retrieved June 23, 2013, from http://www.ncbi.nlm.nih.gov/pubmed/23433725

This research conducted a quantitative review of the nursing violence literature, estimating exposure rates by type of violence, setting, source, and world region. A total of 136 articles provided data on 151,347 nurses from 160 samples. Categories depended on the availability of at least five studies. Exposure rates were coded as percentages of nurses in the sample who reported a given type of violence. Five types of violence were physical, nonphysical, bullying, sexual harassment, and combined (type of violence was not indicated). Setting, time frame, country, and source of violence were coded.

Overall violence exposure rates were 36.4% for physical violence, 66.9% for nonphysical violence, 39.7% for bullying, and 25% for sexual harassment, with 32.7% of nurses reporting having been physically injured in an assault. Rates of exposure varied by world region (Anglo, Asia, Europe, and the Middle East), with the highest rates for physical violence and sexual harassment in the Anglo region, and the highest rates of nonphysical violence and bullying in the Middle East. Regions also varied in the source of violence, with patients accounting for most of it in Anglo and European regions, whereas patients' families/friends were the most common source in the Middle East.

About a third of nurses worldwide indicated exposure to physical violence and bullying, about a third reported injury, about a quarter experienced sexual harassment, and about two-thirds indicated nonphysical violence. Physical violence was most prevalent in emergency departments, geriatric, and psychiatric facilities. Physical violence and sexual harassment were most prevalent in Anglo countries, and nonphysical violence and bullying were most prevalent in the Middle East. Patients accounted for most physical violence in the Anglo region and Europe, and patients' family and friends accounted for the most in the Middle East.

While sexual harassment between health-care workers is noted most often in the literature, it may also come from the patients that nurses care for. On September 6, 2012, EEOC filed suit against a Virginia long-term care agency under Title VII of the Civil Rights Act, alleging that the employer failed to protect a female receptionist from sexual harassment by a resident, which created a "sexually hostile work environment" for her (Boehm, 2013). As with most harassment lawsuits, the employee alleged that she made numerous complaints to her supervisor about the harassment, yet the employer failed to take proper corrective action. Boehm (2013) notes that while sexual harassment is a difficult issue in any employment setting, many nursing homes have residents who act out inappropriately as a result of dementia or Alzheimer disease. Nevertheless, these agencies must take steps to address and minimize the risk of their employees even when it comes from residents.

Indeed, health-care organizations must be alert to sexual harassment and intervene immediately when it is suspected, regardless of the perpetrator. This requires a proactive approach on the part of employers to prevent, detect, and correct instances of harassment. At minimum, organizations must have a plan that outlines temporary steps to deal with such allegations while they are being investigated as well as permanent remedial steps once the investigation has been completed, to ensure that the situation does not recur.

Lastly, nurses must take appropriate action when they witness the harassment of others or when they themselves are the targets of such offenses. When one person makes another uncomfortable in the workplace by the use of sexual innuendoes or jokes or invades another's personal space, this behavior should be recognized and confronted as sexual harassment. Unfortunately, underreporting of the problem is common and nurses often make light of sexually harassing incidents. In addition, Rossheim (2013) notes that while hospital procedure enables direct-care workers to remove themselves from cases where patients are sexually inappropriate, nurses rarely do.

LEARNING EXERCISE 22.6

Confronting Sexual Harassment

You are a new female employee at Valley Medical Center's ICU and love your job. Although only 25 years old, you have been a nurse for 4 years, and the last two were spent in a small critical care unit in a rural hospital. You work the 3 PM to 11 PM shift. Ever since you came to work here, one of the male physicians (Dr. Jones) has been especially attentive to you. At first, you were flattered, but more recently, you have become uncomfortable around him. He sometimes touches you and seems to be flirting with you. You have no romantic interest in him and know that he is married. Last night, he asked you to meet him for an after-work drink and you refused. He is a very powerful man in the unit, and you do not want to alienate him, but you are becoming increasingly troubled by his behavior.

Today, you went to your shift charge nurse and explained how you felt. In response, the nurse said, "Oh, he likes to flirt with all the new staff, but he is perfectly harmless." These comments did not make you feel better. At approximately 7 PM, Dr. Jones came to the unit and cornered you again in a comatose patient's room and asked you out. You said no again, and you are feeling more anxious because of his behavior.

Assignment: Outline an appropriate course of action. What options can you identify? What is your responsibility? What are the driving and restraining forces for action? What support systems for action can you identify? What responsibility does the organization have? Be creative and think beyond the obvious. Be able to support your decisions.

Legislation Affecting Americans with Disabilities

The *Rehabilitation Act of 1973* required all employers with government contracts of more than $25,000 to take affirmative action to recruit, hire, and advance disabled people who are qualified. Similar but less aggressive affirmative action steps were required for other companies doing business with the federal government, with specific requirements depending on the size of the company and the dollar amount of the contract. The Department of Labor was charged with enforcing this act. Although initially there was very slow progress in getting companies to hire those with disabilities, steady progress has been made.

In 1990, Congress passed the *Americans with Disabilities Act* to eliminate discrimination against Americans with physical or mental disabilities in the workplace and in social life. *Disability* is defined as "any physical or mental impairment that limits any major life activity." This includes people with obvious physical disabilities as well as those with cancer, diabetes, HIV or AIDS, and recovering substance abusers.

Veterans Readjustment Assistance Act

The *Veterans Readjustment Act* provides employment rights and privileges for veterans with regard to positions that they held before they entered the armed forces. This act was used by some nurses after the Vietnam War and during the nursing surplus after the Persian Gulf War to gain reemployment after military service. There is a lesser need for nurses implementing this act when veterans return from war during a nursing shortage, because jobs are readily available.

The Occupational Safety and Health Act

The manager needs to be particularly cognizant of legislation imposed by the OSHA and state health licensing boards. OSHA speaks to the employer's requirements to provide a place of employment that is free from recognized hazards that may cause physical harm. The Department of Labor enforces this act. Because it is impossible for the Department of Labor to physically inspect all facilities, most inspections are brought about by employee complaint or employer request. The act allows fines to be levied if employers continue with unsafe conditions.

Since OSHA's inception, many organizations have vehemently criticized the act, and specifically its administration. They have charged that the cost of meeting OSHA standards has excessively burdened American businesses. On the other hand, unions have asserted that the federal government has never staffed or funded OSHA adequately. They have charged that the OSHA has been negligent in setting standards for toxic substances, carcinogens, and other disease-producing agents.

Because the risk of discovery and the fine (if judged guilty) are both low, employers may choose to ignore unsafe working conditions. Nurse-managers are in a unique position to call attention to hazardous conditions in the workplace and should communicate such concerns to a higher authority. Ongoing controversies regarding safety issues include the cost and effectiveness of universal precautions and immunizations against potential bioterrorism. Most states also have occupational and safety regulations. Again, the employer must comply with the more stringent regulations in the case of overlaps. Many state licensing boards have additional health regulations that differ from the federal regulations.

STATE HEALTH FACILITIES LICENSING BOARDS

In addition to health and safety requirements, many state boards have regulations regarding staffing requirements. It is the ultimate responsibility of top-level management to meet the requirements for state licensing. However, all managers are responsible for knowing and meeting the regulations that apply to their unit or department. For example, if the manager of an ICU has a state staffing level that mandates 12 hours of nursing care per patient per day and requires that the ratio of RNs to other staff be 2:1, then the supervisor is obligated to staff at that level or greater. If, during times of short staffing, supervisors are unable to meet this level of staffing, they must communicate this to the upper-level management so that there can be a joint resolution.

The variation in state licensing requirements makes a lengthy discussion of them inappropriate for this book. However, managers must be knowledgeable about state licensing regulations that pertain to their level of supervision.

INTEGRATING LEADERSHIP SKILLS AND MANAGEMENT FUNCTIONS WHEN WORKING WITH COLLECTIVE BARGAINING, UNIONIZATION AND EMPLOYMENT LAWS

Unionization and legal constraints will seem less burdensome if managers remember that both primarily protect the rights of patients and employees. If managers perform their jobs well and work for organizations that desire to "do the right thing" by accepting their social responsibility, they need not fear unionization and legal constraints. If the organization is not unionized, the manager must use the leadership skills of communication, fairness, and shared decision-making to ensure that employees do not feel unionization is necessary. The integrated leader-manager is a role model for fairness, knows unit employees well, and sincerely seeks to meet their needs.

When making decisions that deal with unions and employment legislation, the effective leader-manager always seeks to do what is just. Additionally, he or she seeks appropriate assistance before finalizing decisions that involve sensitive legal or contractual issues. By using these leadership skills, the manager becomes fairer in personnel management, develops increased self-awareness, and develops an understanding of the average individual's need to seek unionization and of the necessity for employment legislation.

The effective manager maintains the required amount of staffing and ensures a safe working environment. The rights of the organization and the employee are protected as the manager uses personnel policies in a nondiscriminatory and consistent manner. The emphasis is on flexibility and the accommodation of employment legislation and union contracts.

KEY CONCEPTS

- Historically, union activity increases during times of labor shortages and economic upswings.

- Although nurses are still roughly twice as likely to be in a union as other occupations, the percentage of nurses as well as total number of nurses in unions nationwide is decreasing.

- Union alliances are becoming increasingly commonplace in health care since increased negotiating power comes with greater membership.

- The ANA acts as a professional association for RNs and as a collective bargaining agent. This dual purpose poses a conflict in loyalty for some nurses.

- People are motivated to join or reject unions as a result of their numerous needs and values.

- Nurses with less than 10% to 15% (equal to about one shift per pay period) of their time as charge nurse are considered staff nurses, while nurses working more than 15% of their professional time as charge nurses are considered supervisors, and therefore, are ineligible for protection under the NLRA.

- Although all managers play an important role in establishing and maintaining effective management–labor relationships, the middle-level manager has the greatest influence on preventing unionization in a nonunion organization.

- Creating a climate in which labor and management can work together to accomplish mutual goals is possible.

- Labor relation laws concern the rights and duties of unions and employers in their relationship with each other.

- Labor standards are regulations dealing with the conditions of the employee's work, including physical conditions, financial aspects, and the number of hours worked.

- State and federal employment legislation often overlap; as a general rule, the employer must abide by the stricter of the two regulations.

- Much of the human rights legislation concerning employment practices came about because of documented discrimination in the workplace.

- Sexual harassment and other types of nonphysical violence are worldwide problems for nurses, with English-speaking countries exhibiting the highest rates of both physical violence and sexual harassment in nursing.

- Although some legislation makes the job of managing people more difficult for managers, it has resulted in increased job fairness and opportunities for women, minorities, the elderly, and the disabled.

ADDITIONAL LEARNING EXERCISES AND APPLICATIONS

LEARNING EXERCISE 22.7

Writing about Employment Laws

Many employment laws generate emotion. Usually, people feel strongly about at least one of these issues. Select one of the following employment laws, and write a 250-word essay on why you support or disapprove of the law. Choose from the *Equal Pay Act of 1963*, equal opportunity laws, affirmative action, sexual harassment, or age discrimination.

LEARNING EXERCISE 22.8

Dilemma Involving an Expired Nursing License

At your long-term care facility, it is a policy that licensed employees have a current, valid medical license. This is in keeping with the state licensing code. It is always difficult to get people to bring their license in to verify that it is current.

You have just come from a meeting with the director, who reminded you that you must not have people performing duties that require a license if the license has expired. You decide to issue a memo stating that you will suspend all employees who have not verified their licenses with you.

Following this, all of the LVNs/LPNs brought their licenses in for verification. However, one of the LVNs/LPNs has an expired license. When questioned, the nurse admits that payment for relicensure was not made until after your memo was received. This nurse delayed payment because of a financial crisis. You call the licensing board and learn it will be 2 weeks before the employee will receive the license in the mail or before web verification of the license is possible. Active license status cannot be verified over the telephone.

(Continued)

You consider the following facts. It is illegal to perform duties that require a license without one. The LVN/LPN had prior knowledge of the licensing laws and hospital policy. The LVN/LPN has been a good employee with no record of prior disciplinary action.

Assignment: Decide what you should do. What alternatives do you have? Provide rationale for your decision.

LEARNING EXERCISE 22.9

How Would You Handle This Petition?

Betty Smith, a unit clerk, has come to see you, the nurse-manager of the medical unit, to complain of flagrant discriminatory practices against female employees of University General Hospital. She alleges that women are denied promotional and training opportunities comparable to those made available to men. She shows you a petition with 35 signatures supporting her allegations. Ms. Smith has threatened to forward this petition to the administrator of the hospital, the press, and the Department of Labor unless corrective action is taken at once. Being a woman yourself, you have some sympathy for Ms. Smith's complaint. However, you believe overall that employees at University General are treated fairly regardless of their sex.

Ms. Smith, a fairly good employee, has worked on your unit for 4 years. However, she has been creating problems lately. She has been reprimanded for taking too much time for coffee breaks. Personnel evaluations that recommend pay raises and promotions are due next week.

Assignment: How should you handle this problem? Is the personnel evaluation an appropriate time to address the petition? Outline your plan and explain your rationale.

REFERENCES

American Nurses Association. (2013). *About ANA*. Retrieved June 22, 2013, from http://www.nursingworld.org/Functional MenuCategories/AboutANA.aspx

Boehm, T. (2013, January). *Harassment by resident*. Provider. Retrieved June 21, 2013, from http://www.providermagazine.com/archives/2013_Archives/Pages/0113/Harassment-By-Resident.aspx

Bump, P. (2013, May 7). *Businesses have the right to remain silent about your right to join a union*. Atlantic Wire. Retrieved August 16, 2013, from http://www.theatlanticwire.com/national/2013/05/businesses-have-right-remain-silent-about-your-right-join-union/64979/

Commins, J. (2012, January 3). *Why do nurses join unions? Because they can*. Strategiesfornursingmanagers.com. Retrieved June 21, 2013, from http://www.strategiesfornursemanagers.com/ce_detail/275275.cfm

Hananel, S. (2013, May 7). *Appeals court strikes down union poster rule*. Bloomberg Business Week News. Retrieved June 22, 2013, from http://www.businessweek.com/ap/2013-05-07/appeals-court-strikes-down-union-poster-rule

Haugh, R. (2006). The new union strategy: Turning the community against you. *Hospitals and Health Networks, 80*(5), 32–37.

Huston, C. (2014a). Collective bargaining and the professional nurse. In C. Huston (Ed.), *Professional issues in nursing* (3rd ed.). Philadelphia, PA: Lippincott Williams & Wilkins 278–291.

Huston, C. (2014b). Diversity in the nursing workforce. In C. Huston (Ed.), *Professional issues in nursing* (3rd ed.). Philadelphia, PA: Lippincott Williams & Wilkins 136–155.

Johnstone, M. (2012). Industrial action and patient safety ethics. *Australian Nursing Journal, 19*(7), 29.

Liu , E. (2013, January 29). *Viewpoint: The decline of unions is your problem too*. Time Ideas. Retrieved June 22, 2013, from http://ideas.time.com/2013/01/29/viewpoint-why-the-decline-of-unions-is-your-problem-too/

Matthews, J. (2010). When does delegating make you a supervisor? *Online Journal of Issues in Nursing, 15*(2), 3. Retrieved June 23, 2013, from http://www.nursingworld.org/MainMenuCategories/ANAMarketplace/ANAPeriodicals/OJIN/TableofContents/Vol152010/No2May2010/Delegating-and-Supervisors.aspx

Mayer, G., & Shimabukuro, J. O. (2012, July 5). *The definition of "supervisor" under the National Labor Relations Act*. Congressional Research Service. Retrieved June 23, 2013, from http://www.fas.org/sgp/crs/misc/RL34350.pdf

Moberg, D. (2013, February 20). *Are mergers the answer for fractious nurses unions?* In These Times. Retrieved June 21, 2013, from http://inthesetimes.com/working/entry/14631/are_mergers_the_answer_for_nurses_unions/.

National Labor Relations Board. (n.d). *Case 09-CA-026348.* Retrieved December 30, 2011, from http://www.nlrb.gov/case/09-CA-026348#casedetails

NLRB v. Health Care & Retirement Corp. (1994). *NLRB v. Health Care & Retirement Corp.*, 114 S. Ct. 1778, May 23, 1994. Retrieved June 23, 2013, from http://www.law.cornell.edu/supct/html/92-1964.ZS.html

Right to Work, Right to Not Join a Union. (2013). Liberty Alliance. Retrieved June 22, 2013, from http://libertyalliance.com/2013/06/right-to-work-right-to-not-join-a-union/

Robertson, K. (2013, January 4). Unions join forces to fight nursing cutbacks. *Sacramento Business Journal.* Retrieved June 22, 2013, from http://www.bizjournals.com/sacramento/news/2013/01/04/unions-join-forces-to-fight-nursing.html?page=all

Rossheim, J. (2013). *How nurses can fight sexual harassment.* Allhealthcare. Retrieved June 22, 2013, from http://allhealthcare.monster.com/benefits/articles/3458-how-nurses-can-fight-sexual-harassment?page=2

Selvam, A. (2012). Striking out: Nurses unions go up against hospitals as year ends. *Modern Healthcare, 42*(1), 14–15.

Service Employees International Union. (2013). *Our union.* Retrieved June 21, 2013, from http://www.seiu.org/our-union/

Spector, P. E., Shou, Z. E., & Che, X. X. (2013, February 19). Nurse exposure to physical and nonphysical violence, bullying, and sexual harassment: A quantitative review. *International Journal of Nursing Studies.* Retrieved June 23, 2013, from http://www.ncbi.nlm.nih.gov/pubmed/23433725

United States Equal Employment Opportunity Commission (USEEOC). (n.d.-a). *Discrimination by type.* Retrieved June 21, 2013, from http://www.eeoc.gov/laws/types/index.cfm

United States Equal Employment Opportunity Commission (USEEOC). (n.d.-b). *Facts about sexual harassment.* Retrieved June 22, 2013, from http://www.eeoc.gov/eeoc/publications/fs-sex.cfm

Warner, K. (2013, January 23). *The real reason for the decline of American unions.* Bloomberg. Retrieved June 22, 2013, from http://www.bloomberg.com/news/2013-01-23/the-real-reason-for-the-decline-of-american-unions.html

Yamada, D. (2013, May 8). *Nurse can proceed with age discrimination claim against employer seeking "rising young stars," federal court holds.* Minding the Workplace. Retrieved June 22, 2013, from http://newworkplace.wordpress.com/2013/05/08/nurse-can-proceed-with-age-discrimination-claim-against-employer-seeking-rising-young-stars-federal-court-holds/

UNIT VII

Roles and Functions in Controlling

23

Quality Control

... the results that pioneering organizations have achieved in leveraging electronic medical records, computerized provider order entry, and other clinical information systems to create evidence-based care processes are demonstrating quite clearly that there is tremendous potential to raise the standard of care.
–Mark Hagland

... because quality health care is a complex phenomenon, the factors contributing to quality in health care are as varied as the strategies needed to achieve this elusive goal.
–Carol Huston

CROSSWALK THIS CHAPTER ADDRESSES:

BSN Essential II: Basic organizational and systems leadership for quality care and patient safety

BSN Essential III: Scholarship for evidence-based practice

BSN Essential IV: Information management and application of patient care technology

BSN Essential V: Health-care policy, finance, and regulatory environments

BSN Essential VI: Interprofessional communication and collaboration for improving patient health outcomes

MSN Essential II: Organizational and systems leadership

MSN Essential III: Quality improvement and safety

MSN Essential IV: Translating and integrating scholarship into practice

MSN Essential V: Informatics and health-care technologies

MSN Essential VI: Health policy and advocacy

MSN Essential VII: Interprofessional collaboration for improving patient and population health outcomes

QSEN Competency: Patient-centered care

QSEN Competency: Teamwork and collaboration

QSEN Competency: Evidence-based practice

QSEN Competency: Quality improvement

QSEN Competency: Safety

QSEN Competency: Informatics

AONE Nurse Executive Competency I: Communication and relationship building

AONE Nurse Executive Competency II: A knowledge of the health-care environment

AONE Nurse Executive Competency III: Leadership

AONE Nurse Executive Competency V: Business skills

LEARNING OBJECTIVES *The learner will:*

- determine appropriate criteria or standards for measuring quality
- collect and analyze quality control data to determine whether established standards have been met
- identify appropriate corrective action to be taken when standards have not been met
- differentiate among process, outcome, structure, and concurrent, retrospective, and prospective audits
- write nursing criteria for process, outcome, and structure audits
- describe key components of total quality management and the Toyota Production System philosophy
- select appropriate quantitative and qualitative tools to measure quality in given situations
- describe the role of organizations such as the Joint Commission (JC), the Centers for Medicare and Medicaid (CMS), the American Nurses Association (ANA), the National Committee for Quality Assurance, and the Agency for Healthcare Research and Quality (AHRQ) in establishing standards of practice and clinical practice guidelines for health-care organizations and health-care professionals
- describe how the work of the *Maryland Hospital Association Quality Indicator Project* is contributing to benchmark work in indicator identification and quality measurement
- analyze the impact of diagnosis-related groups and the prospective payment system on the quality of care of hospitalized patients
- describe national efforts such as Health Plan Employer Data and Information Set and ORYX to standardize the collection of quality care data
- identify the purpose of standardized nursing languages and discuss how creating a common use of terminology/definitions in nursing could improve the quality of patient care
- debate the importance of articulating "nursing-sensitive" outcome measures in measuring the quality of health care
- identify the four evidence-based standards Leapfrog Groups believes will provide the greatest impact on reducing medical errors
- describe characteristics of a "just culture" and discuss why having such a culture is critical to timely and accurate medical error reporting
- analyze (quantitatively and qualitatively) the extent of the quality health-care gains that have occurred since the publication of *To Err Is Human*
- empower subordinates and followers to participate in continuous quality improvement efforts

During the *controlling* phase of the management process, performance is measured against predetermined standards, and action is taken to correct discrepancies between these standards and actual performance. Employees who feel that they can influence the quality of outcomes in their work environment experience higher levels of motivation and job satisfaction. Organizations also need some control over productivity, innovation, and quality outcomes. Controlling, then, should not be viewed as a means of determining success or failure but as a way to learn and grow, both personally and professionally.

This unit explores controlling as the fifth and final step in the management process. Because the management process—like the nursing process—is cyclic, controlling is not an end in itself; it is implemented throughout all phases of management. Examples of management controlling functions include the periodic evaluation of unit philosophy, mission, goals, and objectives; the measurement of individual and group performance against pre-established standards; and the auditing of patient goals and outcomes.

Quality control—a specific type of controlling—refers to activities that are used to evaluate, monitor, or regulate services rendered to consumers. For any quality control program to be effective, certain components need to be in place (Display 23.1). First, the program needs to be supported by top-level administration; a quality control program cannot merely be an exercise to satisfy various federal and state regulations. A sincere commitment by the institution, as evidenced by fiscal and human resource support, will be a deciding factor in determining and improving quality of services.

| DISPLAY 23.1 | Hallmarks of Effective Quality Control Programs |

1. Support from top-level administration.
2. Commitment by the organization in terms of fiscal and human resources.
3. Quality goals reflect search for excellence rather than minimums.
4. Process is ongoing (continuous).

Although the organization must be realistic about the economics of rendering services, if nursing is to strive for excellence, then developed quality control criteria should be pushed to optimal levels rather than minimally acceptable levels. Finally, the process of quality control must be ongoing; that is, it must reflect a belief that the search for improvement in quality outcomes is continuous and that care can always be improved. Although controlling is generally defined as a management function, effective quality control requires managers to have skill in both leadership and management. Leadership roles and management functions inherent in quality control are delineated in Display 23.2.

| DISPLAY 23.2 | Leadership Roles and Management Functions Associated with Quality Control |

LEADERSHIP ROLES

1. Encourages followers to be actively involved in the quality control process.
2. Clearly communicates expected standards of care to subordinates.
3. Encourages the setting of high standards to maximize quality instead of setting minimum safety standards.
4. Embraces and champions quality improvement (QI) as an ongoing process.
5. Uses control as a method of determining why goals were not met.
6. Is active in communicating quality control findings and their implications to other health professionals and consumers.
7. Acts as a role model for followers in accepting responsibility and accountability for nursing actions.
8. Distinguishes between clinical standards and resource utilization standards, ensuring that patients receive at least minimally acceptable levels of quality care.
9. Supports/actively participates in research efforts to identify and measure nursing-sensitive patient outcomes.
10. Creates a work culture that deemphasizes blame for errors and focuses instead on addressing factors that lead to and cause near misses, medical errors, and adverse events.
11. Encourages the use of Six Sigma as the benchmark for QI goals.
12. Establishes benchmarks that mirror those of best-performing organizations and that drive a goal of continuous quality improvement (CQI).

MANAGEMENT FUNCTIONS

1. In conjunction with other personnel in the organization, establishes clear-cut, measurable standards of care and determines the most appropriate method for measuring if those standards have been met.
2. Selects and uses process, outcome, and structure audits appropriately as quality control tools.
3. Accesses appropriate sources of information in data gathering for quality control.
4. Determines discrepancies between care provided and unit standards and uses *critical event analysis* (CEA) or *root cause analysis* (RCA) to determine why standards were not met.
5. Uses quality control findings in determining needed areas of staff education or coaching.

6. Keeps abreast of current government, accrediting body, and licensing regulations that affect quality control.
7. Actively participates in state and national benchmarking and "best practices" initiatives.
8. Continually assesses the unit or organizational environment to identify and categorize errors that are occurring and proactively reworks the processes that led to the errors.
9. Establishes an environment where research evidence and clinical guidelines based on best practices drive clinical decision-making and patient care.
10. Is accountable to insurers, patients, providers, and legislative and regulatory bodies for quality outcomes.
11. Establishes Six Sigma methodology as a goal for every aspect of QI.

To understand quality control, the manager must become familiar with the process and terminology used in quality measurement and improvement activities. This chapter introduces quality control as a specific and systematic process. Audits are presented as tools for assessing quality. In addition, the historical impact of external forces on the development and implementation of quality control programs in health-care organizations is discussed. Key organizations involved in the establishment and monitoring of quality initiatives in the United States are discussed. In addition, quality control strategies, quality measurement tools, benchmarking, and clinical practice guidelines (CPGs) are introduced. Finally, strategies for creating a culture of safety are identified, as are the challenges of changing a system that all too often focuses on individual errors rather than on the need to make system-wide changes.

DEFINING QUALITY HEALTH CARE

Quality measurement and *outcomes accountability* have been buzzwords in health care since the 1980s and continue to be at the forefront of almost every health-care agenda today. Defining and measuring quality of care are essential for health-care providers to demonstrate accountability to insurers, patients, and legislative and regulatory bodies. However, achieving quality care is not just a matter of better training for providers or delivering more care. The problem is multidimensional, and its complexity begins with the very definition of quality care itself.

The Institute of Medicine (IOM) (1994, p. 3) defines *health-care quality* as "the degree to which health services for individuals and populations increase the likelihood of desired health outcomes and are consistent with current professional knowledge." While this classic definition is widely accepted, parts of it merit further examination. The first is the assertion that quality does not exist unless desired health outcomes are attained. Outcomes are only one indicator of quality. Sometimes, patients receive the best possible care with the information available and poor outcomes occur. At other times, poor care may still result in good outcomes. Using outcomes alone as a way to measure quality care then is flawed.

While outcomes are an important measure of quality care, it is dangerous to use them as the only criteria for quality measurement.

The second implication in the IOM definition is that for care to be considered high quality, it must be consistent with current professional knowledge. Staying current in terms of professional knowledge in today's information firestorm is difficult for even the most dedicated providers. To complicate the issue even further, how quality of care is defined and measured often differs between providers and patients. Clearly, it is difficult to find a common definition of quality health care that represents the viewpoints of all stakeholders in the health-care system. What is even more difficult, however, is identifying and elucidating the myriad of factors that play a part in determining whether quality health care exists.

QUALITY CONTROL AS A PROCESS

If defining health-care quality is problematic, then the measurement of health-care quality is even more difficult. To make the process more effective and efficient, the collection of both quantitative and qualitative data is used as well as a specific and systematic process. This process, when viewed simplistically, can be broken down into three basic steps:

1. The criterion or standard is determined.
2. Information is collected to determine if the standard has been met.
3. Educational or corrective action is taken if the criterion has not been met.

The first step, as depicted in Figure 23.1, is the establishment of *control criteria* or *standards*. Measuring performance is impossible if standards have not been clearly established. Not only must standards exist, but leader-managers must also see that subordinates know and understand the standards. Because standards vary among institutions, employees must know the standard expected of them at their organization. Employees must be aware that

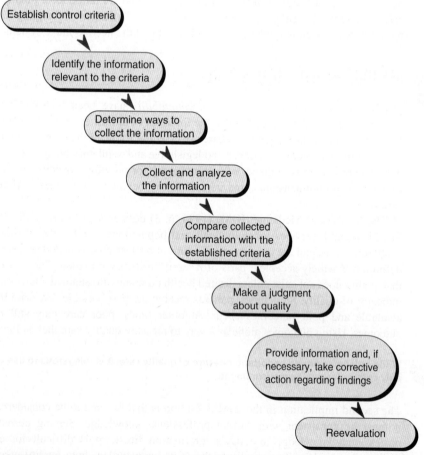

FIGURE 23.1 • Steps in auditing quality control. Copyright ® 2006 Lippincott Williams & Wilkins. Instructor's Resource CD-ROM to Accompany Leadership Roles and Management Functions in Nursing, by Bessie L. Marquis and Carol J. Huston.

their performance will be measured in terms of their ability to meet the established standard. For example, hospital nurses should provide postoperative patient care that meets standards specific to their institution. A nurse's performance can be measured only when it can be compared with a preexisting standard.

Many organizations have begun using *benchmarking*—the process of measuring products, practices, and services against best-performing organizations—as a tool for identifying desired standards of organizational performance. In doing so, organizations can determine how and why their performance differs from exemplar organizations, and use the exemplar organizations as role models for standard development and performance improvement.

 Benchmarking is the process of measuring products, practices, and services against best-performing organizations.

Many states have initiated a best practices program that invites health-care institutions to submit a description of a program or protocol relating to improvements in quality of life, quality of care, staff development, or cost-effectiveness practices. Experts review the submissions, examine outcomes, and then designate a *best practice*. The difference in performance between top-performing health-care organizations and the national average is called the *quality gap*. While the quality gap is typically small in many industries, it is often significant in health care.

The second step in the quality control process includes identifying information relevant to the criteria. What information is needed to measure the criteria? In the example of postoperative patient care, this information might include the frequency of vital signs, dressing checks, and neurologic or sensory checks. Often, such information is determined by reviewing current research or existing evidence.

The third step is determining ways to collect information. As in all data gathering, the manager must be sure to use all appropriate sources. When assessing quality control of the postoperative patient, the manager could find much of the information in the patient chart. Postoperative flow sheets, the physician orders, and the nursing notes would probably be most helpful. Talking to the patient or nurse could also yield information.

The fourth step in auditing quality control is collecting and analyzing information. For example, if the standards specify that postoperative vital signs are to be checked every 30 minutes for 2 hours and every hour thereafter for 8 hours, it is necessary to look at how often vital signs were taken during the first 10 hours after surgery. The frequency with which vital signs are assessed is listed on the postoperative flow sheet and then is compared with the standard set by the unit. The resulting discrepancy or congruency gives managers information with which they can make a judgment about the quality or appropriateness of the nursing care.

If vital signs were not taken frequently enough to satisfy the standard, the manager would need to obtain further information regarding why the standard was not met and counsel employees as needed. This is often done using a process known as computer-aided error analysis (CEA) or root cause analysis (RCA).

In addition to evaluating individual employee performance, quality control provides a tool for evaluating unit goals. If unit goals are consistently unmet, the leader must reexamine those goals and determine if they are inappropriate or unrealistic. There is danger here that the leader, who feels pressured to meet unit goals, may lower standards to the point where quality is meaningless. This reinforces the need to determine standards first and then evaluate goals accordingly.

The last step in Figure 23.1 is reevaluation. If quality control is measured on 20 postoperative charts and a high rate of compliance with established standards is found, the need for short-term reevaluation is low. If standards are consistently unmet or met only partially, frequent reevaluation is indicated. However, quality control measures need to be ongoing, not put forth simply in response to a problem. Effective leaders ensure that quality control is proactive by pushing standards to maximal levels and by eliminating problems in the early stages before productivity or quality is compromised.

 Quality control efforts must be proactive, not solely as a reaction to a problem.

LEARNING EXERCISE 23.1

Designing an Audit Tool

You are a public health nurse in a small, nonprofit visiting nurse clinic. The nursing director has requested that you chair the newly established QI committee because of your experience with developing audit criteria. Because a review of the patient population indicates that maternal–child visits make up the greatest percentage of home visits, the committee chose to develop a retrospective-process audit tool to monitor the quality of initial postpartum visits. The criteria specified that the clients to be included in the audit had to have been discharged with an infant from a birth center or obstetrical unit following uncomplicated vaginal delivery. The home visit would occur not later than 72 hours after the delivery.

Assignment: Design an audit tool appropriate for this diagnosis that would be convenient to use. Specify percentages of compliance, sources of information, and number of patients to be audited. Limit your process criteria to 20 items. Try solving this yourself before reading the possible solution that appears in the Appendix.

THE DEVELOPMENT OF STANDARDS

A *standard* is a predetermined level of excellence that serves as a guide for practice. Standards have distinguishing characteristics; they are predetermined, established by an authority, and communicated to and accepted by the people affected by them. Because standards are used as measurement tools, they must be objective, measurable, and achievable. There is no one set of standards. Each organization and profession must set standards and objectives to guide individual practitioners in performing safe and effective care. *Standards for practice* define the scope and dimensions of professional nursing.

The American Nurses Association (ANA) has been instrumental in developing professional standards for almost 80 years. In 1973, the ANA Congress first established standards for nursing practice, thereby providing a means of determining the quality of nursing that a patient receives, regardless of whether such services are provided by a professional nurse alone or in conjunction with nonprofessional assistants.

 The ANA has played a key role in developing standards for the profession.

Currently, the ANA publishes numerous different standards for nursing practice that reflect different areas of specialty nursing practice (ANA, 2013a). The *Scope and Standards of Practice*—originally published by the ANA in 1991 and revised several times since—provides a foundation for all registered nurses (RNs) in practice. These standards consist of *Standards of Practice* and *Standards of Professional Performance* (Display 23.3). The most recent updates include significant changes such as the incorporation of competency statements in the place of measurement criteria under the standards section and an expanded list of standards of practice (ANA, 2013b).

DISPLAY 23.3	American Nurses Association Scope and Standards of Practice (2nd Edition) (2010)

STANDARDS OF PRACTICE

1. Assessment—The RN collects comprehensive data pertinent to the health-care consumer's health or the situation.
2. Diagnosis—The RN analyzes the assessment data to determine the diagnoses or issues.
3. Outcomes Identification—The RN identifies expected outcomes for a plan individualized to the health-care consumer or the situation.
4. Planning—The RN develops a plan that prescribes strategies and alternatives to attain expected outcomes.
5. Implementation—The RN implements the identified plan.

    Standard 5A. Coordination of Care—The RN coordinates care delivery.

    Standard 5B. Health Teaching and Health Promotion—The RN employs strategies to promote health and a safe environment.

    Standard 5C. Consultation.

    Standard 5D. Prescriptive Authority and Treatment.
6. Evaluation—The RN evaluates progress toward the attainment of outcomes.

STANDARDS OF PROFESSIONAL PERFORMANCE

7. Ethics—The RN practices ethically.
8. Education—The RN attains the knowledge and competency that reflects current nursing practice.
9. Evidence-Based Practice and Research—The RN integrates evidence and research findings into practice.
10. Quality of Practice—The RN contributes to quality nursing practice.
11. Communication—The RN communicates effectively in a variety of formats in all areas of practice.
12. Leadership—The RN demonstrates leadership in the professional practice setting and the profession.
13. Collaboration—The RN collaborates with health-care consumer, family, and others in the conduct of nursing practice.
14. Professional Practice Evaluation—The RN evaluates her or his own nursing practice in relation to professional practice standards and guidelines, relevant statutes, rules, and regulations.
15. Resource Utilization—The RN utilizes appropriate resources to plan and provide nursing services that are safe, effective, and financially responsible.
16. Environmental Health—The RN practices in an environmentally safe and healthy manner.

Source: American Nurses Association (2010). Scope and Standards of Practice (2nd ed.). Silver Spring, MD: American Nurses Association.

In addition, the ANA (2009) publication *Nursing Administration: Scope and Standards of Practice* may be of particular interest to nurse-managers. It too includes *Standards of Practice* as well as *Standards of Professional Performance*. These standards are regarded as authoritative statements describing the duties that nurse administrators are expected to perform competently (p. vii).

Other developed standards reflect such diverse fields of practice as diabetes nursing, forensic nursing practice, home health nursing practice, gerontologic nursing, nursing practice in correctional facilities, parish nursing, oncology nursing, school nursing, psychiatric–mental health nursing practice, nursing informatics, and public health (ANA, 2013a). All of these standards exemplify optimal performance expectations for the nursing profession and have provided a basis for the development of organizational and unit standards nationwide.

Organizational standards outline levels of acceptable practice within the institution. For example, each organization develops a policy and procedures manual that outlines its specific standards. These standards may minimize or maximize in terms of the quality of service expected. Such standards of practice allow the organization to measure unit and individual performance more objectively.

One contemporary effort to establish standards for individual nursing practice has been the development of clinical practice guidelines (CPGs). *CPGs or standardized clinical guidelines* provide diagnosis-based, step-by-step interventions for providers to follow in an effort to promote high-quality care while controlling resource utilization and costs. CPGs, such as those developed by the Agency for Healthcare Research and Quality (AHRQ), are developed following an extensive review of the literature and suggest what interventions, in what order, will likely lead to the best possible patient outcomes. In other words, CPGs should reflect current research findings and best practices.

 CPGs reflect evidence-based practice; that is, they should be based on cutting edge research and best practices.

In 1998, the AHRQ and the U.S. Department of Health, in partnership with the American Medical Association and American Association of Health Plans–Health Insurance Association of America, launched the *National Guideline Clearinghouse* (NGC). The NGC is a free, publicly available comprehensive database of evidence-based CPGs and related documents in one easy-to-access location (AHRQ, 2013). The Web site for this clearinghouse and the key features of the NGC are shown in Display 23.4.

DISPLAY 23.4	**The National Guideline Clearinghouse: Key Components**

1. Structured, standardized abstracts (summaries) about each guideline and its development
2. Editorial insights on current issues of importance to the guideline and/or measure fields including perspectives on trends in guideline and/or measure development, reviews/critiques of guidelines/measures, comments on topics related to evidence-based medicine, or similar themes
3. Guideline syntheses are systematic comparisons of selected guidelines that address similar topic areas. Key elements of each synthesis include a discussion of areas of agreement and difference, the major recommendations and the corresponding strength of evidence and recommendation rating schemes, and a comparison of guideline methodologies. Also presented are the source(s) of funding, the benefits/harms of implementing the guideline recommendations, and any associated contraindications
4. A guideline matrix/utility for filtering NGC content and for comparing attributes of two or more guidelines in a side-by-side comparison
5. Guideline resources such as AHRQ evidence reports; hospital-acquired conditions; complementary Web sites; mobile device resources; and patient education materials
6. Annotated bibliographies from more than 7,100 citations for publications and resources about guidelines. Resources are selected from peer-reviewed journals as well as non-journal sources. Links to PubMed or the original article are provided when available

Source: Agency for Healthcare Research and Quality (2013). National Guideline Clearing House. Retrieved June 23, 2013, from http://www.guideline.gov/about/index.aspx

Newhouse (2010) cautions, however, that many currently endorsed guidelines are largely based on expert opinion rather than research evidence. In addition, she suggests that some guidelines do not include the strength of the evidence on which the guideline is based. This disadvantages the user who assumes that the guidelines are based on credible research evidence. Finally, Newhouse suggests that some guidelines are not useful because they have been influenced by potential bias (conflicts of interest) or because they lack flexibility for a complex and divergent patient population.

In addition, some providers eschew CPGs, arguing that they are "cookbook medicine"; however, the reality is that they likely serve as the best possible guide in caring for specific patient populations that exists today. This does not mean that providers cannot deviate from evidence-based guidelines; they can and do. However, such deviations should be accompanied by the identification of the unique factors of the individual case that calls for that deviation. Other barriers to the implementation of CPGs are noted in Examining the Evidence 23.1.

Examining the Evidence 23.1

Source: *Facilitators and Barriers to the Use of Clinical Practice Guidelines. (2012).* AORN Journal, 96*(6), 668–669.*

The increased emphasis on evidence-based practice has led to the development of CPGs and checklists to help with clinical decision-making and care planning. Guidelines only work if they are used, however, and they must be reviewed and revised as needed. In this study, the researchers sought to identify factors that facilitate or prevent nurses from using CPGs.

The researchers identified three primary facilitators that encourage CPG use: education/orientation/training; communication; and time/staffing/workload. The three primary barriers to CPG use were time/staffing/workload; education, orientation, and training; and communication.

The researchers in this study suggested that almost every working staff nurse can identify with these findings because guidelines and checklists are becoming more prevalent and even mandatory at many facilities. They noted that additional research is needed to determine whether electronic CPGs are used more often and promote better patient care than written guidelines. In addition, nurses should participate in the development of new CPGs, and managers should ensure adequate education and orientation is provided for every new CPG.

AUDITS AS A QUALITY CONTROL TOOL

Where standards provide the yardstick for measuring quality care, audits are measurement tools. An *audit* is a systematic and official examination of a record, process, structure, environment, or account to evaluate performance. Auditing in health-care organizations provides managers with a means of applying the control process to determine the quality of services rendered. Auditing can occur retrospectively, concurrently, or prospectively. *Retrospective audits* are performed after the patient receives the service. *Concurrent audits* are performed while the patient is receiving the service. *Prospective audits* attempt to identify how future performance will be affected by current interventions. The audits most frequently used in quality control include the outcome, process, and structure audits.

Outcome Audit

Outcomes can be defined as the end result of care. *Outcome audits* determine what results, if any, occurred as a result of specific nursing interventions for patients. These audits assume that the outcome accurately demonstrates the quality of care that was provided. Many experts consider outcome measures to be the most valid indicators of quality care, but until the past decade, most evaluations of hospital care have focused on structure and process.

Outcomes reflect the end result of care or how the patient's health status changed as a result of an intervention.

Outcome measurement, however, is not new; Florence Nightingale was advocating the evaluation of patient outcomes when she used mortality and morbidity statistics to publicize the poor quality of care during the Crimean War. In today's era of cost-containment, outcome research is needed to determine whether managed care processes, restructuring, and other new clinical practices are producing the desired cost savings without compromising the quality of patient care.

Outcomes are complex, and it is important to recognize that many factors contribute to patient outcomes. There is growing recognition, however, that it is possible to separate the contribution of nursing to the patient's outcome; this recognition of outcomes that are *nursing-sensitive* creates accountability for nurses as professionals and is important in developing nursing as a profession. Although outcomes traditionally used to measure quality of hospital care include mortality, morbidity, and length of hospital stay, these outcomes are not highly nursing-sensitive. More nursing-sensitive outcome measures for the acute-care setting include patient fall rates, nosocomial infection rates, the prevalence of pressure sores, physical restraint use, and patient satisfaction rates.

Process Audit

Process audits measure how nursing care is provided. The audit assumes a connection between the process and the quality of care. Critical pathways and standardized clinical guidelines are examples of efforts to standardize the process of care. They also provide a tool to measure deviations from accepted best practice process standards.

 Process audits are used to measure the process of care or how the care was carried out and assume that a relationship exists between the process used by the nurse and the quality of care provided.

Process audits tend to be task-oriented and focus on whether practice standards are being fulfilled. Process standards may be documented in patient care plans, procedure manuals, or nursing protocol statements. A process audit might be used to establish whether fetal heart tones or blood pressures were checked according to an established policy. In a community health agency, a process audit could be used to determine if a parent received instruction about a newborn during the first postpartum visit.

In addition, a process audit could be done of the medication reconciliation process used to prevent medication errors at patient transition points. *Medication reconciliation* is the process of comparing the medications a patient is taking (and should be taking) with newly ordered medications (Joint Commission, 2012). The comparison addresses duplications, omissions, and interactions, and the need to continue current medications. The types of information that clinicians use to reconcile medications include (among others) medication name, dose, frequency, route, and purpose (Joint Commission, 2012).

Structure Audit

Structure audits assume that a relationship exists between quality care and appropriate structure. A structure audit includes resource inputs such as the environment in which health care is delivered. It also includes all those elements that exist prior to and separate from the interaction between the patient and the health-care worker. For example, staffing ratios, staffing mix, emergency department wait times, and the availability of fire extinguishers in patient care areas are all structural measures of quality of care.

Structural standards, which are often set by licensing and accrediting bodies, ensure a safe and effective environment, but they do not address the actual care provided. An example of a structural audit might include checking to see if patient call lights are in place or if patients can reach their water pitchers. It also might examine staffing patterns to ensure that adequate resources are available to meet changing patient needs.

LEARNING EXERCISE 23.2

Identifying Structure, Process, and Outcome Measures

You are a charge nurse on a postsurgical unit. Retrospective survey data reveal that many patients report high levels of postoperative pain in the first 72 hours after surgery. You decide to make a list of possible structure, process, and outcome variables that may be impacting the situation. One of the structure measures you identify is that the narcotic medication carts are located some distance from the patient rooms and that may be contributing to a delay in pain medication administration. One of the process measures you identify is that licensed staff are inconsistent in terms of how soon they make their initial pain assessments on postoperative patients as well as the tools they use to assess pain levels. An outcome measure might be the average wait time from the time a patient requests pain medication until it is administered.

Assignment: Identify at least three additional structure, process, and outcome measures for which you might collect data in an effort to resolve this problem. Select at least one of these measures, and specifically identify how you would collect the data. Then, describe how you would use your findings to increase the likelihood that future practice on the unit will be evidence-based.

STANDARDIZED NURSING LANGUAGES

One means of better identifying nursing-sensitive outcomes has been the development of standardized nursing languages. A *standardized nursing language* provides a consistent terminology for nurses to describe and document their assessments, interventions, and the outcomes of their actions. Currently, 12 standardized nursing languages have been approved by the ANA (National Association of School Nurses, 2012) (see Display 23.5.). Three are discussed in this chapter.

DISPLAY 23.5	Standardized Nursing Languages Approved by the American Nurses Association

1. NANDA International (NANDA-I)
2. Nursing Interventions Classification (NIC)
3. Nursing Outcomes Classification (NOC)
4. Clinical Care Classification System (CCC)
5. The Omaha System
6. Perioperative Nursing Data Set (PNDS)
7. International Classification for Nursing Practice (ICNP)
8. Systemized Nomenclature of Medicine Clinical Terms (SNOMED CT)
9. Logical Observation Identifiers Names and Codes (LOINC)
10. Nursing Minimum Data Sets (NMDS)
11. Nursing Management Minimum Data Sets (NMMDS)
12. ABC Codes

Source: National Association of School Nurses (2012). Standardized nursing languages. Retrieved June 23, 2013 from http://www.nasn.org/PolicyAdvocacy/PositionPapersandReports/NASNPositionStatementsFullView/tabid/462/ArticleId/48/Standardized-Nursing-Languages-Revised-June-2012

One of the oldest standardized nursing languages is the NMDS. The NMDS—developed by Werley and Lang—represents efforts lasting more than a decade to standardize the collection of nursing data. With the NMDS, a minimum set of items of information with uniform definitions and categories is collected to meet the needs of multiple data users. Thus, it creates a shared language that can be used by nurses in any care delivery setting as well as by other health professionals and researchers. This data then can be used to compare nursing effectiveness, costs, and outcomes across clinical settings and nursing interventions.

Another tool that helps to link nursing interventions and patient outcomes is the NIC developed by the Iowa Interventions Project, College of Nursing, Iowa City, Iowa. The NIC is a research-based classification system that provides a common, standardized language for nurses; it consists of independent and collaborative interventions of nurses in all specialty areas and in all settings. With 30 diverse classes of care, such as drug management, child bearing, community health promotion, physical comfort promotion, and perfusion management and multiple domains of interventions, the NIC can be linked with the *North American Nursing Diagnosis Association taxonomy*, the NMDS, and nursing outcomes to improve patient outcomes.

Finally, the International Council of Nurses (ICN) has developed the *International Classification for Nursing Practice* (ICNP), a compositional terminology for nursing practice that is applicable globally. The ICNP represents the domain of nursing practice as an essential and complementary part of professional health services, necessary for decision-making and policy development aimed at improving health status and health care (ICN, 2009).

QUALITY IMPROVEMENT MODELS

Over the past several decades, the American health-care system has moved from a *quality assurance* (QA) model to one focused on *quality improvement* (QI). The difference between the two concepts is that QA models target currently existing quality; QI models target ongoing and continually improving quality. Two models that emphasize the ongoing nature of QI include *total quality management* (TQM) and the *Toyota Production System* (TPS).

Quality assurance models seek to ensure that quality currently exists, whereas QI models assume that the process is ongoing and quality can always be improved.

Total Quality Management

TQM, also referred to as *continuous quality improvement* (CQI), is a philosophy developed by Dr. W. Edward Deming. TQM is one of the hallmarks of Japanese management systems. It assumes that production and service focus on the individual and that quality can always be better. Thus, identifying and doing the right things, the right way, the first time, and problem-prevention planning—not inspection and reactive problem-solving—lead to quality outcomes.

TQM is based on the premise that the individual is the focal element on which production and service depend (i.e., it must be a customer-responsive environment) and that the quest for quality is an ongoing process.

Because TQM is a never-ending process, everything and everyone in the organization are subject to continuous improvement efforts. No matter how good the product or service is, the TQM philosophy says that there is always room for improvement. Customer needs and experiences with the product are constantly evaluated. Workers—not a central QA/QI department—do this data collection, thus providing a feedback loop between administrators, workers, and consumers. Any problems encountered are approached in a preventive or proactive mode so that crisis management becomes unnecessary.

Another critical component of TQM is the empowerment of employees by providing positive feedback and reinforcing attitudes and behaviors that support quality and productivity. Based on the premise that employees have an in-depth understanding of their jobs, believe they are valued, and feel encouraged to improve product or service quality through risk-taking and creativity, TQM trusts the employees to be knowledgeable, accountable, and responsible and provides education and training for employees at all levels. Although the philosophy of TQM emphasizes that quality is more important than profit, the resultant increase in quality of a well-implemented TQM program attracts more customers, resulting in increased profit margins and a financially healthier organization. The 14 quality management principles of TQM as outlined by Deming (1986) are summarized in Display 23.6.

DISPLAY 23.6   Total Quality Management Principles

1. Create a constancy of purpose for the improvement of products and service.
2. Adopt a philosophy of continual improvement.
3. Focus on improving processes, not on inspection of product.
4. End the practice of awarding business on price alone; instead, minimize total cost by working with a single supplier.
5. Constantly improve every process for planning, production, and service.
6. Institute job training and retraining.
7. Develop the leadership in the organization.
8. Drive out fear by encouraging employees to participate actively in the process.
9. Foster interdepartmental cooperation, and break down barriers between departments.
10. Eliminate slogans, exhortations, and targets for the workforce.
11. Focus on quality and not just quantity; eliminate quota systems if they are in place.
12. Promote teamwork rather than individual accomplishments. Eliminate the annual rating or merit system.
13. Educate/train employees to maximize personal development.
14. Charge all employees with carrying out the TQM package.

Source: Deming, W. E. (1986). Out of the crisis. Cambridge, MA: MIT Press.

LEARNING EXERCISE 23.3

Deming's 14 Total Quality Management Principles

Think back to the organization for which you have worked the longest. How many of Deming's 14 principles for TQM are used in that organization? Do you believe some of the 14 principles are more important than others? Why or why not? Could an organization have a successful quality management program if only some of the principles are used?

The Toyota Production System

Another more contemporary, customer-focused QI model is the TPS. TPS is a production system built on the complete elimination of waste and focused on the pursuit of the most efficient production method possible (Toyota Motor Company, n.d.). "Toyota members seek to continually improve their standard processes and procedures in order to ensure maximum quality, improve efficiency and eliminate waste. This is known as *kaizen* and is applied to every sphere of the company's activities" (para 3).

Health-care organizations that use TPS would have caregivers not only attempt to directly solve problems at the time they occur, but it would also have them determine the root cause of the problem, so that the likelihood of the problem recurring would be minimized. TPS argues that solving individual problems this way, one at a time and where, when, and with whom they occur, prevents larger problems. Thus, management decisions are based on a long-term philosophy, even at the expense of short-term financial goals.

Implementing TPS, however, is not easy. It usually requires a change in organizational culture, values, and roles since responsibility and accountability for solving problems is so decentralized. In addition, eliminating problems at their root is far different from solving an immediate problem at hand. Thus, adopting TPS in an organization requires a substantial commitment of leadership time and resources. It also requires a tremendous amount of staff preparation and involvement.

WHO SHOULD BE INVOLVED IN QUALITY CONTROL?

Ideally, everyone in the organization should participate in quality control, because each individual is a recipient of the benefits. Quality control gives employees feedback about their current quality of care and how the care they provide can be improved. Engagement of frontline staff appears to be especially critical when implementing or sustaining QI efforts such as TCAB (*Transforming Care at the Bedside*)—a new national program developed and led by the Robert Wood Johnson Foundation and the Institute for Health Improvement (Parkerton et al., 2009). TCAB engages leaders at all levels of the organization, empowers frontline staff to improve care processes, and engages family members and patients in decision-making about their care. The end result is an improvement in patient safety indicators.

Many contemporary organizations, however, designate an individual (frequently a nurse) to be their *patient safety officer*. This strategy is risky, as it may create the impression that the responsibility for quality care is not shared. Therefore, although it is impractical to expect full staff involvement throughout the quality control process, as many staff as possible should be involved in determining criteria or standards, reviewing standards, collecting data, or reporting.

Quality control also requires evaluating the performance of all members of the multidisciplinary team. Professionals such as physicians, respiratory therapists, dietitians, and physical therapists contribute to patient outcomes and therefore must be considered in the audit process. Patients should also be actively involved in the determination of an organization's quality of care. It is important to remember, however, that quality care does not always equate with patient satisfaction.

Patient satisfaction often has little to do with whether a patient's health improved during a hospital stay.

For example, the quality of food, provision of privacy, satisfaction with a roommate, or noisiness of the nursing station may play into a patient's satisfaction with a hospital admission. In addition, patient satisfaction may be adversely affected by long waits for call lights to be answered and for transport to ancillary services such as the radiology department. Even the friendliness of the staff can impact patient satisfaction and perception of quality care. Although these factors are an important component of patient comfort, and therefore quality of care, quality is more encompassing and must always include an examination of whether the patient received the most appropriate treatment from the most appropriate provider in a timely manner.

QUALITY MEASUREMENT AS AN ORGANIZATIONAL MANDATE

Organizational accountability for the internal monitoring of quality and patient safety has increased exponentially the last 30 years. Most health-care organizations today have complete QI programs and are actively working to improve patient outcomes and promote patient safety. Changing government regulations regarding quality control, however, continue to influence QI efforts strongly. Managers must be cognizant of changing government and licensing regulations that affect their unit's quality control and standard setting. This awareness allows the manager to implement proactive rather than reactive quality control.

External Impacts on Quality Control

Although few organizations would debate the significant benefits of well-developed and implemented quality control programs, quality control in health-care organizations has evolved primarily from external influences and not as a voluntary monitoring effort. When

Medicare and Medicaid (government reimbursement for the elderly, disabled, and indigent) were implemented in the early 1960s, health-care organizations had little need to justify costs or prove that the services provided met patients' needs. Reimbursement was based on the costs incurred in providing the service, and no real ceilings were placed on the amount that could be charged for services. Only when the cost of these programs skyrocketed did the government establish regulations requiring organizations to justify the need for services and to monitor the quality of services.

Professional Standards Review Organizations

Professional Standards Review Board legislation (PL 92-603), established in 1972, was among the first of the federal government's efforts to examine cost and quality. *Professional standards review organizations* mandated certification of need for the patient's admission and continued review of care; evaluation of medical care; and analysis of the patient profile, the hospital, and the practitioners.

This new kind of surveillance and the existence of external controls had a huge effect on the industry. Health-care organizations began to question basic values and were forced to establish new methods for collecting data, keeping records, providing services, and accounting in general. Because government programs, such as Medicare and Medicaid, represent such a large group of today's patients, organizations that were unwilling or unable to meet these changing needs did not survive financially.

The Prospective Payment System

The advent of *diagnosis-related groups* (DRGs) in the early 1980s added to the ever-increasing need for organizations to monitor cost-containment yet guarantee a minimum level of quality (Chapter 10). As a result of DRGs, hospitals became part of the *prospective payment system* (PPS), whereby providers are paid a fixed amount per patient admission regardless of the actual cost to provide the care. This system has been criticized as promoting abbreviated hospital stays and services leading to a reduced quality of care. Clearly, DRGs have resulted in increased acuity levels of hospitalized patients, a decrease in the length of patient stay, and a perception by many health-care providers that patients are being discharged prematurely. All of these factors have contributed to growing levels of dissatisfaction by nurses regarding the quality of care they provide.

Critics of the PPS argue that although DRGs may have helped to contain rising health-care costs, the associated rapid declines in length of hospital stay and services provided have resulted in declines in quality of care.

LEARNING EXERCISE 23.4

Quality of Patient Care

How do you define quality of care? Is the quality of your care always what you would like it to be? If not, why not? What factors can you control in terms of providing high-quality care? (Which are internal and which are external?) In your clinical experience, have DRGs affected the quality of care provided? If so, how? Do you see differences in the quality of care provided to clients based on their ability to pay for that care or the type of insurance that they have?

The Joint Commission

The *Joint Commission* (JC) (formerly known as the *Joint Commission for Accreditation of Healthcare Organizations* [JCAHO])—an independent, not-for-profit organization that accredits more than 20,000 health-care organizations and programs in the United States (Joint Commission, 2013a)—has historically had a tremendous impact on planning for quality control in acute-care hospitals. The JC was the first to mandate that all hospitals have a QA program in place by 1981. These QA programs were to include a review of the care provided by all clinical departments, disciplines, and practitioners; the coordination and integration of the findings of quality control activities; and the development of specific plans for known or suspected patient problems. Again, in 1982, the JC began to require quarterly evaluations of standards for nursing care as measured against written criteria.

The JC also maintains one of the nation's most comprehensive databases of sentinel (serious adverse) events by health-care professionals and their underlying causes. A *sentinel event* is defined by the JC (2013c, para 2) as "an unexpected occurrence involving death or serious physical or psychological injury, or the risk thereof. Serious injury specifically includes loss of limb or function. The phrase, 'or the risk thereof' includes any process variation for which a recurrence would carry a significant chance of a serious adverse outcome." Such events are called "sentinel" because they signal the need for immediate investigation and response. Information from the JC sentinel database is regularly shared with accredited organizations to help them take appropriate steps to prevent medical errors (JC, 2013c).

Another JC priority is the development of *RCA* with a plan of correction for the errors that do occur. The JC's (2013c) Sentinel Event Policy provides that organizations that are either voluntarily reporting a sentinel event or responding to the JC's inquiry about a sentinel event submit their related RCA and action plan electronically to the JC whenever such events occur. The sentinel event data are then reviewed, and recommendations are made. The JC defends the confidentiality of the information, if necessary, in court.

Similarly, some organizations use a *failure mode and effects analysis* to examine all possible failures in a design—including sequencing of events, actual and potential risk, points of vulnerability, and areas for improvement (American Society for Quality, n.d.).

ORYX

In the late 1990s, the JC instituted its *Agenda for Change*—a multiphase, multidimensional set of initiatives directed at modernizing the accreditation process by shifting the focus of accreditation from organizational structure to organizational performance or outcomes. This required the development of clinical indicators to measure the quality of care provided. To further this goal, the JC approved a milestone initiative, known as *ORYX*, in February 1997. This initiative integrated outcomes and other performance measures into the accreditation process with data being publicly reported at a Web site known as *Quality Check* (www .qualitycheck.org).

Under ORYX, all organizations accredited by the JC were required to select at least 1 of 60 acceptable performance measurement systems and to begin data collection on specific clinical measures. Organizations could also volunteer for *ORYX Plus*, an effort by the JC to create a national standardized database of 32 performance measures. In addition, the JC began collecting data on outcome measures, including the *sentinel events* overall error rate, the number of reports on possible errors or near misses, hospital readmission rates, and the rate of hospital-acquired infections in an effort to better measure quality of care.

CORE MEASURES

Finally, the JC implemented its core measures program (also called *Hospital Quality Measures*) as part of ORYX in 2002 in an effort to better standardize its valid, reliable, and evidence-based data sets. Hospitals that choose not to participate in the core measures initiative receive a reduction of 2% in their Medicare Annual Payment.

The four areas initially targeted for implementation were acute myocardial infarction, pneumonia, heart failure, and the surgical care improvement project. Other core measures have since been added including children's asthma care, emergency department, hospital-based inpatient psychiatric services, hospital outpatient, immunization, stroke, substance use, perinatal services, tobacco treatment, and venous thromboembolism (Joint Commission, 2013b).

In January 2013, the JC announced that it will expand performance measurement requirements for accredited general medical/surgical hospitals from four to six core measures. (The Joint Commission Expands Performance, 2013). The additional requirements will take effect from January 1, 2014. The current four core measures will be mandatory for all general medical/surgical hospitals that serve specific patient populations. For hospitals with 1,100 or more births per year, the perinatal care measure set will become the mandatory fifth measure set. The sixth measure set (or fifth and sixth measure sets, for hospitals with fewer than 1,100 births per year) will be chosen by all general medical/surgical hospitals from the approved complement of core measure sets (The Joint Commission Expands Performance, 2013). The JC expects that requirements will increase over time, depending on the national health-care environment, emerging national measurement priorities, and hospitals' ever-increasing capability to electronically capture and transmit data (The Joint Commission Expands Performance, 2013).

National Patient Safety Goals

To augment the core measures and promote specific improvements in patient safety, the JC also issues *National Patient Safety Goals* (NPSGs) annually. For example, the NPSGs for 2013 included such things as identifying patients correctly, improving staff communication, using medicines safely, preventing infection, identifying patient safety risks, and preventing mistakes in surgery (The Joint Commission, 2013d). It remains to be seen to what degree compliance with core measures and the NPSGs actually improves patient outcomes. Early research findings are mixed with some studies reporting improved patient outcomes associated with core measures implementation and others finding no difference.

CENTERS FOR MEDICARE AND MEDICAID SERVICES

The *Centers for Medicare and Medicaid Services* (CMS), formerly the Health Care Financing Administration, also plays an active role in setting standards for and measuring quality in health care. With the introduction of the *Medicare Quality Initiative* in November 2001 (now called the *Hospital Quality Initiative* [HQI]), health outcomes were targeted as the data source. As part of the HQI, easy-to-understand data on health-care quality from nursing homes, home health agencies, hospitals, and kidney dialysis facilities are made available to all consumers via a variety of media. The intent is to encourage consumers and their physicians to discuss and make better-informed decisions on how to get the best hospital care, create incentives for hospitals to improve care, and support public accountability (Hospital Quality Initiative, 2008).

Pay for Performance/Quality-Based Purchasing

The CMS, through Medicare, has also established *Pay for Performance (P4P)*, also known as *quality-based purchasing*. P4P initiatives were created to align payment and quality incentives and to reduce costs through improved quality and efficiency. For example, the *Physician Quality Reporting Initiative* allows for payments to health professionals who satisfactorily report quality information to Medicare. In addition, 10 groups began participating in the 4-year *Physician Group Practice Demonstration* in 2005. For each year of the project, the groups could receive up to 80% of the savings they generated for Medicare by preventing complications and hospitalizations. Bonus payments depended on their savings and their quality of care.

Critics of the P4P incentive system suggest, however, that the system has failed to yield the desired results. They state this has occurred for many reasons, including a focus on provider improvement and not achievement, the risk adjustment of provider scores may be imprecise or even inapplicable to certain P4P metrics, small sample sizes result in too few patients who are eligible to be scored for a given metric, and because patients are often treated by multiple physicians (Pay for Performance, 2011).

In addition, they suggest that "P4P may result in better documentation of care, without a concurrent improvement in actual care. In addition, physicians may move their practices to areas where they believe patients can more effectively manage their own care; coordination of care could decline, especially for patients with multiple illnesses; physicians might focus on improving care only in areas addressed by financial rewards; and practice administrative costs could increase" (Pay for Performance, para 13).

Hospital Consumer Assessment of Healthcare Providers and Systems Surveys

The Hospital Consumer Assessment of Healthcare Providers and Systems (HCAHPS) survey is the first national, standardized, publicly reported survey of patients' perspectives of hospital care. Developed by a partnership between AHRQ and CMS beginning in 2002, the 27-item HCAHPS (pronounced "H-caps") survey instrument measures patients' perceptions of their hospital experience and can be conducted by mail, telephone, mail with telephone follow-up, or active interactive voice recognition (HCAHPS Fact Sheet, 2012).

The HCAHPS survey asks medical, surgical, and maternity care patients who have been recently discharged (between 48 hours and 6 weeks) about aspects of their hospital experience including "how often" or whether patients experienced a critical aspect of hospital care, rather than whether they were "satisfied" with the care. Data collected include how well nurses and doctors communicate with patients, how responsive hospital staff are to patients' needs, how well hospital staff help patients manage pain, how well the staff communicates with patients about medicines, and whether key information is provided at discharge (see Examining the Evidence 23.2). In addition, the survey addresses the

Examining the Evidence 23.2

Source: Study Links HCAHPS, Readmission Rates. (2013). Hospital Case Management, 21*(2), 25.*

This study by Press Ganey, a South Bend, IN, health-care performance improvement organization, analyzed hospitals' readmission penalty data and compared it with their performance on the CMS value-based purchasing measures. The study found a strong correlation between 30-day readmissions and performance on the HCAHPS portion of the Value-Based Purchasing Program with 30-day readmission rates decreasing as HCAHPS scores increased.

Press Ganey noted that good communication with patients and family members is a major factor in performance on patient perception of care measures as well as on the hospital's success in preventing 30-day readmissions. The HCAHPS survey asked patients to rate communication with nurses and physicians, responsiveness of the hospital staff, and discharge information, along with questions about cleanliness and quietness of the hospital environment, and pain management. Many of the questions focused on communication and the hospital's effectiveness in engaging patients—factors that also affect patients' ability to care for themselves after discharge and avoid being readmitted.

The researchers concluded that case managers should start discharge planning on admission and communicate frequently with patients and family members during their hospital stay. This will reduce the hospital readmissions that occur as a result of patients not following their discharged instructions, failing to take their medication correctly, and not having the community resources they need to manage after discharge, all of which indicate gaps in communication.

cleanliness and quietness of patients' rooms, the patients' overall rating of the hospital, and whether they would recommend the hospital to family and friends. Ten HCAHPS measures are publicly reported on the Hospital Compare Web site (www.hospitalcompare.hhs.gov) for each participating hospital.

While many hospitals collected information on patient satisfaction for their own internal use, until HCAHPS there were no common metrics and no national standards for collecting and publicly reporting information about patient experience of care. Since 2008, HCAHPS data have been reported publicly making, valid comparisons possible across hospitals locally, regionally, and nationally. This public reporting has created new incentives for hospitals to improve quality of care and has enhanced accountability in health care by increasing transparency of the quality of hospital care (HCAHPS Fact Sheet, 2012).

National Committee for Quality Assurance

Another external force assessing quality control in health-care organizations is the *National Committee for Quality Assurance* (NCQA). The NCQA, a private nonprofit organization that accredits managed care organizations, has developed the *Health Plan Employer Data and Information Set* (HEDIS) to compare the quality of care in managed care organizations. HEDIS 2013 consists of 75 measures across 8 domains of care, which provide numerical and descriptive information about the quality of care, patient outcomes, access and availability of services, utilization, premiums, and the plan's financial stability and operating policies (NCQA, 2013). Future versions are expected to have an even greater number of performance indicators as the growing Medicaid and Medicare segment of the population enrolled in managed care adds more specific performance indicators.

One of the most significant weaknesses of NCQA accreditation, however, is that such accreditation is voluntary. Since 1999, however, Medicare and Medicaid have contracted their managed care plans only with health plans that are accredited by the NCQA. More employers are also adopting this policy with the result that most managed care organizations will need this accreditation in the future to survive fiscally.

Maryland Hospital Association Quality Indicator Project

Another major initiative to measure quality in acute-care settings is the *Maryland Hospital Association Quality Indicator Project* (QI Project). The QI Project—a research project that began in 1985 with 7 acute-care hospitals in Maryland—currently has more than 1,800 acute-care hospitals and other health-care facilities participating. Among facilities accredited by the JC, the QI Project is the performance measurement system most frequently selected for meeting the ORYX requirement. Nearly 1,000 of the project's participants use their QI Project data to meet this JCAHO requirement (Wisconsin Hospital Association, 2003–2013). It is important though to remember that the QI Project is still considered a research project, and as such, the project is not intended to be used to establish performance thresholds or standards of care; however, its benchmark work in indicator identification and measurement is invaluable.

Multistate Nursing Home Case Mix and Quality Demonstration

There has also been a major move to develop quality indicators in long-term care settings. One of the most significant efforts has been the *Multistate Nursing Home Case Mix and Quality demonstration*, funded by the CMS. This demonstration seeks to develop and implement both a case mix classification system to serve as the basis for Medicare and Medicaid payment and a quality-monitoring system to assess the impact of case mix payment on quality and to provide better information to the nursing home survey process.

Report Cards

In response to the demand for objective measures of quality, a number of health plans, health-care providers, employer purchasing groups, consumer information organizations, and state governments have begun to formulate health-care quality report cards. Most states have laws requiring providers to report some type of data. AHRQ has also been exploring the development of a report card for the nation's health-care delivery system.

However, many current report cards do not contain information about the quality of care rendered by specific clinics, group practices, or physicians in a health plan's network. In addition, some critics of health-care report cards point out that health plans may receive conflicting ratings on different report cards. This is a result of using different performance measures and how each report card chooses to pool and evaluate individual factors. In addition, report cards may not be readily accessible or may be difficult for the average consumer to understand.

MEDICAL ERRORS: AN ONGOING THREAT TO QUALITY OF CARE

Many studies over the past 2 decades suggest that medical errors are rampant in the health-care system. The most well known of these studies was likely the 1999 IOM report called *To Err Is Human* (Kohn, Corrigan, & Donaldson, 2000). This report found that between 44,000 and 98,000 Americans die each year as a result of medical errors, making medical errors the eighth leading cause of death in this country, even when the lower estimate was used. The IOM study also looked at the type of errors that were occurring. Medication errors stood out as a particularly high risk, since these errors can lead to patient injuries, often called *adverse drug events*.

Perhaps the most significant contribution of the IOM report, however, was the conclusion that most of these errors did not occur from individual recklessness. Instead, they occurred because of basic flaws in the way that the health delivery system is organized and delivered. The current focus in medical error research is on fixing these flaws and creating and/ or fostering environments that minimize the likelihood of errors occurring. Strategies to create such environments include better reporting of the errors that do occur, the Leapfrog initiatives, reform of the medical liability system, and other point-of-care strategies such as bar coding, smart IV pumps, and medication reconciliation.

Reporting and Analyzing Errors

One critical strategy for addressing errors in the health-care system is the need to increase both the mandatory and voluntary reporting of medical errors. At the unit level, organizational cultures must be created that remove blame from the individual and, instead, focus on how the organization itself can be modified to reduce the likelihood of such errors occurring in the future. Only then will health-care workers feel they can report the errors and near misses they see occurring every day in their clinical practice.

This does not, however, remove individual practitioner responsibility and accountability to do everything they can to provide safe and competent care. This need to find a middle ground between a blame-free culture, which attributes all errors to system failure and says no individual is held accountable, and an overly punitive culture, where individuals are blamed for all mistakes, has been labeled a "*just culture*" (Landro, 2010). Developed by engineer David Marx, a just culture emphasizes finding the middle ground between the two extremes. It also seeks to separate unavoidable error from reckless behavior and unjustifiable risk (Landro).

Ignoring the problem of medical errors, denying their existence, or blaming the individuals involved in the processes does nothing to eliminate the underlying problems.

Legislation is also occurring at the national level to promote both the mandatory and voluntary reporting of medical errors. For example, the *Patient Safety and Quality Improvement Act* was signed into law in 2005. This bill protects medical error information voluntarily submitted to new private organizations (*patient safety organizations*) from being subpoenaed or used in legal discovery and generally requires that the information is treated as confidential.

Federal legislation has also been proposed to protect the voluntary reporting of ordinary injuries and "*near misses*"—errors that did not cause harm this time but easily could the next time. This would be like what is done in aviation, in which near misses are confidentially reported and can be analyzed by anyone.

Health-care organizations also need to do a better job of identifying what errors are occurring, categorizing those errors, and examining and reworking the processes that led to the errors. It is the leader-manager who bears the responsibility for proactively creating a work environment that minimizes these risks.

The Leapfrog Group

In addition, to help minimize risks to patients, the standards and expectations of oversight groups, insurers, and professional groups have been raised. One such effort is the *Leapfrog Group*, a growing conglomeration of non–health-care Fortune 500 company leaders who are committed to modernizing the current health-care system. Based on current research, the Leapfrog Group has identified four evidence-based standards that they believe will provide the greatest impact on reducing medical errors: *computerized physician–provider order entry* (CPOE), *evidence-based hospital referral* (EHR), *ICU (intensive care unit) physician staffing* (IPS), and the use of *Leapfrog Safe Practices* scores (Leapfrog Group, 2013). These strategies and the evidence supporting their use are described more fully in Display 23.7.

Scientific evidence indicates that these Leapfrog initiatives will reduce preventable medical errors. Their implementation is already underway or feasible in the short term;

DISPLAY 23.7   **Evidence-Based Leapfrog Initiatives**

COMPUTERIZED PHYSICIAN–PROVIDER ORDER ENTRY

Requires primary care providers to enter orders into a computer instead of handwriting them. This reduces medication errors based on inaccurate transcription. It also gives providers vital *clinical decision support* via access to information tools that support a health-care provider in decisions related to diagnosis, therapy, and care planning of individual patients.

Evidence: CPOE has been shown to reduce serious prescribing errors in hospitals by more than 50%.

EVIDENCE-BASED HOSPITAL REFERRAL

Suggests that patients with high-risk conditions should be treated at hospitals with characteristics shown to be associated with better outcomes.

Evidence: Referring patients needing certain complex medical procedures to hospitals offering the best survival odds based on scientifically valid criteria, such as the number of times a hospital performs these procedures each year or other process or outcomes data, reduces the patient's risk of dying up to 40%.

(Continued)

INTENSIVE CARE UNIT PHYSICIAN STAFFING

Examines the level of training of ICU medical personnel and suggests that quality of care in hospital ICUs is strongly influenced by (a) whether *intensivists* (doctors with special training in critical care medicine) are providing care and (b) the staff organization in the ICU.

Evidence: IPS has been shown to reduce the risk of patients dying in the ICU by 40%.

LEAPFROG SAFE PRACTICES SCORES

The National Quality Forum (NQF) endorsed safe *practices*, which if utilized would reduce the risk of harm in certain processes, systems, or environments of care. Included in the 34 practices are the 3 initiatives noted above. This fourth initiative assesses a hospital's progress on the remaining 31 NQF safe practices.

Source: Collated from Leapfrog Group. (2013). The Leapfrog Group fact sheet. Retrieved June 24, 2013, from http:// www.leapfroggroup.org/about_us/leapfrog-factsheet and Huston, C. (2014). Medical errors: An ongoing threat to quality health care. In C. Huston (Ed.), Professional issues in nursing: Challenges and opportunities (3rd ed.), Philadelphia, PA: Lippincott Williams & Wilkins.

---

consumers can appreciate their value; and health plans, purchasers, or consumers can easily ascertain their presence or absence in selecting health-care providers.

Leapfrog has also endorsed the use of *bar coding* to reduce point-of-care medication errors. As set forth by the U.S. Food and Drug Administration (FDA), all prescription and over-the-counter medications used in hospitals must contain a *national drug code* number, which indicates its dosage forms and strength. The FDA suggests that a bar code system coupled with a CPOE system would greatly enhance the ability of all health-care workers to follow the "five rights" of medication administration—that the *right* person receives the *right* drug in the *right* dose via the *right* route at the *right* administration time.

In addition, hospitals are increasingly turning to so-called *smart pumps* for intravenous (IV) therapy infusions. These smart pumps have safety software inside an advanced infusion therapy system that prevents IV medication errors through minimum and maximum dose limits as well as preset limits that cannot be overridden at a clinician's discretion.

A Six Sigma Approach

Another approach that has been taken to create a culture of safety management at the institutional level has been the implementation of a *Six Sigma approach*. *Sigma* is a statistical measurement that reflects how well a product or process is performing. Higher sigma values indicate better performance. Historically, the health-care industry has been comfortable striving for three sigma processes (all data points fall within 3 standard deviations) in terms of health-care quality, instead of six (Huston, 2014). This is one reason why health care has more errors than the banking or airline industries, where Six Sigma is the expectation. Organizations should aim for this target by carefully applying the Six Sigma methodology to every aspect of QI.

 The safety record in health care is a far cry from the enviable record of the similarly complex aviation industry.

Reforming the Medical Liability System

Finally, if quality health care is to be achieved, the medical liability system and our litigious society must be recognized as potential barriers to systematic efforts to uncover and learn from mistakes that are made in health care. Organizational cultures need to change for employees and patients to be comfortable in reporting hazards that can affect patient safety without fear of personal risk. Many experts have argued that the culture in health-care organizations must shift from one of blame to one in which errors are identified and responded to in a timely manner.

Are We Making Progress?

Gaps continue to exist between the care that patients should receive and the care they actually receive. This has been borne out in numerous studies including the follow-up IOM study *Crossing the Quality Chasm: A New Health System for the 21st Century*, which found large gaps between the preventive, acute, and chronic care that people should get and what they actually received.

Similarly, a large study by Healthgrades (2008) of 41 million Medicare patient records between 2004 and 2006 in virtually all of the nation's nearly 5,000 nonfederal hospitals reported 238,337 potentially preventable deaths. The overall incident rate was approximately 3% of all Medicare admissions, accounting for 1.1 million patient safety incidents during the 3 years studied. Medicare patients who experienced a patient safety incident had a one-in-five chance of dying as a result of the incident. The study concluded that if all of the hospitals had performed at the level of *Distinguished Hospitals for Patient Safety*, approximately 220,106 patient safety incidents and 37,214 Medicare deaths could have been prevented, saving the US $2.0 billion during the study period.

More recent data from Healthgrades (2013), however, was more encouraging. Hospital quality, as measured by mortality and complication rates, saw significant improvement from 2005 to 2011, although this varied by condition and procedure. For example, from 2005 through 2011, the nation's average in-hospital risk-adjusted mortality rate improved 22% across 16 of the common procedures and conditions studied by Healthgrades, such as chronic obstructive pulmonary disease (COPD), heart failure, and stroke.

Changes in hospital performance during this time frame varied widely by procedure and condition, ranging from a 3.5% increase in the risk-adjusted mortality rate for gastrointestinal surgeries and procedures (performance decline) to a 34.1% improvement in risk-adjusted mortality rate for COPD. Hospital quality also varied significantly across the United States with certain states performing exceptionally well (California and Delaware) and some performing poorly (Alabama and Pennsylvania) (Healthgrades, 2013).

It is clear then that despite all the interventions that have come out from the IOM studies and the multitude of organizations dedicated to QI in health care, progress in addressing the problem of medical errors is limited. Indeed, Wachter (2010) affirms that QI gains in health care in the 15 years since the publication of *To Err Is Human* have been slow to materialize, and he suggests that future changes will also likely be incremental. Yet, he also suggests that we have learned much from the missteps we have taken and that new important and unaddressed areas are now being placed on the patient safety agenda.

 INTEGRATING LEADERSHIP ROLES AND MANAGEMENT FUNCTIONS WITH QUALITY CONTROL

Quality control provides managers with the opportunity to evaluate organizational performance from a systematic, scientific, and objective viewpoint. To do so, managers must determine what standards will be used to measure quality care in their units and then develop and implement quality control programs that measure results against those standards. All managers are responsible for monitoring the quality of the product that their units produce; in health-care organizations, that product is patient care. Managers too must assess and promote patient satisfaction whenever possible.

The manager, however, cannot operate in a vacuum in determining what quality is and how it should be measured. This determination should come from research-based evidence. Demands for hard data on quality have increased as regulatory bodies, patients, payers, and hospital managers have required justification for services provided. Managers must be cognizant of rapidly changing quality control regulations and proactively adjust unit standards to meet these changing needs. Until 2 decades ago, limited attention was given to quality measurement in health care. As we enter the 21st century, however, there is an ever-increasing focus on the quality of care and the standardization of quality data collection and an increased accountability for outcomes from the system level to the individual provider.

Inspiring subordinates to establish and achieve high standards of care is a leadership skill. Leaders are a role model for high standards in their own nursing care and encourage subordinates to seek maximum rather than minimum standards. One way that this can be accomplished is by involving subordinates in the quality control process. By studying direct cause–effect relationships, subordinates learn to modify individual and group performance to improve the quality of care provided.

Vision is another leadership skill inherent in quality control. The visionary leader looks at what is and determines what should be. This future focus allows leaders to shape organizational goals proactively and improve the quality of care. Moreover, the integrated leader-manager in quality control must be willing to be a risk-taker and to be accountable. In an era of limited resources and cost-containment, there is great pressure to sacrifice quality in an effort to contain costs. The self-aware leader-manager recognizes this risk and seeks to achieve a balance between quality and cost-containment that does not violate professional obligations to patients and subordinates.

Winning the war to improve health care will require sustained public interest to create the momentum to systematically change the health-care system in a way that improves quality. Increasing consumer knowledge and participation in health care will be imperative in this effort. In addition, change agents must be able to successfully address the disconnection that still exists between consumers' perceptions of the quality of their own care and the actual quality provided. This dialogue has only just begun.

KEY CONCEPTS

- Controlling is implemented throughout all phases of management.
- Quality control refers to activities that are used to evaluate, monitor, or regulate services rendered to consumers.
- A standard is a predetermined baseline condition or level of excellence that constitutes a model to be followed and practiced.
- Because there is no one set of standards, each organization and profession must set standards and objectives to guide individual practitioners in performing safe and effective care.
- CPGs provide diagnosis-based, step-by-step interventions for nurses to follow in an effort to promote evidence-based, high-quality care and yet control resource utilization and costs.
- Benchmarking is the process of measuring products, practices, and services against those of best-performing organizations.
- The difference in performance between top-performing health-care organizations and the national average is called the quality gap. While the quality gap is typically small in industries such as manufacturing, aviation, and banking, wide variation is the norm in health care.
- CEA and RCA help to identify not only what and how an event happened but why it happened, with the end goal being to ensure that a preventable negative outcome does not recur.

- Outcome audits determine what results, if any, followed from specific nursing interventions for patients.

- Process audits are used to measure the process of care or how the care was carried out.

- Structure audits monitor the structure or setting in which patient care occurs (such as the finances, nursing service structure, medical records, and environmental structure).

- There is growing recognition that it is possible to separate the contribution of nursing to the patient's outcome; this recognition of outcomes that are nursing-sensitive creates accountability for nurses as professionals and is important in developing nursing as a profession.

- Standardized nursing languages provide a consistent terminology for nurses to describe and document their assessments, interventions, and the outcomes of their actions.

- Quality assurance models seek to ensure that quality currently exists, whereas QI models assume that the process is ongoing and that quality can always be improved.

- Quality control in health-care organizations has evolved primarily from external forces and not as a voluntary effort to monitor the quality of services provided.

- Critics of the PPS argue that although DRGs may have helped to contain rising health-care costs, the associated rapid declines in length of hospital stay and services provided have resulted in declines in quality of care.

- The JC is the major accrediting body for health-care organizations and programs in the United States. It also administers the ORYX initiative and collects data on core measures in an effort to better standardize data collection across acute-care hospitals.

- The CMS plays an active role in setting standards for and measuring quality in health care including the HQI and P4P.

- The 27-item HCAHPS survey is the first national, standardized, publicly reported survey of patients' perspectives of hospital care. It measures recently discharged patients' perceptions of their hospital experience.

- The NCQA, a private nonprofit organization that accredits managed care organizations, also developed the HEDIS to compare quality of care in managed care organizations.

- Ideally, everyone in an organization should participate in quality control activities.

- In response to the demand for objective measures of quality, a number of health plans, health-care providers, employer purchasing groups, consumer information organizations, and state governments have begun to formulate health-care quality report cards.

- A plethora of studies across the past 2 decades suggest that medical errors continue to be rampant in the health-care system.

- The Patient Safety and Quality Improvement Act, signed into law in 2005, protects medical error information that is voluntarily submitted to new private organizations (patient safety organizations) from being subpoenaed or used in legal discovery and generally requires that the information is treated as confidential.

- The Leapfrog Group identified four evidence-based standards that they believe will provide the greatest impact on reducing medical errors: CPOE, EHR, IPS, and the use of Leapfrog Safe Practices scores.

- The FDA has suggested that a drug bar code system coupled with a computerized order entry system would greatly decrease the risk of medication errors.

- Historically, the health-care industry has been comfortable with striving for three sigma processes (all data points fall within 3 standard deviations) in terms of health-care quality instead of six (that are adopted by the highest-performing organizations in terms of quality).

- As direct caregivers, staff nurses are in an excellent position to monitor nursing practice by identifying problems and implementing corrective actions that have the greatest impact on patient care.

ADDITIONAL LEARNING EXERCISES AND APPLICATIONS

LEARNING EXERCISE 23.5

Identifying Nursing-Sensitive Outcome Criteria

Some patients get better despite nursing care, not as a result of it. However, the quality of nursing care can affect patient outcomes tremendously. Do you believe that quality nursing care makes a difference in patients' lives? Identify five criteria that you would use to define *quality nursing care*. These criteria should reflect what you believe nurses do (nursing-sensitive) that makes the difference in patient outcomes. Are the criteria you listed measurable?

LEARNING EXERCISE 23.6

Working Short Staffed—Again

You are a staff nurse at Mercy Hospital. The hospital's patient census and acuity have been very high for the last 6 months. Many of the nursing staff have resigned; a coordinated recruitment effort to refill these positions has been largely unsuccessful. The nursing staff is demoralized, and staff frequently call in sick or fail to show up for work. Today, you arrive at work and find that you are again being asked to work short-handed. You will be the only RN on a unit with 30 patients. Although you have two licensed professional nurses/licensed vocational nurses and two certified nursing assistants assigned to work with you, you are concerned that patient safety could be compromised. A check with the central nursing office ascertains that no additional help can be obtained.

You feel that you have reached the end of your rope. The administration at Mercy Hospital has been receptive to employee feedback about the acute staffing shortage, and you believe that they have made some efforts to try to alleviate the problem. You also believe, however, that the efforts have not been at the level they should have been and that the hospital will continue to expect nurses to work short-handed until some major force changes things. Although you have thought about quitting, you really enjoy the work that you do and feel morally obligated to your coworkers, the patients, and even your superiors. Today, it occurs to you that you could anonymously phone the state licensing bureau and turn in Mercy Hospital for consistent understaffing of nursing personnel, leading to unsafe patient care. You believe that this could be the impetus needed to improve the quality of care. You are also aware of the action's political risks.

Assignment: Discuss whether you would take this action. What is your responsibility to the organization, to yourself, and to patients? How do you make decisions such as this one, which have conflicting moral obligations?

LEARNING EXERCISE 23.7

Examining Mortality Rates

You have been the nursing coordinator of cardiac services at a medium-sized urban hospital for the last 6 months. Among the hospital's cardiac services are open-heart surgery, invasive and noninvasive diagnostic testing, and a comprehensive rehabilitation program. The open-heart surgery program was implemented a little over a year ago. During the last 3 months, you have begun to feel uneasy about the mortality rate of postoperative cardiac patients at your facility. An audit of medical records shows a unit mortality rate that is approximately 30% above national norms. You approach the unit medical director with your findings. He becomes defensive and states that there have been a few freakish situations to skew the results but that the open-heart program is one of the best in the state. When you question him about examining the statistics further, he becomes very angry and turns to leave the room. At the door, he stops and says, "Remember that these patients are leaving the operating room alive. They are dying on your unit. If you stir up trouble, you are going to be sorry."

Assignment: Outline your plan. Identify areas in your data gathering that may have been misleading or that may have skewed your findings. If you believe action is still warranted, what are the personal and professional risks involved? How well developed is your power base to undertake these risks? To whom do you have the greatest responsibility?

LEARNING EXERCISE 23.8

Weighing Conflicting Obligations

You are the unit supervisor of a medical–surgical unit. Shauna, an RN on your unit, who graduated 3 years ago from nursing school, has made a number of small errors in the past few months, all of which she has voluntarily reported. These errors included things like missing medications, giving medications late, and on one occasion, giving medications to the wrong patient. No apparent harm has occurred to her patients as a result of these errors and on each occasion, Shauna has responded to your coaching efforts with an assertion that she will be more attentive and careful in the future.

Today, however, Shauna came to your office to admit that she flushed a patient's IV line with 10,000 units of heparin rather than with the 100 units that was ordered. The vials looked similar and she failed to notice the dosing on the label. Shauna reported the error to the patient's physician and filled out the adverse incident report form required by the hospital on all medication errors. At this point, the patient is demonstrating no ill effects from the overdosing, but will need to be monitored closely for the next 24 hours.

You recognize that Shauna's pattern of repetitive medication errors is placing patients at risk. You have some reservations, however, about dealing with Shauna in a punitive way since she openly reports the errors she makes and because none of her errors until today had really jeopardized patient safety. You are also aware, however, that you have an obligation to make sure that the staff caring for your patients are competent and that patients are protected from harm. You are also attempting to establish a unit culture that encourages open reporting, not "shame and blame," so you are aware that your staff are watching closely how you will respond to yet another error on Shauna's part.

Assignment: What will you do to address this error as well as the errors Shauna has made in the past few months? What options are available to you? What obligations do you have to Shauna, to the organization, and to the patients on your unit? How will you create a culture that encourages the open reporting of errors and yet protects patients from potentially unsafe practitioners?

LEARNING EXERCISE 23.9

Avoiding Adverse Events and Medication Errors

Assignment: Interview the patient safety officer or the manager of the risk management department at your local hospital. Use the following questions as a guide to begin the interview. Present a report to your peers regarding your findings.

1. What are the most common causes of medication errors in this facility?

(Continued)

2. Which medications are more commonly involved in medication errors? What factors has this agency identified that cause these errors to occur?

3. What are the most common adverse events affecting patients? What precipitating factors have been identified as increasing the possibility of these adverse events?

4. What new technologies have been adopted to increase patient safety? Examples might be IV smart pumps, bar coding of medications, and computerized physician–provider order entry.

5. How are medication errors or adverse events reported? What safeguards have been built in to encourage voluntary reporting of errors? Do disincentives exist that would discourage someone from reporting such an error?

6. Are staff included in the quality control process? If so, how?

7. For which of the JC core measures are data being collected? What is the process for this data collection?

LEARNING EXERCISE 23.10

Quality Topics for Group Discussion

Assignment: Select one of the topics below for small or large group debate. Generate as many perspectives as possible.

- Support or oppose the proposition that quality in health care should be quantitatively measurable.

- Support or oppose the proposition that public and private sector initiatives during the past 3 decades have been successful in lowering health-care costs while maintaining quality.

- Support or oppose the proposition that traditional natural science study designs, such as the experimental method, are the most appropriate models for testing hypotheses about quality and health-care delivery.

- Support or oppose the proposition that quality in health care should be measured more by client satisfaction than by traditional outcome measures.

- Support or oppose the proposition that downsizing (layoffs of professional RNs) and the increased use of unlicensed assistive personnel are currently affecting the quality of patient care negatively.

LEARNING EXERCISE 23.11

Tracking Down an Infection through Root Cause Analysis

You work in a small, long-term care facility and are often the only RN working on the unit. Many of your patients have indwelling Foley catheters. Recently, several patients have developed bladder infections, after having a unit nosocomial urinary tract infection (UTI) rate of less than 1% for the past year. In fact, the facility has always prided itself on carefully following established evidence-based policies and procedures, both in catheter insertion and in routine catheter care. When you talk to the Chief Nursing Officer about the problem, she asks you to investigate the problem and report back to her. You decide to sit down and make a list of the structure and process indicators you could examine in an attempt to find the cause of the problem.

Assignment: Identify at least eight process and structure variables you could use to determine the cause(s) of the spike in nosocomially acquired UTIs in the facility. Then develop a quality evaluation plan for one of these variables. What data will you collect? What steps will you implement to carry out this quality audit?

REFERENCES

Agency for Healthcare Research and Quality. (2013). *National guideline clearing house.* Retrieved June 23, 2013, from http://www.guideline.gov/about/index.aspx

American Nurses Association. (2010). *Scope and standards of practice* (2nd ed.). Silver Spring, MD: American Nurses Association.

American Nurses Association. (2009). *Nursing administration. Scope & standards of practice.* Silver Springs, MD: Nursesbooks.org

American Nurses Association. (2013a). *Nursing standards.* Retrieved June 24, 2013, from http://nursingworld.org/MainMenuCategories/ThePracticeofProfessionalNursing/NursingStandards.aspx

American Nurses Association. (2013b). *Call for public comment. Nursing: Scope & standards of practice.* Retrieved June 23, 2013, from http://www.nursingworld.org/HomepageCategory/NursingInsider/Archive_1/2010-NI/Jan10-NI/Public-Comment-Nursing-Scope-Standards.aspx

American Society for Quality. (n.d.). *Quality tools. Failure modes and effects analysis (FMEA).* Retrieved June 23, 2013, from http://asq.org/learn-about-quality/process-analysis-tools/overview/fmea.html

Deming, W. E. (1986). *Out of the crisis.* Cambridge, MA: MIT Press.

Facilitators and Barriers to the Use of Clinical Practice Guidelines. (2012). *AORN Journal, 96*(6), 668–669.

HCAHPS Fact Sheet. (2012). *CAHPS–A registered trademark of AHRQ.* Retrieved June 24, 2013, from http://www.hcahpsonline.org/files/HCAHPS%20Fact%20Sheet%20May%202012.pdf

Healthgrades. (2008, April 8). *Medical errors cost U.S. $8.8 billion, result in 238,337 potentially preventable deaths according to HealthGrades Study.* Retrieved March 14, 2010, from http://www.healthgrades.com/media/DMS/pdf/HealthGradesPatientSafetyRelease2008.pdf

Healthgrades. (2013). *American Hospital Quality Outcomes 2013: Healthgrades report to the nation Executive summary.* Retrieved June 24, 2013, from http://c773731.r31.cf2.rackcdn.com/d0/ce/09b1df7b4fb4960b69dcb50313e3/Healthgrades%20American%20Hospital%20Quality%20Report%202013.pdf

Hospital Quality Initiative Overview. (2008, July). *Centers for Medicare & Medicaid Services.* Retrieved June 24, 2013, from http://www.cms.hhs.gov/HospitalQualityInits/Downloads/Hospitaloverview.pdf

Huston, C. (2014). Medical errors: An ongoing threat to quality health care. In C. Huston (Ed.), *Professional issues in nursing: Challenges and opportunities* (3rd ed.). Philadelphia, PA: Lippincott Williams & Wilkins 228–248.

Institute of Medicine. (1994). *America's health in transition: Protecting and improving quality.* Washington, DC: National Academy Press.

International Council of Nurses. (2009, January 26). *International Classification for Nursing Practice (ICNP®) now included as a related classification in the WHO Family of International Classifications.* Retrieved June 23, 2013, from http://www.icn.ch/images/stories/documents/news/press_releases/2009_PR_03_ICNP_now_included_as_a_Related_Classification_in_the_WHO_Family_of_International_Classifications.pdf

(The) Joint Commission. (2013a). *Facts about the joint commission.* Retrieved June 24, 2013, from http://www.jointcommission.org/about_us/fact_sheets.aspx

(The) Joint Commission. (2013b). *Facts about ORYX® for hospitals (National Hospital Quality Measures).* Retrieved June 24, 2013, from http://www.jointcommission.org/facts_about_oryx_for_hospitals/

(The) Joint Commission. (2013c). *Sentinel event policy and procedures.* Retrieved June 24, 2013, from http://www.jointcommission.org/Sentinel_Event_Policy_and_Procedures/

(The) Joint Commission. (2013d). *2013 hospital national patient safety goals.* Retrieved June 25, 2013, from http://www.jointcommission.org/assets/1/6/2013_HAP_NPSG_final_10-23.pdf

(The) Joint Commission. (2012). *Using national patient safety goals effective January 1, 2013.* Retrieved June 24, 2013, from http://www.jointcommission.org/assets/1/18/NPSG_Chapter_Jan2013_HAP.pdf

Kohn, L. T., Corrigan, J. M., & Donaldson, M. S. (Eds.) (2000). Executive summary In: *To err is human: Building a safer health system* (pp. 1–6). Retrieved August 22, 2013, from http://www.nap.edu/openbook.php?record_id=9728&page=R1

Landro, L. (2010, March 16). *New focus on averting errors: Hospital culture.* Wall Street Journal–Digital Network. Health. Retrieved March 17, 2010, from http://online.wsj.com/article/SB10001424052748704588404575123500096433436.html?mod=WSJ_hps_MIDDLEThirdNews.

Leapfrog Group. (2013). *The Leapfrog Group fact sheet.* Retrieved June 24, 2013, from http://www.leapfroggroup.org/about_us/leapfrog-factsheet

National Association of School Nurses. (2012). *Standardized nursing languages.* Retrieved June 23, 2013, from http://www.nasn.org/PolicyAdvocacy/PositionPapersandReports/NASNPositionStatementsFullView/tabid/462/ArticleId/48/Standardized-Nursing-Languages-Revised-June-2012

National Committee for Quality Assurance. (2013). *HEDIS and performance measurement. Measuring performance.* Retrieved June 23, 2013, from http://www.ncqa.org/tabid/59/Default.aspx

Newhouse, R. P. (2010, February). Clinical guidelines for nursing practice. Are we there yet? *Journal of Nursing Administration, 40*(2), 57–59.

Parkerton, P. H., Needleman, J., Pearson, M. L., Upenieks, V. V., Soban, L. M., & Yee, T. (2009, November). Lessons from nursing leaders on implementing TCAB. *American Journal of Nursing, 109*(11), 71–76.

Pay for Performance: An Overview. (January 20, 2011). *Healthcare economist.* Retrieved June 23, 2013, from http://healthcare-economist.com/2011/01/20/pay-for-performance-an-overview/

Study Links HCAHPS, Readmission Rates. (2013). *Hospital Case Management, 21*(2), 25.

The Joint Commission Expands Performance Measurement Requirements. (2013). *Healthcare Purchasing News, 37*(1), 6.

Toyota Motor Company (n.d.). *Toyota production system.* Toyota Motor Corporation. Retrieved June 24, 2013, from http://www.toyota.com.au/toyota/company/operations/toyota-production-system

Wachter, R. (2010, January). Patient safety at ten: Unmistakable progress, troubling gaps. *Health Affairs, 29*(1), 165–173.

Wisconsin Hospital Association. (2003–2013). *What is the Maryland quality indicator project?* Retrieved June 24, 2013, from http://www.wha.org/marylandQIP.aspx

24

Performance Appraisal

... it is a paradoxical but profoundly true and important principle of life that the most likely way to reach a goal is to be aiming not at that goal itself but at some more ambitious goal beyond it.

−Arnold Toynbee

... performance stands out like a ton of diamonds. Non-performance can always be explained away.

−Harold S. Geneen

CROSSWALK THIS CHAPTER ADDRESSES:

BSN Essential II: Basic organizational and systems leadership for quality care and patient safety

MSN Essential II: Organizational and systems leadership

MSN Essential VII: Interprofessional collaboration for improving patient and population health outcomes

QSEN Competency: Teamwork and collaboration

QSEN Competency: Safety

AONE Nurse Executive Competency I: Communication and relationship building

AONE Nurse Executive Competency II: A knowledge of the health-care environment

AONE Nurse Executive Competency III: Leadership

AONE Nurse Executive Competency V: Business skills

LEARNING OBJECTIVES *The learner will:*

- identify and use appropriate performance appraisal tools for measuring professional nursing performance
- identify factors that increase the likelihood that a performance appraisal will develop and motivate staff
- provide feedback regarding peer performance in a constructive and assertive manner
- avoid the halo effect, horns effect, and central tendency errors in conducting performance appraisals
- recognize subjectivity as an ever-present limitation of the performance appraisal process
- describe coaching techniques that promote employee growth in work performance
- gather data for performance appraisals in a systematic manner that is fair and objective
- develop an awareness of biases that influence a person's ability to complete a fair and objective performance appraisal
- differentiate between performance appraisal tools such as rating scales, checklists, essays, self-appraisal, and management by objectives (MBOs)
- identify what conditions should be present before, during, and after the performance appraisal that increase the likelihood of a positive outcome

An important managerial controlling responsibility is determining how well employees carry out the duties of their assigned jobs. This is done through *performance appraisals*, in which work performance is reviewed. Performance appraisals let employees know the level of their job performance as well as any expectations that the organization may have of them. Performance appraisals also generate information for salary adjustments, promotions, transfers, disciplinary actions, and terminations.

In performance appraisals, actual performance, not intent, is evaluated.

None of the manager's actions is as personal as appraising the work performance of others. Because work is an important part of one's identity, people are very sensitive to opinions about how they perform. For this reason, performance appraisal becomes one of the greatest tools an organization has to develop and motivate staff. When used correctly, it can encourage staff and increase retention and productivity; however, in the hands of an inept or inexperienced manager, the appraisal process may significantly discourage and demotivate workers.

In addition, because a manager's opinions and judgments are used for far-reaching decisions regarding the employee's work life, they must be determined in an objective, systematic, and formalized manner as possible. Using a formal system of performance review reduces, but does not eliminate, the appraisal's subjectivity. In addition, the more professional a group of employees is, the more complex and sensitive the evaluation process becomes. The skilled leader-manager who uses a formalized system for the appraisal is better able to build a team approach to patient care.

This chapter focuses on the relationship between performance appraisal and motivation and discusses how performance appraisals can be used to determine the developmental needs of the staff. Emphasis is placed on appropriate data gathering and the types of performance appraisal tools available. The performance appraisal interview is explored, and strategies are presented for reducing appraiser bias and increasing the likelihood that the appraisal itself will be growth-producing. Finally, performance management is introduced as an alternative to the traditional annual performance appraisal. The leadership roles and management functions inherent in successful performance appraisal are shown in Display 24.1.

DISPLAY 24.1	Leadership Roles and Management Functions Associated with Performance Appraisal

LEADERSHIP ROLES

1. Uses the appraisal process to motivate employees and promote growth.
2. Uses appropriate techniques to reduce the anxiety inherent in the appraisal process.
3. Involves employees in all aspects of performance appraisal.
4. Is aware of own biases and prejudices so as to eliminate their influence in the performance appraisal process.
5. Develops employee trust by being honest and fair when evaluating performance.
6. Encourages the peer review process among professional staff.
7. Uses appraisal interviews to facilitate two-way communication.
8. Provides ongoing support to employees who are attempting to correct performance deficiencies.
9. Uses coaching techniques that promote employee growth in work performance.
10. Individualizes performance goals and the appraisal interview as needed to meet the unique needs of a culturally diverse staff.

MANAGEMENT FUNCTIONS

1. Uses a formalized system of performance appraisal.
2. Gathers fair and objective data throughout the evaluation period to use in employee's performance appraisals.

3. Uses the appraisal process to determine staff education and training needs.
4. Bases performance appraisal on documented standards.
5. Is as objective as possible in performance appraisal.
6. Maintains appropriate documentation of the appraisal process.
7. Follows up on identified performance deficiencies.
8. Conducts the appraisal interview in a manner that promotes a positive outcome.
9. Provides frequent informal feedback on work performance.

USING THE PERFORMANCE APPRAISAL TO MOTIVATE EMPLOYEES

Although systematic employee appraisals have been used in management since the 1920s, using the appraisal as a tool to promote employee growth did not begin until the 1950s. This evolution of performance appraisals is reflected in its changing terminology. At one time, the appraisal was called a *merit rating* and was tied fairly closely to salary increases. More recently, it was termed *performance evaluation*, but because the term *evaluation* implies that personal values are being placed on the performance review, that term is used infrequently. Some organizations continue to use both of these terms or others, such as *competency assessment, effectiveness report*, and *service rating*. Most health-care organizations, however, use the term *performance appraisal*, because this term implies an appraisal of how well employees perform the duties of their job as delineated by the job description or some other prespecified criteria.

An important point to consider, if the appraisal is to have a positive outcome, is how the employee views the appraisal. Indeed, Mulvaney, McKinney, and Grodsky (2012) note that both employees and management often view the performance appraisal process as frustrating and unfair. These frustrations are largely attributed to a reliance on performance appraisal instruments that are not job related; have confusing or unclear rating levels; and are viewed as subjective and biased by staff. The result is that both the administration and staff often come to view the performance appraisal process as a painful, annual exercise (Mulvaney et al.). Price (2013) concurs, noting that many managers feel the annual performance appraisal is treated as something of a paper exercise.

Management research has shown that various factors influence whether the appraisal ultimately results in increased motivation and productivity. Some of these factors include the following:

- The employee must believe that the appraisal is based on a standard to which other employees in the same classification are held accountable. This standard must be communicated clearly to employees at the time they are hired and may be a job description or an individual goal set by staff for the purpose of performance appraisal.

- The employee must believe that the appraisal tool adequately and accurately assesses performance criteria directly related to his or her job. For example, Olmstead, Falcone, Lopez, Sharpe, and Michna (2012) shared the story of an Indiana hospital that used a hospital-wide evaluation tool related to the hospital mission statement goals. This tool rated employees on vague criteria such as dignity, quality, and compassion. As a result, the employees regularly challenged managers' evaluations, arguing that the rating categories in the evaluation tool had little to do with actual performance or job requirements.

- The employee should have some input into developing the standards or goals on which his or her performance is judged. This is imperative for the professional employee.

- The employee must know in advance what happens if the expected performance standards are not met.

- The employee needs to know how information will be obtained to determine performance. The appraisal tends to be more accurate if various sources and types of information are solicited. Sources could include peers, coworkers, nursing care plans, patients, and personal observation. Employees should be told which sources will be used and how such information will be weighted.

- The appraiser should be one of the employee's direct supervisors. For example, the charge nurse who works directly with the staff nurse should be involved in the appraisal process and interview. It is appropriate and advisable in most instances for the head nurse and supervisor also to be involved. However, employees must believe that the person doing the major portion of the review has actually observed their work.

- The performance appraisal is more likely to have a positive outcome if the appraiser is viewed with trust and professional respect. This increases the chance that the employee will view the appraisal as a fair and accurate assessment of his or her work performance. A summary of the factors influencing the effectiveness of appraisals can be seen in Display 24.2.

If employees believe that the appraisal is based on their job description rather than on whether the manager approves of them, they are more likely to view the appraisal as relevant.

DISPLAY 24.2	Factors Influencing Effective Performance Appraisal

Appraisal should be based on a standard.
The appraisal tool must adequately and accurately assesses job performance.
Employee should have input into development of the standard.
Employee must know the standard in advance.
Employee must know the sources of data gathered for the appraisal.
Appraiser should be someone who has observed the employee's work.
Appraiser should be someone who the employee trusts and respects.

LEARNING EXERCISE 24.1

Writing about Performance Appraisals

During your lifetime, you probably have had many performance appraisals. These may have been evaluations of your clinical performance during nursing school or as a paid employee. Reflect on these appraisals. How many of them encompassed the six recommendations listed in Display 24.2? How did the inclusion or exclusion of these recommendations influence your acceptance of the results?

Assignment: Select one of the above six recommendations about which you feel strongly. Write a three-paragraph essay about your personal experience as it relates to these recommendations.

STRATEGIES TO ENSURE ACCURACY AND FAIRNESS IN THE PERFORMANCE APPRAISAL

If the goal of the performance appraisal is to satisfy the requirements of the organization, then the performance appraisal is a waste of time. On the other hand, if the employee views the appraisal as valuable, valid and growth-producing, it can have many positive effects. Information obtained during the performance appraisal can be used to develop the employee's potential, to assist the employee in overcoming difficulties that he or she has in fulfilling the job's role, to point out strengths of which the employee may not be aware, and to aid the employee in setting goals.

A performance appraisal wastes time if it is merely an excuse to satisfy regulations and the goal is not employee growth.

Because inaccurate and unfair appraisals are negative and can demotivate, it is critical that the manager use strategies that increase the likelihood of a fair and accurate appraisal. Although some subjectivity is inescapable, the following strategies will assist the manager in arriving at a fairer and more accurate assessment:

1. *The appraiser should develop an awareness of his or her own biases and prejudices.* This helps to guard against subjective attitudes and values influencing the appraisal. The appraiser must always recognize though that all employee reviews involve some subjectivity and Bacal (2013) suggests that we need to stop pretending that our ways of evaluating employee performance are objective.

2. *Consultation should be sought frequently.* Another manager should be consulted when a question about personal bias exists and in many other situations. For example, it is very important that new managers solicit assistance and consultation when they complete their first performance appraisals. Even experienced managers may need to consult with others when an employee is having great difficulty fulfilling the duties of the job. Consultation must also be used when employees work several shifts so that information can be obtained from all of the shift supervisors.

3. *Data should be gathered appropriately.* Many different sources should be consulted about employee performance and the data gathered needs to reflect the entire time period of the appraisal. Frequently, managers gather data and observe an employee just before completing the appraisal, which gives an inaccurate picture of performance. Because all employees have periods when they are less productive and motivated, data should be gathered systematically and regularly.

4. *Accurate record-keeping is another critical part of ensuring accuracy and fairness in the performance appraisal.* Information about subordinate performance (both positive and negative) should be recorded and not trusted to memory. The recording of both positive and negative performance behavior throughout the performance period is also known as *critical incident* recording. The manager should make a habit of keeping notes about observations, others' comments, and his or her periodic review of charts and nursing care plans. Taking regular notes on employee performance is a way to avoid the *recency effect*, which favors appraisal of recent performance over less recent performance during the evaluation period.

When ongoing anecdotal notes are not maintained throughout the evaluation period, the appraiser is more apt to experience the recency effect, where recent issues are weighed more heavily than past performance.

5. *Collected assessments should contain positive examples of growth and achievement and areas where development is needed.* Nothing delights employees more than discovering that their immediate supervisor is aware of their growth and accomplishments and can cite specific instances in which good clinical judgment was used. Too frequently, collected data concentrate on negative aspects of performance. Bacal (2013) agrees, noting that the performance appraisal should move away from "evaluating" the past and move toward improving success in the future.

6. *Some effort must be made to include the employee's own appraisal of his or her work.* Self-appraisal may be performed in several appropriate ways. Employees can be

instructed to come to the appraisal interview with some informal thoughts about their performance, or they can work with their managers in completing a joint assessment. One advantage of *management by objectives* (MBOs)—the use of personalized goals to measure individual performance—is the manner in which it involves the employee in assessing his or her work performance and in goal-setting.

7. The appraiser needs to guard against three common pitfalls of assessment: the *halo effect*, the *horns effect*, and *central tendency*. The halo effect occurs when the appraiser lets one or two positive aspects of the assessment or behavior of the employee unduly influence all other aspects of the employee's performance. The horns effect occurs when the appraiser allows some negative aspects of the employee's performance to influence the assessment to such an extent that other levels of job performance are not accurately recorded. Mackenzie (2013, p. 453) notes that "rating employees more severely than their performance merits will frustrate and discourage workers who will resent unfair assessment of their performance. Likewise, rating employees more favorably than their performance merits cheats them and the department of the benefits of exploring areas for improvement and the opportunities for developing and coaching."

   The manager who falls into the central tendency trap is hesitant to risk true assessment and therefore rates all employees as average. These appraiser behaviors lead employees to discount the entire assessment of their work. Accel-Team (2013) states that some managers equivocate on performance appraisal ratings for fear that subordinates given a high rating may expect immediate rewards and that employees given low ratings will cause trouble. "In such instances, formal performance evaluation reviews have negative consequences, in that they don't just summarize past performance, they can shape future performance" (Accel-Team, para 6).

8. *Finally, reviewers need to guard against a bias known as the Matthew effect.* The *Matthew effect* is said to occur when employees receive the same appraisal results, year after year. Those who performed well early in their employment are likely to do well. Those who struggled will continue to struggle. Often the Matthew effect is compared with the adage "the rich get richer and the poor get poorer." Thus, past appraisals prejudice an employee's future attempts to improve. Display 24.3 provides a summary of performance appraisal strategies.

DISPLAY 24.3   Strategies to Ensure Performance Appraisal Accuracy

Develop self-awareness regarding own biases and prejudices.
Use appropriate consultation.
Gather data adequately over time.
Keep accurate anecdotal records for the length of the appraisal period.
Collect positive data and identify areas where improvement is needed.
Include employee's own appraisal of his or her performance.
Guard against the halo effect, horns effect, central tendency trap, and Matthew effect.

LEARNING EXERCISE 24.2

Planning an Employee's First Performance Appraisal

Mrs. Jones is a new licensed vocational nurse (LVN)/licensed practical nurse (LPN) and has been working the 3 PM to 11 PM shift on the long-term care unit where you are the evening charge nurse. It is time for her 3-month performance appraisal. In your facility, each employee's job description is used as the standard of measure for performance appraisal. Essentially, you believe that Mrs. Jones is performing her job well, but you are somewhat concerned because she still relies on the registered nurses (RNs) even for minor patient care decisions. Although you are glad that she does not act completely on her own, you would like to see her become more independent. The patients have commented favorably to you on Mrs. Jones's compassion and on her follow-through on all their requests and needs.

Mrs. Jones gets along well with the other LVNs/LPNs, and you sometimes believe that they take advantage of her hard-working and pleasant nature. On a few occasions, you believe that they inappropriately delegated some of their work to her. When preparing for Mrs. Jones's upcoming evaluation, what can you do to make the appraisal as objective as possible? You want Mrs. Jones's first evaluation to be growth-producing.

Assignment: Plan how you will proceed. What positive forces are already present in this scenario? What negative forces will you have to overcome? Support your plan with readings from References at the end of this chapter.

PERFORMANCE APPRAISAL TOOLS

Since the 1920s, many appraisal tools have been developed, all of which have been popular at different times. Since the early 1990s, the Joint Commission has been advocating the use of an employee's job description as the standard for performance appraisal. Bacal (2013) cautions, however, that job descriptions may be a poor source for setting employee goals since they are often outdated by the time they are on paper. Instead Bacal suggests that employees be allowed to flesh out job description tasks and to set goals which more specifically address the employee's specific strengths and weaknesses.

The Joint Commission also suggests that employers must be able to demonstrate that employees know how to plan, implement, and evaluate care specific to the ages of the patients they care for. This continual refinement of critical *competencies* for professional nursing practice has a tremendous impact on the tools used in the appraisal process. It is important to remember, however, that competence assessments are not the same as performance evaluations. A *competence assessment* evaluates skill and knowledge; a *performance evaluation* evaluates execution of a task or tasks.

A competence assessment evaluates whether an individual has the knowledge, education, skills, or experience to perform the task, whereas a performance evaluation examines how well that individual actually completes that task.

The effectiveness of a performance appraisal system is only as good as the tools used to create those assessments. An effective competence assessment tool should allow the manager to focus on the priority measures of performance. The following is an overview of some of the appraisal tools commonly used in health-care organizations.

Trait Rating Scales

A *trait rating scale* is a method of rating a person against a set standard, which may be the job description, desired behaviors, or personal traits. The trait rating scale has been one of the most widely used of the many available appraisal methods. Rating personal traits and behaviors is the oldest type of rating scale. Many experts argue, however, that the quality or quantity of the work performed is a more accurate performance appraisal method than the employee's personal traits and that trait evaluation invites subjectivity. Rating scales are also subject to central tendency and halo- and horns-effect errors and thus are not used as often today as they were in the past. Instead, many organizations use two other rating methods, namely, the job dimension scale and the *behaviorally anchored rating scale* (BARS). Display 24.4 shows a portion of a trait rating scale with examples of traits that might be expected in an RN.

DISPLAY 24.4 Sample Trait Rating Scale

Job Knowledge

Serious gaps in essential knowledge	Satisfactory knowledge of routine	Adequately informed on most phases of the job	Good knowledge of all phases of the job	Excellent understanding of the job
1	2	3	4	5

Judgment

Decisions are often wrong on issues	Makes some decision errors	Good decisions	Sound and logical thinker	Makes good, complex decisions
1	2	3	4	5

Attitude

Resents suggestions, no enthusiasm, new ideas accepted reluctantly	Disengaged but cooperative and accepting	Generally cooperative and accepting of new ideas	Openly cooperates and accepts new ideas	Consistently helpful and offers new ideas
1	2	3	4	5

Job Dimension Scales

Job dimension scales require that a rating scale be constructed for each job classification. The rating factors are taken from the context of the written job description. Although job dimension scales share some of the same weaknesses as trait scales, they do focus on job requirements rather than on ambiguous terms such as "quantity of work." Display 24.5 shows an example of a job dimension scale for an industrial nurse.

DISPLAY 24.5 Sample Job Dimension Rating Scale for an Industrial Nurse

JOB DIMENSION 5 4 3 2 1

Renders first aid and treats job-related injuries and illnesses
Holds fitness classes for workers
Teaches health and nutrition classes
Performs yearly physicals on workers
Keeps equipment in good working order and maintains inventory
Keeps appropriate records
Dispenses medication and treatment for minor injuries
(5 = excellent; 4 = good; 3 = satisfactory; 2 = fair; 1 = poor)

Behaviorally Anchored Rating Scales

BARS, sometimes called *behavioral expectation scales*, overcome some of the weaknesses inherent in other rating systems. As in the job dimension method, the BARS technique requires that a separate rating form be developed for each job classification. Then, as in the job dimension rating scales, employees in specific positions work with management to delineate key areas of responsibility. However, in BARS, many specific examples are defined for each area of responsibility; these examples are given various degrees of importance by ranking them from 1 to 9. If the highest-ranked example of a job dimension is being met, it is less important than a lower-ranked example that is not.

Appraisal tools firmly grounded in desired behaviors can be used to improve performance and keep employees focused on the vision and mission of the organization. However, because separate BARS are needed for each job, the greatest disadvantage in using this tool with large numbers of employees is the time and expense. Additionally, BARS are primarily applicable to physically observable skills rather than to conceptual skills. Yet, this is an effective tool, because it focuses on specific behaviors, allows employees to know exactly what is expected of them, and reduces rating errors.

Although all rating scales are prone to weaknesses and interpersonal bias, they do have some advantages. Many may be purchased, and although they must be individualized to the organization, there is little need for expensive worker hours to develop them. Rating scales also force the rater to look at more than one dimension of work performance, which eliminates some bias.

Checklists

There are several types of *checklist* appraisal tools. The *weighted scale*, the most frequently used checklist, is composed of many behavioral statements that represent desirable job behaviors. Each of these behavior statements has a weighted score attached to it. Employees receive an overall performance appraisal score based on behaviors or attributes. Often, merit raises are tied to the total point score (i.e., the employee needs to reach a certain score to receive an increase in pay).

Another type of checklist, the *forced checklist*, requires the supervisor to select an undesirable and a desirable behavior for each employee. Both desirable and undesirable behaviors have quantitative values, and the employee again ends up with a total score on which certain employment decisions are made.

Another type of checklist is the *simple checklist*. The simple checklist comprises numerous words or phrases describing various employee behaviors or traits. These descriptors are often clustered to represent different aspects of one dimension of behavior, such as assertiveness or interpersonal skills. The rater is asked to check all those that describe the employee on each checklist. A major weakness of all checklists is that there are no set performance standards. In addition, specific components of behavior are not addressed. Checklists do, however, focus on a variety of job-related behaviors and avoid some of the bias inherent in the trait rating scales.

Essays

The *essay appraisal method* is often referred to as the *free-form review*. The appraiser describes in narrative form an employee's strengths and areas where improvement or growth is needed. Although this method can be unstructured, it usually calls for certain items to be addressed. This technique does appropriately force the appraiser to focus on positive aspects of the employee's performance. However, a greater opportunity for personal bias undoubtedly exists. In addition, Mackenzie (2013) notes it is complex and time-consuming and the quality of the content may be more reflective of the writing skills of the appraiser than the performance of the employee.

Many organizations combine various types of appraisals to improve the quality of their review processes. Because the essay method does not require exhaustive development, it can quickly be adapted as an adjunct to any type of structured format. This gives the organization the ability to decrease bias and focus on employee strengths.

Self-Appraisals

Employees are increasingly being asked to submit written summaries or *portfolios* of their work-related accomplishments and productivity as part of the *self-appraisal* process.

Portfolios often provide examples of continuing education, professional certifications, awards, and recognitions. The portfolio also generally includes the employee's goals and an action plan for accomplishing these goals.

There are advantages and disadvantages to using self-appraisal as a method of performance review. Although introspection and self-appraisal result in growth when the person is self-aware, even mature people require external feedback and performance validation. Some employees look forward to their annual performance review in anticipation of positive feedback. Asking these employees to perform their own performance appraisal would probably be viewed negatively rather than positively.

 Some employees look on their annual performance review as an opportunity to receive positive feedback from their supervisor, especially if the employee receives infrequent praise on a day-to-day basis.

Some employees undervalue their own accomplishments or feel uncomfortable giving themselves high marks in many areas. In an effort to avoid this potential influence on their rating, managers may wish to complete the performance appraisal tool before reading the employee's self-analysis, or they should view the self-appraisal as only one of a number of data sources that should be collected when evaluating worker performance. When self-appraisal is not congruent with other data available, the manager may wish to pursue the reasons for this discrepancy during the appraisal conference. Such an exchange may provide valuable insight regarding the worker's self-awareness and ability to view himself or herself objectively.

Management by Objectives

MBO is an excellent tool for determining an individual employee's progress because it incorporates both the employee's assessments and the organization. The focus in this chapter, however, is on how these concepts are used as an effective performance appraisal method rather than on their use as a planning technique.

Although seldom used in health care, MBO is an excellent method to appraise the performance of the employee in a manner that promotes individual growth and excellence. The following steps delineate how MBO can be used effectively in performance appraisal:

1. The employee and supervisor meet and agree on the principal duties and responsibilities of the employee's job. This is done as soon as possible after beginning employment.
2. The employee sets short-term goals and target dates in cooperation with the supervisor or manager, and the manager guides the process so that it relates to the position's duties. It is important that the subordinate's goals not be in conflict with the goals of the organization. In setting these goals, the manager must remember that one's values and beliefs simply reflect a single set of options among many. This is especially true in working with a multicultural staff. Professional expectations and values can vary greatly among cultures, and the manager must be careful to resist judgmental reactions and allow for cultural differences in goal-setting.
3. Both parties agree on the criteria that will be used for measuring and evaluating the accomplishment of goals. In addition, a time frame is set for completing the objectives, which depends on the nature of the work being planned. Common time frames used in health-care organizations vary from 1 month to 1 year.
4. Regularly, but more than once a year, the employee and supervisor meet to discuss progress. At these meetings, some modifications can be made to the original goals if both parties agree. Major obstacles that block completion of objectives within the stipulated time frame are identified. In addition, the resources and support needed from others are identified.

5. The manager's role is supportive, assisting the employee to reach goals by coaching and counseling.
6. During the appraisal process, the manager determines whether the employee has met the goals.
7. The entire process focuses on outcomes and results and not on personal traits.

One of the many advantages of MBO is that the method creates a vested interest in the employee to accomplish goals because employees are able to set their own goals. Additionally, defensive feelings are minimized, and a spirit of teamwork prevails. MBO as a performance appraisal method also has its disadvantages. Highly directive and authoritarian managers find it difficult to lead employees in this manner. Also, the marginal employee frequently attempts to set easily attainable goals. However, research has shown that MBO, when used correctly, is a very effective method of performance appraisal.

LEARNING EXERCISE 24.3

Using Management by Objective as a Part of Performance Appraisal

It is time for Nancy Irwin's annual performance appraisal. She is an RN on a postsurgical unit, dealing with complex trauma patients requiring high-level nursing intensity. You are the evening charge nurse and have worked with Ms. Irwin for the 2 years since she graduated from nursing school. Last year, in addition to the regular 1 to 5 rating scale for job expectations, all of the charge nurses added an MBO component to the performance appraisal form. In collaboration with his or her charge nurse, each employee developed five goals that were supposed to have been carried out over a 1-year period.

In reviewing Ms. Irwin's performance, you use several sources, including your written notes and her charting, and your conclusion is that with her strengths and weaknesses, overall she is a better-than-average nurse. However, you believe that she has not grown much as an employee over the past 6 months. This observation is confirmed by a review of the following:

Objective	Result
1. Conduct a mini in-service or patient care conference twice monthly for the 12 mo.	Met goal for the first 2 mo. In the last 10 mo, she conducted only six conferences.
2. Will attend five educational classes related to work; at least one of these will be given by an outside agency.	Attended one surgical nursing wound conference in the city and one in-house conference on TPN.
3. Will become an active member of a nursing committee at the hospital.	Became an active member of the Policies and Procedures Committee and regularly attends meetings.
4. Reduce the number of late arrivals at work by 50% (from 24 per year to 12).	First 3 mo: not late. Second 3 mo: three late arrivals. Third 3 mo: six late arrivals. Last 3 mo: six late arrivals.
5. Ensure that all patients discharged have discharge instructions documented in their charts.	Anecdotal notes show that Ms. Irwin still frequently forgets to document these nursing actions.

Assignment: As Ms. Irwin's charge nurse what can you do to ensure that the current appraisal results in greater growth for her? What went wrong with last year's MBO plan? Devise a plan for the performance appraisal. Try solving this yourself before reading the possible solution that appears in the Appendix.

Peer Review

When peers rather than supervisors carry out monitoring and assessing work performance, it is referred to as *peer review*. Most likely, the manager's review of the employee is not complete unless some type of peer review data is gathered. Peer review provides feedback that can promote growth. It can also provide learning opportunities for the peer reviewers.

The concept of collegial evaluation of nursing practice is closely related to maintaining professional standards.

Although the prevailing practice in most organizations is to have managers evaluate employee performance, there is much to be said for collegial review. Peer review is widely used in medicine and academe; however, health-care organizations have been slow to adopt peer review for the following five reasons:

1. Staff are often poorly oriented to the peer review method and many first-level managers, including team leaders, have had little training in how to conduct a growth-producing performance appraisal. In fact, Keegal (2013) suggests that first-level managers like team leaders often have to learn these skills on the job, supported only by brief management courses with minimal leadership theory.

2. Peer review is viewed as very threatening when inadequate time is spent orienting employees to the process and when necessary support is not provided throughout the process.

3. Peers feel uncomfortable sharing feedback with people with whom they work closely, so they omit needed suggestions for improving the employee's performance. Thus, the review becomes more advocacy than evaluation. Randall and Sharples (2012) agree, noting that leniency in performance appraisal is common and difficult to reduce. This leniency is typically driven by raters' motivation to avoid conflicts with ratees (Examining the Evidence 24.1).

Examining the Evidence 24.1

Source: Randall, R., & Sharples, D. (2012). The impact of rater agreeableness and rating context on the evaluation of poor performance. Journal of Occupational & Organizational Psychology, 85(1), 42–59.

Participants were 230 government employees responsible for administering welfare benefits. Participant agreeableness was measured using the 20 agreeableness items from *Goldberg's International Personality Inventory Pool.* Example items included "I am easy to satisfy" and "I suspect hidden motives in others."

Participants were informed that they were testing an appraisal system developed for a small local manufacturing company and that they would rate the performance of one of the managers from this company using a competency framework. Participants were told by the researcher that they would be required to provide face-to-face feedback individually to the ratee. Participants then received training, completed two practice rating exercises, and were introduced to, but did not interact with, the ratee who vacated the room after being introduced.

The study found that significantly higher ratings were given by raters when raters thought they had to meet face-to-face with the ratees. Raters did not, however, generally give lenient ratings when exposed to inflated self-ratings if future collaboration was not anticipated. The researchers concluded that rater agreeableness exerts a largely independent effect on rating behavior, since the higher the rater's agreeableness the higher the ratings that were given. These effects appeared to be driven by raters' motivation to avoid conflict with ratees.

---

4. Peer review is viewed by many as more time-consuming than traditional superior–subordinate performance appraisals.

5. Because much socialization takes place in the workplace, friendships often result in inflated evaluations, or interpersonal conflict may result in unfair appraisals.

6. Because peer review shifts the authority away from management, the insecure manager may feel threatened.

Peer review has its shortcomings, as evidenced by some university teachers receiving unjustified tenure or the failure of physicians to maintain adequate quality control among some individuals in their profession. Additionally, peer review involves much risk-taking, is time-consuming, and requires a great deal of energy. However, nursing as a profession should be responsible for setting the standards and then monitoring its own performance. Because performance appraisal may be viewed as a type of quality control, it seems reasonable to expect that nurses should have some input into the performance evaluation process of their profession's members.

Peer review can be carried out in several ways. The process may require the reviewers to share the results only with the person being reviewed, or the results may be shared with the employee's supervisor and the employee. The review would never be shared only with the employee's supervisor. The results may or may not be used for personnel decisions. The number of observations, number of reviewers, qualification and classification of the peer reviewer, and procedure need to be developed for each organization. If peer review is to succeed, the organization must overcome its inherent difficulties by doing the following before implementing a peer review program:

- Peer review appraisal tools must reflect standards to be measured, such as the job description.
- Staff must receive a thorough orientation to the process before its implementation. The role of the manager should be clearly defined.
- Ongoing support, resources, and information must be made available to the staff during the process.
- Data for peer review need to be obtained from predetermined sources, such as observations, charts, and patient care plans.
- A decision must be made about whether anonymous feedback will be allowed. This is controversial and needs to be addressed in the procedure.
- Decisions must be reached on whether the peer review will affect personnel decisions and, if so, in what manner.

Peer review has the potential to increase the accuracy of performance appraisal. It can also provide many opportunities for increased professionalism and learning. The use of peer review in nursing should continue to expand as nursing increases its autonomy and professional status. Display 24.6 provides a summary of types of performance appraisal tools.

The 360-Degree Evaluation

An adaptation of peer review, and a relatively new addition to performance appraisal tools, the *360-degree evaluation*, includes an assessment by all individuals within the sphere of

DISPLAY 24.6   Summary of Performance Appraisal Tools

Trait rating scales: Rates an individual against some standard.
Job dimension scales: Rates the performance on job requirements.
Behaviorally anchored rating scales: Rates desired job expectations on a scale of importance to the position.
Checklists: Rates the performance against a set list of desirable job behaviors.
Essays: A narrative appraisal of job performance.
Self-appraisals: An appraisal of performance by the employee.
Management by objectives: Employee and management agree upon goals of performance to be reached.
Peer review: Assessment of work performance carried out by peers.

LEARNING EXERCISE 24.4

Addressing Mary's Change in Behavior

Even in organizations that have no formal peer review process, professionals must take some responsibility for colleagues' work performance, even if informally. The following scenario illustrates the need for peer involvement.

You have worked at Memorial Hospital since your graduation from nursing school. Your school roommate, Mary, has also worked at Memorial since her graduation. For the first year, you and Mary were assigned to different units, but you were both transferred to the oncology unit 6 months ago. You and Mary work the 3 PM to 11 PM shift, and it is the policy for the charge nurse duties to alternate among three RNs assigned to the unit on a full-time basis. Both of you are among the nurses assigned to rotate to the charge position. You have noticed lately that when Mary is in charge, her personality seems to change; she barks orders and seems tense and anxious.

Mary is an excellent clinical nurse, and many of the staff seek her out in consultation about patient care problems. You have, however, heard several of the staff grumbling about Mary's behavior when she is in charge. As Mary's good friend, you do not want to hurt her feelings, but as her colleague, you feel a need to be honest and open with her.

Assignment: A very difficult situation occurs when personal and working relationships are combined. Describe what, if anything, you would do.

influence of the individual being appraised. "The idea is to look at how the employee is perceived by multiple layers of people. This includes physicians, patients, the employees, coworkers, whoever they report to, and employees from other departments with whom they work" (Gallo, Minsley, & Wright, 2009, p. 110). For example, a 360-degree evaluation of a ward clerk or unit secretary might include feedback from the nursing staff, from patients, and from staff from other departments who interact with that individual on a regular basis. In addition, most 360-degree feedback tools include a self-assessment.

Getting feedback from multiple individuals provides a broader, more accurate perspective of the employee's work performance. This divergent thinking suggests that involving additional individuals in the appraisal process provides unique and valuable perspectives that might otherwise not be considered. Luse (2013) notes that no more than 12 individuals should be involved in the process and that it should ideally be done in an online format. Nowack and Mashihi (2012) concur that inviting more, rather than fewer reviewers to participate in the process, makes findings more relevant and useful. In fact, recent research suggests that when two or fewer respondents provide data, rater responses may be inadequate for reliable measurement. The risk, however, with large numbers of reviewers is that it may be difficult to interpret important differences by different raters and to decide what to do with discrepant results. Nowack and Mashihi note the importance of coaches helping ratees fully understand and interpret the meaning of such differences.

DecisionWise (2013) concurs, suggesting that some type of coaching is generally indicated for the individual who receives 360-degree feedback results. Those individuals who receive some type of coaching on their feedback and set goals for development, experience significantly greater performance improvement than those who simply participate in the 360-degree feedback process and receive their feedback reports (DecisionWise).

3D Group (2013) sounds a warning, however, that 360-degree ratings can become tainted by bias if raters know the results could have an affect on the recipient's position in a company. Therefore, some individuals argue it should be used only for developmental purposes. Others argue that if feedback recipients are not held accountable for making behavioral changes based on the results, the 360-degree feedback program loses some of its impact (3D Group).

LEARNING EXERCISE 24.5

The 360-Degree Evaluation

Think of a role you have held which was important to you and which you worked hard at to be successful. This could be a personal role such as being a parent, boyfriend, or girlfriend, or a specific job you have held in the past or at present. Identify at least six individuals you would have chosen to complete a 360-degree evaluation of you in that role. Why did you select these individuals? Might their perceptions have been in conflict? Would these individuals have been likely to give you honest appraisal feedback? If so, how might their feedback have altered how you approached the role or the goals you were trying to achieve?

PLANNING THE APPRAISAL INTERVIEW

The most accurate and thorough appraisal will fail to produce growth in employees if the information gathered is not used appropriately. Many appraisal interviews have negative outcomes because the manager views them as a time to instruct employees only on what they are doing wrong rather than looking at strengths as well.

Managers often dislike the appraisal interview more than the actual data gathering. One of the reasons managers dislike the appraisal interview is because of their own negative experiences when they have been judged unfairly or criticized personally. Indeed, some managers are so uncomfortable with conducting performance appraisals that they find reasons not to do them at all. Stonehouse (2013) notes that at times, it may be that other priorities must take precedence, but the message that is imparted when appraisals are frequently cancelled or postponed is that they are unimportant.

Clearly, both parties in the appraisal process tend to be anxious before the interview; thus, the appraisal interview remains an emotionally charged event. For many employees, past appraisals have been traumatizing. Although little can be done to eliminate the often-negative emotions created by past experiences, the leader-manager can manage the interview in such a manner that people will not be traumatized further.

OVERCOMING APPRAISAL INTERVIEW DIFFICULTIES

Feedback, perhaps the greatest tool a manager has for changing behavior, must be given in an appropriate manner. There is a greater chance that the performance appraisal will have a positive outcome if certain conditions are present before, during, and after the interview.

Before the Interview

- Make sure that the conditions mentioned previously have been met (e.g., the employee knows the standard by which his or her work will be evaluated), and he or she has a copy of the appraisal form.
- Select an appropriate time for the appraisal conference. Do not choose a time when the employee has just had a traumatic personal event or is too busy at work to take the time needed for a meaningful conference.
- Give the employee 2 to 3 days of advance notice of the scheduled appraisal conference so that he or she can prepare mentally and emotionally for the interview.
- Be prepared mentally and emotionally for the conference yourself. If something should happen to interfere with your readiness for the interview, it should be canceled and rescheduled.

- Schedule uninterrupted appraisal time. Hold the appraisal in a private, quiet, and comfortable place. Forward your telephone calls to another line, and ask another manager to answer any pages that you may have during the performance appraisal.

- Plan a seating arrangement that reflects collegiality rather than power. Having the person seated across a large desk from the appraiser denotes a power–status position; placing the chairs side by side denotes collegiality.

During the Interview

- Greet the employee warmly, showing that the manager and the organization have a sincere interest in his or her growth.

- Begin the conference on a pleasant, informal note.

- Ask the employee to comment on his or her progress since the last performance appraisal.

- Avoid surprises in the appraisal conference. The effective leader coaches and communicates informally with staff on a continual basis, so there should be little new information at an appraisal conference. Indeed, Keegal (2013) notes that managers should not wait for the annual appraisal to deal with poor performance, as this allows bad habits to become entrenched and team resentment to grow.

- Use coaching techniques throughout the conference.

- When dealing with an employee who has several problems—either new or long-standing—do not overwhelm him or her at the conference. If there are too many problems to be addressed, select the major ones.

- Conduct the conference in a nondirective and participatory manner. Input from the employee should be solicited throughout the interview; however, the manager must recognize that employees from some cultures may be hesitant to provide this type of input. In this situation, the manager must continually reassure the employee that such input is not only acceptable but is also desired.

- Listen carefully to what the employee has to say and give them your full attention.

- Focus on the employee's performance and not on his or her personal characteristics.

- Avoid vague generalities, either positive or negative, such as "your skills need a little work" or "your performance is fine." Be prepared with explicit performance examples. Be liberal in the positive examples of employee performance; use examples of poor performance sparingly. Use several examples only if the employee has difficulty with self-awareness and requests specific instances of a problem area.

- When delivering performance feedback, be straightforward and state concerns directly so as not to retard communication or cloud the message.

 Indirectness and ambiguity are more likely to inhibit communication than enhance it, and the employee is left unsure about the significance of the message.

- Mackenzie (2013) suggests that since most employees are waiting for the "bad news," it is probably most effective to describe areas for improvement first, followed by the employee's strengths.

- Never threaten, intimidate, or use status in any manner. Differences in power and status interfere with the ability of professionals to form meaningful and constructive relationships. This is not to say that managers should not maintain an appropriate authority–power gap with their employees; it simply suggests that power and status issues should be minimized as much as possible so that the performance appraisal can appropriately focus on the subordinate's performance and needs.

- Let the employee know that the organization and the manager are aware of his or her uniqueness, special interests, and valuable contributions to the unit. Remember that all employees make some special contribution to the workplace.
- Make every effort to ensure that there are no interruptions during the conference.
- Use terms and language that are clearly understood and carry the same meaning for both parties. Avoid words that have a negative connotation. Do not talk down to employees or use language that is inappropriate for their level of education.
- Mutually set goals for further growth or improvement in the employee's performance. Decide how goals will be accomplished and evaluated and what support is needed.
- Plan on being available for employees to return retrospectively to discuss the appraisal review further. There is frequently a need for the employee to return for elaboration if the conference did not go well or if the employee was given unexpected new information. This is especially true for the new employee.

After the Interview

- Both the manager and the employee need to sign the appraisal form to document that the conference was held and that the employee received the appraisal information. This does not mean that the employee is agreeing to the information in the appraisal; it merely means that the employee has read the appraisal. An example of such a form is shown in Display 24.7. There should be a place for comments by both the manager and the employee.

DISPLAY 24.7   Performance Appraisal Documentation Form

Performance appraisal for
Name: _____
Unit: _____
Prepared by: _____
Reason: _____
(Merit, terminal, end of probation, general reviews)
Date of appraisal conference: _____
Comments by employee:

Employee's signature: _____
(Signature of employee denotes that the appraisal has been read. It *does not* signify acceptance or agreement. Space is provided for any comments the employee wishes to make.) Comments by appraiser.
(These comments are to be written at the time of the appraisal conference and in the presence of the employee.)

_____   _____
Employee's signature (Date)   Evaluator's signature (Date)

- End the interview on a pleasant note.
- Document the goals for further development that have been agreed on by both parties. The documentation should include target dates for accomplishment, support needed, and when goals are to be reviewed. This documentation is often part of the appraisal form.
- If the interview reveals specific long-term coaching needs, the manager should develop a method of follow-up to ensure that such coaching takes place.

PERFORMANCE MANAGEMENT

Some experts in human resource management have suggested that annual performance appraisals should be replaced by ongoing *performance management*. In performance management, appraisals are eliminated, and the manager places his or her efforts into ongoing coaching, mutual goal-setting, and the leadership training of subordinates. This focus requires the manager to spend more regularly scheduled face-to-face time with subordinates.

In contrast to the annual performance review, which is often linked to an employee's hire date, the performance management calendar is generally linked to the organization's business calendar. This way, performance planning is coordinated throughout the entire organization, as strategic goals for the year can be identified and subordinates' roles to achieve those goals can be openly discussed and planned. Some organizations, however, view performance management as a continuous cycle. Regardless, all performance-managed organizations identify role-based competency expectations for every employee, regardless of job description. Then, employees can determine how these qualities translate into performance in specific jobs.

COACHING: A MECHANISM FOR INFORMAL PERFORMANCE APPRAISAL

Coaching is described in the literature as "a process through which an individual is provided with one-on-one interaction to either address specific developmental issues and receive feedback on strengths and opportunities for involvement or to receive support and guidance during times of transition in their personal role or throughout the organization" (Karsten & Baggot, 2010, p. 140). In other words, *coaching* conveys the spirit of leaders' and managers' roles in informal day-to-day performance appraisals, which promote improved work performance and team building. Coaching can guide others into increased competence, commitment, and confidence as well as help them to anticipate options for making vital connections between their present and future plans.

Day-to-day feedback regarding performance is one of the best methods for improving work performance and building a team approach.

Manthey (2001) uses the terms *reflective practice* and *clinical coaching* to describe a management strategy that fuses both performance coaching and performance management. In clinical coaching, the manager or mentor meets with an employee regularly to discuss aspects of his or her work. Both individuals determine the agenda jointly with the goal of an environment of learning that can span the personal and professional aspects of the employee's experience. During clinical coaching, employees can discuss things that have made them feel angry or discouraged. They can also get new ideas and information about how to deal with situations from someone who often has experienced the same problems and issues. This shared connection between the manager and the employee makes the employee feel validated and part of a larger team. When coaching is combined with informal performance appraisal, the outcome is usually a positive modification of behavior. For this to occur, however, the leader must establish a climate in which there is a free exchange of ideas.

BECOMING AN EFFECTIVE COACH

The following tactics will assist managers in becoming more effective coaches:

- Be specific, not general, in describing behavior that needs improvement.
- Be descriptive, not evaluative, when describing what was wrong with the work performance.
- Be certain that the feedback is not self-serving but meets the needs of the employee.
- Direct the feedback toward behavior that can be changed.
- Use sensitivity in timing the feedback.
- Make sure that the employee has clearly understood the feedback and that the employee's communication has also been clearly heard.

When employees believe that their manager is interested in their performance and personal growth, they will have less fear of the work performance appraisal. When that anxiety is reduced, the formal performance interview process can be used to set mutual performance goals.

USING LEADERSHIP SKILLS AND MANAGEMENT FUNCTIONS IN CONDUCTING PERFORMANCE APPRAISALS

Performance appraisal is a major responsibility in the controlling function of management. The ability to conduct meaningful, effective performance appraisals requires an investment of time, effort, and practice on the part of the manager. Although performance appraisal is never easy, if used appropriately, it produces growth in the employee and increases productivity in the organization.

To increase the likelihood of successful performance appraisal, managers should use a formalized system of appraisal and gather data about employee performance in a systematic manner, using many sources. The manager should also attempt to be as objective as possible, using established standards for the appraisal. The result of the appraisal process should provide the manager with information for meeting training and educational needs of employees. By following up conscientiously on identified performance deficiencies, employees' work problems can be corrected before they become habits.

Integrating leadership into this part of the controlling phase of the management process provides an opportunity for sharing, communicating, and growing. The integrated leader-manager is self-aware regarding his or her biases and prejudices. This self-awareness leads to fairness and honesty in evaluating performance. This, in turn, increases trust in the manager and promotes a team spirit among employees.

The leader also uses day-to-day coaching techniques to improve work performance and reduce the anxiety of performance appraisal. When anxiety is reduced during the appraisal interview, the leader-manager is able to establish a relationship of mutual goal-setting, which has a greater potential to result in increased motivation and corrected deficiencies. The result of the integration of leadership and management is a performance appraisal that facilitates employee growth and increases organizational productivity.

KEY CONCEPTS

- The employee performance appraisal is a sensitive and important part of the management process, requiring much skill.
- When accurate and appropriate appraisal assessments are performed, outcomes can be very positive.
- Performance appraisals are used to determine how well employees are performing their job. Therefore, appraisals measure actual behavior and not intent.

(Continued)

- Job descriptions often produce objective criteria for use in the performance appraisal.
- There are many different types of appraisal tools and methods, and the most appropriate one to use varies with the type of appraisal to be done and the criteria to be measured.
- The employee must be involved in the appraisal process and view the appraisal as accurate and fair.
- MBO has been shown to increase productivity and commitment in employees.
- Peer review has great potential for developing professional accountability but is often difficult to implement.
- Unless the appraisal interview is carried out in an appropriate and effective manner, the appraisal data will be useless.
- Because of past experiences, performance appraisal interviews are highly charged, emotional events for most employees.
- Showing a genuine interest in the employee's growth and seeking his or her input at the interview will increase the likelihood of a positive outcome from the appraisal process.
- Performance appraisals should be signed to show that feedback was given to the employee.
- Informal work performance appraisals are an important management function.
- Leaders should routinely use day-to-day coaching to empower subordinates and improve work performance.
- In performance management, appraisals are eliminated. Instead, the manager places his or her efforts into ongoing coaching, mutual goal-setting, and the leadership training of subordinates.

ADDITIONAL LEARNING EXERCISES AND APPLICATIONS

LEARNING EXERCISE 24.6

Requesting Feedback from Employees

You are the director of a home health agency. You have just returned from a management course and have been inspired by the idea of requesting input from your subordinates about your performance as a manager. You realize that there are some risks involved but believe that the potential benefits from the feedback outweigh the risks. However, you want to provide some structure for the evaluation, so you spend some time designing your appraisal tool and developing your plan.

Assignment: What type of tool will you use? What is your overall goal? Will you share the results of the appraisal with anyone else? How will you use the information obtained? Would you have the appraisal forms signed or have them be anonymous? Who would you include in the group that is evaluating you? Be able to support your ideas with appropriate rationale.

LEARNING EXERCISE 24.7

Making Appraisal Interviews Less Traumatic

You are the new night-shift charge nurse in a large intensive care unit composed of an all-RN staff. When you were appointed to the position, your supervisor told you that there had been some complaints regarding the manner in which the previous charge nurse had handled evaluation sessions. Not wanting to repeat the mistakes, you draw up a list of things that you could do to make the evaluation interviews less traumatic. Because the evaluation tool appears adequate, you believe that the problems must lie with the interview itself. At the top of your list, you write that you will make sure each employee has advance notice of the evaluation.

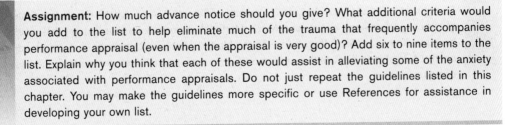

Assignment: How much advance notice should you give? What additional criteria would you add to the list to help eliminate much of the trauma that frequently accompanies performance appraisal (even when the appraisal is very good)? Add six to nine items to the list. Explain why you think that each of these would assist in alleviating some of the anxiety associated with performance appraisals. Do not just repeat the guidelines listed in this chapter. You may make the guidelines more specific or use References for assistance in developing your own list.

LEARNING EXERCISE 24.8

Helping a Seasoned Employee to Grow

Patty Brown is an LVN/LPN who has been employed by your unit for 10 years. She is an older woman and is very sensitive to criticism. Her work is generally of high quality, but in reviewing her past performance appraisals, you notice that during the last 10 years, at least seven times she has been rated unsatisfactory for not being on duty promptly and eight times for not attending staff development programs. Because you are the new charge nurse, you would like to help Patty grow in these two areas. You have given Patty a copy of the evaluation tool and her job description and have scheduled her appraisal conference for a time when the unit will be quiet. You can conduct the appraisal in the conference room.

Assignment: How would you conduct this performance appraisal? Outline your plan. Include how you would begin. What innovative or creative way would you attempt to provide direction or improvement in the areas mentioned? How would you terminate the session? Be able to give rationale for your decisions.

LEARNING EXERCISE 24.9

Could This Conflict Have Been Prevented?

Mr. Jones, a 49-year-old automobile salesman, was admitted with severe back pain. As his primary care nurse, you have established a rapport with Mr. Jones. He has a type A personality and has been very critical of much of his hospitalization. He was also very upset by the level and duration of his pain following his laminectomy. You agreed to ambulate him on your shift three times (at 4:00 PM, 7:00 PM, and 10:30 PM) so that he would need to be ambulated only once during the day shift. He does not care for many of the day staff and feels that you help to ambulate him better than anyone else. You noted the ambulating routine on his nursing orders.

Yesterday, Joan Martin, a day nurse, believed that his bowel sounds were somewhat diminished. She urged him to ambulate more on the day shift, but he refused to do so. (The doctor had ordered ambulation q.i.d.) When Mr. Jones's physician visited, Nurse Martin told him that Mr. Jones ambulated only once on the shift. She did not elaborate further to the doctor. The physician proceeded to talk very sternly with Mr. Jones, telling him to get out of bed three times today. Nurse Martin did not mention this incident to you in the report.

By the time you arrived on duty and received the report, Mr. Jones was very angry. He threatened to sign himself out against medical advice. You talked with his doctor, got the order changed, and finally managed to calm Mr. Jones down. You then wrote a nursing order that read, "Nurse Martin is not to be assigned to Mr. Jones again." When Joan Martin came on duty this morning, the night shift pointed out your notation. She was very angry and went to see the head nurse.

(Continued)

Assignment: Should you have done anything differently? If so, what? Could the evaluation of clinical performance by you and Nurse Martin have been done in a manner that would not have resulted in conflict? If you were Nurse Martin, what could you have done to prevent the conflict? Be able to discuss this case in relation to professional trust, peer review, and assertive communication.

LEARNING EXERCISE 24.10

Addressing Sally's Errors in Judgment

You are a senior baccalaureate nursing student. This is your sixth week of a medical–surgical advanced practicum. Your instructor assigns two students to work together in caring for four to six patients. The students alternate fulfilling leader and follower roles and providing total patient care. This is the second full day that you have worked as a team with Sally Brown.

Last week, when you were assigned with Sally, she was the leader and made numerous errors in judgment. She got a patient up who was on strict bed rest. She made an IV medication error by giving a medication to the wrong patient. She gave morphine too soon because she forgot to record the time in the medication record, and she frequently did not seem to know what was wrong with her patients.

Today, you have been the leader and have observed her contaminate a dressing and forget to check armbands twice when she was giving medications. When you asked her about checking the placement of the nasogastric tube, she did not know how to perform this skill. You have heard some of the other students complain about Sally.

Assignment: What is your obligation to your patients, your fellow students, the clinical agency, and your instructor? Outline what you would do. Provide the rationale for your decisions.

REFERENCES

3D Group. (2013). *January 2013—Future of 360 degree feedback: New study finds increased HR influence.* Retrieved June 26, 2013, from http://www.3dgroup.net/january-2013-future-of-360-degree-feedback-new-study-find-increased-hr-influence.html

Accel-Team (2013). *Self assessment. A system to set your own performance goals.* Retrieved June 27, 2013, from http://www.accel-team.com/techniques/employee_evaluation.html

Bacal, R. (2013). *10 ways to modernize performance management and appraisal for 2013.* Performance Management Health Center. Retrieved June 26, 2013, from http://performance-appraisals.org/Bacalsappraisalarticles/articles/tenways.htm

DecisionWise (2013). *What is 360-degree feedback.* Retrieved June 25, 2013, from http://www.decision-wise.com/what-is-360-degree-feedback.html

Gallo, C. L., Minsley, M. A., & Wright, J. (2009, October). Do patients say good, or not so good, things about your access staff? *Hospital Access Management, 28*(10), 109–112.

Karsten, M., & Baggot, D. (2010, March). Professional coaching as an effective strategy to retaining frontline managers. *Journal of Nursing Administration, 40*(3), 140–144.

Keegal, T. (2013, May). Poor performance: Managing the first informal stages. *Primary Health Care, 23*(4), 31–38.

Luse, K. A. (2013, March/April). Managerial strategies for creating an effective work environment. *Radiologic Technology, 84*(4), 383–397.

Mackenzie, R. (2013, June 1). Supervision and appraisal: How to support staff performance. *Nursing & Residential Care, 15*(6), 452–454.

Manthey, M. (2001). Reflective practice. *Creative Nursing, 7*(2), 3–5.

Mulvaney, M. A., McKinney, W. R., & Grodsky, R. (2012). The development of a pay-for-performance appraisal system for municipal agencies: A case study. *Public Personnel Management, 41*(3), 505–533.

Nowack, K. M., & Mashihi, S. (2012). Evidence-based answers to 15 questions about leveraging 360-degree feedback. *Consulting Psychology Journal: Practice & Research, 64*(3), 157–182.

Olmstead, J., Falcone, D., Lopez, J., Sharpe, L., & Michna, J. (2012). Perioperative employee annual evaluations: A 30-second process. *AORN Journal, 96*(6), 627–633.

Price, B. (2013). Preparing for your annual staff appraisal: Part 2. *Nursing Standard, 27*(21), 42–48.

Randall, R., & Sharples, D. (2012). The impact of rater agreeableness and rating context on the evaluation of poor performance. *Journal of Occupational & Organizational Psychology, 85*(1), 42–59.

Stonehouse, D. (2013). Appraisal and its benefits for the support worker. *British Journal of Healthcare Assistants, 7*(5), 246–249.

25

Problem Employees: Rule Breakers, Marginal Employees, and the Chemically or Psychologically Impaired

… as patient advocates, nurse leaders must help ensure fitness for duty.
—Richard Hader

… difficult employees can make you question why you became a manager in the first place.
—Mark Pipkin

CROSSWALK THIS CHAPTER ADDRESSES:

BSN Essential II: Basic organizational and systems leadership for quality care and patient safety
BSN Essential V: Health-care policy, finance, and regulatory environments
BSN Essential VIII: Professionalism and professional values
MSN Essential II: Organizational and systems leadership
MSN Essential III: Quality improvement and safety
QSEN Competency: Teamwork and collaboration
QSEN Competency: Safety
AONE Nurse Executive Competency I: Communication and relationship building
AONE Nurse Executive Competency II: A knowledge of the health-care environment
AONE Nurse Executive Competency III: Leadership
AONE Nurse Executive Competency IV: Professionalism
AONE Nurse Executive Competency V: Business skills

LEARNING OBJECTIVES The learner will:

- identify the "hot stove" rules described by McGregor to make discipline as fair and growth-producing as possible
- describe the usual steps in progressive discipline
- differentiate between constructive and destructive discipline
- identify factors that must be present to foster a climate of self-discipline in employees
- seek to eliminate rules that are outdated or no longer appropriate in the environments in which they function
- compare and contrast how the disciplinary process may vary between unionized and nonunionized organizations
- analyze situations in which discipline is required and identify appropriate strategies for constructively modifying behavior
- determine appropriate levels of discipline for rule-breaking in specific situations
- develop strategies that assist marginal employees to be contributing members of the workforce

- describe the risk factors that result in an increased risk of chemical addiction in the nursing profession
- identify behaviors and actions that may signify chemical impairment in an employee or colleague
- analyze how personal feelings, values, and biases regarding chemical impairment may alter one's ability to confront and/or help the chemically impaired employee
- recognize the importance of the manager not assuming the role of counselor or treatment provider for employees who are chemically or psychologically impaired

Employees' perceptions vary as to what they owe the organization and what they owe themselves. At times, organizational and individual needs, wants, and responsibilities are in conflict. The coordination and cooperation needed to meet organizational goals require leader-managers to control individual subordinates' urges that are counterproductive to these goals. Subordinates do this by self-control. Managers meet organizational goals by enforcing established rules, policies, and procedures. Leaders do this by creating a supportive and motivating climate and by coaching.

Luse (2013) notes that problem behavior can assume many forms, including blatant insubordination such as an employee refusing to perform a task, not reporting to work on time, or showing disrespect to coworkers or others. Highly problematic behavior is often more subtle, but equally serious. This includes behavior such as undermining fellow team members (e.g., by spreading gossip or participating in exclusionary activities) and creating an unwelcome or hostile workplace.

When employees are unsuccessful in meeting organizational goals, managers must attempt to identify the reasons for this failure and counsel employees accordingly. If employees fail because they are unwilling to follow rules or established policies and procedures or they are unable to perform their duties adequately despite assistance and encouragement, the manager has an obligation to take disciplinary action. However, progressive discipline is inappropriate for employees who are impaired as a result of disease or degree of ability. These employees have special problems and needs that require active coaching, support, and, often, professional counseling to maintain productivity. For employees to be managed most appropriately, managers must be able to distinguish between employees in need of discipline and those who are impaired.

Regardless of the cause, however, supervisors should promptly address inappropriate conduct and poor work performance. Delay only exacerbates such situations. Luse (2013) agrees, noting that employees become disenchanted with their positions and work environment for varied and unique reasons. The disenchantment of a single employee can spread, affecting otherwise satisfied and highly valued employees. When someone is not performing well, everyone knows it. And when management refuses to act, employees may perceive that their leaders lack the resolve necessary to make the organization successful.

Not disciplining an employee who should be disciplined jeopardizes an organization's morale.

This chapter focuses on discipline, coaching, and referral as tools in promoting subordinates' growth and meeting organizational goals. The normal progression of steps taken in disciplinary action and strategies for administering discipline fairly and effectively are delineated. Formal and informal grievances are discussed.

The chapter also focuses on two types of employees with special needs: the marginal employee and the impaired employee. *Marginal employees* are those employees who disrupt unit functioning because the quantity or quality of their work consistently meets only minimal standards at best. This chapter identifies the challenges inherent in working with marginal employees and presents managerial strategies for dealing with these problem employees.

Impaired employees are those who are unable to accomplish their work at the expected level as a result of chemical or psychological disease. While the emphasis in this chapter is on *chemical impairment* (impairment resulting from drug or alcohol addiction), *psychological impairment* is increasingly recognized as a significant problem for employees. The strategies used to deal with both types of impairment typically overlap. This chapter profiles chemical addiction among nurses as well as behaviors common to chemically impaired nurses. Steps in the recovery process and the reentry of the recovering chemically impaired nurse into the workforce are also discussed. Leadership roles and management functions appropriate for use with problem employees are shown in Display 25.1.

DISPLAY 25.1   Leadership Roles and Management Functions in Dealing with Problem Employees

LEADERSHIP ROLES

1. Recognizes and reinforces the intrinsic self-worth of each employee and the role of successful work performance in maintaining a positive self-image.
2. Encourages employees to be self-disciplined in conforming to established rules and regulations.
3. Understands group norms and is able to work within those norms to mold group behavior.
4. Assists employees to identify with organizational goals, thus increasing the likelihood that the standards of conduct deemed acceptable by the organization will be accepted by its employees.
5. Is self-aware regarding the power and responsibility inherent in having formal authority to set rules and discipline employees.
6. Serves in the role of coach in performance deficiency coaching or problem-centered coaching.
7. Assures that the rights and the responsibilities of both the manager and the employee are considered in addressing worker grievances.
8. Is self-aware regarding values, biases, and beliefs about chemical abuse.
9. Uses active listening as a support tool in working with chemically and psychologically impaired subordinates but recognizes own limitations in counseling and refers impaired employees to outside experts for appropriate counseling.
10. Examines the work environment for stressors that contribute to substance abuse and eliminates those stressors whenever possible.
11. Keeps patient safety first and foremost when considering how best to intervene with problem employees.
12. Recognizes that all employees have intrinsic worth and assists them in reaching their maximal potential.

MANAGEMENT FUNCTIONS

1. Discusses clearly all written rules and policies with subordinates, explains the rationale for the existence of the rules and policies, and encourages questions.
2. Clearly identifies performance expectations for all employees and confronts employees when those expectations are not met.
3. Uses formal authority as judiciously as possible so that subordinates have the opportunity to invoke self-discipline.
4. Uses formal authority to administer discipline using a progressive model when employees continue to fail to meet expected standards of achievement.
5. Thoroughly investigates the situation before employee discipline is administered.
6. Consults with either a superior or the human resources department before dismissing an employee.
7. Maintains clear, objective, and comprehensive written records regarding the problem employee's behavior and attempts to counsel.
8. Uses organizational transfers appropriately.

9. Seeks out and completes extensive education about chemical abuse in the work setting; provides these same opportunities to staff.
10. Acts as a resource to chemically or psychologically impaired employees regarding professional services or agencies that provide counseling and support services.
11. Collects and records adequate objective data when suspicious of employee chemical impairment.
12 Focuses employee confrontations on performance deficits and not on the cause of the underlying problem or addiction.
13. Works with the rule breaker, chemically impaired, and/or marginal employee to develop a remedial plan for action; ensures that the employee understands the performance expectations of the organization and the consequences of not meeting these expectations.

CONSTRUCTIVE VERSUS DESTRUCTIVE DISCIPLINE

Discipline involves training or molding the mind or character to bring about desired behaviors. Discipline is often considered a form of punishment but is not quite the same thing as punishment. *Punishment* is an undesirable event that follows unacceptable behavior. Although discipline can have negative consequences, it can be a powerful motivator for positive change since it has an educational component as well as a corrective one.

Scientific management theory viewed discipline as a necessary means for controlling an unmotivated and self-centered workforce. Because of this traditional philosophy, managers primarily used threats and fear to control behavior. This "big stick" approach to management focused on eliminating all behaviors that could be considered to conflict with organizational goals. Although this approach may succeed on a short-term basis, it is usually demotivating and reduces long-term productivity because people will achieve goals only up to the level that they believe is necessary to avoid punishment. This approach is also destructive because discipline is often arbitrarily administered and is unfair either in the application of rules or in the resulting punishment.

In contrast to punishment, discipline is called *constructive discipline* when it assists employee growth. Punishment is frequently inferred when defining discipline, but discipline can also be defined as training, educating, or molding. In fact, the word *discipline* comes from the Latin term *disciplina*, which means teaching, learning, and growing. In constructive discipline, punishment may be applied for improper behavior, but it is carried out in a supportive and corrective manner. Employees are reassured that the punishment given is because of their actions and not because of who they are.

Constructive discipline uses discipline as a means of helping the employee grow, not as a punitive measure.

LEARNING EXERCISE 25.1

Thinking about Growth-Producing versus Destructive Discipline

Think back to when someone in authority such as a parent, teacher, or boss sets limits or enforced rules in such a way that you became a better child, student, or employee. What made this disciplinary action growth-producing instead of destructive? What was the most destructive disciplinary action that you ever experienced? Did it modify your behavior in any way?

SELF-DISCIPLINE AND GROUP NORMS

The highest level and most effective form of discipline is *self-discipline*. When employees feel secure, validated, and affirmed in their essential worth, identity, and integrity, self-discipline is forthcoming. Ideally, all employees have adequate self-control and are self-directed in their pursuit of organizational goals. However, this is not always the case. Instead, group norms often influence individual behavior and make self-discipline difficult. *Group norms* are group-established standards of expected behavior that are enforced by social pressure. The leader, who understands group norms, is able to work within those norms to mold group behavior. This modification of group norms, in turn, affects individual behavior and thus self-discipline.

Although self-discipline is internalized, the leader plays an active role in developing an environment that promotes self-discipline in employees. It is impossible for employees to have self-control if they do not understand the acceptable boundaries for their behavior, nor can they be self-directed if they do not understand what is expected of them. Therefore, managers must discuss clearly all written rules and policies with subordinates, explain the rationale for the existence of the rules and policies, and encourage questions.

Self-discipline is possible only if subordinates know the rules and accept them as valid.

Self-discipline also requires an atmosphere of mutual trust. Managers must believe that employees are capable of and actively seek self-discipline. Likewise, employees must respect their managers and perceive them as honest and trustworthy. Employees lack the security to have self-discipline if they do not trust their managers' motives. Finally, for self-discipline to develop, formal authority must be used judiciously. If formal discipline is quickly and widely used, subordinates do not have the opportunity to invoke self-discipline.

FAIR AND EFFECTIVE RULES

Several guidelines must be followed if discipline is to be perceived by subordinates as growth-producing. This does not imply that subordinates enjoy being disciplined or that discipline should be a regular means of promoting employee growth. However, discipline, if implemented correctly, should not permanently alienate or demoralize subordinates. McGregor (1967) developed four rules to make discipline as fair and growth-producing as possible (Display 25.2). These rules are called "hot stove" rules, because they can be applied to someone touching a hot stove.

DISPLAY 25.2	McGregor's Hot Stove Rules for Fair and Effective Discipline

Four elements must be present to make discipline as fair and growth-producing as possible:
1. Forewarning
2. Immediate consequences
3. Consistency
4. Impartiality

1. All employees must be *forewarned* that if they touch the hot stove (break a rule), they will be burned (punished or disciplined). They must know the rule beforehand and be aware of the punishment.
2. If the person touches the stove (breaks a rule), there will be *immediate consequences* (getting burned). All discipline should be administered immediately after rules are broken.
3. If the person touches the stove again, he or she will again be burned. Therefore, there is *consistency*; each time the rule is broken, there are immediate and consistent consequences.
4. If any other person touches the hot stove, he or she also will get burned. Discipline must be *impartial*, and everyone must be treated in the same manner when the rule is broken.

Most rule-breaking is not enforced using McGregor's rules. For example, many people exceed the speed limit when driving. Generally, people are aware of speed limit regulations, and signs are posted along the roadway as reminders of the rules; thus, there is *forewarning*. There is no, however, *immediacy, consistency,* or *impartiality*. Many people exceed the speed limit for long periods before they are stopped and disciplined, or they may never be disciplined at all. Likewise, a person may be stopped and disciplined one day and not the next even though the same rule is broken. Finally, the punishment is inconsistent because some people are punished for their rule-breaking, but others are not. Even the penalty varies among people.

Imagine what would happen if automobiles were developed that alarmed every time a driver exceeded the speed limit and then transmitted this rule violation to local law enforcement so that a speeding ticket could be issued. The incidence of speeding would decrease dramatically. In addition, drivers would likely accept greater accountability for the speeding tickets they received since they would have been forewarned of the consequences of breaking the speed limit rule and they would know that this rule would be enforced consistently and impartially for all drivers.

If a rule or regulation is worth having, it should be enforced. When rule-breaking is allowed to go unpunished, other people tend to replicate the behavior of the rule-breaker. Likewise, the average worker's natural inclination to obey rules can be dissipated by lax or inept enforcement policies because employees develop contempt for managers who allow rules to be disregarded. The enforcement of rules using McGregor's hot stove rules keeps morale from breaking down and allows structure within the organization.

An organization should, however, have as few rules and regulations as possible. A leadership role involves regularly reviewing all rules, regulations, and policies to see if they should be discarded or modified in some way. If managers find themselves spending much of their time enforcing one particular rule, it would be wise to reexamine the rule and consider whether there is something wrong with the rule or how it is communicated.

LEARNING EXERCISE 25.2

Rule Breakers and Outdated Rules

Part 1: Think back to "rule breakers" you have known. Were they a majority or minority in the group? How great was their impact on group behavior? What characteristics did they have in common? Did the group modify the rule breaker's behavior, or did the rule breaker modify group behavior?

Part 2: Rules quickly become outdated and need to be deleted or changed in some way. Think of a policy or rule that needs to be updated. Why is the rule no longer appropriate? What could you do to update this rule? Does the rule need to be replaced with a new one?

DISCIPLINE AS A PROGRESSIVE PROCESS

Managers have the formal authority and responsibility to take progressively stronger forms of discipline when employees fail to meet expected standards of achievement. However, inappropriate discipline (too much or too little) can undermine the morale of the whole team. Determining appropriate disciplinary action, then, is often difficult, and many factors must be considered.

Discipline is generally administered using a progressive model. This is especially true in unionized organizations. However, even in nonunion organizations, managers should have a disciplinary procedure that is written and well communicated.

Action must be taken when employees continue undesirable conduct, either by breaking rules or by not performing their job duties adequately.

Generally, the first step of the progressive disciplinary process is an *informal reprimand* or *verbal admonishment*. This reprimand includes an informal meeting between the employee and the manager to discuss the broken rule or performance deficiency. The manager suggests ways in which the employee's behavior might be altered to keep the rule from being broken again. Often, an informal reprimand is all that is needed for behavior modification.

The second step is a *formal reprimand* or *written admonishment*. If rule-breaking recurs after verbal admonishment, the manager again meets with the employee and issues a written warning about the behaviors that must be corrected. This written warning is very specific about what rules or policies have been violated, the potential consequences if behavior is not altered to meet organizational expectations, and the plan of action that the employee is expected to take to achieve expected change.

Both the employee and the manager should sign the warning to signify that the problem or incident was discussed. The employee's signature does not imply that the employee agrees with everything on the report, only that it has been discussed. The employee must be allowed to respond in writing to the reprimand, either on the form or by attaching comments to the disciplinary report; this allows the employee to air any differences in perception between the manager and the employee. One copy of the written admonishment is then given to the employee, and another copy is retained in the employee's personnel file. Display 25.3 presents a sample written reprimand form.

DISPLAY 25.3   **Sample Written Reprimand Form**

Employee name

Position _____ Date of hire _____
Person completing report _____
Position _____ Date report completed _____
Date of incident(s) _____ Time _____ rule.
Description of incident(s):
Prior attempts to counsel employee regarding this behavior (cite date and results of disciplinary conferences):
Disciplinary contract (plan for correction) and time lines:
Consequences of future repetition:
Employee comments (additional documentation or rebuttal may be attached):

_____ _____
Signature of individual making the report   Employee signature
Date _____ Date _____
Date and time of follow-up appointment to review disciplinary contract:

The third step in progressive discipline is usually a *suspension from work*, either with or without pay. If the employee continues the undesired behavior despite verbal and written warnings, the manager should remove the employee from his or her job for a brief time, generally a few days to several weeks. Such a suspension gives the employee the opportunity to reflect on the behavior and to plan how he or she might modify the behavior in the future.

TABLE 25.1 Guide to Progressive Discipline

Offense	First Infraction	Second Infraction	Third Infraction	Fourth Infraction
Gross mistreatment of a patient	Dismissal			
Discourtesy to a patient	Verbal admonishment	Written admonishment	Suspension	Dismissal
Insubordination	Written admonishment	Suspension	Dismissal	
Use of intoxicants while on duty	Dismissal			
Neglect of duty	Verbal admonishment	Written admonishment	Suspension	Dismissal
Theft or willful damage of property	Written admonishment	Dismissal		
Falsehood	Verbal admonishment	Written admonishment	Dismissal	
Unauthorized absence	Verbal admonishment	Written admonishment	Dismissal	
Abuse of leave	Verbal admonishment	Written admonishment	Suspension	Dismissal
Violation of safety rules	Verbal admonishment	Written admonishment	Dismissal	
Inability to maintain work standards	Verbal admonishment	Written admonishment	Suspension	Dismissal
Excessive unexcused tardiness[a]	Verbal admonishment	Written admonishment	Dismissal	

[a]The first, second, and third infractions do not mean the first, second, and third time an employee is late but the first, second, and third time that unexcused tardiness becomes excessive as determined by the manager.

The last step in progressive discipline is *involuntary termination* or *dismissal*. In reality, many people terminate their employment voluntarily before reaching this step, but the manager cannot count on this happening. Termination should always be the last resort when dealing with poor performance. However, if the manager has given repeated warnings and rule-breaking or policy violations continue, then the employee should be dismissed. Although this is difficult and traumatic for the employee, the manager, and the unit, the cost in terms of managerial and employee time and unit morale of keeping such an employee is enormous.

When using progressive discipline, the steps are followed only for repeated infractions of the same. At the end of a predesignated period, the slate is wiped clean. For example, although an employee may have previously received a formal reprimand for unexcused absences, discipline for a first-time offense of tardiness should begin at the first step of the process. Also, remember that although discipline is generally administered progressively, some rule-breaking is so serious that the employee may be suspended or dismissed with the first infraction. Table 25.1 presents a progressive discipline guide for managers.

 When using progressive discipline in all but the most serious infractions, the slate should be wiped clean at the end of a predesignated period.

LEARNING EXERCISE 25.3

Deciding Upon Disciplinary Action

You are a supervisor in a neurologic care unit. One morning, you receive a report from the night-shift registered nurses (RNs), Nurse Caldwell and Nurse Jones. Neither of the nurses reports anything out of the ordinary, except that a young head-injury patient has been particularly belligerent and offensive in his language. This young man was especially annoying because he appeared rational and then would suddenly become abusive. His language was particularly

(Continued)

vulgar. You recognize that this is fairly normal behavior in a patient with a head injury, but yesterday morning, his behavior was so offensive to his neurosurgeons that one of them threatened to wash his mouth out with soap.

After both night nurses leave the unit, you receive a phone call from the house night supervisor who relates the following information: When the supervisor made the usual rounds to the neuro unit, Nurse Caldwell was on a coffee break and Nurse Jones was in the unit with two licensed vocational nurses/licensed professional nurses. Nurse Jones reported that Nurse Caldwell became very upset with the head-injury patient because of his abusive and vulgar language and had taped his mouth shut with a 4" piece of adhesive tape. Nurse Jones had observed the behavior and had gone to the patient's bedside and removed the piece of tape and suggested that Nurse Caldwell go get a cup of coffee.

The supervisor observed the unit several times following this, and nothing else appeared to be remiss. Stating that no harm had come to the patient, Nurse Jones was reluctant to report the incident but believed that perhaps one of the supervisors should counsel Nurse Caldwell. You thank the night supervisor and consider the following facts in this case:

- Nurse Caldwell has been an excellent nurse but is occasionally judgmental.
- Nurse Caldwell is a very religious young woman and has led a rather sheltered life.
- Taping a patient's mouth with a 4" piece of adhesive tape is very dangerous, especially for someone with questionable chest and abdominal injuries and neurologic injuries.
- Nurse Caldwell has never been reprimanded before.

You call the physician and explain what happened. The physician believes that no harm was done and agrees with you that it is up to you whether to discipline the employee and to what degree. However, the physician believes that most of the medical staff would want the nurse fired.

You phone the nurse and arrange for a conference with her. She tearfully admits what she did. She states that she lost control. She asks you not to fire her, although she agrees this is a dischargeable offense. You consult with the administration, and everyone agrees that you should be the one to decide the disciplinary action in this case.

Assignment: Decide what you would do. You have a duty to your patients, the hospital, and your staff. List at least four possible courses of action. Select from among these choices, and justify your decision.

DISCIPLINARY STRATEGIES FOR THE NURSE-MANAGER

It is vital that managers recognize their power in evaluating and correcting employees' behavior. Because a person's job is very important to him or her—often as a part of self-esteem and as a means of livelihood—disciplining or taking away a person's job is a very serious action and should not be undertaken lightly. The manager can implement several strategies to increase the likelihood that discipline will be fair and produce growth.

The first strategy the manager must use is to thoroughly investigate the situation that has prompted the employee discipline. A supervisor must investigate all allegations of misconduct even if the misconduct is anonymously reported or initially appears to have no basis.

The manager might ask the following questions: Was the rule clear? Did this employee know that he or she was breaking a rule? Is culture a factor in this rule-breaking? Has this employee been involved in a situation like this before? Was he or she disciplined for this behavior? What was his or her response to the corrective action? How serious or potentially serious is the current problem or infraction? Who else was involved in the situation? Does this employee have a history of other types of disciplinary problems? What is the quality of this employee's performance in the work setting? Have other employees in the organization also experienced the problem? How were they disciplined? Could there be a problem with the rule or policy? Were there any special circumstances that could have contributed to the problem in this situation? What disciplinary action is suggested by organization policies for this type of offense? Has precedent been established? Will this type of disciplinary action keep the infraction from recurring? The wise manager will ask all these questions so that a fair decision can be reached regarding an appropriate course of action.

Another strategy that the manager should use is to always consult with either a superior or the human resources department before dismissing an employee. Most organizations have very clear policies about which actions constitute grounds for dismissal and how that dismissal should be handled. To protect themselves from charges of willful or discriminatory termination, managers should carefully document the behavior that occurred and any attempts to counsel the employee. Managers also must be careful not to discuss with one employee the reasons for discharging another employee or to make negative comments about past employees, which may discourage other employees or reduce their trust in the manager.

Performance Deficiency Coaching

Performance deficiency coaching is another strategy that the manager can use to create a disciplined work environment. This type of coaching may be ongoing or problem-centered. *Problem-centered coaching* is less spontaneous and requires more managerial planning than *ongoing coaching*. In performance deficiency coaching, the manager actively brings areas of unacceptable behavior or performance to the attention of the employee and works with him or her to establish a plan to correct deficiencies. Because the role of a coach is less threatening than that of an enforcer, the manager becomes a supporter and helper. Performance deficiency coaching helps employees, over time, to improve their performance to the highest level of which they are capable. As such, the development, use, and mastery of performance deficiency coaching should result in improved performance for all. The scenario depicted in Display 25.4 is an example of performance deficiency coaching.

| DISPLAY 25.4 | Performance Deficiency Coaching Scenario |

Coach: I am concerned that you have been regularly coming into report late. This interrupts the other employees who are trying to hear report and creates overtime because the night shifts must stay and repeat report on the patients you missed. It also makes it difficult for your modular team members to prioritize their plan of care for the day if the entire team is not there and ready to begin at 0700. Why is this problem occurring?

Employee: I've been having problems lately with an unreliable babysitter and my car not starting. It seems like it's always one thing or another, and I'm upset about not getting to work on time, too. I hate starting my day off behind the eight ball.

Coach: This hospital has a long-standing policy on attendance, and it is one of the criteria used to judge work performance on your performance appraisal.

Employee: Yes, I know. I'm just not sure what I can do about it right now.

Coach: What approaches have you tried in solving these problems?

Employee: Well, I'm buying a new car, so that should take care of my transportation problems. I'm not sure about my babysitter, though. She's young and not very responsible, so she'll call me at the last minute and tell me she's not coming. I keep her, though, because she's willing to work the flexible hours and days that this job requires, and she doesn't charge as much as a formal daycare center would.

Coach: Do you have family in the area or close friends you can count on to help with childcare on short notice?

(Continued)

Employee: Yes, my mother lives a few blocks away and is always glad to help, but I couldn't count on her on a regular basis.

Coach: There are employment registry lists at the local college for students interested in providing childcare. Have you thought about trying this option? Often, students can work flexible hours and charge less than formal daycare centers.

Employee: That's a good idea. In fact, I just heard about a childcare referral service that also could give me a few ideas. I'll stop there after work. I realize that my behavior has affected unit functioning, and I promise to try to work this out as soon as possible.

Coach: I'm sure these problems can be corrected. Let's have a follow-up visit in 2 weeks to see how things are going.

LEARNING EXERCISE 25.4

Writing a Performance Deficiency Coaching Plan

You are the professional staff coordinator of a small emergency-care clinic. Historically, the clinic is busiest on weekend evenings when most drunk-driving injuries, stabbings, and gunshot wounds occur. Many also come to the clinic on weekends to take care of nonemergency medical needs that were not addressed during regular physician office hours. Jane has been an RN at the clinic since it opened 2 years ago. She is well liked by all the employees and provides a sense of humor and lightheartedness in what is usually a highly stressful environment.

Jane has a reputation for being a "party animal." She is known to begin partying after work on Friday night and close down the bars Saturday morning. During the last 3 months, Jane has called in sick five of the seven Saturday evenings that she was scheduled to work. The other employees have worked understaffed on what is generally the busiest night of the week, and they are becoming angry. They have asked you to talk to Jane or to staff an additional employee on those Saturday evenings that Jane is assigned to work.

Assignment: You have decided to begin performance deficiency coaching with Jane. Write a possible coaching scenario that includes the following:

- The problem stated in behavioral terms
- An explanation to the employee of how the problem is related to organizational functioning
- A clear statement of the possible consequences of the unwanted behavior
- A request for input from the employee
- Employee participation in the problem solving
- A plan for follow-up on the problem

Disciplinary problems, if unrecognized or ignored, generally do not go away; they only get worse.

The Disciplinary Conference

When coaching is unsuccessful in modifying problem behavior, the manager must take more aggressive steps and use more formal measures, such as a *disciplinary conference*. After thoroughly investigating an employee's offenses, managers must confront the employee with their findings. This occurs in the form of a disciplinary conference. The following steps are generally part of the disciplinary conference.

Reason for Disciplinary Action

Begin by clearly specifying why the employee is being disciplined. The manager must not be hesitant or apologetic. The role of the manager includes authority. Despite the assignment of authority, novice managers often feel uncomfortable with the disciplinary process and may provide unclear or mixed messages to the employee regarding the nature or seriousness of a disciplinary problem. A major responsibility in this role is evaluating employee performance and suggesting appropriate action for improved or acceptable performance.

In the disciplinary conference, managers must assume the authority given to them by their role.

Levoy (2012) notes, however, that great caution should be used in suggesting the problem is an employee's "attitude" since this presumes the manager can read the mind of the problem employee. Instead, focus on the behaviors that are measurable and specific that provide evidence of that attitude.

Employee's Response to Action
Give the employee the opportunity to explain why the rule was not followed. Allowing employees feedback in the disciplinary process ensures them recognition as human beings. It also reassures them that your ultimate goal is to be fair and promote their growth.

Rationale for Disciplinary Action
Explain the disciplinary action that you are going to take and why you are going to take it. Although the manager must keep an open mind to new information that may be gathered in the second step, preliminary assessments regarding the appropriate disciplinary action should already have been made. This discipline should be communicated to the employee. The employee who has been counseled at previous disciplinary conferences should not be surprised at the punishment, as it should have been discussed at the last conference.

Clarification of Expectations for Change
Describe the expected behavioral change and list the steps needed to achieve this change. Explain the consequences of failure to change. Again, do not be apologetic or hesitant; otherwise, the employee will be confused about the seriousness of the issue. Because they may lack self-control, employees who have repeatedly broken rules need firm direction. It must be very clear to the employee that timely follow-up will occur.

Agreement and Acceptance of Action Plan
Get agreement and acceptance of the plan. Give support, and let the employee know that you are interested in him or her as a person. Remember too that the leader-manager administers discipline to promote employee growth rather than to impose punishment. Although the expected standards must be very clear, leaders impart a sense of genuine concern for and desire to help the employee grow. This approach helps the employee to recognize that the discipline is directed at the offensive behavior and not at the individual. The leader must be cautious, however, not to relinquish the management role in an effort to nurture and counsel. The leadership role is to provide a supportive environment and structure so that the employee can make the necessary changes.

Besides understanding what should be covered in the disciplinary conference, the leader must be sensitive to the environment in which discipline is given. Although the employee must receive feedback about his or her rule-breaking or inappropriate behavior as soon as possible after it has occurred, the manager should implement discipline privately, never in front of patients or peers. If more than an informal admonishment is required, the manager should inform the employee of the unacceptable action, and then schedule a formal disciplinary conference later.

All discipline, even informal admonishments, should be conducted in private.

All formal disciplinary conferences should be scheduled in advance at a time agreeable to both the employee and the manager. Both will want time to reflect on the situation that has occurred. Allowing time for reflection should reduce the situation's emotionalism and promote employee self-discipline, because employees often identify their own plan for keeping the behavior from recurring.

In addition to privacy and advance scheduling, the length of the disciplinary conference is important. It should not be so long that it degenerates into a debate, nor so short that both the employee and the manager cannot provide input. If the employee seems overly emotional or if great discrepancies exist between the manager and the employee's perceptions, an additional conference can be scheduled. Employees often need time to absorb what they have been told and to develop a plan that is not defensive.

Clearly, identifying the need for and conducting disciplinary conferences can be as stressful for the manager as it is for the employee, especially when the unit manager is relatively new or inexperienced in this role. Research conducted by O'donnell, Livingston, and Bartram (2012) underscores the emotional component experienced by frontline managers in addressing performance deficits and disciplining employees (Examining the Evidence 25.1).

Examining the Evidence 25.1

Source: O'donnell, D. M., Livingston, P. M., & Bartram, T. (2012). Human resource management activities on the front line: A nursing perspective. Contemporary Nurse: A Journal for the Australian Nursing Profession, 41 (2), 198–205.

Purposive sampling was used to recruit two groups of nurses from one acute hospital within Eastern Health, the second largest public health service located in Victoria, Australia. Group 1 consisted of nurse unit managers employed within the role for a minimum of 4 weeks. Group 2 consisted of five Ward/Unit nursing staff who had worked a minimum of 6 months, to see if those issues identified by the nurse unit managers were also experienced by those staff who reported directly to them. Overall, nine managers participated in the first focus group and five RNs participated in the second.

Two prominent themes emerged as the key human resource management challenges facing the unit managers in their everyday practice. The first was the management of staff behaviors requiring disciplinary intervention, and the second, retention of staff through staff satisfaction. Participants described a variety of behaviors and actions displayed by nursing staff and groups of nursing staff that required some form of disciplinary action to be commenced by the front-line manager. These behaviors included arriving late to work, manipulation, threats, underperformance, general negativity, bitterness, inappropriate comments/actions, and excluding individual staff nurses from group factions. In some cases, and complicating efforts to modify behavior, the erring behavior was influenced by mental illness and/or substance abuse. All of these behaviors were perceived as placing colleagues and patients at risk.

The term "performance management" was used by participants to describe a range of disciplinary activities aimed at modifying or eliminating problem behavior. The process of performance management was described by the unit managers as "long" and "tedious," an "endless" process that is drawn out over months with an unsatisfactory resolution that tends to benefit the individual at the expense of their colleagues. This intensive process was often complicated by the inclusion of union representation at the request of the erring nurse.

Nurse unit managers recognized that they undertook human resource issues, such as performance management "well some days and not others." The dependent variables included "the baggage [the nurse manager] you bring to work" and their exposure and experience within the role. It was noted that the most junior unit manager felt that as a result of her inexperience, she was perceived as a target by some of the staff with strong and challenging behaviors.

The researchers concluded that future frontline management development opportunities should address the foundational knowledge and skill deficits experienced by nurse-managers prior to or during the transition from clinician to manager. Special attention should be paid to the process of managing undesirable behaviors displayed by staff nurses and developing strategies to assist unit managers to cope with stressors experienced during disciplinary interventions.

The Termination Conference

At times, the disciplinary conference must be a termination conference. Although many of the principles are the same, the termination conference differs from a disciplinary conference in that planning for future improvement is eliminated. The following steps should be followed in the termination conference:

1. *Calmly state the reasons for dismissal.* The manager must not appear angry or defensive. Although managers may express regret that the outcome is termination of employment, they must not dwell on this or give the employee reason to think that the decision is not final. The manager should be prepared to give examples of the behavior in question.
2. *Explain the employment termination process.* State the date on which employment is terminated as well as the employee's and organization's role in the process.
3. *Ask for employee input.* Termination conferences are always tense; raw, spontaneous, emotional reactions are common. Listen to the employee, but do not allow yourself to be drawn emotionally into his or her anger or sorrow. Always stay focused on the facts of the case and attempt to respond without reacting.
4. *End the meeting on a positive note, if possible.* The manager should also inform the employee what, if any, references will be supplied to prospective employers. Finally, it is usually best to allow the employee who has been dismissed to leave the organization immediately. If the employee continues to work on the unit after dismissal has been discussed, it can be demoralizing for all the employees who work on that unit.

TRANSFERRING THE PROBLEM EMPLOYEE

A *transfer* may be defined as a reassignment to another job within the organization. In a strict business sense, a transfer usually implies similar pay, status, and responsibility. Because of the variety of positions available for nurses in any health-care organization, coupled with the lack of sufficient higher-level positions available, two additional terms have come into use: lateral transfer and downward transfer.

A *lateral transfer* describes one staff person moving to another unit, to a position with a similar scope of responsibilities, within the same organization. A *downward transfer* occurs when someone takes a position within the organization that is below his or her previous level. It may be in a nurse's interest to consider a downward transfer because it can increase the chances of long-term career success.

Downward transfers also should be considered when nurses are experiencing periods of stress or role overload. Self-aware nurses often request such transfers. In some circumstances, the manager may need to intervene and use a downward transfer to alleviate temporarily a nurse's overwhelming stress. Another type of downward transfer may accommodate employees in the later stages of their career. In many cases, valued employees who wish to reduce their career roles may be accommodated by a manager's assistance with locating a suitable position for their talent and stature in the profession.

Managers often assist valuable employees who desire a reduced role in their careers to locate a position that will use their talents and still allow them a degree of status.

These *accommodating transfers* generally allow someone to receive a similar salary but with a reduction in energy expenditure. For example, a long-time employee might be given a position as ombudsman to use his or her expertise and knowledge of the organization and at the same time assume a status position that is less physically demanding.

Finally, there is the *inappropriate transfer*. Some managers solve unit personnel problems by transferring problem employees to another unsuspecting department. Such transfers are harmful in many ways. They contribute to decreased productivity, are demotivating for all employees, and are especially destructive for the employee who is transferred.

This is not to say that employees who do not "fit" in one department will not do well in a different environment. Before such transfers, however, both the manager and the employee must speak candidly regarding the employee's capabilities and the manager's expectations. All types of transfers should be individually evaluated for appropriateness.

It is not uncommon for an employee to struggle in one department yet improve his or her performance in a new department or unit.

GRIEVANCE PROCEDURES

Growth can only occur when employees perceive that feedback and discipline are fair and just. When employees and managers perceive "fair" and "just" differently, the discrepancy can usually be resolved by a more formal means called a *grievance procedure*. The grievance procedure is essentially a statement of wrongdoing or a procedure to follow when one believes that a wrong has been committed. This procedure is not limited to resolving discipline discrepancies; employees can use it any time they believe that they have not been treated fairly by management. This chapter, however, focuses specifically on grievances that result from the disciplinary process. Most grievances or conflicts between employees and management can be resolved informally through communication, negotiation, compromise, and collaboration. Generally, even informal resolution has well-defined steps that should be followed.

Formal Process

If the employee and management cannot resolve their differences informally, a formal grievance process begins. The steps of the formal grievance process are generally outlined in all union contracts or administrative policy and procedure manuals. Generally, these steps include the progressive lodging of formal complaints up the chain of command. If resolution does not occur at any of these levels, a formal hearing is usually held. A group of people is impaneled—much in the same way as a jury—to make a determination of what should be done. Such groups are often at risk for favoring the individual employee over the all-powerful institution. This tendency reinforces the need for the manager to have clear, objective, and comprehensive written records regarding the problem employee's behavior and attempts to counsel.

Arbitration

If the differences cannot be settled through a formal grievance process, the matter may finally be resolved in a process known as arbitration. In *arbitration*, both sides agree on the selection of a *professional mediator* who will review the grievance, complete fact-finding, and interview witnesses before coming to a decision.

Although grievance procedures extract a great deal of time and energy from both employees and managers, they serve several valuable purposes. Grievance procedures can settle some problems before they escalate into even larger ones. The procedures are also a source of data to focus attention on ambiguous contract language for labor–management negotiation at a later date.

Perhaps the most important outcome of a grievance is the legitimate opportunity that it provides for employees to resolve conflicts with their superiors.

Employees who are not given an outlet for resolving work conflicts become demoralized, angry, and dissatisfied. These emotions affect unit functioning and productivity. Even if the outcome is not in the favor of the person filing the grievance, the employee will know that the opportunity was given to present the case to an objective third party, and the chances of constructive conflict resolution are greatly increased. In addition, managers tend to be fairer and more consistent when they know that employees have a method of redress for arbitrary managerial action.

Rights and Responsibilities in Grievance Resolution

Employees and managers have some separate and distinct rights and responsibilities in grievance resolution, but many rights and responsibilities overlap. Although it is easy to be drawn into the emotionalism of a grievance that focuses on one's perceived rights, the manager and employee must remember that they both have rights and that these rights have concomitant responsibilities. For example, although both parties have the right to be heard, both parties are equally responsible to listen without interrupting. The employee has the right to a positive work environment but has the responsibility to communicate needs and discontent to the manager. The manager has the right to expect a certain level of productivity from the employee but has the responsibility to provide a work environment that makes this possible. The manager has the right to expect employees to follow rules but has the responsibility to see that these rules are clearly communicated and fairly enforced.

Both the manager and the employee must show goodwill in resolving grievances. This means that both parties must be open to discussing, negotiating, and compromising and must attempt to resolve grievances as soon as possible. The ultimate goal of the grievance should not be to win but to seek a resolution that satisfies both the person and the organization.

In many cases, the manager can eliminate or reduce his or her risk of being involved in a grievance by fostering a work environment that emphasizes clear communication and fair, constructive discipline. Employees can also eliminate or reduce their risk of being involved in a grievance by being well informed about the labor contract, policies and procedures, and organizational rules. If both the employee and the employer recognize their rights and responsibilities, the incidence of grievances in the workplace should decrease. When mutual problem-solving, negotiation, and compromise are ineffective at resolving conflicts, the grievance process can provide a positive and growth-producing resolution to disciplinary conflict.

DISCIPLINING THE UNIONIZED EMPLOYEE

It is essential that all managers be fair and consistent in disciplining employees regardless of whether a union is present. The presence of a union does, however, usually entail more procedural, legalistic safeguards in administering discipline and a well-defined grievance process for employees who believe that they have been disciplined unfairly. Usually, the manager of nonunionized employees has greater latitude in selecting which disciplinary measure is appropriate for a specific infraction. Although this gives the manager more flexibility, discipline among employees may be inconsistent.

On the other hand, unionized employees generally must be disciplined according to specific, preestablished steps and penalties within an established time frame. For example, the union contract may be very clear that excessive unexcused absences from work must be disciplined first by a written reprimand, then a 3-day work suspension, and then termination. This type of discipline structure is generally fairer to the employee but allows the manager less flexibility in evaluating each case's extenuating circumstances.

Another aspect of discipline that may differ between unionized and nonunionized employees is following due process in disciplining union employees. *Due process* means that management must provide union employees with a written statement outlining disciplinary charges, the resulting penalty, and the reasons for the penalty. Employees then have the right to defend themselves against such charges and to settle any disagreement through formal grievance hearings.

Another difference between unionized and nonunionized employee discipline lies in the *burden of proof*, which typically is the responsibility of the employee without union membership but is the responsibility of the manager of the employee who belongs to a union. This means that managers who discipline union employees must keep detailed records regarding misconduct and counseling attempts.

 In disciplinary situations with nonunionized employees, the burden of proof typically falls on the employee. With union employees, the burden of proof for the wrongdoing and need for subsequent discipline falls on management.

Another common difference between unionized and nonunionized employees is that most nonunion employees are classified as at-*will*, meaning that they are subject to dismissal "at the will" of the employer. The *at-will doctrine*, which is applicable in many states, permits an employer to terminate employment for any or no reason and at the discretion of the supervisor. In states that do not subscribe to the employment-at-will doctrine or in organizations that have union representation for employees, employers must have good and legal cause to dismiss an employee.

It must be noted, however, that even when the employment-at-will doctrine is applicable, there are numerous exceptions, and an employer must be knowledgeable of each exception. Such exceptions where at-will dismissal would not apply might include when employment is being terminated based on membership in a protected legal group such as race, sex, pregnancy, national origin, religion, disability, age, or military status.

The contract language used by unions regarding discipline may be quite specific or quite general. Most contracts recognize the right of management to discipline, suspend, or dismiss employees for just cause. *Just cause* can be defined as having appropriate rationale for the actions taken. For just cause to exist, the manager must be able to prove that the employee violated established rules, that corrective action or penalty was warranted, and that the penalty was appropriate for the offense. These contracts also generally recognize the right of the employee to submit grievances when he or she believes that these actions have been taken unfairly or are discriminatory in some way.

Managers are responsible for knowing all union contract provisions that affect how discipline is administered on their units. Managers also should work closely with others employed in human resources or personnel positions in the organization. These professionals generally prove to be invaluable resources in dealings with union employees.

THE MARGINAL EMPLOYEE

Marginal employees are another type of problem employee; however, traditional discipline is generally not constructive in modifying their behavior. This is because marginal employees often make tremendous efforts to meet competencies yet usually manage to meet only minimal standards at best. All organizations have at least a few such employees. Managing these employees then is often a frustrating and tiring task.

 Marginal employees usually do not warrant dismissal, but they contribute very little to overall organizational efficiency.

Managers typically try multiple strategies to deal with marginal employees. One common strategy is simply to transfer the employee to another department, section, or unit. Although some marginal employees may be more successful on one unit than another, more commonly, the problem is simply transferred from one unit to another, and the marginal employee experiences yet another failure.

Other managers choose to dismiss marginal employees or attempt to talk them into early retirement or resignation. Again, this does little to help the marginal employee succeed. Other managers simply choose to ignore the problem and attempt to "work around" the employee. This is not always possible, however, and the end result is frequently resentment from coworkers who have to carry the burden of finishing work the marginal employee was unable to accomplish.

The most time-intensive option in dealing with marginal employees is *coaching*. With this strategy, the manager attempts to improve the marginal employee's performance through active coaching and counseling. While this strategy holds the greatest promise for personal growth in the marginal employee, there is no guarantee that the employee's performance will improve or that the end results will justify the time and energy costs to the manager. The strategy chosen for dealing with the marginal employee often varies with the level of the manager. Ignoring the problem is a passive response and is more frequently used by low-level managers. High-level managers tend to employ the more active measures of coaching, transferring, and dismissal.

The nature of the organization also plays a role in determining what strategy is used to deal with the marginal employee. Government-controlled organizations are more likely to use passive measures, whereas managers in nongovernmental organizations are more likely to use active measures. The size of the organization also influences how managers deal with the marginally productive employee. In larger organizations, the trend has been toward passive managerial coping strategies with marginal employees.

It is important for the manager to remember that each person and situation is different and that the most appropriate strategy depends on many variables. Looking at past performance will help determine if the employee is tired, needs educational or training opportunities, is unmotivated, or just has very little energy and only marginal skills for the job. If the latter is true, then the employee may never become more than a marginal employee, no matter what management functions and leadership skills are brought into play.

Learning Exercise 25.5, which has been solved for the reader (see Appendix), depicts alternatives that managers may consider in dealing with the marginal employee.

LEARNING EXERCISE 25.5

The Marginal Employee

You are the oncology supervisor in a 400-bed hospital. There are 35 beds on your unit that are usually full. It is an extremely busy unit, and your nursing staff needs high-level assessment and communication skills for providing patient care. Because the nursing care needs on this floor are unique and because you use primary nursing, it has been very difficult in the past to float staff from other units when additional staffing has been required. Although you have been able to keep the unit adequately staffed on a day-to-day basis, there are two open positions for RNs on your unit that have been unfilled for almost 3 months.

Historically, your staff members have been excellent employees. They enjoy their work and are highly productive. Unit morale has been exceptionally good. However, in the last 3 months, the staff has begun complaining about Judy, a full-time employee who has been with the unit for about 4 months. Judy has been an RN for approximately 15 years and has worked in oncology

(Continued)

units at other facilities. References from former employers identified Judy's work as competent, although little other information was given. At Judy's 6-week and 3-month performance appraisals, you coached her regarding her barely adequate work habits, assessment and communication skills, and decision-making. Judy responded that she would attempt to work on improving her performance in these areas because working with this unit was one of her highest career goals.

Although Judy has been receptive to your coaching and has verbalized to you her efforts to improve her performance, there has been little observable difference in her behavior. You have slowly concluded that Judy is probably currently working at the highest level of her capability and that she is a marginal employee at best. The other nurses believe that Judy is not carrying her share of the workload and have asked that you remove her from the unit.

Assignment: Use the traditional problem-solving process to help you resolve this issue. Compare your solution to the one in Appendix.

THE CHEMICALLY IMPAIRED EMPLOYEE

Substance misuse involves maladaptive patterns of psychoactive substance abuse, with the substance user continuing use in the face of recurrent occupational, social, psychological or physical problems, and/or dangerous situations. Effective management demands that the organization takes an active role in ensuring patient safety by immediately removing these employees from the work setting. However, managers also have a responsibility to help these employees deal with their disease so that they can return to the workforce in the future as productive employees.

Nursing administrators may face no management problem more costly or emotionally draining than that of nurses whose practice is impaired by substance abuse or psychological dysfunction.

Modlin and Montes (1964) first documented chemical dependency in the health professions in studies in the late 1940s, although Monroe (2009) suggests the public recognition of chemical impairment in nursing profession did not even really begin until 1980, when the National Nurses Society of Addictions established a task force on addiction. Despite this relatively recent examination of the problem of substance abuse in nursing, there is little doubt that chemical dependency has been around as long as alcohol and drugs.

The exact magnitude of chemical impairment in nursing is not known and estimates vary widely, but a review of the literature suggests that somewhere between 8% and 16% of all nurses are chemically impaired. In addition, the chemical impairment rate of health professionals is generally acknowledged as being greater than that of the general public.

Scimeca (2008) suggests that a conservative estimate is that one in ten nurses will develop a problem with drugs and/or alcohol within their lifetime and that the prevalence may be double that. She notes that given the millions of nurses licensed in the United States alone, even the lower assessment of 10% represents nearly 500,000 individuals. If one were to calculate this number on an annual basis over a 70-year span, this would mean that more than 7,000 nurses cross an invisible line into what often becomes a very visible problem each year in this country (Scimeca). Heacock (2013) adds that while the risk of addiction is not limited to any one specialty, the specialties with the highest prevalence of substance abuse uses are intensive care unit, emergency room, operating room, and anesthesia.

Talbert (2009) suggests that several factors have been identified as increasing the risk of substance abuse in nurses, including a family history of emotional impairment, alcoholism, drug use, or emotional abuse, resulting in low self-esteem, overwork, and overachievement. This family history is significant since being in an environment with dependent family members may lead to enabling behaviors, often described as "helping" behaviors. Research by Dittman (2012) concurs, suggesting that having experienced physical or emotional abuse during their formative years was a common finding in male nurses who developed substance abuse problems. These nurses reported chaotic environments in childhood in the form of maltreatment, neglect, denial, and enabling behavior that resulted in an unstable lifestyle.

Stress in the workplace is another reason cited for nurses abusing substances, since overtime, floating, rotating shifts, and workplace bullying can contribute to stress, fatigue, and feelings of alienation (Talbert). Substance use may be one way of coping. Again, research by Dittman (2012) supports these assertions in that substance abusing male nurses reported a need to cover up stress and sensation-seeking behaviors related to medication diversion. Similarly, Heacock (2013) suggests that long hours and stress related to caring for the sick and dying as well as easy access to medications increase the risk of addiction in nursing.

One difference, however, between chemically impaired health professionals and other addicts is that chemically impaired nurses and physicians tend to obtain their drugs of choice through channels such as legitimate prescriptions that were written for them or diversionary measures on the job rather than purchasing them illegally on the street. Since nurses have greater access to undiverted medications (colleagues write prescriptions or prescriptions are forged) and since they are highly experienced in administering medications to others, they sometimes erroneously believe that they have the ability to control their own medication use (Talbert, 2009).

Despite narcotic-dispensing machines, introduced to reduce the diversion of these drugs, workplace theft has been identified as the most frequent source of illegally obtained narcotics. Indeed, one nurse who surrendered her license after being investigated by the Board of Nursing for an addiction to prescription drugs suggested that "In nursing school they really should warn you that you're going to have a buffet of narcotics at your hands that's part of your job" (Jorgensen, 2013, para 3). In fact, the majority of disciplinary actions by licensing boards are related to misconduct resulting from chemical impairment including the misappropriation of drugs for personal use and the sale of drugs and drug paraphernalia to support an addiction (Lillibridge, 2014).

Although alcohol is the most frequently abused substance, meperidine (Demerol) is a common drug of choice, while oxycodone (OxyContin) and clonazepam (Klonopin) are increasing in popularity (National Institute on Drug Abuse, 2013). Other frequently abused chemicals include benzodiazepines such as diazepam (Valium) and narcotic drugs such as morphine and pentazocine (Talwin). Barbiturates may replace alcohol in the workplace so that the employee may feel a similar effect without having alcohol detectable on their breath.

RECOGNIZING THE CHEMICALLY IMPAIRED EMPLOYEE

Although most nurses have finely tuned assessment skills for identifying patient problems, they may be less sensitive to behaviors and actions that may signify chemical impairment in their coworkers. Sensitivity to others and to the environment is a leadership skill. The profile of the impaired nurse may vary greatly, although several behavior patterns and changes are noted frequently. These behavior changes can be grouped into three primary areas: personality/behavior changes, job performance changes, and time and attendance changes. Display 25.5 shows characteristics of these categories.

As the employee progresses into chemical dependency, managers can more easily recognize these behaviors. Typically, in the earliest stages of chemical dependency, the

DISPLAY 25.5 | Characteristic Changes in Chemically Impaired Employees

CHANGES IN PERSONALITY OR BEHAVIORS

- Increased irritability with patients and colleagues, often followed by extreme calm
- Social isolation; eats alone, avoids unit social functions
- Extreme and rapid mood swings
- Euphoric recall of events or elaborate excuses for behaviors
- Unusually strong interest in narcotics or the narcotic cabinet
- Sudden dramatic change in personal grooming or any other area
- Forgetfulness ranging from simple short-term memory loss to blackouts
- Change in physical appearance, which may include weight loss, flushed face, red or bleary eyes, unsteady gait, slurred speech, tremors, restlessness, diaphoresis, bruises and cigarette burns, jaundice, and ascites
- Extreme defensiveness regarding medication errors

CHANGES IN JOB PERFORMANCE

- Difficulty meeting schedules and deadlines
- Illogical or sloppy charting
- High frequency of medication errors or errors in judgment affecting patient care
- Frequently volunteers to be medication nurse
- Has a high number of assigned patients who complain that their pain medication is ineffective in relieving their pain
- Consistently meeting work performance requirements at minimal levels or doing the minimum amount of work necessary
- Judgment errors
- Sleeping or dozing on duty
- Complaints from other staff members about the quality and quantity of the employee's work

CHANGES IN ATTENDANCE AND USE OF TIME

- Increasingly absent from work without adequate explanation or notification; most frequent absence on a Monday or Friday
- Long lunch hours
- Excessive use of sick leave or requests for sick leave after days off
- Frequent calling in to request compensatory time
- Arriving at work early or staying late for no apparent reason
- Consistent lateness
- Frequent disappearances from the unit without explanation

employee uses the addictive substance primarily for pleasure, and although the alcohol or drug use is excessive, it is primarily recreational and social. Thus, substance use usually does not occur during work hours, although some secondary effects of its use may be apparent.

As chemical dependency deepens, the employee develops tolerance to the chemical and must use greater quantities more frequently to achieve the same effect. At this point, the person has made a conscious lifestyle decision to use chemicals. There is a high use of defense mechanisms, such as justifying, denying, and bargaining about the drug. Often, the employee in this stage begins to use the chemical substance both at and away from work. Work performance generally declines in the areas of attendance, judgment, quality, and interpersonal relationships. An appreciable decline in unit morale, resulting from an unreliable and unproductive worker, becomes apparent.

In the final stages of chemical dependency, the employee must continually use the chemical substance, even though he or she no longer gains pleasure or gratification. Physically and psychologically addicted, the employee generally harbors a total disregard for self and others. Because the need for the substance is so great, the employee's personal and professional lives focus on the need for drugs, and the employee becomes unpredictable and undependable in the work area. Assignments are incomplete or not done at all, charting may be sloppy or illegible, and frequent judgment errors occur. Because the employee in this stage must use drugs frequently, signs of drug use during work hours may be seen. Narcotic vials are missing. The employee may be absent from the unit for brief periods with no plausible excuse. Mood swings are excessive, and the employee often looks physically ill.

Research by Dittman (2012, p. 37) concurs, noting that substance abusing male nurses reported that access to medications at this point in their life became a driving force. "Their guiding principles of lying, hiding, denying, diverting, and manipulating affected their families, peers, patients, and profession. Their motivation to continue the competent nurse appearance was based on the underlying concern of how this would affect their lives, not how it would affect others." In addition, addiction clouded their professional compasses since no need was greater than the need for chemical substances (Dittman).

The bottom line is that chemically impaired employees should be removed from the work setting long before they reach this stage. The reality, however, is that the identification of chemical impairment is often very difficult. Nursing school courses generally focus on the physiological effects of alcohol and other drugs, dealing little with the psychological process of addiction and even less with chemical dependency in nurses. Because of this limited knowledge about chemical impairment, many nurses are ill-prepared to deal with chemical impairment.

Confronting the Chemically Impaired Employee

Unlike most alcoholics or IV narcotic users, health-care professionals do not achieve tacit peer acceptance of their addictive behavior. Thus, physicians and nurses are much less likely to admit, even to colleagues, that they are using—much less that they are addicted to—a controlled substance. Frequently, they deny their chemical impairment even to themselves. Indeed, research by Dittman (2012) found that none of the impaired male nurses in the study self-reported their addiction; all were caught in either a medication audit or urine drug screen.

This self-denial is perpetuated because nurses and managers traditionally have been slow to recognize and reluctant to help these colleagues. This is changing. All but a few state boards of nursing now have treatment programs for nurses (discussed later in this chapter), and as managers gain more information about chemical impairment, how to recognize it, and how to intervene, more employees are being confronted with their impairment.

The first step in dealing with the chemically impaired employee actually occurs before the confrontation process. In the data- or evidence-gathering phase, the manager collects as much hard evidence as possible to document suspicions of chemical impairment in the employee. All behavior, work performance, and time and attendance changes presented in the displays in this chapter should be noted objectively and recorded in writing. If possible, a second person should be asked to validate the manager's observations. In suspected drug addiction, the manager also may examine unit narcotic records for inconsistencies and check to see that the amount of narcotic the nurse signed out for each patient is the same as the amount ordered for that patient.

Because few nurses drink alcohol while on duty, managers have to observe for more subtle clues, such as the smell of alcohol on the employee's breath. If the organization's policy allows for it, the manager may wish to require an employee suspected of chemical impairment to undergo immediate drug or alcohol testing. If the employee refuses to cooperate, the organization's policy for documenting and reporting this incident should be followed.

 Proving alcohol impairment is often more difficult than detecting drug impairment, as an employee can generally hide alcoholism more easily than drug addiction.

If at any time the manager suspects that an employee is chemically influenced and thus presents a potential hazard to patient safety, the employee must be immediately removed from the work environment. The manager should decisively and unemotionally tell the employee that he or she will not be allowed to return to the work area because of the manager's perception that the employee is chemically impaired. The manager should arrange for the employee to be taken home so that he or she does not drive while impaired. A formal meeting to discuss this incident should be scheduled within the next 24 hours.

This type of direct confrontation between the manager and the employee is the second phase in dealing with the employee suspected of chemical impairment. Although some employees admit their problem when directly confronted, many use defense mechanisms (including denial) because they may not have admitted the problem to themselves. Indeed, research conducted on nurses with a history of substance abuse suggests that chemically dependent individuals often report becoming masterminds at manipulating all connections to human and professional resources, including family, friends, professional peers, professional superiors, and the rehabilitation process (Dittman, 2012).

Denial and anger should be expected in the confrontation. If the employee denies having a problem, documented evidence demonstrating a decline in work performance should be shared. The manager must be careful to keep the confrontation focused on the employee's performance deficits and not allow the discussion to be directed to the cause of the underlying problem or addiction. These are issues and concerns that the manager is unable to address. The manager also must be careful not to preach, moralize, scold, or blame.

Confrontation always should occur before the problem escalates too far. However, in some situations, the manager may have only limited direct evidence but still may believe that the employee should be confronted because of rapidly declining employee performance or unit morale. There is, however, a greater risk that confrontation at this point may be unsuccessful in terms of helping the employee. If direct confrontation is unsuccessful, it may have been too early; the employee may not have been desperate enough or may still be in denial. In these situations, job performance will probably continue to be marginal or unsatisfactory, and progressive discipline may be necessary. If the employee continues to deny chemical impairment and work performance continues to be unsatisfactory despite repeated constructive confrontation, dismissal may be necessary.

The last phase of the confrontation process is outlining the organization's plan or expectations for the employee in overcoming the chemical impairment. This plan is similar to the disciplinary contract in that it is usually written down and clearly outlines the rehabilitative measures that should be undertaken by the employee and consequences if remedial action is not sought. Although the employee is generally referred informally by the manager to outside sources to help deal with the impairment, the employee is responsible for correcting his or her work deficiencies. Timelines are included in the plan, and the manager and employee must agree on and sign a copy of the contract.

LEARNING EXERCISE 25.6

The Chemically Impaired Colleague

Write a two-page essay that speaks to the following: Has your personal or professional life been affected by a chemically impaired person? In what ways have you been affected? Has it colored the way that you view chemical abuse and chemical impairment? Do you believe that you can separate your personal feelings about chemical abuse from the actions that you must take as a manager in working with chemically impaired employees? Have you ever suspected a work colleague of chemical abuse? What, if anything, did you do about it? If you did suspect a colleague, would you approach him or her with your suspicions before talking to the unit manager? Describe the risks involved in this situation.

The Manager's Role in Assisting the Chemically Impaired Employee

Clearly, the incidence of chemical impairment in health professionals is substantial. On a personal level, a person suffers from an illness that may go undetected and untreated for many years. On a professional level, the chemically impaired employee affects the entire health-care system. Nurses with impaired skills and judgment jeopardize patient care. The chemically impaired nurse also compromises teamwork and continuity as colleagues attempt to pick up the slack for their impaired team member. The personal and professional cost of chemical impairment demands that nursing leaders and managers recognize the chemically impaired employee as early as possible and intervene.

Because of the general nature of nursing, many managers find themselves wanting to nurture the impaired employee, much as they would any other person who is sick. However, this nurturing can quickly become enabling. The employee who already has a greatly diminished sense of self-esteem and a perceived loss of self-control may ask the manager to participate actively in his or her recovery. This is one of the most difficult aspects of working with the impaired employee. Others who have greater expertise and objectivity should assume this role.

The manager must be very careful not to assume the role of counselor or treatment provider for the impaired nurse.

The manager also must be careful not to feel the need to diagnose the cause of the chemical addiction or to justify its existence. Protecting patients must be the top priority, taking precedence over any tendency to protect or excuse subordinates. The manager's role is to clearly identify performance expectations for the employee and to confront the employee when those expectations are not met. This is not to say that the manager should not be humanistic in recognizing the problem as a disease and not a disciplinary problem or that he or she should be unwilling to refer the employee for needed help. Although the manager may suggest appropriate help or refer the impaired employee to someone, a manager's primary responsibility is to see that the employee becomes functional again and can meet organizational expectations before returning to work.

The manager can play a vital role in creating an environment that decreases the chances of chemical impairment in the work setting. This may be done by controlling or reducing work-related stressors whenever possible and by providing mechanisms for employee stress management. The manager also should control drug accessibility by implementing, enforcing, and monitoring policies and procedures related to medication distribution. Finally, the manager should provide opportunities for the staff to learn about substance abuse, its detection, and available resources to help those who are impaired.

LEARNING EXERCISE 25.7

Working Under the Influence

There have been rumors for some time that Mrs. Clark, one of the night nurses on the unit you supervise, has been coming to work under the influence of alcohol. Fellow staff have reported the odor of alcohol on her breath, and one staff member stated that her speech is often slurred. The night supervisor states that she believes "this is not my problem," and your night charge nurse has never been on duty when Mrs. Clark has shown this behavior. This morning, one of the patients whispered to you that he thought Mrs. Clark had been drinking when she came to work last night. When you question the patient further, he states, "Mrs. Clark seemed to perform her nursing duties okay, but she made me nervous." You have decided that you must talk with Mrs. Clark. You call her at her home and ask her to come to your office at 3 PM.

Assignment: Determine how you are going to approach Mrs. Clark. Outline your plan and provide rationale for your choices. What flexibility have you built into your plan? How much of your documentation will be shared with Mrs. Clark?

The Recovery Process

Although most authorities disagree on the name or number of steps in the recovery process, they do agree that certain phases or progressive observable behaviors suggest that the person is recovering from the chemical impairment. In the first phase, the impaired employee continues to deny the significance or severity of the chemical impairment but does reduce or suspend chemical use to appease family, peers, or managers. These employees hope to reestablish their substance abuse in the future.

In the second phase, as denial subsides, the impaired employee begins to see that the chemical addiction is having a negative impact on his or her life and begins to want to change. Frequently, people in this phase are buoyant with hope and commitment but lack maturity about the struggles they will face. This phase generally lasts for about 3 months.

During the third phase, the person examines his or her values and coping skills and works to develop more effective coping skills. Frequently, this is done by aligning himself or herself with support groups that reinforce a chemical-free lifestyle. In this stage, the person realizes how sick he or she was in the active stage of the disease and is often fraught with feelings of humiliation and shame.

In the last phase, people gain self-awareness regarding why they became chemically addicted, and they develop coping skills that will help them deal more effectively with stressors. As a result of this, self-awareness, self-esteem, and self-respect increase. When this happens, the person can decide consciously whether he or she wishes to or should return to the workplace.

State Board of Nursing Treatment Programs

Although chemical dependency can impair nurses' physical, psychological, social, and professional functioning, the problem was largely ignored until the late 1970s and early 1980s. Since that time, assistance occurs primarily in the form of *diversion programs* (also called *intervention or peer assistance* programs). A diversion program is generally a voluntary, confidential program for nurses whose practice may be impaired due to chemical dependency or mental illness.

The goal of a diversion program is to protect the public by early identification of impaired nurses and by providing these nurses access to appropriate intervention programs and treatment services. Public safety is protected by immediate suspension of practice, when needed, and by ongoing careful monitoring of the nurse. In addition to rehabilitating nurses with chemical dependence, most diversion programs also serve nurses impaired by certain mental illnesses such as anxiety, depression, bipolar disorder, and schizophrenia. Some programs cover nurses with physical disabilities as well.

Several factors have led state boards to adopt diversion programs. First, a punitive system creates barriers to reporting and keeps impaired nurses from getting help. Nurse colleagues or practitioners who suspect a nurse is impaired may well hesitate to report something that could cost a nurse his or her job and license. Monroe (2009) agrees, suggesting that coworkers are more likely to intervene and report impairment when supportive alternative-to-dismissal policies are in place. In addition, from an employer's standpoint, the fear of litigation often makes it easier to dismiss a nurse without charges of misconduct. But this practice leaves the nurse, who is at risk for self-harm and for harming patients, free to seek work elsewhere. A board investigation can take months to 2 years, during which time the nurse in question may be able to continue working without restraint. Moving to another state will not, however, allow the nurse to avoid disciplinary action and states typically consider this in granting license reciprocity.

Diversion programs are voluntary and confidential. Besides helping the nurse with recovery, the programs offer assistance to the employers and staff in coping with employee substance abuse. Impaired nurses who refuse participation in diversion programs are subject to disciplinary review by their state board of nursing and possible license revocation. Nurse-leader-managers should advocate for those who are impaired so that they receive appropriate assistance, treatment, and access to fair institutional and legal processes.

The fear of being ostracized by their colleagues has kept many nurses from seeking help even though they knew they were addicted to drugs. Indeed, negative and stigmatizing attitudes continue to surround most individuals experiencing drug and alcohol dependency and this is accentuated for the nursing professional, who is often held to an even higher standard of behavior. Lillibridge (2014) suggests that while nursing is a profession known for its caring nature toward others, we often fail to care for ourselves. She goes on to say that employers must create positive work environments, know their employees so that confrontation can occur early, increase awareness about substance abuse so that nurses are not afraid to ask for help, ensure that an *Impaired Practice Policy* is in place, and provide a process that facilitates reentry into practice following recovery.

LEARNING EXERCISE 25.8

Researching Your State Board of Nursing's Recovery Program

Determine if your state board of nursing offers some type of recovery program for chemically impaired nurses and for mentally ill nurses. You may either call the board or use the Internet. Research the following questions:

- Is the program voluntary and confidential?
- What is the rate of *recidivism*?
- What types of monitoring mechanisms are in place?
- What is the duration of the program?
- Are nurses allowed to continue practicing while completing the treatment program?
- Are there practice restrictions?

Assignment: Write a one-page report of your findings.

The Chemically Impaired Employee's Reentry to the Workplace

Because chemically impaired nurses recover at varying rates, predicting how long this process will take is difficult. Many experts believe that impaired employees must devote at least 1 year to their recovery without the stresses of drug availability, overtime, and shift rotation. Success in reentering the workforce depends on factors such as the extent of the recovery process and individual circumstances. Again, although managers must show a genuine personal interest in their employee's rehabilitation, their primary role is to be sure that the employee understands the organization's right to insist on unimpaired performance in the workplace. The following are generally accepted reentry guidelines for the recovering nurse:

- No psychoactive drug use will be tolerated.
- The employee should be assigned to day shift for the first year.
- The employee should be paired with a successfully recovering nurse whenever possible.
- The employee should be willing to consent to random urine screening with toxicology or alcohol screens.

- The employee must give evidence of continuing involvement with support groups such as Alcoholics Anonymous and Narcotics Anonymous. Employees should be encouraged to attend meetings several times each week.
- The employee should be encouraged to participate in a structured aftercare program.
- The employee should be encouraged to seek individual counseling or therapy as needed.

These guidelines should be a part of the employee's return to work contract. Mandatory drug testing, however, invokes questions about privacy rights and generally should not be implemented without advice from human resources personnel or legal counsel. Humanistic leaders recognize the intrinsic self-worth of each individual employee and strive to understand the unique needs these workers have. If the leader genuinely cares about and shows interest in each employee, employees learn to trust and the helping relationship has a chance to begin.

Managers have the responsibility to be proactive in identifying and confronting chemically impaired employees. Prompt and appropriate intervention by managers is essential for positive outcomes. Organizations have an ethical responsibility to actively assist these employees to return as productive members of the workforce.

INTEGRATING LEADERSHIP ROLES AND MANAGEMENT FUNCTIONS WHEN DEALING WITH PROBLEM EMPLOYEES

The leader recognizes that all employees have intrinsic worth and assists them in reaching their maximal potential. Because individual abilities, achievement drives, and situations vary, the leader recognizes each employee as an individual with unique needs and intervenes according to those specific needs. In some situations, such as frequent rule-breaking, discipline may be the most effective tool for ensuring that employees succeed. In the case of the chemically or psychologically impaired employee, there is a need to balance the concern for patient safety with concern for the health of the employee (Lillibridge, 2014). Assisting the employee to get the treatment needed is a primary management responsibility.

Constructive discipline then requires leadership and management skills. In administering discipline, the leader actively shapes group norms and promotes self-discipline. The leader also is a supporter, motivator, enabler, and coach. The humanistic attributes of the leadership role make employees want to follow the rules of the leader and thus the organization. In dealing with the employee with special needs (the marginal employee, those who are psychologically or chemically impaired), the leader serves more as a coach and resource person than as a counselor, disciplinarian, or authority figure.

The manager, however, must enforce established rules, policies, and procedures, and although good managerial practice greatly reduces the need for discipline, some employees still need external direction and discipline to accomplish organizational goals. Discipline allows employees to understand clearly the expectations of the organization and the penalty for failing to meet those expectations. The manager's primary obligation is to see that patient safety is assured and that productivity is adequate to meet unit goals. The manager uses the authority inherent in his or her position to provide positive and negative sanctions for employee behavior in an effort to meet these goals.

The effective leader-manager blends these unit productivity needs and human resource needs; however, selecting and implementing appropriate strategies to meet both goals is difficult. The leader-manager believes that each employee has the potential to be a successful and valuable member of the unit and intervenes accordingly to meet each employee's special needs.

KEY CONCEPTS

- It is essential that managers are able to distinguish between employees who need progressive discipline and those who are chemically impaired, psychologically impaired, or marginal employees so that the employee can be managed in the most appropriate manner.

- Discipline is a necessary and positive tool in promoting subordinate growth.

- The optimal goal in constructive discipline is assisting employees to behave in a manner that allows them to be self-directed in meeting organizational goals.

- To ensure fairness, rules should include McGregor's "hot stove" components of forewarning, immediate application, consistency, and impartiality.

- If a rule or regulation is worth having, it should be enforced. When rule-breaking is allowed to go unpunished, groups generally adjust to and replicate the low-level performance of the rule-breaker.

- As few rules and regulations as possible should exist in the organization, all rules, regulations, and policies should be regularly reviewed to see if they should be deleted or modified in some way.

- Except for the most serious infractions, discipline should be administered in progressive steps, which include verbal admonishment, written admonishment, suspension, and dismissal.

- In performance deficiency coaching, the manager actively brings areas of unacceptable behavior or performance to the attention of the employee and works with him or her to establish a short-term plan to correct deficiencies.

- The grievance procedure is essentially a statement of wrongdoing or a procedure to follow when one believes that a wrong has been committed. All employees should have the right to file grievances about disciplinary action that they believe has been arbitrary or unfair in some way.

- The presence of a union generally entails more procedural, legalistic safeguards for administering discipline and a well-defined grievance process for employees who believe that they have been disciplined unfairly.

- Because chemical and psychological impairment are diseases, traditional progressive discipline is inappropriate because it cannot result in employee growth.

- The profile of the impaired nurse may vary greatly, although typically behavior changes are seen in three areas: personality/behavior changes, job performance changes, and time and attendance changes.

- Nurses and managers traditionally have been slow to recognize and respond to chemically impaired colleagues.

- Confronting an employee who is suspected of chemical impairment should always occur before the problem escalates and before patient safety is jeopardized.

- The manager should not assume the role of counselor or treatment provider or feel the need to diagnose the cause of the chemical addiction. The manager's role is to clearly identify performance expectations for the employee and to confront the employee when those expectations are not met.

- Strategies for dealing with marginal employees vary with management level, the nature of the health-care organization, and the current prevailing attitude toward passive or active intervention.

ADDITIONAL LEARNING EXERCISES AND APPLICATIONS

LEARNING EXERCISE 25.9

Determining an Appropriate Action When Proof Is Unavailable

You are the supervisor of a pediatric acute-care unit. One of your patients, Joey, is a 5-year-old boy who sustained 30% third-degree burns, which have been grafted and are now healing. He has been a patient in the unit for approximately 2 months. His mother stays with him nearly all the waking hours and generally is supportive of both him and the staff.

(Continued)

In the last few weeks, Joey has begun expressing increasing frustration with basic nursing tasks, has frequently been uncooperative, and in your staff's opinion has become very manipulative. His mother is frustrated with Joey's behavior but believes that it is understandable given the trauma he has experienced. She has begun working with the staff on a mutually acceptable behavior modification program.

Although you have attempted to assign the same nurses to care for Joey as often as possible, it is not possible today. This lack of continuity is especially frustrating because the night shift has reported frequent tantrums and uncooperative behavior. The nurse whom you have assigned to Joey is Monica. She is a good nurse but has lacked patience in the past with uncooperative patients. During the morning, you are aware that Joey is continuing to act out. Although Monica begins to look more and more harried, she states that she is handling the situation appropriately.

When you return from lunch, Joey's mother is waiting at your office. She furiously reports that Joey told her that Monica hit him and told him he was "a very bad boy" after his mother had gone to lunch. His mother believes that physical punishment was totally inappropriate, and she wants this nurse to be fired. She also states that she has contacted Joey's physician and that he is on his way over.

You call Monica to your office where she emphatically denies all the allegations. Monica states that during the lunch hour, Joey refused to allow her to check his dressings and that she followed the behavior modification plan and discontinued his television privileges. She believes that his accusations further reflect his manipulative behavior. You then approach Joey, who tearfully and emphatically repeats the story that he told to his mother. He is consistent about the details and swears to his mother that he is telling the truth. None of your staff was within hearing range of Joey's room at the time of the alleged incident. When Joey's doctor arrives, he demands that Monica be fired.

Assignment: Determine your action. You do not have proof to substantiate either Monica or Joey's story. You believe that Monica is capable of the charges but are reluctant to implement any type of discipline without proof. What factors contribute the most to your decision?

LEARNING EXERCISE 25.10

What Type of Discipline Is Appropriate?

Susie has been an RN on your medical–surgical unit for 18 months. During that time, she has been competent in terms of her assessment and organizational skills and her skills mastery. Her work habits, however, need improvement. She frequently arrives 5 to 10 minutes late for work and disrupts report when she arrives. She also frequently extends her lunch break 10 minutes beyond the allotted 30 minutes. Her absence rate is twice that of most of your other employees. You have informally counseled Susie about her work habits on numerous past occasions. Last month, you issued a written reprimand about these work deficiencies and placed it in Susie's personnel file. Susie acknowledged at that time that she needed to work on these areas but that her responsibilities as a single parent were overwhelming at times and that she felt demotivated at work. Every day this week, Susie has arrived 15 minutes late. The staff are complaining about Susie's poor attitude and have asked that you take action.

You contemplate what additional action you might take. The next step in progressive discipline would be a suspension without pay. You believe that this action could be supported given the previous attempts to counsel the employee without improvement. You also realize that many of your staff are closely watching your actions to see how you will handle this situation. You also recognize that suspending Susie would leave her with no other means of financial support and that this penalty is somewhat uncommon for the offenses described. In addition, you are unsure if this penalty will make any difference in modifying Susie's behavior.

Assignment: Decide what type of discipline, if any, is appropriate for Susie. Support your decision with appropriate rationale. Discuss your actions in terms of the effects on you, Susie, and the department.

LEARNING EXERCISE 25.11

Discipline and Insubordination

You are the coordinator of a small, specialized respiratory rehabilitation unit. Two other nurses work with you. Because all of the staff are professionals, you have used a very democratic approach to management and leadership. This approach has worked well, and productivity has always been high. The nurses work out schedules so that there are always two nurses on duty during the week, and they take turns covering the weekends, at which time there is only one RN on duty. With this arrangement, it is possible for three nurses to be on duty 1 day during the week, if there is no holiday or other time off scheduled by either of the other two RNs.

Several months ago, you told the other RNs that the state licensing board was arriving on Wednesday, October 16, to review the unit. It would, therefore, be necessary for both of them to be on duty because you would be staying with the inspectors all day. You have reminded them several times since that time.

Today is Monday, October 14, and you are staying late preparing files for the impending inspection. Suddenly, you notice that only one of the RNs is scheduled to work on Wednesday. Alarmed, you phone Mike, the RN who is scheduled to be off. You remind him about the inspection and state that it will be necessary for him to come to work. He says that he is sorry that he forgot about the inspection but that he has scheduled a 3-day cruise and has paid a large, nonrefundable deposit. After a long talk, it becomes obvious to you that Mike is unwilling to change his plans. You say to him, "Mike, I feel this borders on insubordination. I really need you on the 16th, and I am requesting that you come in. If you do not come to work, I will need to take appropriate action." Mike replies, "I'm sorry to let you down. Do what you have to do. I need to take this trip, and I will not cancel my plans."

Assignment: What action could you take? What action should you take? Outline some alternatives. Assume that it is not possible to float in additional staff because of the specialty expertise required to work in this department. Decide what you should do. Give rationale for your decision. Did ego play a part in your decision?

REFERENCES

Dittman, P. (2012). Mountains to climb: Male nurses and their perspective on professional impairment. *International Journal For Human Caring, 16*(1), 34–41.

Heacock, S. (2013, January 6). *Nurses and substance abuse.* Nursetogether. Retrieved June 29, 2013, from http://www.nursetogether.com/nurses-and-substance-abuse

Jorgensen, D. (2013, April 25). *Prescription drug abuse among nurses.* Keloland TV. Retrieved June 29,

2013, from http://www.keloland.com/newsdetail.cfm/prescription-drug-abuse-among-nurses/?id=147176

Levoy, B. (2012). How to deal with problem employees. *Podiatry Management, 31*(5), 47–48.

Lillibridge, J. (2014). Impaired nursing practice. What are we doing about it? In C. Huston (Ed.), *Professional issues in nursing* (3rd ed.). Philadelphia, PA: Lippincott Williams & Wilkins 266–277.

Luse, K. A. (2013). Managerial strategies for creating an effective work environment. *Radiologic Technology, 84*(4), 383–397.

McGregor, D. (1967). *The professional manager.* New York, NY: McGraw-Hill.

Modlin, H. C., & Montes, A. (1964). Narcotics addiction in physicians. *American Journal of Psychiatry, 121,* 358–363.

Monroe, T. (2009, May). Educational innovations. Addressing substance abuse among nursing students: Development of a prototype alternative-to-dismissal policy. *Journal of Nursing Education, 48*(5), 272–278.

National Institute on Drug Abuse (NIDA). (2013, May). *Drug Facts: Prescription and over-the-counter medications.* Retrieved August 22, 2013, from http://www.drugabuse.gov/publications/drugfacts/prescription-over-counter-medications

O'donnell, D. M., Livingston, P. M., & Bartram, T. (2012). Human resource management activities on the front line: A nursing perspective. *Contemporary Nurse: A Journal for the Australian Nursing Profession, 41*(2), 198–205.

Scimeca, P. D. (2008) *Unbecoming a nurse. Bypassing the hidden chemical dependency trap.* Staten Island, NY: Sea Meca, Inc.

Talbert, J. (2009, February). Substance abuse among nurses. *Clinical Journal of Oncology Nursing, 13*(1), 17–19.

Solutions to Selected Learning Exercises

The following are possible solutions for challenging situations presented in various Learning Exercises throughout the book.

LEARNING EXERCISE 9.6

A Busy Day at the Public Health Agency
Here is how one nurse handled interruptions and still had time for lunch.

Time	Task	Rationale
8:00 AM	Assign lunch breaks: 11:30–12:30–receptionist 12:30–1:30–clerical worker 12:00–1:00–you	Because you have a lunch engagement at noon, make sure other employees know when their lunch times must be.
	Finish reports	Because reports are due tonight, this would be the immediate task to be accomplished. Plan to finish these by 9 AM.
8:30 AM	Supervisor's request	Ask her when she needs the information. Tell her an estimate using primary diagnoses is now available but that an accurate figure that includes secondary diagnoses must wait until you have time to go through your 150 family case files, which will be next week.
9:00 AM	Client with pregnant daughter	The pregnancy takes priority over the chest clinic drop-ins. Ask the receptionist to start the paperwork on drop-ins while you spend 30 min with the mother.
9:30 AM	Phone call	Delegate this to the receptionist.
9:30 AM	Dental clinic referral	Delegate this duty to the clerical worker.
10:00 AM	Client call	Because this person is confused and you do not have available information, ask that he come in at 10 AM tomorrow with his bills.

(Continued)

Time	Task	Rationale
10:45 AM	Families with food vouchers	Ask receptionist to finish paperwork and interviews on the families. Then quickly review information and sign vouchers. These families should not have had such a long wait. Make a note to find out what happened, and later counsel office staff about the delay.
11:45 AM	Drug call	Talk with client. Make a referral to a local drug clinic, and make an appointment for a part-time psychiatrist at the clinic. Do not get too involved on the phone with the client because it is better to make the appropriate referrals.

LEARNING EXERCISE 12.3

Cultures and Hierarchies

Below is an analysis of how one might approach a problem involving a nonnursing department but affecting the nurses' work and the nursing staff.

Analysis: Data Assessment

1. A copy of the organization chart was given to you when you were hired. The formal structure is a line-and-staff organization. The housekeeping department head is below the nursing director and the nursing section supervisor but at the same level as the immediate clinic supervisor. The housekeeping department head reports directly to the maintenance and engineering department head.

2. The county administrator has stated that she has an open-door policy. You do not know if this means that bypassing department heads is acceptable or merely that the administrator is interested in the employees. An important reason for not skipping intermediate supervisors when communicating is that they must know what is going on in their departments. A manager's position, value, and status are strengthened if he or she serves as a vital and essential link in the vertical chain of command.

3. You have twice attempted to talk with your immediate supervisor; however, whether you followed up regarding your supervisor's action on the complaint is unclear.

4. You are a new employee and therefore probably do not know how the formal or informal structure works. This newness might render the complaints less credible.

5. Possible risks include creating trouble for the housekeeping staff or their immediate supervisor, being labeled a troublemaker by others in the organization, and alienating your immediate supervisor.

6. Before proceeding, you need to assess your own values and determine what is motivating you to pursue this issue.

Alternatives for Action

There are many choices available to you.

1. You can do nothing. This is often a wise choice and should always be an alternative for any problem-solving. Some problems solve themselves if left alone. Sometimes, the time is not right to solve the problem.

2. You can talk with the county health administrator. Although this involves some risk, the possibility exists that the administrator will be able to take action. At the very least, you will have unburdened your problem on someone.

3. You can talk directly with the individual housekeepers by using "I" messages, such as, "I get angry when the housekeeping staff take naps, and the bathrooms are dirty." Perhaps, if feelings and frustrations were shared, you would learn more about the problem. Maybe there is a reason for their behavior; maybe they only socialize during their breaks. This alternative involves some risk: The housekeepers might look on you as a troublemaker.

4. Have all the evening staff sign a petition and give it to the immediate supervisor. Forming a coalition often produces results. However, the supervisor could view this action as overreacting or meddlesome and might feel threatened.

5. Go to the housekeeping staff's department head and report them. In this way, you are saving some time and going right to the person who is in charge. However, this might be unfair to the housekeepers and certainly will create some enemies for you.

6. Follow up with the immediate supervisor. You could request permission to take action yourself and ask how best to proceed. This would involve your immediate supervisor and keep her informed. However, it also shows that you are willing to take risks and devote some personal time and energy to solving the problem.

Selecting an Alternative

This problem has no right answer. Under certain conditions, various solutions could be used. Under most circumstances, it is more fair to others and efficient for you to select the third alternative listed. However, because you are new and have little knowledge of the formal and informal organizational structure, your wisest choice would be alternative 6. New employees need to seek guidance from their immediate supervisors.

For this follow-up session with the supervisor to be successful, you need to do the following:

1. Talk with the supervisor during a quiet time.

2. Admit to personally "owning" the problem without involving colleagues.

3. Acknowledge that legitimate reasons for the housekeepers' actions may exist.

4. Request permission to talk directly with the housekeepers. Role-play an appropriate approach with the supervisor.

You must accept the consequences of your actions. However, your attempt to correct the problem may motivate your supervisor to pursue the problem directly with the housekeeping staff's supervisor. If this is the action your supervisor takes, you should ask to speak with the housekeeping staff directly first. If, after talking with the housekeeping staff, you decide a problem still exists and you elect to address that problem, then you should return to your immediate supervisor before proceeding.

Analysis of the Problem-Solving

Would you have solved this problem differently? What are some other alternatives that could have been generated? Have you ever gone outside the chain of command and had a positive experience as a result?

LEARNING EXERCISE 13.6

Turning Lemons into Lemonade

This is the strategy that Sally Jones used to solve the conflict between her and Bob Black. In analyzing this case, one must forego feelings of resentment regarding Bob's obvious play for control and power. In reality, what real danger does his empire building pose for the director of nursing? Is not Sally really just ridding herself and her staff of clerical duties and interruptions?

A certain amount of power is inherent in the ability to hire. Employees develop a loyalty for the person who actually hires them. Because Sally Jones or her designee will still actually make the final selection, Bob's proposal should result in little loss of loyalty or power.

Let us look at what the real Sally Jones did to solve this conflict. When she was able to see that Bob was not stripping her of any power, Sally was capable of using some very proactive strategies. Here was a chance for her to appear compromising, thereby increasing her esteem in the CEO's eyes and gaining political clout in the organization.

When she met with Jane Smith and Bob, Sally began by complimenting Bob on his ideas. Then she suggested that because nurses were in the habit of coming to the nursing department to apply for positions and because human resources offices were rather cold and formal places, stationing the new personnel clerk in the nursing office would be more convenient and inviting. Sally knew that the human resources department lacked adequate space and that the nursing office had some extra room. She went on to say that because some of her unit clerks were very knowledgeable about the hospital organization, Bob might want to interview several of them for the new position. Although an experienced unit clerk would be difficult to replace, Sally said she was willing to make this sacrifice for the new plan to succeed.

The CEO, very impressed with Sally's generous offer, turned to Bob and said, "I think Sally has an excellent idea. Why don't you hire one of her clerks and station her in the nursing office?" Jane then said to Sally, "Now, do we understand that the clerk will be Bob's employee and will work under him?"

Sally agreed with this because she felt she had just pulled off a great power play. Let us examine what Sally won in this political maneuver.

1. She gained by not competing with Bob, therefore not making him her enemy.
2. She gained by impressing the CEO with her flexibility and initiative.
3. She gained a new employee.

Although the new employee would be working for Bob with the salary charged to his cost center, the clerk would be Sally's former employee. Because the clerk would be working in the nursing office, she would have some allegiance to Sally. In addition, the clerk would be doing all the work that Sally and her assistants had been doing and at no cost to the nursing department.

When Sally first received Bob's memo, she was angry; her initial reaction was to talk to the CEO privately and complain about Bob. Fortunately, she did not do this. It is nearly always a political mistake for one manager to talk about another behind his or her back and without his or her knowledge. This generally reflects unfavorably on the employee, with a loss of respect from the supervisor.

Another option Sally had was to compete with Bob and be uncooperative. Although this might have delayed centralizing the personnel department, in the end Bob undoubtedly would have accomplished his goal, and Sally would not have been able to reap such a great political victory.

The later effects of this political maneuver were even more rewarding. The personnel clerk remained loyal to Sally. Bob became less adversarial and more cooperative with Sally on other issues. The CEO gave her a sly grin later in the week and said, "Great move with Bob Black." This case might be concluded by saying that this is an example of someone being given a lemon and then making lemonade.

LEARNING EXERCISE 21.3

Conflicting Personal, Professional, and Organizational Obligations

The following is conflict resolution strategy used by you when the nursing office supervisor (Carol), who considers you to be competent and responsible, asked you to help cover the workload in the delivery room. Although this supervisor believes you can do the job, you think that you do not know enough about labor and delivery nursing to be effective. Here are some strategies you can use to resolve the conflict.

Analysis: You need to examine your goal, the supervisor's goal, and a goal on which you can both agree. Your goal might be protection of your license and doing nothing that would bring harm to a patient. Carol's goal might be to provide assistance to an understaffed unit. A possible supraordinate goal would be for neither you nor Carol to do anything that would bring risk or harm to the organization.

The following conflict resolution strategies were among your choices:

Accommodating. Accommodating is the most obvious wrong choice. If you really believe you are unqualified to work in the delivery room, this strategy could be harmful to patients and your career. Such a decision would not meet with your goal or the supraordinate goal.

Smoothing or avoiding. Because you have little power and no one is available to intervene on your behalf, you are unable to choose either of these solutions. The problem cannot be avoided, nor will you be able to smooth the conflict away.

Compromising. In similar situations, you might be able to negotiate a compromise. For instance, you might say, "I cannot go to the delivery room, but I will float to another medical–surgical area if there is someone on another medical–surgical unit who has OB experience." Alternatively, you could compromise by stating, "I feel comfortable working postpartum and will work in that area if you have a qualified nurse from postpartum that can be sent to the delivery room." It is possible that either solution could end the conflict, depending on the availability of other personnel and how comfortable you would feel in the postpartum area. Often, someone attempting to solve problem, such as the supervisor in this case, becomes so overburdened and stressed that other alternatives are not apparent.

Collaborating. If time allows and the other party is willing to adopt a common goal, this is the preferred method of dealing with conflict. However, the power holder must view the other as having something important to contribute if this method of conflict management is to be successful. Perhaps, you could convince Carol that the hospital and she could be at risk if an unqualified registered nurse (RN) was assigned to an area requiring special skills. Once the supraordinate goal is adopted, you and Carol would be able to find alternative solutions to the problem. There are always many more ways to solve a problem than any one person can generate.

Competing. Normally, competing is not an attractive alternative for resolving conflict, but sometimes it is the only recourse. Before using competition as a method to manage this conflict, you need to examine your motives. Are you truly unqualified for work in the delivery room, or are you using your lack of experience as an excuse not to float to an unfamiliar area that would cause you anxiety? If you are truly convinced that you are unqualified, then you possess information that the supervisor does not have (a criterion necessary for the use of competing as a method of conflict resolution). Therefore, if other methods for solving the conflict are not effective, you must use competition to solve the conflict. You must win at the expense of the supervisor's losing. You risk much when using this type of resolution. The supervisor might fire you for insubordination or, at best, she may view you as uncooperative.

(Continued)

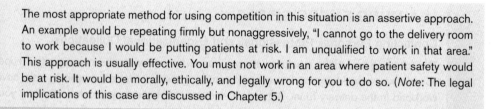

The most appropriate method for using competition in this situation is an assertive approach. An example would be repeating firmly but nonaggressively, "I cannot go to the delivery room to work because I would be putting patients at risk. I am unqualified to work in that area." This approach is usually effective. You must not work in an area where patient safety would be at risk. It would be morally, ethically, and legally wrong for you to do so. (*Note:* The legal implications of this case are discussed in Chapter 5.)

LEARNING EXERCISE 21.4

An Exercise in Negotiation Analysis

Analysis: A head nurse's goal is to be sure that all patients receive safe and adequate care. However, some hidden agendas may exist. One might be that the head nurse does not want to relinquish any authority or does not want to devote energy to the change that has been proposed. The staff nurses have goals of job satisfaction and providing more continuity of care; however, their hidden agenda is probably the need for more autonomy and control of the work setting.

If the conflict is allowed to escalate, the staff nurses could begin to disrupt the unit because of their dissatisfaction, and the head nurse could transfer some of the "ringleaders" or punish them in some other way. The head nurse is wise in reconsidering these nurses' request. By demonstrating a willingness to talk and negotiate the conflict, the staff will view the head nurse as cooperative and interested in their job satisfaction.

The staff nurses must realize that they are not going to obtain everything they want in this conflict resolution nor should they expect that result. To demonstrate their interest, they should develop some sort of workable policy and procedure for patient care assignments, recognizing that the head nurse will want to modify their procedure. Once the plan is developed, the nurses need to plan their strategy for the coming meeting. The following may be their outline:

1. Select as a spokesperson a member of the group who has the best assertive skills but whose approach is not abrasive or aggressive. This keeps the group from appearing overpowering to the head nurse. The other group members will be at the meeting lending their support but will speak only when called on by the group leader. Preferably, the spokesperson should be someone who the head nurse knows well and whose opinion is respected.

2. The designated leader of the group should begin by thanking the head nurse for agreeing to the meeting. In this way, the group acknowledges the authority of the head nurse.

3. There should be a sincere effort by the group to listen to the head nurse and to follow modifications to their plan. They must be willing to give up something as well, perhaps some modification in the staffing pattern.

4. As the meeting progresses, the leader of the group should continue to express the goal of the group—to provide greater continuity of patient care—rather than focus on how unhappy the group is with the present system.

5. At some point, the nurses should show their willingness to compromise and offer to evaluate the new plan periodically.

Ideally, the outcome of the meeting would be some sort of negotiated compromise in patient care assignment, which would result in more autonomy and job satisfaction for the nurses, enough authority for the head nurse to satisfy ongoing responsibilities, and increased continuity of patient care assignment.

LEARNING EXERCISE 23.1

Designing an Audit Tool

When writing audit criteria, first define the patient population as clearly as possible so that information can be retrieved quickly. In this case, eliminate patients who had complicated births, births of abnormal newborns, cesarean section births, and home births because these patients will need more assessment and teaching. The performance expectations should be set at 100% compliance with an allowance made for reasonable exceptions. One hundred percent is recommended because if any of these criteria are not recorded in the patient's record, remedial actions should be taken.

Select the patient's record as the most objective source of information. It should be assumed that if criteria were not charted, they were not met. Audit 30 charts to give the agency enough data to make some assumptions but not too many as to make it economically burdensome to review records. An audit form that could be developed follows:

NURSING AUDIT FORM FOR VISITING NURSES

Nursing Diagnosis: Initial home visit within 72 hours after uncomplicated vaginal delivery, with normal newborn, occurring in a birth center or obstetrical facility

Source of Information: Patient's record

Expected Compliance: 100%, unless specific exceptions are noted

Number of Records to Be Audited: 30

After the audit committee reviews the records, a summary should be made of the findings. A summary could look like this:

SUMMARY OF AUDIT FINDINGS

Nursing Diagnosis: Initial home visit, within 72 hours after uncomplicated delivery, with normal newborn, occurring in a birth center or obstetrical facility

Number of Records Audited: 30

Date of Audit: 7/6/2014

Summary of Findings: 100% compliance in all areas except recording of mother's temperature (50% compliance) and of newborn's temperature (70% compliance)

Suggestions for Improving Compliance: Remind nurses to record temperature of mother and infant in record, even if normal. Time might be a factor in initial home visit because temperatures for both were generally recorded on subsequent visits. Committee agrees that temperatures on mother and baby should be taken during first home visit and suggests an in-service and staff meeting regarding this area of noncompliance.

Signed, Chair of the Committee _____

The summaries should be forwarded to the individual responsible for quality improvement, in this case the director of the agency. At no time should individual public health nurses be identified as not having met the criteria. Quality improvement must always be separated from performance appraisal.

LEARNING EXERCISE 24.3

Using Management by Objective as a Part of Performance Appraisal

Analysis: This case could have several different approaches, depending on whether motivation or change theory or another rationale was being implemented to support the decisions. In reality, a manager may employ several different theories to increase productivity. However, this case

(Continued)

will be solved by using only performance appraisal techniques to demonstrate that they can also serve as an effective method to control productivity.

There are several aspects that seem to stand out in the information presented in this case. First, it appears that Ms. Irwin is a person who needs to be reminded. She functions well in Objective 3 because she received monthly reminders of the meetings, and since she worked with a group of people, she was able to make a real contribution to this committee. The similarities among the other four objectives are that (a) they all required Ms. Irwin to work alone to accomplish them and (b) there were no built-in reminders.

Rather than viewing this performance appraisal critically, the charge nurse should expend her energy in developing a plan to help Ms. Irwin succeed in the coming months. Nothing is as depressing or demotivating to an employee as failure. The following plan concentrates only on the management by objective (MBO) portion of Ms. Irwin's performance appraisal and does not center on the rating scale of job performance.

Prior to the Interview

1. Ask Ms. Irwin to review her objectives from last year and to come prepared to discuss them.

2. Set a convenient time for you and Ms. Irwin and allow adequate time and privacy.

At the Interview

1. Begin by complimenting Ms. Irwin on meeting Objective 3. Ask her about her work on the committee, what procedures she is working on, and so forth.

2. Review each of the other four objectives and ask for Ms. Irwin's input. Withhold any evidence or criticism at this point.

3. Ask Ms. Irwin if she sees a pattern.

4. Tell Ms. Irwin that MBO often works better if objectives are reviewed on a more timely basis, and ask how she feels about this.

5. Suggest that she keeps her unmet four objectives, and add one new one.

6. Work with Ms. Irwin in developing a reminder or check point system that will assist her in meeting her objectives.

7. Do not sympathize or excuse her for not meeting objectives.

8. End on a note of encouragement and support: "I know that you are capable of meeting these objectives."

Rationale

1. Gives the employee opportunity for individual problem-solving and personal introspection.

2. Shows interest in and respect for the employee.

Rationale

1. Shows interest in and support of the employee.

2. Allows the employee to make her own judgments about her performance.

3. Guide the employee into problem-solving on her own.

4. This is an offer to assist the employee in achieving improved performance and is not a punitive measure. It allows the employee to have input.

5. Employees should be encouraged to meet objectives unless they were stated poorly or were unrealistic.

6. Again, this helps the employee to succeed. Do not simply tell employees that they should do better; help them to identify how to do better.

7. The focus should remain on growth and not on the status quo.

8. Employees often live up to their manager's expectations of them, and if those expectations are for growth, then the chances are greater that it will occur.

LEARNING EXERCISE 25.5

The Marginal Employee

As the nursing supervisor of a 35-bed oncology unit in a 400-bed hospital, this is how you may solve the problems posed by a marginal employee (Judy) on your staff.

1. *Identify the problem*: The marginal performance of one employee is affecting unit morale.

2. *Gather data to analyze the causes and consequences of the problem.* The following information should be gathered and considered:

   - Judy has been an RN for 15 years and probably has always been a marginal employee.
   - Judy states she is highly motivated to be an oncology nurse.
   - Judy has been coached on several occasions regarding how she might improve her performance and no improvement is evident.
   - It is difficult to recruit and retain staff nurses for this unit.
   - The unit is already short of two full-time RN positions.
   - Judy's performance is not unsatisfactory; it is only marginal.
   - The other nurses on the floor considered Judy's performance to be disruptive enough to ask you to remove her from the floor.

3. *Identify alternative solutions.*

   Alternative 1—Terminate Judy's employment.

   Alternative 2—Transfer Judy to another floor.

   Alternative 3—Continue coaching Judy, and help her identify specific and realistic goals about her performance.

   Alternative 4—Do nothing and hope the problem resolves itself.

   Alternative 5—Work with the other staff nurses to create a work environment that will make Judy want to be transferred from the unit.

4. *Evaluate the alternatives.*

   Alternative 1—Although this would provide a rapid solution to the problem, there are many negative aspects to this alternative. Judy, although performing at a marginal level, has not done anything that warrants discipline or termination. Although some staff members have requested her removal from the unit, this action could be viewed as arbitrary and grossly unfair by a silent minority. Thus, employees' sense of security and unit morale could decrease even more. In addition, it would be difficult to fill Judy's position.

   Alternative 2—This alternative would immediately remove the problem from the supervisor and would probably please the staff. This alternative merely transfers the problem to a different unit, which is counterproductive to organizational goals. This might be an appropriate alternative if the supervisor could show that Judy could be expected to perform at a higher level on another unit. It is difficult to predict how Judy would feel about this alternative. Judy is probably aware of the other staff's frustration with her, and a transfer would provide at least temporary shelter from her colleagues' hostility. In addition, although Judy would be pleased that she was not dismissed, she would appropriately view the transfer as her failure. This recognition is demoralizing, and the opportunity for her to fulfill a long-term career goal would be denied.

(Continued)

Alternative 3—This alternative requires a long-term and time-consuming commitment on the part of the manager. There is inadequate information in the case to determine whether the supervisor can make this type of commitment. In addition, there is no guarantee that setting short-term, specific, and realistic goals will improve Judy's work performance. It should, however, increase Judy's self-esteem and reinforce her supervisor's interest in her as a person. It also retains an RN who is difficult to replace. This alternative does not address the staff's dissatisfaction.

Alternative 4—There are few positive aspects to this alternative other than that the supervisor would not have to expend energy at this point. The problem, however, will probably snowball, and unit morale will get worse.

Alternative 5—Although most would agree that this alternative is morally corrupt, there are some advantages. Judy would voluntarily leave the unit, and the supervisor and staff would not have to deal with the problem. The disadvantages are similar to those cited in Alternative 1.

5. *Select the appropriate solution.* As in most decisions with an ethical component, there is no one right answer, and all the alternatives have desirable facets. Alternative 3 probably presents the least number of undesirable attributes. The cost to the supervisor is in time and effort. There is really little to lose in attempting this plan to increase employee productivity, because there are no replacements to fill the position anyway. Losing Judy by dismissal or transfer merely increases the workload on the other employees due to short staffing. It also cannot help the employee.

6. *Implement the solution.* In implementing Alternative 3, the supervisor should be very clear with Judy about her motives. She also must be sure that the goals they set are specific and realistic. Although the staff may continue to verbalize their unhappiness with Judy's performance, the supervisor should be careful not to discuss confidential information about Judy's coaching plan with them. The manager should, however, reassure the staff that she is aware of their concerns and that she will follow the situation closely.

7. *Evaluate the results.* The supervisor elected to review her problem solving 6 months after the plan was implemented. She found that although Judy was satisfied with her performance and appreciative of her supervisor's efforts, her performance had not improved appreciably. Judy continued to be a marginal employee but was meeting minimal competency levels. The supervisor did find, however, that the staff seemed more accepting of Judy's level of ability and rarely verbalized their dissatisfaction with her anymore. In general, unit morale increased again.

Index

Note: Page numbers followed by *d* indicate displays, those followed by *f* indicate figures, and those followed by *t* indicate tables.

RRS1311